ON RECORD 1986 G. BROWN

CONTENTS

ON RECORD ENTRIES ARE
NOT ORDERED ALPHABETICALLY,
BUT ORGANIZED INTUITIVELY—
A MIXTURE OF SEGUES BY
MUSICAL GENRE OR STYLE.

007 INTRODUCTION

008 HUEY LEWIS & THE NEWS
010 BRUCE HORNSBY & THE RANGE
012 STEVE WINWOOD
014 TINA TURNER
016 THE PRETENDERS
018 GENESIS
020 PETER GABRIEL
022 DURAN DURAN
024 DEPECHE MODE
026 THE HUMAN LEAGUE
028 ART OF NOISE
030 THE FIXX
032 HOWARD JONES
034 BILLY IDOL
036 JULIAN LENNON
038 CYNDI LAUPER
040 STACEY Q
042 BERLIN
044 BANANARAMA
046 BANGLES
048 THE B-52'S
050 R.E.M.
052 GAME THEORY
054 GUADALCANAL DIARY
056 GEORGIA SATELLITES
058 BODEANS
060 CROWDED HOUSE
062 BILLY JOEL
064 PAUL SIMON
066 JACKSON BROWNE
068 JIMMY BUFFETT
070 JOHN FOGERTY
072 BOB SEGER & THE SILVER BULLET BAND
074 JOHN PRINE
076 BONNIE RAITT
078 JOE COCKER
080 THE MOODY BLUES
082 GTR
084 PETER FRAMPTON
086 CHICAGO
088 BOSTON
090 JOURNEY
092 38 SPECIAL
094 VAN HALEN
096 DAVID LEE ROTH
098 BON JOVI
100 CINDERELLA
102 POISON
104 RATT
106 METALLICA
108 JUDAS PRIEST
110 IRON MAIDEN
112 HEAR 'N AID
114 STRYPER
116 TESLA
118 GLASS TIGER
120 EIGHT SECONDS
122 STABILIZERS
124 JOHN EDDIE
126 PETER CASE
128 GRAHAM NASH
130 RICHARD THOMPSON
132 LEO KOTTKE
134 GERARD McMANN
136 RIC OCASEK
138 IGGY POP
140 DAVID + DAVID
142 TIMBUK 3
144 THE SMITHEREENS
146 THE RAINMAKERS
148 WANG CHUNG
150 ORCHESTRAL MANOEUVRES IN THE DARK
152 PET SHOP BOYS
154 NEW ORDER
156 THE SMITHS
158 BIG AUDIO DYNAMITE
160 BEASTIE BOYS
162 JEAN BEAUVOIR
164 BILLY OCEAN
166 FREDDIE JACKSON

168 JEFFREY OSBORNE
170 JERMAINE STEWART
172 KOOL & THE GANG
174 CLUB NOUVEAU
176 STEEL PULSE
178 BAD BRAINS
180 GONE
182 STEVE EARLE
184 LYLE LOVETT
186 GARY MORRIS
188 ANNE MURRAY
190 MARIE OSMOND
192 THE FABULOUS THUNDERBIRDS
194 ERIC JOHNSON
196 ROY BUCHANAN
198 THE BLUESBUSTERS
200 TAJ MAHAL
202 LITTLE RICHARD
204 YELLOWJACKETS
206 JEFF LORBER
208 ANDREAS VOLLENWEIDER
210 JANET JACKSON
210 MADONNA
210 PATTI LABELLE
214 TOP GUN
214 LIONEL RICHIE
214 PRINCE & THE REVOLUTION
218 ROLLING STONES
218 QUEEN
218 THE FIRM
222 ERIC CLAPTON
222 PAUL MCCARTNEY
222 ROD STEWART
226 DARYL HALL
226 DENNIS DEYOUNG
226 BENJAMIN ORR
230 NEIL YOUNG
230 STEVE MILLER BAND
230 EDDIE MONEY
234 VAN MORRISON
234 ELVIS COSTELLO
234 JOE JACKSON
238 ROBBIE NEVIL
238 ROBERT TEPPER
238 DANNY WILDE
242 STAN RIDGWAY
242 TONIO K.
242 BILLY BRAGG
246 PETER CETERA
246 NEIL DIAMOND
246 CHRIS DE BURGH
250 BELINDA CARLISLE
250 MARILYN MARTIN
250 LINDA RONSTADT
254 SAMANTHA FOX
254 E.G. DAILY
254 DEBBIE HARRY
258 'TIL TUESDAY
258 LONE JUSTICE
258 DEVICE
262 TALKING HEADS
262 THE CALL
262 HONEYMOON SUITE
266 TRIUMPH
266 KANSAS
266 BLUE ÖYSTER CULT
270 KRAFTWERK
270 TOTO
270 EMERSON, LAKE & POWELL
274 EUROPE
274 NEW KIDS ON THE BLOCK
274 DON JOHNSON
278 LET'S ACTIVE
278 NU SHOOZ
278 WAX
282 WHAM!
282 CULTURE CLUB
282 A-HA
286 WORLD PARTY
286 XTC
286 BIG COUNTRY
290 THE BLOW MONKEYS
290 COMMUNARDS
290 DOUBLE
294 PUBLIC IMAGE LTD
294 DOCTOR & THE MEDICS
294 SIGUE SIGUE SPUTNIK
298 EURYTHMICS
298 ARETHA FRANKLIN
298 ANITA BAKER
302 GRACE JONES
302 MELI'SA MORGAN
302 GWEN GUTHRIE
306 TRAMAINE
306 SHIRLEY MURDOCK
306 MELBA MOORE
310 POINTER SISTERS
310 S.O.S. BAND
310 REGINA
314 LUTHER VANDROSS
314 GREGORY ABBOTT
314 COLONEL ABRAMS
318 GEORGE CLINTON
318 GAVIN CHRISTOPHER
318 CARL ANDERSON
322 READY FOR THE WORLD
322 MIDNIGHT STAR
322 LOOSE ENDS
326 SYLVESTER
326 FIVE STAR
326 NEW EDITION
330 RUN-D.M.C.
330 WHODINI
330 JUICE
334 OZZY OSBOURNE
334 YNGWIE MALMSTEEN
334 DARK ANGEL
338 SLAYER
338 MEGADETH
338 METAL CHURCH
342 RAMONES
342 HÜSKER DÜ
342 ROKY ERICKSON
346 DWIGHT YOAKAM
346 RANDY TRAVIS
346 GEORGE STRAIT
350 WAYLON JENNINGS
350 EARL THOMAS CONLEY
350 THE O'KANES
354 ALABAMA
354 RESTLESS HEART
354 THE BELLAMY BROTHERS
358 REBA MCENTIRE
358 CRYSTAL GAYLE
358 TANYA TUCKER
362 JEAN-MICHEL JARRE
362 ROBERT CRAY
362 ALBERT COLLINS
366 WYNTON MARSALIS
366 BOB JAMES/DAVID SANBORN
366 MILES DAVIS
370 KENNY G
370 TONY BENNETT
370 DIANE SCHUUR
374 CLASS OF '55
374 ROBIN WILLIAMS
374 BILL COSBY
378 AC/DC
378 BLACK SABBATH
378 DUMPTRUCK
379 CAMEO
379 SALT 'N PEPA
379 THE 2 LIVE CREW
380 HANK WILLIAMS, JR.
380 JOHNNY CASH & WAYLON JENNINGS
380 EDDY RAVEN
381 AL JARREAU
381 MICHAEL JOHNSON
381 PETER, PAUL & MARY

382 ACKNOWLEDGMENTS

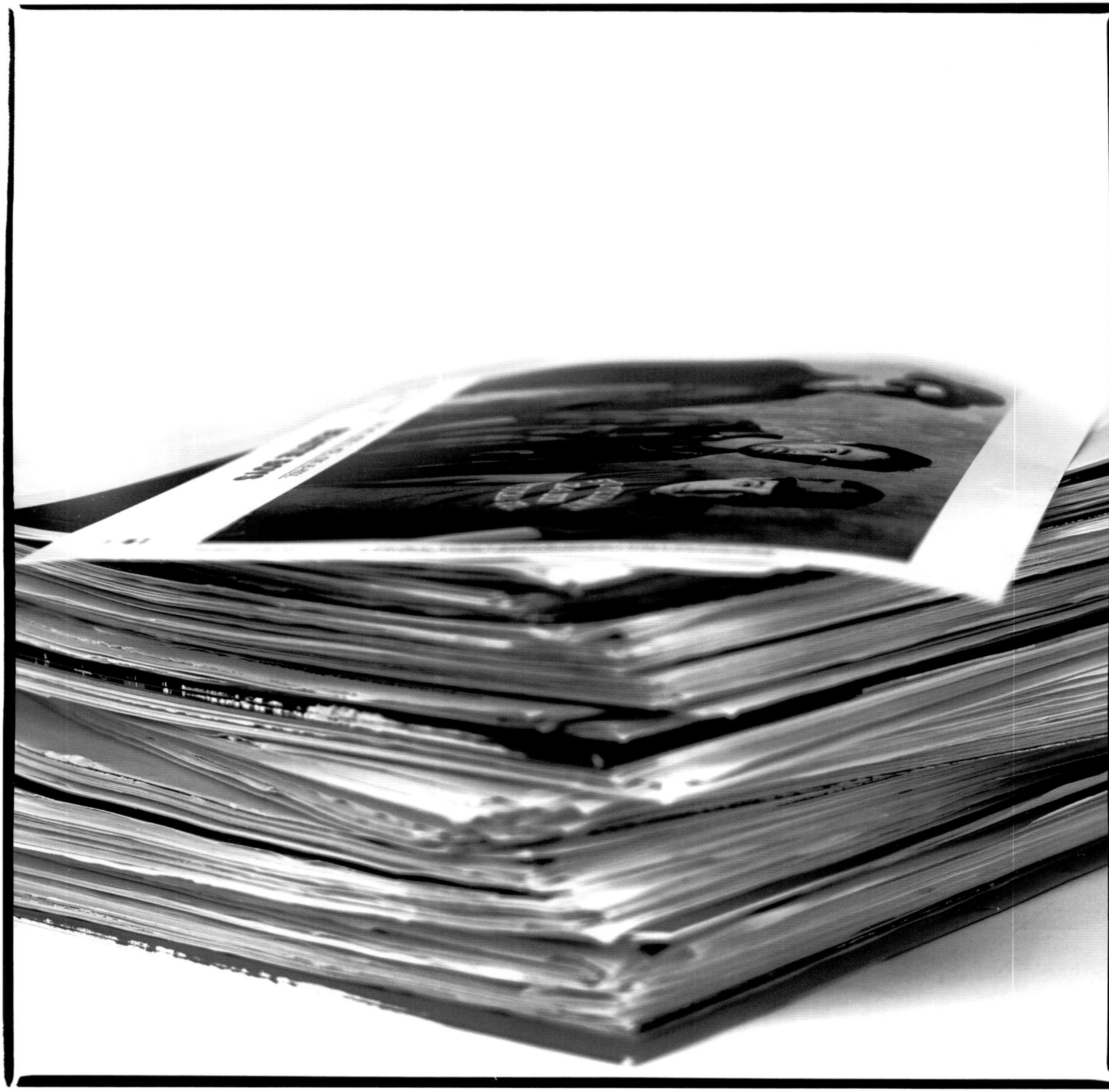

PHOTOGRAPH BY STEPHEN COLLECTOR

ON RECORD VOL.8 1986

WHEN ASKED about the best or worst interview I ever conducted, I choose to be definitive about my most memorable—and shortest—exchange.

I was contacted by a national magazine to orchestrate a photo shoot of the inimitable James Brown—the Hardest Working Man in Show Business, Soul Brother No. 1, Mr. Dynamite and one of my musical heroes—when he was scheduled to perform in Denver, my town. He was back on top after a few years of declining record sales, having had success with the Grammy-winning hit single "Living in America," featured prominently in the film *Rocky IV*.

We would take his portrait at the Turn of the Century, a somewhat goofy venue—a converted grocery store that hosted a variety of Las Vegas entertainers. A huge curtain bifurcated the floor plan. On one side was a stage and seating amid faux glamour décor. The other side housed dressing rooms and production storage, presumably in the former produce section.

On the anointed day, I arrived at 4 p.m. with Stephen Collector, a marvelously skilled photographer. We went to the backstage side of the curtain and set up a makeshift studio. After two hours, members of the band started showing up. They were young cats, cutting up, tuning up, readying for the show. Another hour passed, and the guys suddenly stood up, walked around the curtain, took the stage and started playing.

Steve and I looked at each other in panicked disbelief. The show was starting! And we hadn't seen hide nor hair of a road manager, a handler or a publicist, much less our subject. How in the Godfather of Soul's name did this happen? What the heck were we supposed to do?

And then, from down the corridor, strutting in his burnt-orange jumpsuit, came the diminutive, stocky superstar. James Brown walked right up and planted himself in front of me. With the band vamping just feet away on the other side of the curtain, it was so loud that I pointed to the stool we had carefully positioned and spoke/shouted, "Mr. Brown, just take a seat and we'll do this very quickly!"

He shook his head briskly, like a kid refusing a spoonful of beets. My anxiety doubled. It was *loud*. I leaned in close. "Mr. Brown, we'll be done in a matter of seconds!" He shook his head again. I got right in his ear. "Mr. Brown, you just need to sit for a few frames. Is something wrong?" I stood back.

He looked up at me and barked politely. "I cain't! *Mypantsaretootight!!*"

Oh! *Oh!* "No problem, Mr. Brown," I said, snatching the stool away. "Please *stand* here for just a second." He did. Steve snapped a few frames. Mr. "Please, Please, Please" said, "Bless you," walked around the curtain and started singing. The entire discourse took 30 seconds.

Arguably, more important things happened in 1986. The Rock and Roll Hall of Fame held its first induction ceremony in Cleveland, with many musical pioneers attending. USA for Africa's "We Are the World" won both Record of the Year and Song of the Year at the Grammy Awards. A tour bus carrying Metallica crashed in Sweden, killing bassist Cliff Burton. I also got to access something most fans didn't—the opportunity to go to all the concerts and get all the new releases and press kits. I was and am a very lucky boy. Please allow me to share. —**G. Brown**

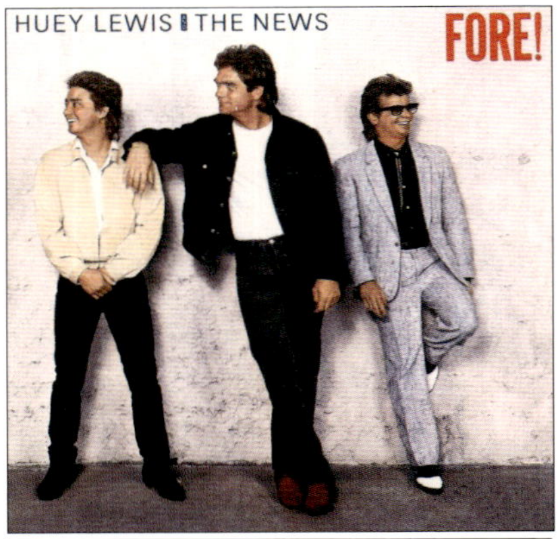

Billboard 200: *Fore!* (No. 1)
Billboard Hot 100: "Stuck with You" (No. 1); "Hip to Be Square" (#3); "Jacob's Ladder" (No. 1); "I Know What I Like" (#9); "Doing It All for My Baby" (#6)

Huey Lewis & the News' fourth album, *Fore!* matched the success of *Sports* and sailed to No. 1 on the charts.

IT WAS apparent from the titles of the smash albums *Sports* and *Fore!* that Huey Lewis & the News harbored an interest in athletics. Of course, Lewis didn't want that to override the music, but he couldn't conceal his glee concerning certain side effects of his fame. Over the course of a tour, he racked up his share of what he called "cheese"—the opportunities to hang out with some of the biggest names in sports.

For instance? Muhammad Ali sent a pair of autographed boxing gloves along with a request for tickets. MVP Don Mattingly of the New York Yankees spent his night off in Detroit watching the Sugar Ray Leonard-Marvin Hagler fight with Lewis. In Cincinnati, manager Pete Rose told the band to come by and take batting practice with the Reds. Lewis worked out with the Celtics' Larry Bird in Boston, and he played golf regularly with Joe Montana and Dwight Clark of his hometown San Francisco 49ers.

"Music? Fuggetaboutit!" Lewis chortled. "I mean, Muhammad Ali is calling me on the phone? Fuggetaboutit!"

But Lewis wasn't overwhelmed by his good fortune—he and his band of friendly, down-to-earth guys had rated as superstars themselves ever since *Sports* sold 9 million copies and spawned five Top 20 singles. What intrigued Lewis were the parallels between the careers of athletic figures and rock stars. After the success of *Sports*, Lewis and his cohorts had to prove they could do it again—not unlike a sports team coming off its best season.

"*Fore!* was the hardest record we'll ever have to make," he admitted. "The expectations were tough—we had never released a record with that kind of pressure before." But on the strength of the No. 1 hits "Stuck with You" and "Jacob's Ladder"—the album spawned five Top 10 singles in all—*Fore!* sold 5 million copies and removed the commercial restraints. Then Lewis faced the demands of constant touring.

"Because our record now stays on the charts for a year, now we've got to tour for a year. And invariably, we play the same show over and over, because the entire production crew of 55 people doing sound and lights is geared to that. A certain complacency wants to set in."

Lewis got a boost from an unexpected source. "(Bruce) Springsteen came by the Paris gig, and for two hours we just rapped it down. He really is a simple, great guy—it's not an act. He starts telling me how much he's played since he started out—he's played San Francisco as much as I have, and I live there.

"So I asked him, 'Isn't it a drag once in a while going up onstage and doing it?' And he said to me, dead serious, 'First of all, you've got to remember that there's one guy out there who's never seen you before, and you've gotta play the show for him. Second of all, there are thousands of guys who would trade jobs with you in a second.' And it sounds corny, but it really helped me out. Whenever I start to lose my focus, I kick myself. I say, 'Geez, you're lucky—you'd better get out and do your job." ■

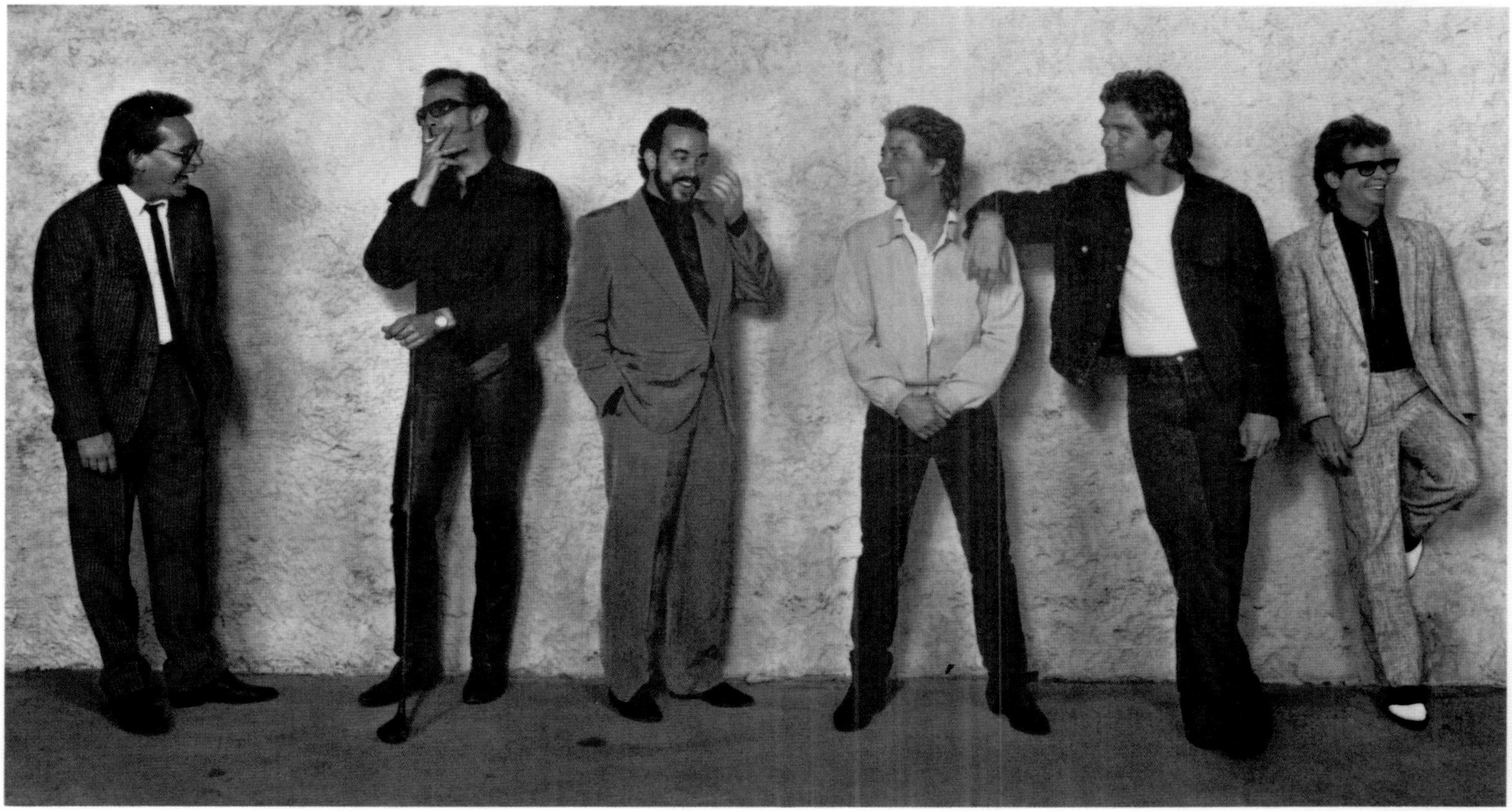

PHOTOGRAPHY—BENNETT HALL

HUEY LEWIS and the NEWS

Chrysalis™
Cassettes, Records & Compact Discs

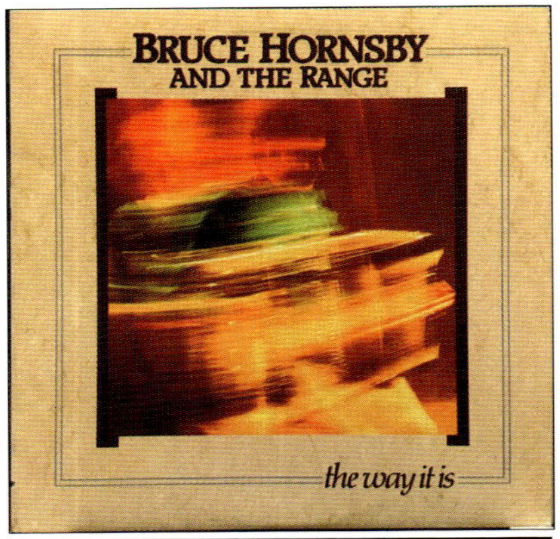

Billboard 200: *The Way It Is* (#3)
Billboard Hot 100: "The Way It Is" (No. 1); "Mandolin Rain" (#4); "Every Little Kiss" (#14)

Proving that perseverance did pay, Bruce Hornsby & the Range netted the Grammy Award for Best New Artist.

NOT SURPRISINGLY, the No. 1 song in the country belonged to someone named Bruce. The twist? It wasn't that Springsteen guy—it was Bruce Hornsby & the Range, whose debut album, *The Way It Is*, was flying out of record stores, propelled by the socially conscious title track, as well as "Mandolin Rain" and "Every Little Kiss," which radio programmers were citing as huge request items.

It seemed like ages in pop music since anyone had heard acoustic piano—much less an accordion—over a synthesizer. Such instrumentation wasn't a gimmick, but a careful integration of Hornsby's Virginia roots with his craft. The alchemy resulted in an enchanting blend of imaginative songwriting with contemporary chops—his influences were along the lines of the Band (he was writing songs with Robbie Robertson), bluegrass, folk and even Stephen Foster, but the piano break in "The Way It Is" owed more to Keith Jarrett. In that No. 1 song, Hornsby wrote "about having compassion for people. The lyrics talk about narrow-mindedness, bigotry and a status quo that never seems to change. To me that's very wrong."

"The other Bruce" had been described as "Jackson Browne if he was from Appalachia." "But better to be compared to Jackson than to Tony Orlando," the tall, self-effacing singer-songwriter said with a laugh. "The satisfying thing is that my stuff isn't really standard. There's a certain vindication in finally getting my music out and seeing it get attention, because I couldn't get signed for years."

Like most apparent overnight sensations, Hornsby actually had paid his dues. After enjoying success with the Bruce Hornsby Band in and around the Southeast, he moved to Los Angeles and made an important contact—Huey Lewis. They eventually did work together—Lewis produced three tracks and sang on *The Way It Is*—but Hornsby's career took its own turn before Lewis became a studio benefactor.

"It's funny—when Huey became famous, we thought having him involved would really do it for me, but frankly, that wasn't what banged the door down," he explained. "I'd been kicking around L.A. for five years, and I was really tired of the game. I was in a square-peg-round-hole thing, trying to fit into radio trends or whatever. I wasn't enjoying it, and I was tired of not playing acoustic piano.

"So last year I made a real organic tape, just myself playing piano, drums and synth bass, and I sent it to independent labels because I didn't think any major label would have any interest in something that sounded nothing like the radio—that's all synthesizers and drum machines. But the tape leaked out to the majors, and they went for it, just reacting to the music. It shows you that sometimes, if you follow your nose and do an honest trip and not try to get the Duran Duran haircut, maybe that can work." ■

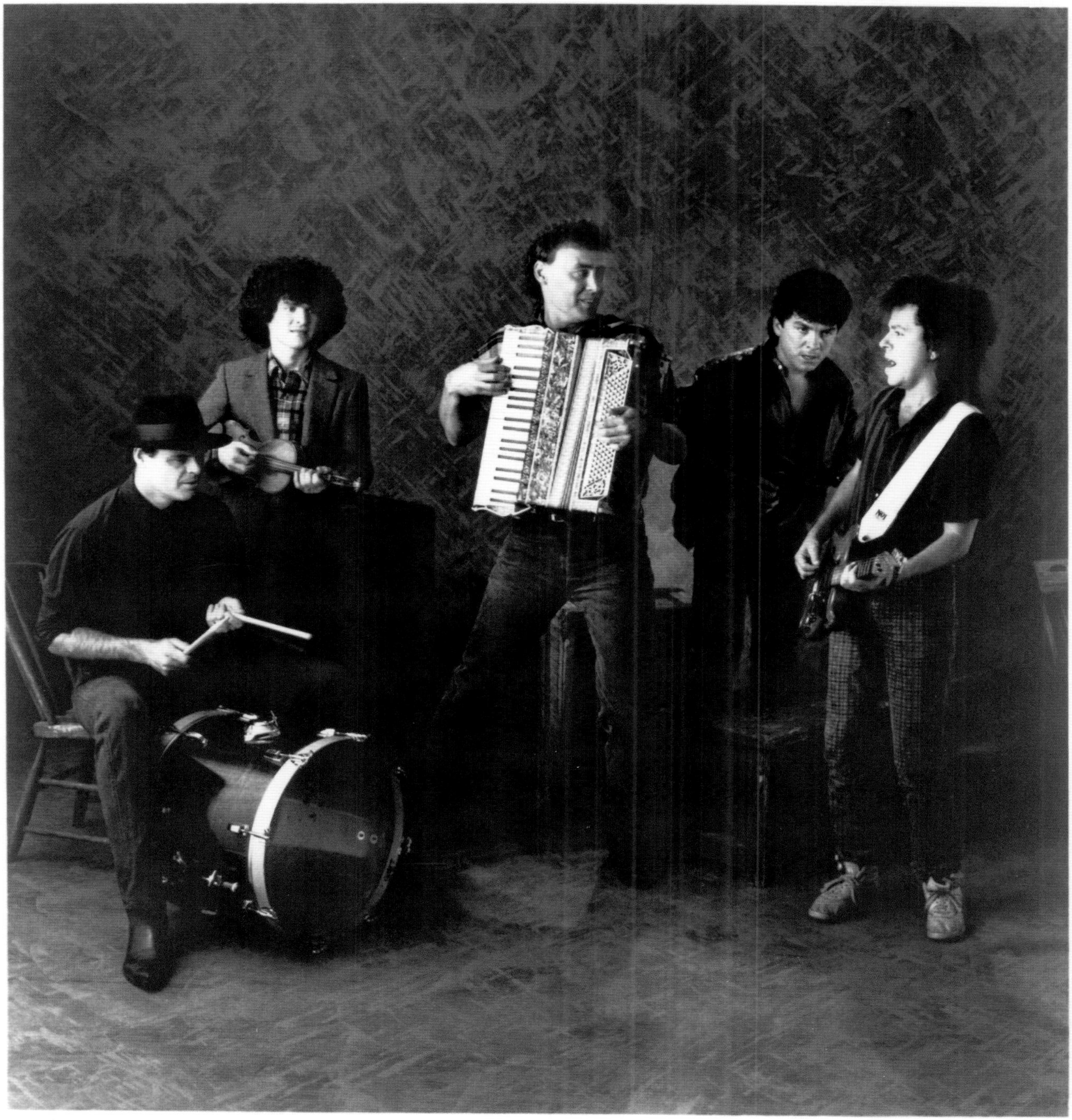

Photo Credit: PHILIP SALTONSTALL Photography

BRUCE HORNSBY
AND THE RANGE

RCA Records and Cassettes

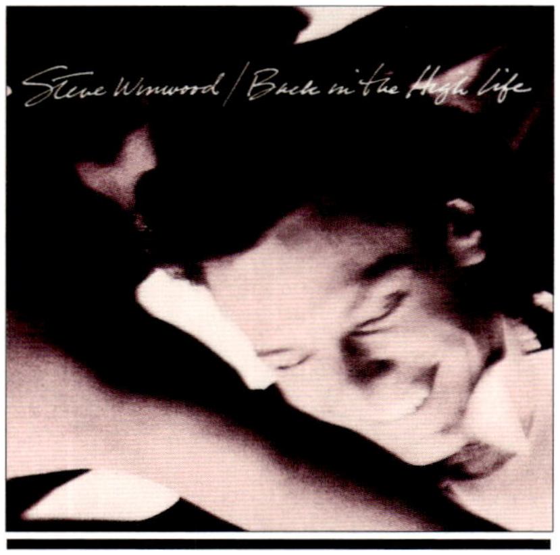

Billboard 200: *Back in the High Life* (#3)
Billboard Hot 100: "Higher Love" (No. 1); "Freedom Overspill" (#20); "Back in the High Life Again" (#13); "The Finer Things" (#8)

Steve Winwood recorded *Back in the High Life*, earning three Grammys and ascending charts with "Higher Love."

THE VOICE heard in the early Spencer Davis Group, and later, in Traffic and Blind Faith, Steve Winwood waited 13 years to put out a record under his own name. His ensuing solo career included the hits "While You See a Chance" and "Valerie."

"I was very pleased with my efforts on *Arc of a Diver* and *Talking Back to the Night*," the English singer, songwriter and multi-instrumentalist said. "It was as if I was proving a point to myself—that I could make all-solo albums. I also have a real interest in recording techniques, programming and engineering. But I found that I wasn't spending enough time simply playing, writing and singing. I wanted to concentrate more on those things."

The meticulously crafted pop production of *Back in the High Life*, Winwood's first album in four years, showcased his white soul warmth, and he returned to working with other artists for inspiration and input. "It differs greatly from my last two solo albums," Winwood said. "I made a conscious decision to use another producer, Russ Titelman, a great engineer by the name of Tom Lord-Alge, and some tremendous musicians and singers. I played less."

Back in the High Life featured appearances by Joe Walsh (the single "Split Decision"), Nile Rodgers, James Taylor (the title track), Dan Hartman, James Ingram ("The Finer Things") and Chaka Khan on "Higher Love," which won a Grammy for Record of the Year.

"I still use a lot of synthesizers and electronics—I try to make them sound as natural as possible," Winwood said. "But I can understand people being down on them, because they can be used in a very irritating way." ■

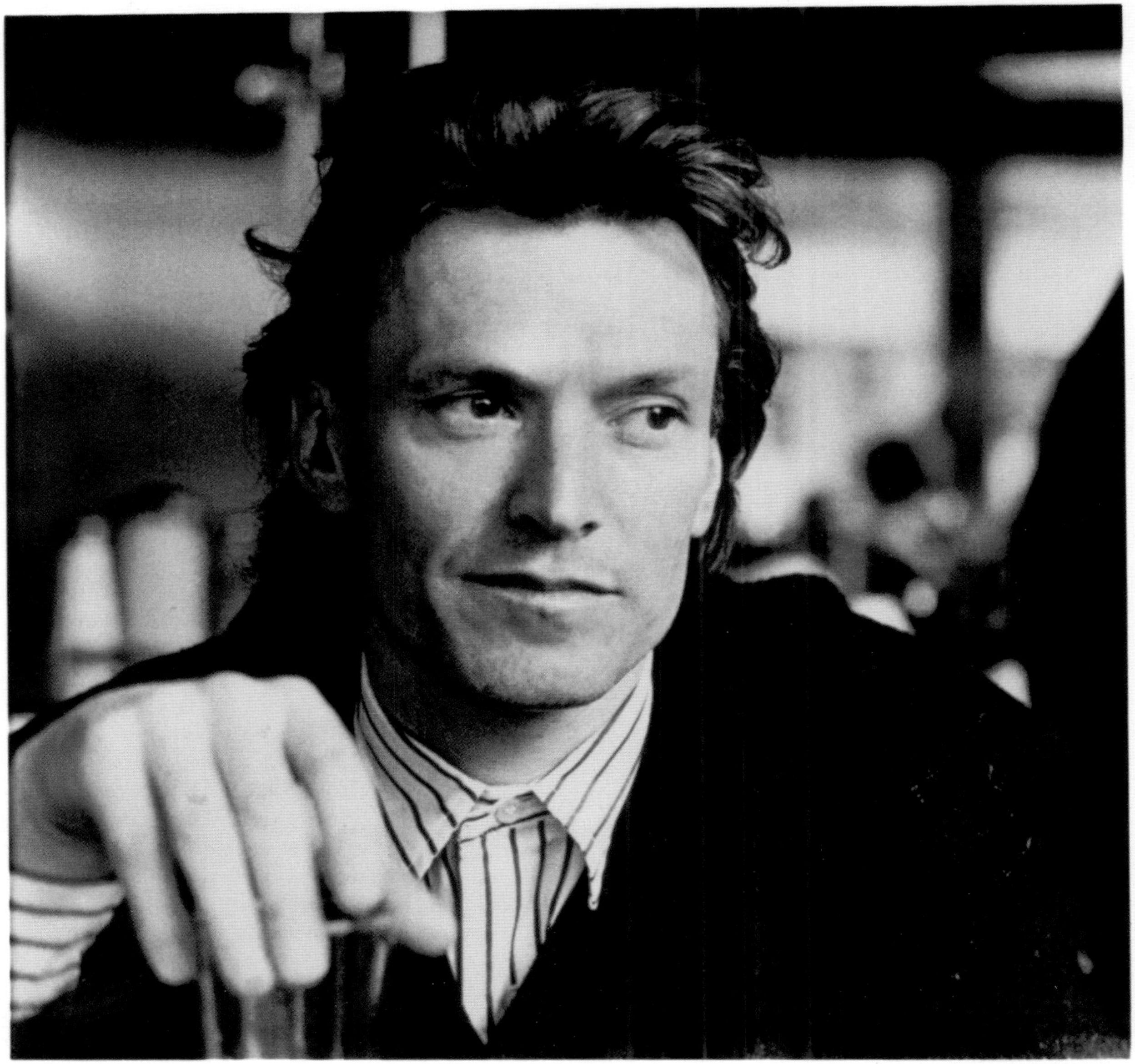

Photo Credit: Arthur Elgort

STEVE WINWOOD

ISLAND

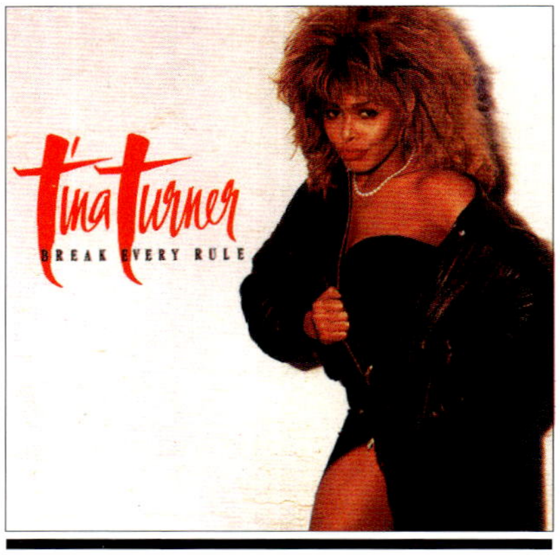

Billboard 200: *Break Every Rule* (#4)
Billboard Hot 100: "Typical Male" (#2); "Two People" (#30); "What You Get Is What You See" (#13); "Break Every Rule" (#74)

Asserting herself, veteran entertainer Tina Turner concluded a phase of her long career with *Break Every Rule*.

WHILE MANY stars had announced retirements from the stage and then returned, Tina Turner insisted that her decision to stop touring was final. She cited the years of roadwork that had marked her career, with the Ike & Tina Turner Revue and when her *Private Dancer* album topped the world's charts in 1984.

"I've been around long enough," the sexy godmother of rock 'n' roll laughed. "I'm leaving people with enough—they've got video tapes to play now! In living my life, performing has been my line of work for my security. Now that I've secured myself, I don't want to travel anymore."

A showbiz survivor, Turner was on her own from the beginning, after her parents left her with sharecropper cousins in Nutbush, Tennessee, when she was 3 years old. At 16, Turner (née Anna Mae Bullock) went to rejoin her mother in East St. Louis, Illinois. Her sister brought her to the Club Manhattan where the hottest band in town was playing—the Kings of Rhythm, led by a guitarist named Ike Turner.

Anna Mae approached Turner to sing with his band, but he ignored her. One night she simply took hold of a microphone and started to belt out a B.B. King tune at her table. Ike stopped playing the organ, ran off the stage and told her, "I didn't know you could really sing. What else do you know?"

After the two married in 1958, Ike gave Anna Mae (whom he renamed Tina) her professional career with the Ike & Tina Turner Revue, scoring a string of R&B hits—and starting her hellish lifestyle as his virtual prisoner. In 1975, having endured ferocious beatings from Ike, she split from him and, after a year off, launched a solo career. "Everybody thought I was struggling," she recalled. "But I was having a *good* time."

The break came in 1984 with *Private Dancer*, a landmark album that transformed Turner into a star. She then accepted the role of Aunty Entity, the despotic boss of a post-holocaust Dodge City in the movie *Mad Max Beyond Thunderdome*. She sang on the historic USA for Africa recording of "We Are the World," performed with Mick Jagger at Live Aid and acted with David Bowie in a Pepsi commercial.

On her *Break Every Rule* album, the quintessential sassy soul shouter schmoozed with Phil Collins (drums on the big hit "Typical Male") and Stevie Winwood (synthesizer on "Afterglow"). Turner hadn't abandoned her potent sex symbol image onstage—the package still included the wild mane of hair, the still-formidable set of legs, the nonstop shouting and twisting and shaking of her moneymaker—never sluttish, just *hot*, cavorting around in her unique crablike gait.

"My work is exercise," she mused about her youthful appearance. "It's a physical exercise for the heart, all the perspiration that the body needs. It's worked for me over a long period of time—I would have to be in shape after 27 years. Yeah, I get colds, I have minor little illnesses and all, but I'm basically quite fit. Now, if I hadn't been working..." ■

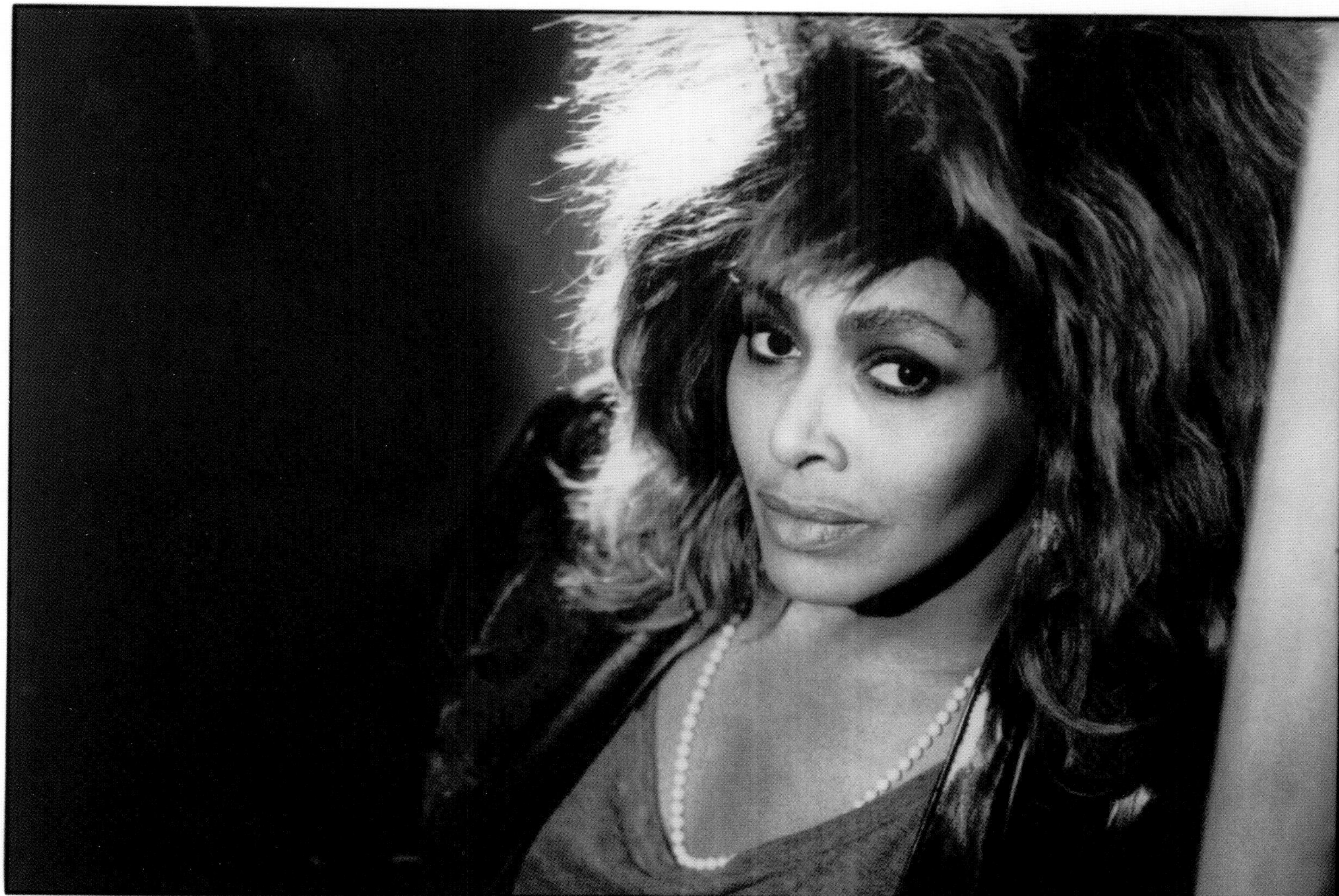

Photography: Paul Cox, 1986

Tina Turner

Capitol Records

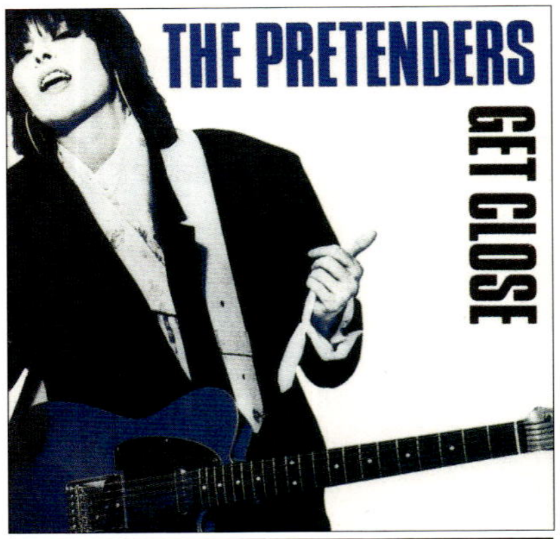

Billboard 200: *Get Close* (#25)
Billboard Hot 100: "Don't Get Me Wrong" (#10); "My Baby" (#64)

The Pretenders' "Don't Get Me Wrong" and "My Baby" both reached No. 1 on the mainstream-rock charts.

EVER SINCE the Pretenders emerged from the post-punk blast of 1979, lead singer and songwriter Chrissie Hynde had an image as the sexy rocker with the thorny personality.

"I seem to be threatening to everybody, and I don't know why that is," Hynde said. "There's this attitude that women in music or business have to be really tough to make it in a man's world. I never found that a problem—I just complained and nagged everyone to death until I got my own way. I try to work in a capacity as one of the band members, but people expect me to have Hell's Angels with crossbows opening the door."

Some of that reaction came from the perception of how Hynde ran her band. Since she was the only original member of the group left—drug overdoses killed guitarist James Honeyman-Scott and bassist Pete Farndon, and former drummer Martin Chambers was dismissed in 1985—the job of fellow Pretender didn't seem to offer much job security. But Hynde's energies had kept the devastated group together.

"We're a guitar-based band, and by losing the bass player and guitar player, we were cut off at the ankles," she said. "And when you make any changes in a band, it's got to come down to the music. That's what happened with Martin, who was a fantastic showman. But when we took a couple of years off, he wasn't playing. And I don't think he realized it, but I could certainly hear the difference."

On *Get Close*, the Pretenders' fourth album, many fans sensed a slight departure. Hynde, who was married to Jim Kerr, lead singer of Simple Minds, had a daughter in 1985. Before that, a long-term affair with Ray Davies of the Kinks had produced daughter Natalie, age 4. Such material as "My Baby" and "Hymn for Her" seemed to be direct reflections of motherhood, but Hynde railed at such easy classification.

"I was making more references to that sort of thing in the beginning," she said. "On our first album, I had a song called 'Lovers of Today' which mentioned 'me and my baby,' and I really meant a little baby—it's like a lullaby. And the song 'Kid' was also on that album. So in the meantime I have a couple of kids, and suddenly all roads lead back to the maternity ward."

Still, Hynde admitted that parenting had affected her craft. "I keep having babies between albums, and it not only makes it hard to hold the guitar in those last months of pregnancy, but you're not in a rock 'n' roll mode mentality," she said. "At 35, I still hear, 'You used to write about this hellcat rock 'n' roll image.' When you have a formula that works in this business, people want you to keep repeating yourself. If you change directions even slightly, it kind of makes them nervous."

And so Hynde, who admitted to being mired in the Sixties, didn't mind standing out from the competition. "All I ever wanted to do was play guitar in a band—I haven't had too many career aspirations outside of that. Every day I have to think, 'Am I the coolest band in town?' In my mind, I always take it back to where I first started rehearsing the Pretenders, and I believe we can still shake the walls down." ■

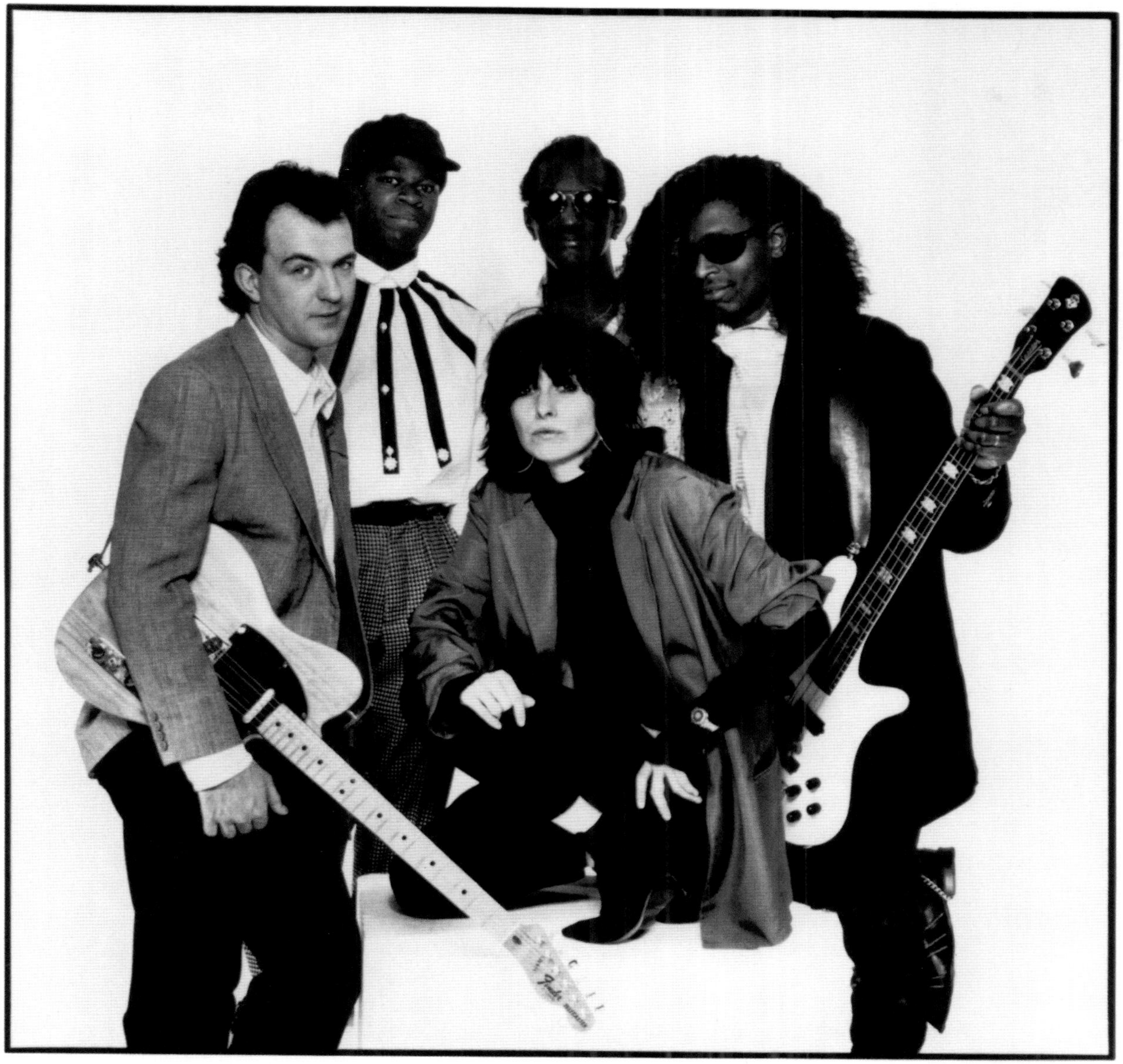

Photo Credit: Davis & Starr

PRETENDERS

SIRE™

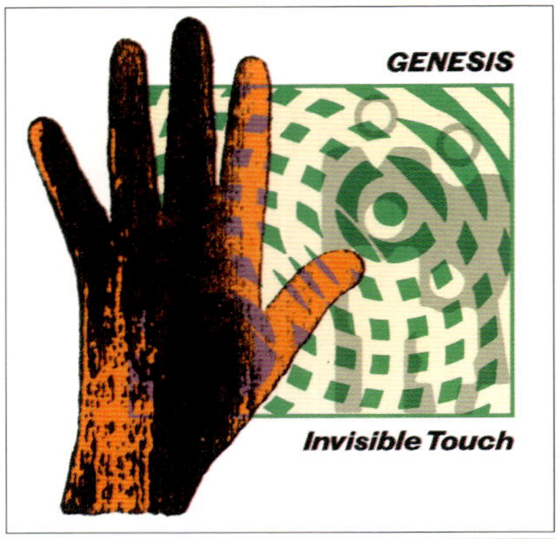

Billboard 200: *Invisible Touch* (#3)
Billboard Hot 100: "Invisible Touch" (No. 1); "Throwing It All Away" (#4); "In Too Deep" (#3); "Land of Confusion" (#4); "Tonight, Tonight, Tonight" (#3)

Genesis reached a high point of popularity with *Invisible Touch*, which generated five Top 5 singles in America.

SOMETHING UNEXPECTED happened to Genesis after the British trio's self-titled 1983 album—drummer and vocalist Phil Collins became a household word. Collins parlayed his fuzzy voice and commercial ear into a Grammy-winning solo album (*No Jacket Required*), No. 1 duets ("Easy Lover" with Philip Bailey, "Separate Lives" with Marilyn Martin) and production work (for Eric Clapton) into the kind of fame that only a handful of artists attained.

Such individual success usually spelled doom for the sturdiest bands—but most bands weren't Genesis. The other two founding and ongoing members—guitarist and bassist Mike Rutherford and keyboardist Tony Banks—and Collins gathered in England and recorded the 16th Genesis album overall, *Invisible Touch*.

"We tease him—it's natural, really," Banks added. "We just want to prevent him from becoming too much of an all-around entertainer—that's his only danger, I think, being held back a little artistically sometimes."

The three Genesis members had sustained the band over a decade and a half through their friendship, as well as a steady growth in popularity and continued musical exploration. "But people find it very hard to understand what goes on," Rutherford admitted. "Who has been going for as long as we have, done all the stuff away from the group, gotten back together to make records and gone off again? I suppose our aim as three individuals is to give everyone the chance to do all the things they want to do."

Rutherford and Banks had also used the last hiatus from Genesis to launch successful solo projects. Rutherford spearheaded a new group dubbed Mike + the Mechanics, and the album had spawned two sizable hits in "Silent Running" and "All I Need Is a Miracle." Banks used the break in the Genesis schedule to score *Quicksilver*, a movie starring Kevin Bacon as an urban bicycle messenger.

But when the ball rang for a Genesis album, both artists promptly reunited with Collins. "This is one of the things we enjoy doing the most," Collins noted, "just turning the tape machines on and turning our instruments on and just going for it. You never quite know what's going to happen. It's just the three of us chopping away, fine-tuning and honing down all these ideas."

Invisible Touch became a worldwide success, the best-selling Genesis album in the US. The album's five singles—the No. 1 title track, "Throwing It All Away," "Land of Confusion," "In Too Deep" and "Tonight, Tonight, Tonight"—reached the Top 5, making Genesis the first group and foreign act to achieve the feat.

"We get something in Genesis that none of us can do on our own, material that's unique to the combination of the three people," Rutherford said. "The papers are always saying that it's our farewell album, but when we sit down to write, the ideas are pouring out by the third day. As long as that happens, we're all up for it. When that stops happening, we'll stop. But it's happened every time for the last 16 albums." ■

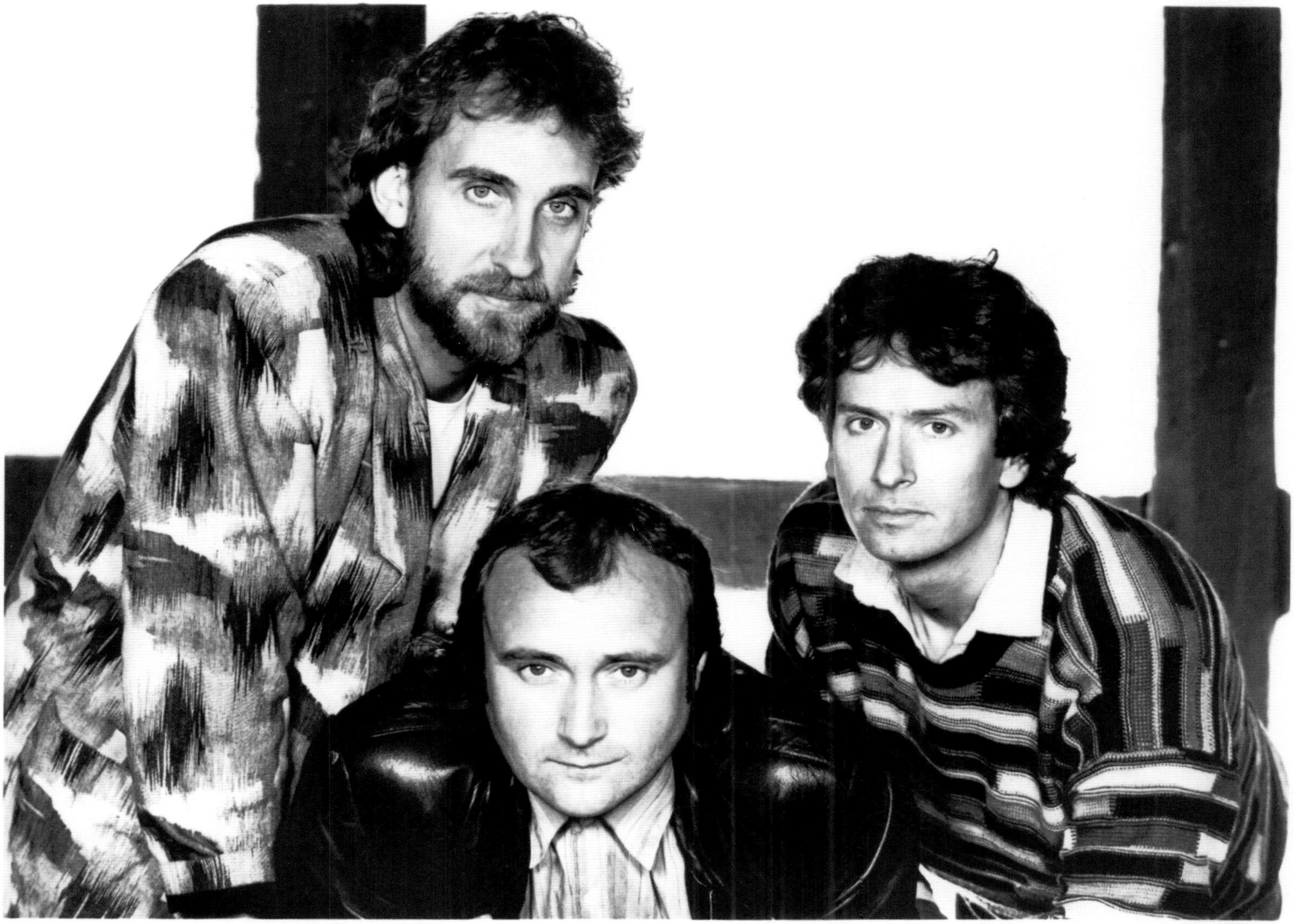

MIKE RUTHERFORD   PHIL COLLINS   TONY BANKS

GENESIS

ATLANTIC

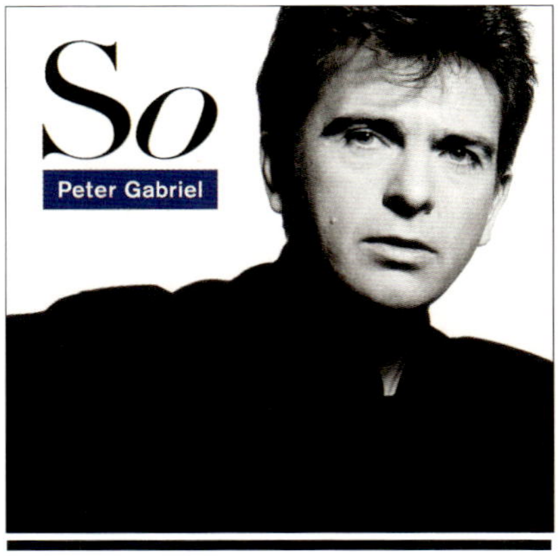

Billboard 200: *So* (#2)
Billboard Hot 100: "Sledgehammer" (No. 1); "Don't Give Up" (#72); "Big Time" (#8); "In Your Eyes" (#26)

Numerous sources of inspiration, both musical and visual, illuminated Peter Gabriel's new experiences on *So*.

EVER SINCE co-founding Genesis as a teenager, Peter Gabriel had developed an expansive cultural palette, and during his seven-year tenure as the band's lead vocalist and frontman, audiences had come to expect the unexpected from him. Still, Gabriel stunned the rock world in 1975 by announcing his departure from one of British rock's premier musical units. His solo career proved to be no less exhilarating and uncompromising. The Top 40 hit "Shock the Monkey" signified Gabriel's sound in his Eighties heyday.

So, his fifth studio album, indulged in craggy vocals, thumping percussion and sparse melodies melded with layers of esoteric electronic atmospheres. It featured contributions from numerous drummers. "Rhythm is the spine of the music, and it dictates the shape of the body that forms around it," Gabriel said. "Conventional rock rhythms tend to lead to conventional rock writing, which is why I look to other cultures for alternative inspiration."

The hit single "Sledgehammer," whose stunning animated video won a record nine MTV awards, was "an attempt to recreate some of the spirit and style of the music that most excited me as a teenager—Sixties soul. The lyrics of many of those songs were full of playful sexual innuendo, and this is my contribution to that songwriting tradition. It is also about the use of sex as a means of getting through a breakdown in communication."

For all his art-rock aspirations, Gabriel was a consummate pop artist when he wrote the classic "Don't Give Up," a duet with Kate Bush, about personal struggle. "I watched the programs on the effect of unemployment on relationships and home life and this triggered an idea for the lyric. A photograph taken by Dorothea Lange showing the American Dustbowl Depression, entitled 'In This Proud Land,' also provided inspiration. The song is closer to gospel and country & western than anything I have previously written. I kept the lyric within that tradition. It is also the reason that the woman is taking the supportive role. Although the man loses his sense of self-worth, and cannot take the support offered, it is a song about hope."

"Big Time" was "a satirical story of a basic human urge. In this lyric a man from a small town achieves all his ambitions, with all parts of his life, personality and anatomy growing larger than life and consequently extremely heavy." Youssou N'Dour, the Senegalese singer, joined Gabriel for the end part of "In Your Eyes." "One of the things that intrigued me as I learned a little about African songs was that many love lyrics were ambiguous.

"At the end of the day, if I had a choice between writing and recording music or performing it live, it would always be writing, because I'm a writer first of all. I look down at the trouser line and think, 'It's about time to get out on the road,' because that's what always shrinks my waist." ■

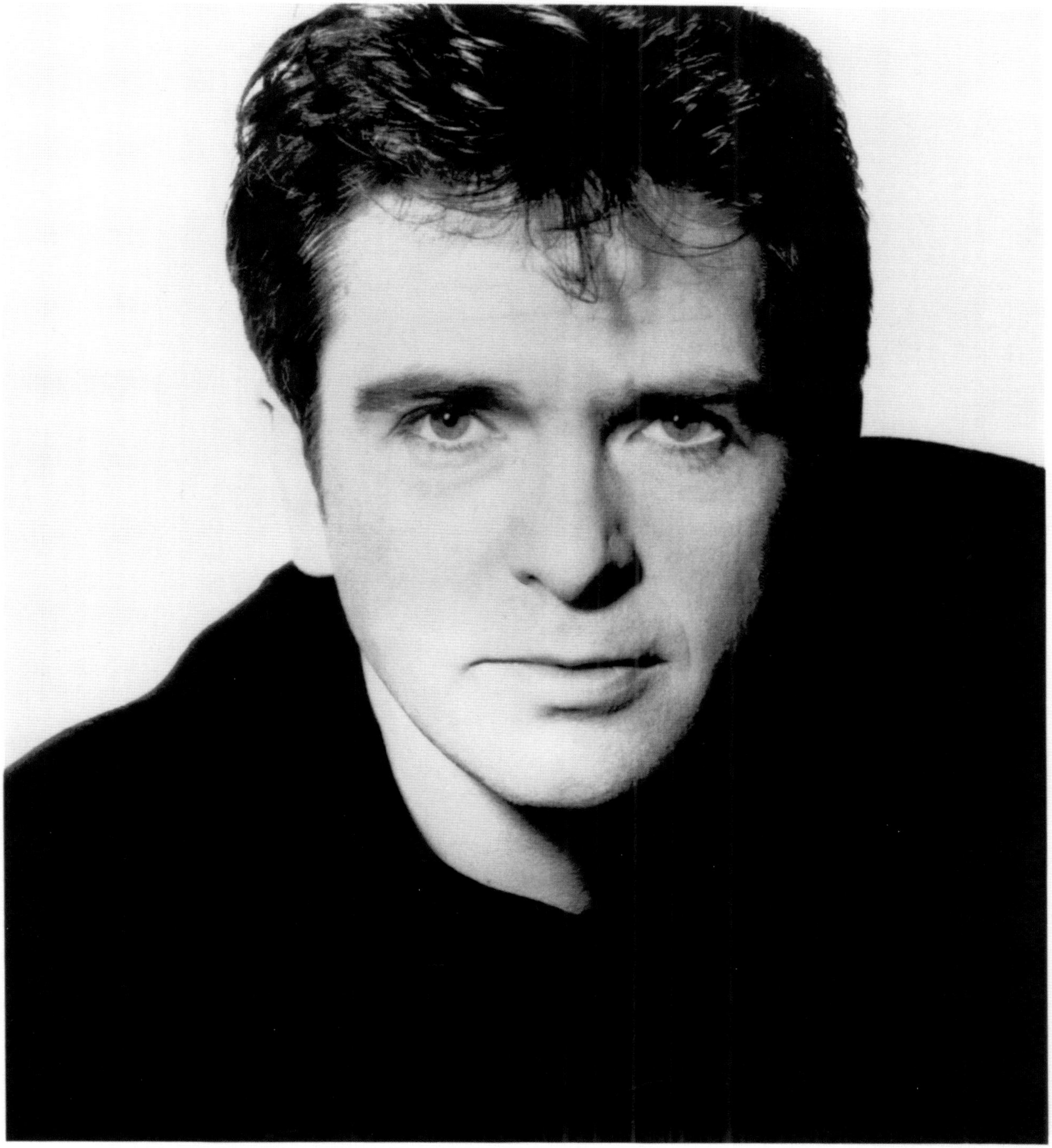

Photo Credit: Trevor Key

PETER GABRIEL

GEFFEN RECORDS

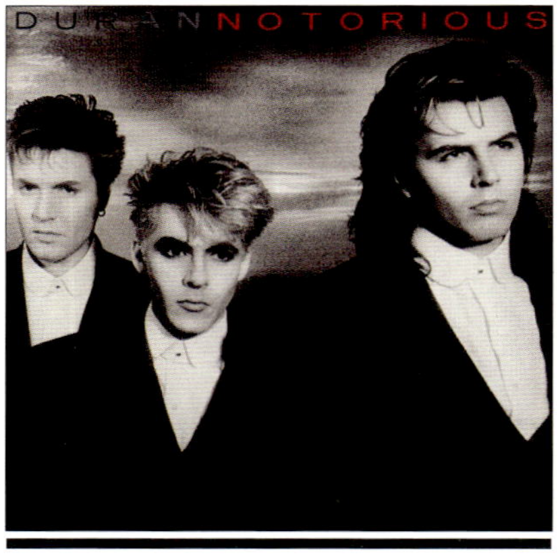

Billboard 200: *Notorious* (#12)
Billboard Hot 100: "Notorious (#2); "Skin Trade" (#39); "Meet El Presidente" (#70)

Deflated by the unsettling loss of two original members, Duran Duran answered back with the *Notorious* album.

THE MEMBERS of Duran Duran became famous in the early Eighties, with their synthesizer-driven new wave music, compounded by an emphasis on visual presentation, often appearing in makeup and pirate shirts. Their photogenic qualities and flashy videos yielded three platinum albums and a raft of hit singles—"Hungry Like the Wolf," "Rio," "Girls on Film" and "The Reflex."

By 1986, the pretty-boy pop phenomenon had changed its tune—it was a revamped, musically mature group, and the members wanted their squealing teeny-bopper following to know it.

"A lot of people are still behaving the same way crowds did three years ago," bassist John Taylor said. "They react in the usual way without reacting to what they're seeing. But we're not the first band that's had that problem. It's an educational process—if you like Duran Duran for the right reasons, then what we're doing now is infinitely better than anything we've done before. It should be—we're working harder at it."

To pare down its image and cross over to an older, more sophisticated audience, the original quintet had broken up and reunited as a trio. The seeds for the transition were sown in 1985, when Duran Duran fractionalized into two outside projects. John Taylor and guitarist Andy Taylor formed Power Station, while singer Simon LeBon, keyboardist Nick Rhodes and drummer Roger Taylor created Arcadia. Both splinter groups enjoyed hits that year, Power Station with "Some Like It Hot" and "Get It On," and Arcadia with "Election Day."

When the five players reconvened the following Christmas, Roger Taylor announced his retirement from the music business. After recording sessions for the *Notorious* album had commenced, Andy Taylor departed for a solo career. "You should be able to turn everything that you do into a positive experience," John Taylor reflected. "I'm very proud of the Power Station record, and I made it at a time when I was not particularly happy with the direction that Duran Duran was going in. All I know is that by the time Simon, Nick and I got back together working again it was better balanced, and we knew what we wanted from each other."

To record *Notorious*, produced by Nile Rodgers, the three remaining members recruited some stellar players, notably drummer Steve Ferrone and ex-Missing Persons gu tarist Warren Cuccurullo. They emerged from the studio with a funky, big-band sound unlike anything on previous albums.

"Duran Duran mastered the art of commercial success very quickly, but we've only started mastering the art of making records," Taylor said. "I mean, I hadn't picked up a guitar until I was 17." ■

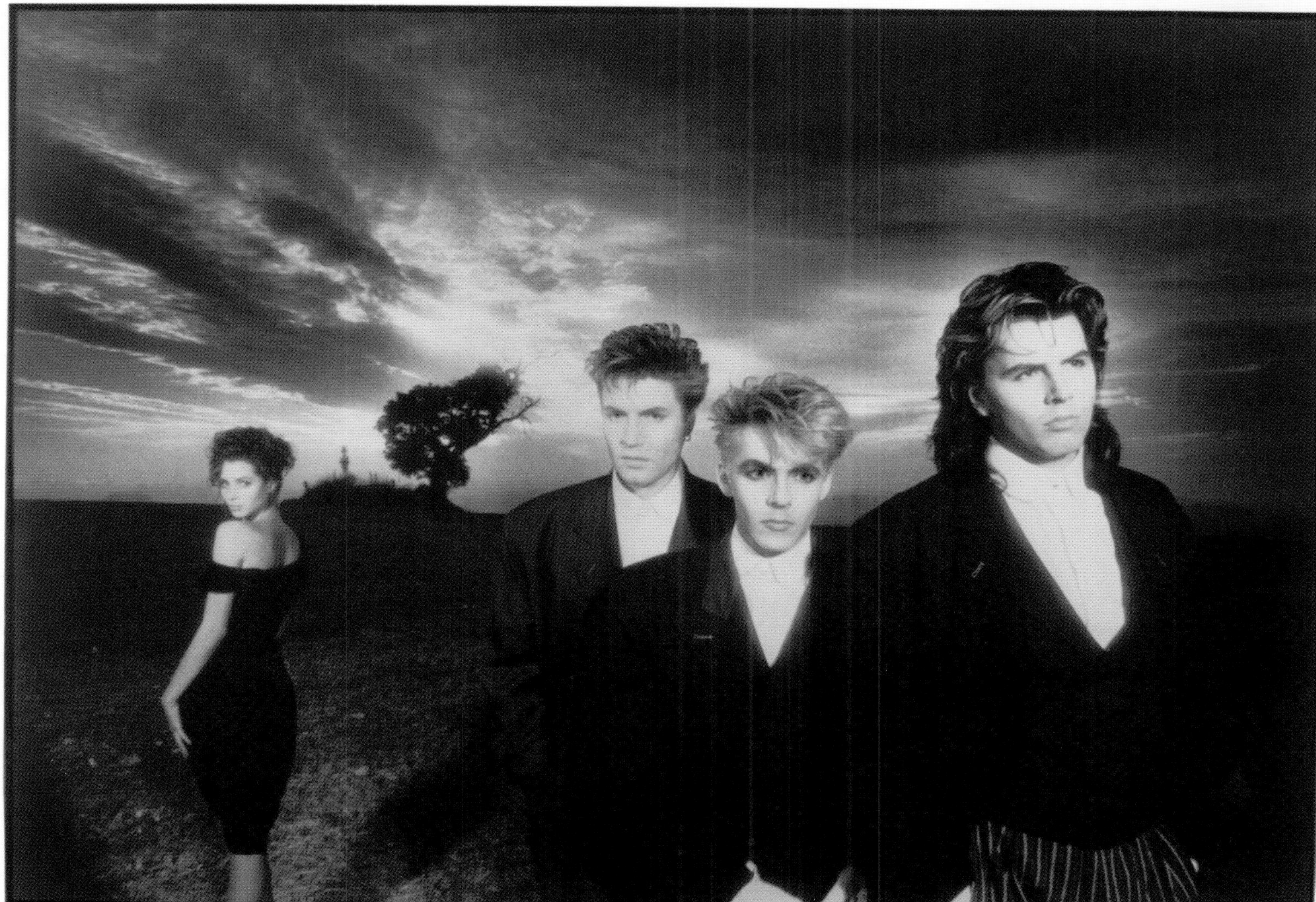

Photo: John Swannell / 1986

Simon Le Bon Nick Rhodes John Taylor

DURAN DURAN

Capitol Records

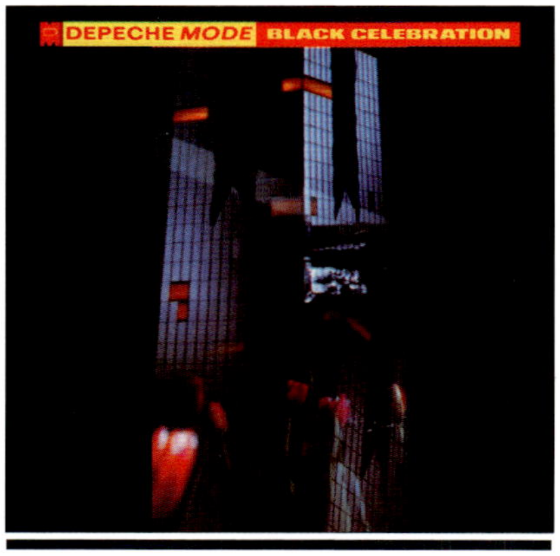

Billboard 200: *Black Celebration* (#90)

Depeche Mode's *Black Celebration* ratified the synth-pop outfit as a force within the electronic music scene.

IT CAME as something of a surprise, but in terms of sheer numbers of concert seats sold, on both sides of the Atlantic, Depeche Mode ranked among the top draws of the mid-Eighties.

The band then emerged with *Black Celebration*, the first collection of new material in more than two years. The album shifted music style, blending warm tones with its usual clangs and beeps to create some sleek, brooding textures. One writer termed the record "a perfect soundtrack for tentative love in the Industrial Age." Guitar freaks called them purveyors of "post-modernistic pop for the so-called space age."

The band didn't mind. "I don't understand it," founding member Martin Gore shrugged. "But it sounds like a nice term, anyway."

So underneath the trappings of teenage fandom (black fingernail polish, bleached hair, leather accessories) and the ominous obsessions of Gore's love songs—"I may be setting myself up as a target, but all of the lyrics come from things I feel personally"—Depeche Mode had proved that it wasn't so one-dimensional after all, gaining solid entry with a whole new generation of listeners. "Stripped," "A Question of Lust" and "A Question of Time" (the music video was directed by Anton Corbijn) were British hits and international successes.

"Depeche Mode is a democracy," Gore explained. "That stops me from writing everything in one direction. We still believe in an old-fashioned song style with lots of melody—we can be really poppy one minute or we can sound harder or moodier."

Following the release of the atmospheric *Black Celebration*, Depeche Mode embarked on an extensive American tour, selling out concert halls with a speed and thoroughness that surprised industry veterans. How could a British "cult band" trending toward somber wistfulness get fans lined up around the block across the heartland?

"We've noticed a difference in the attitude of American people. Prior to this, we always felt we were fighting a losing battle. We were always asked, 'Why aren't you a rock band? Why don't you use guitars?' But suddenly we have respect, we're selling tickets and records. We aren't doing anything different—the public is just becoming more aware of our kind of electronic music." ■

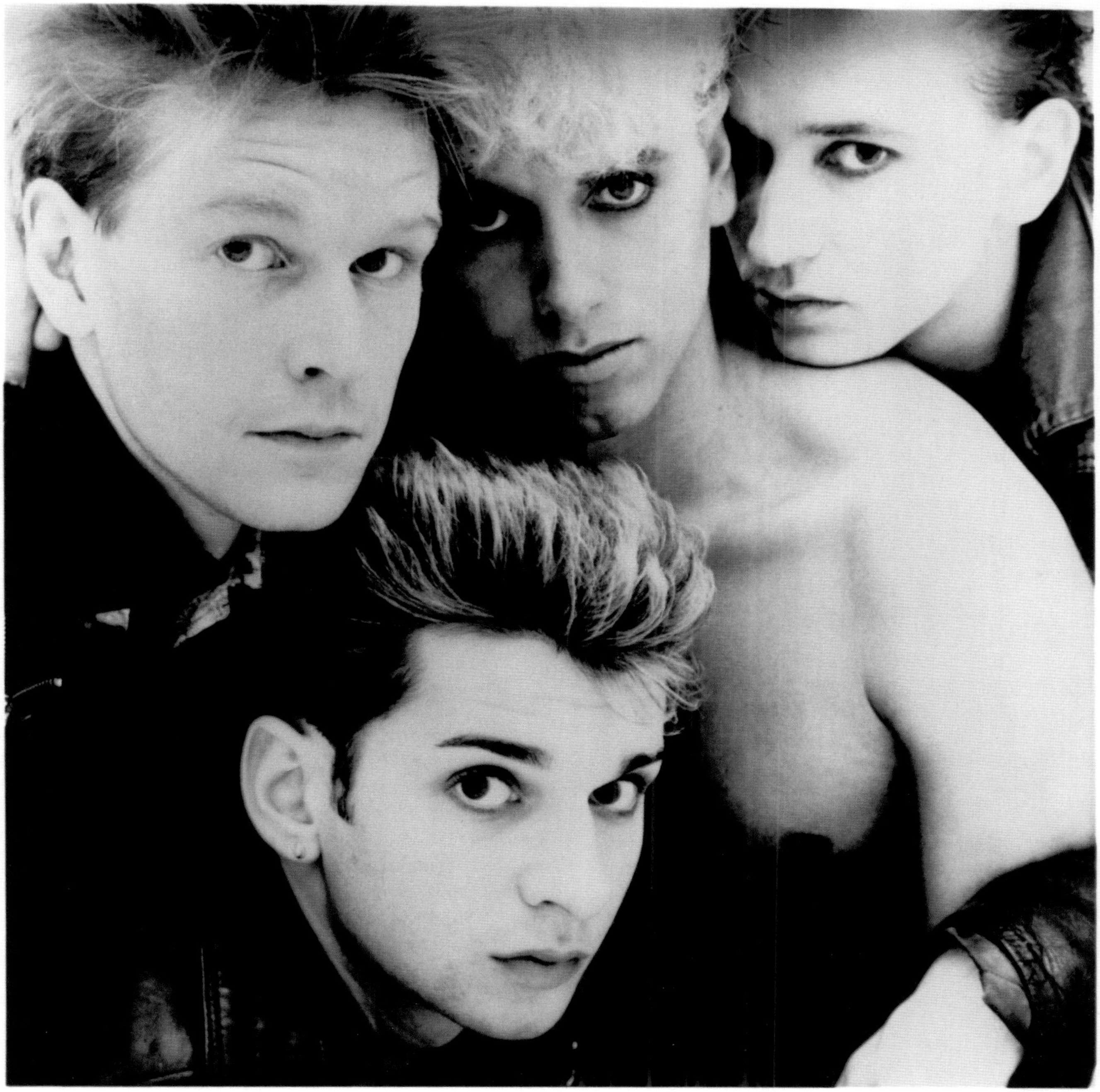

DEPECHE MODE

MUTE RECORDS

SIRE™

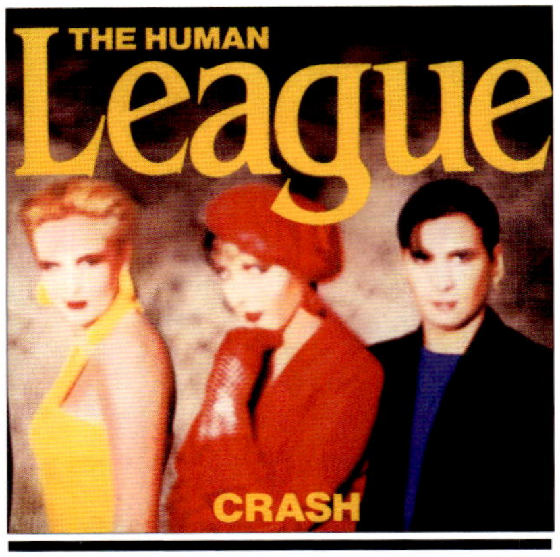

Billboard 200: *Crash* (#35)
Billboard Hot 100: "Human" (No. 1); "I Need Your Loving" (#44)

The Human League resurfaced with *Crash*, and the plaintive "Human" soon peaked at the top of the US charts.

THE HUMAN League could have been dismissed as just another casualty of the early Eighties British Invasion, when electronic pop band after electronic pop band scored a hit or two in the United States and then quickly faded from sight. The group fit right into that pattern—a No. 1 hit in 1982 with "Don't You Want Me," two follow-ups in "(Keep Feeling) Fascination" and "Mirror Man," and then a slide into oblivion.

But the Human League hadn't disappeared. As the members readily admitted, nothing happened very fast for them. *Crash* followed a period of some unrest.

"We've made two albums since 'Don't You Want Me'—it just happens that they each took two years to make," leader Philip Oakey explained. "And it did get a bit depressing, actually, but we kept on working."

For *Crash*, the Human League endured a false start with Colin Thurston, the veteran Duran Duran producer who proved incapable of giving them a dance album. But the band's fortunes changed when they teamed up with the hot songwriting and producing duo of Jimmy Jam and Terry Lewis, in the wake of the dance-music *meisters*' success with Janet Jackson's *Control*. Together, they created *Crash* and the group's No. 1 hit, "Human."

"We were very familiar with their work, but we never even thought about asking to work with them because we though they only did stuff that they'd written themselves," Oakey recalled. Yet the Human League became the first non-American, non-Black pop act with whom Jam and Lewis had ever worked. "We've always been sort of Black-based anyway," Oakey noted.

And Oakey should have known—he was the only original member left in the Human League, which formed in Sheffield in 1977 to explore the possibilities of electronic music. "We were actually just a punk band using synthesizers instead of guitars," he said. "We were more punky than other groups because we wouldn't even learn the guitar."

When fellow founders Martyn Ware and Ian Marsh left to establish Heaven 17, Oakey recruited the players who remained the core of Human League—bassist Ian Burden and Joanne Catherall and Susan Sulley, two girl dancers he spotted in a Sheffield disco. Ironically, that "less musical" version of the band rocketed instantly to stardom with "Don't You Want Me." With the chart-topping success of "Human," the Human League was ready to cement its American reputation.

"Now there's no tapes or sequencers or drum machines onstage—we used to do that in the old Human League, and I saw that destroy the band," Oakey said. "Now every note or sound is made by someone onstage at the time. It's really just an old-fashioned band. It's taken a while, but I feel like we're finding ourselves again. We allowed ourselves to become a studio group, and people want a live group. If we can become a live group, we'll be huge." ■

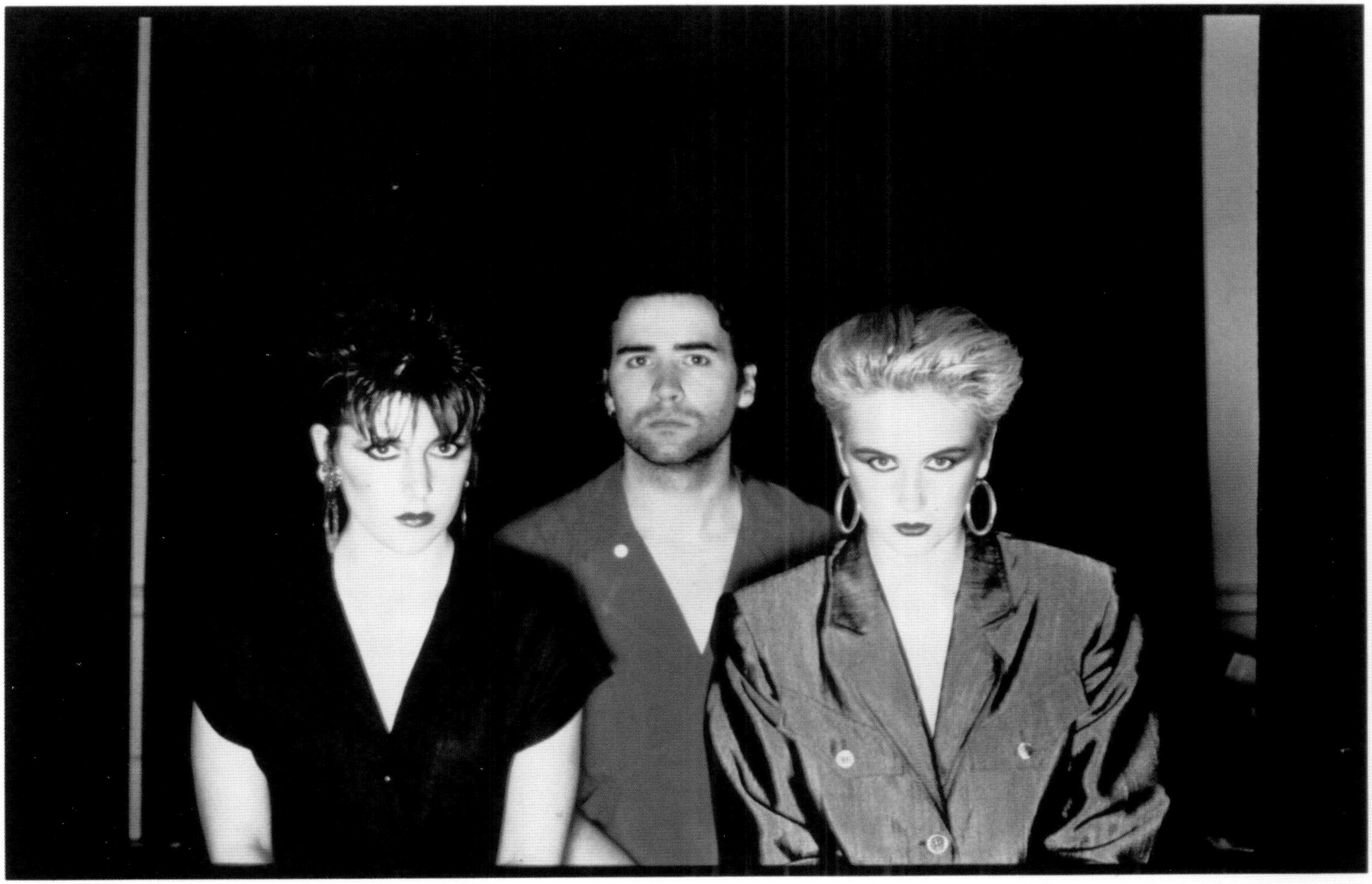

JOANNE CATHERALL PHILIP OAKEY SUSAN SULLEY

THE HUMAN LEAGUE

A&M RECORDS
Printed in U.S.A.

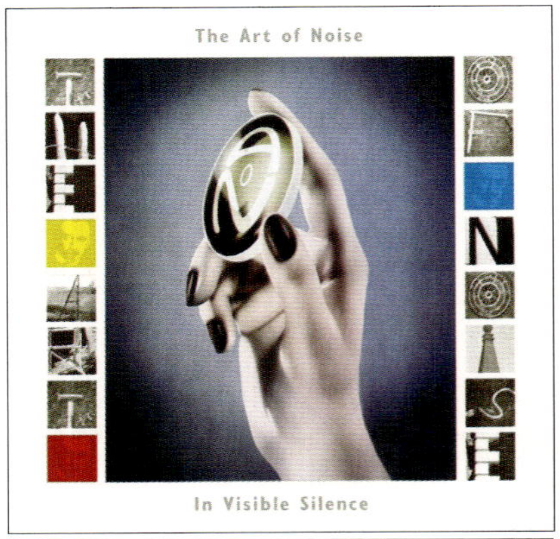

Billboard 200: *In Visible Silence* (#53)
Billboard Hot 100: "Peter Gunn" (#50)

Guitar legend Duane Eddy recreated his classic riff on Art of Noise's canny update of the "Peter Gunn" theme.

STYLIZING AND playing up high-tech dance music, Art of Noise didn't qualify as a typical pop band. The reclusive English trio was comprised of behind-the-scenes studio wizards who claimed to have no preset roles, other than collaborating to spring new instrumental creations on the public. The concept originated when engineer Gary Langen linked up with producer Trevor Horn to record the Buggles' 1979 hit "Video Killed the Radio Star," in which the production was catchier than the performance.

"Things had become a bit boring for me because I didn't like working with punk bands in the studio," the exuberant Langen recalled. "Then I bumped into Trevor, and he wanted to do this funny sort of recording—keep everything real small, isolate the drums and make certain things real loud in the mix. People kept saying, 'You can't do that!' We kept saying, 'Well, yes, we can—here it is!"

Langen continued to work with Horn on ABC's *The Lexicon of Love* and Yes' *90125*, albums that were more impressive for the all-around cleverness of sound than the material. At the same time, Langen became friendly with Anne Dudley, a session keyboardist, and Jonathan "J.J." Jeczalik, a Fairlight programmer-player. When Langen's five-year working relationship with Horn and his ZTT Records came to an acrimonious end—"I needed a change, and Trevor took too long to make records"—he formed Art of Noise with Dudley and Jeczalik.

The appealing cacophony of "Beatbox" reached No. 1 on the US dance charts, and more hits followed—"Legs," "Paranoimia" (featuring the tones of computerized TV star Max Headroom) and particularly "Peter Gunn," a reworking of guitarist Duane Eddy's 1960 hit instrumental. The group persuaded Eddy to come out of retirement to contribute his distinctive twangy guitar line, and the version was awarded a Grammy for Best Rock Instrumental performance.

"Any other band would have been criticized for a cop-out," Langen noted gleefully. "But nobody can ascertain right or wrong for whatever we do—you either accept it or you don't. Art of Noise is really quite modular—basically, we're three units that will slot together in lots of different ways."

Indeed, Dudley and Jeczalic went out on tour promoting the group's *In Visible Silence* album while Langen remained in New York to handle promotional work and mix Billy Idol's *Whiplash Smile*. "In two years' time, when we've amassed more finances, then we can do something far more extravagant, and that's when it will need all hands on deck," Langen explained. "But for now, we decided there was really no reason for me to go out—I just taught a guy how to do the sound. There are eight people onstage, so that keeps the whole thing really faceless—nobody knows who's in Art of Noise!

"But it's not half a dozen geezers sitting there playing keyboards, either. There are not tapes, no pre-programmed sequences—everything is in fact played. So from that standpoint, it's very rock 'n' roll." ■

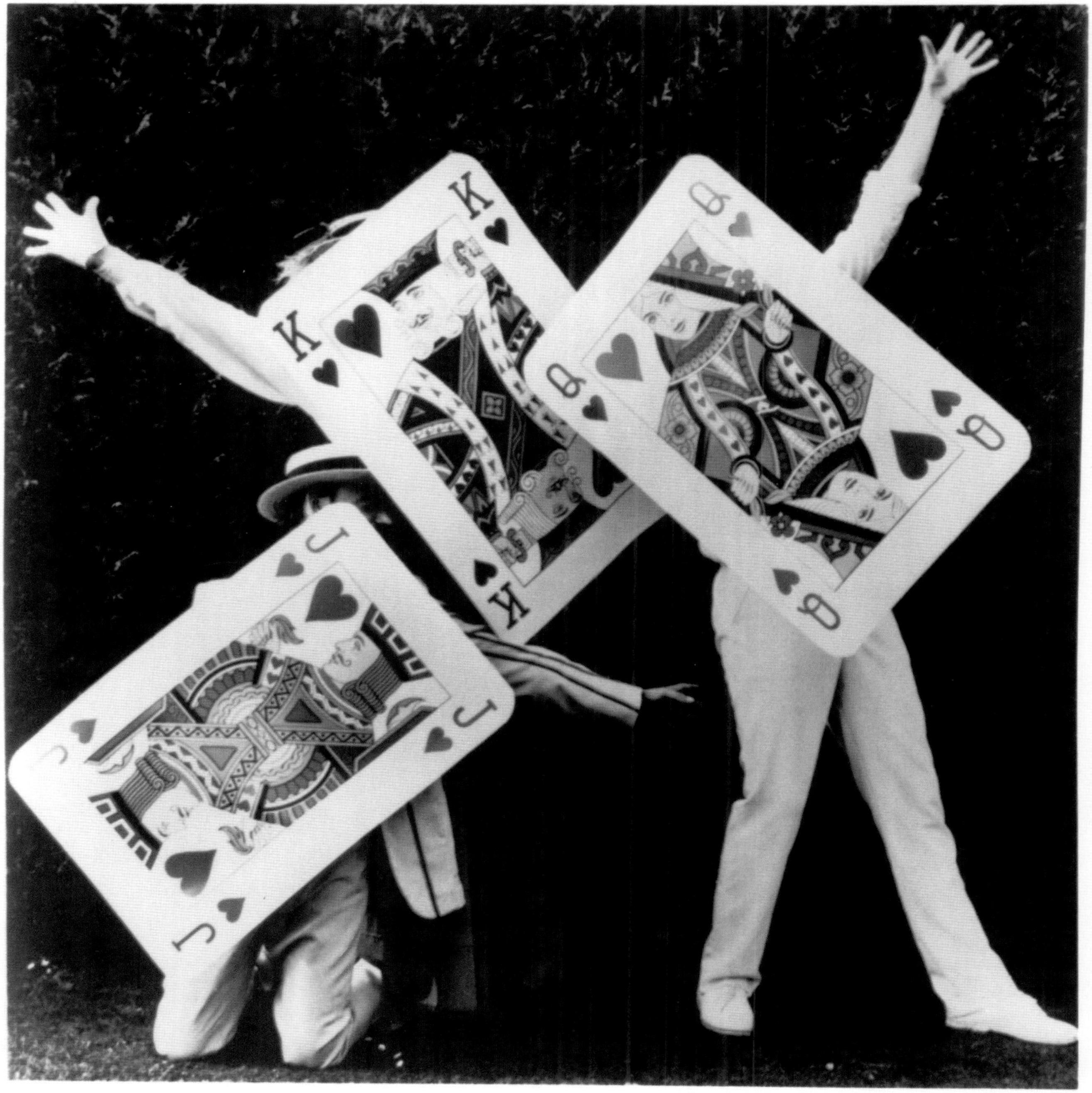

THE ART OF NOISE

Chrysalis

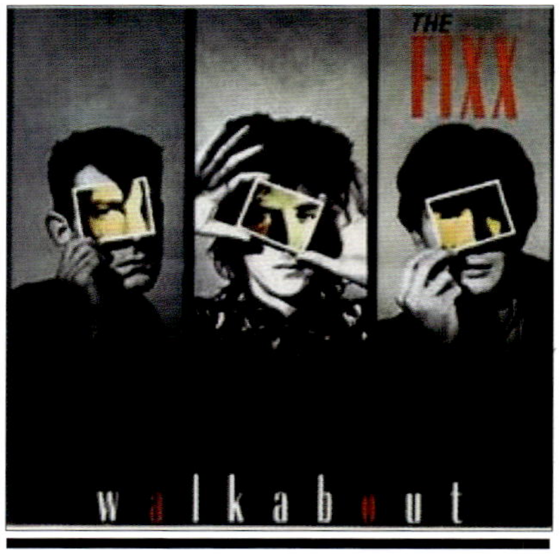

Billboard 200: *Walkabout* (#30)
Billboard Hot 100: "Secret Separation" (#19)

The Fixx kept its sound intact for *Walkabout,* featuring the soothing summertime single "Secret Separation."

THERE HAD been a high attrition rate among the post-new wave generation of rock bands, but one of the survivors was the Fixx. The band's breakthrough singles, "One Thing Leads to Another," "Saved by Zero," "Red Skies," "Stand or Fall" and "Deeper and Deeper" had become radio standards.

Walkabout, the British band's fourth album, added to that commercial legacy. Two factors separated the album. One was the studio touch of Rupert Hine, who once again had captured the band's bright rhythms and ringing guitar sound in a slick yet subtle setting.

"We've gotten so much from the relationship—he's a musician himself, aware of what music can do, and he keeps up those ideals," founding member Adam Woods (drums) said. The other new twist in evidence on *Walkabout* was a more positive lyrical stance. "My work in the past has been quite gloomy," vocalist Cy Curnin admitted with a smile. The difference? The birth of his first child (a son) imbued him with a growing sense of hope, optimism and belief in self.

"It changed my whole view—while one future ends, another goes on," he reflected. "It suddenly hit me that there's a danger in bringing everything down, because there's always something to put in its place.

"We also took a long period of time off. We separated and traveled on our own, and we saw how things are changing all the time. Before, we traveled around but we never really experienced where we were. I started writing constructively, because that's how I was feeling and that's what people need in their lives. The media isn't going to touch certain things. To them, good news is made up by bad events, because good events don't make good news. So it left me with a whole new spectrum to use as inspiration."

The impressive result was the hypnotic "Secret Separation," a No. 1 hit on *Billboard*'s Album Rock Tracks chart. The maturing five-piece band was settled in for the long haul.

"You can say you're going for a hit album or a Top 40 single or whatever, but in the end you're going for overall popularity regardless of the channel for sale," Woods said. "As long as people get to hear your work, that's the main thing." ■

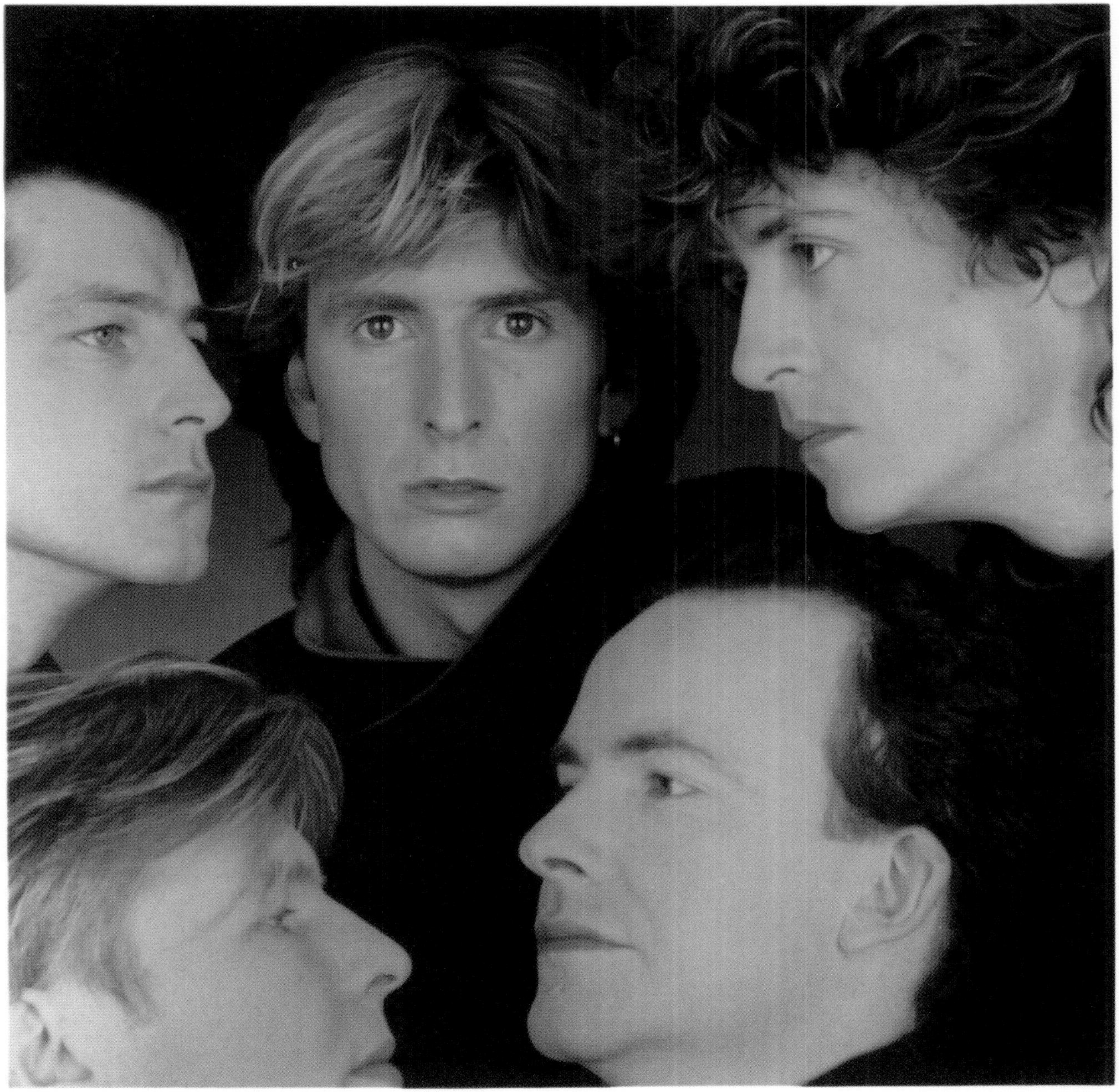

THE
FIXX

.MCA RECORDS

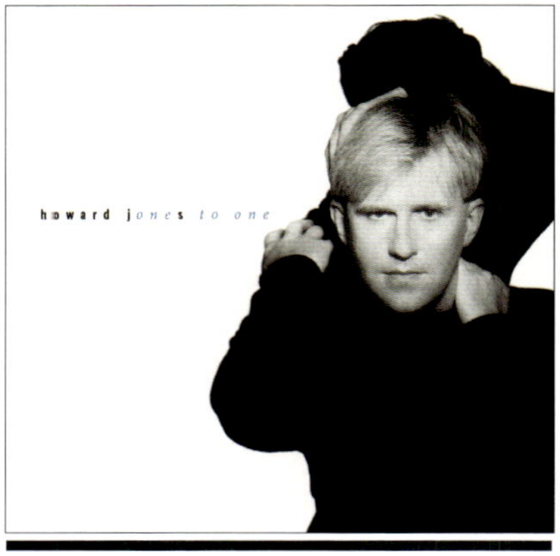

Billboard 200: *One to One* (#59)
Billboard Hot 100: "You Know I Love You...Don't You?" (#17);
"All I Want" (#76)

One to One, a more reflective work, brought Howard Jones another hit with "You Know I Love You...Don't You?"

RIDING INTO America on a spate of press clippings and the success of his 1984 debut album, Howard Jones was hailed as a musician espousing the positive nature of the human condition. On his first US tour, he was a one-man aural whirlwind, a skinny English elf with a cockatoo coiffure, controlling his trusty array of sophisticated electronic keyboards. A mime provided diversions and visual song interpretations.

The techno-pop artist had since established himself as a fixture on the US charts, offering synthesizer-based songs that were danceable without sounding disco-fied, thought-provoking without being pretentious—"What Is Love?," "New Song," "Life in One Day," "Like to Get to Know You Well" and "Things Can Only Get Better."

Jones' technical abilities, which reflected his early background in classical music, had attracted a series of capable producers. He recorded his first two albums—*Human's Lib* and *Dream into Action*—with Rupert Hine (the Fixx, Tina Turner). "With all the new gear coming out, it's so exciting and fun to make records in ways nobody has done before," Jones admitted. "The piano has always been my instrument, but I've made a conscious attempt to write music that's dressed in the musical clothes of the day."

In 1986, Jones released *Action Replay*, an EP of remixes that featured a new version of "No One Is to Blame." Genesis and solo star Phil Collins re-recorded and mixed the song over the course of two weekends to give Jones a Top 5 single, his biggest US hit. On *One to One*, his third album, Jones collaborated with Arif Mardin, the famed R&B producer. The album yielded "You Know I Love You...Don't You?"

Jones' lyrics continued to reflect his philosophy of practical idealism. "It's good to be aware of what's going on in the world around you, but you can have the greatest effect within your immediate environment," he mused. "If you're going to have a go at trying to change things for the better, you've got to start by affecting the people you work with, at school, in your life, and upholding some kind of values.

The mild-mannered Brit had gleaned enough studio know-how to start producing his own albums. "I think I've got the confidence now," he said. "And that's all production is, trusting your instincts. I might need some help on the dance re-mixes and stuff like that, but if I do, I'll be more than willing to throw up the white flag for help."

Jones' fans had eased him into stardom. "I didn't know back then what my career would be like, but I'm quite happy where it's at," he concluded. "The thing that makes me the happiest is that my audience seems to have grown along with me." ■

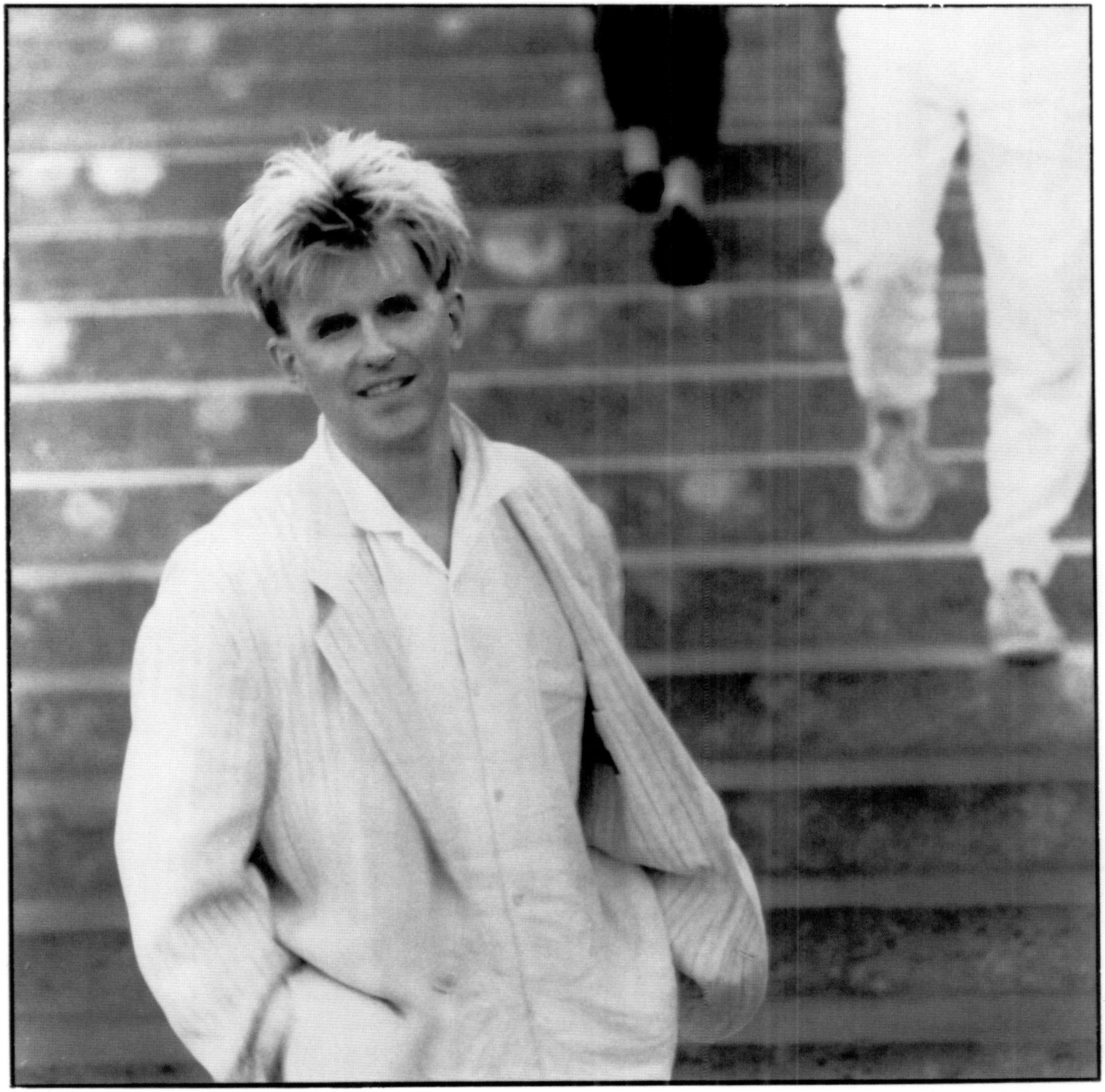

PHOTO CREDIT: SIMON FOWLER/1986

howard jones

ELEKTRA

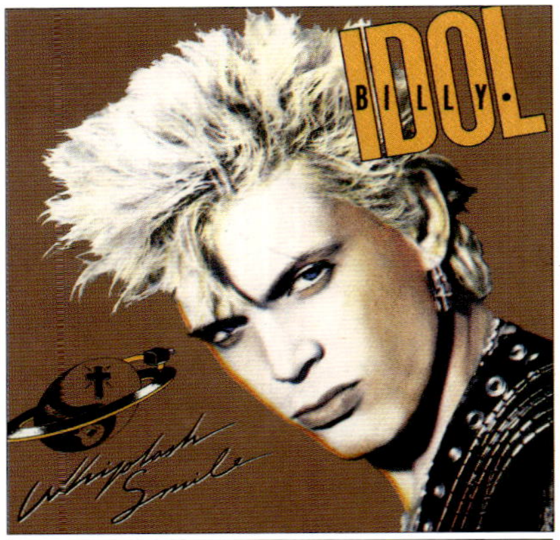

Billboard 200: *Whiplash Smile* (#6)
Billboard Hot 100: "To Be a Lover" (#6); "Don't Need a Gun" (#37); "Sweet Sixteen" (#20)

Billy Idol came out of hiding, and *Whiplash Smile* earned rhapsodic reviews as well as raves from his peers.

EMERGING FROM the London punk rock scene in the Seventies as a member of Generation X, Billy Idol subsequently embarked on a solo career and, with the 1983 breakthrough *Rebel Yell*, became one of MTV's leading hitmakers, resulting in international recognition.

Then he disappeared. Rumors flew that the former William Broad was seriously ill, even that he had died mysteriously. But the singer finally put such talk to rest, returning with a new album. On *Whiplash Smile*, Idol's collaboration with guitarist Steve Stevens yielded another batch of snarling, metal-edged dance-rock tracks. But lyrically, Idol could be heard probing his personal emotions, no longer content with the empty raised-fist sentiments of his early material. Why?

"Ever since we stopped the 'Rebel Yell' tour, I've been fighting to stay me," Idol said. "I don't want to stop being a normal person. It's not good to be a rock star all the time. There's been a lot of pressure to put out records faster, but I told everyone they're going to have to wait. I'm gonna have to live and do my record and be someone for real.

"I've recently tried to deal with more things that I think about personally. My old manager has drifted off, and I haven't seen him for a year and a half. Me and my girlfriend kind of split up—she went off to do this career thing. I can sing about those things. I'm not the only one they happen to. Everybody loses something they love."

Idol ended the album with a fabulous cover of William Bell's "To Be a Lover," a song he first heard covered by reggae artist George Faith. "I did forget to be a lover," he said. "I was always eager to push everything away to make my dreams come true. When it came to the end of the album, what did I do? I recorded my favorite song. It showed me where I wanted to go."

Idol's fans had seemingly accepted his maturation, as "To Be a Lover" cracked the Top 10. But he claimed his peace of mind was no longer dependent on maintaining commercial acceptance. "It doesn't matter about money, having it or not having it," he said. "I'm still living on the edge—my edge, which is whether I'm down or whether I'm up." ■

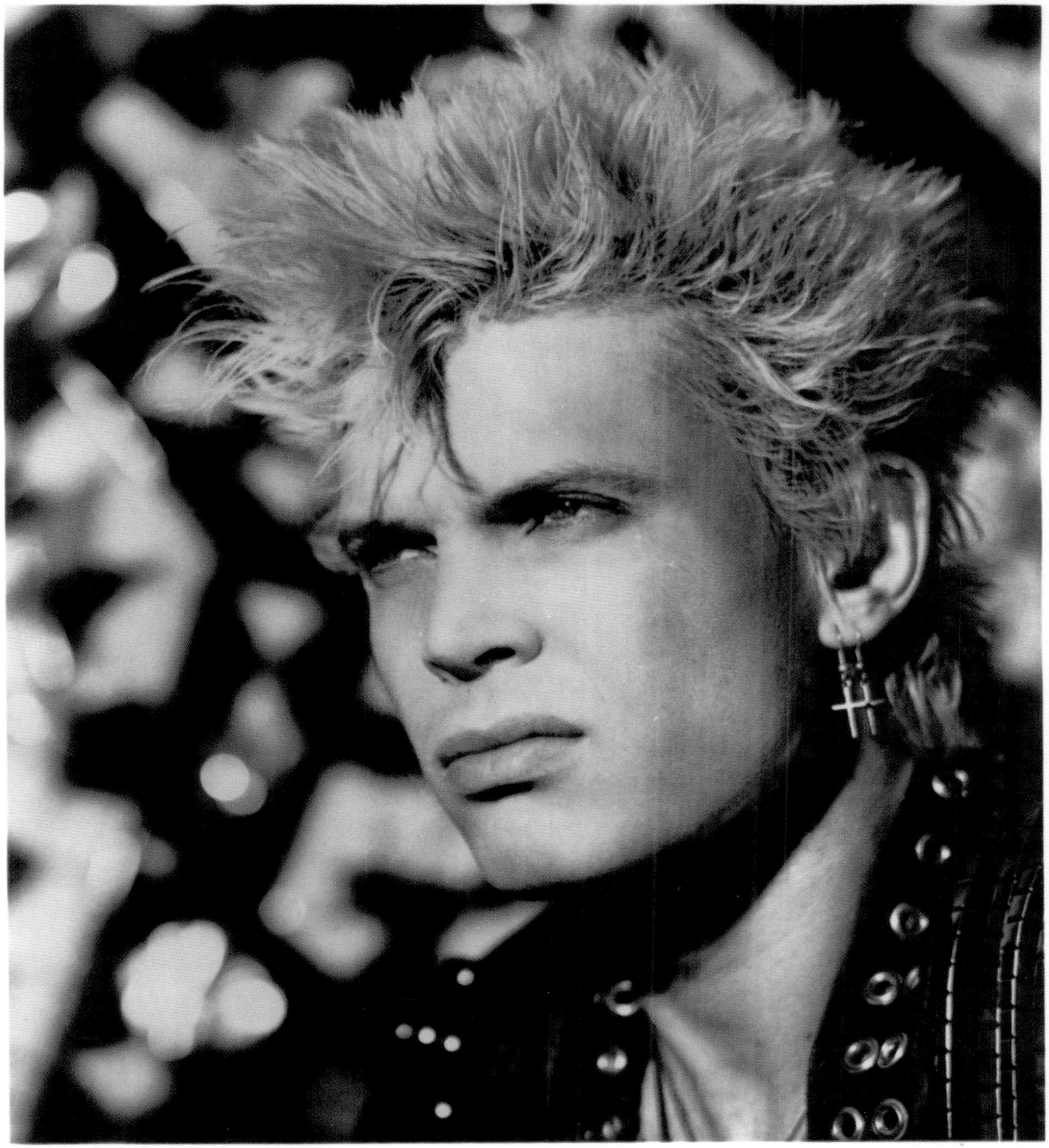

Photo Credit: Albert Sanchez/Visage

BILLY IDOL

BILLY IDOL

Chrysalis™

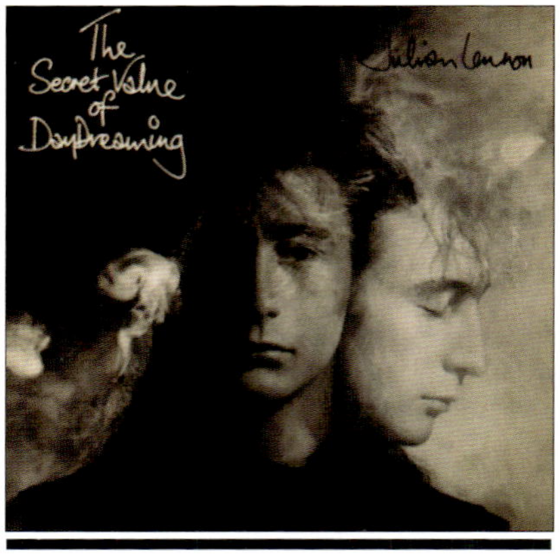

Billboard 200: *The Secret Value of Daydreaming* (#32)
Billboard Hot 100: "Stick Around" (#32)

In Julian Lennon's *The Secret Value of Daydreaming*, the follow-up to his hit debut, "Stick Around" stood out.

AFTER JOHN Lennon's murder in 1980, his son, Julian Lennon, decided to follow in his footsteps and begin a singing career. His 1984 debut *Valotte* spawned two hits (the title track and "Too Late for Goodbyes") and earned him a Grammy nomination for Best New Artist.

But the young Lennon found himself in a no-win situation. He was committed to developing his own skills as a tunesmith, but he knew—and the public knew—that there was no denying his vocal and stylistic similarities to his father. He could accept or deny his heritage—either way, someone was bound to accuse him of copping out. He also surprised many by going on tour following the release of *Valotte*, so early in his career.

"I was surprised as hell, too," he said with a laugh. "I had decided in my head to go out after the second album, when I would have more material behind me. But the first album was doing so well, my agent said, 'Listen, this would be a good time to grab them, while you've got their attention.' It was a pretty short decision time—like two days—because of the scheduling that had to be done. So I thought, 'Yeah, I'll push myself,' and I did it.

"And I'm glad that I did, because now, just two years down the line, I feel comfortable onstage. Whereas if I hadn't done it, now I'd be going through all that nervousness, being scared out of my brains. Obviously, I've had to learn about performing, but it hasn't felt like a learning process. It's just a question of becoming more comfortable in your surroundings, of the situations you have to deal with."

Lennon's *The Secret Value of Daydreaming* reached the Top 30, but the album didn't come close to matching the success of *Valotte,* although the single "Stick Around" was a No. 1 single on the album rock charts. When the follow-ups "This Is My Day" and "Want Your Body" failed in the market, Lennon made a big decision to disappear for a year.

"I'm going to get out of the limelight for a bit, make people a bit inquisitive again, wonder where I've gone and what I'm doing," he explained. "I'm going to listen to other music a bit more—get around, try a few directions instead of the basic boy/girl stories. I'll think things over and hopefully write some hot stuff that will shock the hell out of people again.

"I've got plenty of time ahead of me, although I'll be yearning to do things while I see everything else going on—all the other bands playing, all the other records coming out. That's the only problem—I'll want to come back after a week!" ■

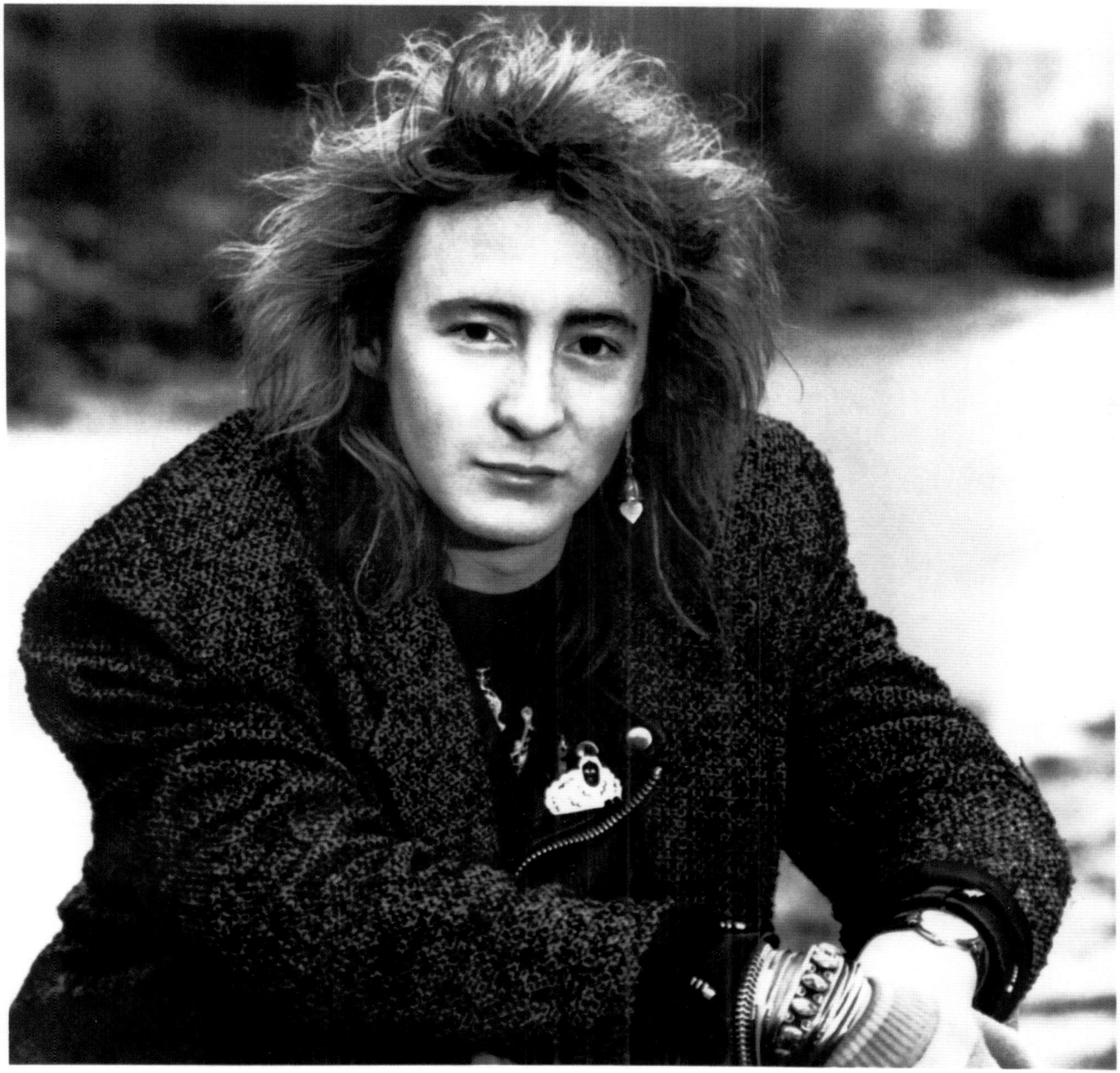

Julian Lennon

ATLANTIC

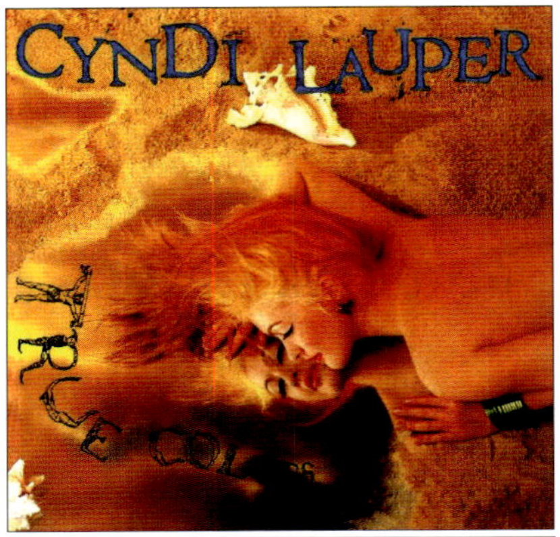

Billboard 200: *True Colors* (#4)
Billboard Hot 100: "True Colors" (No. 1); "Change of Heart" (#3); "What's Going On" (#12); "Boy Blue" (#71)

Cyndi Lauper managed to sustain her instant fame with *True Colors*, deemed to be a solid sophomore effort.

IN 1984, Cyndi Lauper's first solo record made her a household name—*She's So Unusual* sold more than 3 million copies and spun off four consecutive Top 5 singles. With her remarkably big voice, quirky sartorial style and zany exuberance, she smashed the stereotype for female vocalists and won countless hearts.

The massive exposure eventually posed a classic dilemma—what would Lauper do for an encore? Was she merely another of pop music's flashes-in-the-pan, the loony female behind "Girls Just Wanna Have Fun?" Or was she an artist with long-range potential, with the insight to write more songs like "Time After Time"?

With the *True Colors* album, Lauper's status as one of rock's premier vocalists was reaffirmed. The record accurately reflected her sensitivity and professionalism, traits she'd worked years on developing. The title track was a No. 1 single, and "Change of Heart" peaked at #3. She was casting an eye toward future projects, "looking for surprises that will make for a great experience. That's what I look forward to when I do anything."

Hence she was making her acting debut in the movie *Vibes* alongside Jeff Goldblum. She planned to marry her manager David Wolff as soon as they found the time—"We don't want to wake up the next day and have to go to a sound check." She continued her fundraising efforts for multiple sclerosis research with former wrestling maven Captain Lou Albano.

"When I was 17, I was trying to get a job and not doing too good," she concluded. "There was this older woman, a Gray Panther, the most beautiful woman I'd ever seen. She said, 'You wanna go to Europe, you wanna go here and there—travel and see your country. Experience the people.' And I never forgot that. Now I'm doing what I want, singing across the country and seeing a lot of ethnic backgrounds and colors. And I'm finding out what makes this country great." ■

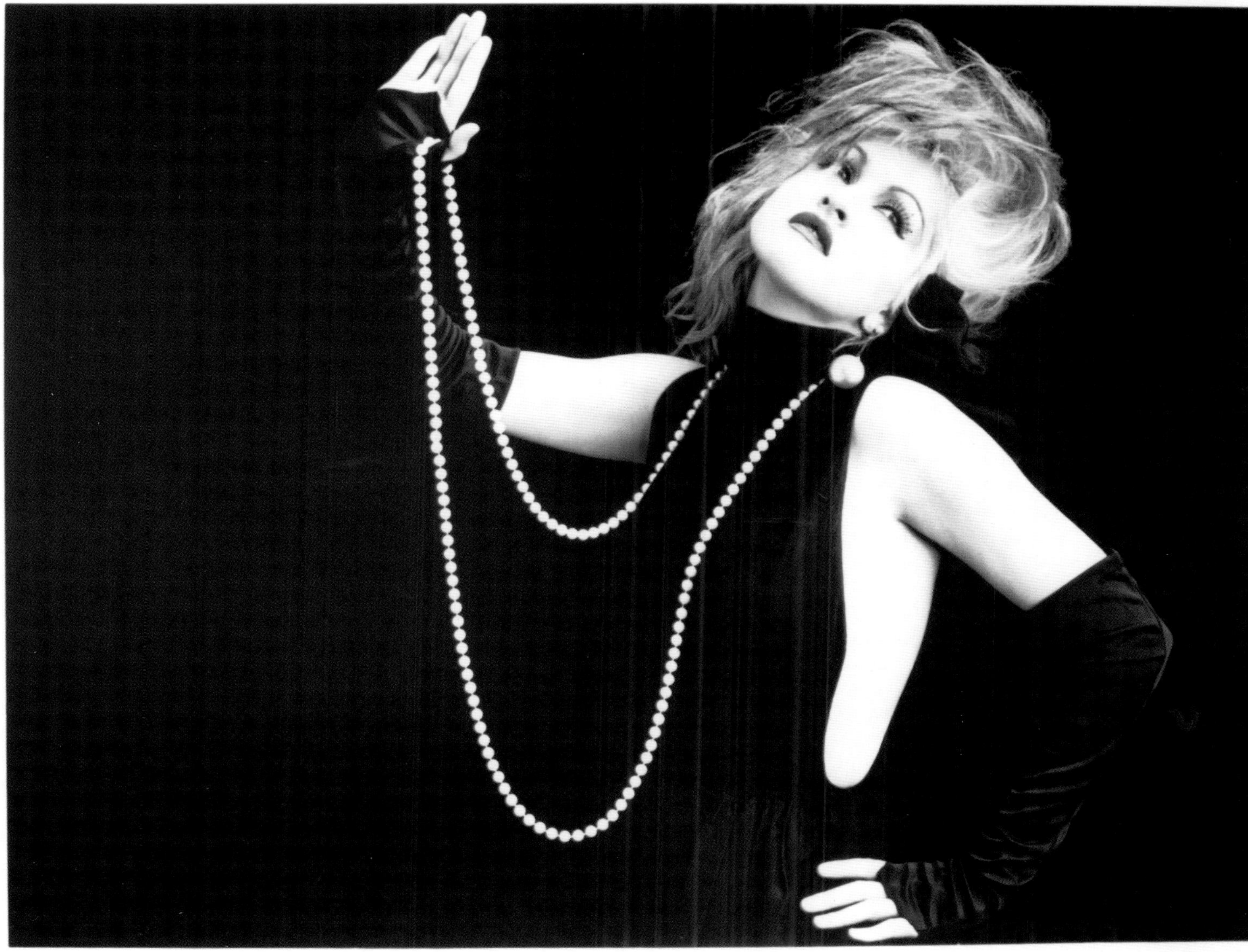

Photo: Annie Leibovitz

CYNDI LAUPER

Portrait

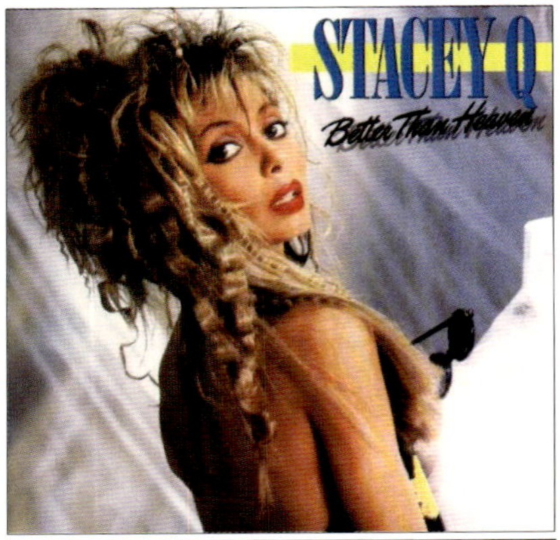

Billboard 200: *Better Than Heaven* (#59)
Billboard Hot 100: "Two of Hearts" (#3); "We Connect" (#35)

Creating catchy, high-tech dance fare, Stacey Q found favor with a top-selling pop single, "Two of Hearts."

WITH "TWO of Hearts" and "We Connect," Stacey Q scored a pair of high-energy dance hits—a surprising development for someone who came to singing almost by accident. Born Stacey Swain, a native of Southern California, she had always wanted to dance, and she attended classical ballet school for 11 years. "I remember asking my mother for lessons when I was three," she insisted, "but she made me wait until I was five."

A close friend, record producer Jon St. James, became the catalyst for her recording career. "In 1981 I had just come off the road riding elephants with Ringling Bros. Barnum & Bailey Circus, and I had a really good job with Marriott Hotels," she recalled. "Some friends were recording in a studio owned by Jon. I started cleaning up after his sessions, and one day he asked me to help him out on background vocals. It wasn't like they called me up with a job—I was just there."

St. James produced Stacey's brand of "technodance" music, as he called it, catching her Madonna-ish sultriness. She began recording for several independent labels under the names Q (the moniker was derived from the gadget-making James Bond character), the band SSQ and, finally, Stacey Q. "Two of Hearts" became an essential ingredient of every club's playlist, a major label picked up on its early signs of success, and the response was worldwide—#3 on the *Billboard* Hot 100 and the Top 20 in seven other countries.

The song led the way for another dance smash, "We Connect," and her debut album, *Better Than Heaven,* passed the gold mark in US sales. Stacey Q had the opportunity to perform both singles on the television sitcom *The Facts of Life*, where she guest-starred as Cinnamon, an aspiring singer. ■

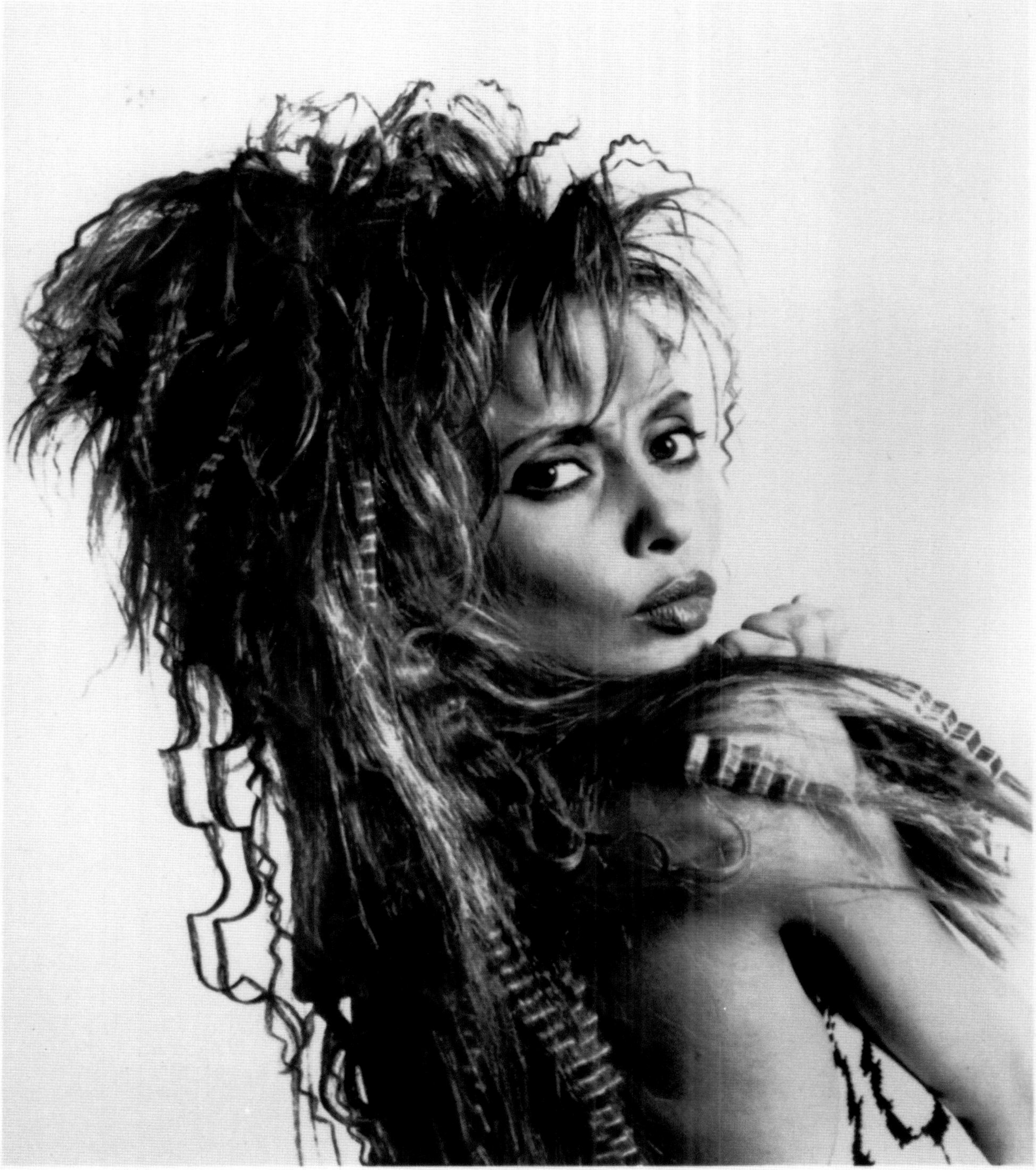

STACEY Q

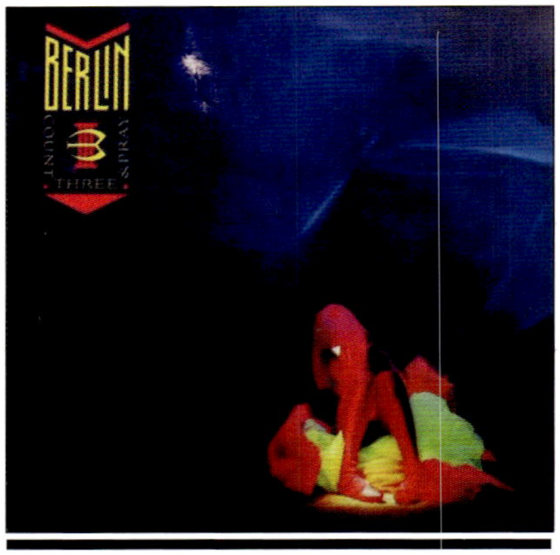

Billboard 200: *Count Three & Pray* (#61)
Billboard Hot 100: "Take My Breath Away" (No. 1); "Like Flames" (#82)

"You Take My Breath Away" suddenly became Berlin's biggest single and a prodigious international success.

OF THE various rock acts that launched careers during the early Eighties synth-pop heyday, Berlin seemed most qualified to become a trivia question. Granted, the band debuted auspiciously with "Sex (I'm A…)," a danceable ditty that also doubled as audio pornography—singer Terri Nunn recited a litany of rude moans and tasteless lyrics that attracted plenty of attention. And the Los Angeles-based band managed to produce another album (*Lovelife*) and single ("No More Words"), while a tour revealed Nunn to be an energetic, hard-working performer instead of a little tease.

But when more than two years passed out of the charts and out of the limelight (an eternity in pop music terms), Berlin was accorded flash-in-the-pan status. That standing changed, however, thanks to *Top Gun*, 1986's top-grossing movie. Berlin performed a song for the soundtrack titled "You Take My Breath Away"—and the hauntingly mawkish ballad hit No. 1 on the charts and went on to take home the Academy Award for Best Original Song. The band duly returned with a new album, *Count Three and Pray*.

"It's just been a long process of trying to get it right," Berlin founder John Crawford explained. "Our troubles started when we got done touring in 1984." Three members of Berlin quit when recordings made with the touring group proved to be disappointing. The remaining trio—Crawford, drummer Rob Brill and the singing Nunn—began re-evaluating Berlin. They traveled to England and linked up with Andy Richards, one of the British masterminds behind the ZZT/Trevor Horn studio sound (Art of Noise, Frankie Goes to Hollywood). The goal was to combine a high-tech manner of recording with the live feel of a human rhythm section, but five months in the studio failed to yield the desired results—"When it came down to decision-making, Andy couldn't relate to doing a track without using a machine."

The majority of songs were finally rerecorded in Los Angeles with producer Bob Ezrin (Alice Cooper, Pink Floyd). Guitar parts were contributed by guests ranging from Ted Nugent to the Cars' Elliot Easton to Pink Floyd's David Gilmour.

Count Three and Pray also included "You Take My Breath Away," penned by Giorgio Moroder, the band's former producer. Rumors persisted that Berlin was a last-ditch choice to record the song.

"I heard CBS was pressing for one of their acts to do it (CBS Records had the *Top Gun* soundtrack rights; Berlin recorded for rival Geffen Records)," Crawford admitted. "They wanted Aimee Mann from 'Til Tuesday to do it. But we were finally offered 'Danger Zone' (which wound up being a hit for Kenny Loggins) or 'You Take My Breath Away.' We chose 'Breath' because Terri obviously sounds great singing it—she gets you in that dark, weird mood.

"I'm proud that the song sounds different than the rest of Top 40—it's really worlds away from what we were doing. Also, a No. 1 single's a good way to come back." ■

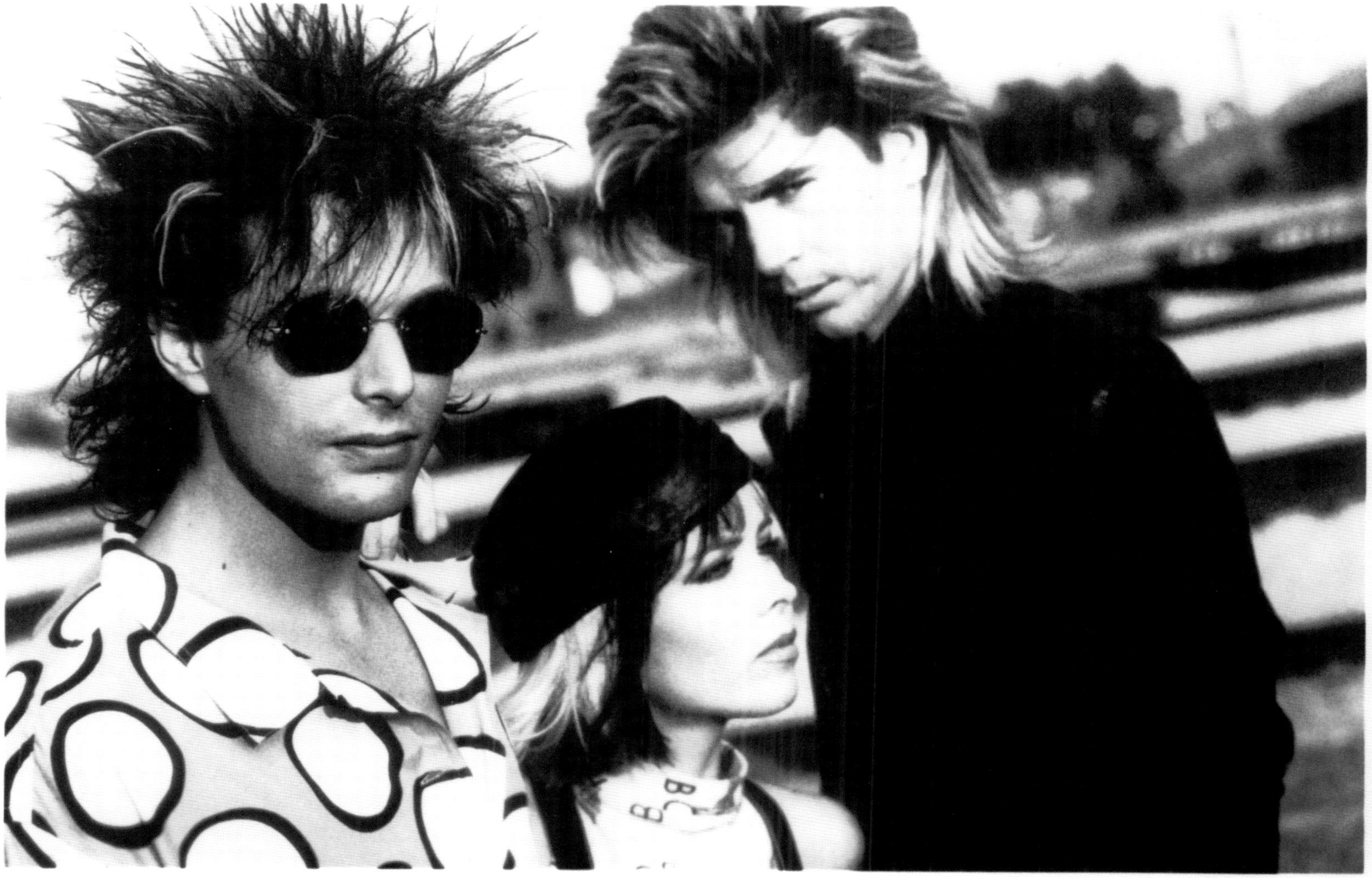

BERLIN

M.F.C. MANAGEMENT
1428 So. Sherbourne Drive
Los Angeles, CA 90035
(213) 652-6993

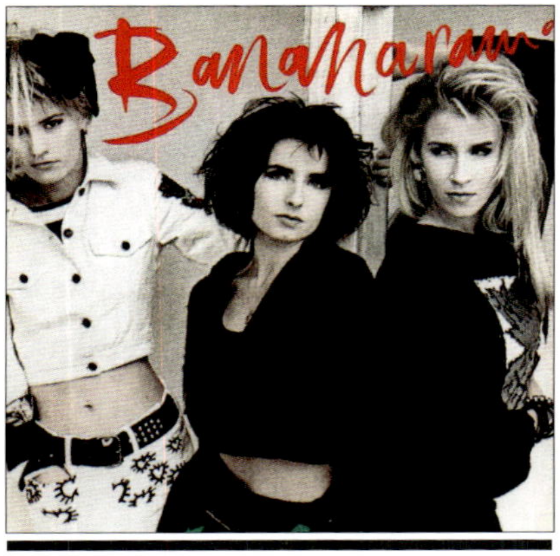

Billboard 200: *True Confessions* (#15)
Billboard Hot 100: "Venus" (No. 1); "More Than Physical" (#73); "A Trick of the Night" (#76)

The girl group Bananarama fashioned a worldwide blockbuster with a dance-pop cover version of "Venus."

HERALDED AS one of the most successful all-girl groups in British history, Bananarama had scored nine Top 40 UK hits in four years. Childhood friends Keren Woodward and Sarah Dallin joined forces with Siobhan Fahey in 1979 when they were just 18, first gaining notoriety in London singing with Fun Boy Three, a popular English band that had splintered off from the Specials. FB3 later returned the favor by producing and backing Bananarama on the girls' earliest singles.

"We just had the cheek to have a go at it," Dallin said. "Punk was long gone by then, but it was that scene that enabled us to get up and try it."

For their first real album, the three Bananarama members teamed up with producers Tony Swain and Steve Jolley (of Spandau Ballet fame). Over lush, highly arranged backing, they crooned such UK smashes as "Shy Boy" and "Robert De Niro's Waiting," and scored an American winner when "Cruel Summer" was heard in the film, *The Karate Kid*, in 1984.

The hit-making team of Stock, Aitman & Waterman (Dead or Alive, Rick Astley) programmed the group's next series of dance-oriented singles, and a hot-blooded interpretation of Shocking Blue's 1969 hit, "Venus," became Bananarama's first US chart-topper. The assortment of producers had yielded little uniformity of sound, but the charming ensemble's vocals and mock-Supremes arrangements provided distinctive character.

Yet the trio battled the perception that someone was behind Bananarama providing songs and fashion.

"I find it a great insult when people can't believe that three reasonably attractive girls can actually have any brains and hold down a career of their own," Dallin stated. "We put Bananarama together—the videos and the way we look are all our ideas. We co-write with our producers because we don't play any instruments, but we're not bimbos or puppets.

"Although the first few years, even though we were immediately successful, it was hard to think of this as a career. We managed ourselves and were very disorganized. Now it feels right." ■

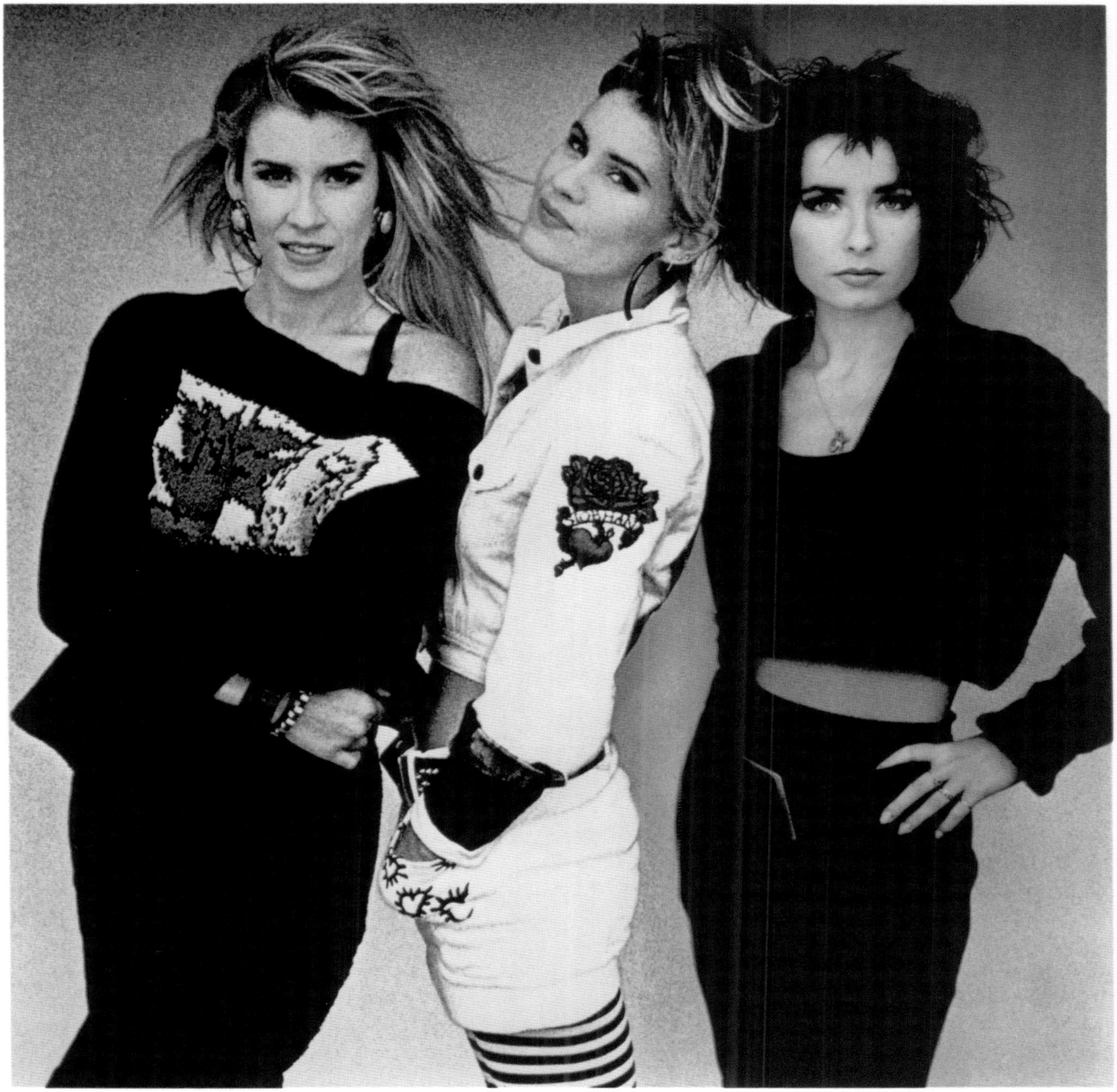

BANANARAMA

LONDON

PolyGram Records

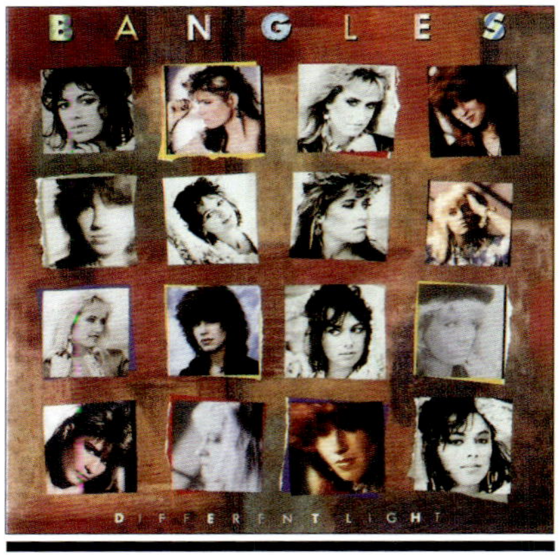

Billboard 200: *Different Light* (#2)
Billboard Hot 100: "Manic Monday" (#2);
"If She Knew What She Wants" (#29);
"Walk Like an Egyptian" (No. 1);
"Walking Down Your Street" (#11)

The ebullient Bangles exploded with *Different Light*, featuring "Manic Monday" and "Walk Like an Egyptian."

WHO WERE the Bangles? The general pop audience was aware of the band through the lilting "Manic Monday" (a hit penned by "Christopher," a pseudonym for Prince) and "Walk Like an Egyptian," which topped the singles chart for six weeks. But the Bangles still found themselves having to explain who they *weren't*.

"It's gone from, 'Oh, you're women, you're from Los Angeles—you're the Go-Go's!' to 'Oh, I heard someone say you're like the Beatles—you're the Beatles!' to 'Hey, what is all this Sixties stuff?'" guitarist Vicki Peterson lamented. "But we expected it, and we'll deal with it. Hopefully we'll gain our own identity."

The members of the Bangles—Peterson, her sister Debbi Peterson on drums, guitarist Susanna Hoffs and bassist Michael "Micki" Steele—knew from the beginning that a rock band composed of four females would be cause for undue attention (which is where the Go-Go's comparisons came in). But over the course of two albums—1984's *All Over the Place* and 1986's *Different Light*—the Bangles had exhibited first-rate songwriting and rich, four-part vocal harmonies (which is where the Beatles/Sixties comparisons came in).

"But the whole Sixties thing has always been there—we can't help it," Peterson said. "It's what we first learned to love when we were very small children listening to the radio, which our parents had on 24 hours a day. It's like if you're raised a Catholic—it never quite leaves you. We're not trying to sound like 1966—there's no point in that. But when you pick up a guitar, something is going to come out of you that you're comfortable with."

So who were the Bangles, really? "I would like to be perceived as a rock 'n' roll band that plays pop music," Peterson replied. "When we're onstage, we do a lot of running around, a lot of sweating, a lot of screaming. It's fun and energetic. But on the other hand, we're playing songs within a pop structure with intertwining vocals and harmonies going over the top of noisy guitars."

The Bangles easily proved Peterson's point. While the defunct Go-Go's came across in concert as a rock 'n' roll slumber party, the Bangles were much more straightforward, balancing their feminine voices with a gutsy guitar sound.

"People who only know us because of 'Manic Monday' are usually surprised to see a band that rocks out," Peterson said, "and there's also a ton of folk rock in us that hasn't shown itself yet. When Susanna, Micki and I were in high school, the in thing to do was play a guitar and sing Joni Mitchell songs. There were some girls who knew every John Denver lick. We'd go to the park and teach each other new chords. But we didn't iron our hair—we were allowed to look like Carole King." ■

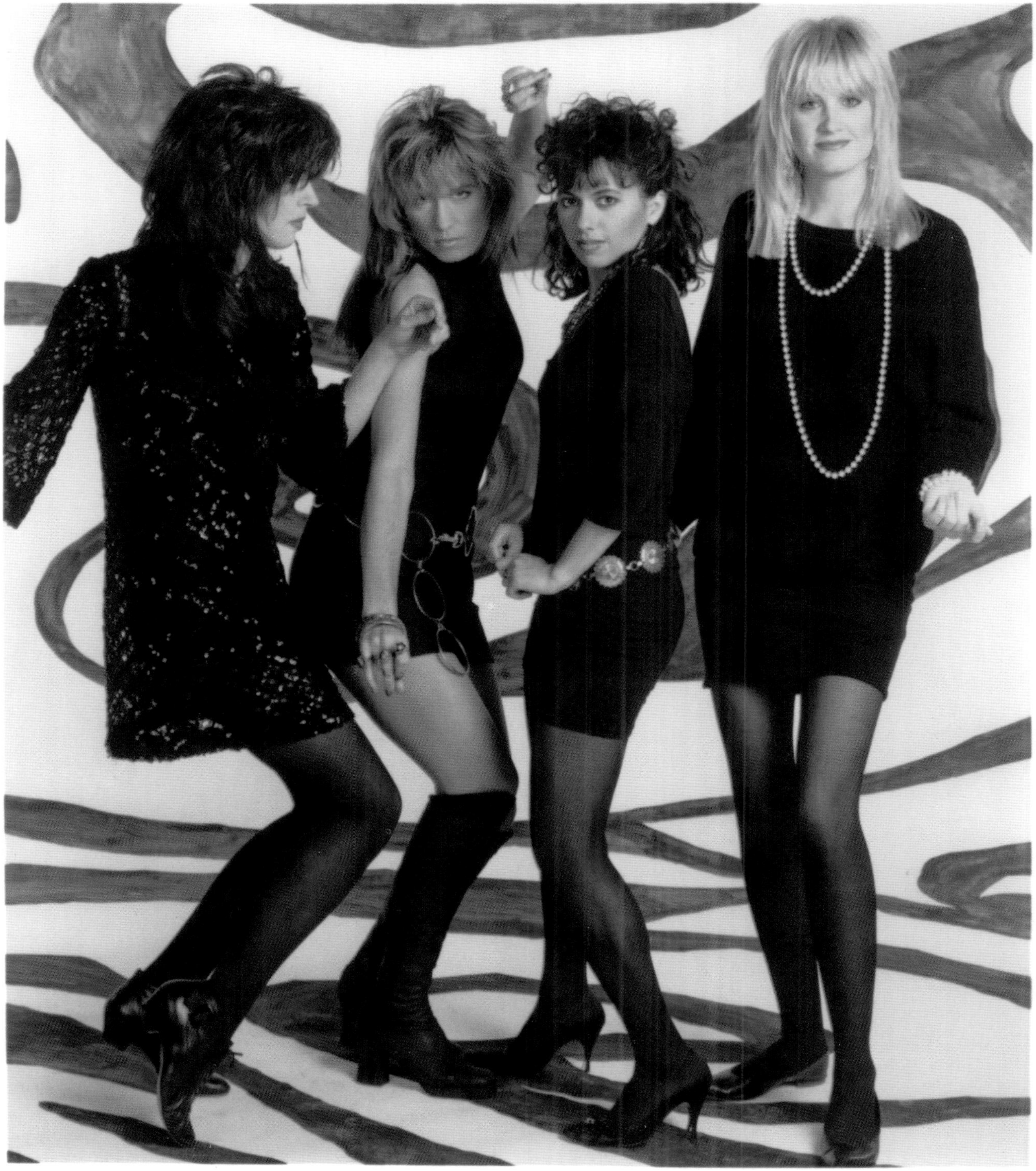

Photo Credit: Raul Vega

Michael Steele Vicki Peterson Susanna Hoffs Debbi Peterson

BANGLES

Columbia

8512

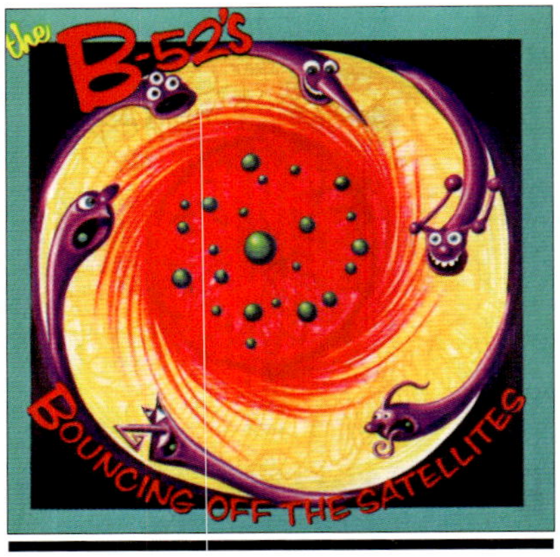

Billboard 200: *Bouncing off the Satellites* (#85)

The B-52's eventually loosed the *Bouncing off the Satellites* album following guitarist Ricky Wilson's passing.

EVER SINCE "Rock Lobster" appeared on the musical menu in 1979, the B-52's had reigned as the new wave scene's masters of kitsch. Musically, they pitted surreal lyrics against sci-fi/beach-blanket rhythms, revving up their own highly danceable 160-beats-per-minute formula. In their polyester duds and tacky wigs ("B-52" was Southern slang for a bouffant hairdo), the Georgia bohemians devised a fractured Sixties junk-store look.

But after 1983's musically adventurous *Whammy!* album failed to generate the expected response, the B-52's disappeared from recording for three years. The group returned with *Bouncing off the Satellites*, and the question arose: Was this still the trashiest band extant? Indubitably, considering such efforts as "Girl from Ipanema Goes to Greenland."

"We're still hip," band member Fred Schneider said with feigned amazement. "But we don't perceive our music as throwaway songs—we put a lot into it. Some songs are sillier than others, but there's more to it than novelty numbers."

Certainly, the record represented a concerted move to dispel the offbeat image they'd fostered. "Our music is a novelty in that it's not what you normally hear, Top 40 schlock," Schneider admitted. "But this album has ballads, some environmental things, just different ways of working together. And that's why people find us constantly new."

"Summer of Love" benefited from an exceptional dance remix, but the mirthful songs and nutty cover artwork belied some heavyhearted feelings, as *Bouncing off the Satellites* closed a chapter on the B-52's career—guitarist Ricky Wilson died from AIDS-related illness in October 1985 following the recording session.

"He was like family—we'd been together 10 years," Schneider said. "The album would have been out last December, but when Ricky passed away, we weren't interested and we put things off. The record had more of a sunny, summer feel, so we waited until this year."

With Wilson's death, the B-52's had been expected to go on hiatus, but Schneider and the other remaining B-52's—Keith Strickland, Kate Pierson and Cindy Wilson, Ricky's sister—were intent on forging ahead.

"With Ricky gone, we weren't really in the frame of mind to do a tour," Schneider said. "We didn't know how to replace Ricky—we couldn't replace Ricky. All of us were five parts of a whole, and with Ricky gone it really leaves something missing. But we're going to start working on new material real soon. We'll try different things and come up with something. If people still want us, we'll be back." ■

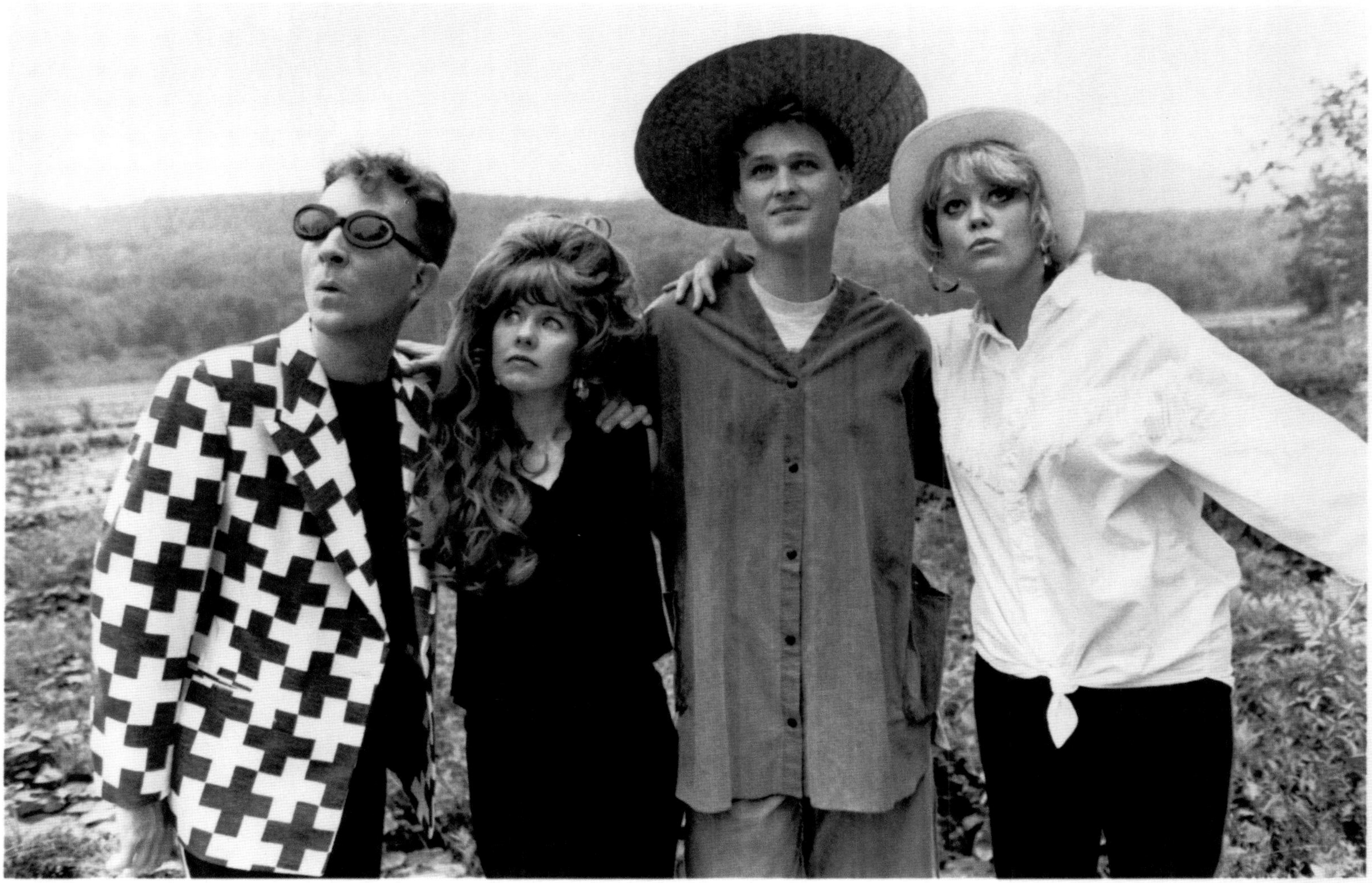

PHOTO CREDIT LAURA LEVINE

the B-52's

WARNER BROS.

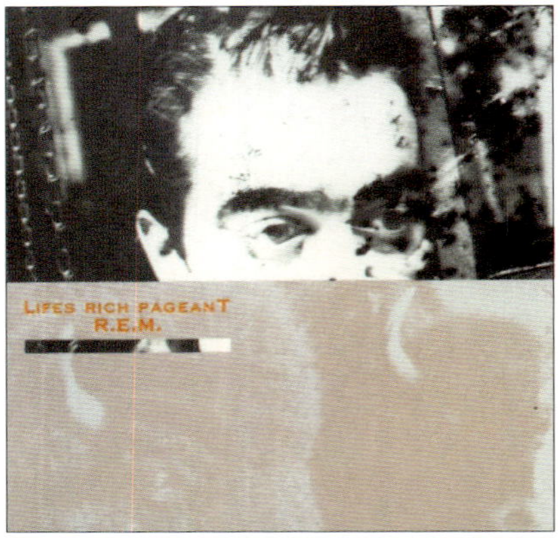

Billboard 200: *Lifes Rich Pageant* (#21)
Billboard Hot 100: "Fall on Me" (#94)

On R.E.M.'s *Lifes Rich Pageant*, a milestone album, the underground darlings learned to rock with confidence.

SINCE THEIR inception as a band in 1982, the members of R.E.M.—four college chums from Athens, Georgia—had been critical favorites. But some observers had grown impatient for the group to top *Murmur*, its signature debut album. One major rock magazine claimed the band's appeal had diminished considerably now that the guys had reached young adulthood.

Others targeted the choice of new producer Don Gehman (of John Cougar Mellencamp fame), who gave R.E.M. its best shot to date for an accessible record with the *Lifes Rich Pageant* album. Gehman sharpened the drum sound and cleaned up Michael Stipe's pebbles-in-the-mouth vocal style, and the aural demystification miffed those who previously heralded the band's obscurantist tendencies.

But the members were nothing but honest about their increasing fortunes. The single "Fall on Me" garnered them the most radio airplay of their career, another breakthrough for a band interested in creating a body of work, building its reputation through releases every year.

Mike Mills, R.E.M.'s ever-friendly bass player, set the record straight. For one thing, he said, the use of Gehman wasn't a decision based on mimicking Mellencamp's hit sound. "That had very little to do with it," Mills insisted. "Once we met Don and did some preproduction down in Athens, that just did it for me. It was obvious that the guy's approach was in line with ours—working with the band instead of on the band. We did want to have an edge, to rock a little more."

And the band maintained its underground charm, considering the single "Superman," an obscurity from the Clique circa 1969 (the act's one hit was the Tommy James-produced "Sugar on Sunday"). "Superman" featured Mills in his first official lead singing role, but he argued the call. "Hey, I sing on almost every song," he said.

"Peter (Buck, guitarist) handed me the record about five years ago and said, 'Listen to this, you're gonna love it,'" Mills recalled. "I don't know where he got it—he'll buy anything with a cool title. We figured we were the only people in the world who knew about it, so Bill (Berry, drummer) and I did the song in our cover band, the Corncobwebs. Michael heard us rehearsing and he thought we'd written it, but we had to tell him differently."

So no matter what the band's detractors were saying, it was business as usual for R.E.M. "I don't see us going away," Mills said. "If we can keep writing or finding the songs, we'll be okay." ■

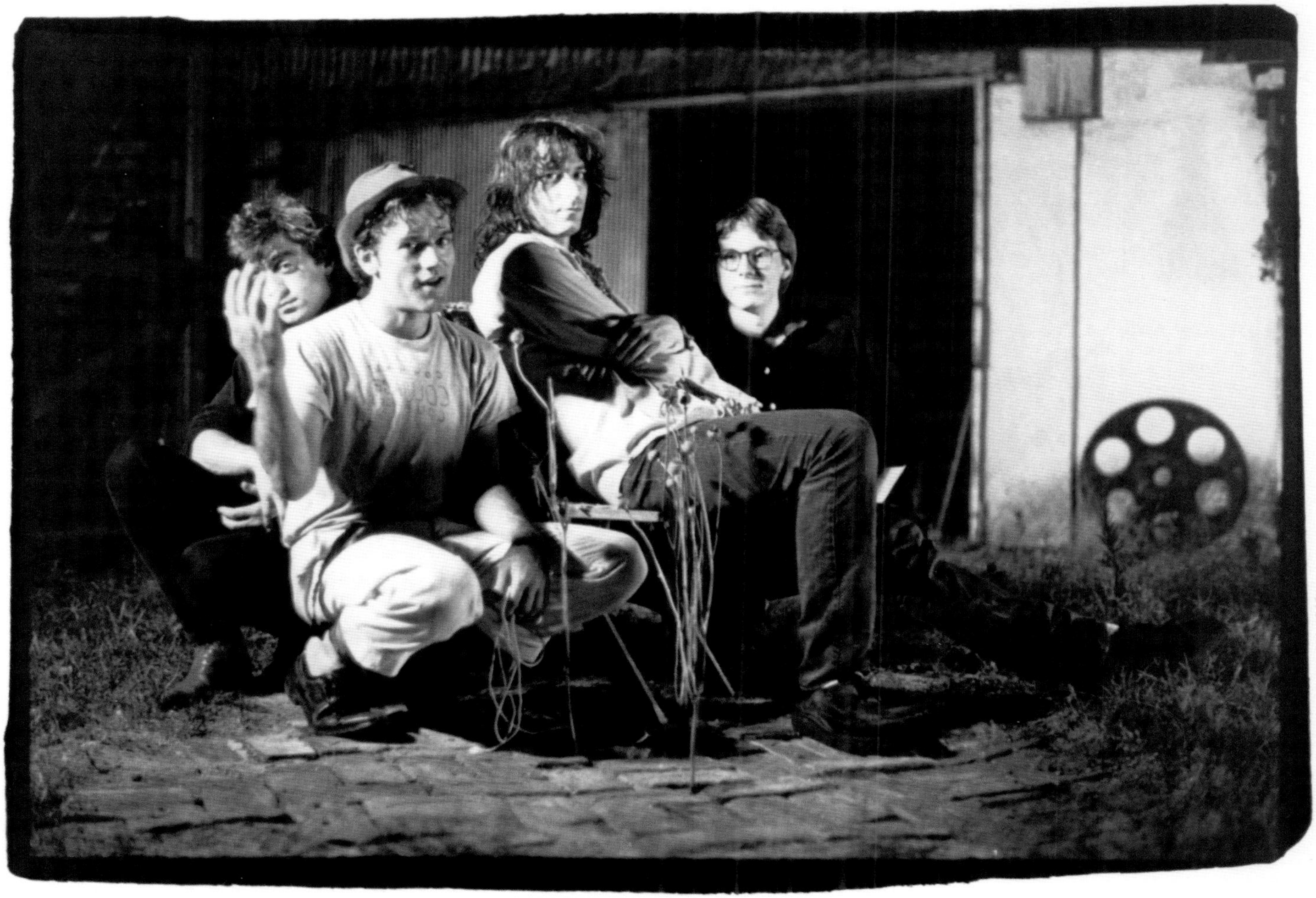

R.E.M.

Michael Stipe   Bill Berry   Mike Mills   Peter Buck

I.R.S.

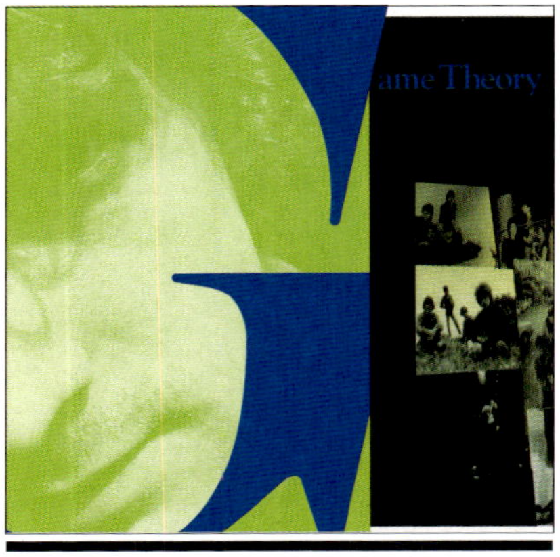

A sturdy power-pop set, **Game Theory**'s *The Big Shot Chronicles* won over an ardent underground audience.

GAME THEORY originated in Davis, California, "about an hour and twenty years northeast of San Francisco," band founder Scott Miller said. Noted primarily for its veterinary school, it was the place where several bands had emerged onto the club and college radio scene. But Game Theory hit a bad patch. Two of the members had become parents-in-waiting, and the balance of the lineup was discouraged by mediocre turnouts at live performances. Miller declared the Game over and moved to San Francisco.

But the offer of a record contract persuaded the singer and guitarist to reform the band. *The Big Shot Chronicles* was produced by Mitch Easter, the underground "new pop" genius of choice (R.E.M.). The sound built on the band's framework—densely layered rhythm guitars and ringing harmonies framed Miller's "close-to-the-bones" pop tunes.

Tracks like "Erica's Word," a popular college radio track, "I've Tried Subtlety" and the tuneful "Regenistraen" demonstrated Game Theory's new level of musical maturity. The band's hooky yet unconventional melodies, literate and often witty lyrics and crafty approach to arrangements and aural montage set it apart from its peers.

"In the late Sixties, experimental pop bands like ourselves got on the charts," Miller said. "But times change. Now the bands that make it all have an even form and style. But R.E.M. was in the Top 10 the last time I looked, so I have hope." ■

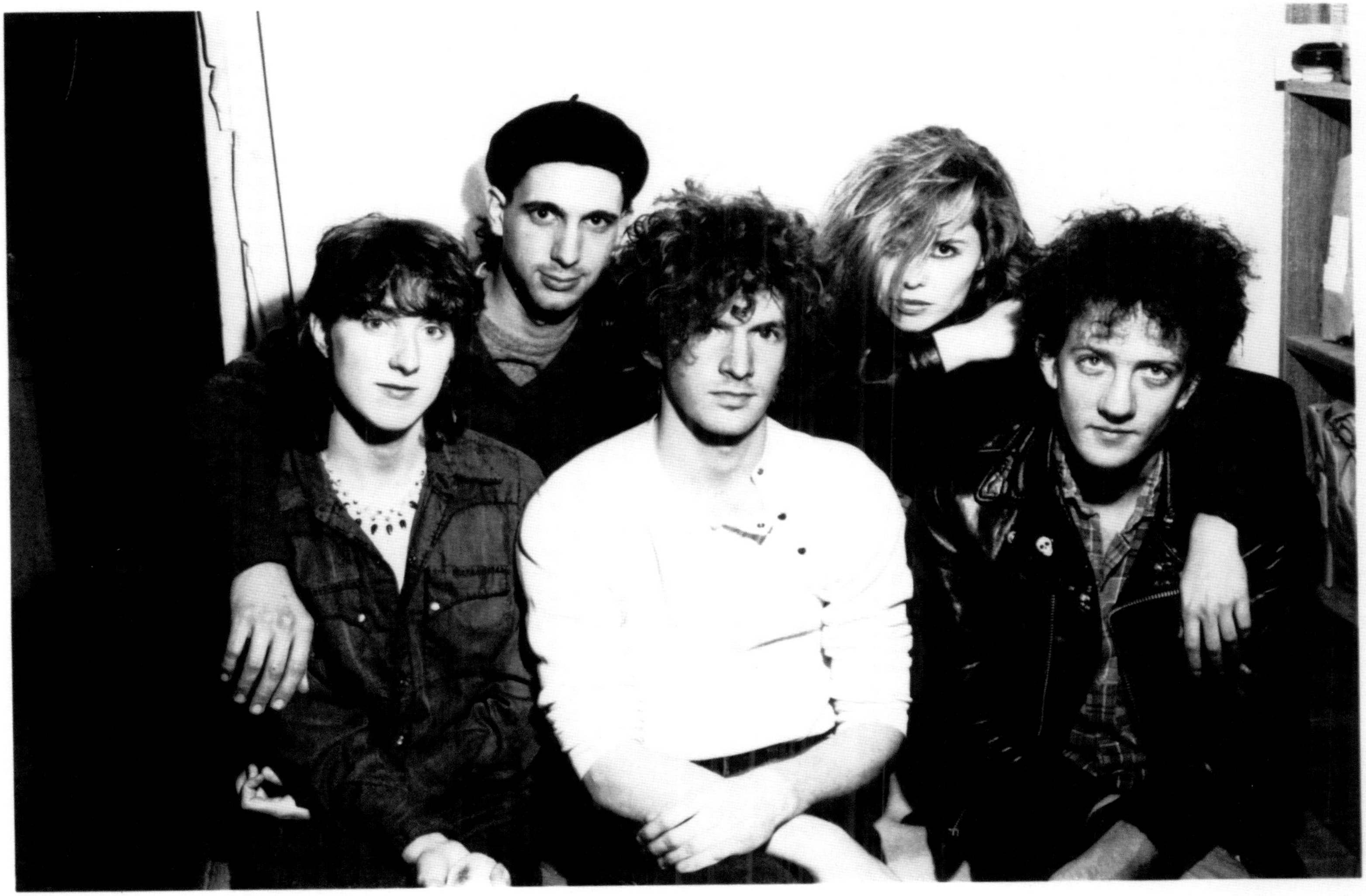

Game Theory

RATIONAL RECORDS

L–R Shelley LaFreniere, Guy Gassuan,
Scott Miller, Donette Thayer, Gil Ray

ENIGMA

ENIGMA RECORDS
P O BOX 2428
EL SEGUNDO CA 90245
213-640-6869

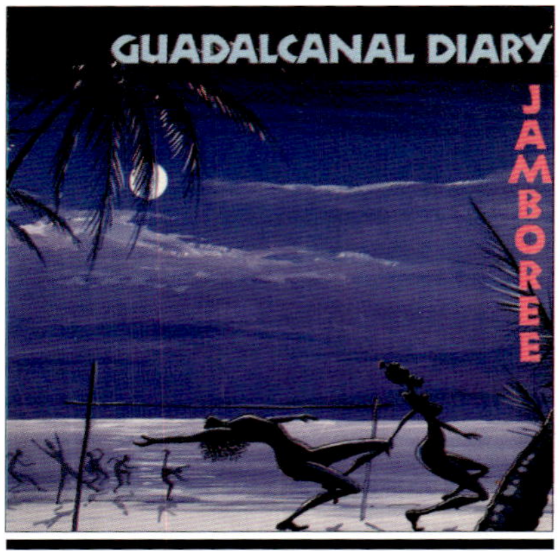

The eclectic *Jamboree* made it harder for critics to hang an easy label on Georgia rockers Guadalcanal Diary.

INEVITABLY COMPARED to fellow Georgians R.E.M., Guadalcanal Diary first came to national attention with *Walking in the Shadow of the Big Man*, an outstanding independent effort (it was recorded and mixed in a mere 50 hours) from a young band with a vision.

Yet the album's folk-rock flavor and acoustic guitars didn't resemble the sound and energy of Guadalcanal Diary's live act, which was ignited by lead singer and guitarist Murray Attaway, a convincing performer who commanded crowds without resorting to teen-macho clichés.

The group had a much bigger budget to record the *Jamboree* album, which was produced by Rodney Mills (the man behind 38 Special's hits).

"It was a real learning experience for me," bassist Rhett Crowe recalled. "Rodney's a bass player, too, and he told me in so many words, 'You're gonna have to play better!'"

Mills got results that were more sonically tailored to the band. "This record has much more of our personalities in it," leader Attaway offered. "We tried to evoke a feeling, rather than a story." But the record still didn't capture his antics or the electricity he generated in concert.

"He's always been a real strong, self-assured personality, never very shy," Crowe noted. "But he's realized his potential through playing onstage. And I feed so much off the audience at live shows—when you're sitting in a studio, it's like being in a hospital by comparison. I don't think we'll ever get that energy until we get the chance to record a live album." ■

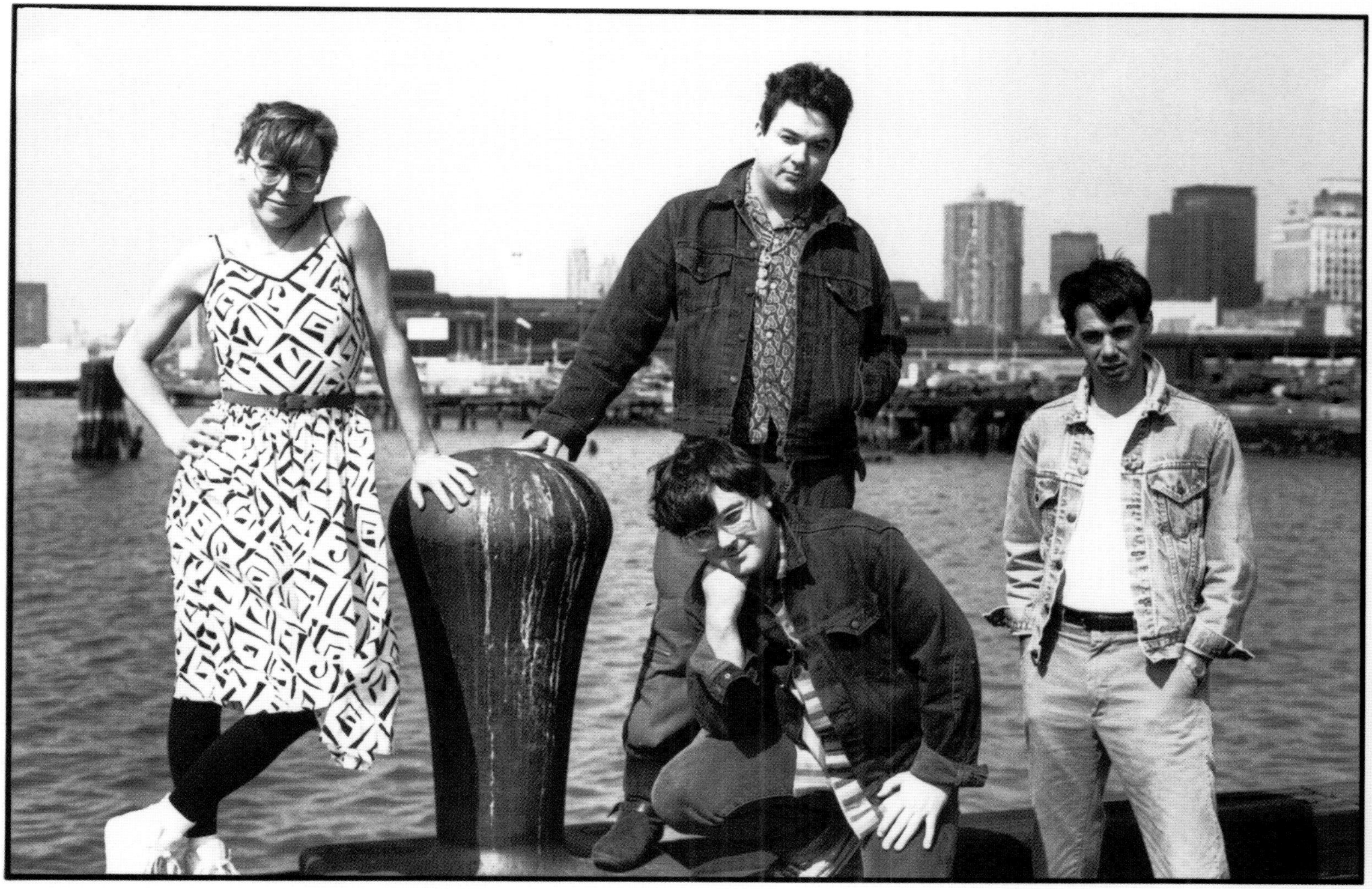

PHOTO CREDIT: MALLORY HATTIE/1986

RHETT CROWE JEFF WALLS (STANDING) JOHN POE (FAR RIGHT) MURRAY ATTAWAY (KNEELING)

GUADALCANAL DIARY

ELEKTRA

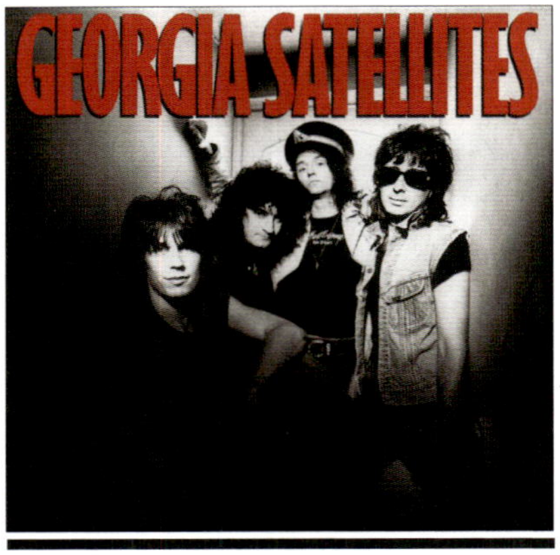

Billboard 200: *Georgia Satellites* (#5)
Billboard Hot 100: "Keep Your Hands to Yourself" (#2); "Battleship Chains" (#86)

Georgia Satellites' insouciant "Keep Your Hands to Yourself" brought back the raunchy essence of rock 'n' roll.

"THERE WAS a drummer in the band who couldn't play very well, but he had a hilarious personality," guitarist Rick Richards said of the song's genesis. "Once he ran into an old girlfriend in a bar, and she shut him down—'Don't touch me, don't look at me, keep your hands to yourself.' Dan (Baird, singer and guitarist) was watching the whole time, laughing like hell." Richards missed the incident, unfortunately—"I was probably in another area of the bar, mentally and physically."

So Baird was moved to write a song mixing mid-period Rolling Stones guitar jangle with Chuck Berry wit, arriving at a sing-along chorus: "Don't give me no lines, and keep your hands to yourself!'" Folks liked it when the band performed the tune in bars, but a demo tape was turned down by every major record company. The group even broke up for a time, but their road manager refused to say die—he took out a loan and released the demo in England, where the British rock press reacted favorably.

Only then did an American label express interest, but the band remained convinced that their album would only get released as a tax write-off. Plastic dance sounds and poseur pop were sending record companies into a frenzy, and the Georgia Satellites weren't that type of act—the four friends were jeans-and-T-shirt types badly in need of haircuts, just your basic garage-band proponents of guitar-based rock 'n' roll.

But that kind of American roots-rock was reborn when "Keep Your Hands to Yourself" started catching a few ears, and the group's fortunes immediately snowballed. The follow-up single, "Battleship Chains," was equally impressive. When the Satellites had temporarily given up on their career before landing a record deal, Baird traveled to North Carolina to work with a group called the Woodpeckers. And he left with their best song.

"'Battleship Chains' is one of the happiest, catchiest songs I'd heard in a long time," Richards admitted. "Actually, the Woodpeckers weren't too excited about us doing it—they cut it first, it was their signature tune. But hopefully when some money starts rolling in, they'll feel better about it." ■

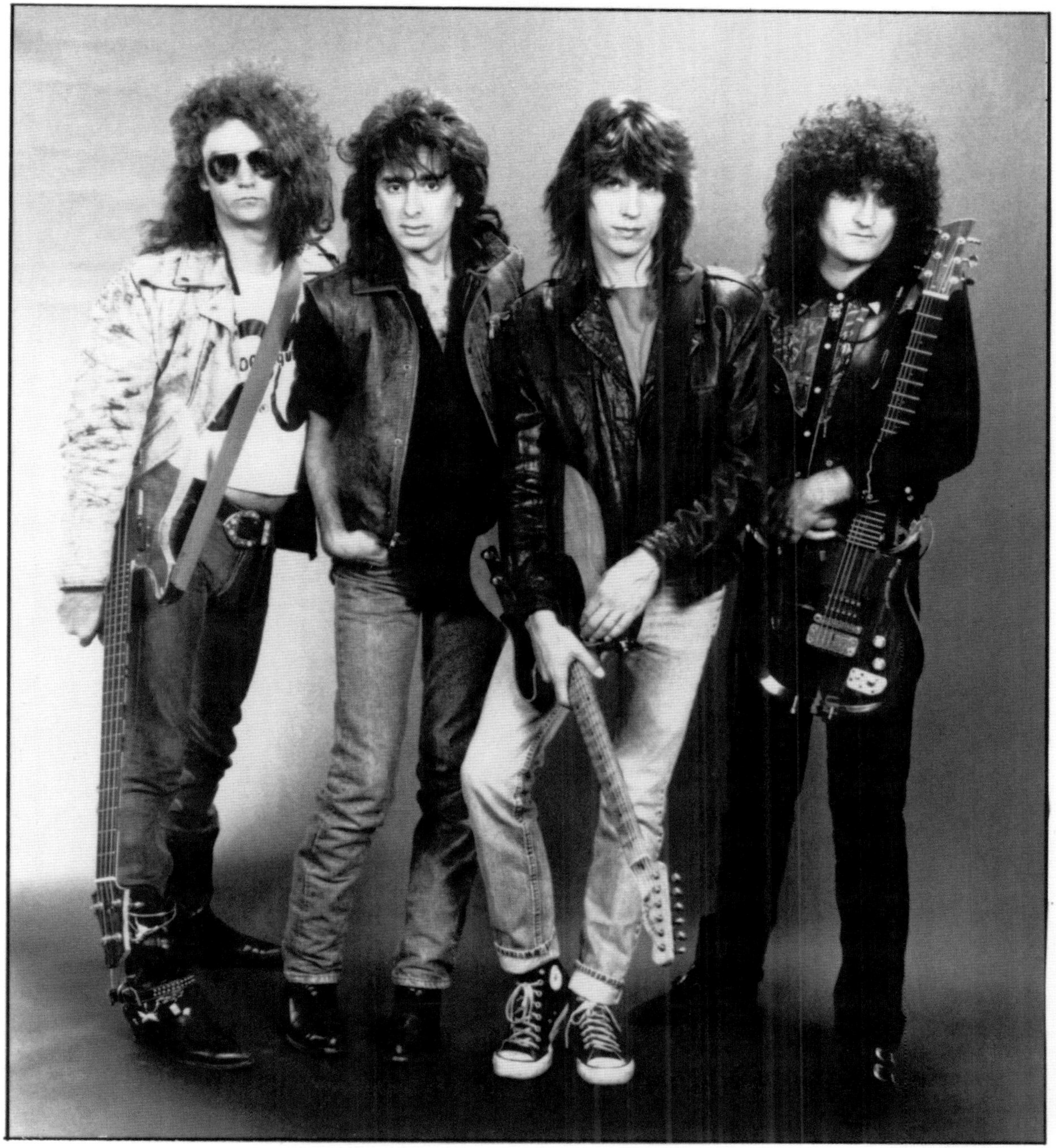

PHOTO CREDIT: MARK WEISS/1986

RICK PRICE MAURO MAGELLAN DAN BAIRD RICK RICHARDS

GEORGIA SATELLITES

PRAXIS INTERNATIONAL

ELEKTRA

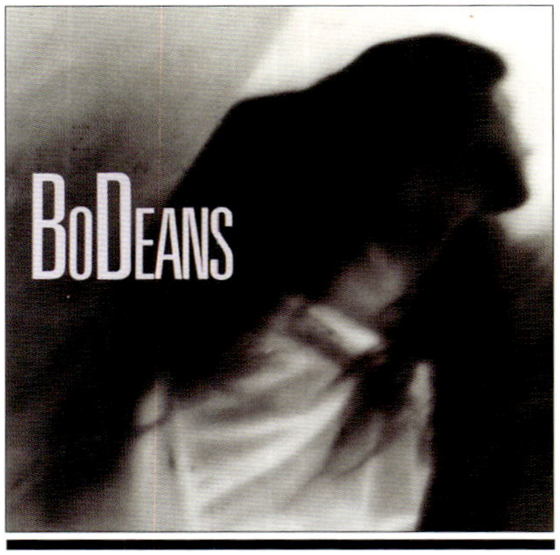

Billboard 200: *Love & Hope & Sex & Dreams* (#115)

For their lack of pretention and bristly vocal interplay, BoDeans were lauded as Midwestern roots-rock saviors.

UPON THE release of their first album, BoDeans received more attention than most acts managed in a career. Profiles in such journalistic bastions as *Rolling Stone* and even *Time* were quick to herald the band's *Love & Hope & Sex & Dreams* as the best debut of the year.

It was heady stuff for a traditional guitar-bass-drums lineup hailing from Waukesha, Wisconsin, a small town that had probably just gotten MTV. So why the inordinate amount of consideration?

"Why not us?" Sammy BoDean (a.k.a. Sammy Llanas—all four members had adopted the same surname, *à la* Ramones) retorted. "At least we're not trying to leap on any bandwagon—we think there's more to us than just that."

Love & Hope & Sex & Dreams, under the guidance of cult-hero producer T-Bone Burnett, filtered the band's considerable feel for older sources through an understated modern sheen. The real key to the group's homey sound was the dual vocals of former high-school chums Sammy and Beau BoDean (Kurt Newman)—they both handled leads, but it was their plaintive harmonies that invited comparisons to the Everly Brothers.

"I have this high bizarre voice, and Kurt has a low bizarre voice," Sammy said. "We fill in the gaps, give each other tones to work off. It's just blind luck that it works."

To back up the album's rave notices, the band toured for the first time by driving across North America, with the usual wearying results. Of course, a backlash had already formed. Some folks intensely disliked BoDeans—they insisted the band was overrated and one-dimensional, and they found Sammy's scruffy nasal crooning downright irritating.

But it was foolish to underestimate such tight, straightforward songs as "Fadeaway," "She's a Runaway" and "Angels"—or to read anything into the name BoDeans. At first, people figured it to be a contraction of Bo Diddley and James Dean.

"Now everybody's jumping on the Jethro Bodine (from television's *The Beverly Hillbillies*) thing," Sammy said. "It really has nothing to do with it. That show is where I first heard the name and got the idea—we like the sound of the word, but that's as far as it goes.

"At first we called ourselves 'da BoDeans,' like you would say 'the BoDeans' in New Jersey. But people didn't get it—they called us 'the da BoDeans.' So when we released our record, we dropped it. It was kind of frustrating, actually." ■

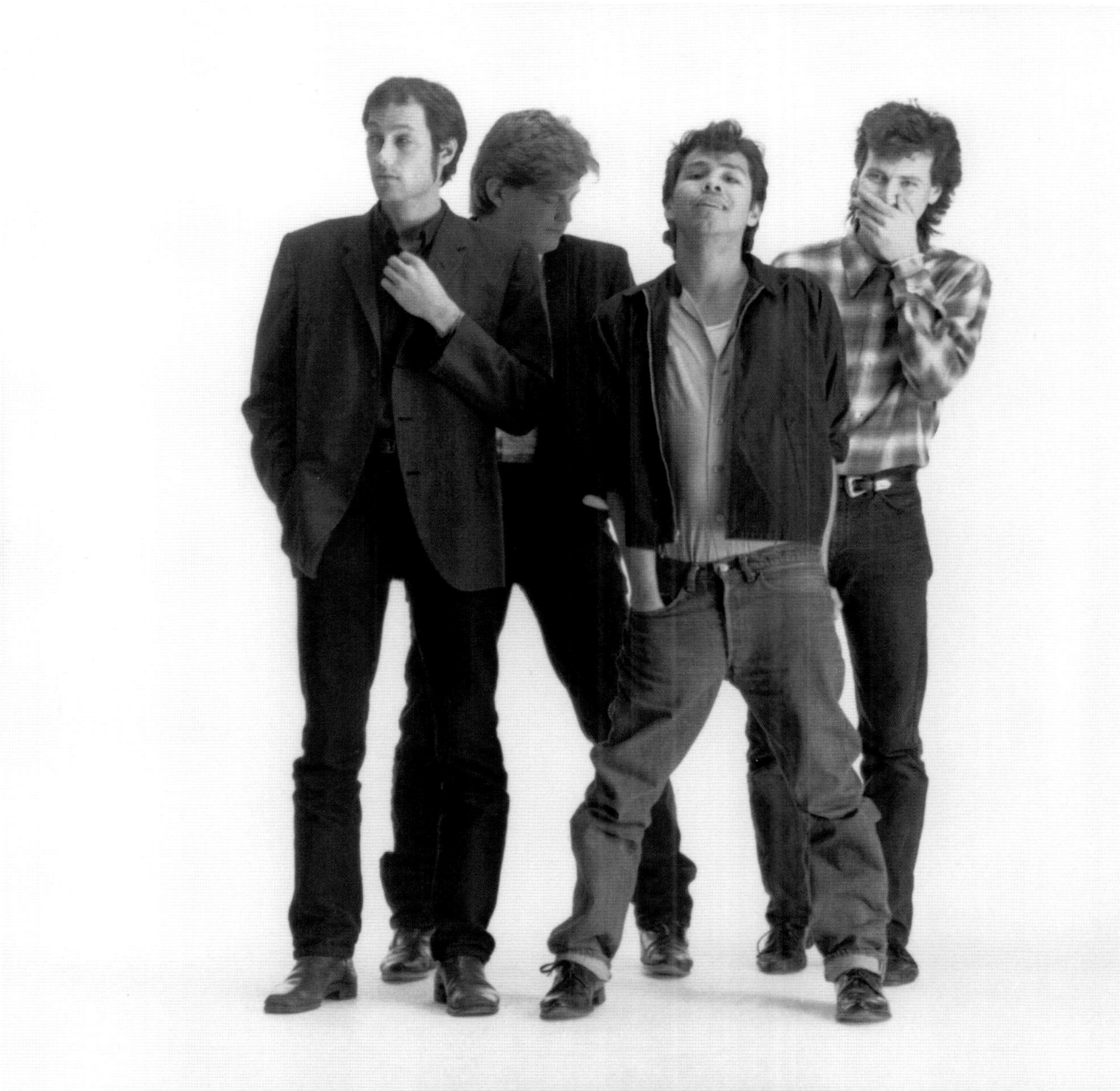

Photo Credit: Francis Ford

BODEANS

Slash™

WARNER BROS.

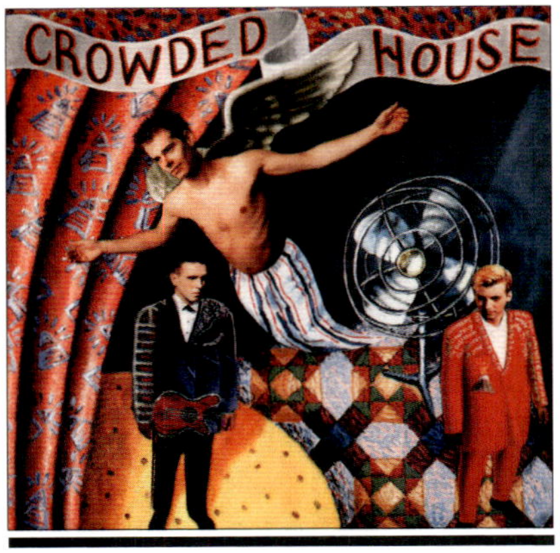

Billboard 200: *Crowded House* (#12)
Billboard Hot 100: "Don't Dream It's Over" (#2);
"World Where You Live" (#65); "Something So Strong" (#7)

Two Top 10 hits, "Don't Dream It's Over" and "Something So Strong," came from Crowded House's first album.

IT SPORTED a wonderful melody, a terrific vocal and an economic performance—in other words, "Don't Dream It's Over" deserved its acclaim as the type of pop masterpiece Paul McCartney wished he still could write. That was heady praise for the humble members of Crowded House.

"It's a compliment, but I think it misses the point," singer Neil Finn said. "There's a certain tradition to the songs I write that is linked to the Sixties pop song—having a clear concise melody, having a song structure as opposed to a dance or disco structure. And the Beatles are the most obvious and consistent exponents of that style of songwriting. But I can't take those comparisons seriously because, for me, the Beatles remain the best pop band that's ever been. I just can't consider that my stuff measures up."

Crowded House had its beginnings in Split Enz, a New Zealand outfit fronted by Neil's brother Tim. When Split Enz formed in 1972, it was primarily known for the members' bizarre, eccentric appearance and geometric extremes in music. Five years later, Neil joined Tim in Split Enz and immediately contributed such Australian chart-toppers as "I Got You," "One Step Ahead" and "History Never Repeats," and by the early Eighties Split Enz had achieved minor status in the US.

When Split Enz called it a day following a 1984 tour of Australia, Finn and drummer Paul Hester recruited bassist Nick Seymour and moved to Los Angeles to rehearse and record. The trio holed up in a tiny Hollywood house that became a popular hangout for hordes of people—hence the band's moniker. Crowded House entered the studio with Mitchell Froom, who contributed lean production and keyboard parts to the band's debut album.

Crowded House was released to a few excellent reviews and no commercial attention. "It was frustrating," Finn admitted. "I was not wanting to be cynical about this new band, and yet I obviously had benefit of some experience with Split Enz. We were asked to do a lot of promotion for the album before we sensed any real direction from the record company. I was pretty nervous and anxious about that, because I didn't feel there was a concerted effort to make the record a hit."

But after a five-month wait, the record company decided to release "Don't Dream It's Over" as a single, and the band's career took off. "It was left so long because they were reluctant to release a ballad first," Finn said. "It seems to be a rule of thumb not to do that, but in our case it worked out really well. It just shows you that there are no rules."

"Something So Strong" and "World Where You Live" also scaled the charts, and Crowded House was widely regarded as the best pop outfit to emerge in recent years.

"The album found its legs, and the band is a lot stronger having done all this touring," Finn said. "And if in 10 years' time I've made as many good albums as the Beatles, then maybe I'll sit back and not be bothered by those comparisons." ■

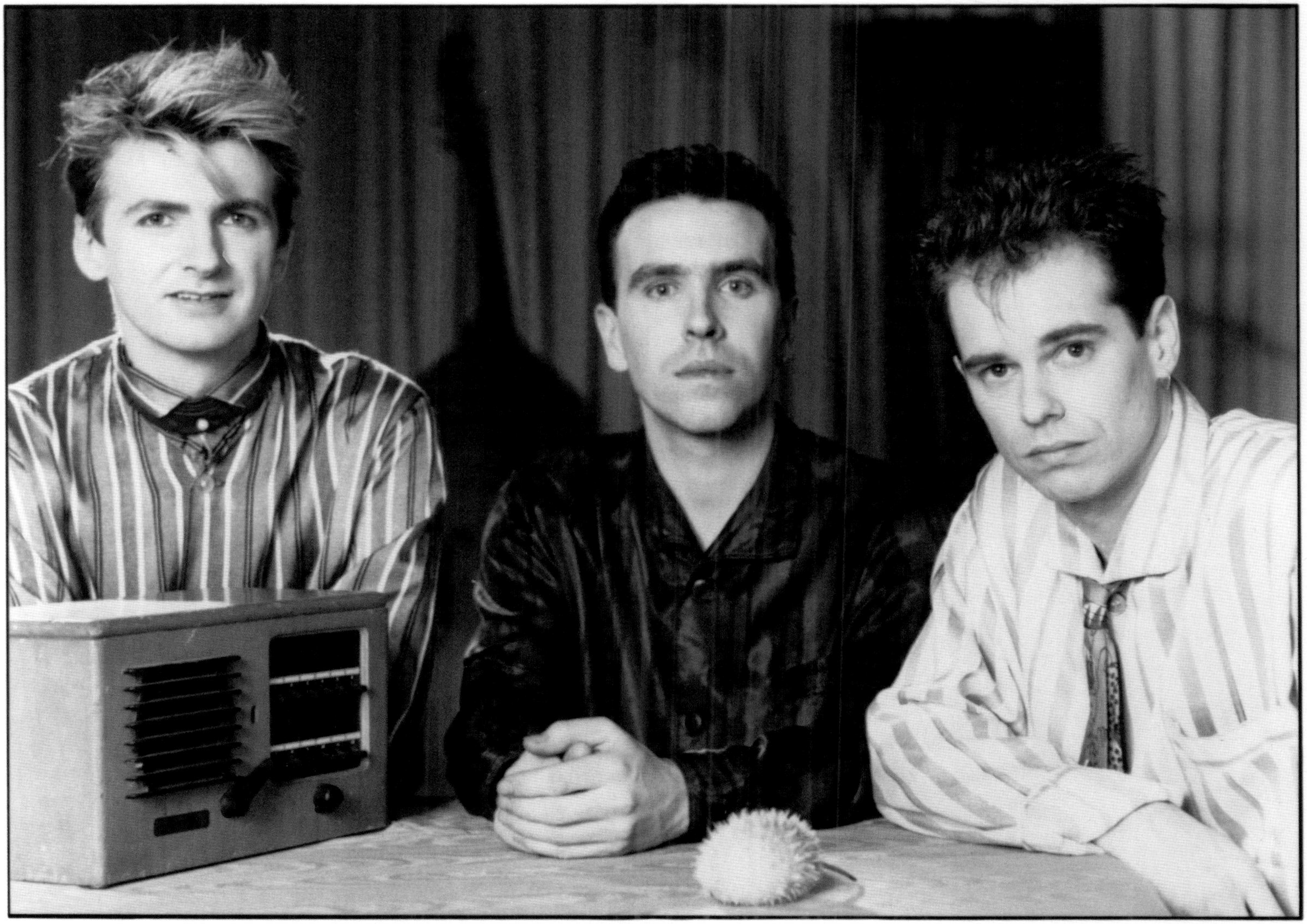

Photo: Dennis Keeley / 1986

Neil Finn Nick Seymour Paul Hester

CROWDED HOUSE

Capitol RECORDS

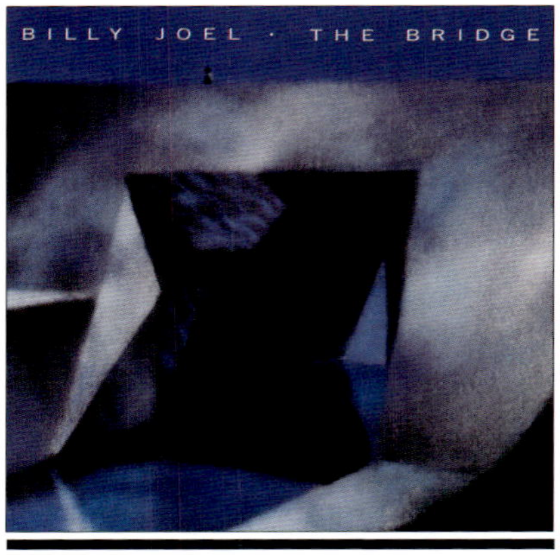

Billboard 200: *The Bridge* (#7)
Billboard Hot 100: "Modern Woman" (#10); "A Matter of Trust" (#10); "This Is the Time" (#18); "Baby Grand" (#75)

The Bridge, a protean collection of songs incorporating several guest musicians, was another hit for Billy Joel.

ON HIS tenth album, Billy Joel couldn't echo the flavor of 1983's *An Innocent Man*—a recording on which the popular singer-songwriter had channeled the styles of music he'd loved as a footloose adolescent.

"I think a lot of people thought I was going to write about Christie (Brinkley), getting married, having a baby, and there are some songs on the album about life experience," Joel said. "But there are songs that have nothing to do with me at all, just fictionalized, where I've invented a character."

Produced by Phil Ramone, *The Bridge* yielded the hits "A Matter of Trust" and "Modern Woman," which also appeared on the soundtrack to the film *Ruthless People*. The ballad "This Is the Time" topped the adult contemporary charts. "Big Man on Mulberry Street" was adapted for television by the producers of a popular series, *Moonlighting*. The album included guest appearances by Ray Charles, Steve Winwood and Cyndi Lauper.

"You should learn something on every album, and if you haven't, then you haven't done a good one," Joel said. "I learned I could write with somebody else. I got to the last song and had terrible writer's block. It lasted about three weeks—I walked around the studio, I banged against the wall, I kicked things. I didn't shave—that was like my penance, 'I'm not going to shave until I write something.' Remember, I got a new baby and I couldn't pick her up and kiss her because I would scratch up her face. It was just a mess.

"Cyndi was recording downstairs (at the studio), and she says, 'Bill, what's the matter, you look like you're going out of your mind, you're climbing the walls.' She was great—she got one of those yellow legal pads and says, 'You sit down at the piano and play, and I'll write down the words you throw out,' I thought I was saying a lot of gibberish, but when she showed it to me, the title came out—'Code of Silence.' She asks, 'What are you being silent about?' and it really got me to thinking. She actually stimulated a lot of the writing, suggested a lot of things, pinpointed what should happen with the song.

Charles, one of Joel's idols (and for whom his daughter Alexa Ray was named), sang a duet with him on the song "Baby Grand."

"I learned I could hold my own as a singer," Joel said. "We flew out to Los Angeles for the session—we had 24 string players, an arranger, conductor, rhythm section, and in walked Ray Charles. I almost went into a freeze-up. We played piano on the basic track and it worked out fine. Then it was time to sing and I didn't know how much of this soul thing I could get into because now I'm staring at this guy I've been trying to sing like. I can't do Ray Charles because there's Ray Charles.

"So I started to sing like this little white kid from the suburbs. And Ray heard me, and he started to sing like a little white kid from the suburbs. So we stopped, and Phil said, 'No, no, kid, you gotta go after him, you gotta get Ray to sing like Ray, because he's following your cue.' Now, I'm not a great believer in my own voice, but Ray got into it." ■

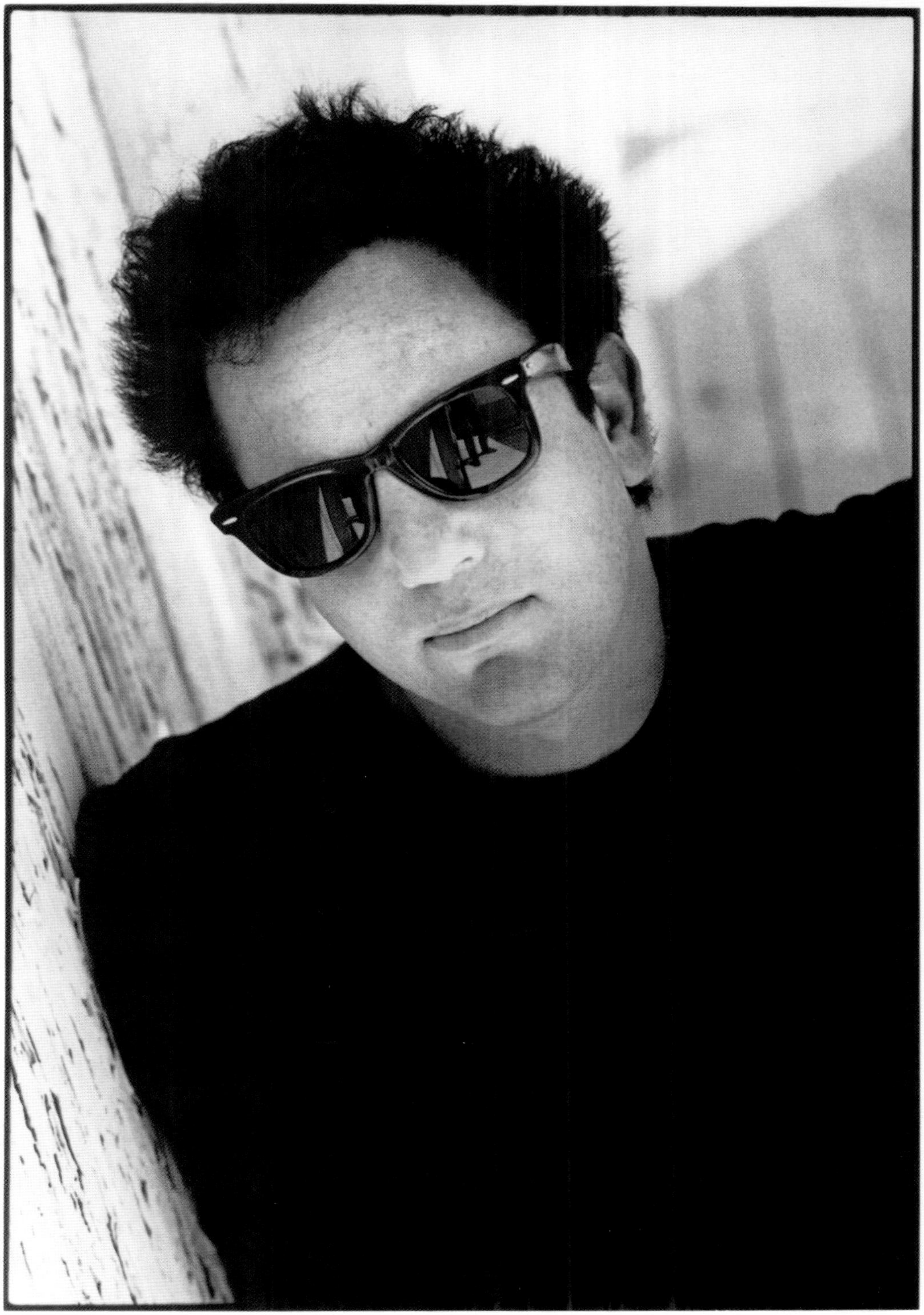

PHOTOGRAPH: PATRICK DEMARCHELIER

BILLY JOEL

Columbia

8607

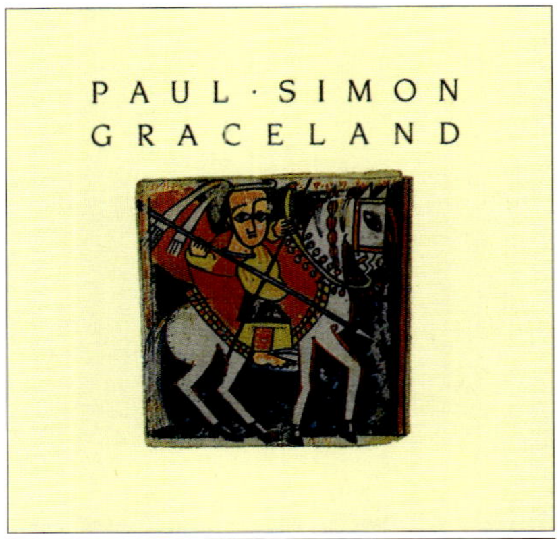

Billboard 200: *Graceland* (#3)
Billboard Hot 100: "You Can Call Me Al" (#23); "Graceland" (#81); "The Boy in the Bubble" (#86)

Inspired by the township music of South Africa, Paul Simon's *Graceland* gratified old fans and captivated new ones.

PAUL SIMON had an interest in the way songs from many cultures could be brought into prevailing pop forms. The Andean echoes of the Simon & Garfunkel hit "El Condor Pasa" and the reggae bounce of his early solo recording "Mother and Child Reunion" were some of the ways Simon had used music and musicians from around the world to broaden musical horizons and create hits in the process.

"I think one of the most important—and entertaining—things any artist can do is try to bridge cultures, to find the common bond and enhance it," Simon explained. "That's one of the things music does better than any other form of communication, and it's certainly the foundation for the songs on this album."

Simon's approach took on a whole new dimension with *Graceland*. Combining his sagacious songwriting with the unexposed mbaqanga music of South Africa, he forged a compelling amalgam that sold millions worldwide.

"A friend gave me a cassette called *Accordion Jive*," Simon explained. "It was fascinating music—accordion, drums, bass and guitar, primitive yet modern sounding, and in a way, very familiar. It reminded me of early blues, like Mississippi John Hurt, and vintage rock 'n' roll from Atlantic's golden era. I listened to it the whole summer and began making up melodies around these basic grooves. Eventually I was able to trace down its point of origin and found out that it was South Africa."

Simon visited Johannesburg, recording with many South African musicians and groups, notably Ladysmith Black Mambazo. He then wrote songs inspired by the recordings, collaborating with African and American artists and brilliantly transferring the creative energy into a whole new context. "These artists are enormously gifted, and there's no question that, in time, they could have as significant an impact on popular music as, say, reggae had in the Seventies," Simon enthused.

Graceland acquainted a global market to South African rhythms and reopened a discourse about the political and social turmoil of that troubled country. It received the Grammy Award for Album of the Year and also the Grammy for Record of the Year for the title track.

"The world is a shrinking place," Simon said. "It's no longer a question of whether other cultures will affect what's going on in this country. It's only a question of how." ■

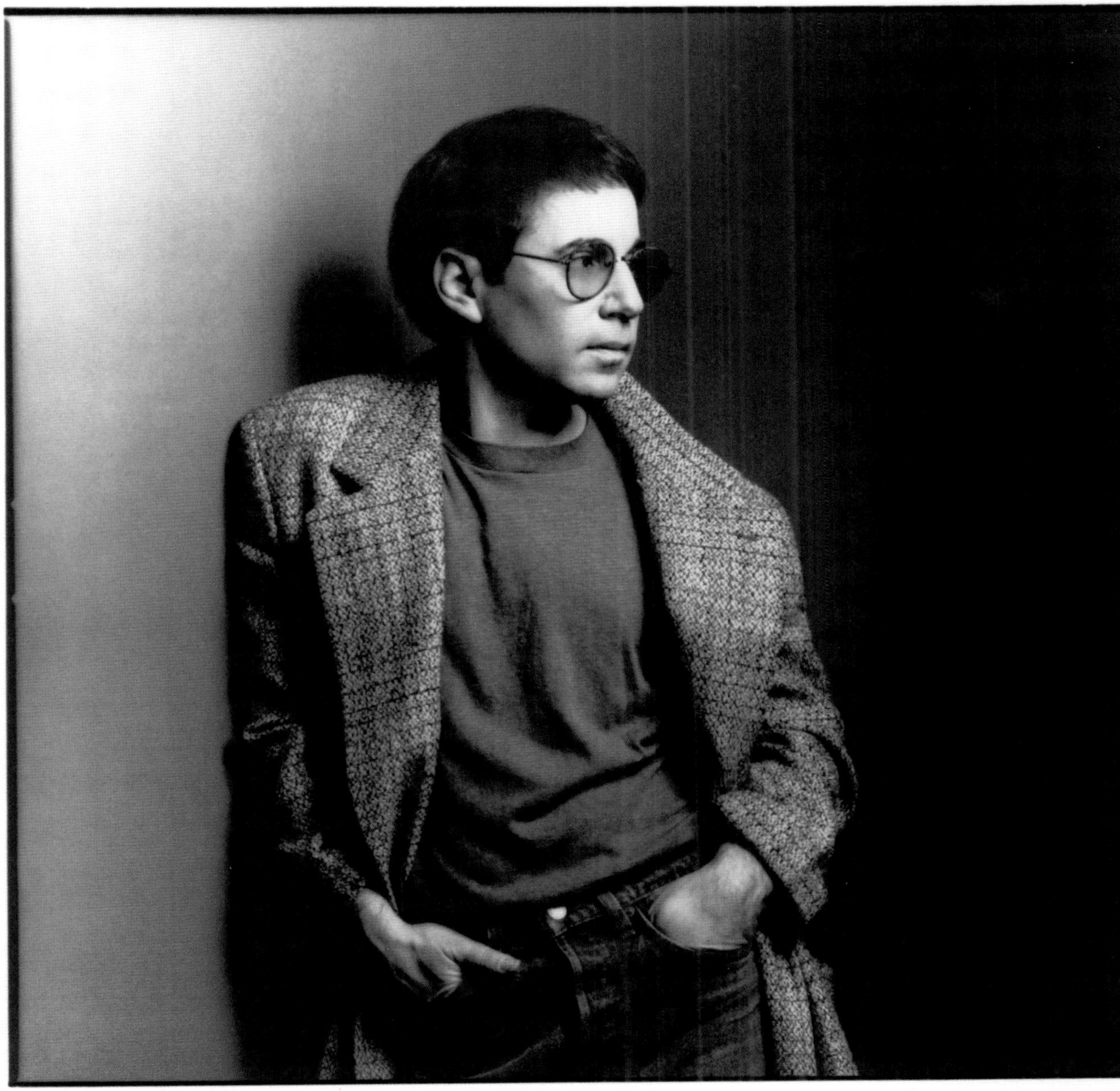

Photo Credit: Gary Heery

PAUL SIMON

WARNER BROS.

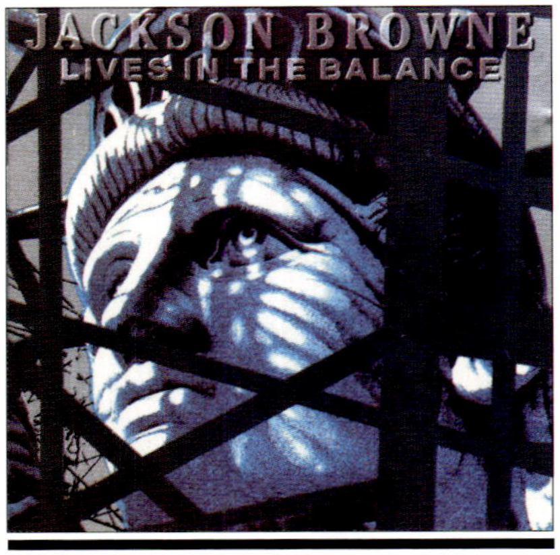

Billboard 200: *Lives in the Balance* (#23)
Billboard Hot 100: "For America" (#30); "Lives in the Balance" (#70)

With *Lives in the Balance*, Jackson Browne spelled out his suspicions of the Reagan administration's policies.

OF ALL the singer-songwriters from the movement's Seventies heyday, Jackson Browne was a master of elevating the emotional landscape on the hard road to romance, down to the small, significant details. "I'm earnest to a fault," the creator of such classic albums as *The Pretender* and *Running on Empty* said. "'Ernie' would be a suitable nom de plume for me."

Most rock performers found themselves in a quandary when they attempted to combine music with any sort of political or educational tone, but Browne had set his finely observed songs on a new course. As an outspoken critic of US foreign policy and a strong supporter of Amnesty International, he bared his conscience with the searing *Lives in the Balance*, an album far removed from his earlier romanticism. His stance as a disillusioned patriot became evident when he offered such bold and assertive tunes as "For America" and the title track, a harsh indictment of American involvement in Central America, addressing the political turmoil and what he felt was the waste of human life and stateside indifference.

Browne made two unusual moves. He released a self-financed video of "Lives in the Balance," and he sent a letter to radio programmers around the country, asking that the song be made available "especially for high-school and college-age (listeners) to encourage them to think about what's happening in Central America and examine closely what they are being told by our government and the major news media. Many of them hardly know where Central America is, let alone the difference in our government's positions towards El Salvador and Nicaragua."

Browne had no commercial motivation behind his video release. The album already had run its sales course of a half-million copies, a respectable figure but not one to encourage his record label to pour more money into promotion. "They look at a video in terms of advertisement for the album," Browne said. "But if you look at video as an art form, it's never too late. And I wanted to make one as a parting shot. This is a timely song, about what's on page one of every paper in the world. Somebody wrote that 'Lives' was more of a speech than a song. If that's the way they look at it, I guess it was a speech that had to be made.

"I'll continue to care about Central America, but I don't know how many songs one can write about the subject. I feel good about my country. There are very few countries where what's going on now could take place, the examination of an administration, holding it up to public scrutiny. I think we're very fortunate to live in America. But with that good fortune comes responsibility." ■

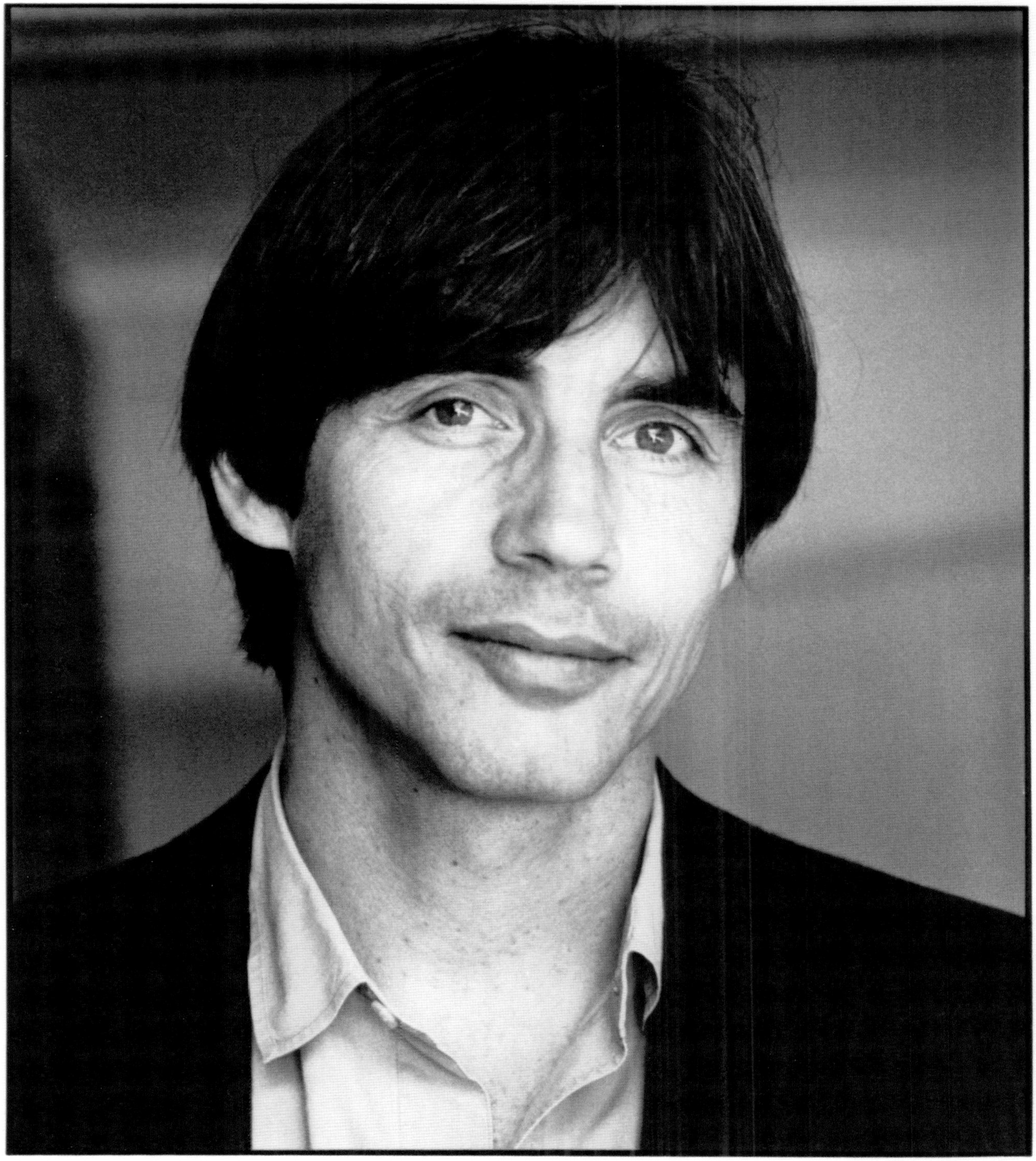

PHOTO CREDIT: HENRY DILTZ/1985

JACKSON BROWNE

ASYLUM

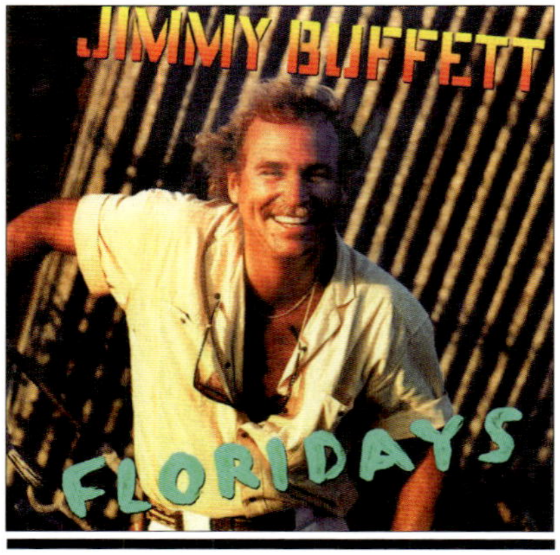

Billboard 200: *Floridays* (#67)

Backed by his Coral Reefer Band, Jimmy Buffett featured all sides of his free and easy character on *Floridays.*

BY THE Eighties, singer Jimmy Buffett's annual albums had stopped going gold and platinum, and he briefly tried the country market. But by the middle of the decade, it was his yearly summer tours that were filling his bank account, and Buffett's colorful fans would turn his concerts into Mardi Gras-like affairs.

"Parrotheads are Jimmy Buffett fanatics," Buffett explained. "They know every word to every song I ever wrote. They seem to be relatively normal most of the time—but when they come to my shows, they put on their 'feathers' and go nuts."

Buffett's Caribbean-flavored tales of ocean breezes and swaying palms, perfect settings for his chug-a-lug ideology. Shirts were off, imbibing was heavy. "I haven't seen this much white meat since Thanksgiving," Buffett surmised.

Floridays, produced by keyboardist Michael Utley, who spearheaded Buffett's Coral Reefer Band, maintained his usual upbeat atmosphere for his following of "cultural outpatients." The eclectic work blended calypso, salsa and country with Stax-Volt horns, but neither "I Love the Now" (co-written with actress Carrie Fisher) or "Creola," the album's two singles, charted. Radio had ignored Buffett's music in the Eighties.

"I'm not bitching about it, but I've been fighting a battle," he said. "In this day and time, quality product doesn't necessarily generate radio airplay the way it used to, before the advent of video. Now it's a matter of fighting for a slot. If you get one hit, then everything else will fall into place. So, there's a sound that programmers look for, and it's disheartening that you can't make your music the way you would naturally."

But Buffett continued to succeed on his own terms on the road. And he'd been peddling a longtime project—his script for *Margaritaville*, a movie based on his hit song, was completed. But it wasn't any closer to getting made.

"We were close to getting it in production," Buffett shrugged. "And then another movie, *Club Paradise*, came out a few months ago, and the storyline was unbelievably similar to our screenplay—and I sent mine out five years ago. The movie industry is one that I'll never understand.

"Anyway, *Club Paradise* bombed—so now no studio is going to touch a similar property with a ten-foot pole. At this point, we're considering a rewrite. But tell you what, I think I'm just gonna go back to writing songs." ■

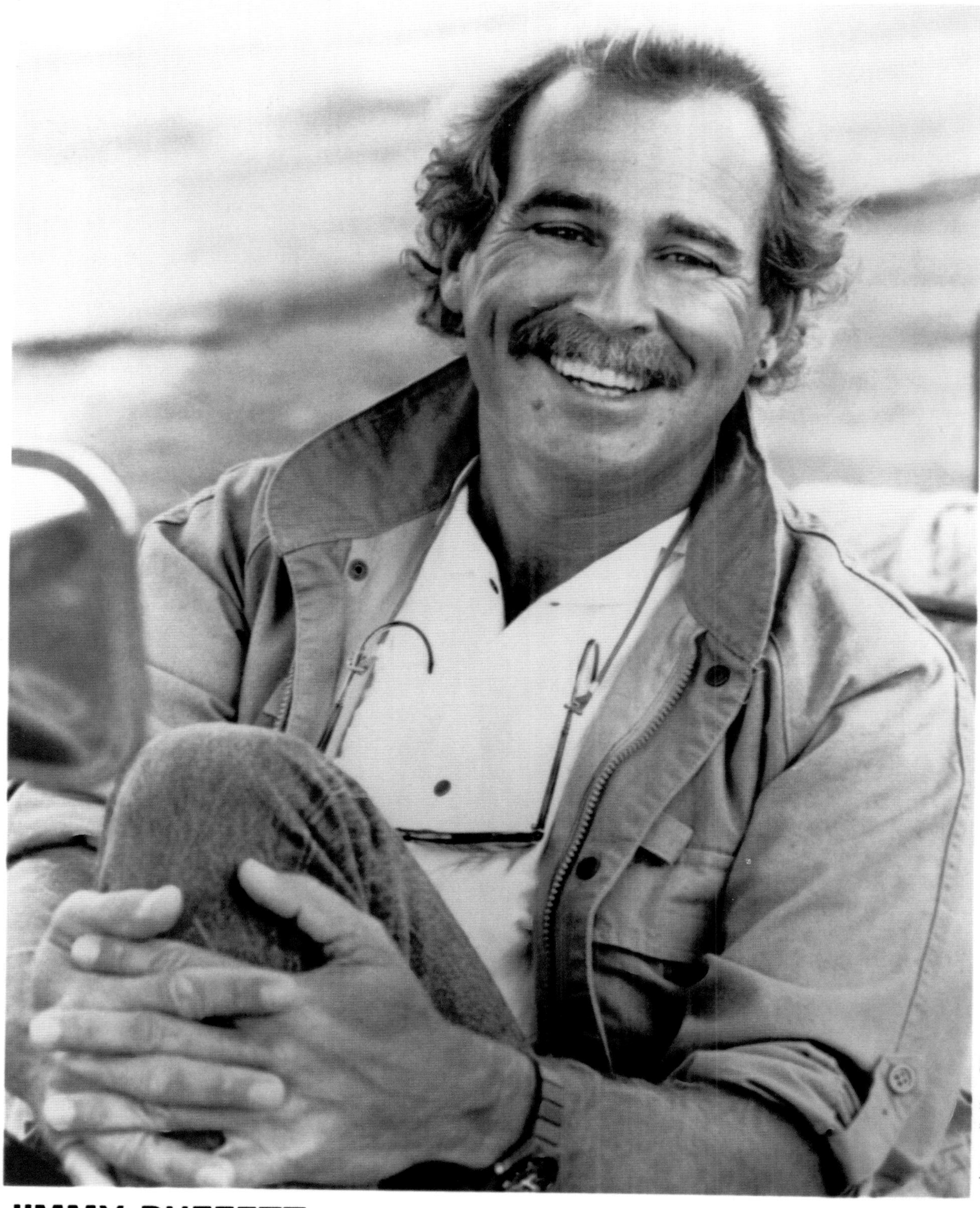

photo credit: Henry Diltz

JIMMY BUFFETT

MCA RECORDS

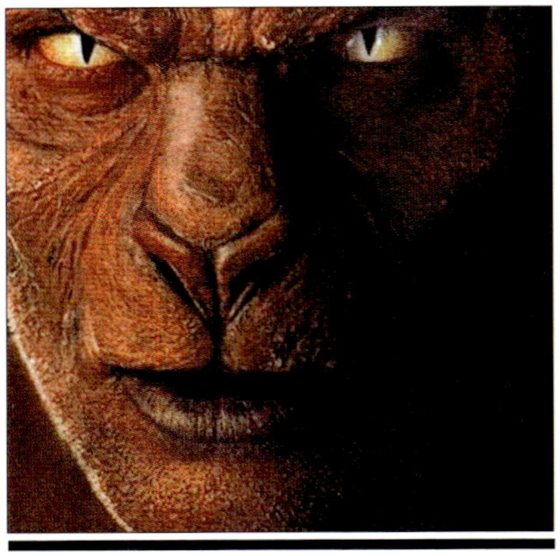

Billboard 200: *Eye of the Zombie* (#26)
Billboard Hot 100: "Eye of the Zombie" (#81)

The cross *Eye of the Zombie*, the sequel to his blockbuster *Centerfield*, put the kibosh on John Fogerty's revival.

INCREDIBLY, IN less than two years in the late Sixties, Creedence Clearwater Revival produced five Top 10 albums. John Fogerty's songwriting, guitar work and hoarse, soulful singing with CCR placed him in the ranks of his generation's premier music legends.

Yet his solo career had been mysterious and disappointing. After Creedence disbanded in 1972, he stubbornly refused to put even a cent in the pocket of his nemesis, Fantasy Records chairman Saul Zaentz, who owned the publishing rights to the old Creedence music. Fogerty dropped from the public eye and ear, reemerging in a big way in with 1985's multiplatinum *Centerfield*, which pushed him back into the spotlight. Writing every song and playing every instrument, he produced the hits "Old Man Down the Road," "Rock and Roll Girls" and the title track, a classic ode to baseball.

But Zaentz sued Fogerty for libel and slander (for the bitter "Zanz Kant Danz," a track on *Centerfield*), and plagiarism (Zaentz contended that "Old Man Down the Road" was borrowed from a Creedence hit, which Fantasy owned).

The angry *Eye of the Zombie*, recorded with a backing band, was significantly less successful than its predecessor. "I wanted to do a record that was darker, a little moodier," Fogerty admitted.

"I get real uncomfortable when people call me the keeper of the roots-rock flame," he said. "I don't like to carry that mantle around. I'd much rather make use of whatever's out there to create the best possible songs. Microchips, computers, synthesizers and digital samplers are just ways to make sounds people are going to remember, that they're going to want to hear again. When I use technology, it's filtered through my own musical approach. I'm not just bowing at the feet of electronics, but by the same token I'm not stubbornly holding on to Fifties rock 'n' roll as the last good thing that happened in pop music."

Fogerty toured behind *Eye of the Zombie*, but he refused to play any CCR material. Bruised after the album's relative commercial failure, he went back into seclusion for another decade. ■

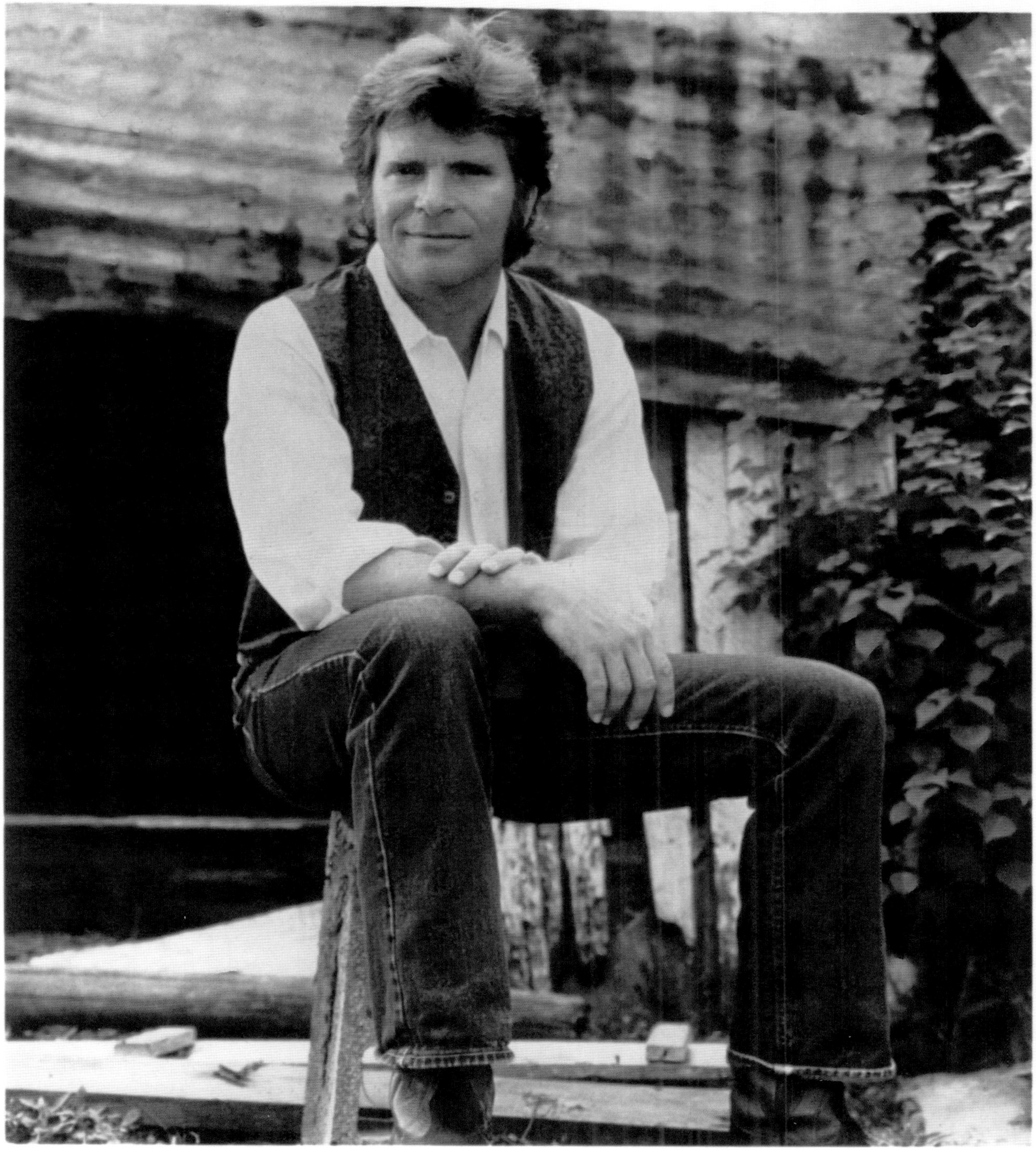

Photo Credit: Craig Dietz

JOHN FOGERTY

WARNER BROS.

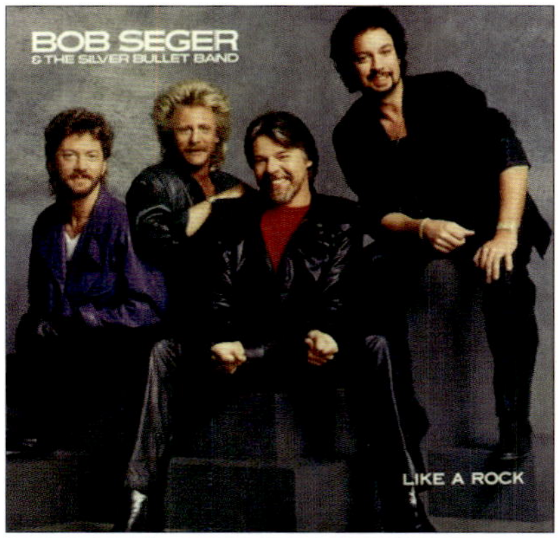

Billboard 200: *Like a Rock* (#3)
Billboard Hot 100: "American Storm" (#13); "Like a Rock" (#12); "It's You" (#52); "Miami" (#70)

Bob Seger & the Silver Bullet Band were eyeing the end of the road—"the road" being a grueling tour circuit.

NO ONE questioned Bob Seger's right to semi-retirement as he entered his third decade of rock 'n' roll. Before his national breakthrough in 1979, he'd already had 14 years of hard work behind him at high-school dances, church socials and, finally, theaters and arenas in his native Midwest.

Now the congenial singer was heralded as the elder statesman of heartland rock, a down-to-earth artist who continued to offer his music without pose or pretense. *Like a Rock*, his Top 5 multiplatinum album, took stock of the human wreckage mounting in the face of contemporary drug use in "American Storm," and the title track became a No. 1 mainstream rock hit.

But success had had its downside. There was the fatigue of his raw performance style.

"I think people knew the old legs just won't bounce around like they used to, the old voice just won't hold up," the veteran rocker said. "I never say 'never,' you know. I don't want to be like Frank Sinatra or Elton John or David Bowie who say, 'Naw, I'm never gonna do it again'—and then three years later, they're out again. That's why I don't want to say one way or another. If I do tour again, it will be much smaller."

And Seger rated *Like a Rock* as one of the most difficult projects of his career. Besides the technical challenges that were presented in producing himself for the first time, he also dealt with a string of personal disasters, including breakups with two girlfriends.

"It put me in a pretty different place for a while, and it wasn't real happy territory to be in," he said. "I was in the studio for 11 straight months, and then I went straight out on the road, doing about 106 dates on the North American tour. It'll be almost two years since I've even spent a month in Michigan. Next time, I want to be just another member of the band. There's too much going on out on the street for me to get locked into a studio again."

But the collective success of Seger and his band had given them a reasonable voice in what they would or wouldn't do. For instance, they declined an offer from Coors Brewing, which saw a potential tie-in with the "Silver Bullet" ad campaign for Coors Light beer.

"My manager saw it and said, 'Ooh, I bet they'll want us,'" Seger chuckled. "They offered me unbelievable, ungodly money to do three years' worth of commercials with my band, showing up in the Silver Bullet Bar. They offered the moon and the sun and a few constellations besides—I wouldn't have to lift a spoon ever again. But I had to turn them down—we just don't do commercials."

Later, "Like a Rock," a song about pride and consistency, would become familiar through its incessant use in a long-running Chevrolet truck ad campaign, which Seger chose to support struggling American auto workers. But his only plans were to continue in his uncalculated ways. "I haven't had a home life in a long time. I want to buy a house, sell my old one—just a lot of domestic stuff that I've completely ignored for two years. In other words, I want to do stuff like everybody else does." ■

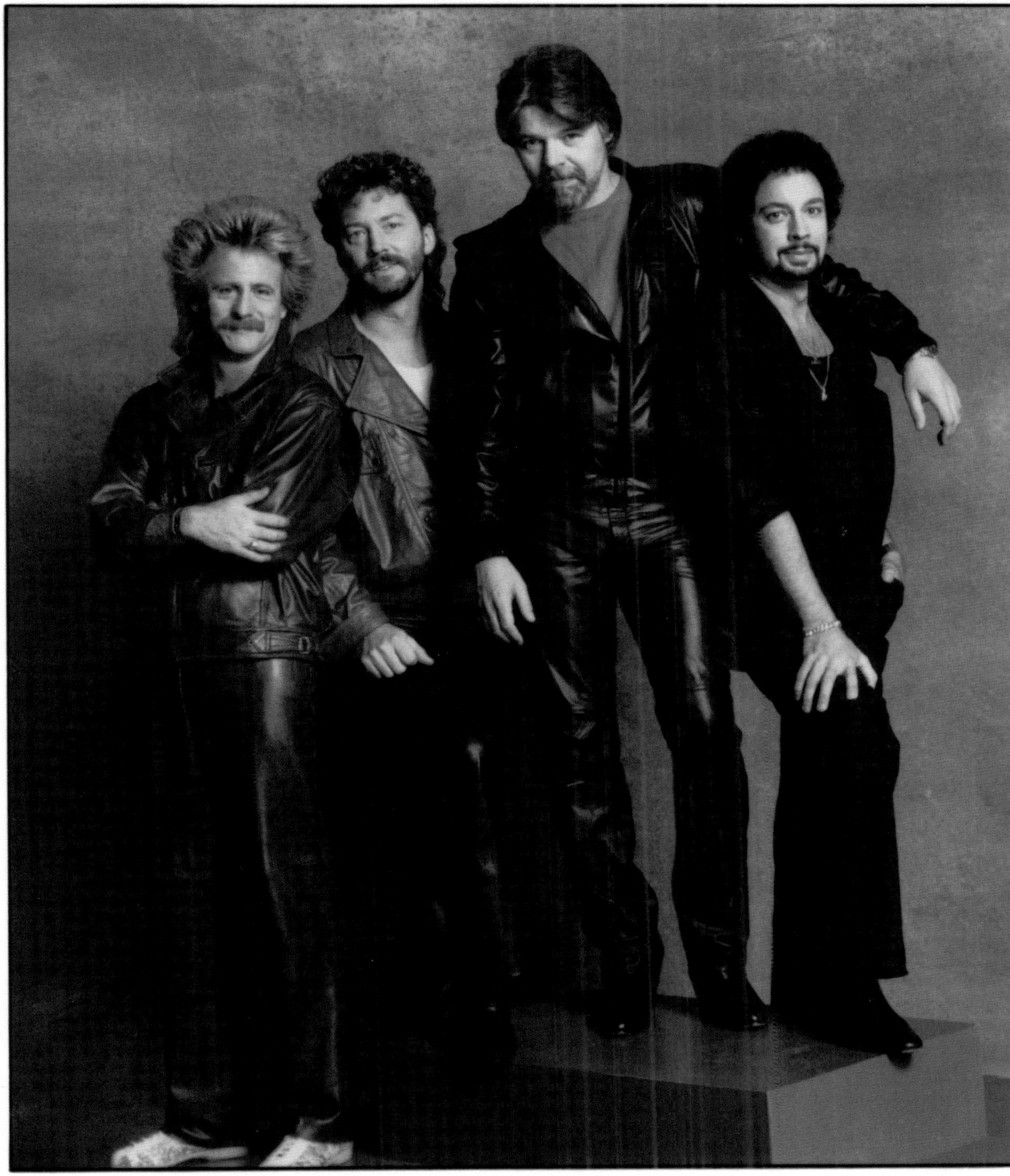

Photo: Aaron Rapoport / 1986

Chris Campbell Craig Frost Bob Seger Alto Reed

BOB SEGER
& THE SILVER BULLET BAND

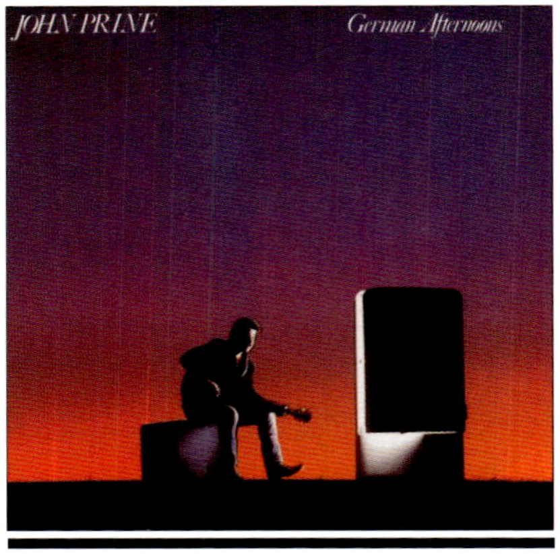

German Afternoons earned John Prine a second Grammy nomination, for Best Contemporary Folk Recording.

THROUGH SONGS that were simultaneously detailed and funny, John Prine had forged a reputation as a respected songwriter and performer, responsible for some of the past decade's most articulate and moving music. But the man who gave the world "Dear Abby" and "Illegal Smile" had a more unconventional image—as a "respected record company president" releasing albums on his own Oh Boy Records.

The independent approach to the music business suited him just fine. "I feel like I own this little hardware store—I make the music, I design the album covers, I follow everything all the way through," he enthused. "And the people I sell it to are the people who enjoy it—it's like we made a deal without those middlemen twirling their mustaches. It makes me want to work more than I ever did before."

The formation of Oh Boy partially resulted from Prine's move to Nashville from Chicago. "My girlfriend was living (in Nashville) and became my bass player," he explained. "Then I married her and lost a bass player but gained a wife. That's the reason I moved in the first place—it was a total accident on my part. If she'd have been from Idaho, I'd probably be eating a lot of potatoes now."

But Prine ensconced himself in the Nashville musical community, and the title of *German Afternoons*, his tenth album, was full of meaning—at least to him. "It's one of those days where you go out around one o'clock to get a burger, and you run into somebody you see all the time and have a beer with them. And somebody else comes in that you both kind of know but not that well. And because this third person comes in, you start buying each other beers. And the next thing you know, you're late for dinner. That's a German afternoon. A lot of the songs were written under that kind of duress—'What happened to the day?'"

But where did the phrase itself come from? "Oh, I just made it up—I like the sound of it," he laughed. "I got into the habit of telling my friends, 'Let's go have a German afternoon.' These things have to start somewhere."

German Afternoons featured acoustic bluegrass players such as New Grass Revival's Sam Bush and harkened back to the traditional country-influenced sound of Prine's *Sweet Revenge*. A remake of "Paradise," which appeared on his debut album in 1971, benefited from the updated musical direction. "Anytime I run into musicians that play fiddle and mandolin, we always end up singing 'Paradise,'" Prine noted. "I've been changing it over the years in my shows, and it's become more upbeat. So, I cut it again."

The offbeat "Linda Goes to Mars" was typical of Prine's exquisite vision, as were a couple of covers—A.P. Carter's "Lulu Walls" and "They'll Never Take Her Love from Me," made famous by Hank Williams. But it was "Speed of the Sound of Loneliness" that became an instant classic for many Prine fans. "The phrase sounds a little too heavy for my taste," Prine said of the ballad. "But on the other hand, I didn't have a co-writer to blame it on." ■

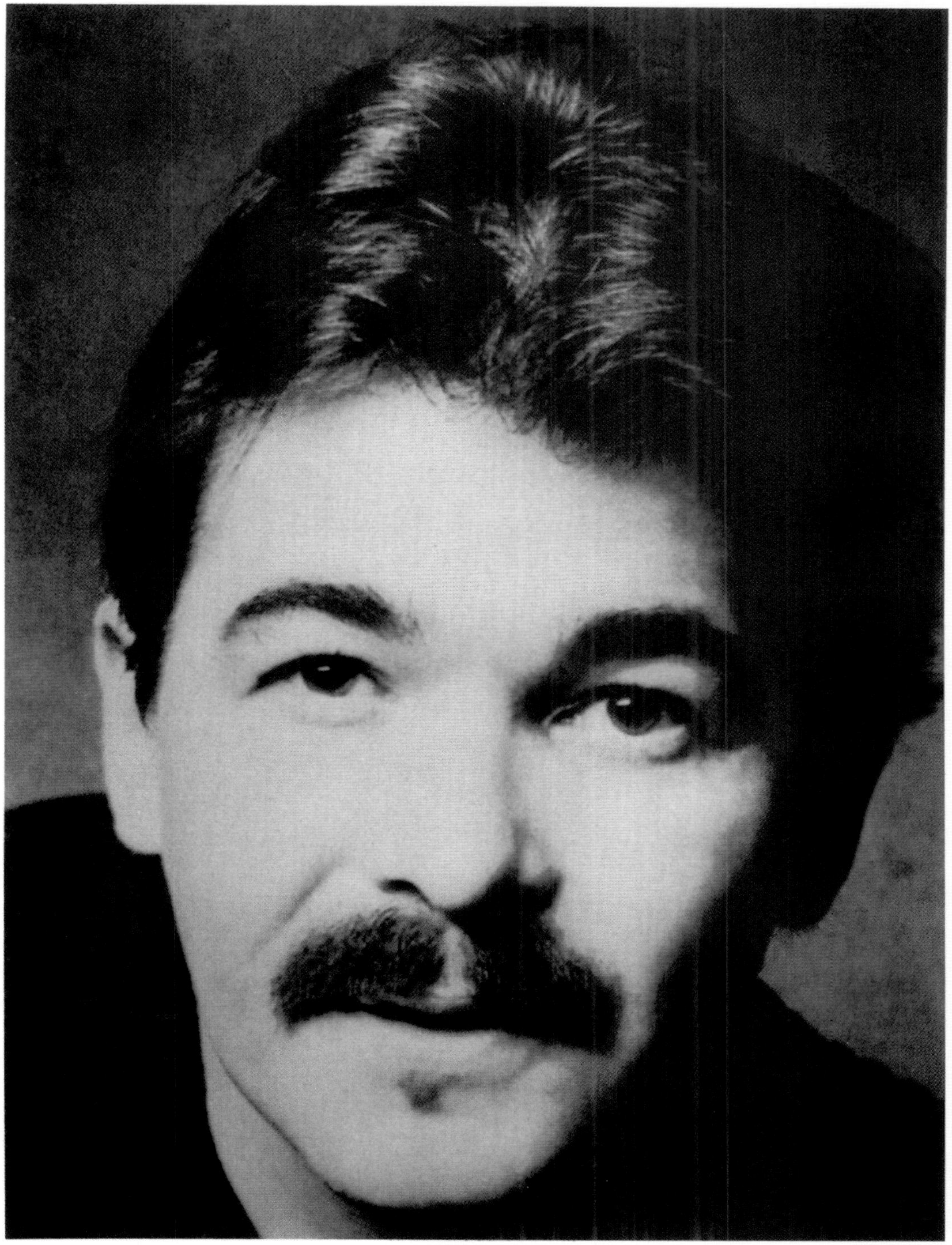

John Prine

Variety Artists
4120 Excelsior Boulevard Minneapolis Minnesota 55416
(612)925-3440

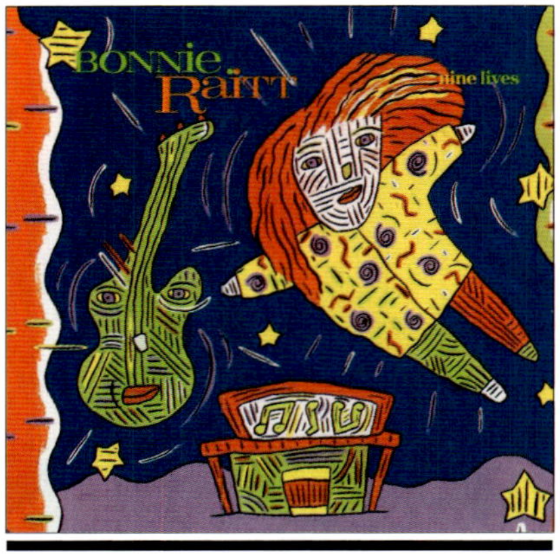

Billboard 200: *Nine Lives* (#115)

Bonnie Raitt remained an artist who commanded fan allegiance in a business usually run by chart positions.

EMERGING IN the Seventies as an authentic white blues performer, Bonnie Raitt had created a respected recording legacy by mingling contemporary and folk-oriented songs into her repertoire. Given the recent success of other blues-derived artists such as the Fabulous Thunderbirds and Robert Cray, Raitt was a likely candidate for a commercial renaissance.

"No Way to Treat a Lady" was the premier track from *Nine Lives*, Raitt's first album since 1982's *Green Light*. But stalwart fans were surprised to learn that the song was written by pop star Bryan Adams.

"I have real eclectic tastes," Raitt said. "Ever since my first album, there's always been some rockers and R&B songs and folk songs and blues songs. And there's always been some people who like only one style and think I've sold out if I try another. They don't realize that I've never tried to stay with one type of music—I'd be bored to death. I just pick songs that I like. I worry about what kind of music they are later."

Nine Lives combined tracks from 1983 sessions and others recorded in 1985. The project was delayed by a squabble with Raitt's longtime record label, Warner Bros., which had unceremoniously dropped her from the artist roster several years before finally agreeing to release *Nine Lives*. "My record label messed up my ability to make a living—I did my job and they didn't support me," she said. "I just stayed out on the road while the lawyers figured it out."

In the interim, Raitt had devised a dual touring career—working with an electric band and playing special acoustic folk-blues concerts accompanied only by a guitarist. "We do a lot of (country-blues legend) Sippie Wallace songs, a lot of ballads from the older days. Anyone who comes to see 'No Way to Treat a Lady' is going to feel a little short-changed. But if you want to come and see me, you've got to like all different sides of me. The wildest people I attract wear mink-lined Birkenstocks."

"No Way to Treat a Lady" garnered Raitt her third Grammy nomination, for Best Female Rock Performance, but sales never followed, and *Nine Lives* failed to erase the memory of previous albums that had been designed to make her a star with a homogenized sound that was too slick to accommodate her native funkiness. The album ended Raitt's long association with Warner Bros. Records. ■

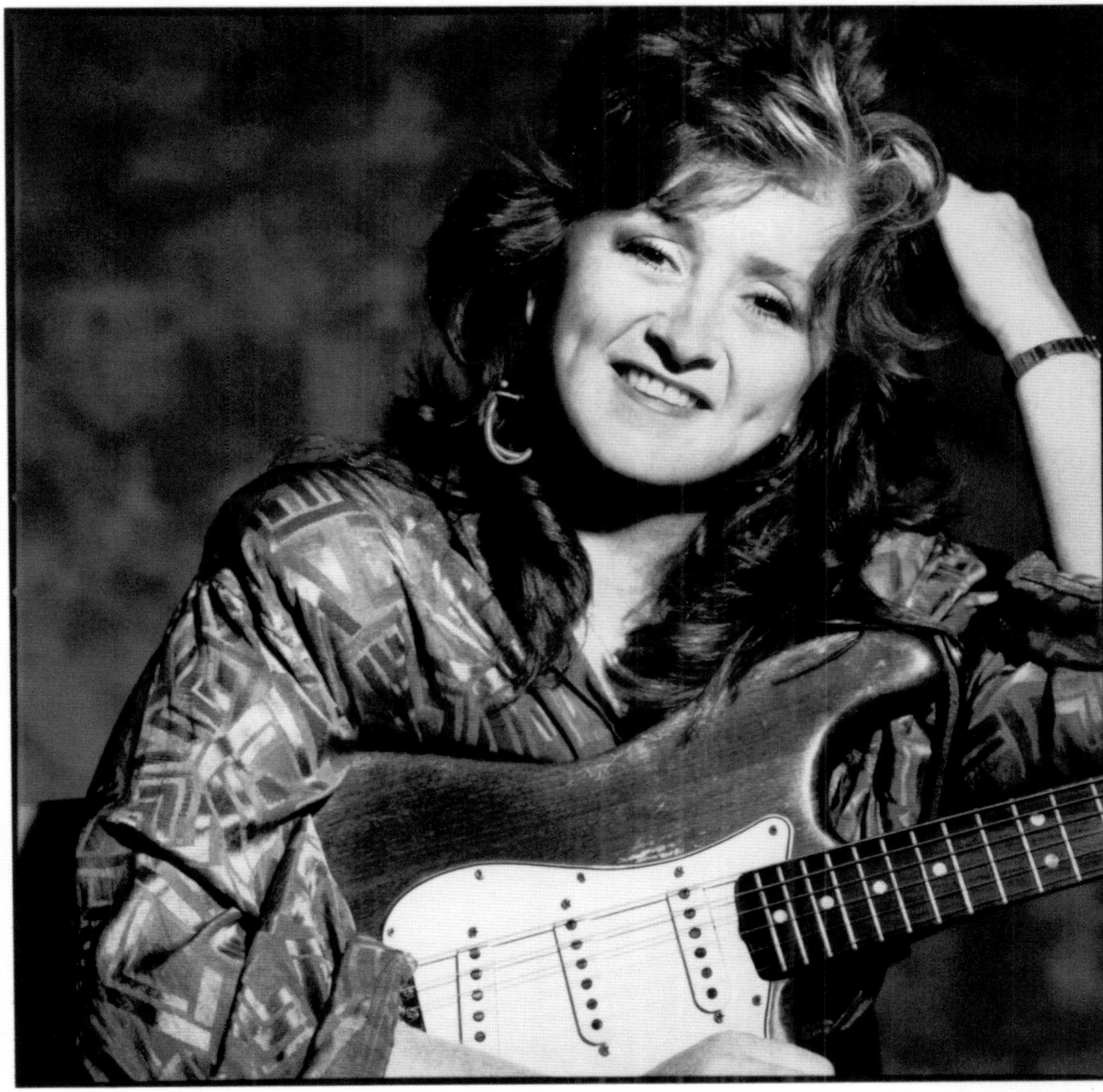

Photo Credit: Chris Cuffaro

BONNIE RAITT

WARNER BROS.

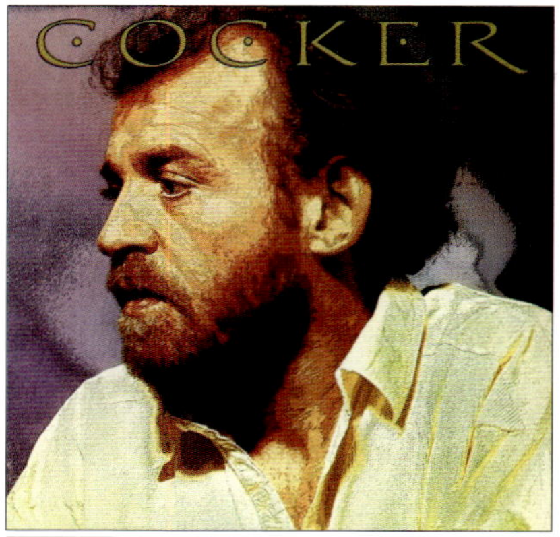

Billboard 200: *Cocker* (#50)
Billboard Hot 100: "Shelter Me" (#91)

"You Can Leave Your Hat On" was Joe Cocker's latest interpretation of an irresistible Randy Newman number.

ONE OF the few artists who could claim hit songs during the Sixties, Seventies and Eighties, Joe Cocker had enjoyed a long, complex career—it had never been sweeter than now.

"On the last tour in Europe, I found kids in the audience who grew up with my music through their parents who were teenagers in the Sixties and early Seventies," Cocker said proudly. "My music's sort of been handed down from one generation of young people to the next."

Cocker made an unforgettable American debut at the Woodstock Festival in 1969, performing the Beatles' "With a Little Help from My Friends," his body alive with spasmodic motion, hands flailing on phantom instruments. He put together a peculiar tribe of musicians with another exponent of blues rock, Leon Russell, for the famed Mad Dogs and Englishmen tour. A hit version of Billy Preston's "You Are So Beautiful" followed.

The dedicated blues rocker was introduced to a somewhat different audience when he teamed up with Jennifer Warnes on "Up Where We Belong," for the soundtrack to the 1982 hit film *An Officer and a Gentleman*. The ballad not only shot to No. 1 on the pop charts but also garnered a Grammy and an Academy Award.

"When people heard that song, they wondered what had happened to the old gravel-belter, that I'd softened up," Cocker said. "But I'll always return to my soul base. Doing those poppy songs doesn't suit me."

On *Cocker*, the track "Shelter Me" was written especially for Cocker by Nick Di Stefano. He continued to illuminate the work of Randy Newman, putting his indelible stamp on "You Can Leave Your Hat On," which was also used in the famous striptease scene featured in the Adrian Lyne film *9½ Weeks* (Newman's "Guilty" was a Cocker hit from 1972).

"I was looking for blues-based songs," he explained. "Meaningful songs—meaningful not necessarily in lyrics but in feeling. They're hard to find. I sifted through thousands of songs and at one point I thought we'd never find enough."

It had been an ofttimes bumpy road for Cocker, but his efforts hadn't turned his head.

"I still get a little crazy," he said. "I haven't particularly mellowed, but I am taking it easier. I'm not quite as berserk as I used to be. I try to pace myself now." ■

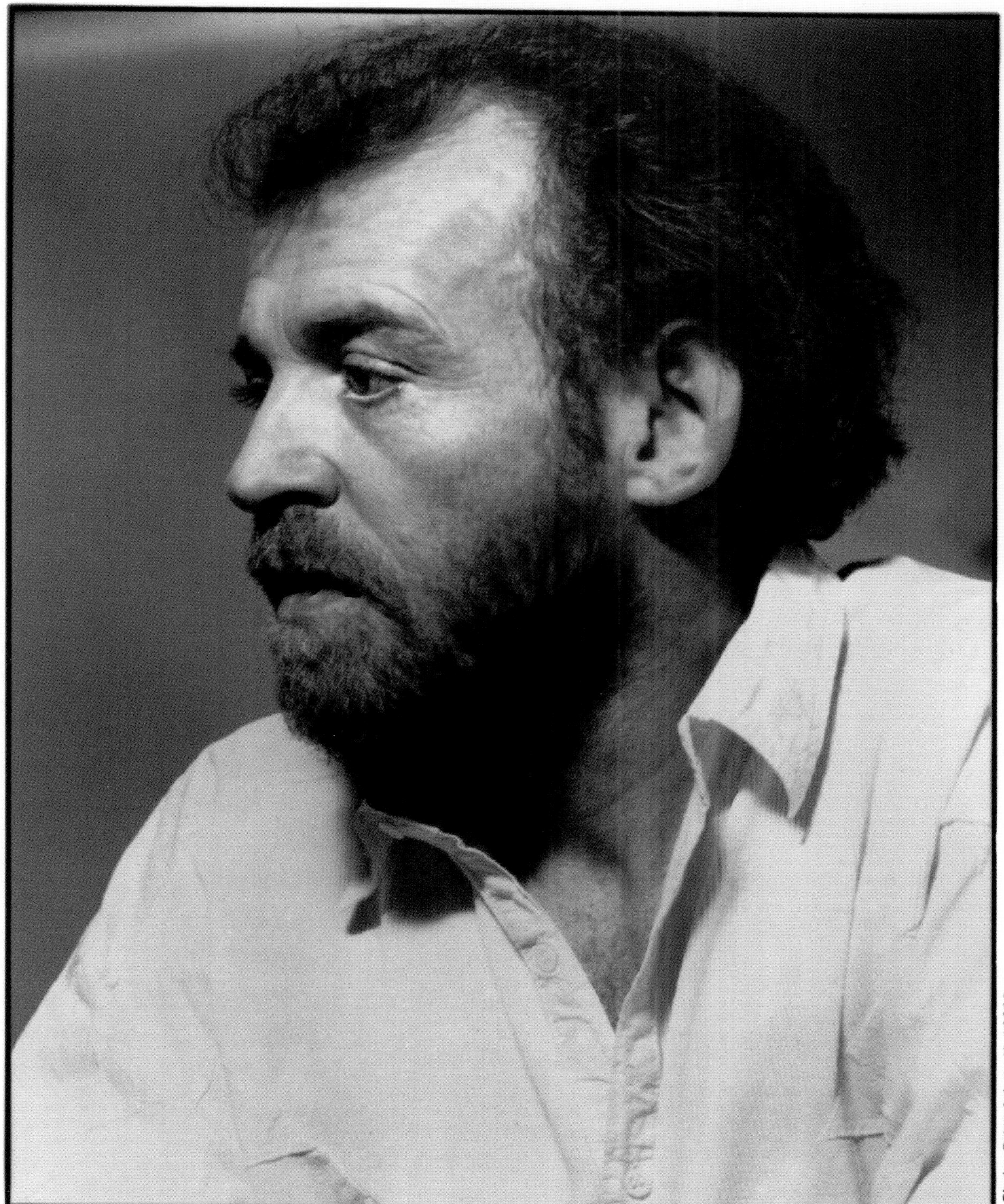

Photo: Peter Ashworth / 1986

JOE COCKER

Capitol RECORDS

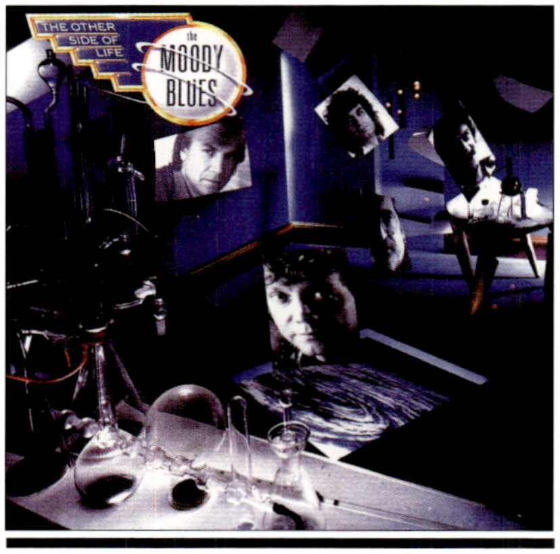

Billboard 200: *The Other Side of Life* (#9)
Billboard Hot 100: "Your Wildest Dreams" (#9); "The Other Side of Life" (#58)

The Moody Blues enjoyed renewed success with *The Other Side of Life* and the hit track "Your Wildest Dreams."

IN THE mid-Sixties, the Moody Blues conceived of their illustrious music-with-a-message approach—*Days of Future Passed* went on to be acknowledged as a milestone in orchestral rock with the classics "Nights in White Satin" and "Tuesday Afternoon."

"The timing of our image was just right," guitarist Justin Hayward said. "As a band, we were going through a lot of psychedelic and religious experiences—and then a couple of months later, it seemed a whole generation decided to change as well. We were very aware of a double meaning in our songs. There was always an 'I-love-you-baby-come-to-bed' meaning, and a spiritual meaning as well."

Two unique factors intersected with the Moodies' success. One was the prominence of overly obsessive fans. "We'd regularly get nice people who said they had traveled to the concert in a spaceship. I'd say, 'Where is it?' and they'd say, 'In the parking lot, where else?' They always told me that unless I could acquire enough faith, I couldn't see it.

"There was an occasion in Texas where this guy really believed the world was going to end, and that the Moody Blues would save things when we came to town to play—our music was going to set up a 'cosmic vibration.' He started this big countdown, got on television and everything. The day of the concert, we played our gig, everyone had a lot of fun, and the world didn't end. The next morning, he was completely incensed. He felt that we'd really let him down! We came out of our hotel and he was yelling, 'You bums!'"

The other element was the Moodies' pioneering use of the Mellotron, a keyboard/tape banks instrument to record sprawling, ambitious soundscapes. "It had an orchestral sound to it, pre-synthesizers," Hayward said. "It was temperamental and incredibly difficult to play. I think we were the only band that got it together to get onstage. But it was a unique mood setter, a perfect blend for the songs we were writing."

No band survived two decades without suffering through dispiriting times, and the Moodies lapsed when they embarked on individual projects. They eventually returned to the group format, enjoying a milestone in 1981 when *Long Distance Voyager* hit No. 1.

The Other Side of Life put the group back into the Top 10, retaining features of the old Moody Blues style—appealing melodies, complex vocal arrangements and an elegantly symphonic feel. The album also yielded "Your Wildest Dreams," the band's first Top 10 single since the reactivated "Nights in White Satin" in 1972—and awakened a new generation of fans to the music. But the members were through with the days of nutty fans ("The locny element has gone on to other things") and out-of-tune Mellotrons ("The sound is digital now rather than mechanical, but you still can't beat the old tinny sound").

"We've brought more personal satisfaction to ourselves by making our music accessible to a wider audience," Hayward said. "We've become less intense as people, about taking our music so seriously. We've learned to enjoy what we do, and that's the key to the whole thing. The Moody Blues will continue as long as it's a pleasure." ■

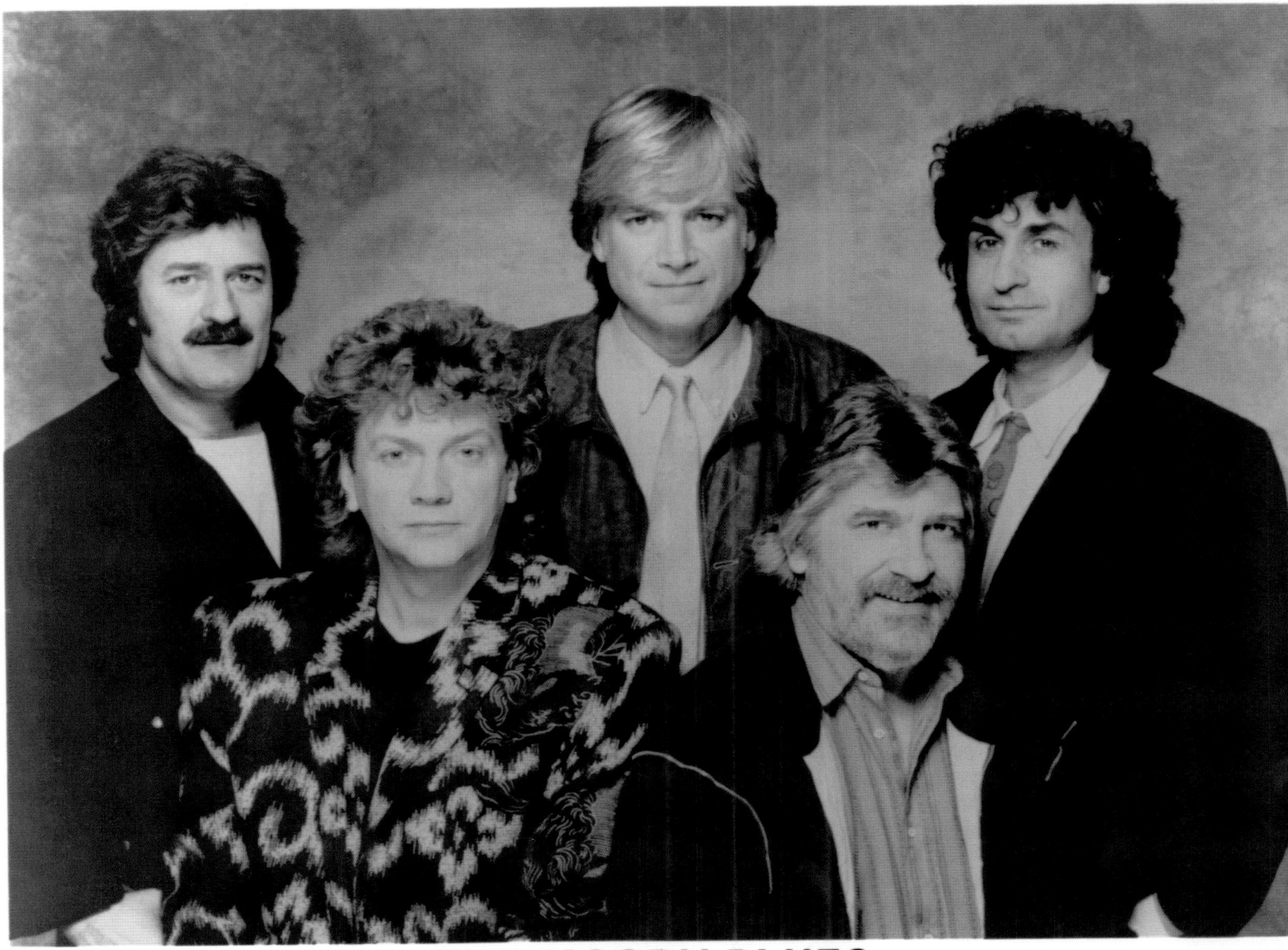

THE MOODY BLUES

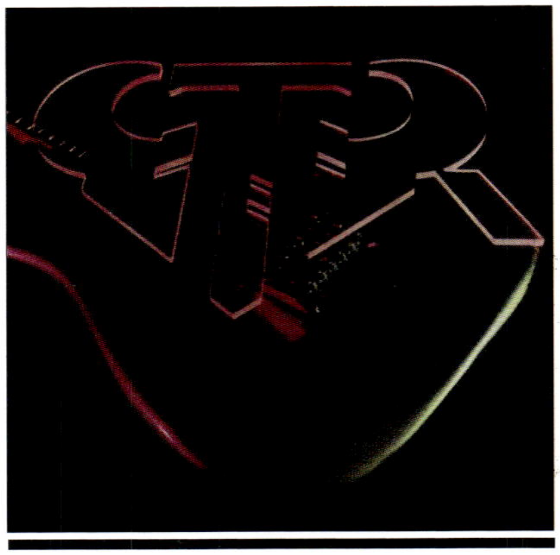

Billboard 200: *GTR* (#11)
Billboard Hot 100: "When the Heart Rules the Mind" (#14); "The Hunter" (#85)

The supergroup GTR brought together Steve Howe and Steve Hackett, a pair of innovative, influential guitarists.

ON PAPER, it was a progressive rock fan's dream come true. GTR—an abbreviation for guitar—was a new group that paired Steve Howe, the former six-string virtuoso with Yes, and Steve Hackett, who played with Genesis during that band's art-rock heyday.

"Steve and I spoke at some point in the Seventies—we acknowledged each other's presence here and there—but we didn't have any real communication until GTR," Howe said. "It could have turned out to be one of those duet albums, but as it happened we talked about songwriting, and piecing a few of our songs together."

The rock press and radio received no shortage of GTR hype. "The guitar equivalent of the *Ben-Hur* chariot race," one press release stated. "If the guitar is the ultimate rock instrument, GTR just may be the ultimate rock band," said another. Fans salivated at the prospect of two guitarists of such distinction facing off for orchestrated battles.

And then came the album. *GTR* ranked as a letdown. The problem wasn't with the playing—Howe and Hackett were undeniably great technicians. But they had applied their skills to formulaic pop rock in the tradition of Asia (Howe founded that group between his stints with Yes and GTR). There was no innovation, no assertion of either guitarist's distinct style.

"Well, the idea is to make something accessible, right?" singer Max Bacon countered. "People don't want to hear guitar solos anymore—it's too self-indulgent. And I happen to have what you'd call a very commercial voice."

GTR recruited Bacon from the heavy-metal band Bronz, but it was obvious that there was no real chemistry in GTR, only a new manufactured framework to attract dyed-in-the-wool Howe fans. The anthemic "When the Heart Rules the Mind" managed to receive video coverage and airplay, but an infamous review of the album consisted of only three letters: "SHT." GTR stayed together for a year. ■

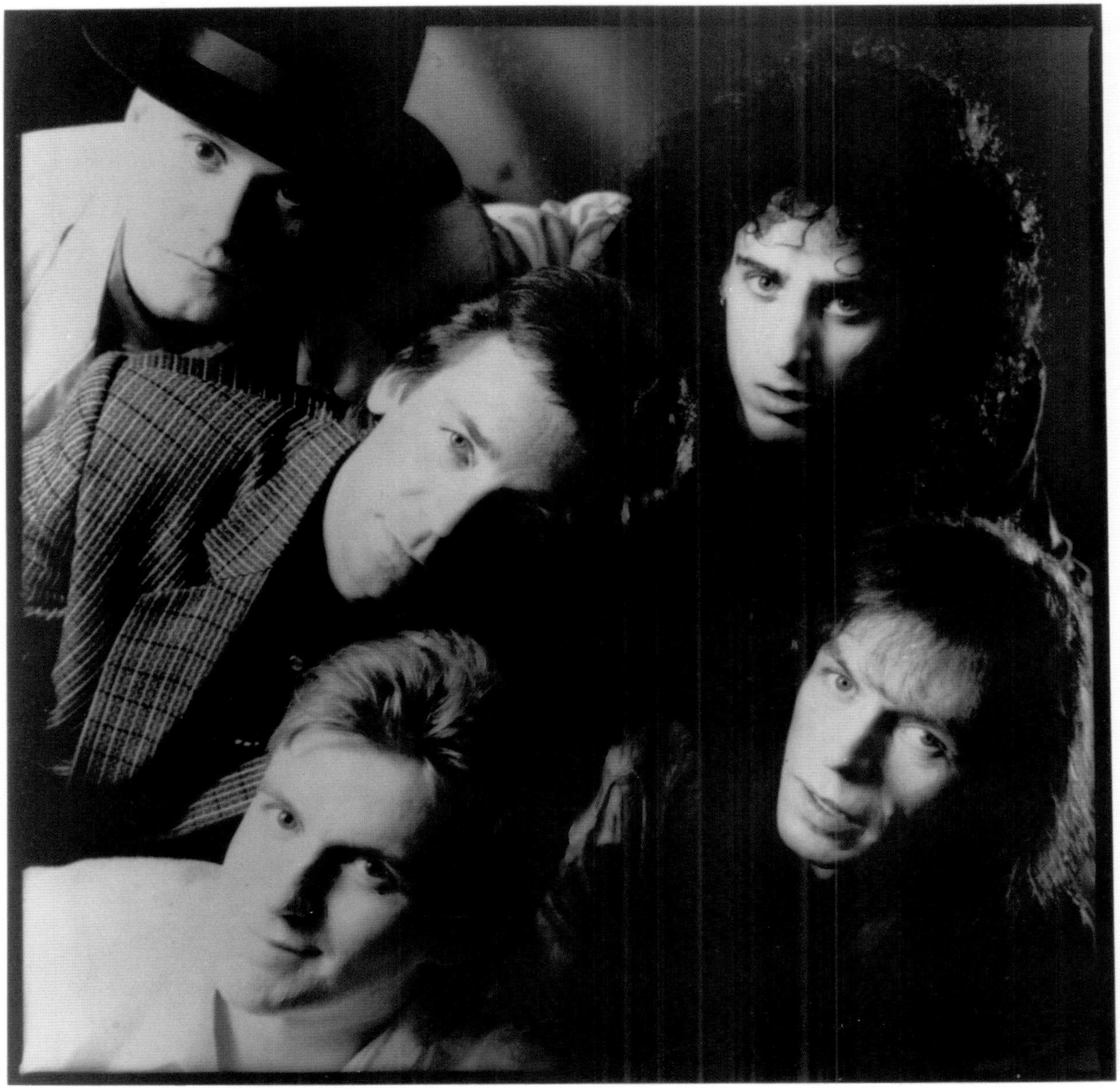

Management: Brian Lane

Premier Talent Agency

ARISTA™

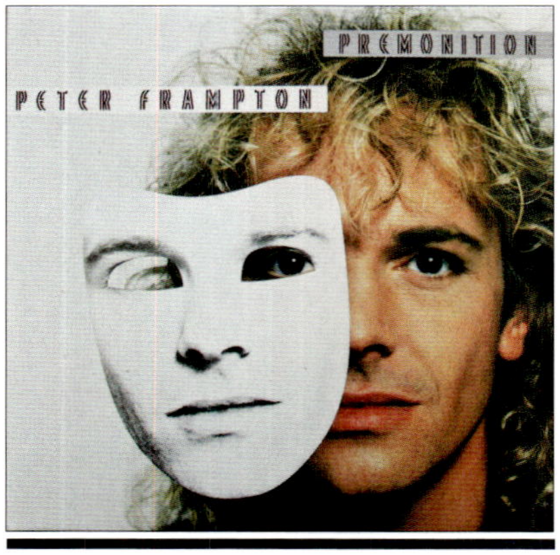

Billboard 200: *Premonition* (#80)
Billboard Hot 100: "Lying" (#74)

The former golden boy of easy-listening rock, Peter Frampton insisted he still had things to say on *Premonition.*

IN THE mid-Seventies, there was no bigger star on the rock music scene than Peter Frampton. Following stints with the Herd and Humble Pie, as well as years on the road opening for other acts, he blew up in the summer of 1976 with the live double-album *Frampton Comes Alive*. His pop-star good looks and seductive electric guitar style attracted more than 8 million record buyers.

Yet Frampton's career went into an abrupt tailspin. His manager at the time coerced him into releasing *I'm in You*, a wimpy follow-up album that catered to teenyboppers rather than his rock following. His appearance in the turgid musical film version of *Sgt. Pepper's Lonely Hearts Club Band* cemented his fate. In his own words, Frampton had come to be perceived as a "pop music cartoon," and he fell from critical and commercial grace. Following 1982's *The Art of Control* album, he dropped out of sight.

"I didn't think people were taking me seriously," the guitarist said. "The press and the public thought I had let them down—and on face value, they were right. But they didn't know what was going on behind the scenes. The image came about through mistakes I had made. I was going against my gut instincts."

But Frampton had launched a comeback with the release of *Premonition*, spawning a minor hit single in "Lying." The return to rock's front lines followed a regrouping for the 36-year-old guitarist. "If you think back, I hadn't really taken an extended break since I was 16 with the Herd," he explained. "For many years, it was write-record-tour, write-record-tour, with only 10 days' vacation. What I should have done is taken time right after the live album. But we can't redo the past, and I don't wish to."

During his break from the public eye, the British rocker married and settled down in New York. "I just enjoyed being at home for a while, because you have to do normal things or you run out of ideas. So, for the first few years, I just helped my wife bring up our daughter."

But Frampton resurfaced in 1984 on a Thelonious Monk tribute album with guitarist Chris Spedding, a move he called "purely selfish—it pushed me as a musician." Soon after, he received a call from former Dixie Dregs guitarist Steve Morse to play on the title track of Morse's *Stand Up* album and to perform a duet at Carnegie Hall. It dawned on Frampton that he was still in demand as a musician.

"It was surprising to me, considering my credibility had definitely been damaged by the publicity," he recalled. "But it made me realize what I really wanted to do—to play the guitar, which is what got me into the whole thing in the first place." The confessed "gadget freak" had kept up with sequencing and sampling and the new technology of making records, and *Premonition* applied contemporary production to his trademark sound.

"I've got a new philosophy," he said. "Before, I lost the enjoyment factor along the way because I said yes begrudgingly to a lot of things. Now, success to me means that I'm enjoying what I'm doing, so I feel successful right now. If pop stardom happens all over again, I'm not going to say no. But I will say no to a lot of other things." ■

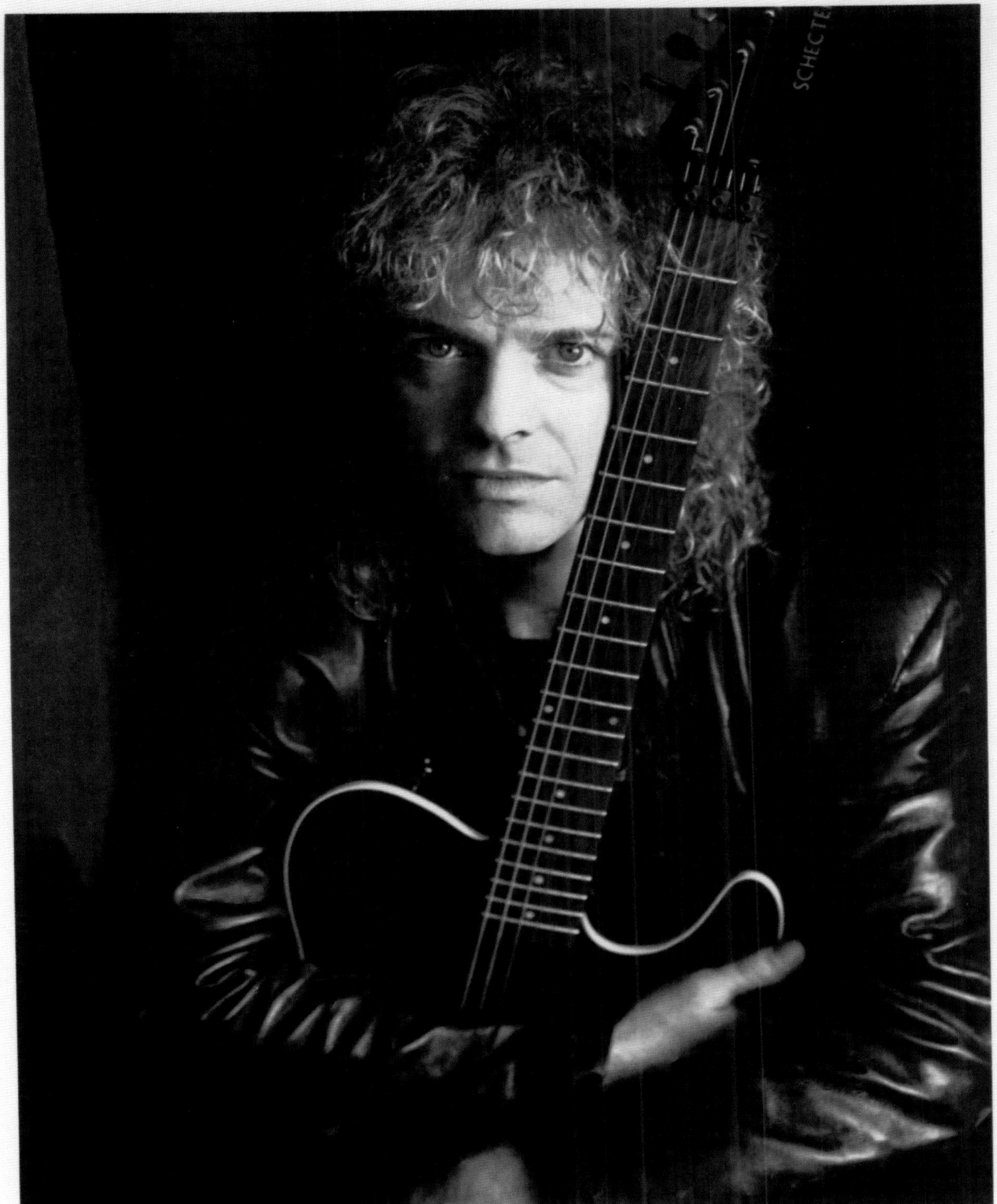

PETER FRAMPTON

ATLANTIC

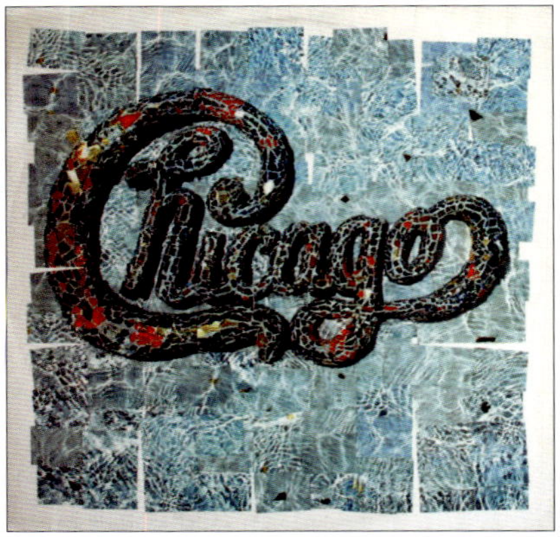

Billboard 200: *Chicago 18* (#35)
Billboard Hot 100: "25 or 6 to 4" (#48); "Will You Still Love Me?" (#3); "If She Would Have Been Faithful..." (#17); "Niagara Falls" (#90)

Secure in their hit-making abilities, the members of Chicago made the first album minus co-founder Peter Cetera.

THE MOST distinguishable element in Chicago's hit sound had been Peter Cetera's voice. His winsome singing had marked the rock group's Top 10 entries ("You're the Inspiration," "Hard Habit to Break"). But following 1984's smash *Chicago 17* album, Cetera announced he was embarking on a solo recording and acting career. The rest of the band wasn't left to languish—after two decades together, the remaining members had learned a thing or two about enduring.

"We'd still be doing the same things with or without Peter," trumpeter Lee Loughnane shrugged. "Writing music. Recording our 18th album. Going on tour with it. We knew for a long time it was going to happen. We just didn't know when. There are still five original guys out of seven. Peter is the only one who actually chose to leave the band."

Loughnane was alluding to the loss of guitarist Terry Kath, who accidentally shot and killed himself in 1978. "We survived that, too, and that was unexpected," Loughnane noted. Indeed, at that point Chicago regrouped and went on to enjoy renewed success and acclaim in the Eighties.

Chicago had never totally relied on a single individual's talent. While Cetera achieved considerable solo success (the hits "Glory of Love" and "The Next Time I Fall"), Chicago still drew on outstanding vocal contributions from keyboardists Robert Lamm and Bill Champlin. The group decided it needed a tenor to fill out the vocal spectrum, however, and recruited Jason Scheff, the son of Jerry Scheff, the longtime bassist with Elvis Presley's band.

"I didn't think I'd ever be able to work with a band like Chicago, because I didn't think there'd be any place for me," the soft-spoken Scheff said. "I was just writing songs as part of a publishing deal—it was a good way to get people talking about me. A few months later, the record company called my publisher looking for songs for Peter Cetera's solo album, possibly someone to collaborate with him. My publisher told them about this new guy—me."

The story then assumed fairy-tale proportions. Scheff's tape circulated among record company executives (Chicago and Cetera shared the same label), producers and band member, who thought Scheff sounded like the guy who could replace Cetera in Chicago. "Some people think our voices are similar," Scheff recalled. "But maybe it comes from all the time I spent singing Top 30, trying to sound like records from Michael Jackson to Sting. Now I'm just relaxing and singing like I sing."

On *Chicago 18*, the Los Angeles-based band continued to benefit from the studio guidance of Grammy Award-winning producer David Foster. "He tells us we're one of the bands that got him involved in pop music," Loughnane said. And it was Foster who convinced the band to remake an old Chicago song—a new high-tech version of "25 or 6 to 4." Still, the song failed to duplicate the success of the original. There was more of a traditional Chicago performance on a power ballad, the Top 3 "Will You Still Love Me," and the Top 20 "If She Would Have Been Faithful..." ■

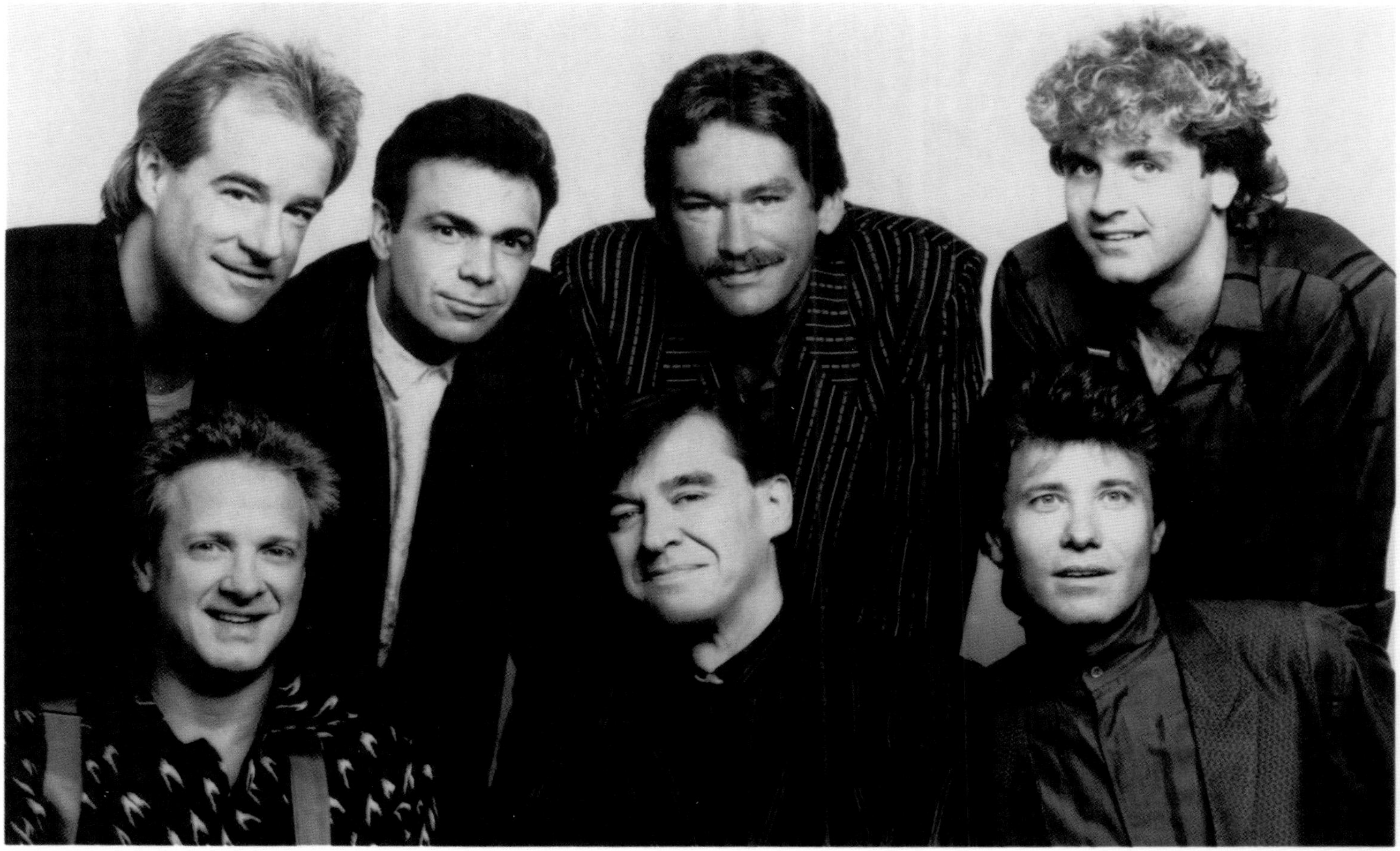

Photo Credit: Guy Webster

JAMES PANKOW DANNY SERAPHINE BILL CHAMPLIN JASON SCHEFF

LEE LOUGHNANE WALT PARAZAIDER ROBERT LAMM

CHICAGO

Full Moon

WARNER BROS.

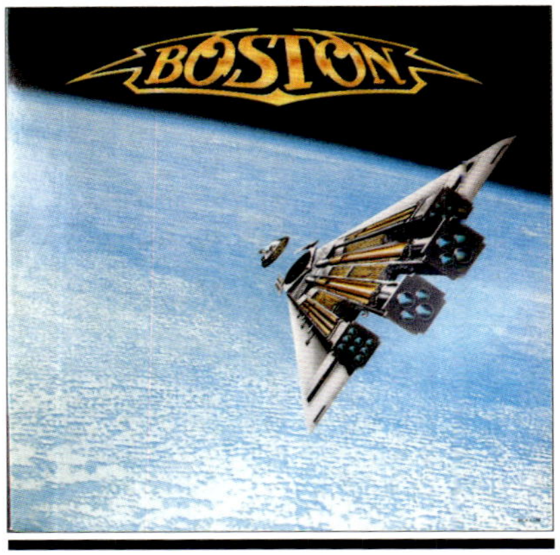

Billboard 200: *Third Stage* (No. 1)
Billboard Hot 100: "Amanda" (No. 1); "We're Ready" (#9);
"Can'tcha Say (You Believe in Me)" (#20)

Wired to call the tune as he pleased, Tom Scholz produced Boston's hit album *Third Stage* at his own pace.

IF ANY American rock band had associated itself with technology, it was Boston. Consider the background of group leader Tom Scholz—a former consultant for Polaroid, a graduate of MIT and the holder of several dozen patents. His engineering skills had aided him immeasurably as the architect of the band's signature sound, a blend of his shimmering, orchestrated guitar parts and perfectly harmonized passages pitted against the high, soaring vocals of Brad Delp. Released in 1976, *Boston* became the fastest-selling rock debut up to that time—the polished, epic-scaled sonics dominated rock radio, imitated but never duplicated by other bands.

Scholz spent over two years working on the follow-up, *Don't Look Back*. He only released the album because of intense label pressure. Dissatisfied with the results, he vowed not to release another record until he could work without duress. Many matters had to be resolved in court, but Scholz worked with attorneys and kept tinkering with an album. After winning a legal battle with his recording label, Scholz finally felt comfortable releasing *Third Stage*—eight years after the band's previous album.

The liner notes gave an indication of Scholz's lifestyle during the recording of *Third Stage*. 175 light bulbs "burnt out before I did," and he claimed to have punched the "record" button a million times on 100 reels of tape. During Boston's hiatus, Scholz marketed the Rockman, a micro gizmo that electronically duplicated many of his patented guitar sounds. What did his musical partner do in that time?

"I produced a couple of children," the affable Delp said. "I spent a lot of time with my family, although it was a guilty pleasure to have that much time off. It certainly wasn't something Tom or I planned. It isn't a wise business move to retire for six years, but I enjoyed my leisure time more than Tom did. My golf game is a lot more polished."

When the time came to lay down his vocal tracks, however, Delp was a diligent collaborator, working for days with Scholz in the studio to perfect a single verse of any given song. "Tom has an amazing ability to concentrate where most people couldn't do it," Delp said. "He starts with something in his mind, and if it's not coming out, he doesn't stop until it does."

Third Stage sold a quick 4 million. "Amanda" peaked at No. 1, and "We're Ready" and "Can'tcha Say" were also hit singles. To tour, Scholz and Delp recruited a new group of players and were pleased with the way the lineup sounded. Given the public's response, they wanted to get the unit in the studio. "Who knows," Delp said, "maybe we'll hear another Boston album before this decade is over." It took another eight years. ■

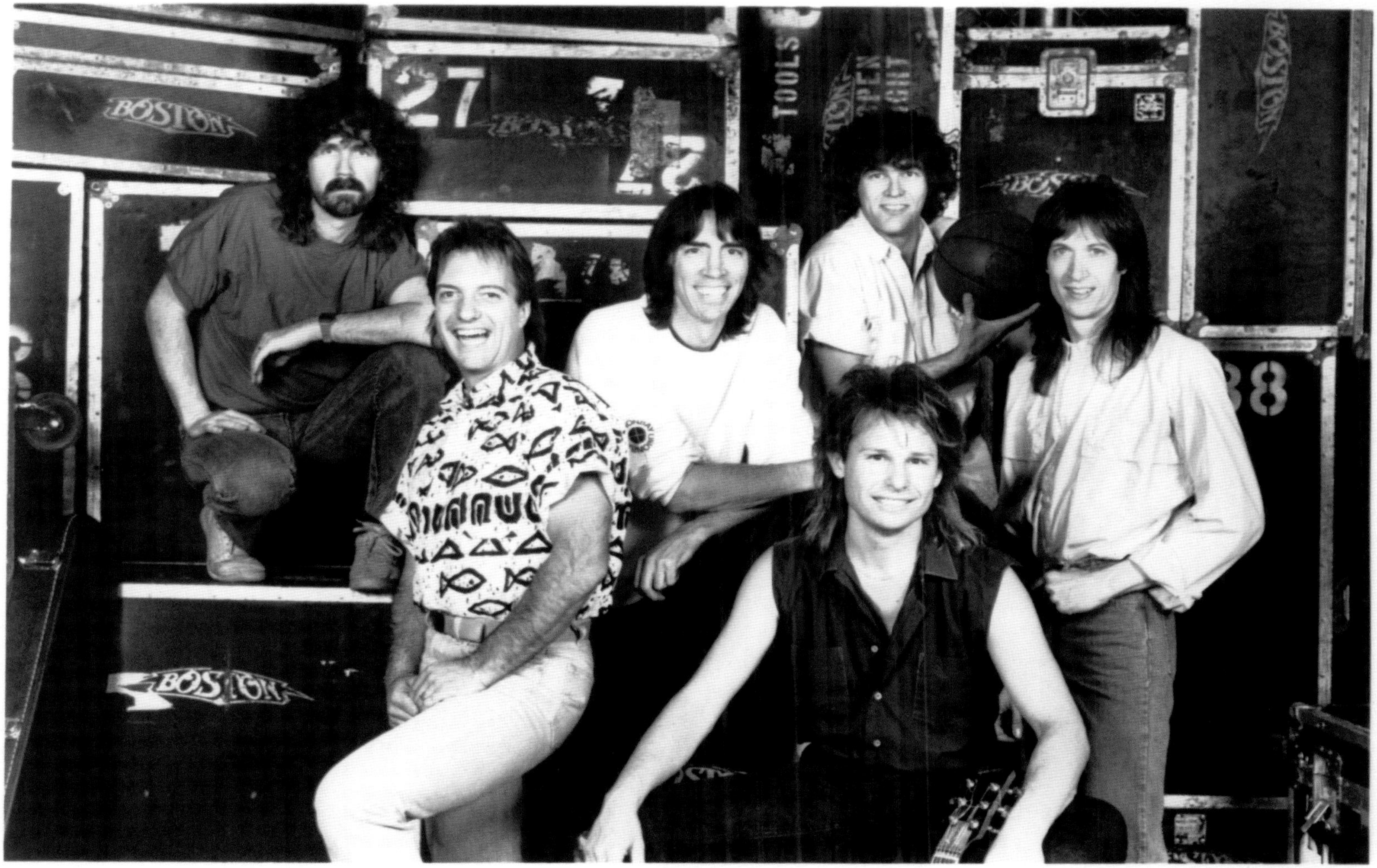

BRAD DELP DOUG HUFFMAN TOM SCHOLZ JIM MASDEA DAVID SIKES GARY PIHL

BOSTON

MCA RECORDS

PHOTO / RON POWNALL

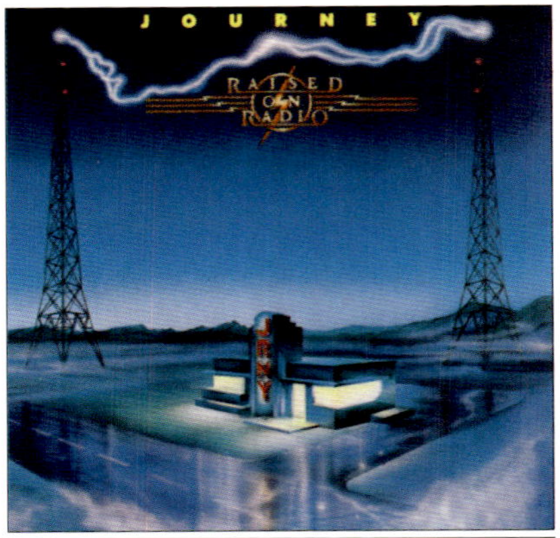

Billboard 200: *Raised on Radio* (#4)
Billboard Hot 100: "Be Good to Yourself" (#9); "Suzanne" (#17); "Girl Can't Help It" (#17); "I'll Be Alright Without You" (#14); "Why Can't This Night Go on Forever" (#60)

The five members of Journey reconvened to make *Raised on Radio*–and the band soon pared down to a trio.

IT WAS a rock 'n' roll given that even the best of bands could break up under lifestyle and business pressures. Jonathan Cain summed it up—"It can be similar to a marriage. Or a divorce."

Cain was the keyboard player in Journey, one of the most popular and undeniably influential bands of the early Eighties. He was snapped up as a replacement for original keyboardist Gregg Rolie in 1981, and he helped the group scale commercial heights with anthemic rockers and sweeping power ballads on such albums as *Escape* and *Frontiers*.

But the hit machinery led to acrimony, and in the three years since the last Journey tour, the group had endured some nearly fatal pressures. Singer Steve Perry recorded a solo album, *Street Talk*, that sold more than 2 million copies and spawned the hits "Oh, Sherrie" and "Foolish Heart." Suddenly a full-time Perry solo career seemed like an obvious course of action, and rumors began surfacing about his parent band.

"Journey didn't exist as a band for a while," Cain admitted. "Steven had some problems, we had some problems and we had to sit down and work them out just like a family."

Guitarist Neal Schon and Cain had already started writing the music for *Raised on Radio*, Journey's 11th album, before Perry made the decision to return to the band and produce the record. Both camps were aware of the many groups that had copied the Journey sound, and they wanted to avoid becoming a caricature of themselves. So they headed into the R&B direction they had investigated on "Ask the Lonely," the group's contribution to the platinum-selling soundtrack for the film *Two of a Kind*. During his solo exercise, Perry had become enamored of singing in that style, so new Journey material wound up sounding very Motown.

But when the band entered the studio to record *Raised on Radio*, problems arose with original bassist Ross Valory and drummer Steve Smith. Smith had played mostly jazz during his time off, and the new Journey tunes were steeped in pop values.

"There was just a distance there after the hiatus, and you either work it out or it's irreconcilable differences," Cain said. "We were after the best record possible. It was unfortunate that Steve Perry had to call the shots as producer; the decision really tore him up emotionally—Steve Smith was one of his biggest fans. But we backed him as a band; it was unanimous. We're certainly taking care of him and Ross. Journey finished *Raised on Radio* with a hired rhythm section. The cohesive, well-crafted album produced four Top 20 singles, but sales didn't match *Escape* or *Frontiers*. The members of Journey weren't surprised.

"Not in this marketplace," Cain said. "If all the disco stuff is what the people want, they can have it. I think the business is in big trouble right now. There's just too much music available, and people are using it like elevator music—turn it on and turn it off. People who will sit down and listen will find that our album is quality, not trendy. We're still Journey—we haven't changed our style." ■

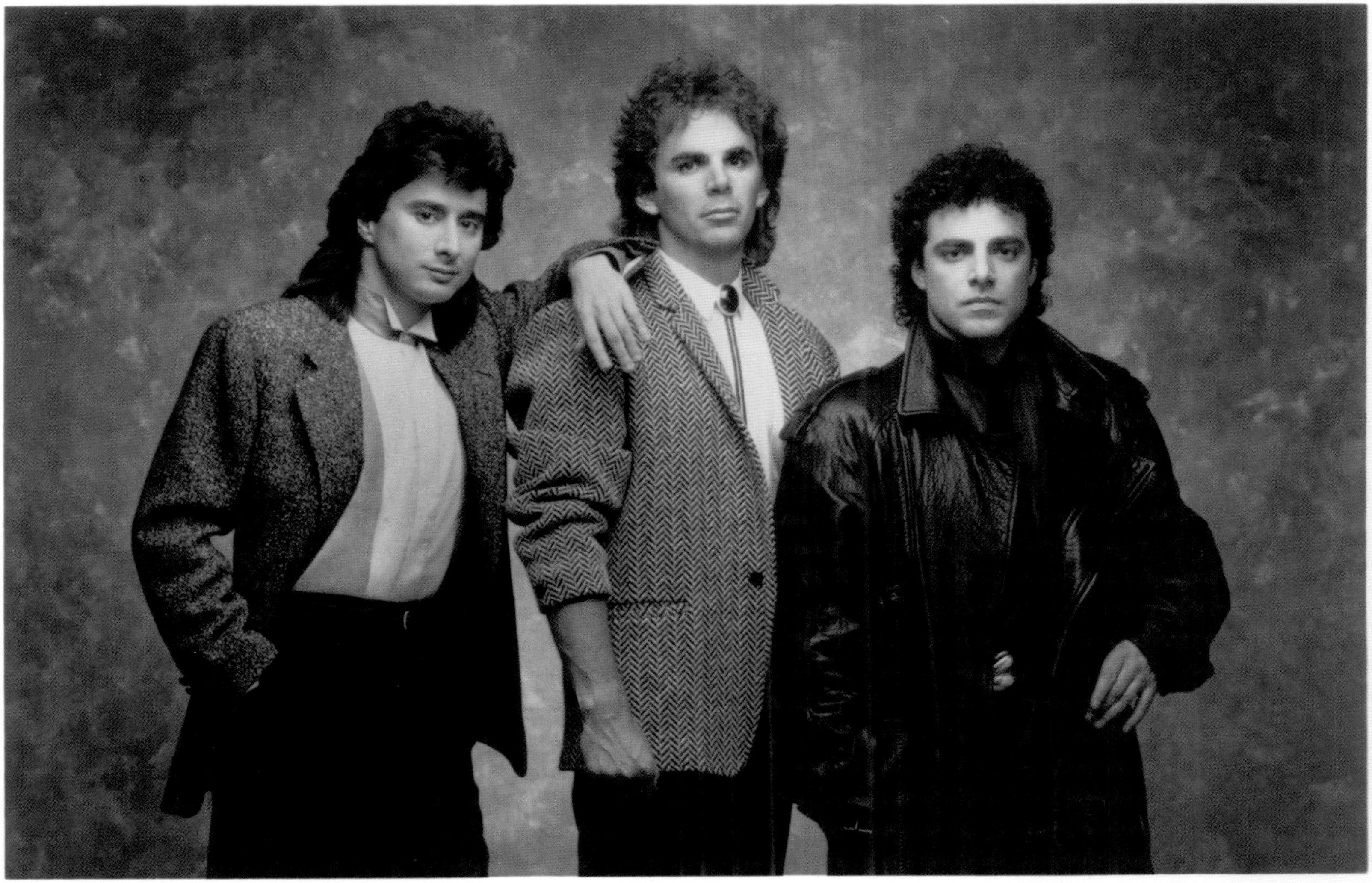

Steve Perry Jonathan Cain Neal Schon

HERBIE HERBERT
MANAGEMENT, INC.

JOURNEY

Columbia
8603

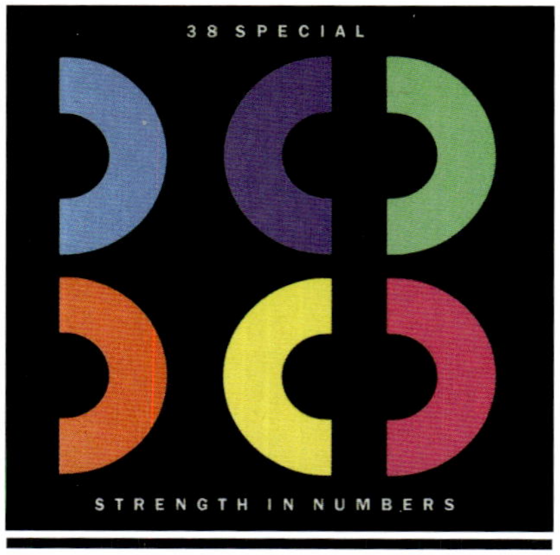

Billboard 200: *Strength in Numbers* (#17)
Billboard Hot 100: "Like No Other Night" (#14); "Somebody Like You" (#48)

Strength in Numbers sported "Like No Other Night," another example of 38 Special's radio-friendly songcraft.

FROM THEIR onetime status as just another Southern rock anachronism, the members of 38 Special had evolved into a potent hit-making machine during the Eighties. The group's songwriting talent was based on a confluence of styles, from British rock to contemporary bands like the Cars.

"Growing up in Jacksonville, Florida, we were very fortunate to be able to rub shoulders with some great musicians," vocalist, guitarist and songwriter Don Barnes said. "We only had to walk down the street to hear the Allman Brothers play. We also learned a lot from Lynyrd Skynyrd's Ronnie Van Zant, especially his competitive spirit. But when we went home, we'd wear out the grooves on our Beatles records, too."

A strong identity was gradually established as 38 Special racked up smash singles ("Fantasy Girl," "Caught Up in You," "Hold On Loosely") and platinum albums. The *Strength in Numbers* album featured a lean, stripped-down sound courtesy of new producer Keith Olsen. "Like No Other Night" was a model 38 Special showcase—a memorable melody, layered vocals, shimmering guitars and plenty of crunch.

"There's still a certain bit of aggression that goes with being underdogs from the South—it brings out that guitar-in-your-face type of attitude," Barnes admitted. Yet many of the band's original fans—the young male battering rams enthralled with hot guitar moves—felt betrayed by 38 Special's move away from their Southern boogie roots.

"But Molly Hatchet stayed with one mode of music, trying to fill Lynyrd Skynyrd's shoes, and they faded away because they weren't ready to change," Barnes countered. "We wanted to find our own way. We always fought that stigma of being 'bikers with guitars and no good sense.' We're living testament that you can do something with yourself if you stick with it—there is hope. You just have to look at the whole puzzle. If you can be positive and a little naïve about it all, you'll find some way to make it work." ■

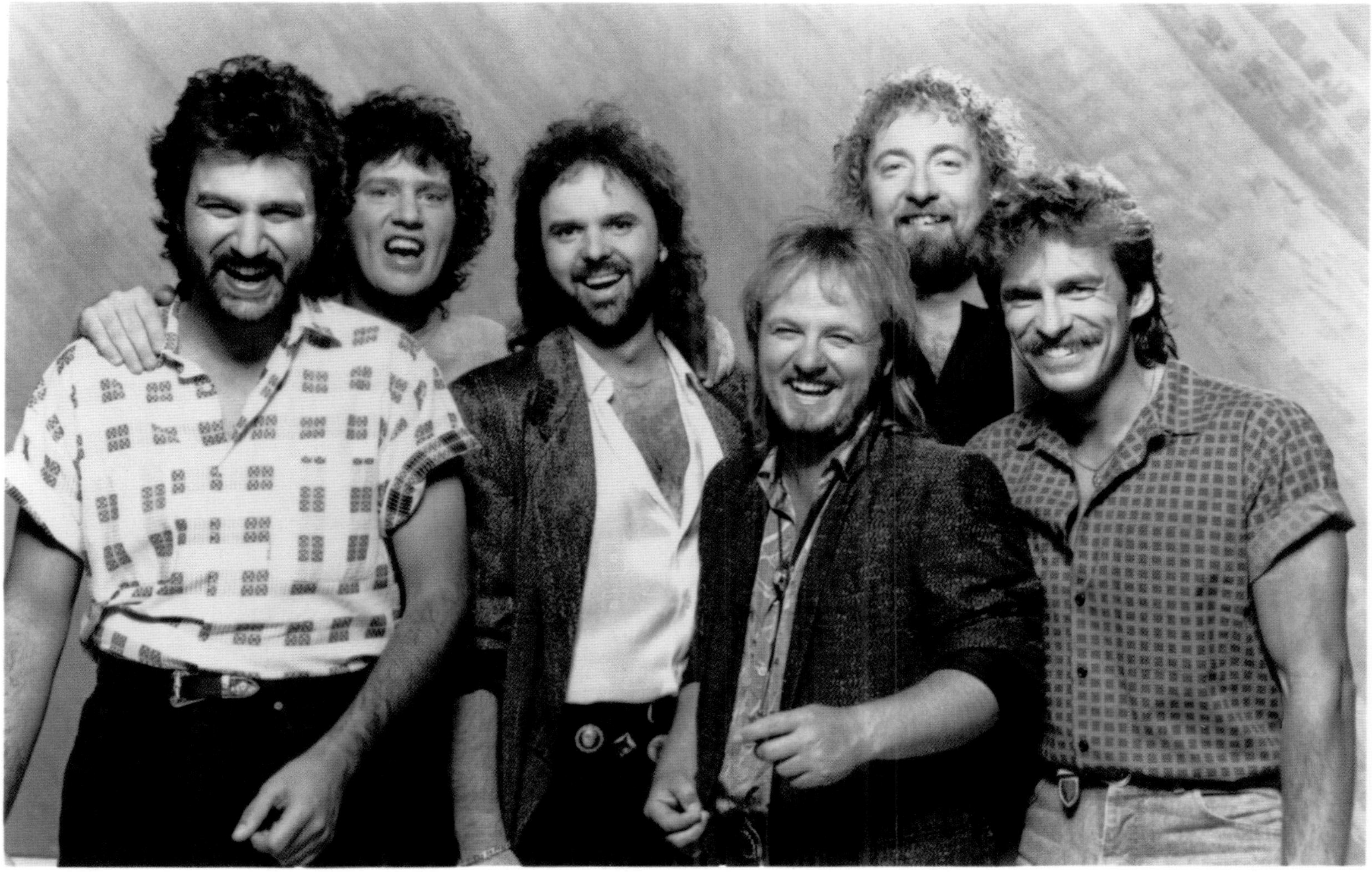

Jeff Carlisi Steve Brookins Don Barnes Donnie Van Zant Larry Junstrom Jack Grondin

38 SPECIAL

Management:
The Mark Spector Company, Inc.
(213) 319-1410

A&M RECORDS
Printed in U.S.A.

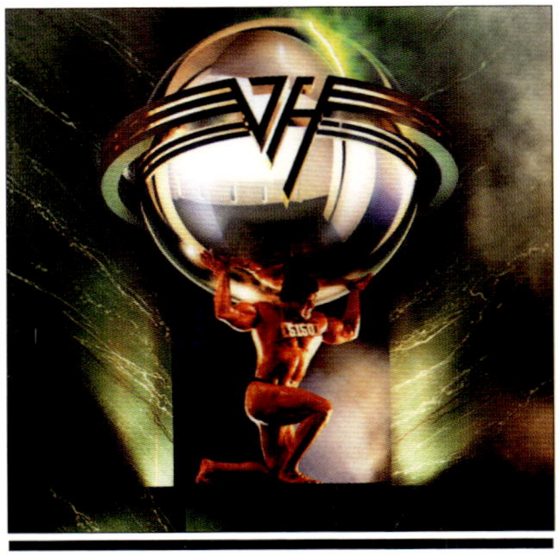

Billboard 200: *5150* (No. 1)
Billboard Hot 100: "Why Can't This Be Love" (#3); "Dreams" (#22); "Love Walks In" (#22)

An even larger wave of fans gave Van Halen and new singer Sammy Hagar their first-ever No. 1 album, *5150*.

WHEN SINGER David Lee Roth announced his exit from Van Halen in 1985, it seemingly signaled the end of the band's six-album reign as America's top hard-rock attraction. Guitarist Eddie Van Halen was miffed about Roth's manner of departure, but the focus finally shifted from acrimony to music. By naming Sammy Hagar as Roth's replacement, Van Halen had been revitalized. Some playfully tagged the new unit as "Van Hagar," but the group preferred to be known as the "real" Van Halen.

And rightfully so, as *5150*—also the name of guitarist Eddie Van Halen's home studio and the Los Angeles Police Department code for the criminally insane—became the first No. 1 album in the band's history (the 10-times platinum *1984* had been stuck at #2 behind Michael Jackson's *Thriller*). It was obvious that the members of Van Halen were having fun again, a far cry from the sullen attitudes that marked their last days with Roth.

Even if Fred Flintstone sang lead, Van Halen was still noteworthy for the awesome instrumental skills of Eddie Van Halen, who continued to combine his electrifying technique with potent ideas. In addition, drummer Alex Van Halen and bassist Michael Anthony had developed over the years into a surprisingly sophisticated rhythm section.

Hagar added a new dimension to the Van Halen sound. Ironically, when the band was signed to Warner Bros. Records back in 1977, he was the label's choice to be the vocalist (unbeknownst to the group members). Hagar gave up a longstanding solo career to come aboard belatedly, and his enthusiasm had visibly moved his new cohorts.

"On the record, he really made a difference," Eddie noted. "It's like Arnold Schwarzenegger's book *Stay Hungry*—it's no longer 'You feel like working?' 'Nah, let's wait until tomorrow. Or let's wait until next year!' With Sammy, his energy is just contagious. He's a great guy, a great worker. Absolutely nothing like . ." And he dissolved into laughter.

Certainly Hagar possessed a wider vocal range than his predecessor, which he displayed on such songs as "Dreams" (featuring a grand piano intro played by Eddie) and "Love Walks In," a pretty but powerful ballad. As a result, *5150* had attracted a whole new pop audience for Van Halen.

"My only problem with that is the terminology," Eddie commented. "To me, music is music, and if it's good, it's pop. I think it's funny that Led Zeppelin was considered the ultimate heavy-metal band of all time, and half of their music was acoustic. Whenever you reach a certain point of success, some people are going to find fault—'Oh, you've sold yourself, you've gone mainstream.' Well, mainstream only means that you're successful at what you do." ■

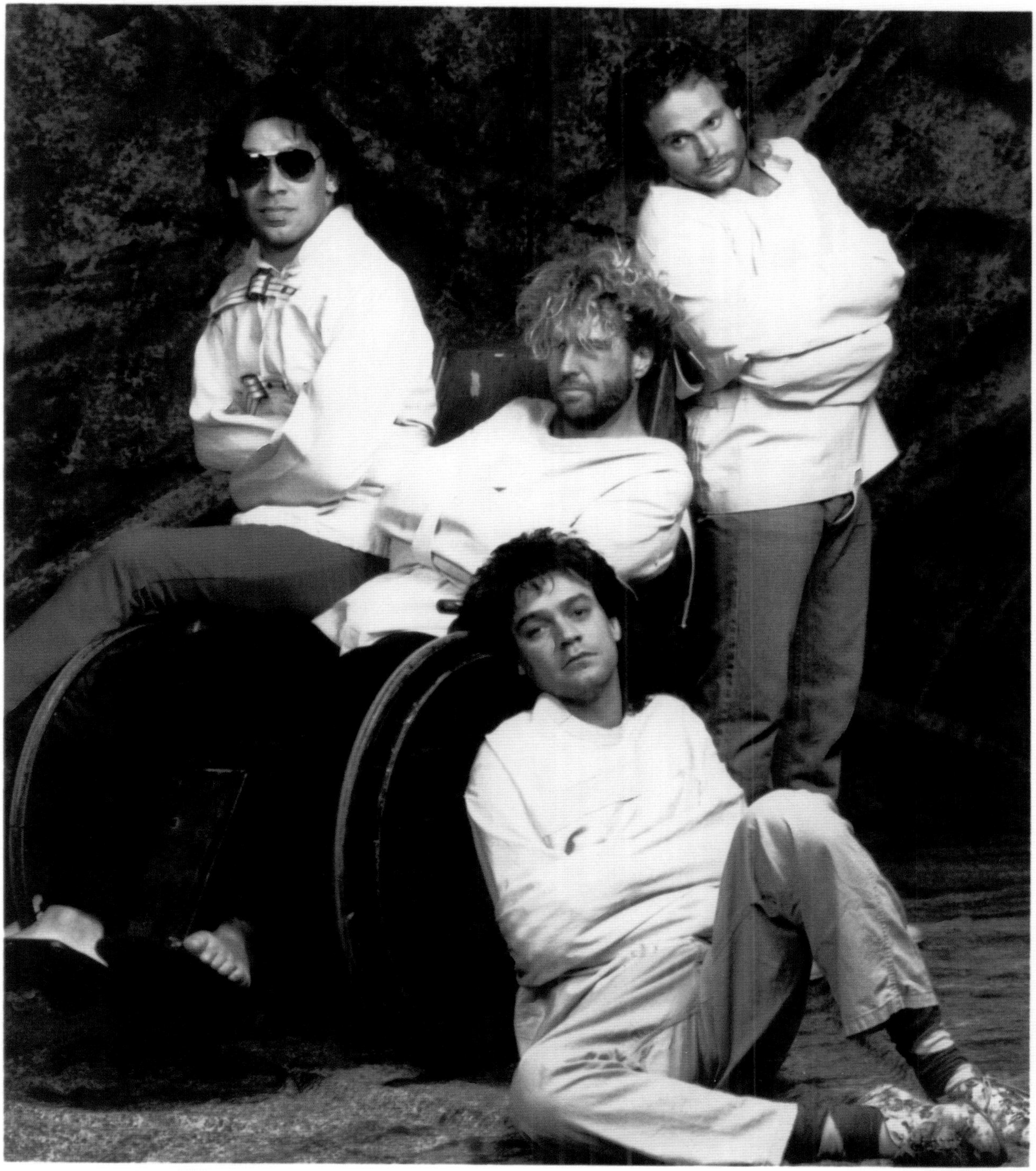

Photo Credit: Bonnie Schiffman

WARNER BROS.

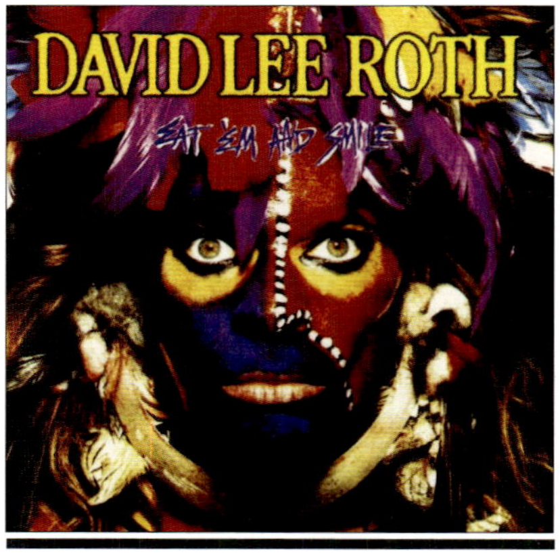

Billboard 200: *Eat 'Em and Smile* (#4)
Billboard Hot 100: "Yankee Rose" (#16);
"Goin' Crazy!" (#66); "That's Life" (#85)

Bitter about exiting Van Halen, flamboyant frontman David Lee Roth took solo flight with *Eat 'Em and Smile.*

THE GLORY days of Van Halen had permanently ensconced the band in the highest echelons of hard rock's hierarchy, the most important act of a generation. Swaggering lead singer David Lee Roth's ribald wit and flair for unabashed showmanship got as much attention as guitarist Eddie Van Halen's nimble fingers. "If all the world's a stage," Roth once said, "then I want better lighting."

But despite Van Halen's success, a creative rift developed between the vocalist and the virtuoso. Roth quit Van Halen in 1985, and the immediate result was a wealth of bad-mouthing between him and his ex-bandmates in the rock press.

"Ed Van Halen without a guitar in his hands is a crummy human being," Roth said. "There's an ego problem with the Van Halens—they don't have one. *I'm* the guy with a huge ego. I feel perfectly comfortable starting over. I'll break bread with anyone who needs their bread broken."

Roth's unstoppable enthusiasm and outrageous charisma continued unabated. He assembled a crackerjack band, siding with superstar guitarist Steve Vai, bassist Billy Sheehan and the renowned drummer Gregg Bissonette, and released his debut solo album, *Eat 'Em and Smile.*

A return to a hard-rock sound for Roth from Van Halen's synthesizer-influenced *1984*, "Yankee Rose" was recorded as a tribute to the Statue of Liberty, which was completing a major renovation for the centenary of its 1886 dedication.

"I've always written songs where you were never sure whether I was talking about a girl or a car, or a girl or an engine part," Roth said. "In 'Yankee Rose,' I picture the Statue of Liberty as an actual person, as she was walking by the candy store and I was being sexy to her—'She's a real state of independence/Ain't she pretty when her rockets glare/She can still prove it any night that her flag is still there.' What we have is lascivious patriotism."

"Goin' Crazy!" was the would-be theme to a film script that was planned around Roth's solo debut. "This was the title track for the movie that was gonna be," he explained. "The lyric is obviously a Californian side—'Well, here I'm rollin' down another sunny highway, guess I've been in the sun too long/I'm goin' coconuts, but at least I'm goin' my way, I'll probably be here when the sun goes down.' It's sort of like a Jimmy Buffett song, but at 138 beats per minute. It would be real good to listen to on a boat." ■

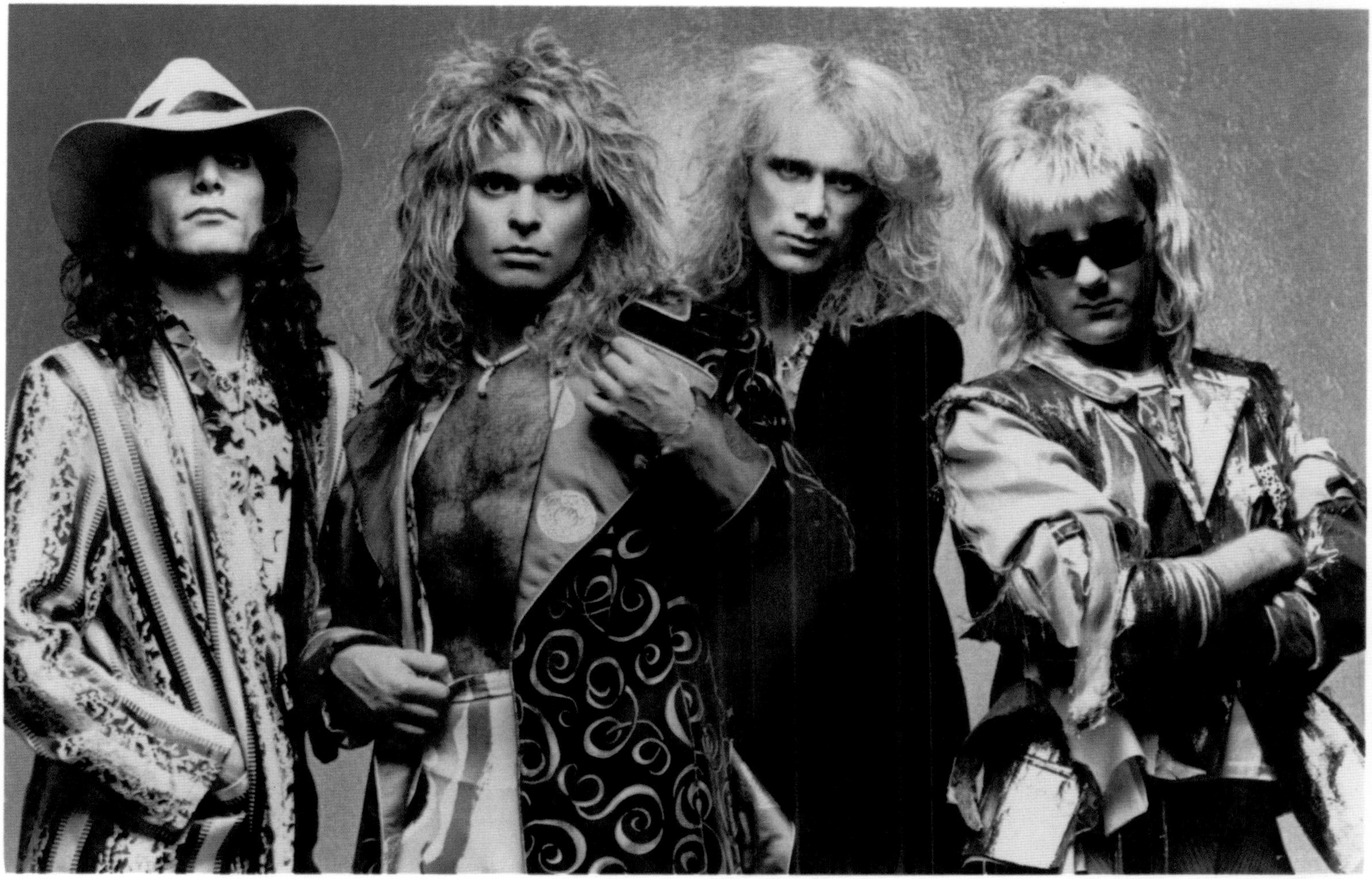

Photo Credit: Neil Zlozower

STEVE VAI DAVID LEE ROTH BILLY SHEEHAN GREG BISSONETTE

DAVID LEE ROTH

WARNER BROS.

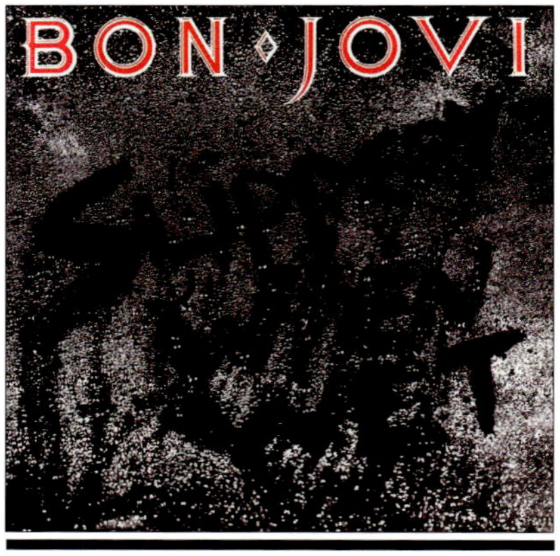

Billboard 200: *Slippery When Wet* (No. 1)
Billboard Hot 100: "You Give Love a Bad Name" (No. 1); "Livin' on a Prayer" (No. 1); "Wanted Dead or Alive" (#7)

The pop-metal of *Slippery When Wet* established Bon Jovi as one of the biggest American bands on the planet.

DISMISSED BY many as another second-echelon rock band, Bon Jovi found itself caught in the album/tour circuit with nothing special to recommend it. But that was before the explosive success of *Slippery When Wet*. The New Jersey-based group's third album reached No. 1 on the strength of the back-to-back chart-topping singles "You Give Love a Bad Name" and "Livin' on a Prayer."

Leader Jon Bon Jovi planned to front his band over the long haul, but he'd been totally floored by the massive commercial success and global recognition. "Nobody in their wildest dreams thought the album would be selling in the millions," he mused. "I mean, I couldn't make up rumors this outrageous!"

That was especially true following 1985's *7800 Fahrenheit*, the band's second album, which Bon Jovi described as "one fight after another to get recorded. There were technical problems, and we had to finish fast because we had dates booked in Japan." The experience made the band—Bon Jovi, guitarist Richie Sambora, keyboardist David Bryan, bassist Alec John Such and drummer Rico Torres—determined to make an album that accurately reflected the band's live sound.

Holing up in a Vancouver studio with producer Bruce Fairbairn, who had crafted hit sounds for Loverboy, Bon Jovi emerged with the immaculate, crunching sonics of *Slippery When Wet*. But improved production alone couldn't explain the album's overwhelming acceptance. The group had turned to songwriting partner Desmond Child to help pen emotive power ballads and walloping rockers about teen angst, raging hormones and the struggle of growing up and finding your place in the world.

"You Give Love a Bad Name" and "Livin' on a Prayer" were obvious hits, although the band didn't think as much initially. "If it had been up to me, some of the songs that made the record wouldn't have," Bon Jovi revealed. "When we wrote 'Livin' on a Prayer,' I said to Richie, 'Maybe we can get this on a soundtrack or something,' because I never thought it was right for the band."

Educating a new generation of rock fans was a real responsibility, and given the need for bands who looked good, acted professional and cranked out catchy songs, why not Bon Jovi? Most parents could tolerate Jon Bon Jovi as a rock 'n' roll role model—he was an anti-drug spokesman, a guy who rocked out loud and hard without being profane or obnoxious.

"I want kids to come to our shows without being confronted by anything that's going to hurt them or us in the long run," he insisted. "It's just easier to sing and sweat and smile and raise your hands, just the idea of 'Here we are, this is entertainment'—nothing more, nothing less, nothing overly political or socially conscious. Because to me personally, rock 'n' roll is supposed to be fun, not a way to save the world. I'm not saying that's right or wrong—it's just how I always felt about it as a kid playing records." ■

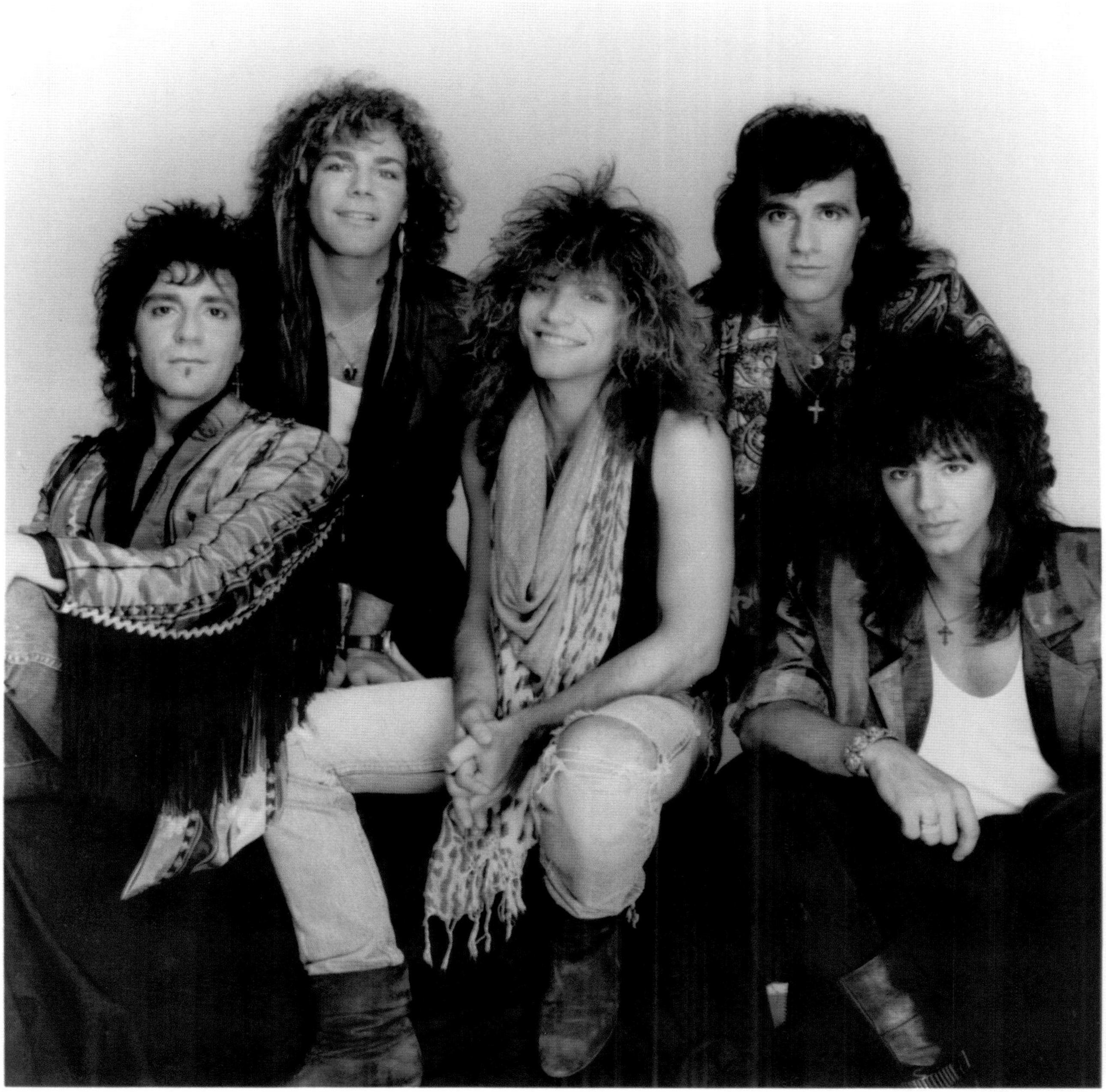

Photo credit: PATRICK HARBRON

BON JOVI

mercury

PolyGram Records

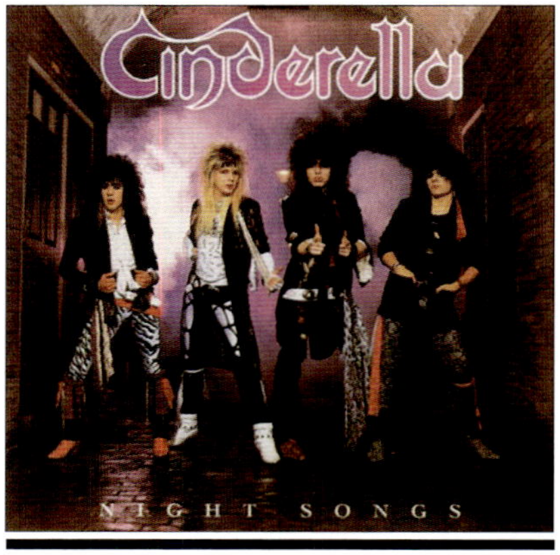

Billboard 200: *Night Songs* (#3)
Billboard Hot 100: "Nobody's Fool" (#13); "Somebody Save Me" (#66)

With the power ballad "Nobody's Fool," glam-metal outfit Cinderella broke through to surprising pop success.

WITH THE Top 3 status of a debut album, *Night Songs*, it was apparent that the band Cinderella was leading a fairy-tale existence. The role of Prince Charming had been played by Jon Bon Jovi, who discovered the rough-sounding quartet in a Philadelphia club. Prior to Bon Jovi's involvement, Cinderella leader Tom Keifer had suffered through stints with several inferior bands, pining for a happy ending.

"Before Jon saw us, we were just rehearsing and making demo tapes, trying to get a deal on our own," Keifer explained. "When Jon saw us in a bar one night, that made things click. Even though we weren't really ready at that point, he saw a band that had the potential to go a long way."

Bon Jovi championed the group to his record company, and after a couple of personnel changes, Cinderella's dedication to Seventies-style rock paid dividends when Andy Johns offered to produce *Night Songs*. Among his engineering credits, Johns listed the Rolling Stones and Led Zeppelin—two bands Keifer cited as his greatest influences.

Cinderella brought a couple of standout songs to the sessions—the roaring Aerosmith-derived "Shake Me" best represented the group's sound, but it failed to chart as a single. It was the hard-edged power ballad "Nobody's Fool" that attracted precious radio airplay. "We figured that song would be a crossover tune for us, and that's just how it worked out," Keifer said.

Night Songs went on to reach multiplatinum sales levels, catapulting Cinderella from the East Coast club circuit onto a rollercoaster ride of arenas playing to more than a million fans. "We'll be staying on the road until we see the big money, and I'm going to buy a house," Keifer concluded. "I've paid enough dues to respect what I've learned, so I think I'm taking all of this pretty well so far." ■

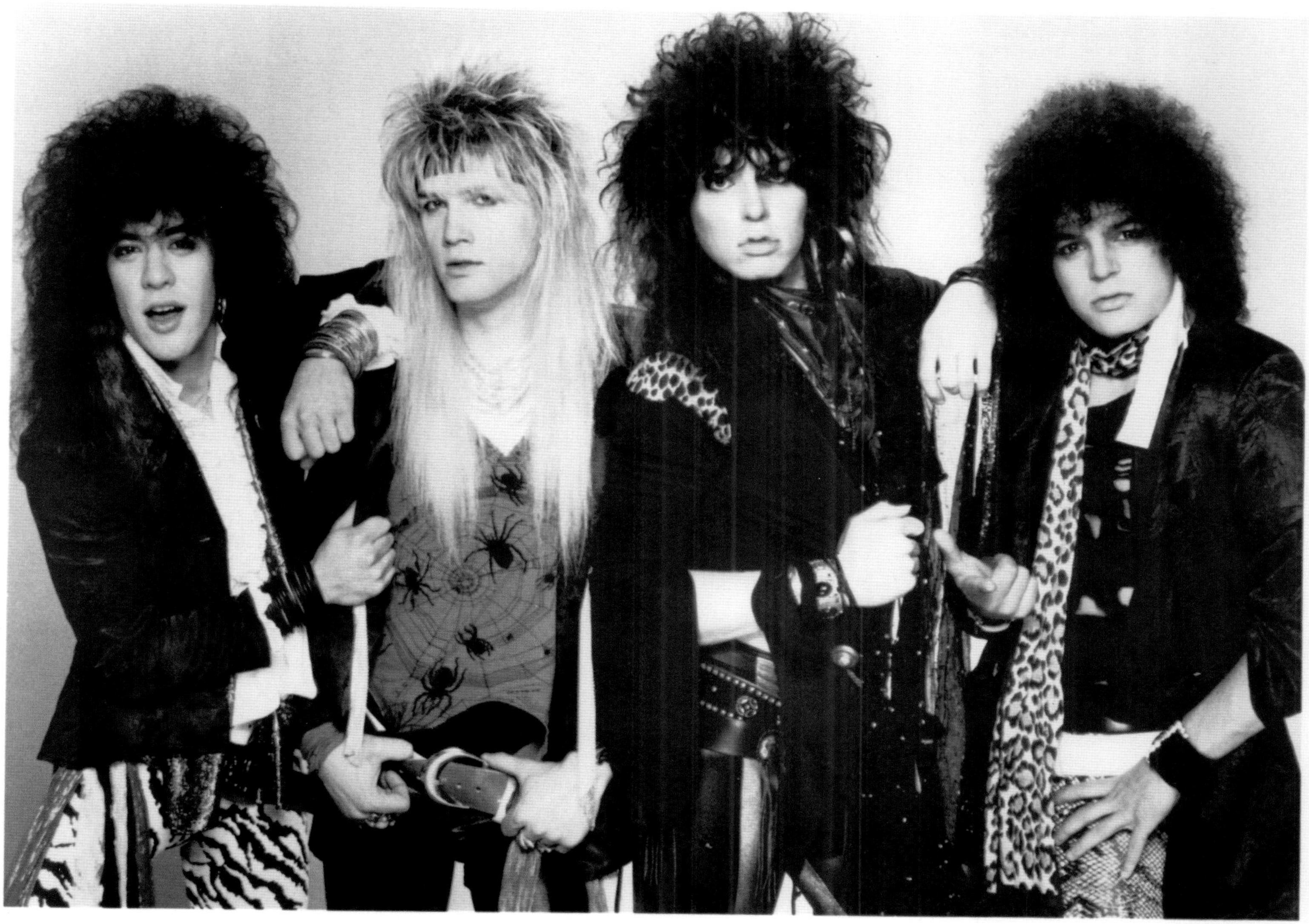

Photo Credit: Mark Weiss

Jeff LaBar Eric Brittingham Tom Keifer Fred Coury

Cinderella

mercury

PolyGram Records

Management: Larry Mazer

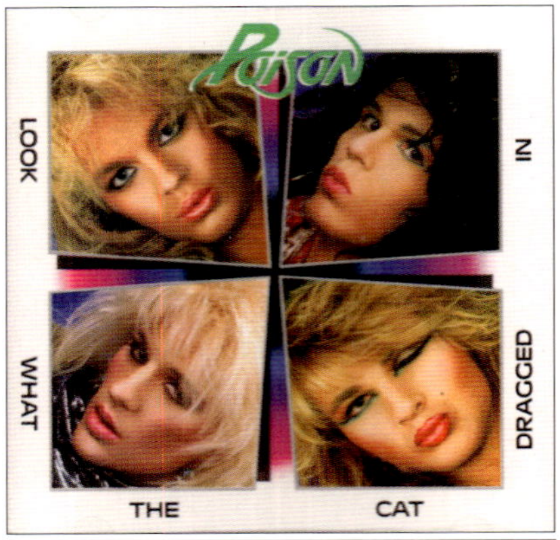

Billboard 200: *Look What the Cat Dragged In* (#3)
Billboard Hot 100: "Talk Dirty to Me" (#9); "I Want Action" (#50); "I Won't Forget You" (#13)

A debut album of peacocky post-punk posturing was enough reason to keep the band Poison on the shelves.

FOLLOWING THE tradition established by Van Halen, Mötley Crüe and Ratt, a street level buzz had surrounded Poison, the top-drawing local band in Los Angeles. The members credited their marketing savvy—after moving to L.A. from Harrisburg, Pennsylvania, they blanketed the town with self-promoting flyers following concerts by other bands.

"We figured if we were going to sleep in the streets, it may as well be someplace warm," drummer Rikki Rockett said of the band's move to California. "We brought an East Coast way of doing things with us. Where we're from, you don't just play three or four times a month and think you're cool. We go out and play several times a week."

But instead of espousing the usual studded-leather look that was prevalent among L.A. bands, Poison had made makeup, scarves and jewelry the important elements of its image, a throwback to the glam-rock bands of the Seventies. Yet every major label roundly ignored Poison. "They never even thought about us long enough to hate us," bassist Bobby Dall observed.

The quartet finally received its big break when they were signed to Enigma. Poison recorded a Kiss/Aerosmith/Alice Cooper-influenced debut album, *Look What the Cat Dragged In*, in an astounding 12 days.

"Talk Dirty to Me," the best example of Poison's hard-working-but-fun-loving attitude, evolved into a hit on rock radio and a No. 1 request on MTV, and the album cracked the Top 3. The band basked in the thrill of being newly discovered and living out fantasies (joined onstage by heroes like Kiss' Paul Stanley).

"All we needed was a chance for something to go right," singer Bret Michaels assured. "Poison isn't a resurgence of glitter-rock—that heavy concept 'I'm from Mars' stuff like David Bowie and the New York Dolls. We're glam rock, which just means dressing for success. Too many bands have this violent 'to hell with the world' look, and I just don't feel that way—I'm loving what I'm doing right now."

The album's first cut, "Cry Tough," was about "making your dreams come true, and that goes for any kind of dream that anybody has," Rockett noted. "This just happens to be ours. We already think we're something, and if we act like it and wish hard enough, we will be." ■

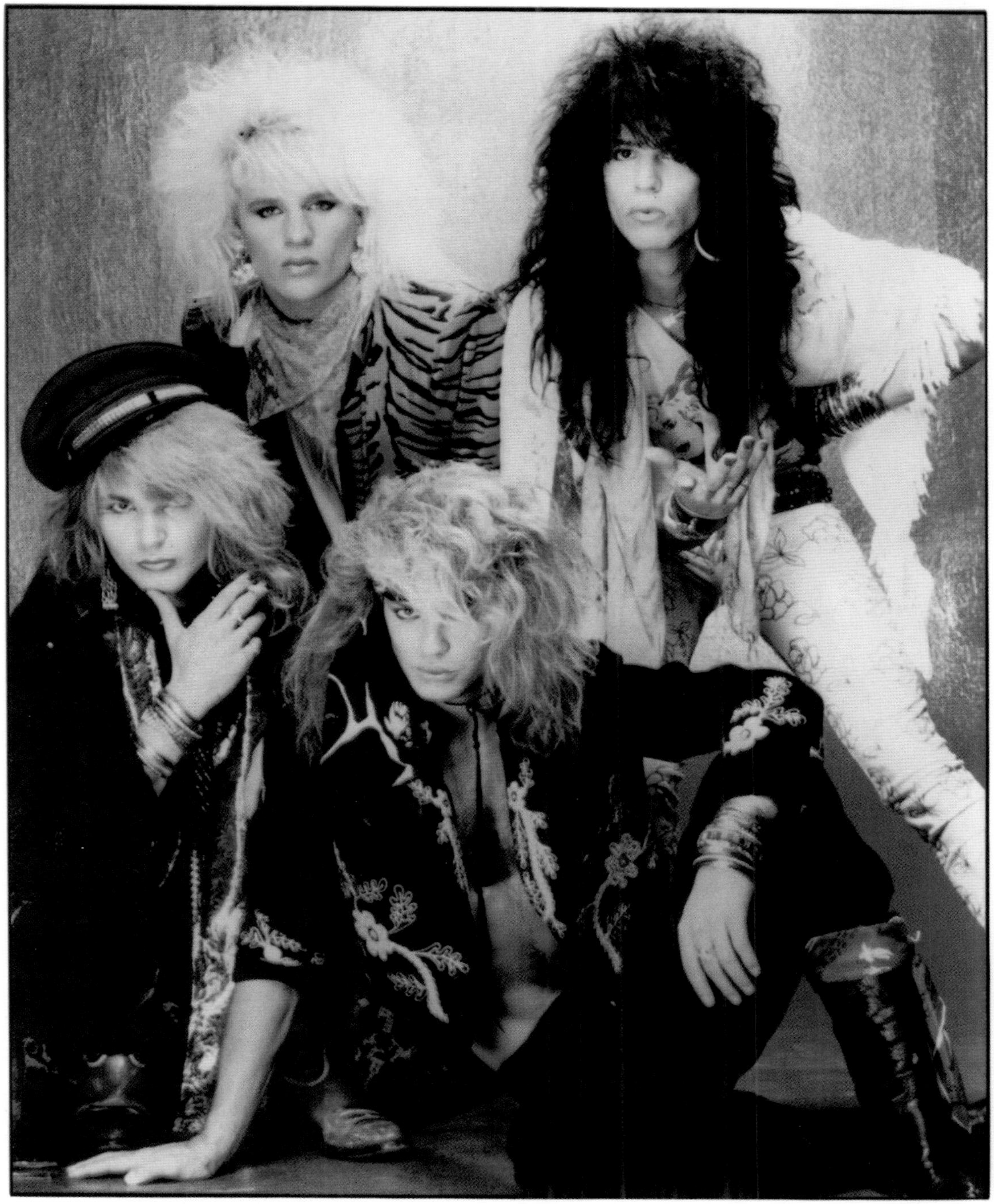

Photo: Neil Zlozower / 1986

Rikki Rockett C.C. DeVille Bret Michaels (sitting) Bobby Dall

Capitol Records

POISON

ENIGMA RECORDS

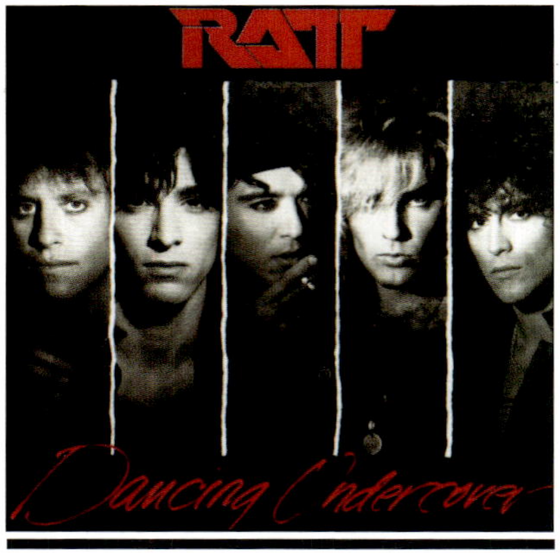

Billboard 200: *Dancing Undercover* (#26)

Dancing Undercover didn't meddle with Ratt's pop-metal formulation, polished to a "tt" by producer Beau Hill.

WITH "ROUND and Round," a hit that sported one of the all-time sharpest metal-pop hooks, the band Ratt broke onto the heavy-metal scene in 1984.

"That was a grand moment, and I wouldn't change a thing," guitarist Robbin Crosby said. "But the song cast a shadow on the band. We're not really a singles band—we're from that metal wave of 1983-84."

Radio hadn't really supported Ratt's newer work, even though the third album, *Dancing Undercover*, kept the Los Angeles group's streak of consecutive platinum albums alive, and the video "Dance" was a Top 10 staple on MTV for several months. So Ratt was content with touring, dragging around a big production that sported the usual *Star Wars*-caliber lighting. The band teamed up with Poison for a hard-rock extravaganza, calling it the (what else?) "Ratt/Poison" tour, which sent uninformed parents scurrying to check under their sinks.

"We don't make music for radio anyway," singer Stephen Pearcy said. "It's not gonna ruin our lives if they don't play Ratt—there are plenty of other good bands that get much less exposure than us."

The best thing about the Ratt pack remained that they were all big, athletic guys, not the usual mincing twerps draped in Spandex and leather. Crosby picked up the guitar in fifth grade, but soon dropped it when he became obsessed with baseball. "I had a chance to go to college and play ball," he said, "but I decided to rock 'n' roll instead."

Crosby then formed Ratt with fellow "cement pirates" from the L.A. rock scene, and the lineup had remained the same since. The members had finally managed to distance themselves from the Aerosmith comparisons that marked their early work. They were established enough that they no longer needed to use comedian Milton Berle in their videos (Berle's son Marshall managed the group).

And Ratt's visual presence earned the band its first motion picture appearance—in *The Golden Child*, starring Eddie Murphy, the group made a brief cameo performing "Body Talk," featured on *Dancing Undercover*. ■

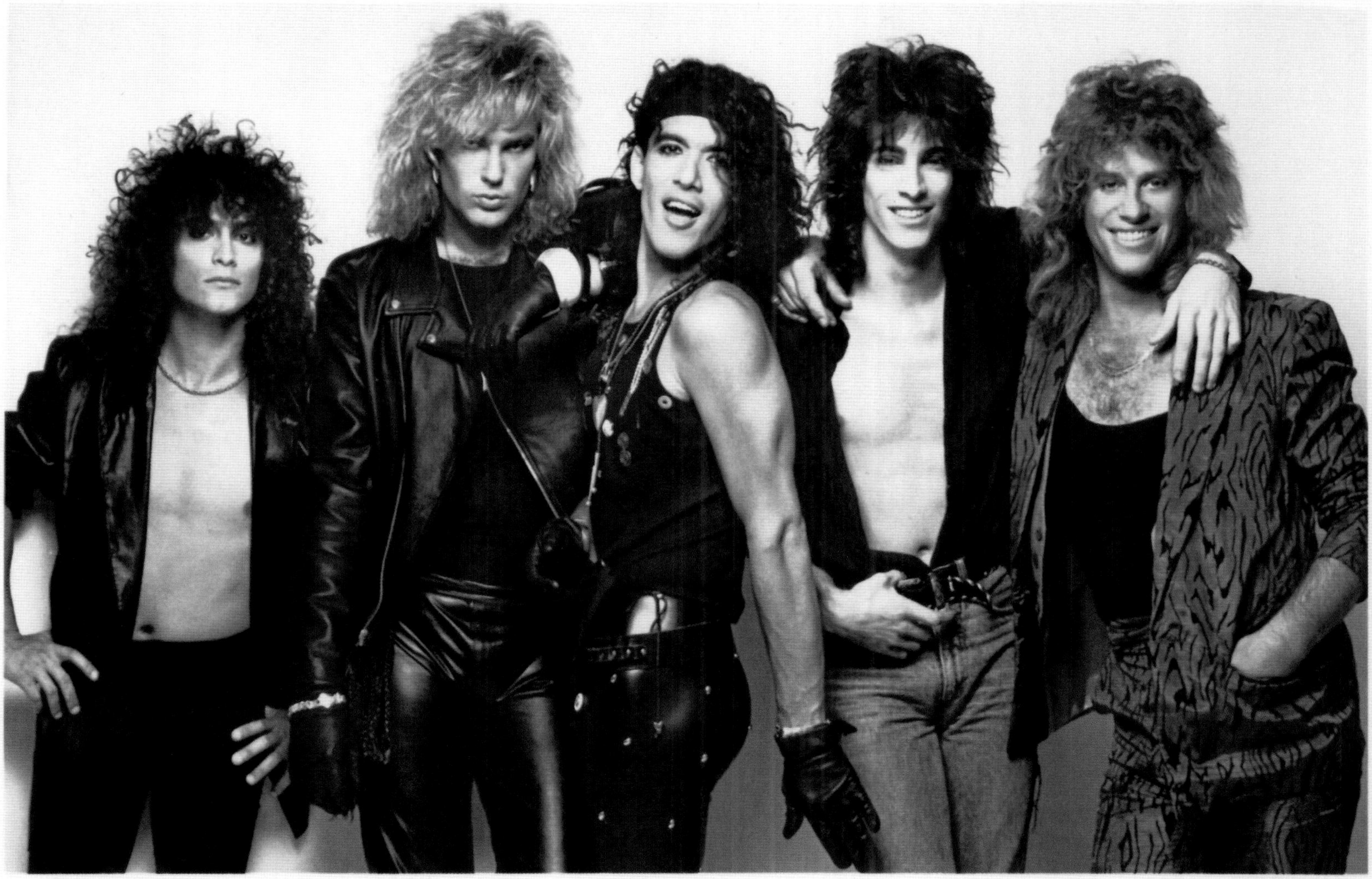

JUAN CROUCIER ROBBIN CROSBY STEPHEN PEARCY WARREN DeMARTINI BOBBY BLOTZER

RATT

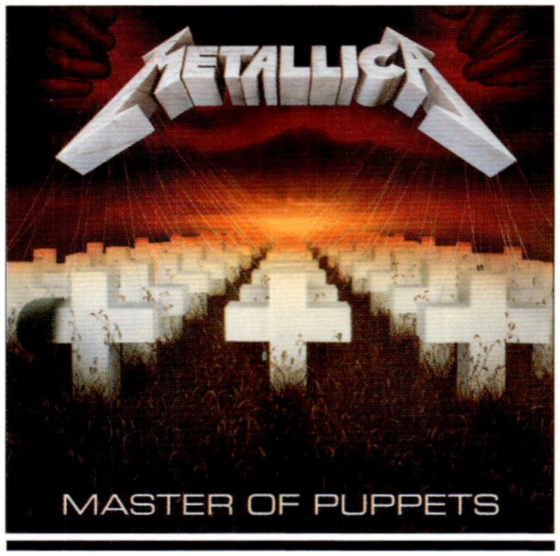

Billboard 200: *Master of Puppets* (#29)

Master of Puppets came to be Metallica's last album to feature bassist Cliff Burton, who died in a bus accident.

THEY HAD never made a rock video. They did not receive radio airplay. What the members of Metallica purveyed was the most brutal, thrashing heavy-metal music imaginable. And yet the maverick band was selling records at the rate of 150,000 a week. Metallica's third album, *Master of Puppets*, reached the Top 30 and platinum status, while the other two albums were still on the charts. What was happening here?

"It's all about the underground," drummer Lars Ulrich replied. "It's all word-of-mouth."

Metallica—Ulrich, singer and guitarist James Hetfield, bassist Cliff Burton and guitarist Kirk Hammett—had filled a void with an intriguing new brand of speed metal, aided by a severe lull in the metal genre. Kids with any degree of musical sophistication could see through Mötley Crüe's let's-party posturing, Def Leppard had disappeared since the breakthrough *Pyromania* album of 1984, and Iron Maiden hadn't followed it's huge 1985 tour with another project.

While those other groups had predicated their appeal on bombastic stage shows, Metallica worked the other side of the street—no special effects or lasers, no medieval imagery or pretense, just heads-down, full-bore metal with some surprisingly complex and subtle sections thrown in for good measure. Also, Metallica's lyrical themes weren't the usual look-at-my-crotch stuff indigenous to the metal genre.

"Most of my lyrics are about manipulation," Hetfield said. "Repression in 'Welcome Home (Sanitarium),' drugs in 'Master of Puppets.' I'm interested in all the different levels you see it in society."

Kids also liked Metallica because the Bay Area band members looked and acted like them. Metallica hadn't been swayed by success, continuing to grant interviews to even the most obscure metal fanzines. Ulrich pointed out that Metallica's music wasn't always so readily accepted, but now the band was having the last laugh with its radical melding of punk and metal—*Master of Puppets* was hailed as a thrash-metal masterpiece.

"We get all kinds of fans—skinheads, punks, headbangers. It just depends on where we're playing," Hetfield said. "We get a lot of people who say, 'I hate metal—you're the only metal band that I like.' And that's great. It means we're not the stuff that they're used to."

But amidst the good fortune, tragedy struck the band. On a promotional tour in Scandinavia, travelling late at night with most of the band asleep in their bunks, the tour bus ran off the road and crashed into a ditch, instantly killing bassist Cliff Burton. The band's first Japanese tour had already been booked.

"It puts pressure on us to get it back together," Ulrich said. "I know Cliff, more than anyone else in the band, would have been the first guy to give us a kick in the ass, and wouldn't want us to sit around. This is what he wants us to do." ■

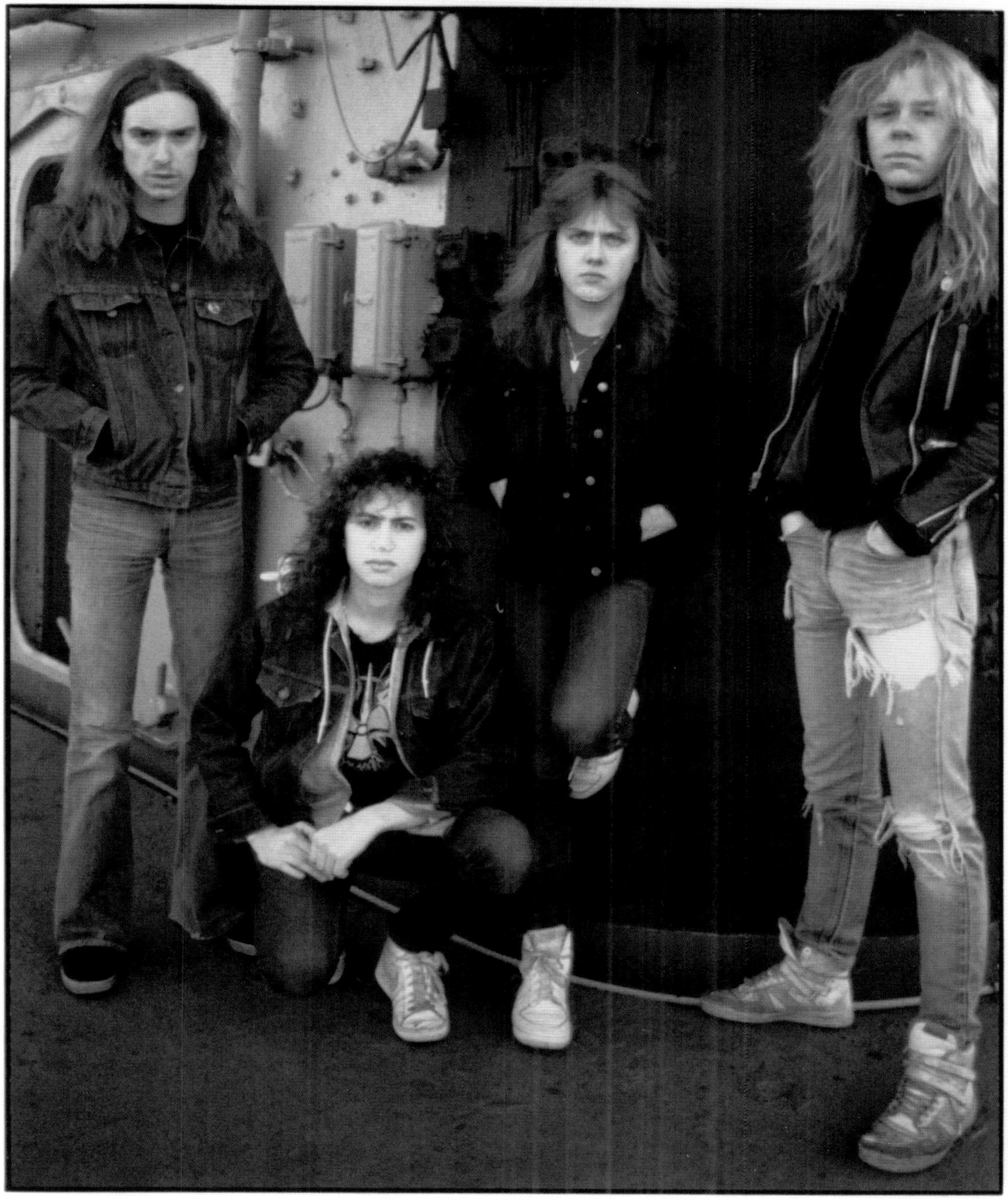

PHOTO CREDIT: ROSS HALFIN/1986

CLIFF BURTON KIRK HAMMETT LARS ULRICH JAMES HETFIELD

METALLICA

ELEKTRA

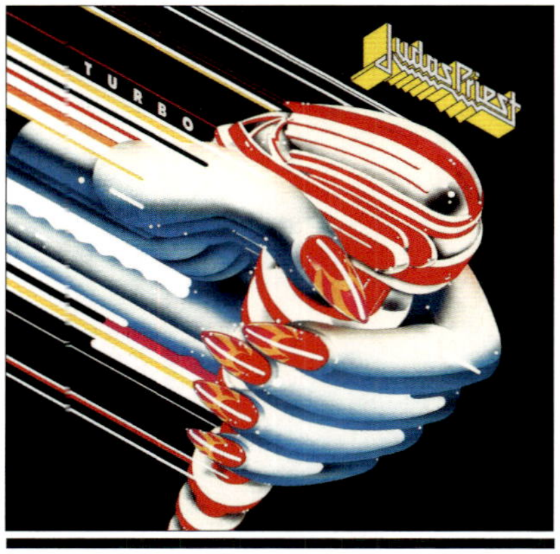

Billboard 200: *Turbo* (#17)

Retooling its heavy-metal sonics to be more accessible, Judas Priest forged a new path with the *Turbo* album.

WITH THE exception of hormone-fueled males, most people dismissed heavy-metal music as so much grunting and flailing. But there was something more going on with Judas Priest.

For one thing, the five-piece British band was managed by Bill Curbushley, who was considered a rather astute judge of talent—he'd only handled one other band in his career, an outfit named the Who. Even without Curbushley's coaching, the Priest had sold millions of albums during the last decade. And songs such as "Locked In" and "Turbo Lover" from the band's 10th album, *Turbo*, got substantial rotation on MTV while other metal acts couldn't buy time on the radio. The album sported a totally modern metal sound, courtesy of digital recording techniques—here was one metal band that was actually worth hearing on compact disc.

"People think that all heavy-metal music entails is simply plugging in and thrashing away," singer Rob Halford allowed. "But there's an incredible amount of sophistication that goes into the production these days. And I think our talents as musicians are more sophisticated, too."

For instance? Well, the unexpectedly mild-mannered Halford was known for his multi-octave vocal range. But he was still shrieking—Judas Priest reigned as the fastest and heaviest band on the block, so what else could the guy do to vie with the clangor of K.K. Downing and Glenn Tipton? The leather-and-studs pretense aside, the two guitarists truly believed that a heavy-metal classification didn't limit their musical scope—their integration of guitar synthesizers was the single most interesting facet of *Turbo*. But Judas Priest didn't expect its human-battering-ram fans to pick up on such subtleties. ■

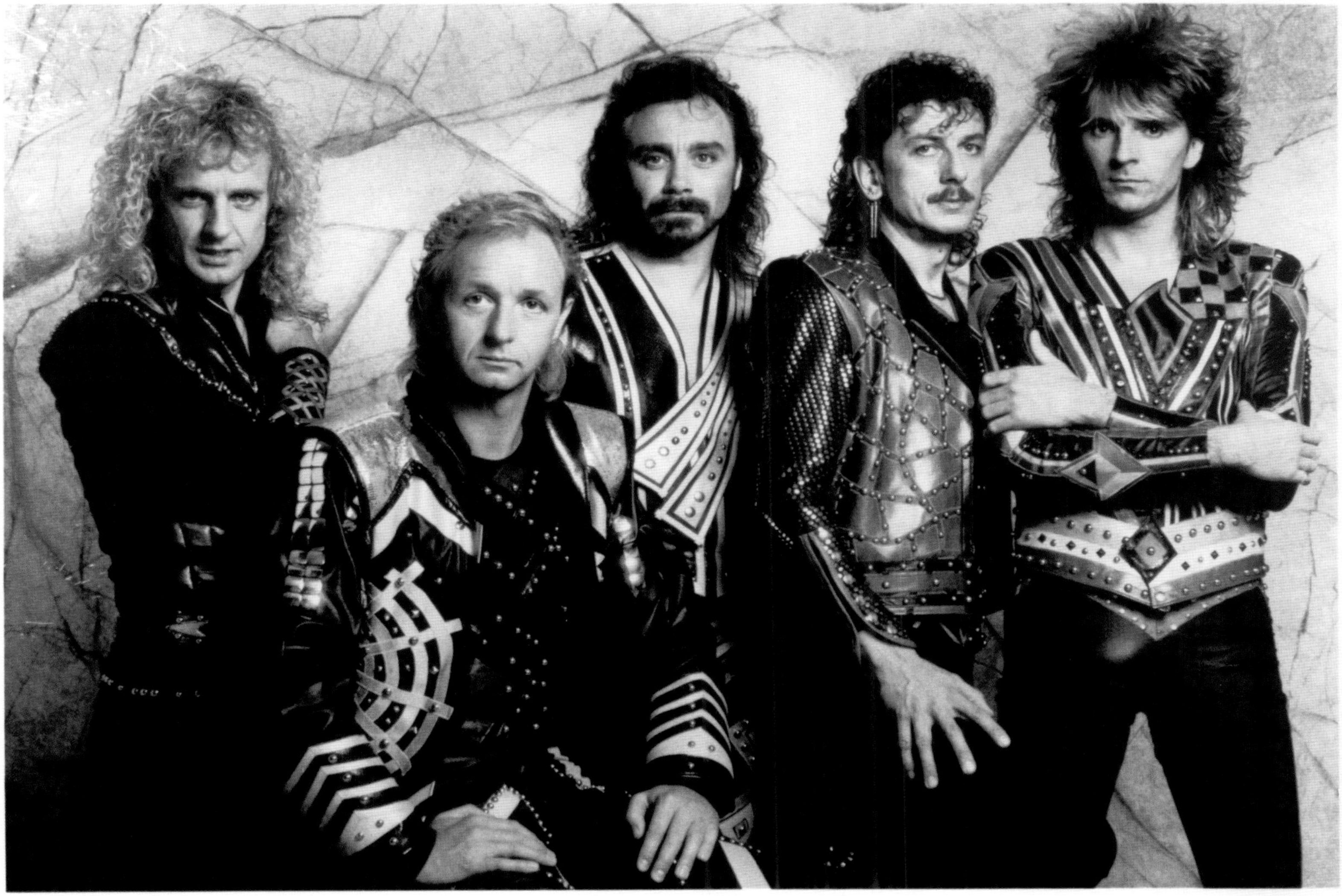

PHOTOGRAPH: RANDEE ST NICHOLAS

JUDAS PRIEST

Columbia

8604

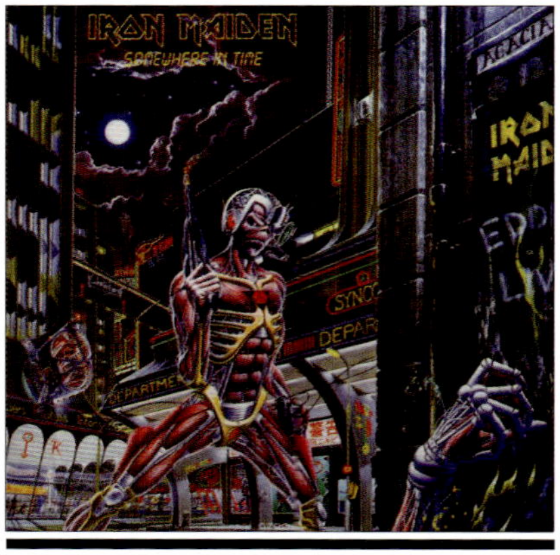

Billboard 200: *Somewhere in Time* (#11)

Iron Maiden's popularity in the worldwide metal community went to the next level due to *Somewhere in Time*.

IRON MAIDEN had forged a special niche on the music scene. Here was a band with more than 60 gold and platinum albums from 17 countries, an act voted No. 1 by heavy-metal fans from Japan to Spain.

But hordes of otherwise ardent music consumers couldn't name a single Iron Maiden song, since radio programmers in the United States and Europe continued to snub the British group despite its overwhelming popularity.

"I can't understand it myself," bassist Steve Harris noted. "We've always felt our albums had two or three tracks that radio could play—we've never been commercial, but there are catchy choruses on quite a few of our songs. Some people say the material is too lengthy, but it could be edited. There's no real excuse for them not playing Iron Maiden—when one of our albums comes out, it goes straight up the charts. So we must have the biggest cult following in the world."

And "in the world" wasn't an exaggeration—following four global tours, Iron Maiden had established itself as an international act that crossed cultural and language barriers. On the previous tour, the group had performed nearly 300 concerts in 28 countries, traveling behind the Iron Curtain to play for thousands of fans in Yugoslavia, Hungary and Czechoslovakia. But they had been strictly forbidden to play in Gdansk, Poland, the home of the anti-authoritarian Solidarity trade union.

However, the authorities did allow the group to perform there in support of the *Somewhere in Time* album—ironically, through radio airplay. "We were actually invited by promoters there," Harris marveled. "We said, 'Why us?' and they said, 'You're the most popular rock band in Poland.' We said, 'Well, how can you gauge it if no one sells records?' They said, 'You get played on the underground radio.' And that's the only place in the world we get played on the radio. It's really weird."

Even in the Polish People's Republic, Iron Maiden records were now getting distribution. "It won't matter because you can't take the money out of the country anyway," Harris said, "but it's nice that the fans won't have to pay two weeks wages for a black-market copy." ■

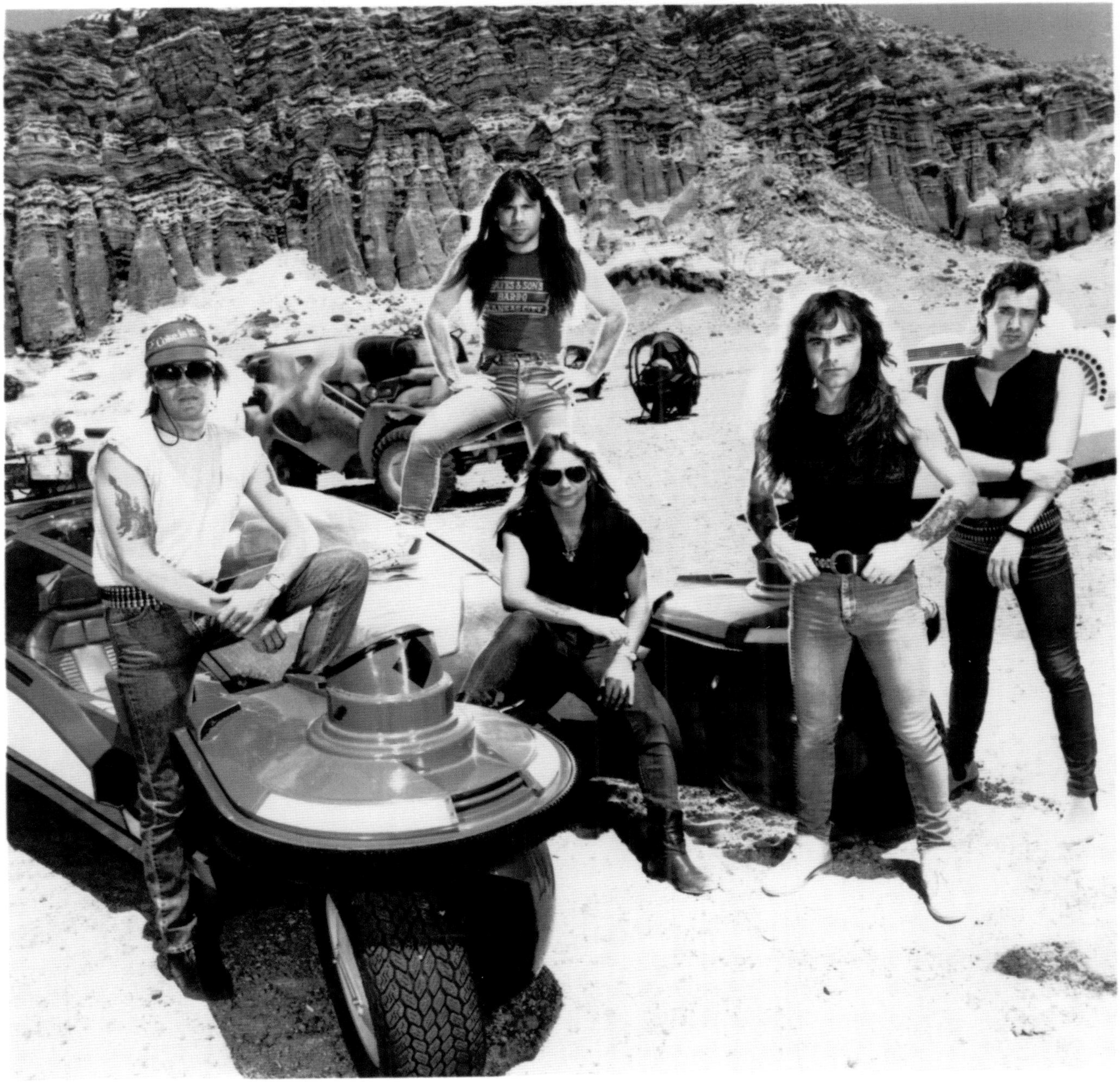

JENSEN COMMUNICATIONS
PUBLIC RELATIONS
(213) 841-3343

IRON MAIDEN

Capitol RECORDS

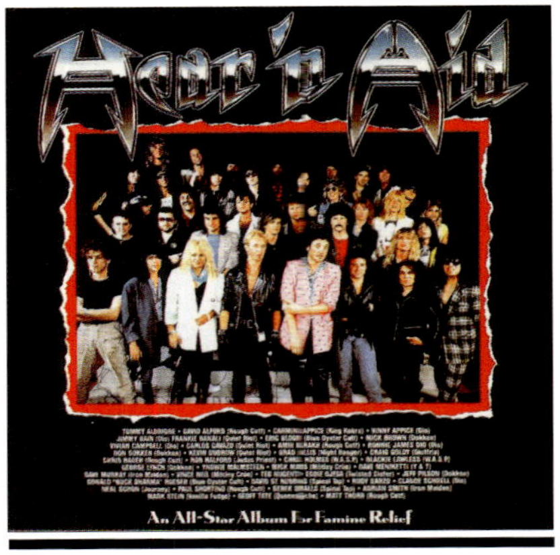

Hear 'n Aid, an all-star assembly of heavy-metal artists, recorded the track "Stars" to help fight world hunger.

THE GREGARIOUS "high priest of heavy metal," Ronnie James Dio wasn't as sinister as his appearance might indicate. It was he and his band Dio who organized Hear 'n Aid, the hard-rock equivalent to USA for Africa or Band Aid.

A large ensemble of 40 heavy-metal musicians came together at A&M Studios—where "We Are the World" was recorded—to lend their musicianship and support for charity. The participants recorded a benefit single, "Stars," a seven-minute anthem which featured a relay of seven vocal solos and one three-and-a-half-minute guitar solo executed by 11 stellar players taking turns.

"The whole idea is that we don't think of ourselves as anything other than human beings," Dio said, "and we're trying to rectify whatever sins we might have committed within our excesses as stars to give instead of take."

"Stars" was the centerpiece of *Hear 'n Aid*. The rest of the compilation album was filled out with mostly rare, unreleased material donated by the artists—five live tracks and two studio offerings from a few top acts. Proceeds were donated to world famine relief projects. ■

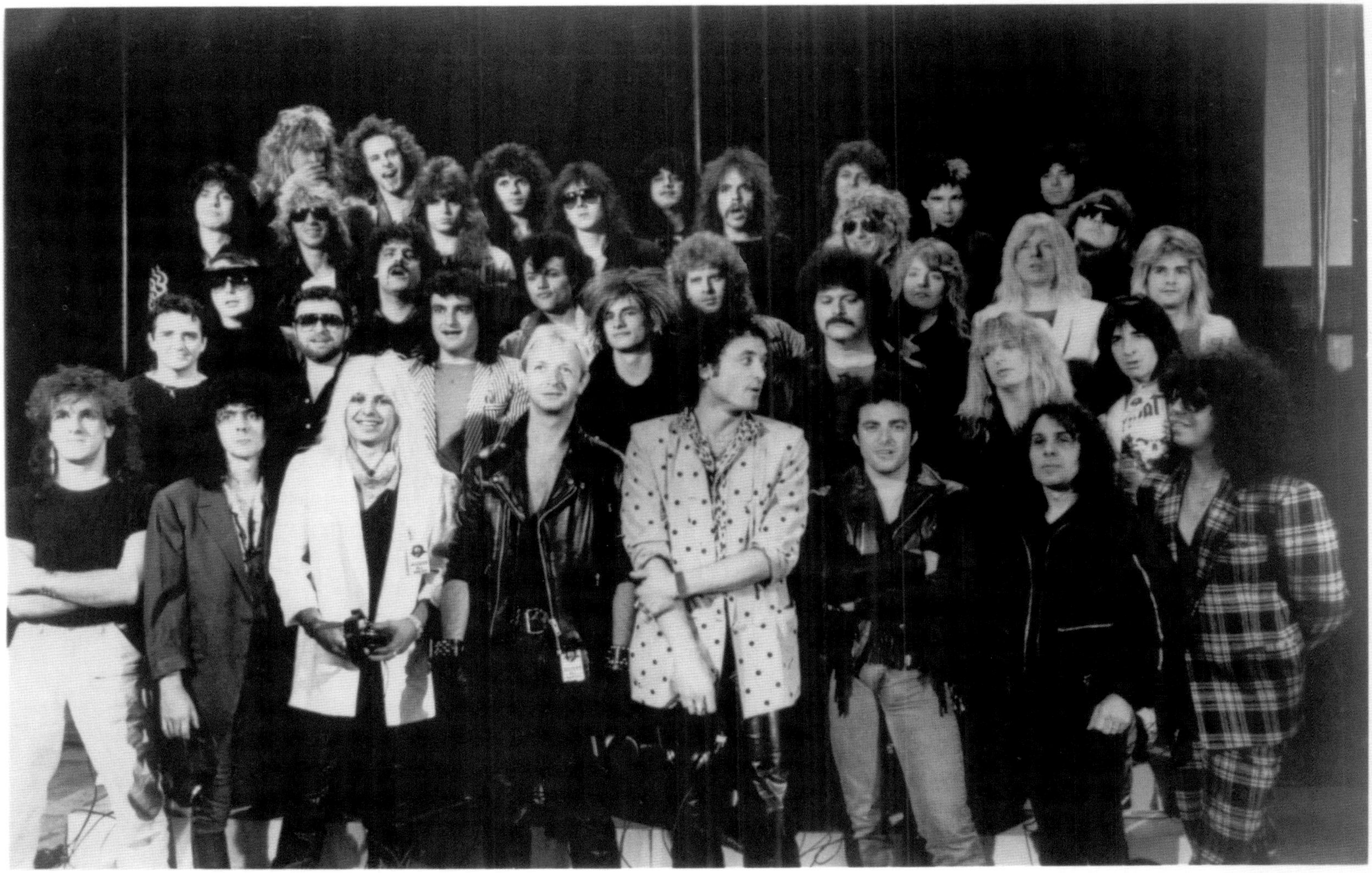

HEAR 'N AID

PolyGram Records

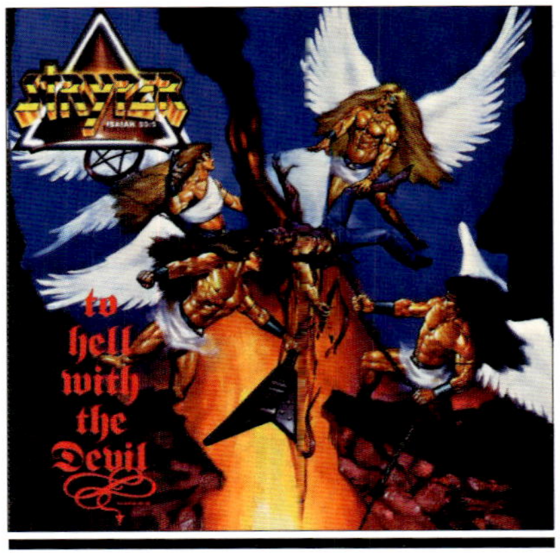

Billboard 200: *To Hell with the Devil* (#32)
Billboard Hot 100: "Honestly" (#23)

A presence on MTV, Christian pop-metal outfit Stryper broke into the mainstream with *To Hell with the Devil.*

IT WAS the hoariest cliché in show biz—"You gotta have an angle"—and Stryper had a doozy. Mixing Spandex and spikes with God's word, the group made a mark as the premier Christian heavy-metal band, its success substantiated as the *To Hell with the Devil* album gained Top 40 and platinum sales status, while the singles "Calling on You," "Free" and the syrupy power ballad "Honestly" became the most requested videos on MTV.

The four guys in Stryper—brothers Michael (guitar) and Robert (drums) Sweet, bassist Tim Gaines and guitarist Oz Fox—said they wouldn't settle for tickling the ears of the already converted; they wanted to play to the kids who needed the message the most, doing away with the first two elements of the classic sex-and-drugs-and-rock-'n'-roll equation.

"We knew the name *To Hell with the Devil* would be perfect—it says exactly what we are trying to do with our music," Robert Sweet said. "We are celebrating God in our songs instead of the Devil and the negative influences in rock music."

To Hell with the Devil advanced Stryper's previous metallic crunch, with a full sound that rivaled the best hard rock. Kids were willing to give the band a chance as a Jesus-loves-you novelty, but in performance they found an act that hit the gospel harder than the guitars.

"We're just trying to be professional," Gaines said. "Everyone hits on the fact that we're a Christian band, and it doesn't matter if we can play or not."

Ironically, Stryper took even more heat from factions in the religious community. The Rev. Jimmy Swaggart, a television evangelist, ripped the band in his *Evangelist* newsletter, where he claimed to have attended a Stryper show in Baton Rouge, Louisiana. Swaggart attacked everything from the band's attire to "the general feeling of the concert." After witnessing Stryper's ritual of throwing miniature Bibles to the crowd, Swaggart said, "Sad to say, most of them were not even picked up."

"As far as we know, he wasn't even there," the soft-spoken Gaines said. "People got crazy to pick up the Bibles. It disappointed us because we love the guy. But frankly, we don't care what he thinks, because God is telling us what to do."

Stryper's message certainly satisfied the Christian crowd, and the band's good looks got them a long way with younger female fans. Except for substituting "Jesus saves" for the typical "party all night" slogans and the Bible tossing, the musical shtick was the same as, say, Bon Jovi or Poison.

But that enabled Stryper to sell albums, Gaines noted. "And that's God again." ■

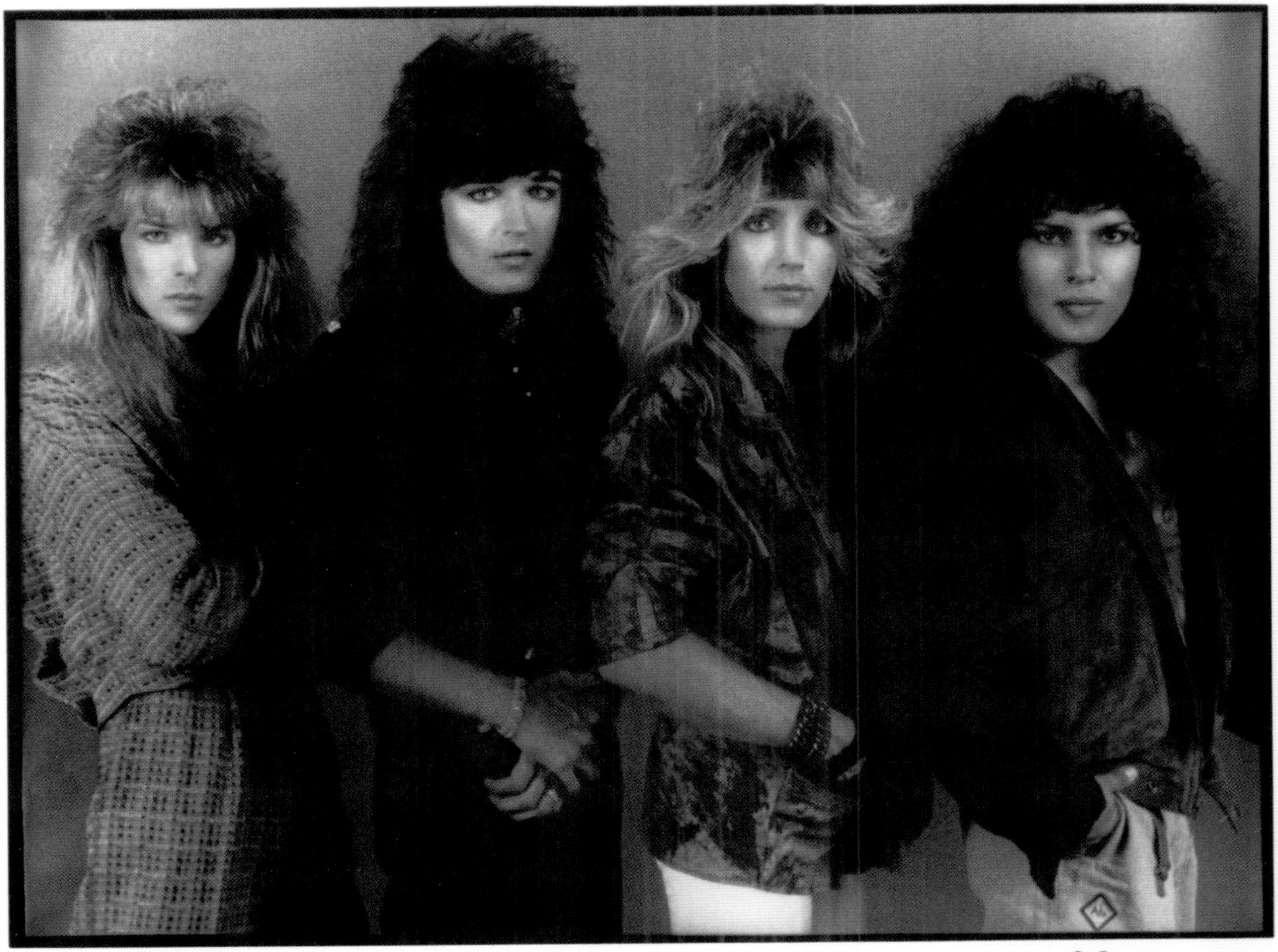

Photo: Suzan Carson/Artist Publications

Timothy Gaines **Michael Sweet** **Robert Sweet** **Oz Fox**

ENIGMA RECORDS
ENIGMA RECORDS, a division of
The Enigma Entertainment Corporation
1750 East Holly Avenue, Post Office Box 2428
El Segundo, California 90245-1528 USA
tlx 503809 fax 213/640-9342

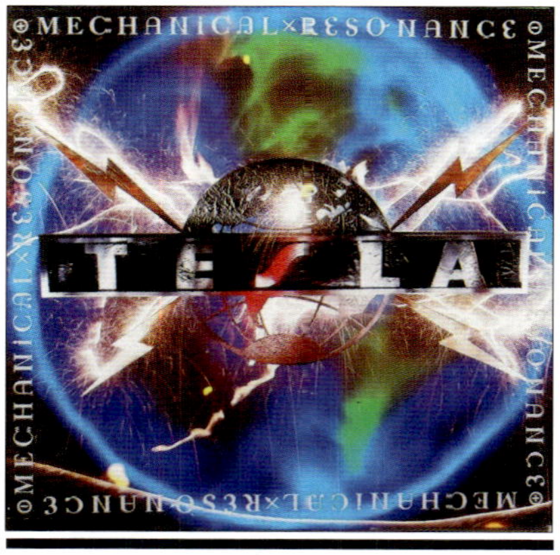

Billboard 200: *Mechanical Resonance* (#32)
Billboard Hot 100: "Little Suzi" (#91)

The mighty *Mechanical Resonance* album introduced the band Tesla's memorable brand of no-gimmick rock.

THE HARD-ROCK rookie band of the year, Tesla took its name from Nikola Tesla, an eccentric electrical inventor, and titled its album *Mechanical Resonance* for his theory that the earth could be split open like an apple using sound waves. Fans across America embraced the tracks "Modern Day Cowboy" and "Little Suzi"—both sharply executed exercises in Van Halen-isms.

Not bad for five unknowns from Sacramento, California. The group could ascribe its humble beginnings to bassist Brian Wheat and guitarist Frank Hannon, two friends who wanted to get a club band together. They met Jeff Keith, who had accrued some singing chops at his day job by screaming along to the radio in an 18-wheel transfer truck.

"Sacramento was the Big Apple as far as I was concerned," Keith said. "Hey, I'm an Okie at heart. It shows in the way I dress—I'm no fashion statement, that's for damn sure."

Guitarist Tommy Skeoch joined Tesla in 1984, and suddenly the band was in Guam, making money playing at a club near the military bases—"We wrote songs, got tight, kicked back," Keith recalled. By the time they returned to the Sacramento metal circuit, Tesla had recruited drummer Troy Lucketta and decided to go all-out for a record contract. The band was discovered by talent scouts and signed to a label shortly thereafter.

It kicked off a succession of hassles with management, lawyers and the business side of the music industry, but Tesla emerged with a hit album. *Mechanical Resonance* was produced by Steve Thompson, who had remixed dance singles for folks like Madonna. Tesla gained exposure on the road as well, opening tours for David Lee Roth (who reportedly selected the group after seeing its video), Alice Cooper and Def Leppard—nice work for a group that purposefully tried not to contrive an image for itself.

"Everybody has their own opinion about what is and isn't heavy metal," Keith said. "To me, we're a straight-ahead, good-time hard-rock band."

The quintet refuted the notion that the lineup was hand-selected by some record company executive and groomed for success.

"Hey, Frank and I started the band, and if anybody's done the picking of players, it's us," Wheat assured. "We didn't get along with our first guitar player, our first singer quit, and our first drummer got married, so we had to replace them, that's all. We're the same band that made the demo tapes that got us signed to a record deal. We're not Menudo!" ■

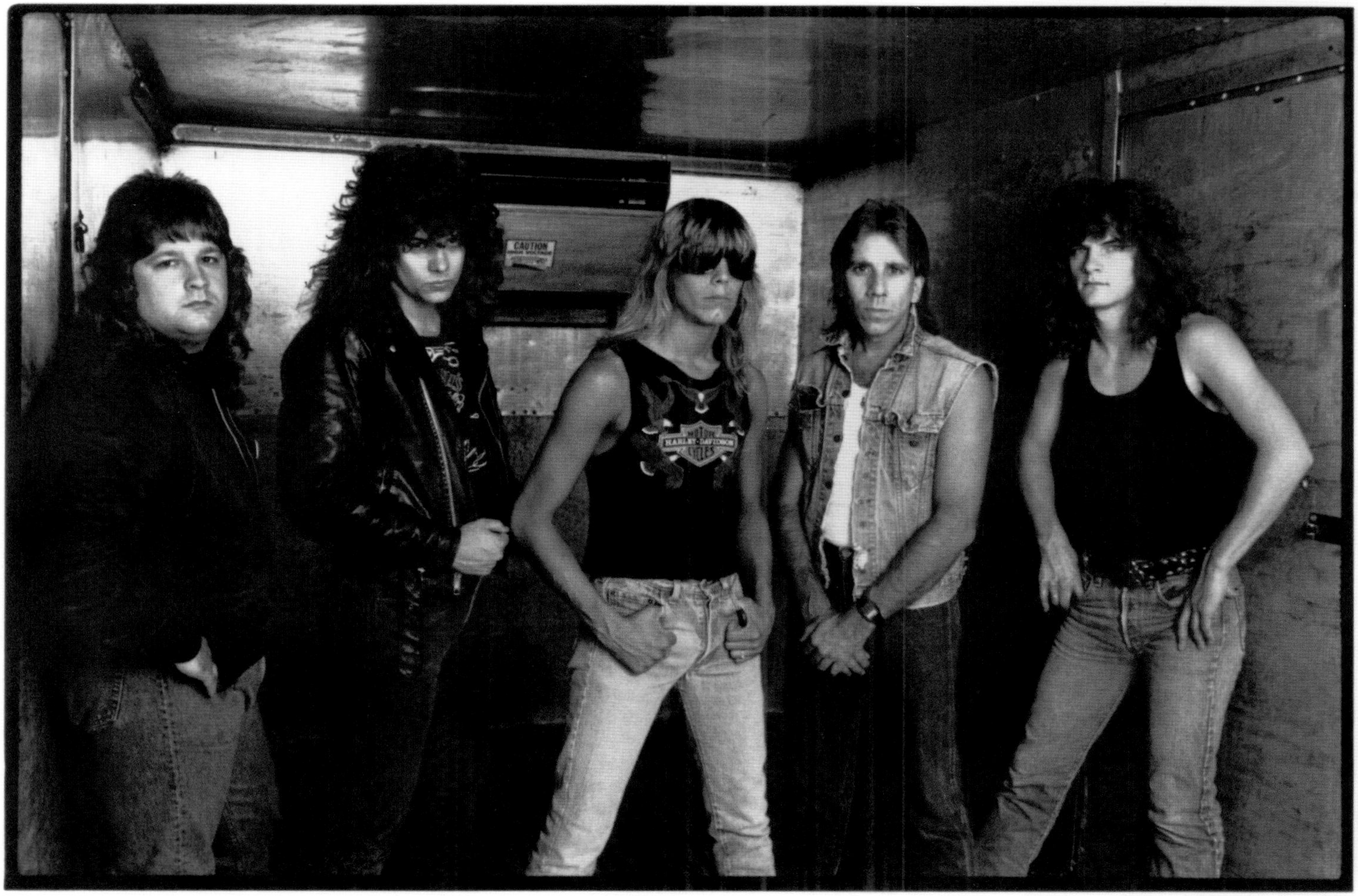

Photo Credit: Ross Halfin

BRIAN WHEAT TOMMY SKIS JEFF KEITH TROY LAQUETTA FRANK HANNON

TESLA

GEFFEN RECORDS

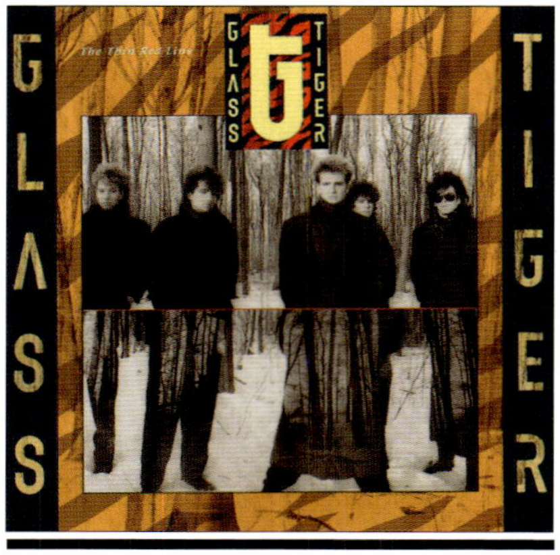

Billboard 200: *The Thin Red Line* (#27)
Billboard Hot 100: "Don't Forget Me (When I'm Gone)" (#2); "Someday" (#7); "I Will Be There" (#34)

Glass Tiger hit the airwaves with two pleasurable singles, "Someday" and "Don't Forget Me (When I'm Gone)."

AFTER TOURING the bar circuit for several years, Glass Tiger secured interest from a major label, and recorded a debut album, *The Thin Red Line*, in the quintet's native Canada. Assisting Glass Tiger in translating their music's potential was Jim Vallance, known for his songwriting and arranging work with Bryan Adams. *The Thin Red Line* marked his first foray into solo production.

"Jim was originally approached by our label to write and arrange with us," vocalist and lyricist Alan Frew recalled. "He had been involved to some extent with production before, but this was his first real assignment."

The entire band composed music, sharing credits with Vallance on "Don't Forget Me (When I'm Gone)." "We walked into Jim's house and my eyes just about popped out of my head when I saw his home studio," keyboardist Sam Reid said. "As a result of my getting my hands on some of the equipment, we started the music track to 'Don't Forget Me' within a half an hour after we arrived."

"Usually, I write and sing scratch lyrics and then rework them, but this song was so happy and up-tempo that Jim talked me into leaving them as is," Frew added. "He was right—it's done great."

Adams, Vallance's old friend, made a memorable cameo singing backup vocals in his signature rasp, and the song reached No. 1 in the Canadian charts and #2 in the US. The follow-up single, "Someday," also reached the Top 10 in the US charts and won a Juno Award (the Canadian equivalent of the Grammys) n the Single of the Year category.

"There's a slight tongue-in-cheek element to the lyrics," Frew said. "When you hear me sound like I'm a loser at love, sometimes I do a twist where I'm the one who caused the break-up. It's difficult having a relationship with someone when ycu're in a band." ■

GLASS TIGER

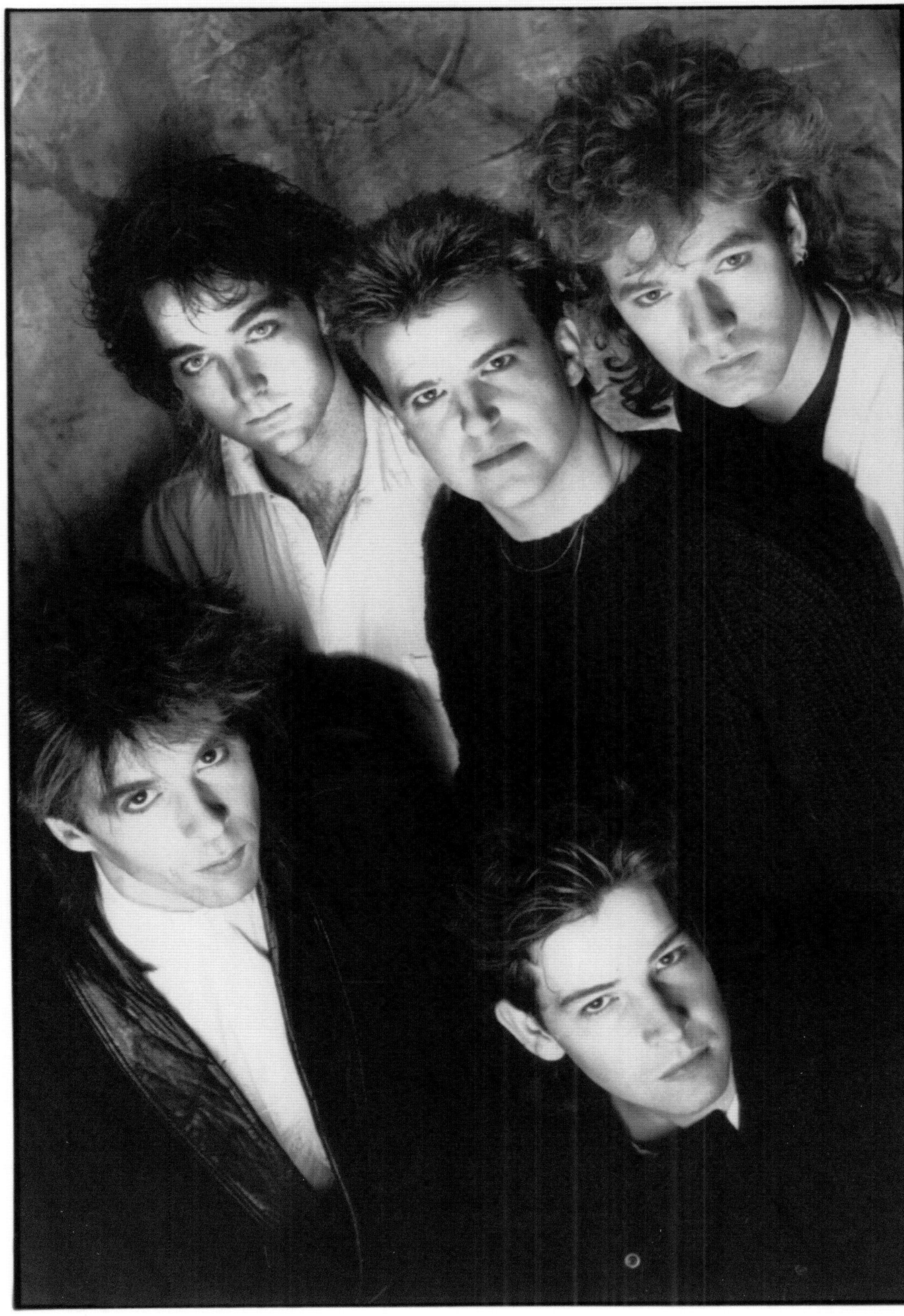

PHOTOGRAPH: BETH BAPTISTE/1986

MAN HAT TAN™

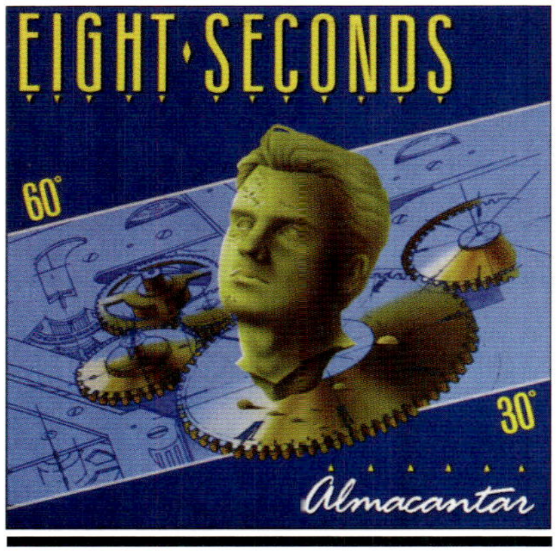

Billboard Hot 100: "Kiss You (When It's Dangerous)" (#72)

Canadian band Eight Seconds caught a few breaks, including business with distinguished producer Rupert Hine.

FORMED IN 1982 in their native Ottawa, the members of Eight Seconds contrived their name by modifying the late Andy Warhol's statement that "in the future, everyone will be famous for 15 minutes."

"Before he died, he said because the media move faster now, fame is more fleeting—it's probably closer to 8½ seconds than 15 minutes," Brazilian-born singer and lyricist Andres del Castillo joked. "So we were only off by a half-second."

Eight Seconds' fortunes changed when the original version of "Where's Bula" won a local FM rock station's contest. First place awarded them the production of a music video, which was subsequently aired on Canada's influential MuchMusic channel and MTV's *Basement Tapes* show.

Almacantar, the band's major label debut album, was produced by Rupert Hine, best known for his success with the Fixx, Howard Jones and Tina Turner. Hine had caught the act at an outdoor Canada Day festival, and his interest created a buzz for the new wave group. "I got to like the music on a personal level," the Englishman said, "and I thought, we ought to be able to do something with these guys."

The quintet had a burgeoning hit single with "Kiss You (When It's Dangerous)," which got radio exposure in US markets. The song was typical of Eight Seconds' pleasant, synthesized sound, reminiscent of Hine's work with *Reach the Beach*-era Fixx. ■

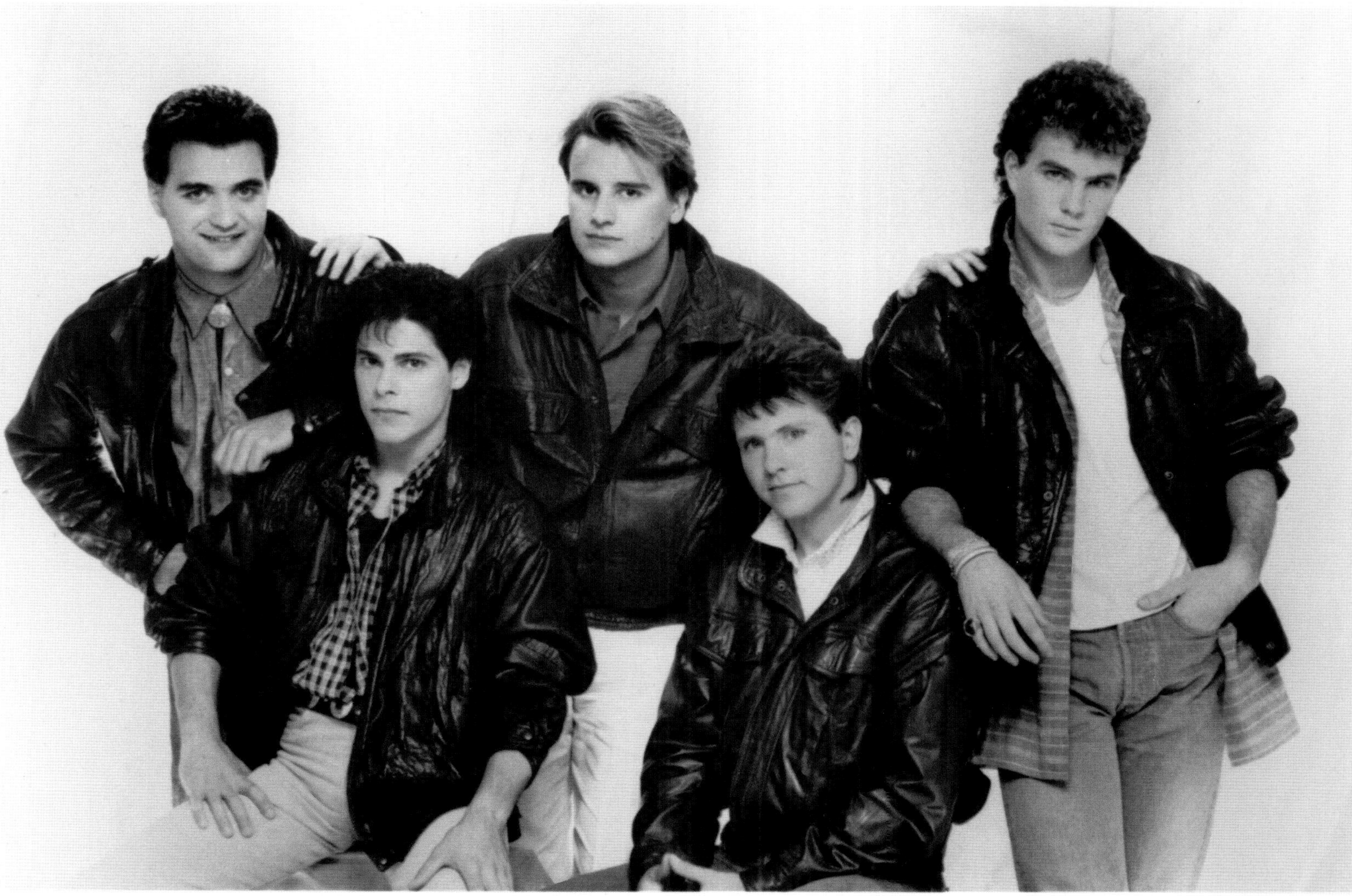

EIGHT SECONDS

polydor

PolyGram Records

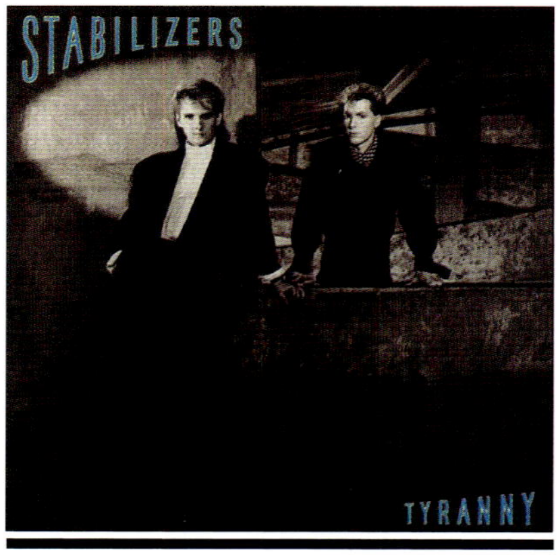

Billboard Hot 100: "One Simple Thing" #93)

A jewel of a single, "One Simple Thing" offered the duo Stabilizers a modicum of achievement and notoriety.

SINGER DAVE Christenson and multi-instrumentalist Rich Nevens, the twosome known as Stabilizers, met while part of the Erie, Pennsylvania, club scene, and they quickly put together a successful musical chemistry. "I was taken with the fact Rich is originally from England," Christenson explained. "He's into technology, putting songs and great chord progressions together. My department is thinking up lyrics. It's a nice arrangement because we fill in each other's shortcomings."

After making homemade demos of songs on a little four-track machine, "Underground" became a hit on the local Top 40 station, and Christenson and Nevens found themselves playing to 1,000 people a night. Stabilizers got signed and moved to Los Angeles to record their first album. *Tyranny* debuted when their record company was busy hyping superstar Bruce Springsteen's live album. So "One Simple Thing," a catchy single that got heavy airplay initially at some rock radio stations, lost momentum.

Ironically, the potential acceptance of "One Simple Thing"—a melodically charged slice of synth-pop—had bugged both Stabilizers. "I have a hard time taking the song seriously, mainly because we built it in the studio at the last minute," Christenson divulged. "We arrived in California with two songs and went right in the studio. I think people just assumed we had more—but we didn't!"

"One Simple Thing" featured a video directed by David Fincher, and Stabilizers performed on *American Bandstand*. "We want to play on the fact that we're not Depeche Mode," Christensen said. "I have a real hard time with all of that 'sullen image' stuff—we like to smile. I just want to write good songs for a long time."

But the follow-up single, "Tyranny " failed to chart when the band wanted to record another album rather than promote the song. A corporate acquisition of the record company led to the band being dropped, and the Stabilizers disappeared from public view. ■

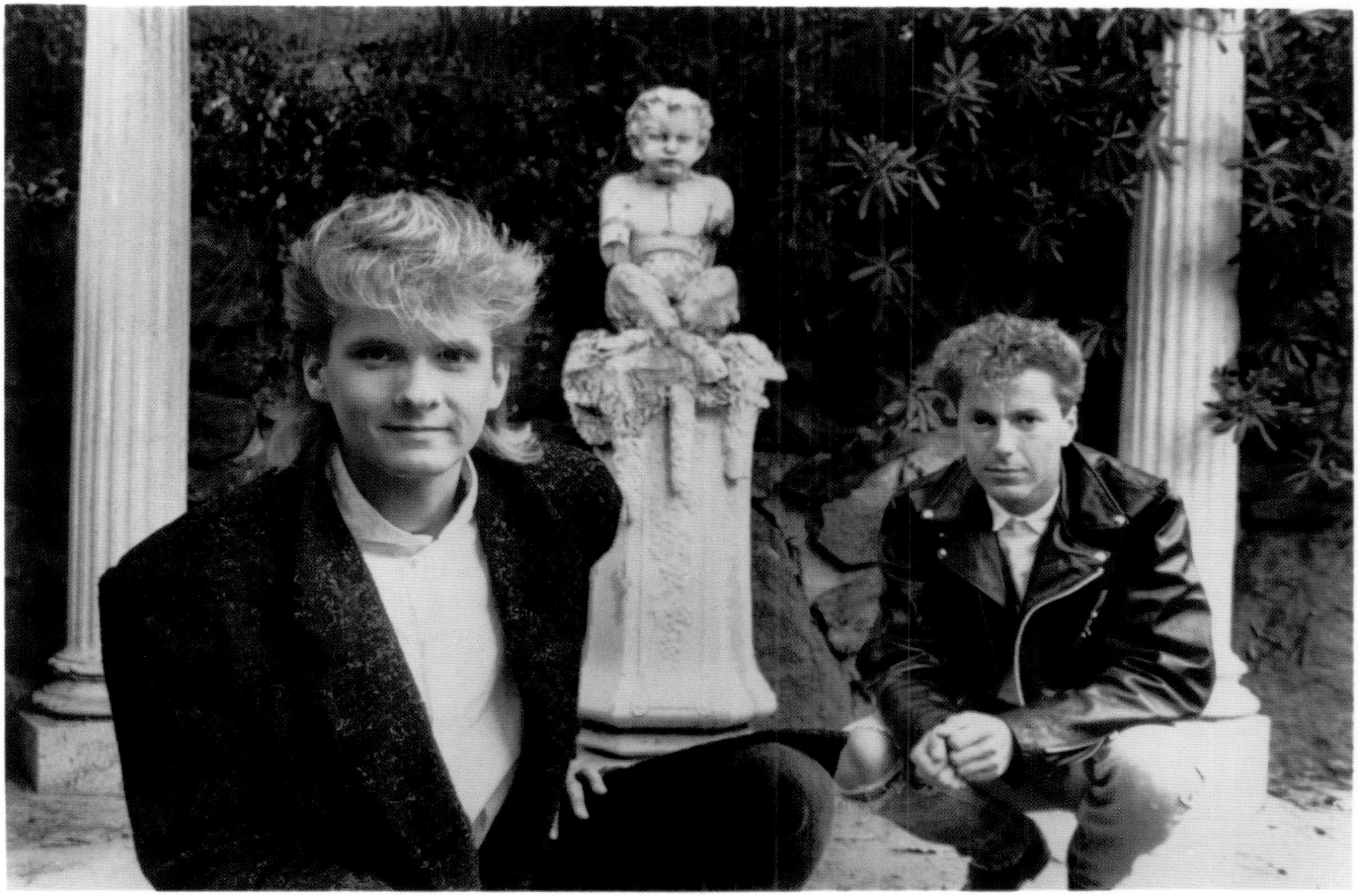

PHOTO CREDIT: ANDY ROSEN

DAVE CHRISTENSON RICH NEVENS

STABILIZERS

LARRY MARKS
HEDRON MANAGEMENT
10880 WILSHIRE BLVD.
L.A. CA. 90024
(213) 475-7171

Columbia

8612

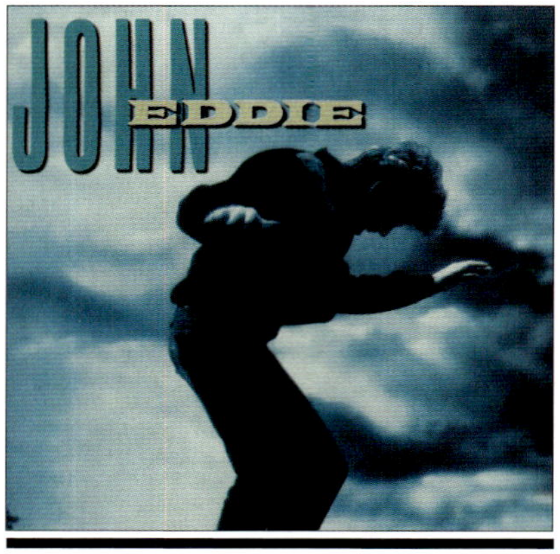

Billboard 200: *John Eddie* (#83)
Billboard Hot 200: "Jungle Boy" (#50)

Like many New Jersey rockers of his generation, John Eddie gathered his inspiration from Bruce Springsteen.

IN JUNIOR high, John Eddie gained a clear-eyed appreciation of what he could do when he saw Bruce Springsteen at a Camden City College concert.

"It wasn't like when Bruce saw Elvis Presley and he knew what he wanted to do in his life," Eddie recalled. "I knew what I wanted to do before I ever saw Bruce—he just showed me there was a way to do it."

Eddie became a legend in the little clubs of New Jersey, Pennsylvania and Delaware, the circuit where Springsteen had once made his name. By 1982, he owned a regular gig at Asbury Park's legendary Stone Pony, and Springsteen jammed with him onstage. He started attracting the attention of record companies and signed with Columbia Records—the home of Springsteen, who had blown up with *Born in the USA*.

The label replaced Eddie's long-time backup band, the Front Street Runners, to record his self-titled debut album. There were hard feelings, but he backed the decision.

"We were going to use a studio band, and I said, 'Yeah, great, sure, whatever,'" Eddie said. "But then I would call up and say, 'Look, what do you think about Max Weinberg (a member of Springsteen's E Street Band)? I think he's a really great rock n' roll drummer.' And they would say, 'Well, sure, let's check it out,' And it turned out he wanted to do it."

John Eddie featured other heavyweight musicians—Springsteen guitarist Nils Lofgren, ex-Faces keyboardist Ian McLagan and respected session pianist Greg Phillinganes. The swaggering single "Jungle Boy" was a middling success.

"When I was in the eighth grade, there was that Gary Glitter song, 'Rock and Roll Part 2,' an instrumental, and all the kids in the cafeteria would be banging on the lunch tables to it," Eddie said. "It got so bad they finally took the jukebox out of the cafeteria. Well, that song has always been on my mind—I wanted to write one just like it. That's what 'Jungle Boy' was for me, my attempt at 'Rock and Roll Part 2.' I really love the way it came out, but it's not going to be there for me until I hear those kids banging on the lunch table." ■

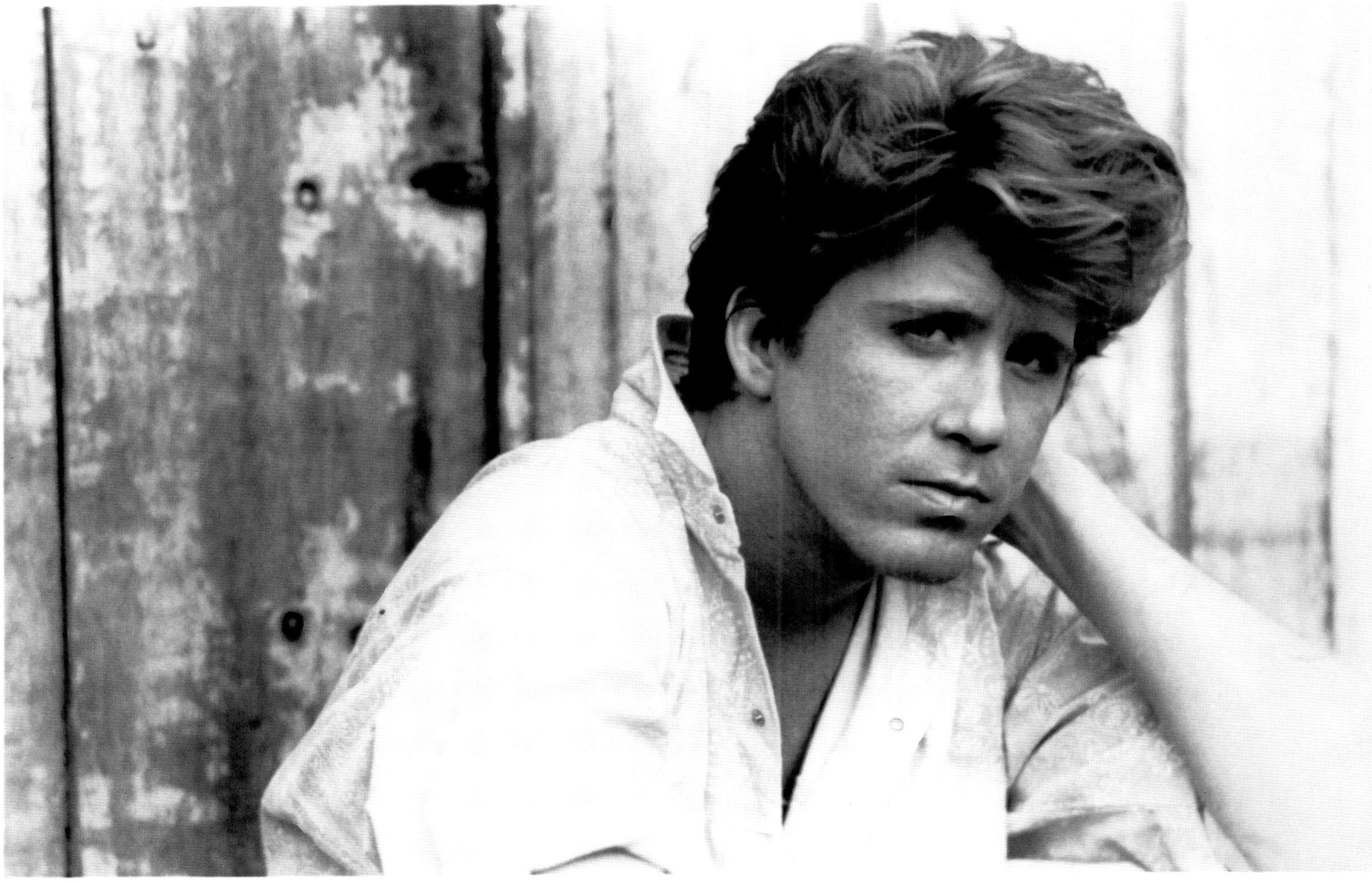

CHAMPION
ENTERTAINMENT
ORGANIZATION INC
130 WEST 57TH STREET, NEW YORK, N.Y. 10019

JOHN EDDIE

Columbia
8604

PHOTOGRAPH: JANET VAN HAM

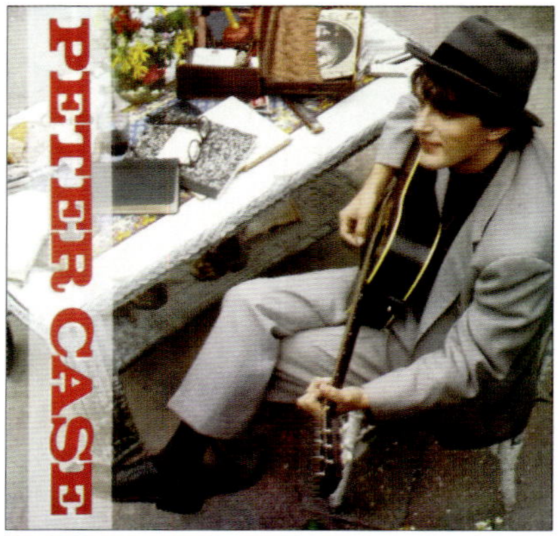

Disbanding the Plimsouls, Peter Case toured as a solo act, armed only with his acoustic guitar and harmonica.

IN HIS ill-fitting thrift-shop suit and horn-rimmed glasses, Peter Case looked more like a disheveled Clark Kent than a pop superman. But, as he sang in his song "Steel Strings," "Do you want a man of steel, or do you want a man that's real?"

Case spent the better part of a decade in pursuit of traditional pop stardom, first as a member of the Nerves, a California band, and then as the leader of the Plimsouls, an exceptional power-pop group that never received its commercial due. The Plimsouls reached an artistic peak with a 1983 single, "A Million Miles Away," but when the song stiffed in the marketplace, Case started considering a musical change of pace.

"That record was well-received, by the few people who received it," he laughed. "But all the terrible things that can happen to a band happened to us in that period—management problems, personal problems. The whole big-time rock 'n' roll world lost its charm for me. I wanted to escape the economic pressures and get better at what I do, strip it down to the essentials—you know, singing and playing. Simplicity."

Case's frustrations deepened when the Plimsouls started performing a song titled "Sorry," and rock audiences insisted on hearing it as "Party." So, the Plimsouls disbanded, and Case immediately began playing as a solo performer around Los Angeles. "I'd wanted to do it for a while. It was a return to when I first started playing coffeehouses in San Francisco when I was 18."

And while Case still wasn't making a lot of money, he was thrilled with the renewed sense of communication he had with listeners. "Most music these days is geared for short attention spans, based on overstimulation every few seconds," he mused. "It misses the subtleties about life. I like great storytellers, mystery, real power, not a bunch of slogans strung together."

Cut by producer T-Bone Burnett with Mitchell Froom, *Peter Case*, his first solo album, was released on a major label, highlighted by the track "Old Blue Car." Case crossed the country playing at the drop of a hat for anyone who was interested in listening, performing his slightly skewed guitar/vocals/harp tunes on the nation's malls. "But I don't think what I'm doing now is that much different," he insisted of his street-playing persona. "I've played club gigs for a lot less people."

It took a special moxie to get up in front of a crowd with nothing but an acoustic guitar and a few songs to win people over, singing his "post-atomic folk music" for chump change.

"But I just think of the music I'm trying to put across and concentrate on that—I can't please everyone," he said. "When you grow, some folks don't want to see you change. I can't do anything but pray for those people. There are enough people doing the rock 'n' roll party thing—they don't need me to do it. So now I'm taking my own music around, and I got plenty of time." ■

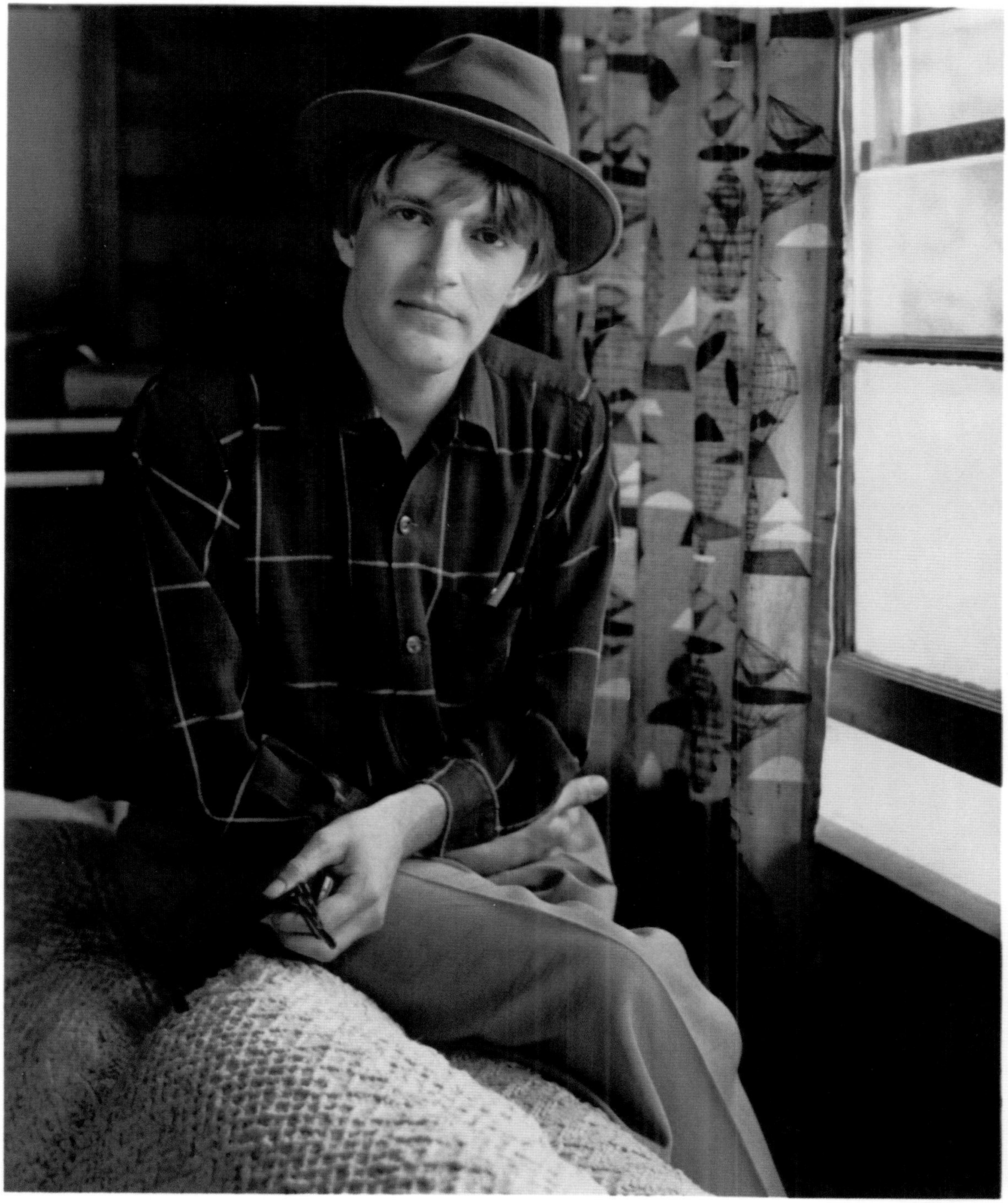

Photo Credit: Stephen Rothfeld

PETER CASE

GEFFEN RECORDS

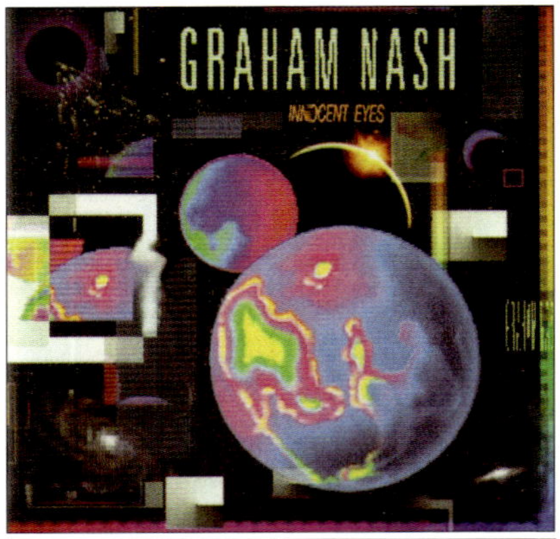

Billboard 200: *Innocent Eyes* (#136)
Billboard Hot 100: "Innocent Eyes" (#84)

Noting musical trends, Graham Nash returned to his solo career with *Innocent Eyes*, his first album in six years.

FIRST RISING to stardom in the Sixties as a founding member of the Hollies, Graham Nash went on to make even greater musical history as a cornerstone of Crosby, Stills & Nash and Crosby, Stills, Nash & Young. Those legendary harmony ensembles had always been Nash's first love, and he unselfishly saved his best compositions—"Marrakesh Express," "Teach Your Children," "Our House" and "Just a Song Before I Go," all hits when released as singles—for those groups rather than solo activities.

"By their very form, songs can dictate where they really should go," Nash said. "'Teach Your Children' was a very obvious CSN song, y'know?"

On his own, Nash's unpretentious style had carried him, but he delivered a surprise with his *Innocent Eyes* album. In a move to sound more contemporary, he surrounded his characteristically keening tenor with electronic instrumentation and drum machines.

"I've had people tell me that my record company put the wrong album in the sleeve," Nash said. "But I take it as a compliment. I wanted to shake people up, make an album that made them say, 'Wait a second!' God, it's 1986 and so many people keep asking me about Woodstock. It's like answering questions about World War II or something."

So the old dog had learned some new techno-tricks, and he made another departure, recording several songs by outside writers. *Innocent Eyes* had been delayed by Crosby, Stills & Nash tours over the past few summers, but Nash no longer had that excuse, as Crosby was serving time in a Texas jail on charges of drug and gun possession.

"I guess we could still tour with (actress) Mary Crosby instead," Nash said with a chuckle before turning serious. "You've got to understand, they really don't want to deal with him at all. So many times, the judge said, 'We don't want to send you to jail. Wise up and lay low—be a good boy for two months, we can get you off our hands and forget this whole thing.' But he wouldn't do that—he got arrested in Mill Valley, he got arrested in Orange County, he kept getting headlines. He forced them to have to deal with him.

Despite Crosby's ongoing problems, Nash continued to defend him like a true friend, although articles quoted Nash extensively as being fed up and angry with the situation.

"He'll never forgive me for that," Nash lamented. "The articles were tremendously accurate in terms of presenting the dark side, but what they didn't tell you is how many people he's made happy with his music over the last 20 years, how much compassion the man has, how bad it is for him. They were very closed-ended—they didn't give a way out or give any hope.

"People have got to realize that it's Crosby who's going through this. It's worse for him than anyone can write about, because he's there in a Texas penitentiary stewing inside a cell. It must be hard to come down. We've all been high, and it's tough to face the fact that you're a human being with failings and weaknesses. I just want him to know that I'll be there, ready and willing to make music with him, when he decides to change his life." ■

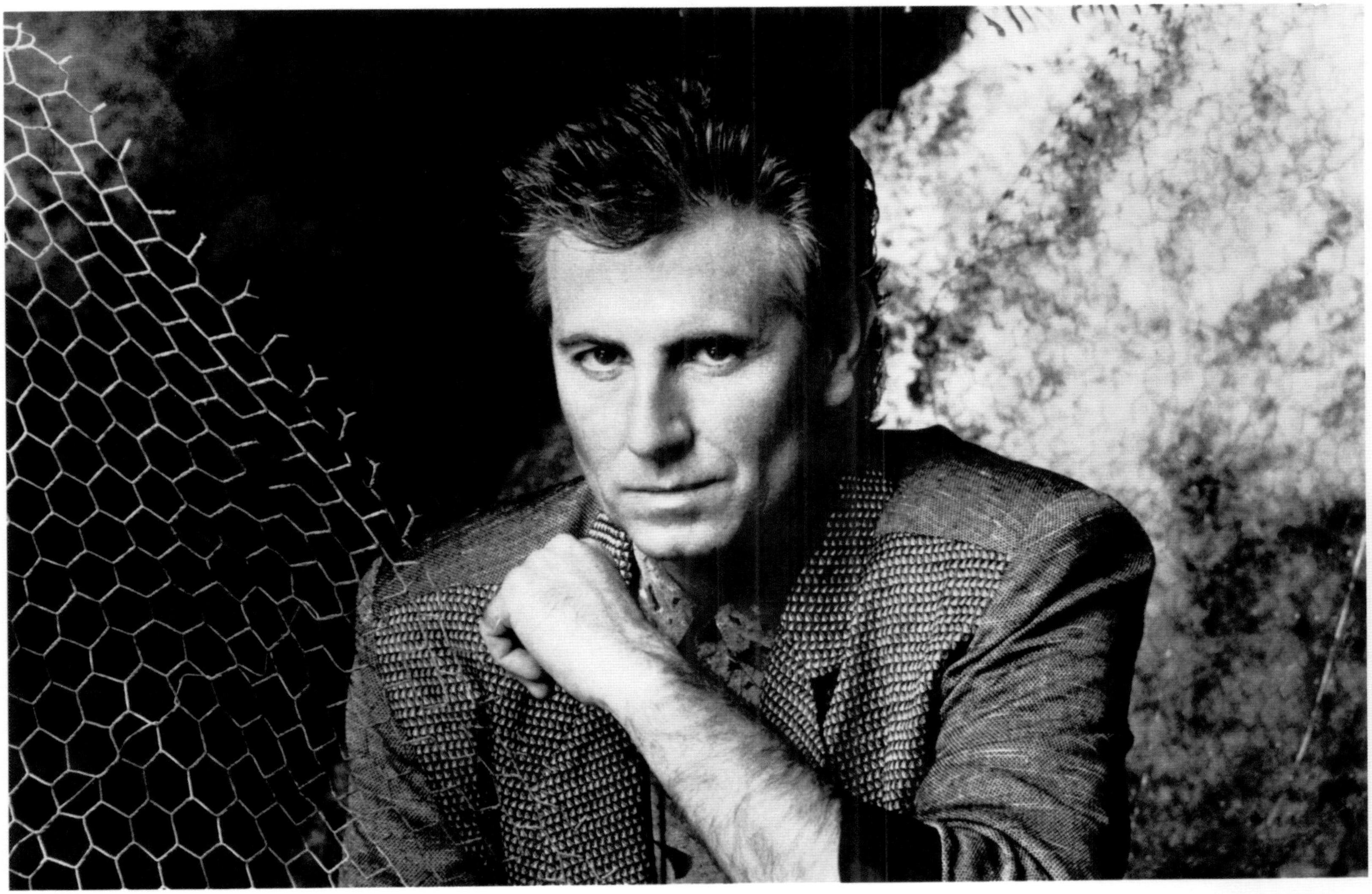

GRAHAM NASH

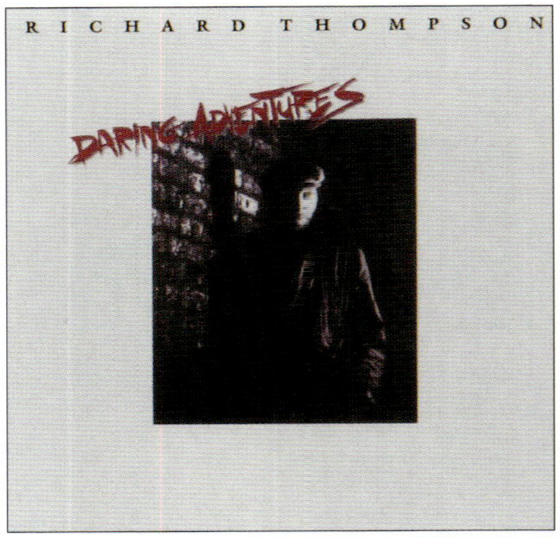

Billboard 200: *Daring Adventures* (#142)

Made with an American band and producer, *Daring Adventures* aimed to broaden Richard Thompson's audience.

SLOWLY BUT surely, the American adult rock audience was discovering that Richard Thompson deserved its attention. Here was a guitarist of exquisite taste, a warm and endearing vocalist—a more eccentric version of Dire Straits' Mark Knopfler, or Britain's answer to Fleetwood Mac's Lindsey Buckingham.

But while those analogies provided an easy musical reference point, they were somewhat unfair. Thompson's recording career had spanned nearly two decades. He got his start circa 1969 as lead guitarist with Fairport Convention, the seminal English folk-rock group that gained critical acclaim for an emotional commitment to traditional song forms.

It was a series of records with wife Linda that cemented Thompson's reputation as a unique talent, culminating in 1982's *Shoot Out the Lights*, a classic album driven by epic songwriting, Linda's majestic singing and Richard's extraordinary guitar work. Of course, just as it started to give the Thompsons some overdue recognition, they divorced. They were last seen together on a concert swing through America, tossing musical invectives at each other from opposite sides of the stage.

"That was a rough tour," Thompson said. "Linda and I had already decided to split up our marriage, but we were forced to go on with the tour or we would have lost all our money. So somehow we managed to go through with it."

Thompson then embarked on a solo career, and *Daring Adventures* was the expected exhibition of tasteful material and impeccable vocal and guitar work, bolstered by livelier production from keyboard player Mitchell Froom.

"I'm basically a good-natured person," Thompson insisted. "My songs aren't exactly sunny, but that's just my way of working things out." "Valerie," a raucous "Celtic rockabilly" tune, got more attention on American radio than any of his other singles, and the sad "How Will I Ever Be Simple Again" emerged as one of his best-loved numbers. But Thompson tread the road of commercial promise warily.

"I heard a few stations are playing 'Valerie,'" he shrugged. "If it helps sell the album, that's fine. But at this late stage, I no longer expect big things. I've grown quite used to doing things at my own pace." ■

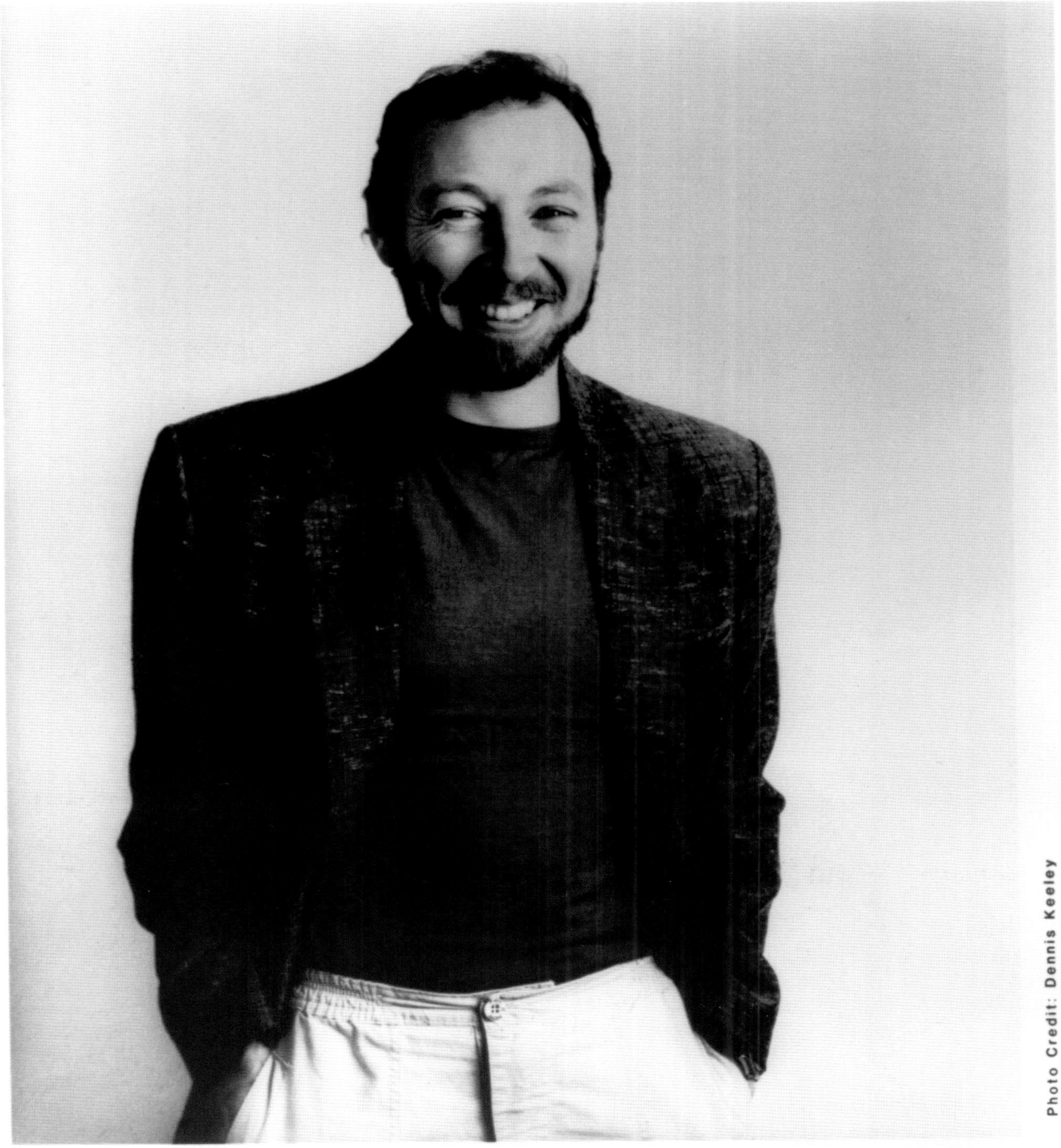

Photo Credit: Dennis Keeley

RICHARD THOMPSON

polydor

PolyGram Records

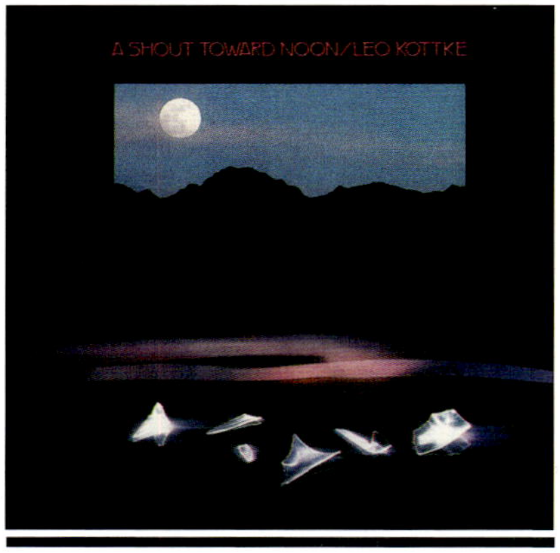

The invigoration of acoustic music in the Eighties prompted renewed affection for Leo Kottke's guitar artistry.

EVER SINCE he snuck out of Minnesota in the early Seventies, Leo Kottke's skills as an acoustic guitarist were irrefutable. He wasn't just fast and dexterous—when he started layering complex countermelodies into his playing, his two hands produced the sound of four. Kottke had spent his career recording for major and minor labels. After a self-imposed three-year hiatus, he finally unveiled his 14th album, *A Shout Toward Noon.*

In the past, Kottke had remained on the folk periphery, attempting to please his record companies by recording every type of album, from solo acoustic to orchestral arrangements. But the reflective *A Shout Toward Noon* offered a twist—it was recorded for Private Music, a new-age music label founded by Tangerine Dream's Peter Baumann. The album's sound didn't herald a major departure for Kottke—it was just his guitar and some occasional cello and synthesizer. Yet the talented performer found himself being marketed in a category that conjured up hot-tub-and-granola cliches.

Still, Kottke accepted his status as a musical black sheep. "It's like being a ball bearing on the point of a needle," he mused. "Business people always try to figure where I fit—and I don't."

However flawed, the new-age tag benefited Kottke—for the perceived yuppie consumers who appreciated excellence, he was a natural hero, committed to the simple virtues of harmony and melody found in country, folk and blues influences. "At least 'new age' is a little broader as a category," he noted. "It's made instrumental music imaginable to the record industry—they can make money on it."

And Kottke remained the quintessential mellow artist. While he'd never taken a guitar lesson, he'd spent recent years studying the complete fingerboard to help his improvisational playing, "learning theory and then forgetting it, so I can be myself without using my brains," he explained. "I think that type of preparation goes for my singing, too."

Which begged the question—would his new instrumental music label let him sing? Fans had come to expect an infrequent vocal offering, although Kottke downplayed the emotive, resonant power of his voice. "I've got three songs with lyrics right now—three more than I had three years ago," was all he said on the matter. In concert, he used his voice to his advantage in one other way, delivering nutty but articulate anecdotes between songs. No other guitarist ever sounded so knowledgeable about rotary nose-hair clippers. ■

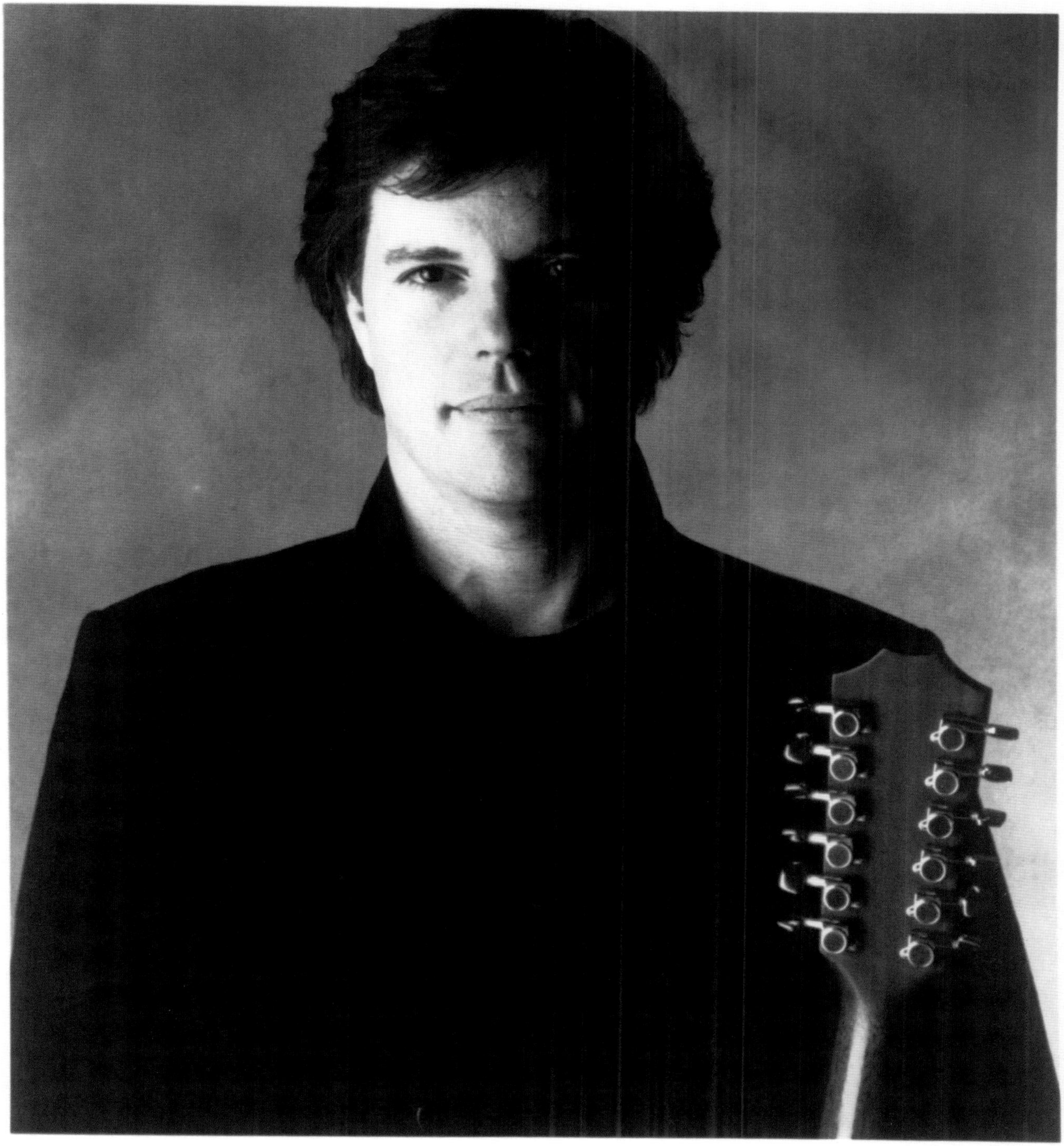

MONTEREY
PENINSULA
ARTISTS
Carmel, California 93921

Leo Kottke

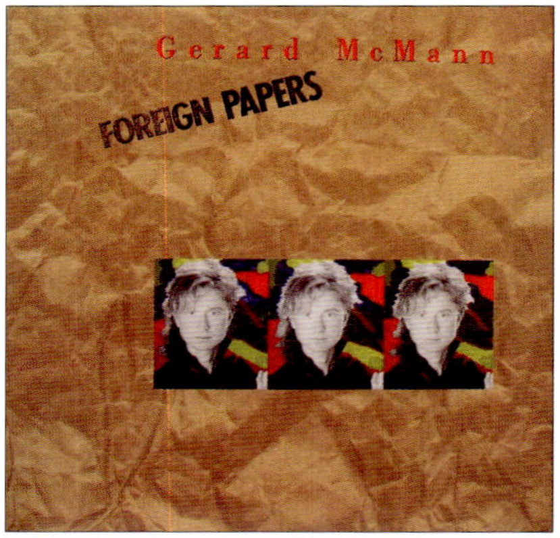

Gerard McMann returned with *Foreign Papers*, an album built on the promise he showed as a young musician.

DURING THE mid-Seventies, Gerard McMahon was the creative force behind Gerard, a 10-piece aggregation known in Colorado for melding sweet pop sensibilities with the roar of a big band. After attending a showcase for another act one evening, Chicago producer James William Guercio walked out mesmerized by Gerard's opening set. The resultant Guercio-produced album, *Gerard*, was released on Caribou Records.

"I'm not ashamed of it, but it's like reading old letters that you wrote—'Did I say that to that girl? How corny could I be?'" McMann recalled. "It's silly to be that way, because it was just part of a growth pattern. It was a beginning as far as record-making."

McMann settled in New York after spending much time in Los Angeles and Europe, establishing himself in industry circles as a hit songwriter. He wrote "Is That You" for Kiss as well as making contributions to the movie soundtracks for *Fast Times at Ridgemont High* and *All the Right Moves*. The publishing royalties sustained him.

"It's been my saving grace, just a result of my being around for a while," he explained. "I don't have a publishing company that pushes my songs; I just go out and do it myself. And now I can make a living off some of them, because a lot of those movies just keep on running. Thank God for HBO!"

But the multitalented performer simultaneously forged his own recording career. As a solo act, McMahon had released the critically acclaimed *Blue Rue* album and the less successful *No Looking Back* in the early part of the Eighties, after which he signed with Atlantic Records and issued *Foreign Papers*, adopting the name Gerard McMann.

Unfortunately, *Foreign Papers*' release coincided with a glut of superstar product, making it harder for McMann's album to get exposure. But he refused to worry. "I care about my record, but I can't think about it too much," he said. "A lot of artists get into that, 'Omigod, is it a hit, is my life over?' frame of mind, and it's counterproductive. I'm a fatalist, so I figure if it's gonna be, it's gonna be. I'm moving on to the next thing."

Still, there was plenty of excitement in McMann's life. Director Joel Schumacher (*St. Elmo's Fire*) had expressed an interest in his acting career, and McMann hoped for a role in a major film. He soon recorded a gothic rock anthem, "Cry Little Sister," for the soundtrack of *The Lost Boys*, Schumacher's vampire movie.

The British-born singer's bigger worry had been explaining the streamlining of his surname to his parents. "When I was a little kid, I didn't even know how to say my name after a while," McMahon/McMann said with a laugh. "I come from an Irish family that says if you change your name, you're disowned, and my father was a little shocked at first. But he finally understood. I just said, 'Dad, at least they'll pronounce it right.'" ■

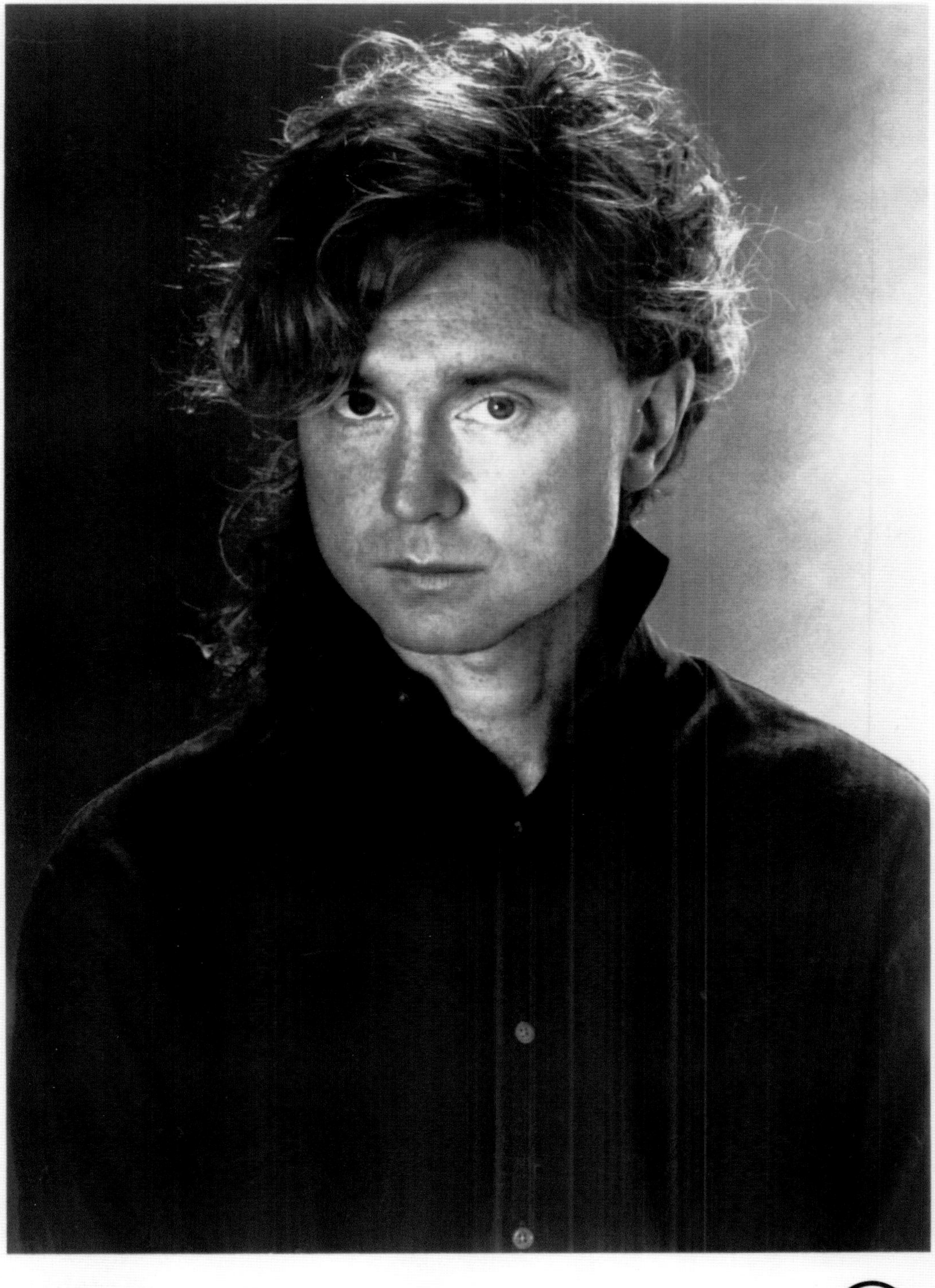

GERARD McMANN

ATCO

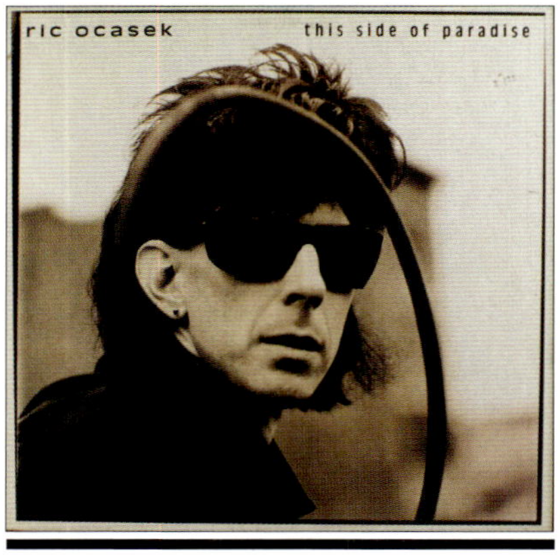

Billboard 200: *This Side of Paradise* (#31)
Billboard Hot 100: "Emotion in Motion" (#15); "True to You" (#75)

Ric Ocasek of the Cars established his second solo endeavor with the gentle "Emotion in Motion," a Top 20 hit.

AMERICA'S FIRST new-wave band to attain massive commercial success during the late Seventies and early Eighties, the Cars were steered by Ric Ocasek, a lanky, steel-eyed fellow with obsidian hair delivering songs with unusual lyrics and mock aloofness.

In 1982, he'd taken a sabbatical to commence work on his first solo record. The follow-up, *This Side of Paradise*, didn't veer too far off the Cars' path. Cars bandmates Greg Hawkes, Elliot Easton and Benjamin Orr played on the album, as did Tears for Fears' Roland Orzabel and producer Chris Hughes, as well as guitarists Tom Verlaine and Steve Stevens. The track "Emotion in Motion," which reached No. 1 on the mainstream rock charts, reaffirmed Ocasek's mastery of a smart, artful and accessible style.

Shifting gears, the soft-spoken Ocasek had also launched a second career as a sought-after producer for other modern-rock groups. He'd produced an album by the influential synth-punk trio Suicide in 1980 and was also working with Bad Brains (*Rock for Light*), Romeo Void (*Benefactor*) and Suicide's Alan Vega. Lou Reed and Iggy Pop had to go elsewhere in search of a producer while Ocasek buckled down on *This Side of Paradise*.

"First of all, I look for bands whose songs and lyrics I like, who are special in the way they sound," he explained. "I try to maintain their integrity. I would never prostitute a band. I'm a little more jaded about the business aspects, but I don't even mention those to the bands I produce. I want them to feel optimistic and have the fun of the climb. It's better to be naïve when you're first starting out and not have a good handle on how music is just a sales war to record companies.

"I think bands feel comfortable that I've already done it. I'm in a band, and I do write songs. They usually relate to me and probably trust me for those reasons. And they should, because I'm not really doing it for the money. I'm doing it for the love of music." ■

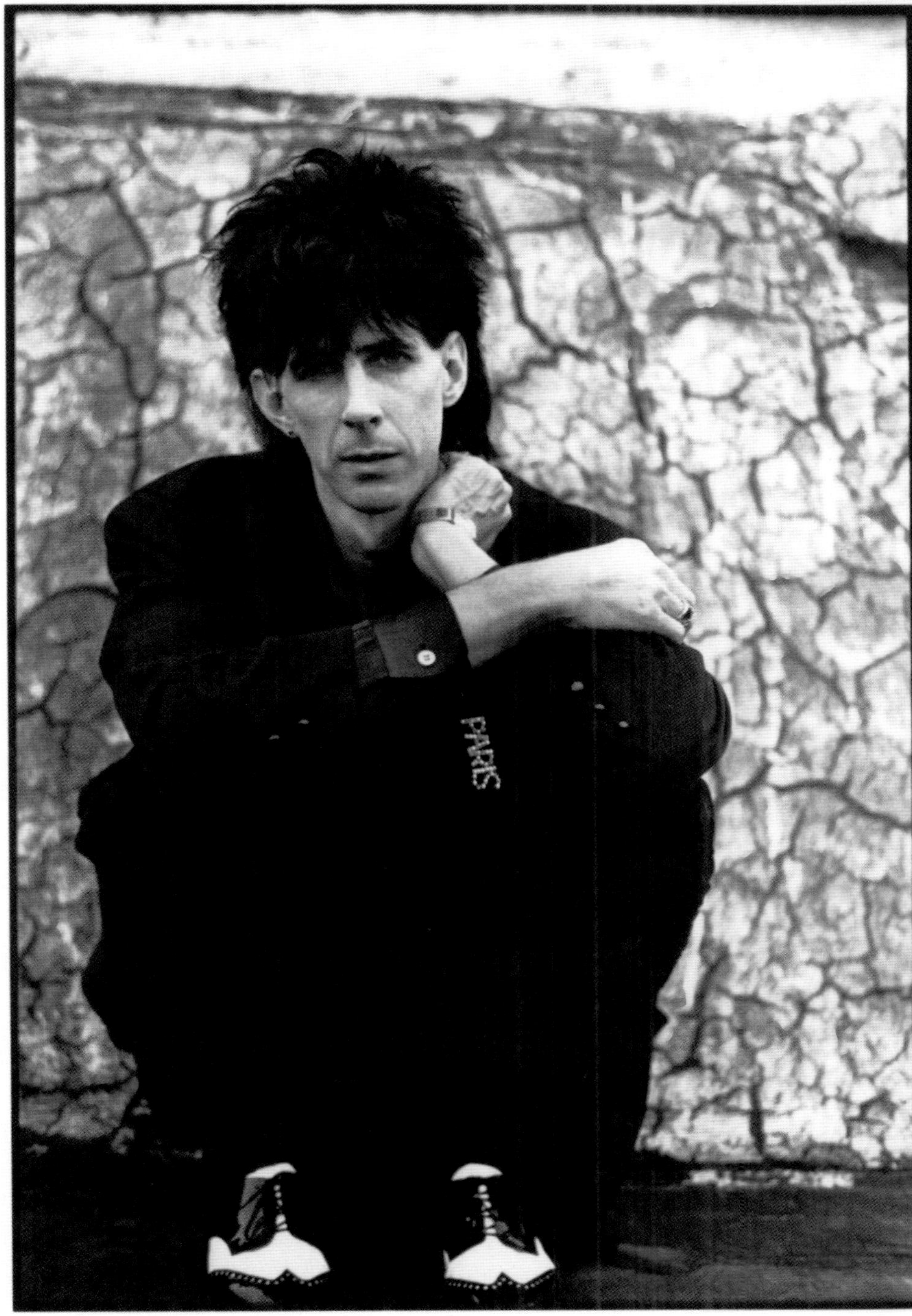

Photo Credit: Arthur Elgort

RIC OCASEK

GEFFEN RECORDS

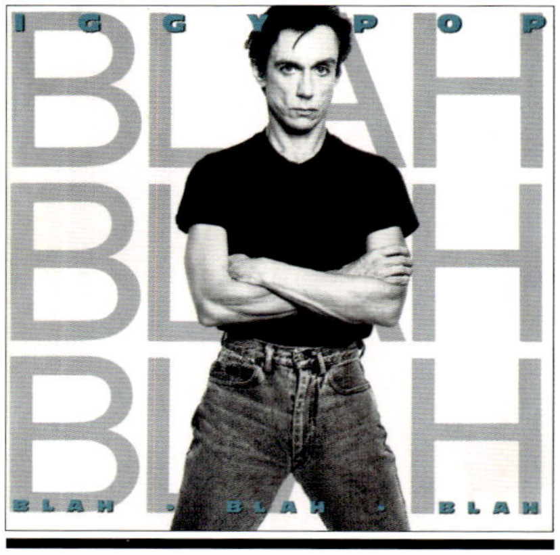

Billboard 200: *Blah-Blah-Blah* (#75)

The doyen of unhinged performances, a revitalized Iggy Pop courted the rock mainstream with *Blah-Blah-Blah*.

IN 1969, Iggy Pop earned his rock 'n' roll notoriety with the release of *The Stooges*, fronting the greatest "stoopid-rock" band in history. While such songs as "I Wanna Be Your Dog" served to doom the group to cult status, Iggy deliberately spurned conventional popularity with his demented stage demeanor—taunting audiences until he got assaulted, shattering glasses on the floor and belly-flopping on the shards, and then pulling off the scabs off from the previous night's gig/abuse.

Because of such outrageous acts, the music world always expected the Michigan native to be the next rock 'n' roll casualty. But Iggy went on to forge a substantial career without ever being entirely tamed. With guitarist James Williamson, he recorded 1973's *Raw Power*, a seminal heavy-metal album of that era. David Bowie became Iggy's patron in the late Seventies and funneled his excesses onto several albums.

The only frontier left for Iggy had been an actual hit record, and his time had arrived—*Blah-Blah-Blah* became his highest-charting album in history, and he was even on the radio with the tune "Real Wild Child (Wild One)" (it was Top 10 in England as well). The success was the product of a straighter, saner Iggy.

"It's a sparkling sunny day, and I just had fruit and granola for breakfast," he mused. "I feel much the same today as when I was 20 years old. And there were times 10 years ago when I felt about 1,000 years old."

Those old days still haunted Iggy occasionally. "Someone will say, 'Well, 10 years ago me and my friends would go to shows to see which way you'd hurt yourself,' but it was never the majority of my appeal," Iggy, aka James Osterberg, insisted. "Those kind of overblown expectations generally come from lazy people who feel they ought to act as if they're familiar with what I do, so they know a quick five lines for cocktail parties—'Oh, Iggy, of course, he's the godfather of punk,' or 'Oh, Iggy, of course, he was contrary to flower power way back when,' blah, blah, blah."

Thus the inspiration for *Blah-Blah-Blah*, an album which reunited Iggy with Bowie and ended a four-year recording hiatus. "He directs me almost like I'm an actor. It used to get so mixed up—he was almost like an alter ego. It tends to be a little more separate now. I was under tremendous pressure to make a good record, no question about it. My ability to communicate everyday concerns to people was being called into question, and that's why I took a few years off, to get to know my society again. I put all of my own savings into it. David and I were roadies for the whole thing—we did all the heavy lifting, the cord connecting, the runs to the music store when things broke."

Iggy remained an animated performer, but with a maturity that was never in evidence before. "The last four years have been a good exercise in discipline for me, investing effort into something in the hopes that it will pay off," he admitted. "But hey, it's not like I'm jogging or anything—I was eating granola in the days when I was puking onstage. I think I've done a pretty good job of my own style of rock 'n' roll. It's been sort of an achievement just to stick around." ■

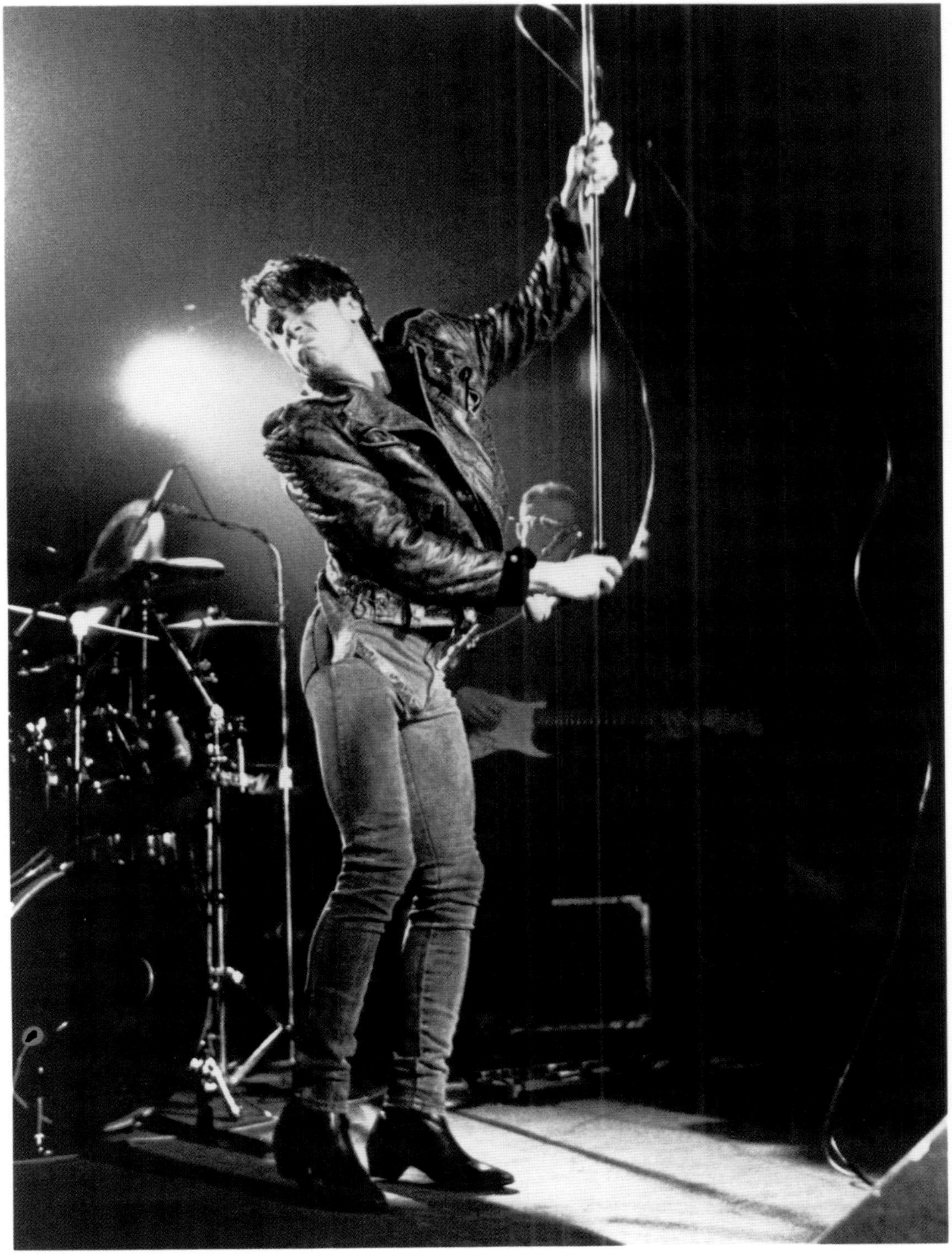

Photo Credit Paul McALPINE

CONTACT: JLM PUBLIC RELATIONS
(212) 673-2626

COLLINS & TAYLOR MANAGEMENT
(212) 683-1902

IGGY POP

A&M RECORDS

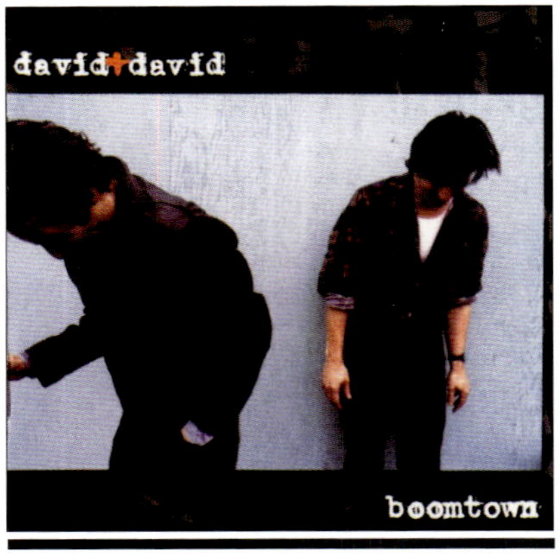

Billboard 200: *Boomtown* (#39)
Billboard Hot 100: "Welcome to the Boomtown" (#37);
"Ain't So Easy" (#51)

David + David joined forces to make *Boomtown*, a sleek, pointed song cycle about the nether realms of L.A. life.

ONE OF the year's most striking new acts, David + David heralded an arresting hit song, "Welcome to the Boomtown," a vignette of the various losers and liars who populated Los Angeles. There was Handsome Kevin, who "got a little offtrack/Took a year off of college, and he never went back/Now he smokes much too much, he's got a permanent hack/Deals dope out of Denny's, keeps a table in the back." Or Cristina, one of Hollywood's upwardly mobile, who "drives a 944/Satisfaction oozes from her pores/She keeps rings on her fingers, marble on her floor/Cocaine in her dresser, bars on her doors."

The jaded resignation of the lyrics bore the mark of L.A. native David Baerwald, while his partner, David Ricketts, structured the sensuous, hypnotic instrumentation. As evidenced by their debut *Boomtown* album, David + David purveyed intelligent, idiosyncratic material that was a notch above the typical Top 40 fare. But surprisingly, the two musicians had never played a note together live.

"I was raised in Philadelphia, but I moved to California seven years ago," Ricketts explained. "I was introduced to David (Baerwald) by a mutual friend, and I spotted him at parties over the years. He wasn't a friend who I saw all the time—he was in a garage band and so was I. He stopped working with his group three years ago, and at that time I had dropped out to put together a home studio. We spent a day working together, and it was okay.

"Then David was asked to write a song for a movie—a movie that doesn't even exist anymore—and he rang me back up to use the studio. We got together to give it another shot, and it was just something that we wanted to continue—we decided we could write tunes together."

Baerwald's lyrical vision wasn't the immediate attraction, Ricketts allowed. "I thought he was crafty with words, but they weren't as in-depth as they would become. But when you're starting out, you're just glad when something seems to work. I don't share his view of Los Angeles 100 percent—I'm not him, I wasn't raised there. But he comes by his experiences honestly, and that's what I like about this collaboration. We spark each other."

After a mere three weeks of working in tandem, the duo took a long shot—they gave a demo tape to the brother of a temporary secretary in the A&R department of A&M Records. Amazingly, Baerwald's nicotine-hampered singing and Ricketts' affecting musical backdrops received an immediate reaction—a record deal, working with producer Davitt Sigerson on *Boomtown*. "Davitt's job was to translate the music to 24-track complexities since we were used to working on a four-track in my home," Ricketts explained.

The sudden notoriety had elicited a few pangs of jealousy from people who had worked with them individually in past years, Ricketts admitted. "But we really did work hard for this—it wasn't like getting discovered at Schwab's drugstore. As far as the attention goes, things are still pretty much as they were—we're going to the same places, driving the same cars. But it feels like, 'Whoa, maybe we're really on the map here!'" ■

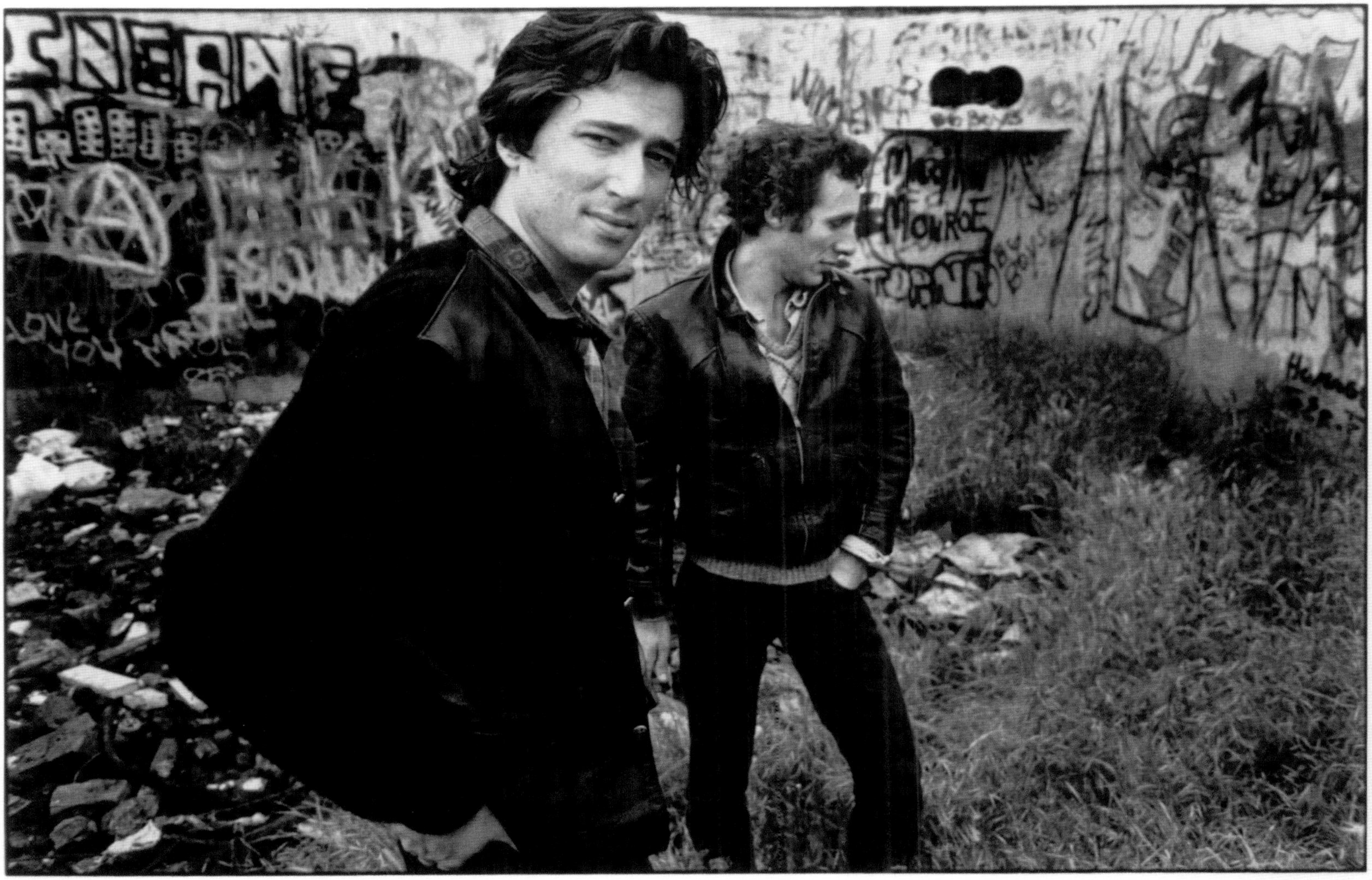

David Ricketts David Baerwald

M.F.C. MANAGEMENT

(213) 652-6993

david + david

A&M RECORDS

Printed in U.S.A.

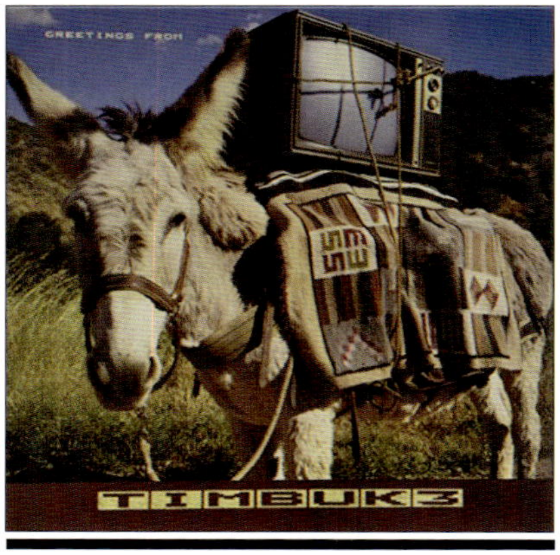

Billboard 200: *Greetings from Timbuk 3* (#50)
Billboard Hot 100: "The Future's So Bright, I Gotta Wear Shades" (#19)

"The Future's So Bright, I Gotta Wear Shades" infiltrated the Top 20, a boon for the duo "plus one" Timbuk 3.

NOT JUST a hit song and yuppie catch phrase, "The Future's So Bright, I Gotta Wear Shades" also served as a dictum for the band that created it. No one had considered the members of Timbuk 3—Pat MacDonald and Barbara K, a husband-and-wife duo from Austin, Texas—as likely candidates for success. After all, Timbuk 3 was more like a trio, with the third member being T3 (or T3PO), their "jambox," a big cassette player/boombox that provided prerecorded drum and bass parts.

The act originated in Wisconsin, where Pat and Barbara were peripheral members of the Madison music scene. Bands formed and broke up around them, the most notable being a folk/new wave outfit called the Essentials. When that group disbanded, the pair decided to pursue a musical vision that incorporated everything from rock to country to hip-hop. They became Timbuk 3 with the addition of T3, creating the rhythm tracks they heard in their heads.

T3's audition was rather cut and dried. "It had to have great bass response, and it couldn't be too huge to carry around," the male member of the low-key duo recalled. "We wound up with a JVC."

They set off for New York to try out their new concept as street singers. "It was basically a trial run to have some fun," Pat explained. "We were using crude rhythm tracks and acoustic guitars."

But an insurmountable problem—"It was cold!"—precipitated a move to Austin, where they settled at the Hole in the Wall, a club where they refined their presentation. Yet their unorthodox grafting of techno beats to countrified songs still didn't fit in. "During breaks in our set, Barbara would change tapes in the jambox while I'd switch harmonicas," Pat mused, "and all the while patrons would be hooting for Jerry Jeff Walker songs."

Fate intervened in the form of *The Cutting Edge*, MTV's monthly new music documentary program produced by I.R.S. Records. Dispatched to film a special Austin installment, the I.R.S. crew stumbled upon Timbuk 3. A debut album, *Greetings from Timbuk 3*, provided a forum for the low-key duo's groove appeal and Pat's blunt observations of society's idiosyncrasies.

"Somebody had asked Barbara, 'How's it goin'?' and she said, 'The future's so bright, I gotta wear shades,'" he chuckled. "I just said 'Whoa!' and wrote the song after that."

The blues-boppin' skewering of the status quo attained anthem-like status. Timbuk 3 looked to their own bright future—Pat and Barbara loaded up T3 ("It's no longer under warranty"), their 3-year-old son Devin, a babysitter, guitars, harmonicas and violins into a van and embarked on a tour of America. The only associate missing from the entourage was Ears. "She's the donkey who appears on our album cover and the 'Shades' video," Barbara said. "She's a nice, casual animal—but she's got her own career to think about." ■

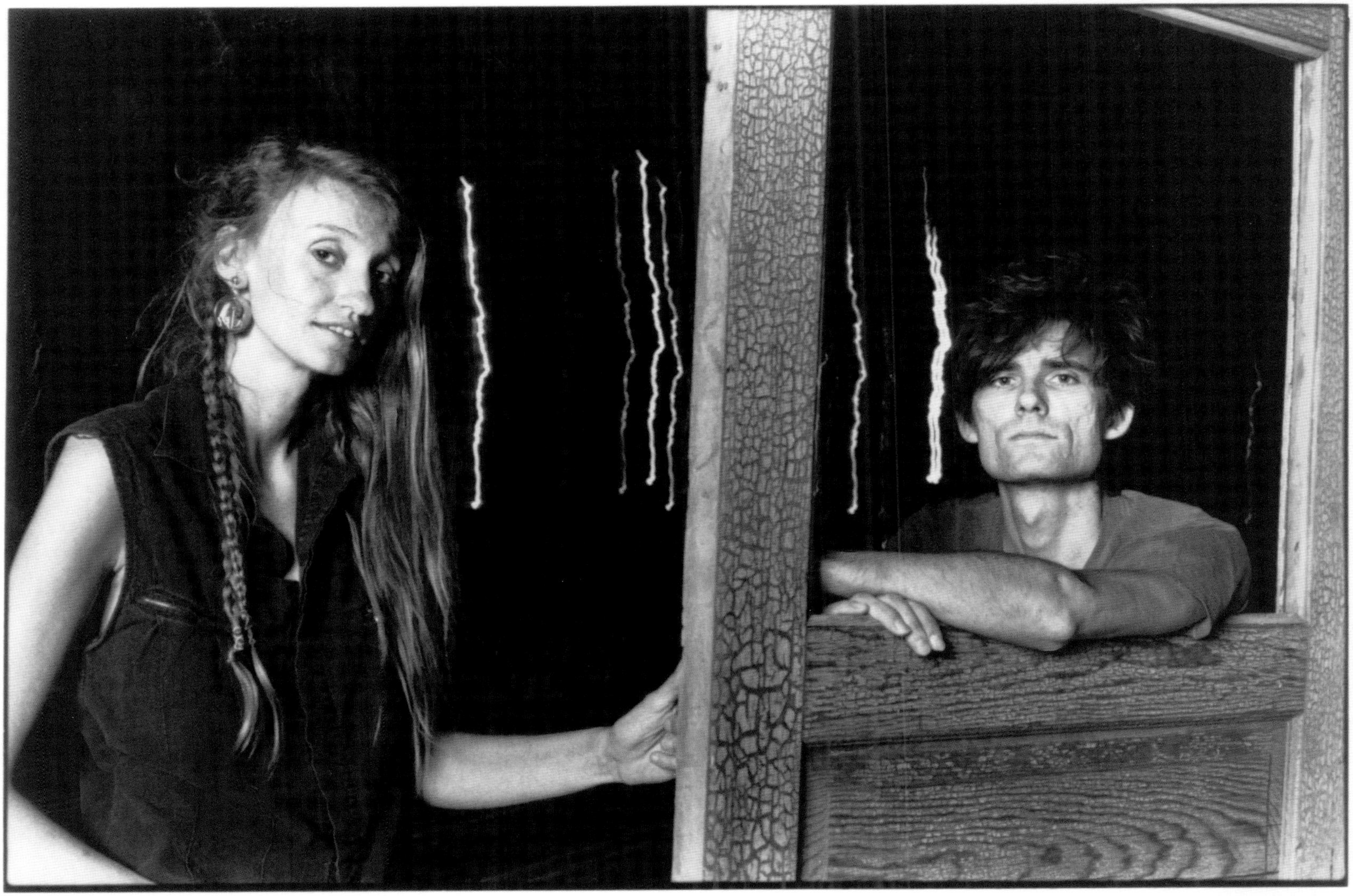

TIMBUK 3

BARBARA K   PAT MACDONALD

I.R.S.

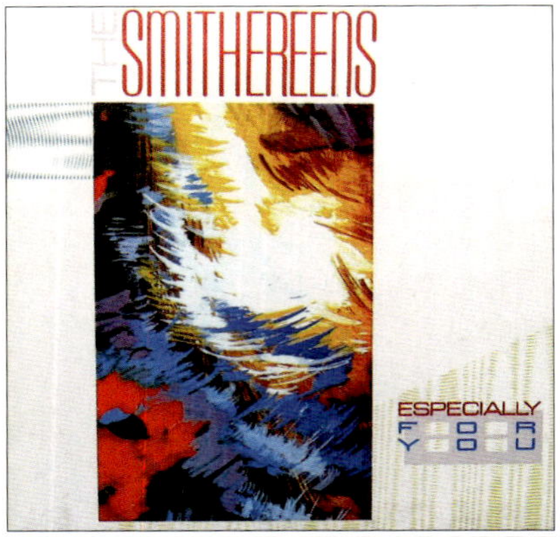

Billboard 200: *Especially for You* (#51)

The Smithereens made their bow, establishing a brand of exceptional pop-rock expertise on *Especially for You*.

IT WAS tough for any new act to gain recognition, but the Smithereens had the goods with an outstanding single, "Blood and Roses." Four long-time friends formed the New Jersey-based act in March of 1980 and had since refined a balance of rock energy and pop intuition on the East Coast club circuit.

"We also played a lot of concerts, opening for whoever was popular at the time," leader Pat DiNizio explained. "Unfortunately, our opportunities were limited—we didn't have a record deal or a booking agent, and there wasn't anyone in the business particularly interested in what we were doing. So we just hung in there, determined to make it eventually."

The band even spent a year as the backup band to legendary songwriter Otis Blackwell (Elvis Presley's "Return to Sender," Jerry Lee Lewis' "Great Balls of Fire"). "Otis' tendency was to go more toward a lounge act, but we refused to let him do that—what people saw was an authentic rock 'n' roll show," DiNizio noted proudly. "We cut two albums with him, rarities that he only sold at the gigs."

Don Dixon, who worked on R.E.M.'s early recordings, produced *Especially for You*, the Smithereens' first rock 'n' pop album. In addition to "Blood and Roses," it contained "Behind the Wall of Sleep" and "In a Lonely Place," a smoky duet between DiNizio and fellow East Coast club artist Suzanne Vega. DiNizio and his bandmates—Dennis Diken (drums), Mike Mesaros (bass) and Jim Babjak (guitar)—were ready to be heard from.

"I don't want to be anybody's idea of a next big thing—you really have to believe in what you're doing to keep at it for seven years with virtually no success," DiNizio concluded. "The style of the band hasn't changed, but our perspective has. We're fortunate to have gotten a few breaks, a little bit of luck recently. Now we want to take it from there and see if the audience grows. The goal was never to be an arena act—the goal is just to do this as a living, to make records and tour." ■

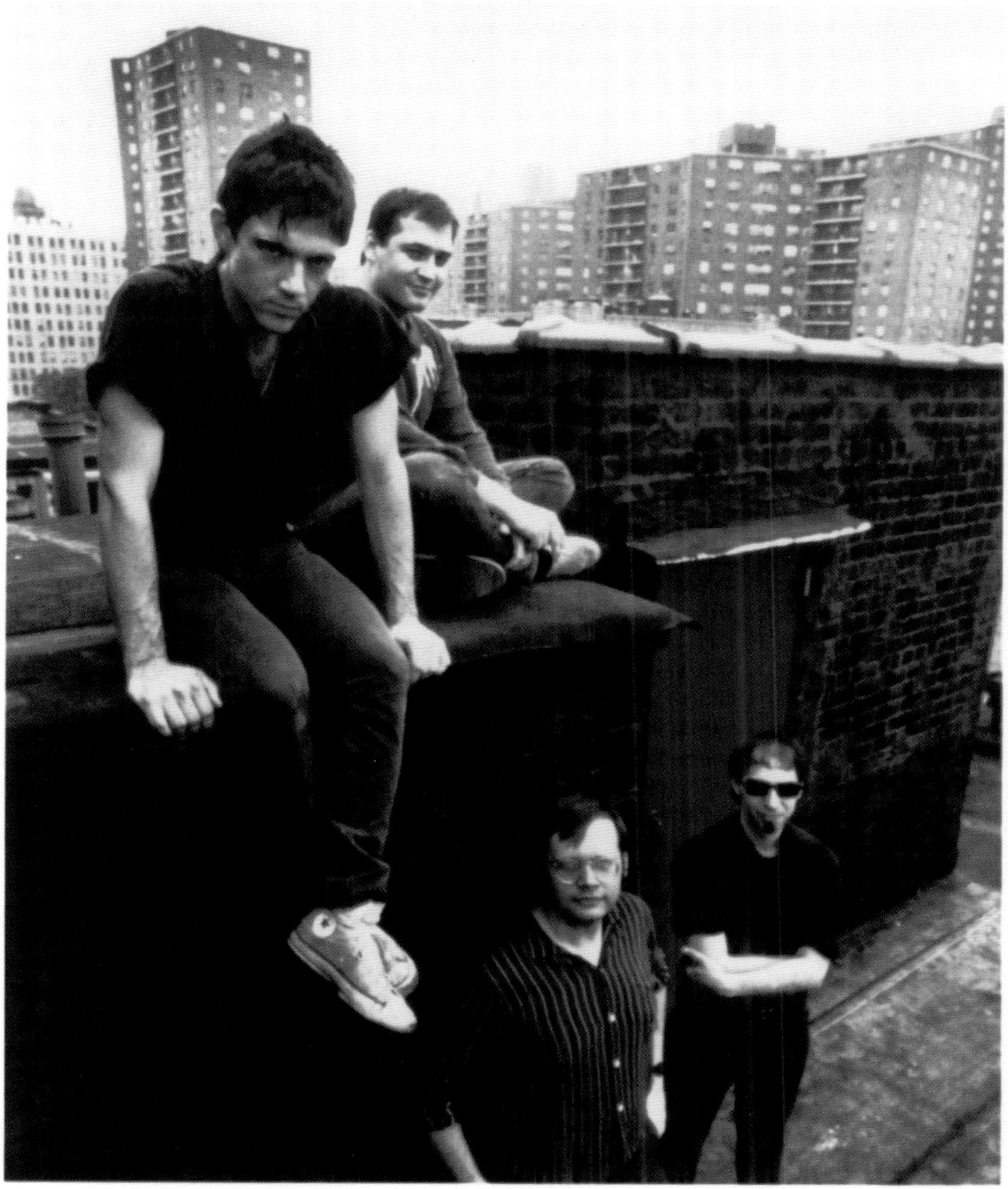

Left to Right: MICHAEL MESAROS JIM BABJAK DENNIS DIKEN PAT DINIZIO

THE SMITHEREENS

ENIGMA RECORDS

ENIGMA RECORDS
1750 East Holly Avenue, Post Office Box 2428
El Segundo, California 90245-1527 USA
Distributed by Capitol Records, Inc.

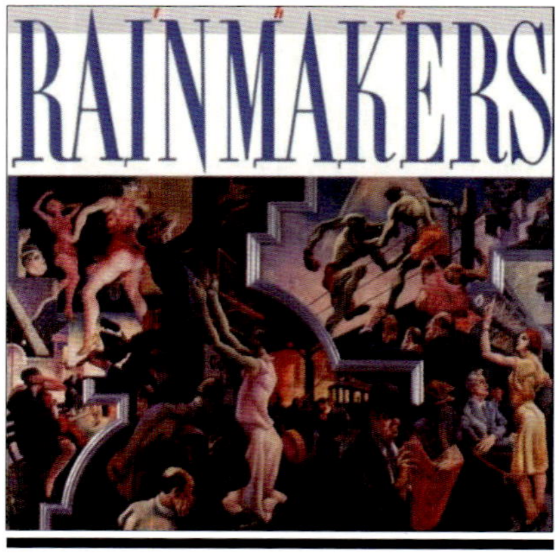

Billboard 200: *The Rainmakers* (#85)

The Rainmakers' "Let My People Go-Go," a rockin' salvo of salvation, was the heart of their major label debut.

AS EVERY aspiring Midwestern rocker surmised—if you really wanted to make it, you had to move to either coast. Rarely was a band signed to a recording deal out of, say, Kansas City. But K.C.'s Rainmakers had managed to garner national attention on their own terms.

"It's been tough—the music industry ignores Kansas and Missouri when they're looking for talent," lead singer, songwriter and guitarist Bob Walkenhorst noted. "No one recognizes any bands that come from Kansas City. You say 'Shooting Star' and they go 'Huh?' But we decided that, instead of disguising the fact that we're from the Midwest, we embrace it, celebrate it. Somehow we've made it work for us."

Circa 1983, Walkenhorst, guitarist Steve Phillips and bassist Rich Ruth began playing Top 40 covers around the Kansas City area as Steve, Bob & Rich. But the trio quickly metamorphosed into an act to be taken seriously. First came a name change to the Rainmakers ("Before that, no one could remember us—it was always 'You're Steve, Bob &...Rich? Bruce?'"). Next they became a quartet with the addition of drummer Pat Tomek, and Walkenhorst, who had been playing stand-up drums, moved out front.

"We had kept things stripped down to a trio for financial reasons, and it sounded fine," Walkenhorst said. "But I got tired of not being able to move around the stage—I couldn't go anywhere. And when I finally saw Bruce Springsteen perform, I said, 'Look, guys, we gotta start doing this right.'"

But the biggest factor in the band's burgeoning success had been Walkenhorst's development into a provocative songwriter. Part court jester and part Missouri mule, he unabashedly termed the Rainmakers' muscular pop style of wit and common sense "oddball." "People notice right away—'These guys sound different, they look different and they're talking about things no one else is talking about.'"

The band's style was gloriously represented on the single "Let My People Go-Go," a pithy parable wherein God revealed the secret of creation by talking like Little Richard—"Secret words in a secret room/ He said a womp bop a lu bop a lop bam boom."

"I wrote if fast," Walkenhorst recalled. "I remember singing it up in the attic—'Moses went up to the mountain high/To find out from God why did you make us why?' I said, 'Whoa, that sounds so corny!' So I wrote another verse."

The Rainmakers piled up a stack of good reviews, and horror master Stephen King quoted the group in a novel, *The Tommyknockers*.

"We're just another twangy American band," Walkenhorst concluded with a refreshing lack of pretense. "Now a lot of groups—the Long Ryders, BoDeans, Del Fuegos—insist, 'Oh, we're not part of that American roots-rock scene.' But I'll admit it—Creedence Clearwater Revival is it for me." ■

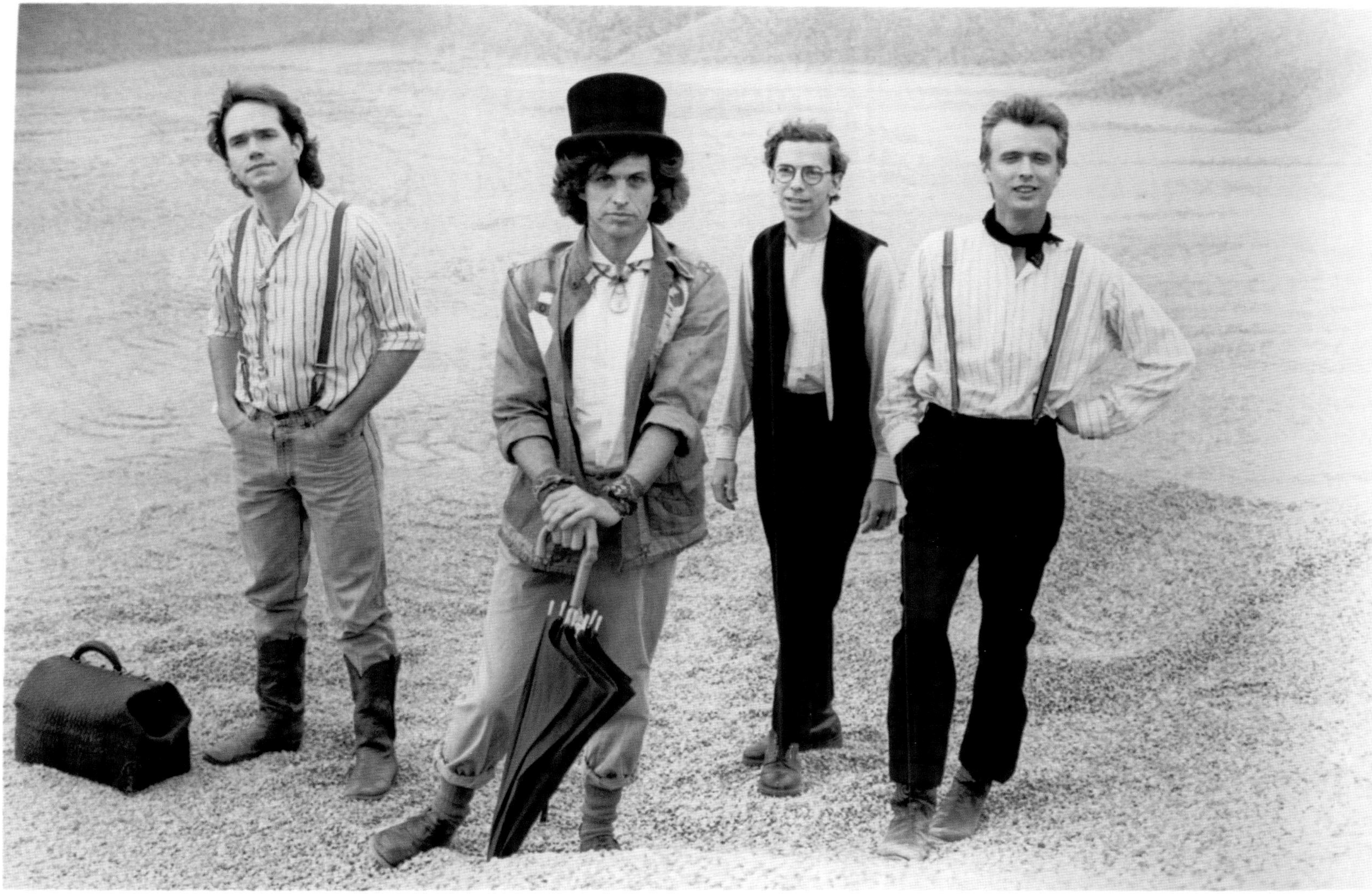

the RAINMAKERS

mercury

PolyGram Records

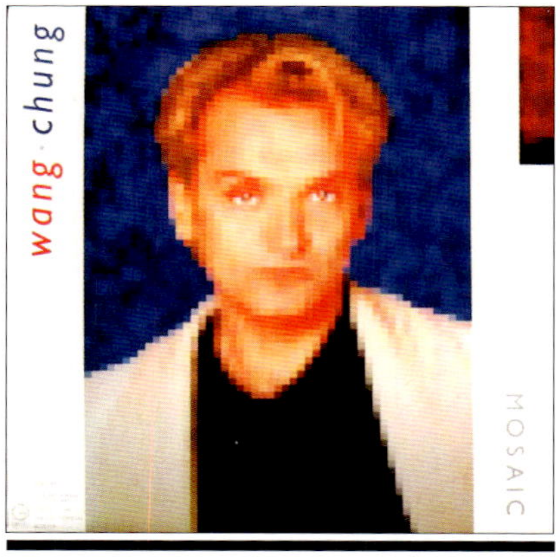

Billboard 200: *Mosaic* (#41)
Billboard Hot 100: "Everybody Have Fun Tonight" (#2); "Let's Go" (#9); "Hypnotize Me" (#36)

With the iconic new-wave hit "Everybody Have Fun Tonight," Britain's Wang Chung called for a worldwide party.

THE COMMERCIAL triumph of Wang Chung's pop hit "Everybody Have Fun Tonight" owed to the song's wide-ranging appeal—it was smart enough to get adults on the dance floor, catchy enough for kids to sing along.

But as with most acts that were blessed with a smash, the British duo of Jack Hues and Nick Feldman still had no idea how they did it.

"We originally wrote it as a slow song, much more ironic," Hues said. "But we wound up speeding it up in the studio—I never expected it to be such a success.

Much of the credit went to Peter Wolf, not the former J. Geils Band singer but the Viennese writer and producer who had also guided Starship to the top of the charts. "We were stunned when we heard 'We Built This City,'" Hues recalled. "While we didn't care for the song, we were totally knocked out by Peter's gleaming production—something was happening every second."

Wolf soon helped Hues and Feldman create their own chart-topper. It didn't hurt that he played up the band's name as a catch phrase in the chorus ("Everybody have fun tonight/Everybody Wang Chung tonight"). When reminded of the tradition of such self-aggrandizing hit singles, from Freddie & the Dreamers' "Do the Freddie" to Chaka Khan's "I Feel for You," Hues broke up laughing. "I've been told it's a trick that everybody tries once in their career," he divulged. "You either pull it off or you blow it."

There wasn't much in Wang Chung's pre-"Everybody" career to suggest the new success. The classically trained Hues and the self-taught Feldman first collaborated as Huang Chung, a capable band that lacked identity and top-drawer songs on a 1981 album. A spelling modification to Wang Chung and the hit "Dance Hall Days" gained them entry with an American pop audience. Working as a duo from that point, they followed up with the soundtrack to director William Friedkin's film *To Live and Die in L.A.*

And then "Everybody Have Fun Tonight" exploded. Ironically, the song made Wang Chung stars in America but not in their native England. Television exposure was crucial for Top 40 success in the UK, but the BBC banned the tune's innovative video—and not because of sex or violence. A doctor retained by the broadcaster's screening committee said the clip—an adventure in split-second editing that produced a bizarre, animated effect of Hues and Feldman jittering their way through a performance—could trigger epileptic fits.

"It's absolutely ludicrous," Hues said. "The BBC feels the video has too many frames per second. It's made us sad and frustrated that we couldn't get attention at home." ■

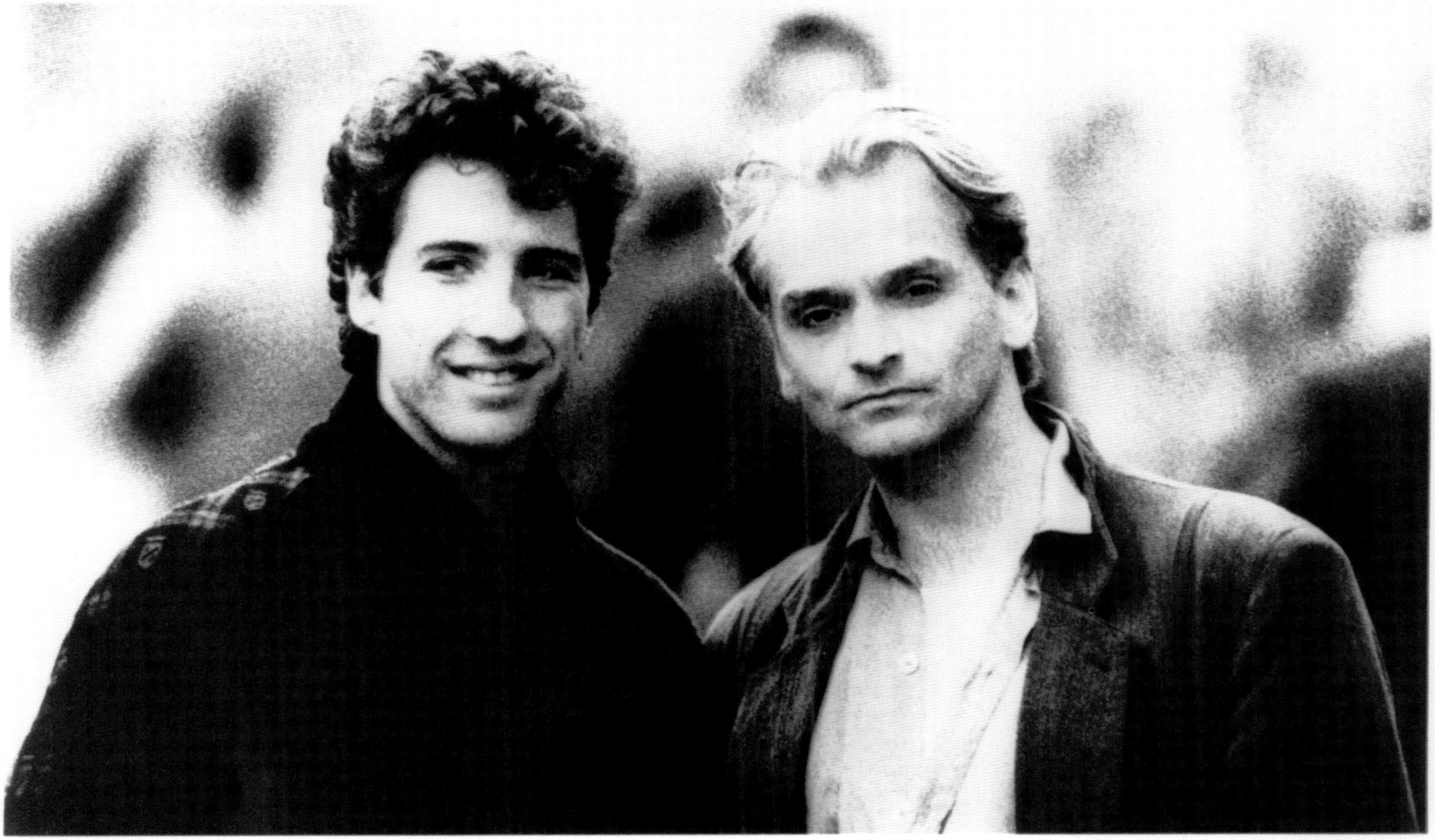

NICK FELDMAN JACK HUES

WANG CHUNG

GEFFEN RECORDS

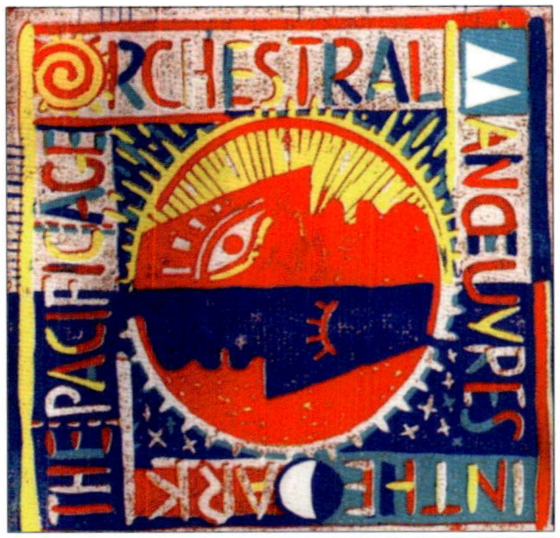

Billboard 200: *The Pacific Age* (#47)
Billboard Hot 100: "(Forever) Live and Die" (#19)

Revealing a shift in the musical braintrust, *The Pacific Age* was a US hit for Orchestral Manoeuvres in the Dark.

WHEN THE trend toward synthesizer-based music was cresting in the early Eighties, Orchestral Manoeuvres in the Dark—the British duo of Andy McCluskey and Paul Humphreys—pioneered their own breakthrough. With Humphreys programming and playing electronic keyboards, and McCluskey singng the melodies and playing bass, a streak of UK hits such as "Souvenir," "Joan of Arc," "Enola Gay" and "Maid of Orleans" ensued. But OMD's polished synth-pop and electronic-tape experiments never reached a mass audience in the US.

"At the time, we didn't know what we were doing," McClusky laughed. "We loved Kraftwerk, we couldn't play guitars—we just did our thing. But the idea of two guys onstage with a synth and a tape machine was a pretty bizarre notion for a band. But that style dominated that time. Now look how many successful duos there are in electronic music."

Naturally, with the synth-pop genre no longer as fashionable, Orchestral Manoeuvres in the Dark was enjoying its biggest success in the States. "If You Leave," from 1985's *Pretty in Pink* soundtrack, cracked the Top 5, and "(Forever) Live and Die," from the album *The Pacific Age*, established OMD on radio playlists.

"We'd been frustrated to the point of just about giving up on selling records in America," McCluskey said. "It was nice to turn it around. Some people have been trying for a long time to write off us and bands who use synths. I don't think it's really important—we just do what we feel like doing, and sometimes we sound more electronic than others."

Orchestral Manoeuvres in the Dark had grown into a six-person unit, adding multi-instrumentalists on guitar, percussion, brass and keyboards to augment its sound. "Paul and I still write the material, but we found the band format worked very well on last year's tour," McCluskey said. The results could be heard on *The Pacific Age*, OMD's fullest-sounding recording to date.

"Over the years a lot of people have said we're more dynamic onstage than on record," McCluskey said. "We took it to heart and decided to be a little less precious. So, it's almost like we've got two audiences now—people who've known us on record for years, and those who only know the last couple of hit singles. But we've consciously chosen not to abandon the cult audience—we're still playing some of the old songs." ■

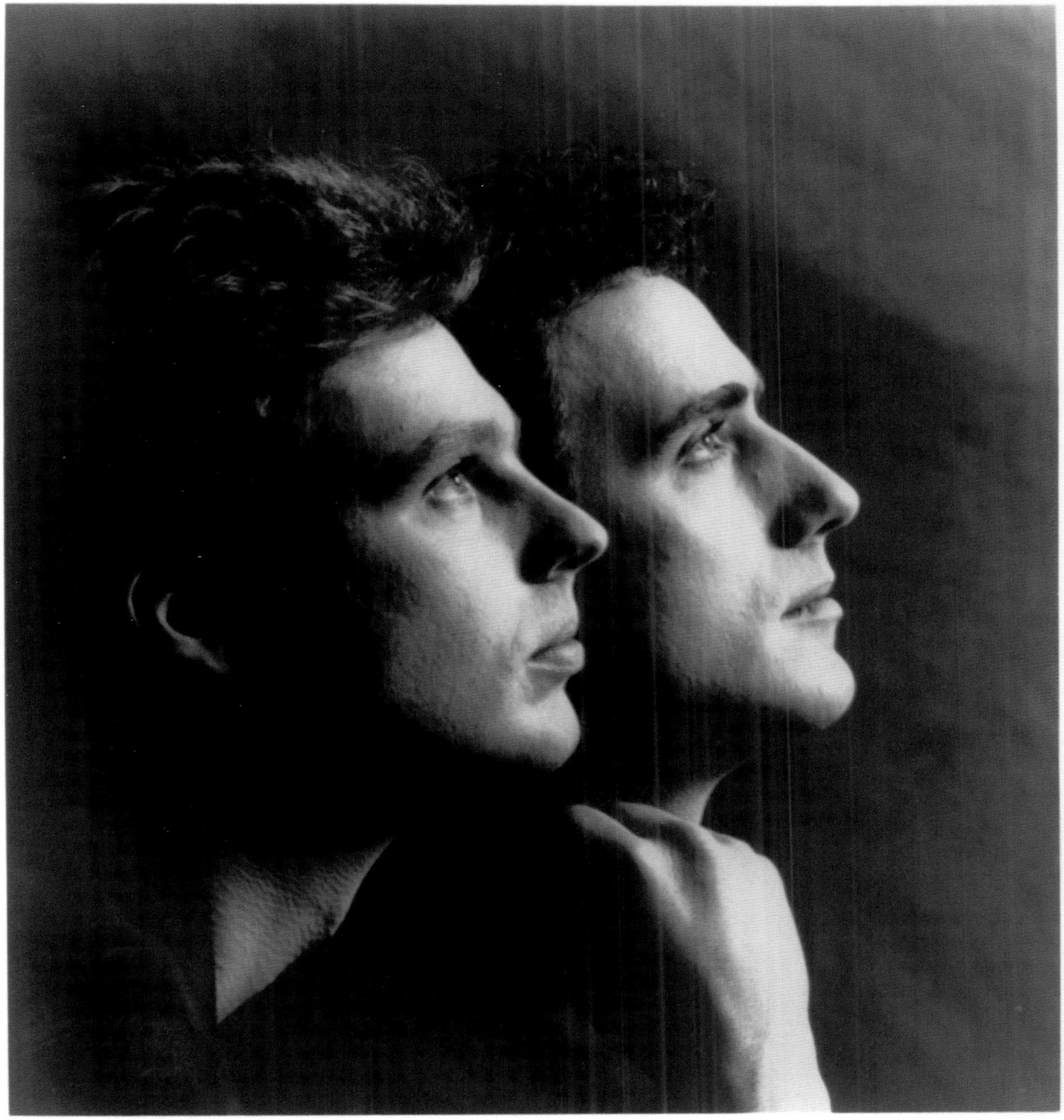

Paul Humphreys Andy McCluskey

OMD

ORCHESTRAL MANOEUVRES IN THE DARK

A&M RECORDS
Printed in U.S.A.

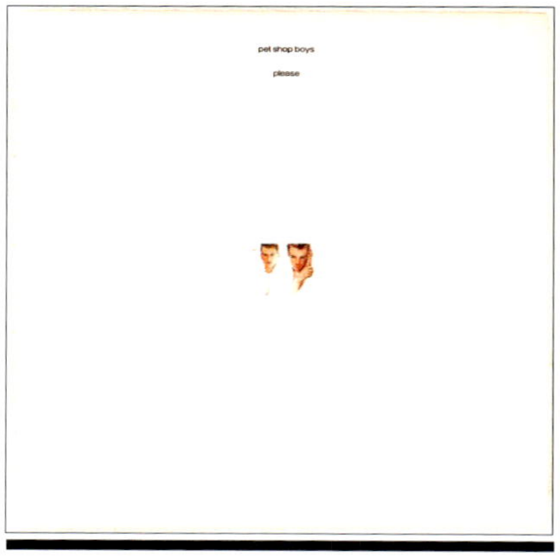

Billboard 200: *Please* (#7)
Billboard Hot 100: "West End Girls" (No. 1); "Opportunities (Let's Make Lots of Money)" (#10); "Love Comes Quickly" (#62); "Suburbia" (#70)

Pet Shop Boys' *Please*, a debut album of affecting dance beats, went platinum in the US and their native UK.

A NEW duo from Great Britain, Pet Shop Boys took the American airwaves by storm with two brilliantly crafted, danceable hits—"West End Girls" and "Opportunities (Let's Make Lots of Money)," continuing a wave of popularity that had already made them stars in Britain and across Europe

Newcastle-born singer Neil Tennant and keyboardist Chris Lowe, who grew up in the seaside town of Blackpool, comprised the innovative duo. They began their musical partnership after meeting in a King's Road music shop. Tennant became a journalist on the staff of the UK pop magazine *Smash Hits*, and Lowe was an architecture student with a yearning to make music. The pair shared an enthusiasm for high-energy Euro-disco (particularly obscure Italian dance records).

"We had a really terrible cassette recorder, and we used to record cassette-to-cassette live," Tennant said. "You really don't need very much at all to write a song.

While on a magazine assignment in New York to interview the Police, Tennant hunted down dance-records producer Bobby "O" Orlando, who cut the first version of "West End Girls." Released in Britain, the track gained the newly launched Pet Shop Boys some attention, but some legal hassles with Orlando slowed progress for a time before they released "Opportunities (Let's Make Lots of Money)."

Learning that a New York newspaper wrote that the band's name was slang for gay male prostitutes who were into S&M, Tennant was surprised. "That's news to me," he said. "We truly called ourselves after some of Chris' friends who worked in an Ealing pet store. That slightly dubious connotation is quite amusing."

When it first became apparent that "West End Girls" was still a club favorite in London, Pet Shop Boys re-recorded the tune with producer Stephen Hague and achieved an evocative No. 1 hit. *Please*, the English duo's debut album, relied on a mix of sophisticated melodies, unrelenting grooves and witty, socially conscious lyrics, generating a series of hit singles—a recut "Opportunities (Let's Make Lots of Money)," "Suburbia" and "Love Comes Quickly."

According to Tennant, the album's title was chosen "because it's got so many implications—pleading, polite, subservient, sarcastic and petulant, and it looks good written down"—not to mention providing a ready joke by which a fan going into a record store had to say, "Can I have the Pet Shop Boys album, *Please*?"

"It's a bit of a cliché, but I think we're honest," Tennant offered, "We don't sing like we're Black, pretend we're the Isley Brothers. We deal with music that's inherent to us. We sing about paying bills, keeping a roof above your head, things in people's lives. We stay down-to-earth." ■

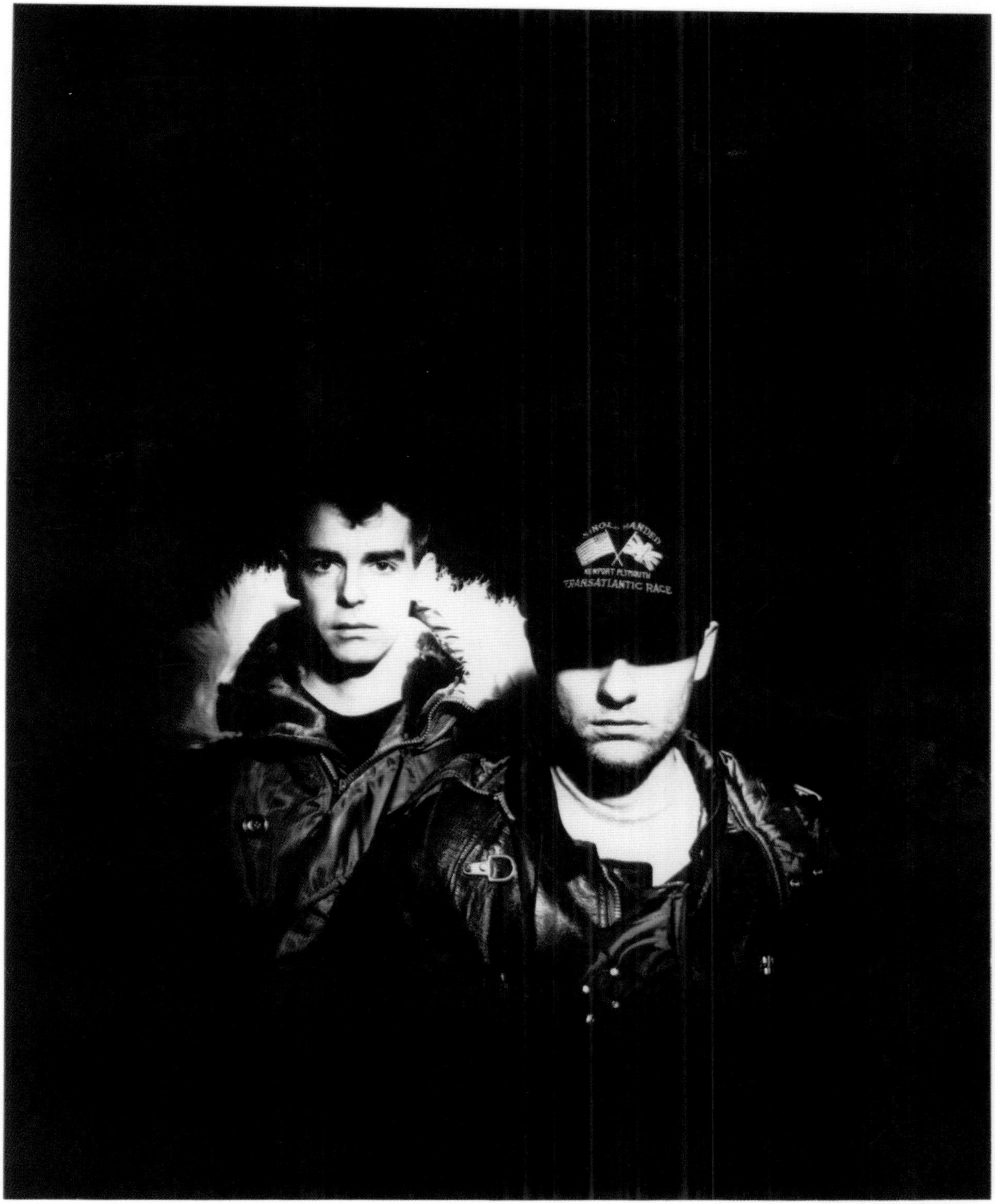

 PHOTOGRAPHER: ERIC WATSON

PET SHOP BOYS

PARLOPHONE

Billboard 200: *Brotherhood* (#117)

The luminous single "Bizarre Love Triangle" commenced New Order's attempt at a transatlantic breakthrough.

FEW BANDS in rock music had a history as intriguing as New Order. The group started out circa 1977 as Joy Division, a British act specializing in grim, desperate, tortured songs. Despite the gloom-and-doom connotations, the act managed to come up with a classic pop record of the era, 1980's "Love Will Tear Us Apart."

But on the eve of the band's first tour of the United States, lead singer Ian Curtis was found dead in his home, a suicide by hanging. After several months of uncertainty and depression, the remaining members—drummer Stephen Morris, bassist Peter Hook and guitarist Bernard Albrecht—added keyboardist Gillian Gilbert, delved heavily into electronics and forged ahead as New Order. Such drama made the band's American breakthrough even more special. The unsettling part was that most of the group's following had little or no knowledge of the emotional past.

"We have a lot of new fans who have only picked up the last record or two—they don't know anything about Joy Division," Morris noted. "But that's all right—we're not a history course. What we've done before certainly has a bearing on what we do now—it's a progression. But if people are interested, they can still find out about the old stuff. And besides, the new fans tend to be the ones who jump about the most in concert, and we like that."

Despite New Order's reputation as a standoffish bunch given to one-word responses to questioning (members maintained an interview embargo until 1983), Morris was genuinely compliant in discussing the group's *Brotherhood* album, which extended the band's union of shimmering production values to smart, meaningful songs.

"There was a lot of head scratching the day we went into the studio," Morris allowed. "We only had half the album written—we just made the rest up. But it's just instinct after working together so long. We're not very self-conscious—we just do what we do, trying different things to make it interesting."

The group ended up assembling tracks into what Morris termed "an acoustic side and an electric side." A remix of "Bizarre Love Triangle" got surprising international attention, a situation that amused him.

"It's like listening to someone else's record the first few times you hear it," he said. "With remixes, you've already done what you can do with the song, done it your way. Then you send it off for some producer to remix and you go, 'That's not what I would have done!' But you've already heard what you would have done. I think remixes are getting a bit over the top—who needs four versions of the same song?"

New Order embarked on its most extensive US tour with tons of technology in tow. "It's just the four of us," Morris assured. "A lot of our show is preprogrammed, of course—it takes ages to set up, and it's a precarious occupation because sometimes it doesn't work. But most of the time—touch wood—we're doing all right with it. Things aren't programmed to minute detail. We can improvise—or make mistakes!" ■

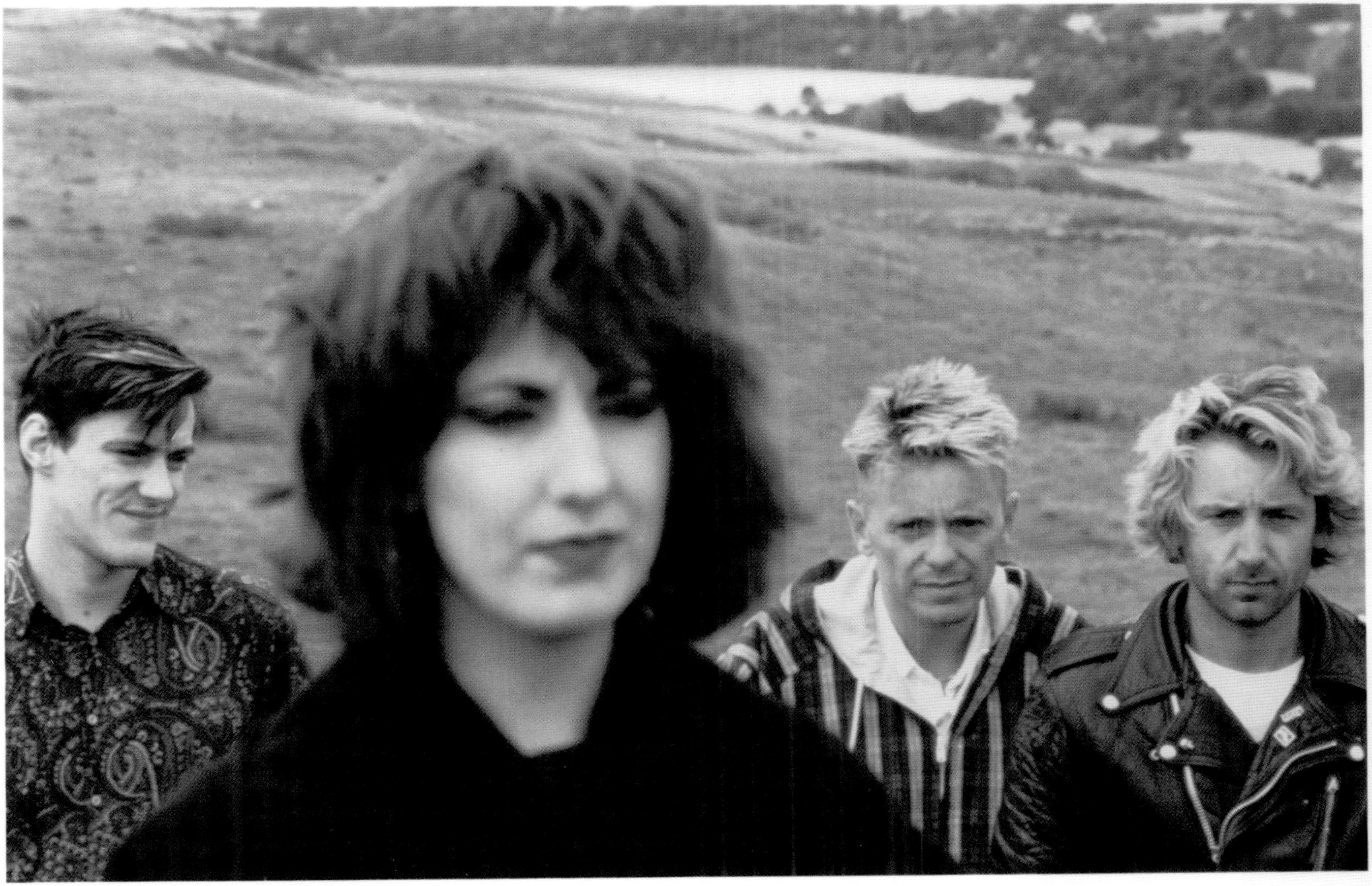

STEPHEN MORRIS GILLIAN GILBERT BERNARD SUMNER PETER HOOK

NEW ORDER

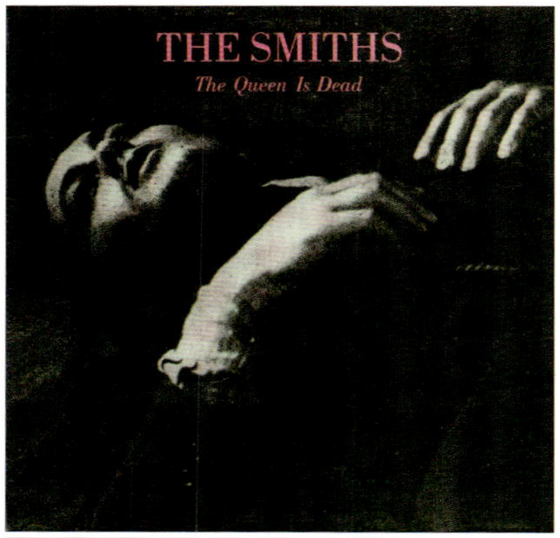

Billboard 200: *The Queen Is Dead* (#70)

The Smiths' *The Queen Is Dead* featured the English band's acclaimed "There Is a Light That Never Goes Out."

THE LEAD singer for the Smiths, Morrissey was perhaps the most eccentric rocker to come along in years. He used to perform with a hearing aid, even though his ears were in fine condition. He was rumored to be gay, although he would only admit to being celibate for the past five years. He was the first to admit that his singing style was somewhat monotonous.

But in his native England, Morrissey's droning vocals had led him to stardom. The Smiths had recently topped the "best group" rankings in the major UK papers, and Morrissey (no first name, please), had become the spokesman for a generation sagging under unemployment and other social ills.

In America, Morrissey's first-person railings against society had established a fervent following but had yet to find a mainstream audience. Nevertheless, the uncompromising Smiths didn't modify their dour outlook for *The Queen Is Dead*, their third album.

"For some curious political reason, music has been forced to portray total escapism—to convey life as it isn't really lived by people in the world," the singer noted. "And it's something that persistently infuriates me. If you go against the grain of this belief and become troublesome, people really don't want you to break through."

The Smiths were formed in 1982 when guitarist Johnny Marr approached Morrissey to collaborate. "I was 23 when it happened," Morrissey recalled. "I had to do it because I had reached a desperate period. I was prepared. I've been an avid record collector since I was very young, so I was drenched in all aspects of music. The obvious thing for me was music journalism, but I was rejected by literally all the magazines in England. Now they hound me for pieces of information. It's a very curious turn of events."

Morrissey's idiosyncratic demeanor had led detractors to dismiss the Smiths as another pretentious, self-consciously arty band. But fans alternately described the band's music as "inviting and disturbing" and "soul-baring," and Marr's unique, atypical contributions on guitar were considerable. Morrissey's list of personal heroes included James Dean, Oscar Wilde and the New York Dolls.

"It's curious to see things from the other side," he said. "If you make records, the world assumes that you have a perfectly clear, clever, worthwhile view of every issue imaginable. Sometimes I'm forced to comment on things that I otherwise wouldn't want to touch upon. But this stresses the importance of popular music in people's lives now. Music figures are more important than anyone else—athletes, actors, et cetera."

The single "The Boy with the Thorn in His Side" and the track "There Is a Light That Never Goes Out" established the Smiths' cult following in the US, and attention beyond Morrissey's expectations. "It's been hysteria in some areas, and I'm saddened because it hasn't been chronicled in any way," the singer lamented. "Average people who don't care that much about music have no notion of who the Smiths are. They don't feel the Smiths are a big group—and we are." ■

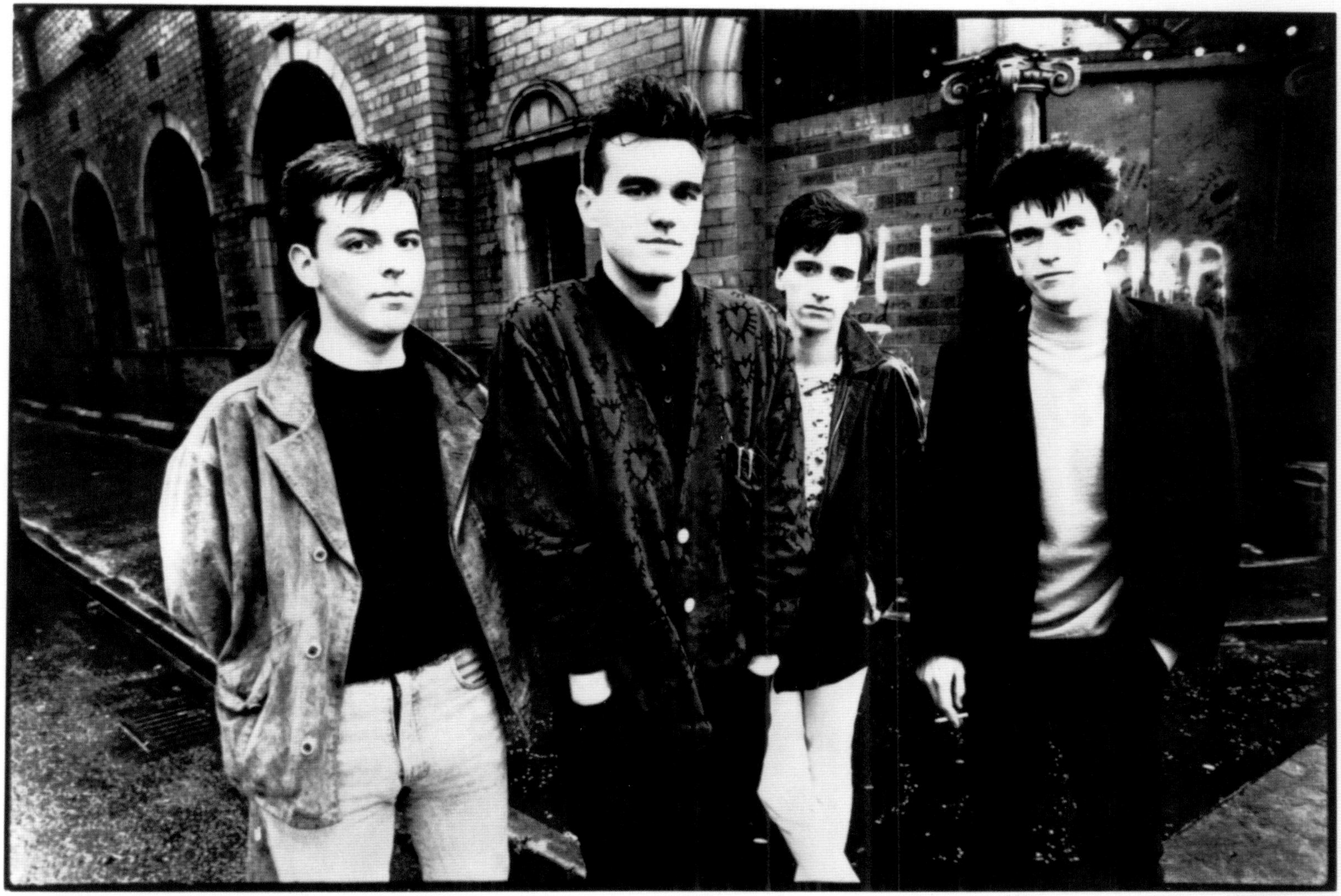

Photo Credit: Steve Wright

THE SMITHS

SIRE™

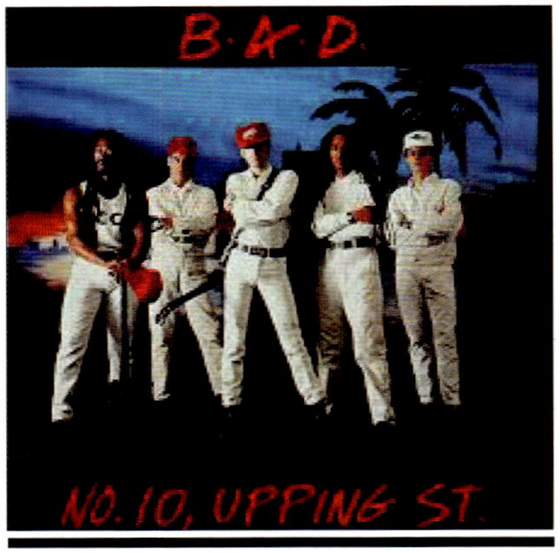

Billboard 200: *No. 10, Upping St.* (#119)

Guitarist Mick Jones had the feeling B.A.D.–Big Audio Dynamite, his post-Clash outfit–was better than good.

IN 1983, the Clash, perhaps the most politically and musically inspiring band to emerge from the British punk scene, unceremoniously ousted guitarist Mick Jones, reportedly because he was more committed to a pop-star lifestyle than he was to the group's leftist rhetoric. While the Clash eventually became a sad caricature of its former radical self and dissolved, Jones achieved vindication by shaping his political convictions into the mixed-race Big Audio Dynamite.

Don Letts had emerged as Jones' main collaborator, and together they fostered one of rock's truly original sounds. Letts, who was credited with "F/X" (effects) on B.A.D.'s albums, masterminded the group's trademark synthesized sonic effects and tape loops. He also contributed a cinematic sense of visual detail—short sound and dialogue bites from movies and television were inserted into the songs, creating a unique spirit and personality.

Jones approached Letts for his new band despite the latter's lack of formal training. "I didn't want a musician; I just wanted someone to talk to," Jones said. "We took colored stickers and put them on the keyboard to show him what to play. He's not technically capable, but he's an ideas man, just like in film. His effects reflect what's going on around us, walking down the streets of London hearing all the stuff coming out of different shops."

The group's second release, *No. 10, Upping St.*, was an infectious, cross-cultural blend of influences ranging from hard rock to hip-hop to third world. The diverse textures were exemplified on "C'mon Every Beatbox," a rap-meets-Eddie-Cochran workout that was both high-tech and street-smart. B.A.D.'s funk-reggae strains were supplemented by Jones' perceptive lyrics, alternately meaningful and satirical—"Sightsee M.C.!" sharply detailed the deteriorating state of British society.

"We have to show that music is still accessible to people," Jones said. "I don't want it to be something that anybody else couldn't do. That's why I never endorse equipment—it's just too expensive for young kids who want to make music."

Clash fans were intrigued that Jones had patched up his relationship with Joe Strummer, his co-founder and partner in the Clash who helped write and produce five songs on *No. 10, Upping St.* But Jones wanted no part of a Clash reunion.

"B.A.D. is a band in the present, happening now," he insisted. "We fit in with what's going on in 1986 just as the Clash fit into their time. I thought it might be different this time—I thought I was going to go over like Michael Jackson or George Michael, one of those Michaels. I thought we'd go over big. But it's pretty much the same deal. I don't know why. It must be because of me." ■

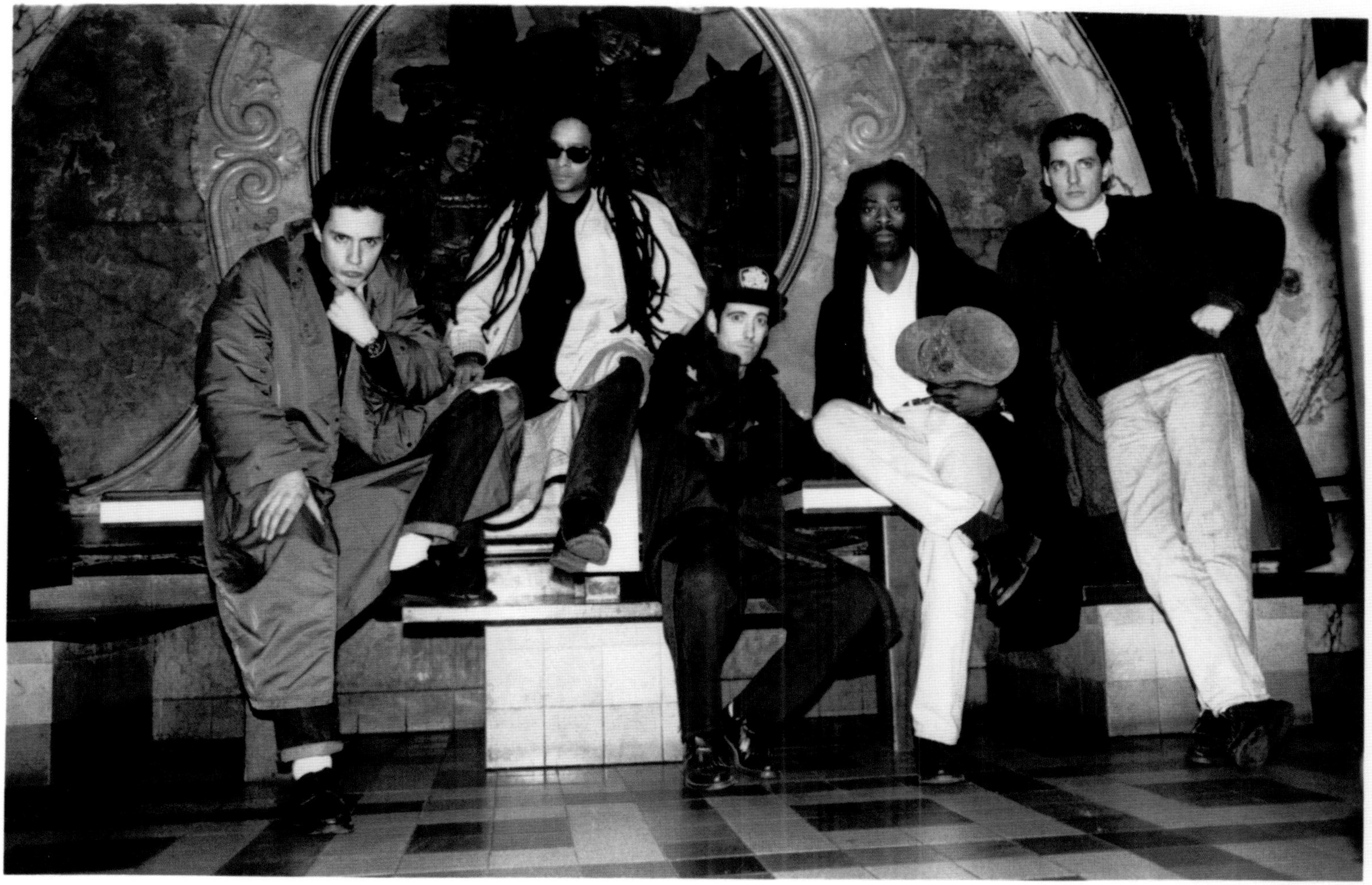

PHOTOGRAPH: JOSH CHEUSE

From left DAN DONOVAN, DON LETTS, MICK JONES, LEO 'E-ZEE KILL' WILLIAMS, GREG ROBERTS

BIG AUDIO DYNAMITE

Columbia

8610

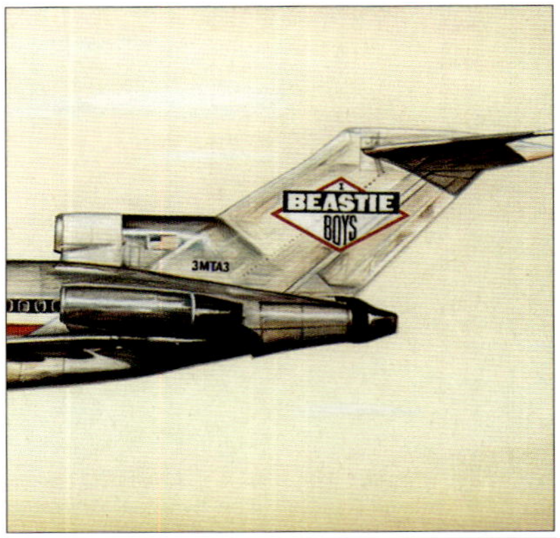

Billboard 200: *Licensed to Ill* (No. 1)
Billboard Hot 100: "Brass Monkey" (#48);
"(You Gotta) Fight for Your Right (To Party!)" (#7)

Beastie Boys incited "(You Gotta) Fight for Your Right (To Party!)" in a barrage of beer swilling and bong hits.

IT WAS self-evident that the young Beastie Boys prided themselves on being exaggeratedly abrasive and obnoxious. The surprise? The three troublemakers had become the biggest new stars on the music scene by wedding loud metal guitar riffs to rap rhymes and beats. A bratty anthem, "(You Gotta) Fight for Your Right (To Party!)," ruled the country, and *Licensed to Ill*, the group's debut album, was a best-selling collection of cartoonish odes to hedonism.

How did a trio of upper-middle-class Jewish kids from New York—King Ad-Rock (Adam Horovitz), MCA (Adam Yauch) and Mike D (Michael Diamond)—arrive at such a formula for success, accurately described by one source as "noisy, nasty, loud, lewd, gross and ideologically damn unsound"? Mike D did his best to sound controversial, but when he seemed to be trying a bit too hard, he revealed how new he was to the game.

"I might only be 19 now, but we've been doing this since I was 13," Mike D assured. "As far as a kids' scene, there hasn't been one in New York until now. Punk was for kids in England, but in New York it was for older people—Talking Heads, all that stuff. We really liked the very first rap records—Sugarhill Gang, things like that—but we were always a hardcore punk band. We still are, that's our attitude—our music is probably louder now than it's ever been."

The Beasties took their crack at "hardcore rap" by teaming up with producer/DJ Rick Rubin, who went on to found his own Def Jam Records, the nation's leading rap label. Def Jam's distribution deal with corporate giant CBS Records had been largely responsible for the Beasties' acceptance.

"But nobody at CBS really understands us—we were banned from their New York offices for doing gross stuff," Mike D chortled. "Now they just get the records in the stores and give us money." Although the group claimed to have complete control over their product, CBS reportedly succeeded in lobbying for some tamed-down lyrics and titles on *Licensed to Ill*.

But no one mistook the Beastie Boys' crowd-baiting shows for recitals—an arena tour featured caged, scantily-clad go-go girls, a huge six-pack of Budweiser tallboys and a 20-foot hydraulic phallus. The Beasties continued to add fuel to the fire with rumors of trashed hotel rooms, offensive actions and general low-life behavior (i.e., their contract called for a rainbow assortment of condoms to be placed in the dressing room after every show).

Their every-parent's-nightmare music was the happening thing—"Brass Monkey" got a barrage of requests at radio, and "It's the New Style" and "Paul Revere" defined Beastie-ality. *Licensed to Ill* became the first rap album to top the *Billboard* album chart.

"We've done the record we wanted, and now all the doors are open to us," Mike D concluded. "We can do anything—a movie, a sitcom, even urinating on people." ■

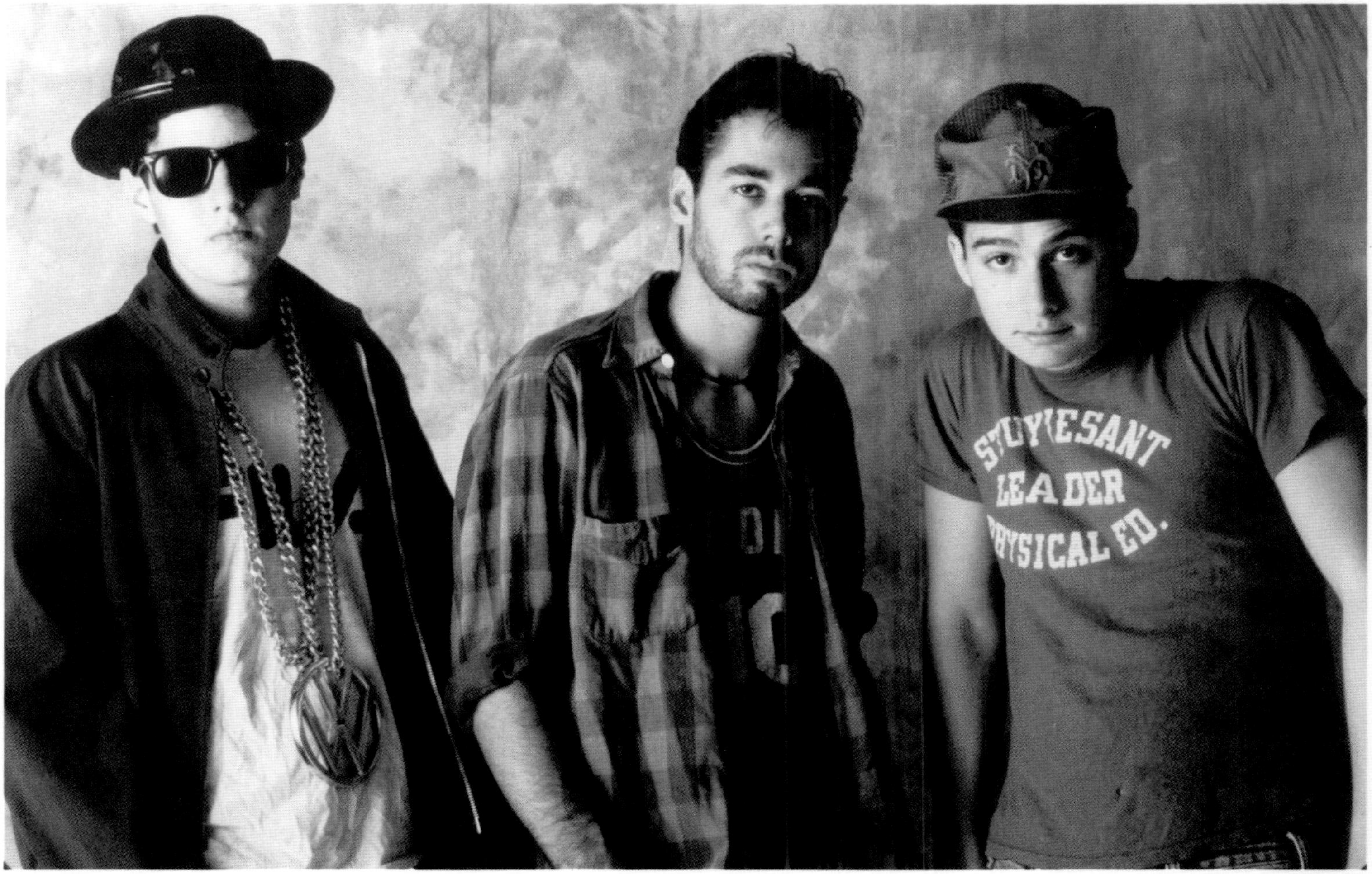

From left MIKE D, MCA, KING AD-ROCK.

PHOTOGRAPH: SUNNY BAK

Def Jam recordings
Rush Artist Management
40 East 19th Street
N.Y , N.Y 10003
212.420.4770

BEASTIE BOYS

Columbia
8610

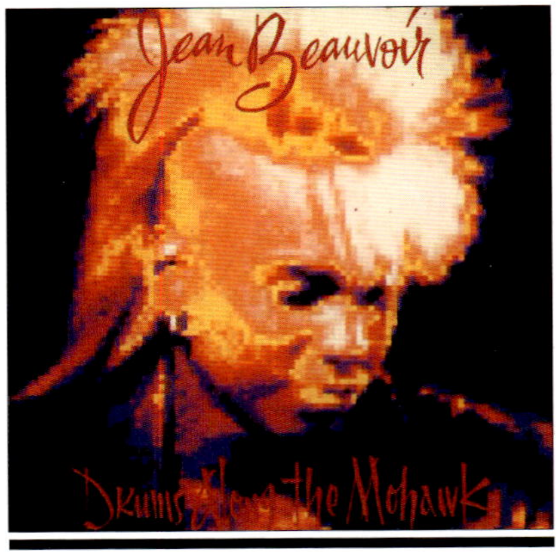

Billboard 200: *Drums Along the Mohawk* (#93)
Billboard Hot 100: "Feel the Heat" (#73)

Crazily crested, leather-clad Jean Beauvoir pushed the button on his solo career with the tune "Feel the Heat."

A SOUGHT-AFTER songwriter and producer, Jean Beauvoir's "Feel the Heat" emerged as a summertime hit single—a considerable accomplishment for someone who got his start with the decidedly non-musical Wendy O. Williams and the Plasmatics. It certainly helped that Sylvester Stallone grabbed "Feel the Heat" as the de facto theme for his movie *Cobra*.

"It's a song about pressure," Beauvoir said. "I wrote it before I had a record deal, when everybody's trying to tell you to go this way, write these kinds of songs, do this and that. You try to follow your own instincts, but you don't know if it's the right way. A lot of people go through that feeling, no matter what their job, and it's one of the most confusing things about life."

Beauvoir also played bass with Little Steven & the Disciples of Soul before embarking on his own career. On his controversial days of auto-destruction as a Plasmatic, he said, "I was looking join a band and I saw an ad for the Plasmatics. I didn't know anything about them, but I auditioned and they eventually said, 'If you want the job, it's yours.' I was really held back (musically), but the band had its purpose—it was a theatrical show, and the music was just a soundtrack for all the mania going on."

Beauvoir, who was of French and Haitian descent, produced, composed, arranged and performed the entirety of his debut album, *Drums Along the Mohawk*. After finishing it, he went back in the studio to produce the Ramones' *Animal Boy* album. But he made a more immediate impact sporting a conspicuous blond Mohawk haircut.

"I had a stripe in my hair when I joined the Plasmatics, but I immediately went for a Mohawk. I was 17, so I was open to anything. It started out as an image thing, but when my career got serious after a while, I didn't know what to do to change it. It became a part of me. I still get other people with crazy haircuts at my shows, but there are other types of fans—little girls who like your clothes, older people who like the lyrics. It's pretty wide-ranging these days." ■

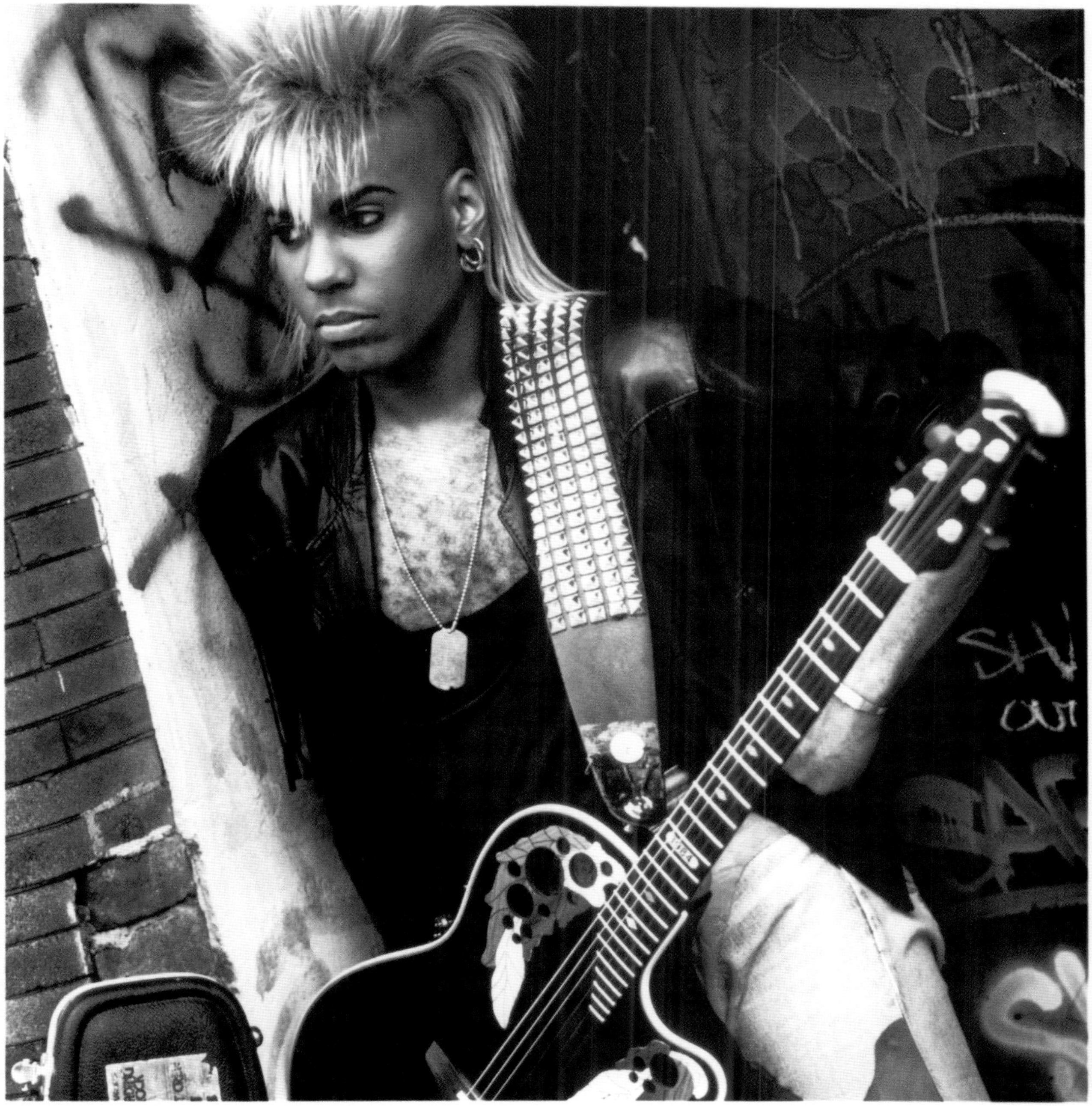

PHOTOGRAPH: CAROLINE GREYSHOCK

Jean Beauvoir

Columbia

8605

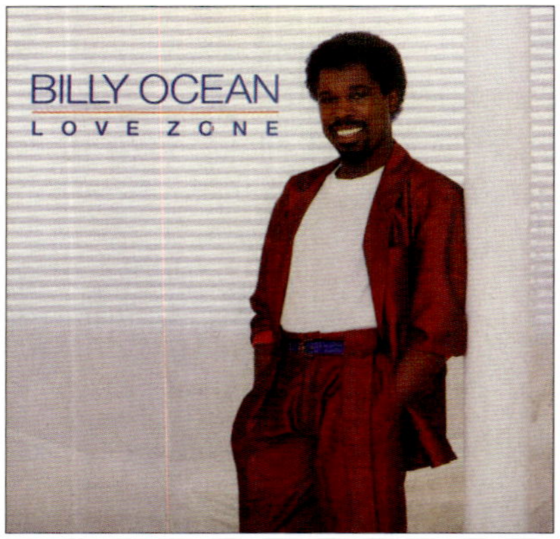

Billboard 200: *Love Zone* (#6)
Billboard Hot 100: "When the Going Gets Tough, the Tough Get Going" (#2); "There'll Be Sad Songs (To Make You Cry)" (No. 1); "Love Zone" (#10); "Love Is Forever" (#16)

A quick succession of hits propelled Billy Ocean's *Love Zone* release to the heights of the R&B and pop charts.

BEGINNING HIS litany of Top 10 singles in 1984 with the breakthrough songs "Caribbean Queen (No More Love on the Run)" and "Loverboy," Billy Ocean quickly joined the elite ranks of platinum-selling recording artists in America. The Trinidadian-British singer-songwriter then contributed the smash "When the Going Gets Tough, the Tough Get Going" to the soundtrack of the movie *Jewel of the Nile*.

That song also appeared on his album *Love Zone*, which featured "There'll Be Sad Songs (To Make You Cry)," which hit the No. 1 spot on the pop, R&B and adult contemporary charts, and the sultry, easy-rocking title track.

Such commercial acceptance couldn't happen to a more gentlemanly artist. Ocean entrusted his career to two men—his record company chief, Clive Caulder, and his manager, Laurie Jay, "a really simple situation that works for me." For *Love Zone*, the duo teamed the artist with Barry Eastmond (formerly Lena Horne's musical director and more recently Freddie Jackson's producer) and Wayne Brathwaite. The collaboration yielded a wealth of romantic ballads as opposed to the up-tempo dance tracks that marked *Suddenly*, Ocean's previous album.

"I've got to work with other people—I'm not disciplined enough to know when to stop something, and that's the key to production," he explained. "We wanted an album that was different but not too different—but I write with good songs in mind anyway. You have to please the people at the record company—when you have three or four songs they like, you know you're on the right track."

Although his concerts built up gradually to include his dance-oriented hits, Ocean favored the slower material where he could stretch his vocal capabilities. "The interesting thing is that the ballads go down so well," he enthused. "'Sad Songs,' 'Suddenly'—there's still excitement, but of a different nature, and the crowd joins right in." A highlight of his sets was a duet with backup singer P.P. Arnold (who had enjoyed considerable solo success in the UK in the Sixties) on the Beatles' "The Long and Winding Road." ■

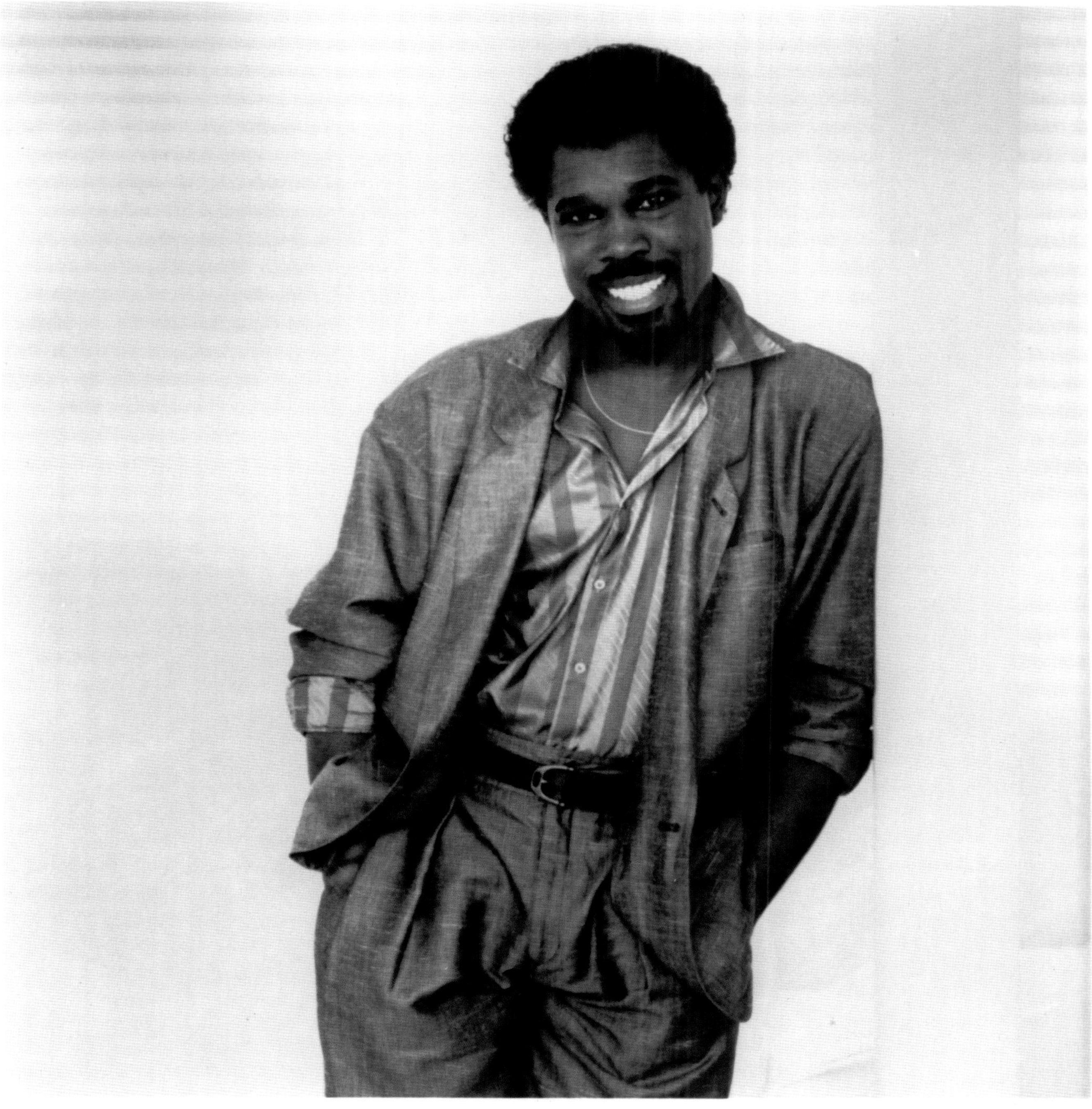

-BILLY OCEAN-

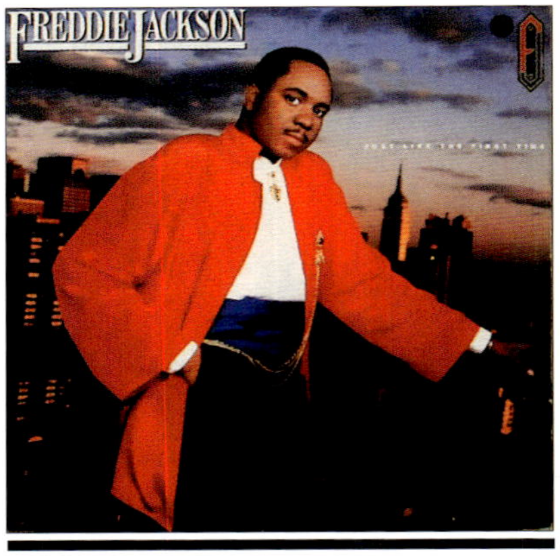

Billboard 200: *Just Like the First Time* (#23)
Billboard Hot 100: "Tasty Love" (#41);
"Have You Ever Loved Somebody" (#69); "Jam Tonight" (#32)

On *Just Like the First Time*, Freddie Jackson, a frequenter of the R&B charts, stuck to urban contemporary fare.

FREDDIE JACKSON had been a showstopper since birth—his mother, a gospel performer, went into labor during a concert. He was trained from an early age, singing at the famed White Rock Baptist Church. "I always knew I wanted to be a singer," Jackson recounted. "I grew up in Harlem, and I watched three shows a day in the Apollo."

Through his dues-paying years, he sang for numerous local bands—one of which, LJE, teamed him with his long-time friend Paul Lawrence, who would become his record producer and songwriting partner. He moved to the West Coast and sang with the funk band Mystic Merlin, but soon returned to New York and played nightspots. Singing star and Tony Award winner Melba Moore helped develop Jackson's career.

He burst on the recording scene in 1985 with his debut album, *Rock Me Tonight*, which topped the Black music charts for 16 weeks.

"Well, I do have an answering machine now and a lot more relatives than I ever was aware of before," Jackson laughed. "But I'm not unhappy about that. It tells me that I've accomplished something positive. Of course, I had my hopes and dreams, but I never thought it would happen on the first album. I just wanted to be able to call my friends and say, 'Listen to me on the radio!'"

Jackson continued his dominance of the R&B charts with his second album, *Just Like the First Time*, as the singles "Tasty Love," the ballad "Have You Ever Loved Somebody" and the up-tempo "Jam Tonight" all made No. 1. "Ballads live," Jackson noted. "They have longevity and they put you in the circuit for longevity as a performer. Even in the church choir, they always gave me slow songs to sing."

Jackson's impassioned vocal technique was an extension of his message. "They say I have bedroom eyes—and I work them as much as I can!" Jackson admitted. "I love giving romance and being romanced. I like pretty things, nice things, women who are beautiful on the inside as well as the outside. Sharing things like fine restaurants, giving flowers, drinking fine wine and champagne—it's nice. I'm a gentleman. A real lady should be treated gently, and I don't seem to lose anything by doing that." ■

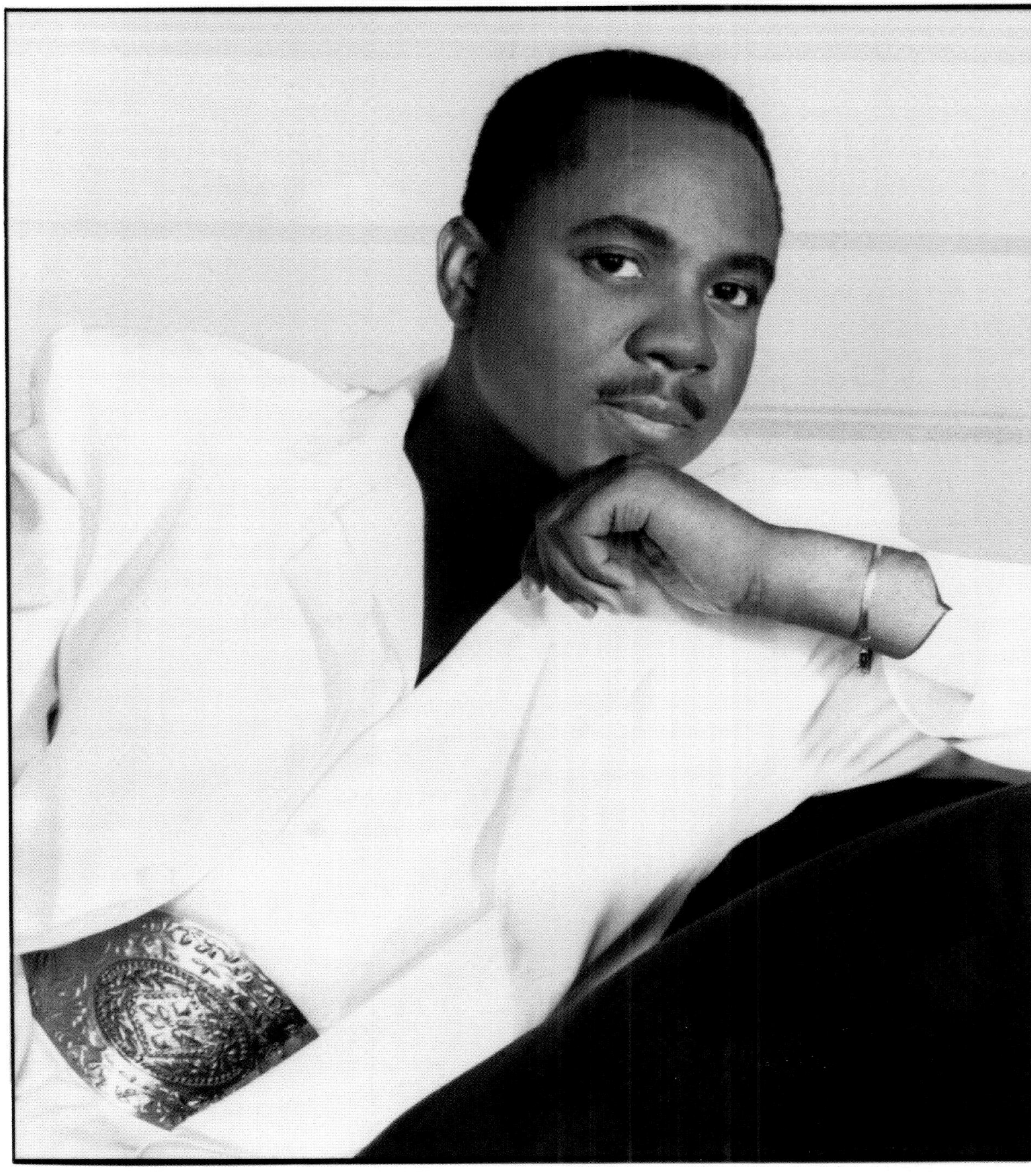

Photo: Carol Weinberg / 1986

FREDDIE JACKSON

Capitol Records

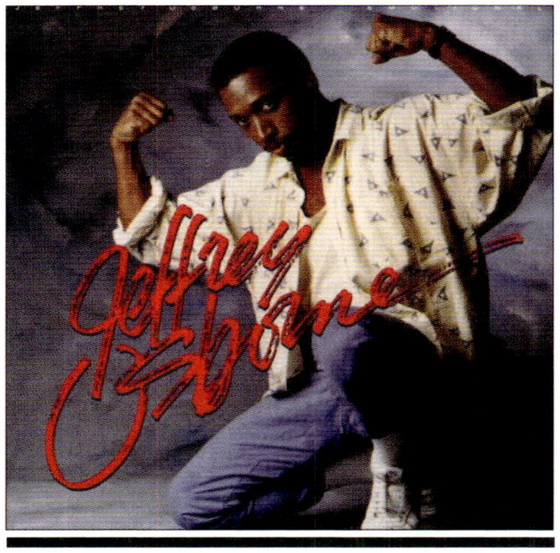

Billboard 200: *Emotional* (#27)
Billboard Hot 100: "You Should Be Mine (The Woo Woo Song)" (#13)

A hefty solo hit, "You Should Be Mine (The Woo Woo Song)," landed for Jeffrey Osborne, previously of L.T.D.

GREAT VOCALISTS dominated the contemporary soul charts, but when it came to jams about l-o-v-e, Jeffrey Osborne glided right by the rest of the big-voiced balladeer competition.

Osborne served a decade-long musical apprenticeship as drummer and eventually leader and vocalist with L.T.D., a slick R&B ensemble that broke a hit with 1977's "(Every Time I Turn Around) Back in Love Again." In recent years he'd launched a solo career with an impressive array of ballads—from the smooth sounds of "On the Wings of Love" to the steamy duet "The Last Time We Made Love" (with Joyce Kennedy).

The key to his burgeoning success had been promoting his strong, emotional, seductive voice. "It's the common denominator to what I do," Osborne said. "I've worked a long time on identity, being able to sing and have people know exactly who it is." As radio airplay suggested, Osborne's songs were usually distinct as well. "Depth and simplicity are the two keys," he noted.

Osborne was enjoying some new challenges—the songwriting and production side of record-making. While several tracks on the *Emotional* album were produced by Richard Perry of Pointer Sisters fame, including the hit single "You Should Be Mine (The Woo Woo Song)," Osborne wound up taking control of the project with some additional help. Still, his overriding image remained that of a sex symbol.

"I am a romantic—all my songs are about love," the happily married singer admitted. "It's quite refreshing to walk onstage and hear the screams. To tell you the truth, I think the concerts would be pretty boring if it weren't for the women—men don't make much noise. My wife is very much in my corner—she's secure and we share a common goal, which is success. Love songs have worked for me, and it's been very healthy. I don't think there's a male vocalist alive who wouldn't want to appeal to the opposite sex. If they say they don't, they're lying or there's something wrong with them." ■

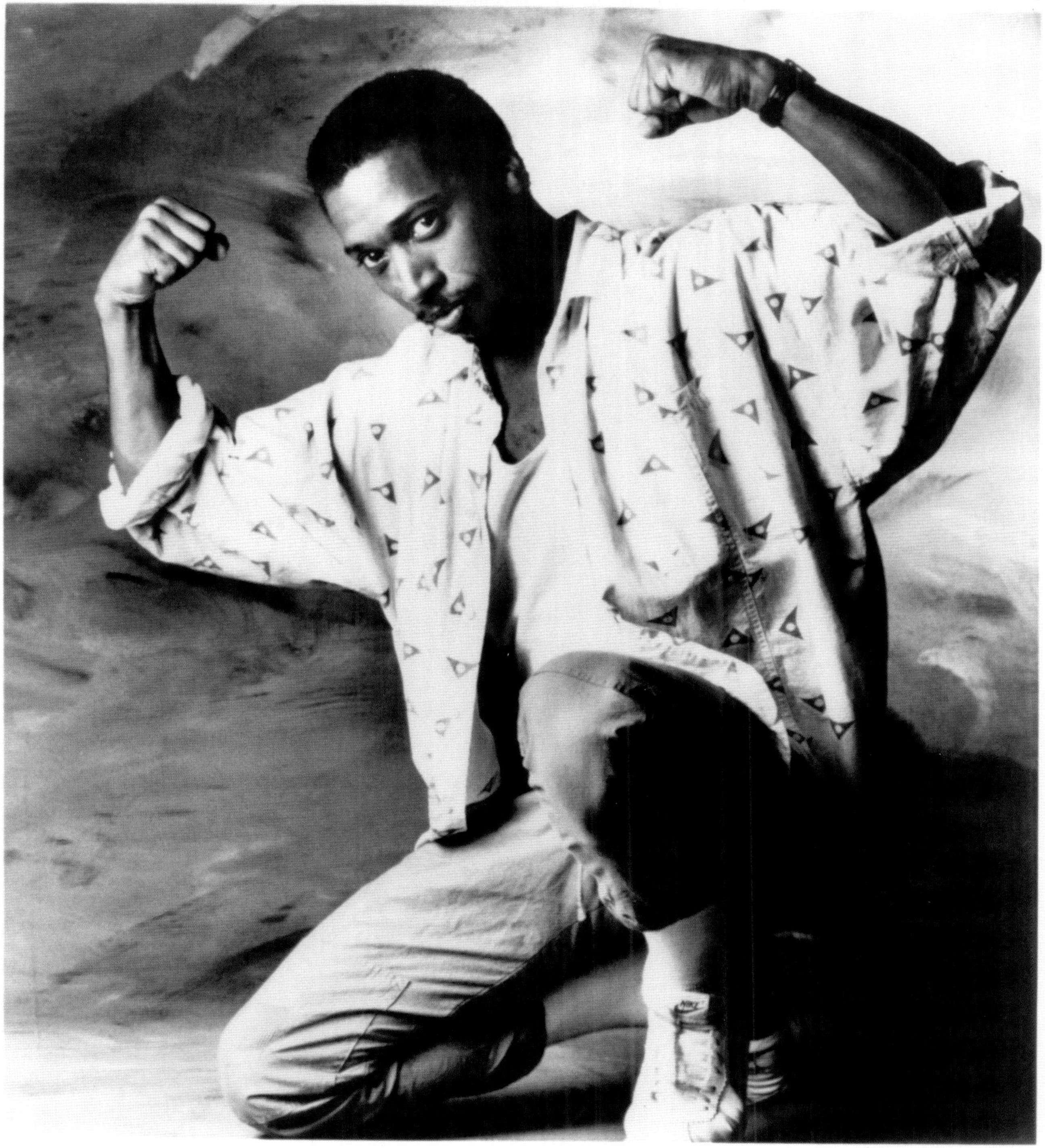

JEFFREY OSBORNE

DIRECTION: JACK NELSON & ASSOCIATES
(213) 465-9905

TRIAD ARTISTS, INC.
LITERARY & TALENT AGENCY

A&M RECORDS
Printed in U.S.A.

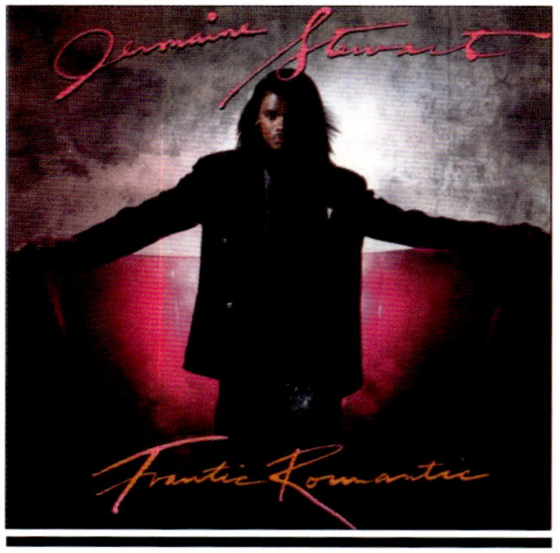

Billboard 200: *Frantic Romantic* (#32)
Billboard Hot 100: "We Don't Have to Take Our Clothes Off" (#5); "Jody" (#42)

Owing to the AIDS epidemic, "We Don't Have to Take Our Clothes Off" spurred Jermaine Stewart's popularity.

WITH AN ultra-hip demeanor, Jermaine Stewart acquired a reputation with "We Don't Have to Take Our Clothes Off," a charting pop, R&B and dance record. Was he a troubadour for the new age of celibacy?

"I hadn't planned on getting labeled a 'goody two-shoes,'" he laughed. "I'm a singer and musician who's into all sorts of things. 'We Don't Have to Take Our Clothes Off' has a positive message and helps some people—you know, be selective about who you're with. But on the other hand, no, I'm not Mister Morality."

Stewart had performed in various capacities prior to his breakthrough. While growing up in Chicago, he sang in church on Sunday and danced on the city's locally produced edition of *Soul Train* as a teen. "Every year I'd go down and compete in the Black Expo dance contest, and every year I won," he said. "So one time some people from the *Soul Train* show were down there and they invited me on."

At the end of the school year, Stewart went to Los Angeles on vacation and earned a spot on the new national version of *Soul Train*, wowing viewers with his innovative dance moves and unique fashion ideas. He also honed his craft as a dancer and occasional background vocalist with various acts, helping out Shalamar on the road. He befriended Culture Club, providing back-up vocals on the group's hit, "Miss Me Blind." Bassist Mikey Craig helped with the demos that got Stewart a recording contract.

Frantic Romantic included "We Don't Have to Take Our Clothes Off," co-written by Narada Michael Walden, composer of Aretha Franklin's recent hit, "Freeway of Love." A second single, the steamy "Jody," was inspired by his friend and former Soul Train dancemate Jody Watley.

The owner of one of pop's funkiest 'dos had never played in concert—he used backing tapes in performances. "I learn a lot from doing live-to-track dates," he insisted. "My music is a liberated style that has no color barrier. I'm Jermaine and that's it." ■

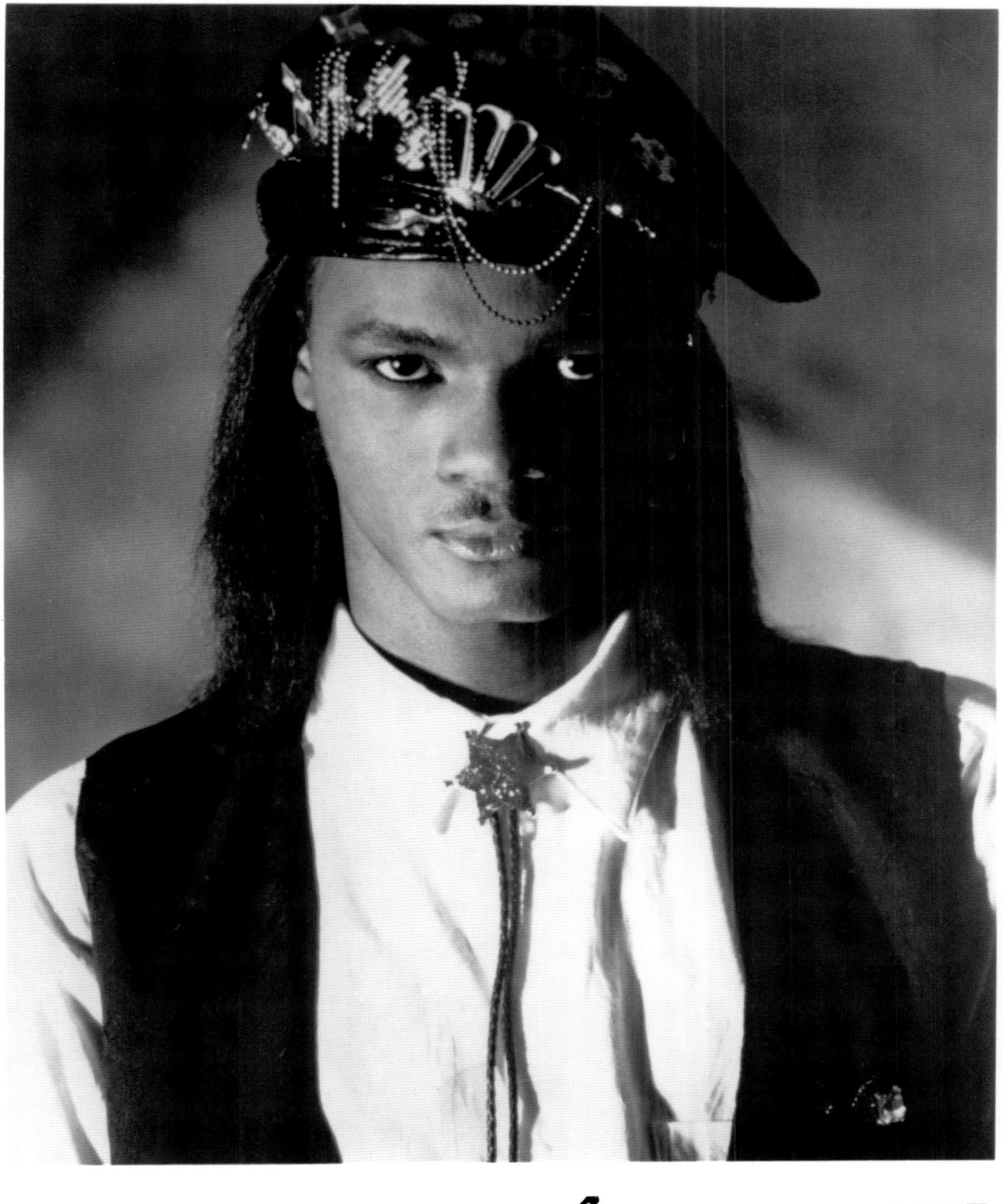

NORBY WALTERS ASSOC.
212-245-3939

Jermaine Stewart

10
ARISTA™

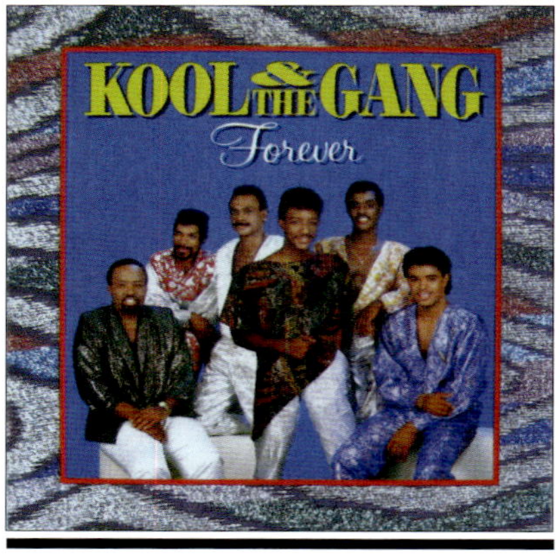

Billboard 200: *Forever* (#25)
Billboard Hot 100: "Victory" (#10); "Stone Love" (#10); "Holiday" (#66); "Special Way" (#72)

Forever, Kool & the Gang's 17th album, perpetuated the R&B group's succession of gold and platinum records.

STATISTICALLY SPEAKING, the top hit-making act of the early Eighties wasn't a member of the Michael Jackson/Prince/Lionel Richie clique. It was Kool & the Gang, the New Jersey funksters who had charted 14 songs in the Top 40 in the decade. That litany of hits included such standards as "Celebrate," "Joanna" and "Cherish."

Two major singles released from the nine-piece band's *Forever* album, "Victory" and "Stone Love," reached the Top 10 on the pop, R&B and adult contemporary charts. The ensemble embarked on a US tour that included the group's "Kool to Stay in School" campaign, an ambitious national program designed to improve school attendance, conceived by singer James "J.T." Taylor and bassist Robert "Kool" Bell.

"I'm in the music business, and that takes an education," Bell explained. "A lot of teenagers look up to rock stars and movie stars, and they think that you just have to be a good musician or actor, that you don't need a good education. That's a mistake. We have lawyers and accountants, and we have to know about copyrights, publishing, marketing and mathematics. That calls for an education to do business. It's just like General Motors—they sell cars, we sell records."

That was the underlying sentiment behind "Victory," the key anthem from *Forever*. "It's about success in life," Bell explained. "It starts out sounding like it's about a game, but it's about much more. When you go out to accomplish things, it's a victory, whether you're trying to become a champion at baseball or football or going after a diploma.

"Hey, you work 12 years and get through high school, that's a victory. There are a lot of things that relate to victory in life. We're telling people that if they work hard enough and believe in themselves, they can succeed. And the one big key to that success is education."

After the tour, Taylor amicably left the group for a solo career. ■

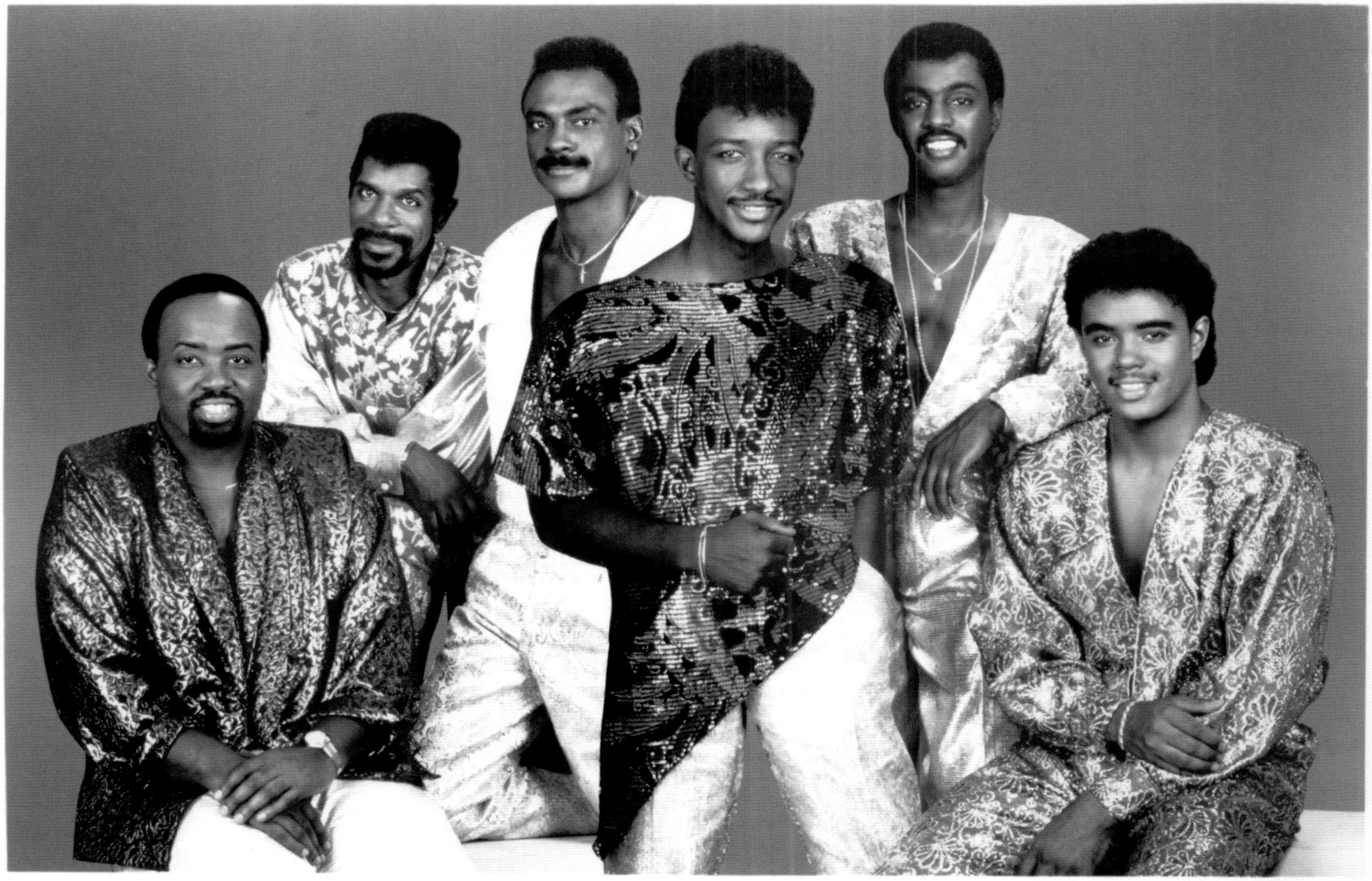

KOOL & the GANG

mercury

PolyGram Records

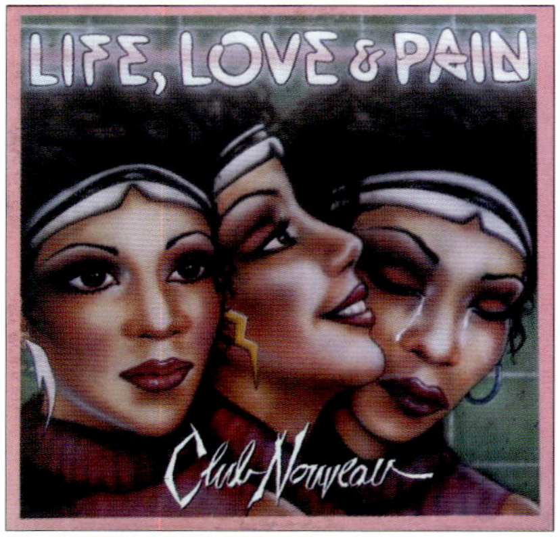

Billboard 200: *Life, Love & Pain* (#6)
Billboard Hot 100: "Lean on Me" (No. 1);
"Why You Treat Me So Bad" (#39)

Club Nouveau was notable for both a No. 1 re-creation of Bill Withers' "Lean on Me" and the pluck of Jay King.

IN 1985, with producer and performer Jay King at the helm, a little-known Bay Area group called Timex Social Club recorded a tune called "Rumors." The song went on to sell more than a million copies and became one of the most successful independently produced singles of the Eighties. But the band splintered at that point.

"From the time we were slaves, Black people have been taught by white people to hate each other," King opined. "And the band didn't trust my intuition. An older white guy came along and said, 'Jay is a young Black kid, the industry isn't gonna respect him. I can make you happen, come with me'—and they did."

So King found himself on his own, burning with the desire to prove he was the smarts behind the band. He formed Club Nouveau and recorded the dance sensation and "Rumors" soundalike "Jealousy," "Situation #9" and then "Lean on Me," an out-of-the-box hit that emerged as a gold-certified single. The lighthearted version of Bill Withers' classic won a Grammy award for Best R&B Song. *Life, Love & Pain*, the debut album, reached #2 on the soul album charts.

King was riding high again, producing and arranging commercial funk-pop material—melodic hooks set to a big hard-rap beat—on his own Sacramento-based King Jay Records with partners Thomas McElroy and Denzil Foster. "I never learned to make records," King admitted. "I just listened to them a lot and knew I wanted to make them." King's expertise was more that of a businessman than of a formally trained musician, but he dismissed his image as a cocky newcomer on the music scene.

"Anytime a Black man has a direction and is self-assured and confident, they're gonna make him look arrogant. But they can't push me around. This is very much an industry where people use other people. My philosophies are totally different—music has no color. People just want to have good, positive songs. I'm a leader, very assertive, aggressive and ambitious. I have a lot of young people around me, and I instill the same ideals in them. I control everything around me." ■

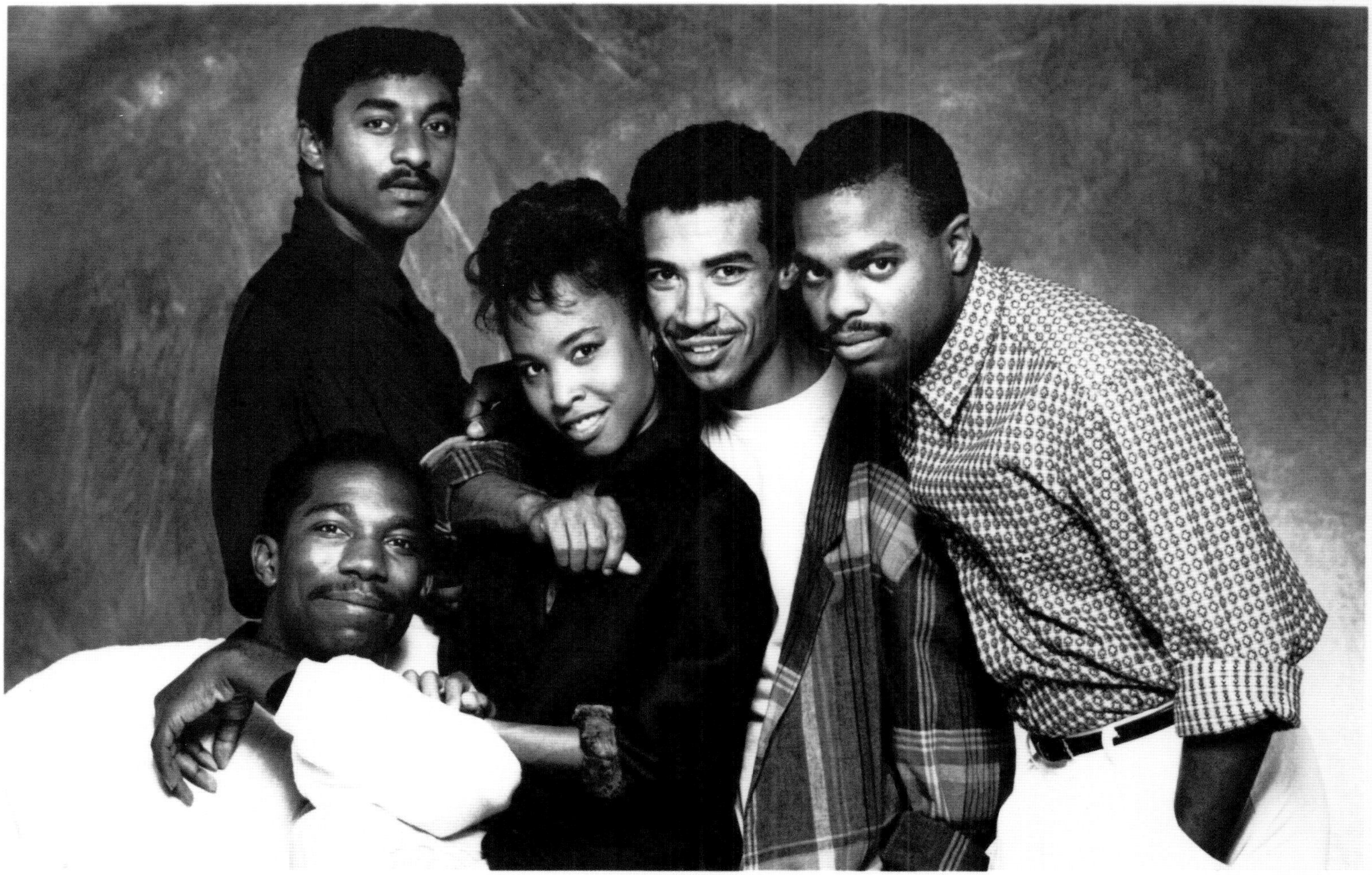

Photo Credit: Chris Cuffaro

DENZIL FOSTER SAMUELLE PRATER VALERIE WATSON JAY KING THOMAS McELROY

CLUB NOUVEAU

WARNER BROS.

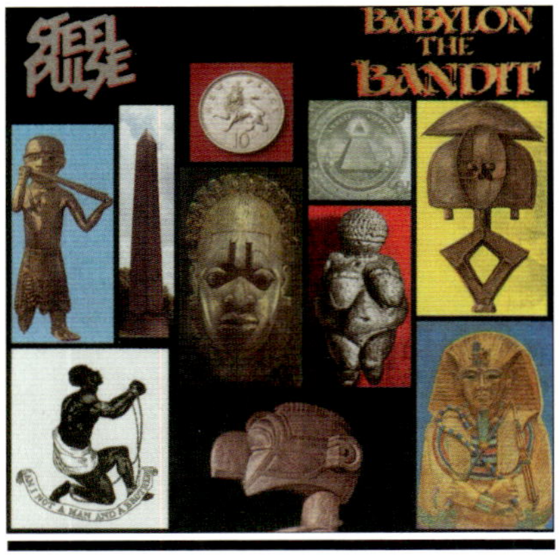

Crafting world-class reggae, Britain's long-lived Steel Pulse scored a Grammy Award for *Babylon the Bandit*.

A ROOTS-REGGAE band from England, Steel Pulse had a commitment to being politically minded. On *Babylon the Bandit*, the group pinpointed the dilemmas existing in the communities of the ethnic minorities and third-world countries across the globe.

"It is right to say that the people of these communities have been, in general, brainwashed and robbed of their natural birth rights," frontman David Hinds said. "To be specific, I mean prevented from practicing their native culture and therefore reduced to attitudes of narrow-mindedness."

Steel Pulse pursued a more mainstream vein for the album, with polished, synth-focused dance elements. The highlight was the forceful "Not King James Version."

"Western history has never given the African much credit for his achievement in developing the human race," Hinds explained. "This false impression has been echoed throughout schools and other sources of education for centuries. For example, Christopher Columbus' so-called discovery of America, when Indians had inhabited the land long before his supposed visit. Also, take the case of Pablo Picasso—his claim to fame with the style of Cubism included direct copies of various African masks.

"From these sources of information, the concept of 'Not King James Version' was born. Rasta has always believed that the Bible, although positive in many ways, was and is still used to misguide the African away from his heritage."

Steel Pulse won the Grammy for Best Reggae Album, the first time the award went to a non-Jamaican outfit. The explicit crossover sound alienated some of the band's older fans, but the title of *Babylon the Bandit* summed up Steel Pulse's lyrical concept.

"You must remember that the term 'Babylon' has been applied to a system of negative things, irrespective of race—Babylon continually robs and rapes the earth of its beauty," Hinds said. "Nevertheless, we are confident of the victory of good over evil, for confrontation with the liberation posse and its defeat, which is eminent and inevitable. Praise Jah." ■

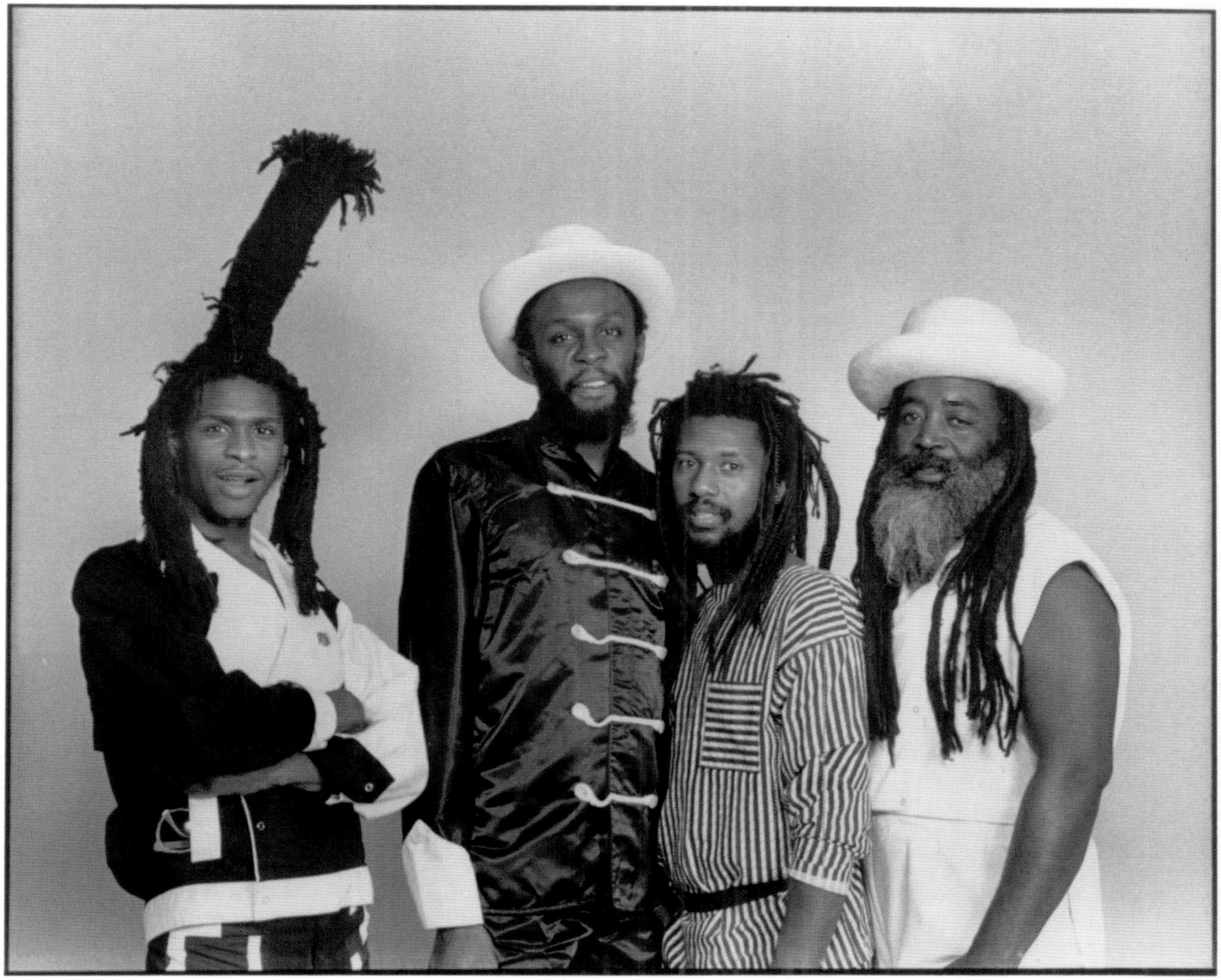

PHOTO CREDIT: EBET ROBERTS/1985

DAVID HINDS SELWYN BROWN PHONSO MART N STEVE NESBITT

STEEL PULSE

ELEKTRA

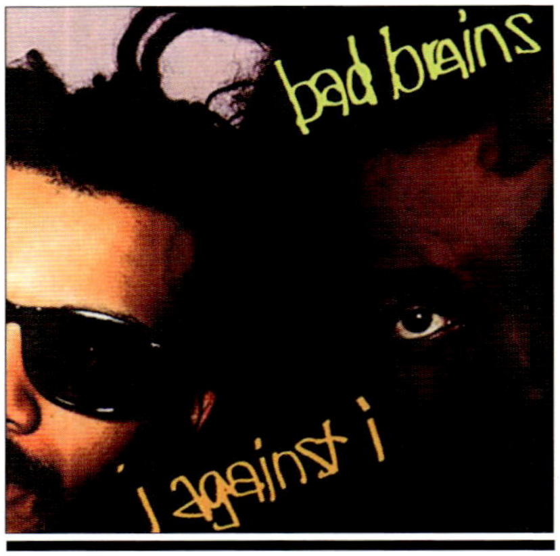

Mixing hardcore punk with funk, reggae and heavy metal, Bad Brains recorded the definitive *I Against I* album.

RHYTHMIC INTENSITY had made Bad Brains a cult sensation across the US. The four members hailed from Washington, D.C., where they languished in the city's jazz-rock fusion scene before hearing the Sex Pistols in 1977. With the zeal of the newly converted, they vowed to get their own brand of punk off the ground, but the area's club owners blacklisted them.

"From the beginning, they didn't want us happening," bassist Darryl Jenifer said. "They were afraid, I guess, of the style of our music, the color of our skin, how we looked."

So the band—Jenifer, H.R. (vocals), Dr. Know (guitar) and Earl Hudson (drums)—relocated to New York City, where the group became enamored of reggae music and the Rastafarian creed in 1980.

"It wasn't a gimmick for us," Jenifer insisted. "It's all normal stuff—you're growing up, you realize something, you start checking it out, it changes you. We were into being positive, so we figured we needed to know more about where that energy comes from, the Jah/God trip, whatever."

Jenifer maintained that reggae music and hardcore punk were "the same thing, the same trip to me." But the blend made for offbeat performances. Bad Brains pounded a room with cathartic blitz-rock while singing a message of unity, justice and love for Jah (the Rastafarian name of God)—a religious and political commitment that wasn't usually a priority among hardcore crowds.

"But that's our duty, to spread a little bit of it around on that scene, too—to be positive and energetic instead of the devil trip all the time," Jenifer said. "When the slam-dancing started, it was just the result of the energy and the vibes."

Bad Brains could have been dismissed as underground darlings if it weren't for *I Against I*, an outstanding album that harnessed the band's roaring sound. The track "Sacred Love" was evidence of the band's ongoing hassles in its hometown. When D.C. police cracked down on resident Jamaicans, they assumed H.R. was a Rasta and busted him on a marijuana-possession charge. The "Sacred Love" vocal track was recorded over the phone from jail. "We had to finish the record," Jenifer said with a shrug.

But despite such difficulties, *I Against I* was a superbly recorded hard-rock release that was superior to the usual output from SST Records (the maverick home of Black Flag and other hardcore acts). The album was produced and engineered by a studio team whose credits included work with such commercial elites as Whitney Houston and Diana Ross.

"Take it to the next step? Maybe that's the worst thing that could happen to us," Jenifer said. "But I want to live off this, too. Regardless of all the capitalism trips people talk about, an artist has to make money for his work. We shouldn't be tapped as a sellout by the hardcore crowd just because we want to pay the rent. We've had some nibbles from major record companies. Maybe they'll turn into bites." ■

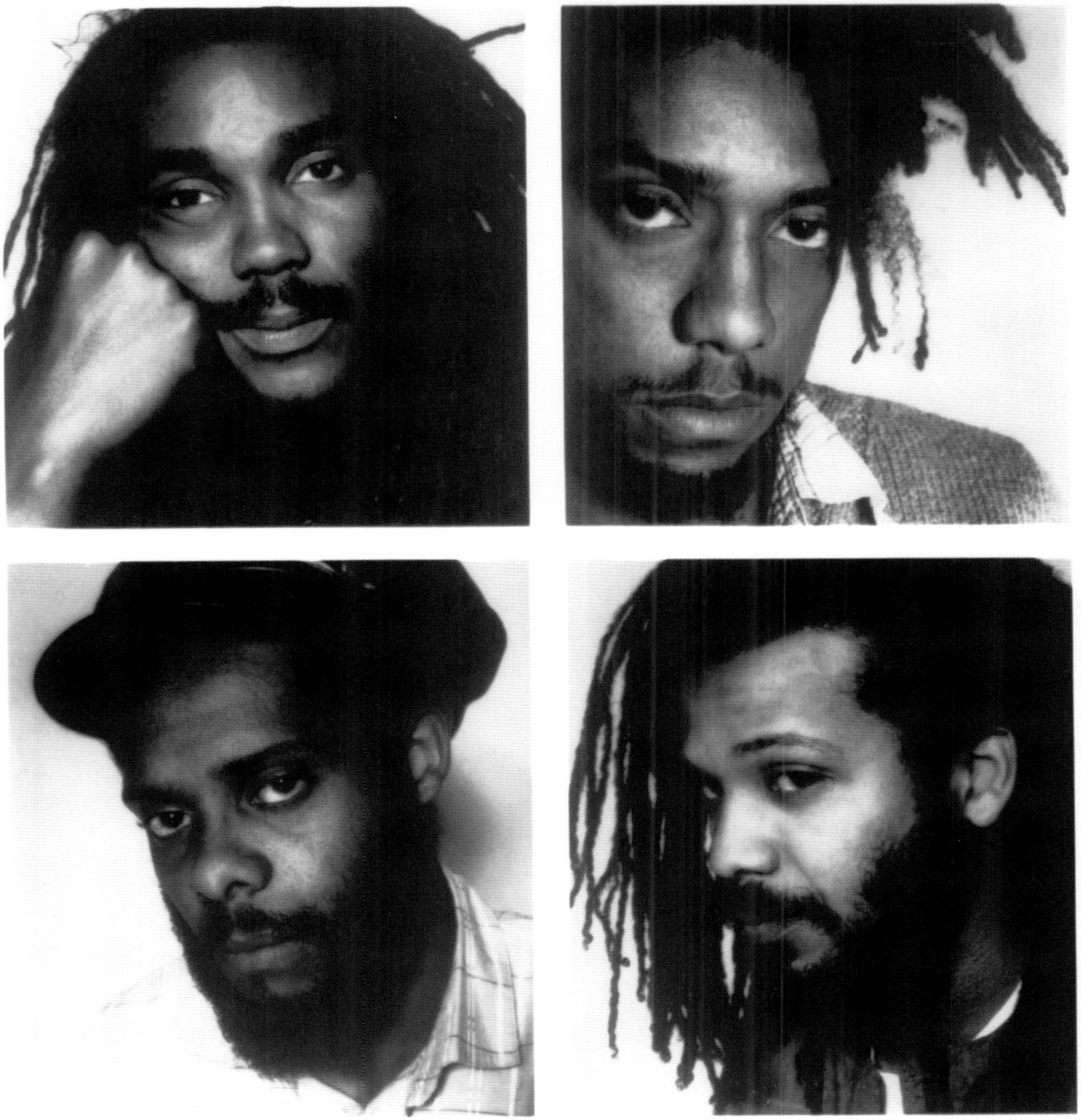

bad brains

Distribution, Publicity, Accounts;
(213) 676-0110
Booking, Tour Publicity:
(213) 618-0797
P.O. Box 1, Lawndale, CA 90260 USA.

As Pictured DARRYL H.R.
EARL DR. KNOW

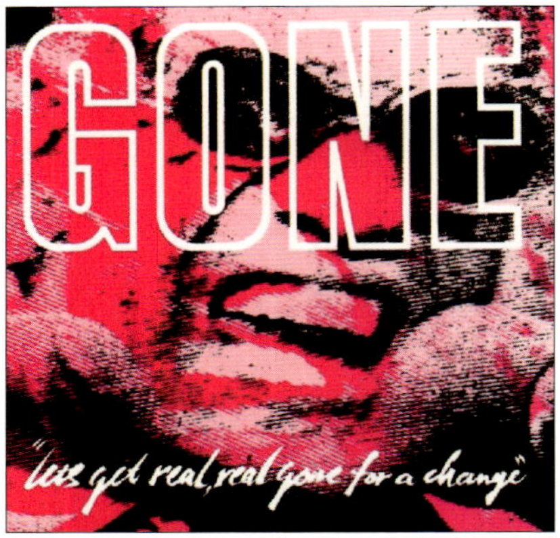

Hurting for an outlet for his increasingly instrumental compositions, Black Flag's Greg Ginn organized Gone.

IN RECENT years, Black Flag had gained national prominence as California's premier hardcore band. But at the same time, guitarist Greg Ginn had gradually expanded on the group's thrashing sound to pioneer a dialogue between punk and jazz modes. Ginn took a big step forward by forming an auxiliary group, Gone, as a showcase for his improvisational leanings.

"I had been doing instrumental stuff with Black Flag for quite a while," Ginn said. "But the group wasn't active enough on that level, so I started Gone." The trio opened more than 100 shows on a Black Flag tour, with Ginn pulling double duty with both bands. But his most inventive playing occurred with Gone's rhythm section of drummer Sim Caine and bassist Andrew Weiss, who had played together in a New Jersey band called Regressive Aid.

"Nobody in the group is stuck in a certain category, and I like being able to write music and not have to worry about how it's going to fit in," Ginn said. "I'd rather just work on music that I like and not have it judged in that way."

On the band's debut album, *Let's Get Real, Real Gone for a Change* (which the trio recorded after three weeks together), Gone sounded like Black Sabbath tackling the King Crimson catalog, with Ginn's densely textured chording incorporating everything from heavy-metal force to jazzy improvisation. Gone's musical vision deserved wider recognition, but it wasn't forthcoming on SST Records, the maverick label that distributed releases by Black Flag, Gone and other underground acts. Yet Ginn, a partner in SST, had no desire to go elsewhere.

"The music I play doesn't really fit it, and so many people that see us never hear any kind of instrumental music," he said. "But I actually like that element, and I think that's why Gone has done better than I would have expected. More people are interested in checking us out since the current cultural climate tends to more literal forms in music, even on the underground level. Even college radio has gotten real conservative."

Continuing to work in new musical territory, Ginn went even further than Gone. He opened the band's shows with his own solo set featuring guitar synthesizers, sequencers, a Linn drum machine and a MIDI bass unit. ■

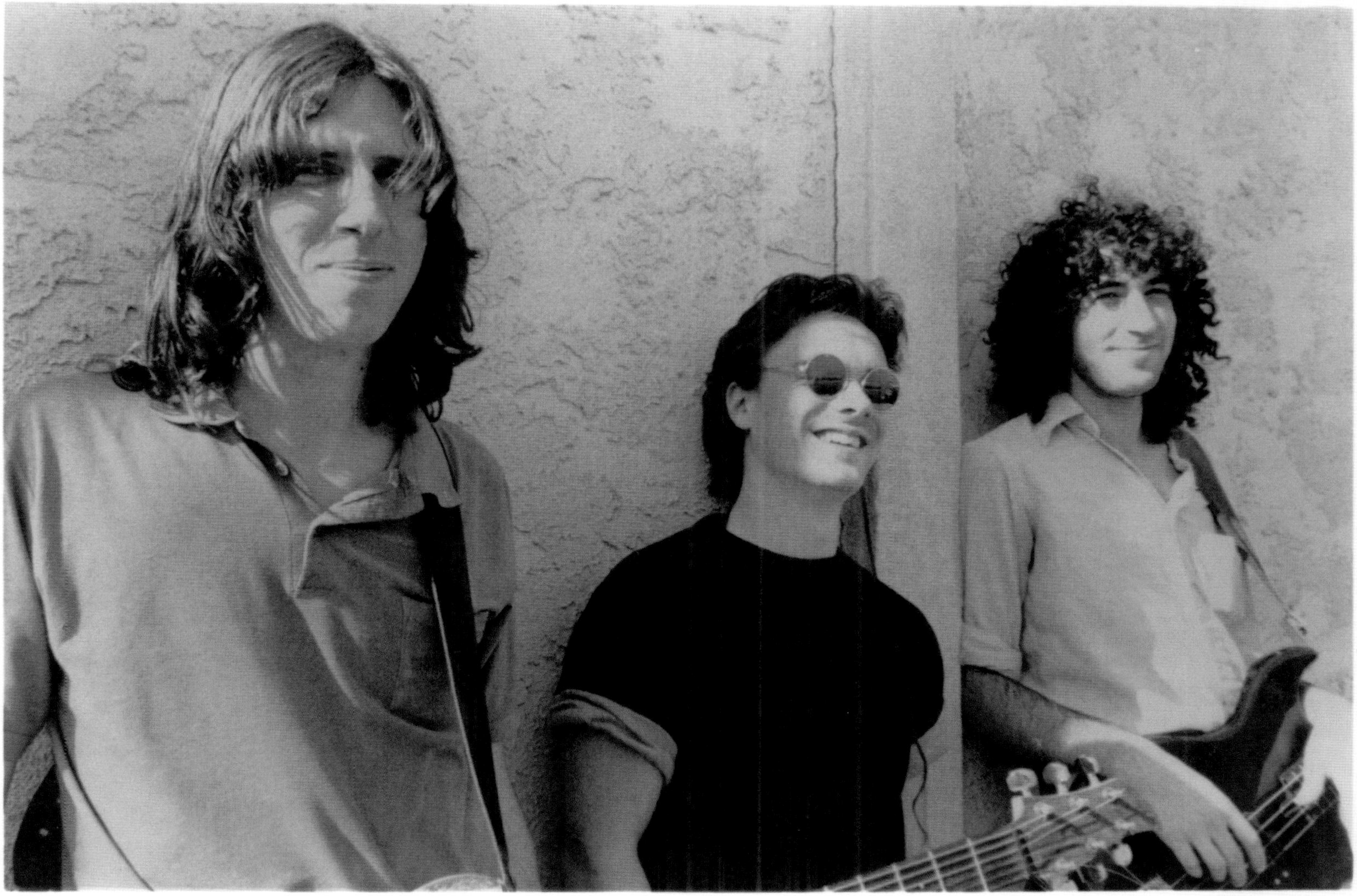

GONE

Photo: Naomi Petersen

(Please run a photo credit.)

SST RECORDS

(US) P.O. Box 1, Lawndale, CA 90260
Office: (213) 676-0110
Booking: (213) 618 0797
(UK) 208 Bravington, London W9
Office/Booking: (01) 278-3331

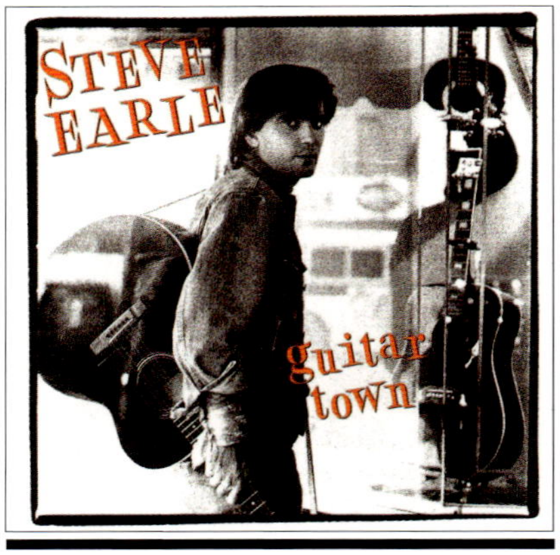

Billboard 200: *Guitar Town* (#89)

With *Guitar Town*, his breakthrough record, Steve Earle tried to stake his claim in Nashville as a major talent.

GUITAR TOWN, Steve Earle's debut album, was greeted with unanimously favorable reviews, and the critical huzzahs eventually translated into a No. 1 album on the country charts. But Earle was heralded by rock listeners as well. The Dukes, his five-piece band, could slip into full throttle at a moment's notice. And because Earle wrote about Reaganomic suffering and small-town restlessness, he stood up to comparisons with such names as Springsteen, Mellencamp and Fogerty just as easily as with a young Merle Haggard.

Earle, a refreshingly unaffected good ol' boy with blue-collar emotions, was quick to declare his intentions. "I'm a country singer—I don't think there's any doubt about that," he insisted in a down-home drawl. "I will always record in Nashville, mainly because I'll always live in Nashville. It's a songwriter's town, and the reason for me to make records doesn't have anything to do with being rock or being country—it has to do with songs. People talk about a resurgence of American music or roots music, but the resurgence of the singer-songwriter is the most important trend in music in the last couple of years. People like Lyle Lovett and Nanci Griffith—songs as literature. Kids are listening to lyrics again."

Earle's apparent overnight success was preceded by a dozen years of struggling for a break. Originally from San Antonio, Texas, he left home at 16 and bounced around Houston and Austin before moving to Nashville at 19. He stated he had done "almost everything for a short period of time—framed houses, hung billboards, cowboyed, worked offshore. But I don't remember ever wanting to be anything but a musician."

And while he had achieved rapid commercial success melding rock and country styles—"I expected to fall in the cracks like everyone else before me," he said—his artistic ascent hadn't been without problems.

"Some people misconstrue my politics as being right-wing," he noted. "It gets irritating, because *Guitar Town* is probably the most anti-Reagan record that came out this year. But it happens because I write in the first person a lot. People should be more understanding and kinder toward the people they label as 'rednecks'—those folks don't have time like songwriters and journalists to sit around and drink and talk about politics. They don't have the time to analyze things—they go to work, they come home, they get the headlines off the news and they lash out at the first thing that seems to be the problem. I don't try to pass myself off as being working-class—I'm not. My parents work, but I've lived a bohemian lifestyle all of my life. I've never had a straight job longer than three months." ■

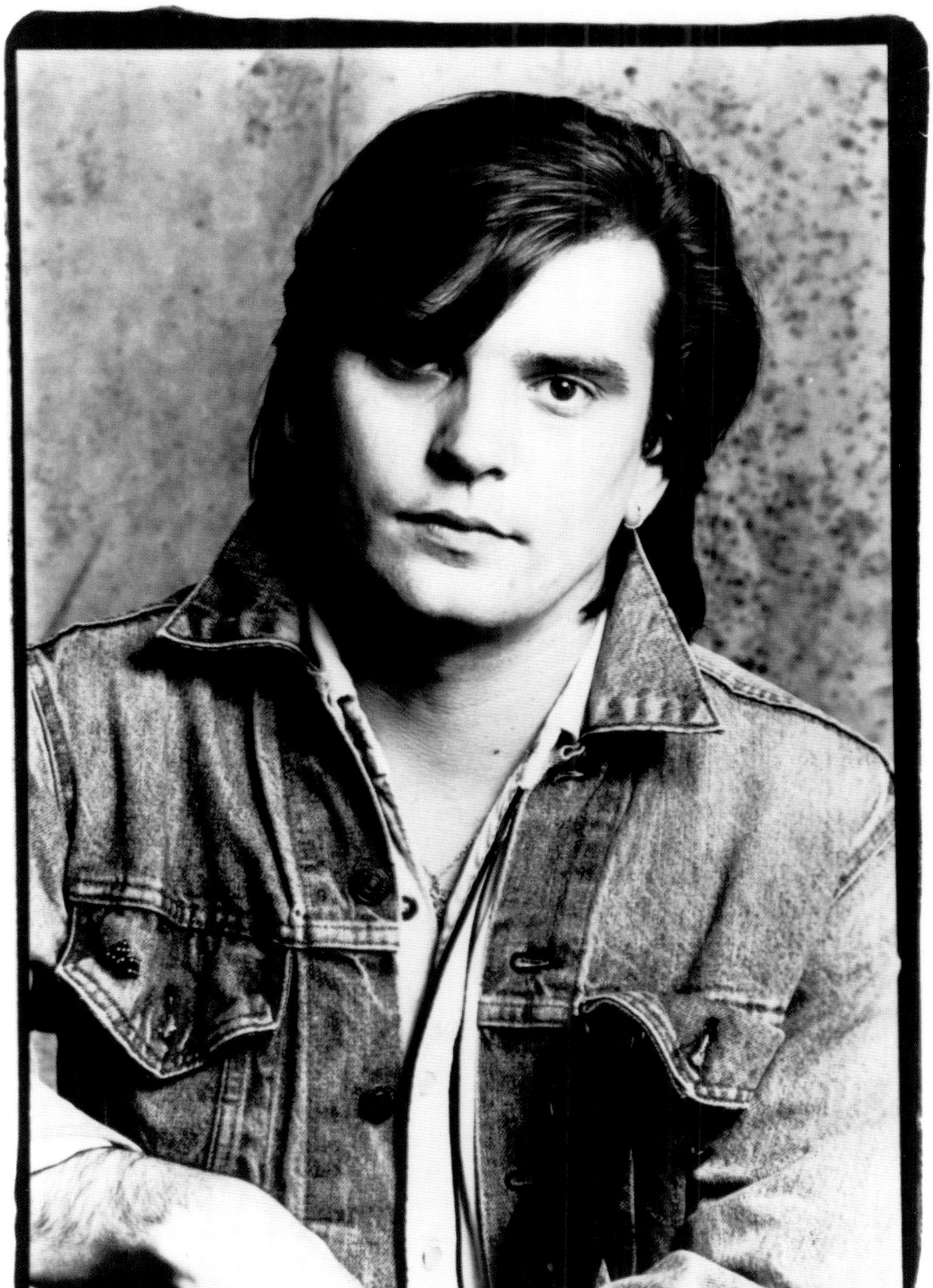

STEVE EARLE MCA RECORDS

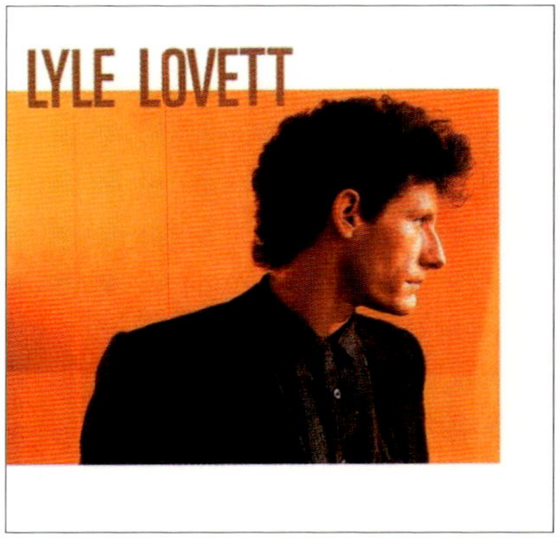

Lyle Lovett's debut release distinguished the Texas native as an original singer-songwriter of the first rank.

THE CALIBER of strong-voiced acoustic performers had fallen off since the Seventies, when such outstanding songwriters as Jesse Winchester, Ry Cooder, Steve Goodman and John Prine launched their careers. But a fresh talent had arrived who invited favorable comparisons to those artists—Lyle Lovett.

While friends and fans thought of him as a folk performer, and while a few of his songs reflected Eagles-like rock influences, Lovett was marketed as one of the new breed of young country artists. The strategy worked—"Farther Down the Line" and "Cowboy Man" climbed the country charts. But while Lovett readily accepted the tag, his songs offered decidedly non-cowboy perspectives. "God Will," a brooding ballad, detailed a lover's lack of forgiveness, and "If I Had a Boat" favored witty wordplay.

In 1984, the fourth-generation Houstonian had gone to Nashville to peddle a demo tape. The country establishment was often criticized for being unreceptive to new talent, but Lovett's steely singing and lyrical finesse got him a quick contract from MCA Records.

"I always felt my songs were the strong point," he said. "I never thought of myself as a singer, only to the extent of presenting my songs. When people would hear my tape and go, 'Well, who is that singing?' it made me feel great. My only training was in parochial-school choir."

And since the release of the *Lyle Lovett* album, favorable word-of-mouth on the newcomer had exploded. His appeal differed from that of Dwight Yoakam and Steve Earle, two other bright new country acts—whereas they shared a reliance on band interplay and a few hillbilly touches, Lovett's focused on lyrics, perceptive and sophisticated in matters of both romance and social satire. His sharp observations were those of a journalist—he'd majored in journalism at Texas A&M—and a poet.

The basic tracks for *Lyle Lovett* were produced independently by Lovett and a nightclub band from Phoenix headed by J. David Sloan. MCA staff producer Tony Brown simply added a few touches on the original tapes, such as a fiddle part on "Cowboy Man." Lovett humbly downplayed his studio vision.

"I just tried to take the songs I'd been playing solo in clubs and make them sound like something you'd hear driving around in your car," he said. "I'm not one of those crazy guys who can crank out a song every week. I really sweat about each one. Every time I write a song, I feel like that's the last one I'll ever write. I'm not a drinker—I think the central thing to what I do is the song, and any of that stuff just makes me stupid, so I try to keep straight to work.

"And I'm lucky—I'm getting to do what I want. I've been playing around Texas for eight years, throwing my P.A. in the back of my truck and driving somewhere, setting it up myself and playing. I know how difficult it is to sell yourself. Now I'm asked, 'What's the hardest thing about dealing with this attention?' Hey, I have more help now than I ever had in my life. Things couldn't be more wonderful." ■

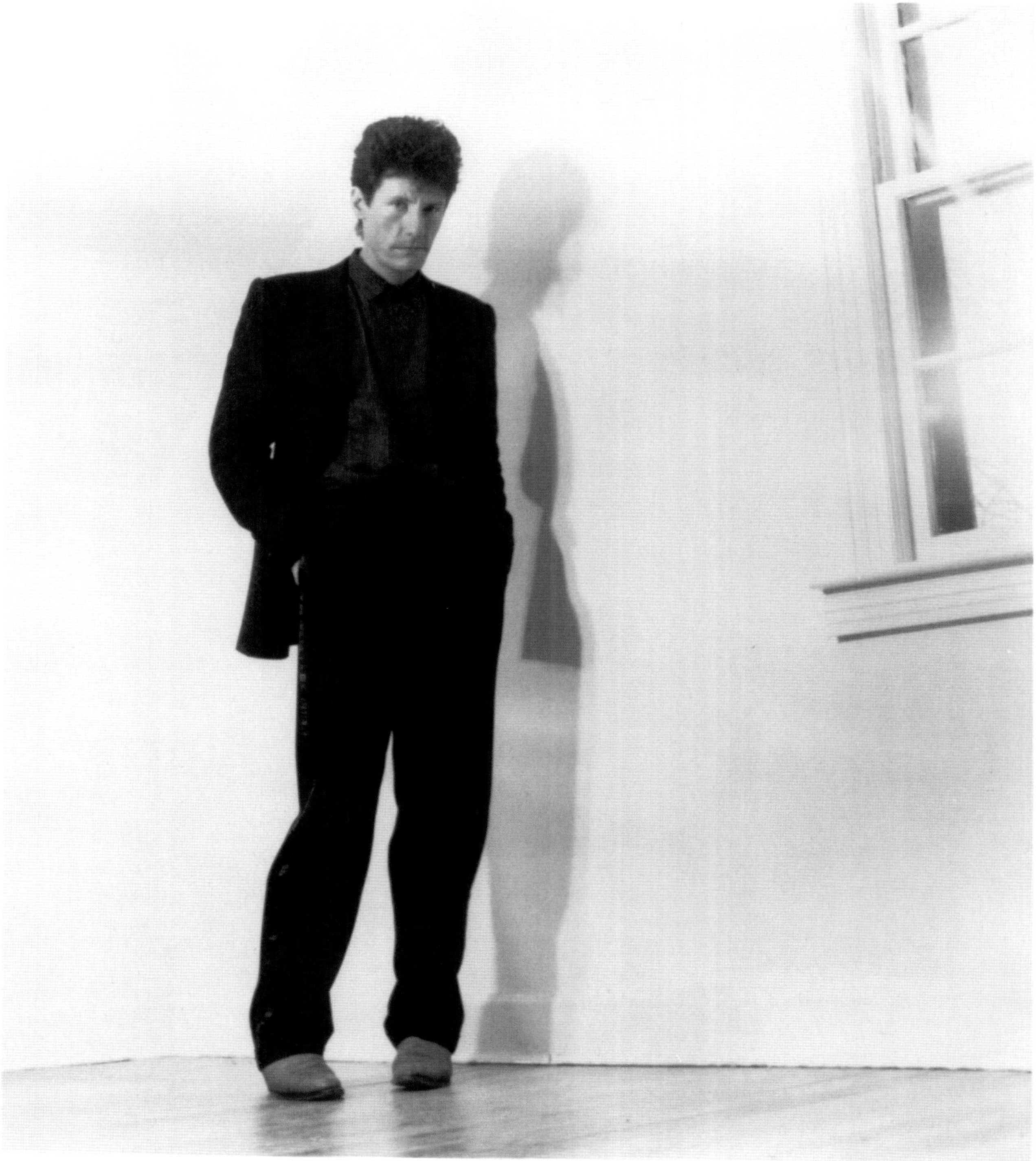

credit: Peter Nash

Lyle Lovett

MCA RECORDS

CURB RECORDS

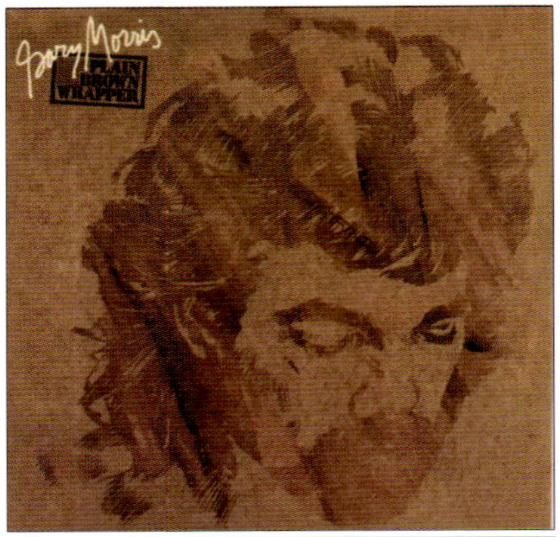

Experiencing a spate of hits on the country music charts, Gary Morris recorded the *Plain Brown Wrapper* album.

THROUGHOUT HIS youth in Fort Worth, Texas, Gary Morris was exposed to all kinds of music, but he focused mainly on athletics. He had intended to enroll in college and play football, but the summer after finishing high school, he and two buddies went to Colorado.

"That was the beginning of my singing career," Morris said. "We stopped at a bar in Colorado Springs called the Golden Bee. We asked the bartender if we could do a few songs. We stood up on some tables and did 'Gentle on My Mind,' 'Early Morning Rain' and 'Visions of Sugar Plums.' The audience just went crazy. We collected $35 in tips and quickly translated that figure into what we could make singing 20 songs. We thought, 'This is it!'"

The trio traveled on to Boulder, where Morris rented an apartment and got a job as a construction worker. They also sang at a bar called the Three Kings "for beer and cheeseburgers." Instead of heading to college that fall, Morris turned his attention to singing and performing. For several years, he fronted a trio that entertained in Denver. He also gained valuable studio experience, singing and writing jingles for companies such as Coors Beer and Frontier Airlines.

He formed a seven-piece country-rock band, Breakaway, which became a popular attraction in the Rocky Mountain states. After three years of trying to land a recording contract with the band, Morris headed for Nashville, where he established himself as a brand-name solo artist with the records "Headed for a Heartache" and "The Love She Found in Me." He achieved the greatest notoriety for his original recording of "The Wind Beneath My Wings," which won Song of the Year awards from both the Country Music Association and the Academy of Country Music

His *Plain Brown Wrapper* was a pleasant surprise, a personal collection of selected oldies ("Honeycomb," a version of the 1957 best-seller by Jimmie Rodgers) and new originals with clean, crisp acoustic flavorings. It showed off the finest players—Jerry Douglas played dobro and Mark O'Connor played mandolin and fiddle. "Fifteen years ago, it would have been considered pop music," Morris said, "But I think it's right in the middle of what should be considered country music in 1986."

"Leave Me Lonely" became his fourth country No. 1. "I was playing somewhere, and it was at a moment when I was being approached by too many fans at one time and I just wanted to be left alone. You know, enough is enough."

The album cover artwork for *Plain Brown Wrapper* was plain and simple. "I keep getting flack about being a 'sex symbol,' so this cover is just a pen-and-ink drawing. The rest of the album is plain brown, so I don't think anybody is going to buy the album for the cover. It'll be a nice test." ■

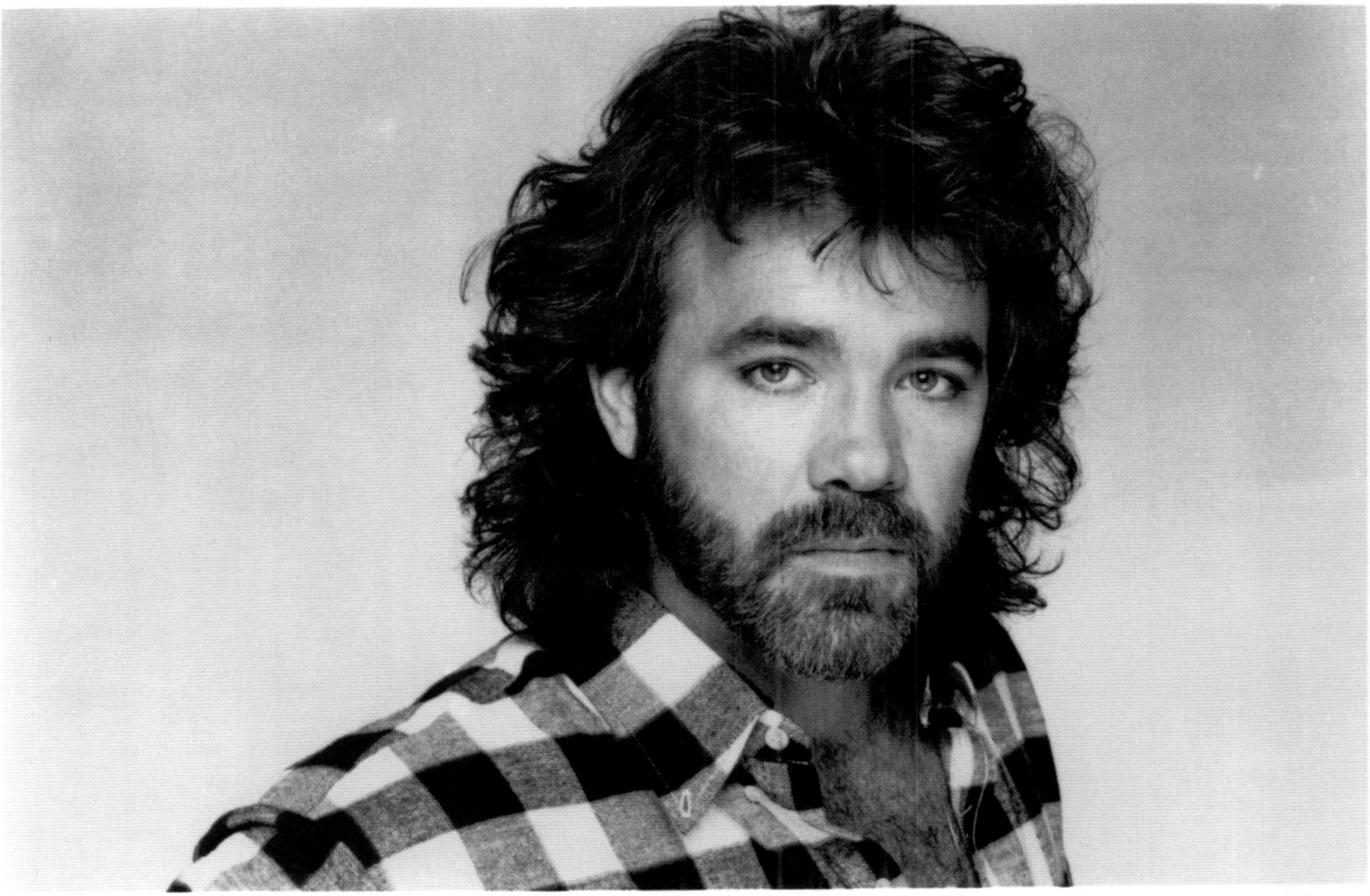

photo credit: RANDEE ST. NICHOLAS

Gary Morris

WARNER BROS.

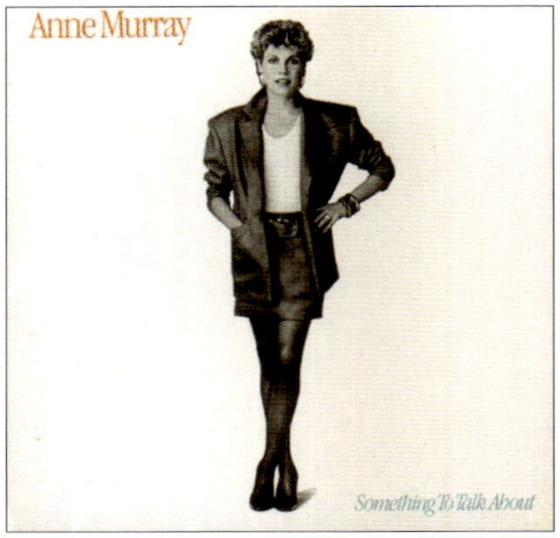

Billboard 200: *Something to Talk About* (#68)
Billboard Hot 100: "Now and Forever (You and Me)" (#92)

An international star for 15 years, Anne Murray asserted her artistic inclinations on *Something to Talk About*.

FOR HER signature song, 1970's "Snowbird," Anne Murray had been the first Canadian female solo singer to reach No. 1 on the US charts and the first to earn a gold record. That success kicked off a string of subsequent hits that simultaneously charted in both pop and country.

"People tend to categorize me as a country singer—and that's right, when I'm singing a country song," Murray said. "But I can do a lot more. I want to stay contemporary and be around in this business for a long, long time. And you can't do that and get to a whole lot of people just singing country music."

The gold-certified *Something to Talk About* marked a departure, as Murray worked with three different accomplished producers on the album—Canadian David Foster, Munich-based Jack White and New York-based Keith Diamond.

"I've tended to work with the same producer for a long time—Brian Ahern for seven albums, then two with Tom Catalano, and nine with Jim Ed Norman," Murray said. "It was time for a change.

"Starting in 1978, my career took right off with 'You Needed Me,' and for the next few years I had hit after hit. They were all kind of ballad-y, and it's really hard to look a gift horse in the mouth—you get on a roll like that, and you don't want to change things. I was certainly not one to turn my back on the success I was having and start experimenting at that time. But music moves on to something else, and you've got to change with it. I've had a history of pop success in the past, and there's no reason that it shouldn't happen again."

"Now and Forever (You and Me)" was Murray's tenth No. 1 hit on the country singles chart, and it crossed over to the pop chart, her first to do so since 1983. Foster wrote the music with Jim Vallance, who was also Bryan Adams' songwriting partner, and Nashville's Randy Goodrum penned the lyrics.

"I think that my audience is ready for the change," Murray said. "I've been working up to it for the last couple of albums, and I don't think it's going to turn anybody off. The vocals are way up front—you can hear every word that I'm singing. If the vocals were buried and all you could hear was a bunch of noise, I can see how people might be upset. And if they are, I'm sorry. But this is what I have to do." ■

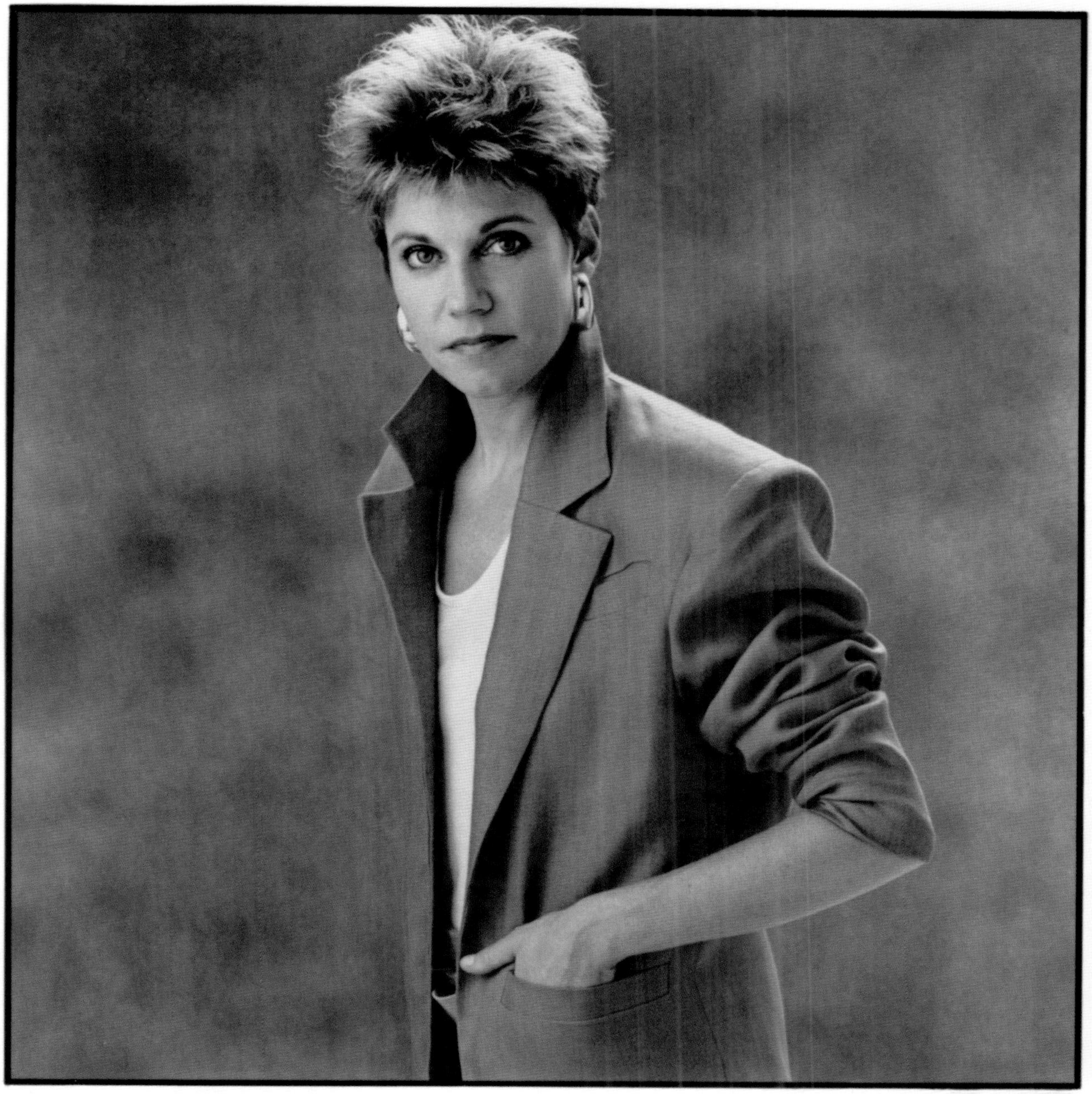

Photo: Nigel Dixon, Toronto / 1986

Anne Murray

Capitol Records

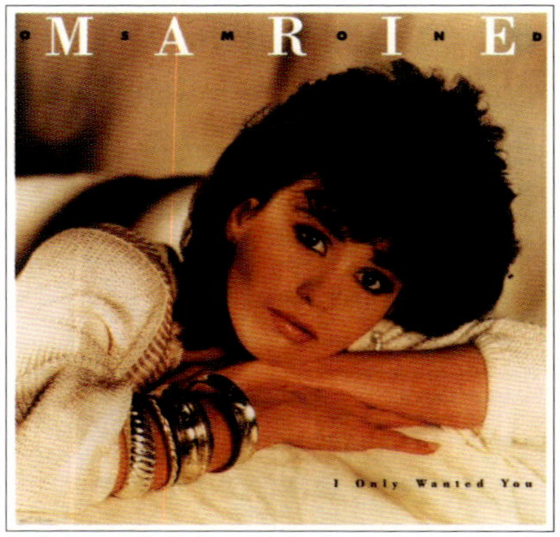

After a number of years away from recording, Marie Osmond charmed the surprised country music community.

ALL AMERICA remembered Marie Osmond, one of America's most popular entertainers since she was three years old, appearing before millions on television's *The Andy Williams Show*. She toured with the Osmonds, her famous siblings. And at the tender age of 13 she recorded "Paper Roses," arranged and produced by country great Sonny James. The single went gold, and country audiences loved her.

Two years later, she and her older brother Donny had their own weekly television variety show. For four seasons, *Donny & Marie* was a primetime hit, and she became a role model for many teenage girls.

"I grew up on national TV," Osmond said. "It may have seemed glamorous, but it's a lot of work—and to have to grow up at the same time is challenging and difficult. There was a lot of criticism, and people can say things that hurt. I learned to brush it off when they'd say I was 'goody-goody' (for her Mormon faith). If that means I'm happy, then fine. I'm the one who has to look in the mirror and like what I see."

After the series, Osmond began delving into dramatic acting in television movies-of-the-week. Yet she wanted to pursue a return to country music. "Musically, I've always been a little bit country. On the *Donny & Marie* show, I was the country entity. When Donny went more progressive, that's when we stopped recording together.

Now a divorced mother of a three-year-old, she sang about real love and hurting. Contemporary country was a difficult sound to dissect, but Osmond emphasized mainstream textures appealing to a broader audience.

"There are many different styles of country—just like rock goes from the Stones to Lionel Richie. I'm not traditional country like a Tammy Wynette. I can't go in that direction and have credibility—it'd be like Loretta Lynn singing 'In-A-Gadda-Da-Vida.' I won't try to be what I'm not."

In 1985, Osmond's *There's No Stopping Your Heart* and her duet with Dan Seals on "Meet Me in Montana" both went to No. 1 on the country charts. She then recorded *I Only Wanted You* and reached No. 1 with "You're Still New to Me," a duet with Paul Davis.

"This time, having success is different," Osmond said. "When you're young, you're not always qualified to make your own decisions. For the most part, you do what you're told. But now I have the opportunity to pick the songs and do them the way I want. I feel like the last 23 years in show business has been one growing experience—rubbing shoulders with great people and learning about myself—and taking all that information and absorbing it. And now, it's 'Let's go for it!'" ■

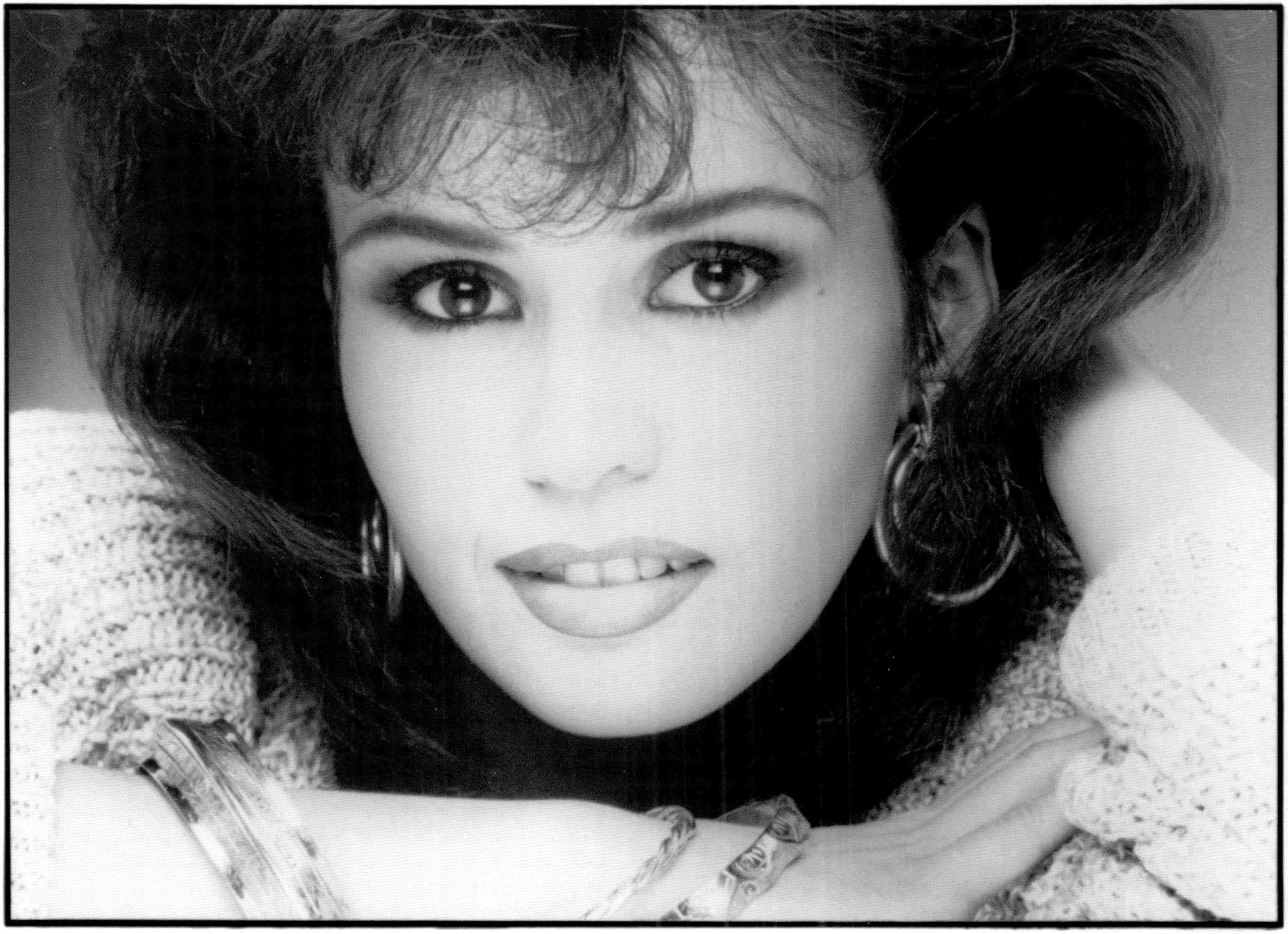

Photo: Charles Bush / 1986

O·M·S·A·M·R·O·I·N·E·D

(MARIE OSMOND)

Capitol RECORDS

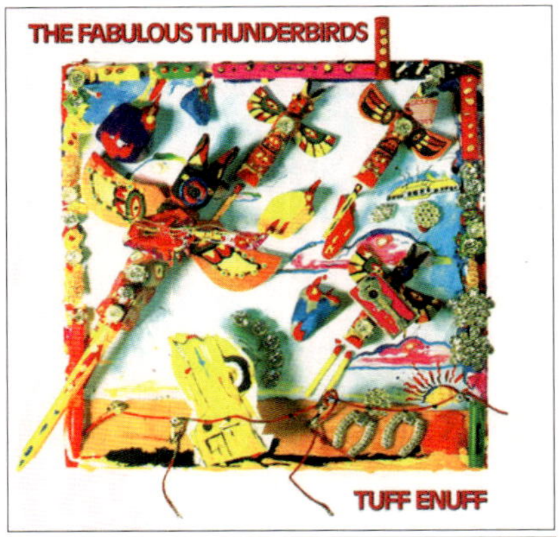

Billboard 200: *Tuff Enuff* (#13)
Billboard Hot 100: "Tuff Enuff" (#10); "Wrap It Up" (#50)

The Fabulous Thunderbirds hit the charts with *Tuff Enuff*, a celebration of American blues, R&B and rock 'n' roll.

SINGER AND harmonica player Kim Wilson and guitarist Jimmie Vaughan founded the Fabulous Thunderbirds in Austin, Texas, in 1974. As the house band at Antone's, the city's premier blues club, the T-Birds sharpened their own sound while backing and jamming with many of the music's true greats—Muddy Waters, Jimmy Rogers, Jimmy Reed, Eddie Taylor, Buddy Guy and Albert Collins.

By 1979, the T-Birds had recorded their first in a series of well-received albums. The band then signed to a new label and released *Tuff Enuff*, a commercial breakthrough produced by Dave Edmunds. The title single shot into the Top 10, and Wilson had figured out some tricks.

"In my limited estimation—I've got a string of one—you need something with a hook that the milkman's going to be singing on his route. And there's a certain beat that has worked ever since Jimmy Reed made records, a kind of soul beat. The Stax stuff and James Brown had it. And 'Tuff Enuff' definitely has it. There are different variations, but every hit record you hear has that beat."

"Tuff Enuff" was featured in the soundtracks of the films *Gung Ho* and *Tough Guys*. A spirited cover of the Sam & Dave scorcher "Wrap It Up" enjoyed notoriety, and the instrumental "Down at Antone's" was nominated for a Grammy award. Wilson noted no pressure to repeat that success. "We've always had pressure just to survive, to pay the bills," he said. "This kind of pressure really isn't much compared to that. It's such a great feeling to broaden the Thunderbirds audience to a point where we can't play those small places anymore."

The band toured with Stevie Ray Vaughan, brother of Jimmie. Wilson encountered no problems making the jump from smoky nightclubs to arenas. "You can still turn a big hall into a beer joint, create a giant party atmosphere and concentrate on everybody having a good time," he insisted. "You know, have a guy out there selling ribs or something." ■

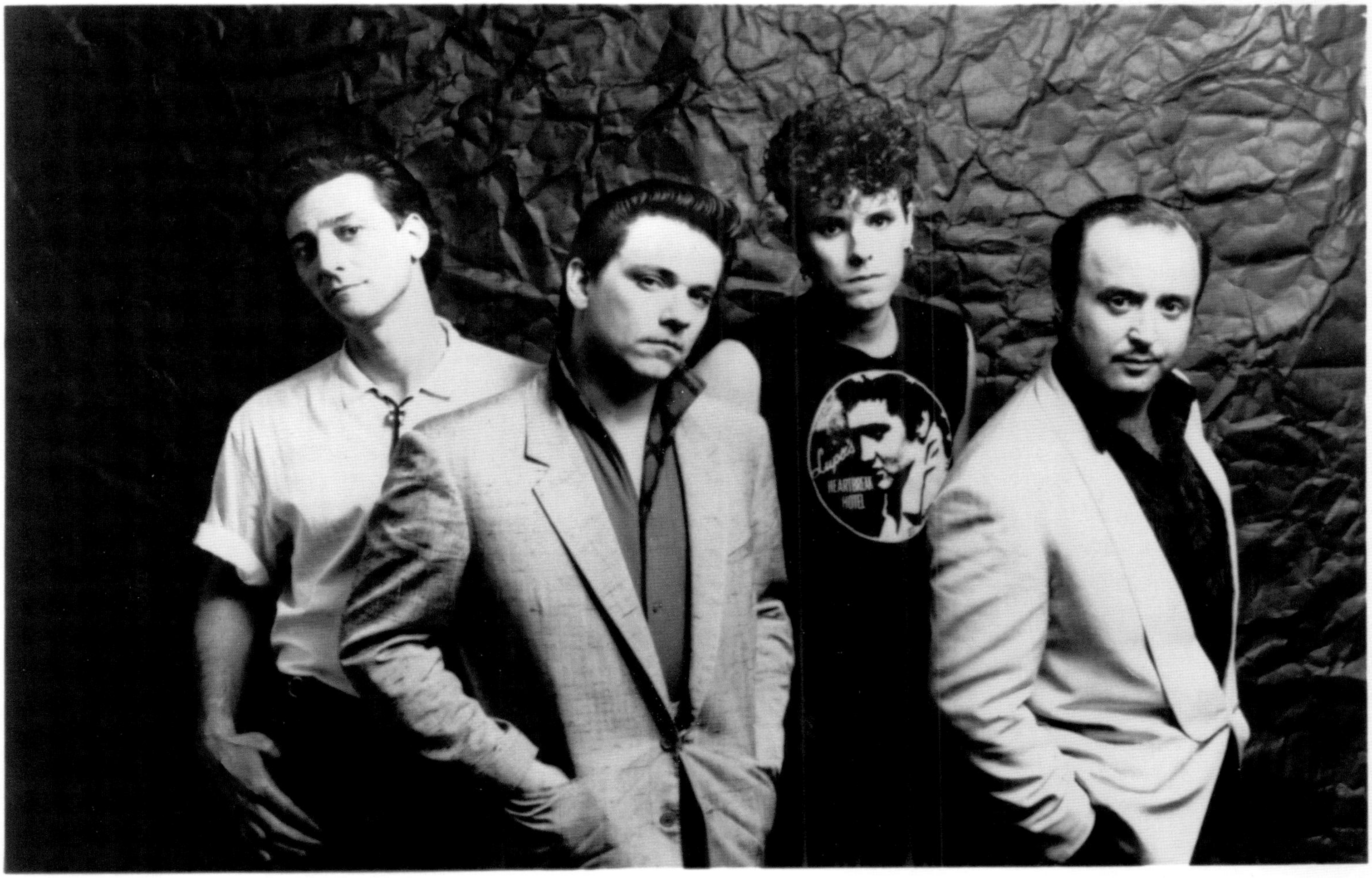

Fran Christina   Jimmie Vaughan   Preston Hubbard   Kim Wilson

THE FABULOUS THUNDERBIRDS

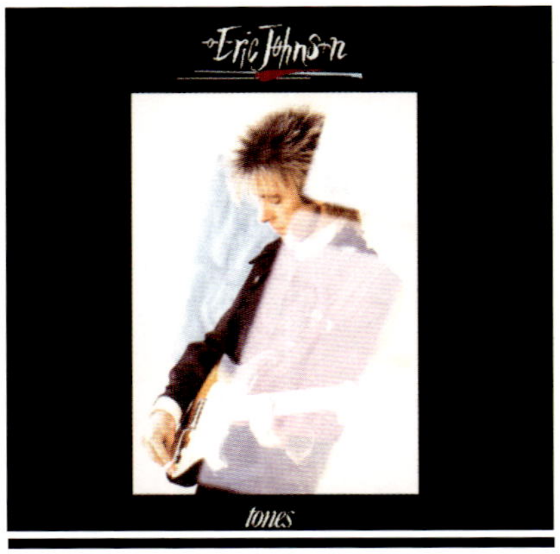

Tones, Eric Johnson's debut solo album, showcased the electric guitar great's expressive array of sweet chops.

CARRYING AROUND the reputation of "guitar virtuoso" could be a burden, and Eric Johnson was the latest to feel the weight. The hype generated by his record company was quick to place him in such rarified company as Jimi Hendrix, Django Reinhardt and Johnny Winter. And since Johnson hailed from Austin, Texas, he was already fighting comparisons with another good-ol'-boy guitar virtuoso, Stevie Ray Vaughan.

Johnson had heard enough. "There are so many guitarists, it's really difficult to say, 'This guy's a good player, this guy's a bad player,'" the soft-spoken Johnson said. "My only goal is to be as well-rounded as possible."

Such sentiments were in evidence on Johnson's debut album, *Tones*. The showcase confused some listeners with its eclecticism. While Johnson tossed off the expected lightning-fast fretting on the instrumental "Zap" (which was nominated for Best Rock Instrumental Performance at the Grammy Awards), he also tackled the Windham Hill-like moodiness of "Desert Song" and the pop arrangement of "Bristol Shore."

"There are parts of the record that don't spell out 'hot licks' verbatim," he said. "I tried to have some subtle, textured stuff as well as some hot playing. I'm not a Stevie Wonder vocalist, and I imagine there are a lot of songwriters better at writing hit songs. So I have to rely on my strength, which is playing in a wide range of styles."

Johnson established his reputation by performing on various sessions (records by Carole King and Cat Stevens), but he had always intended to lead his own band and create his own music. Yet the outlet and opportunity for such freedom weren't easy to come by. While Vaughan was exploding onto the national scene, Johnson was stifled back in Austin due to a contractual obligation with Bill Ham, the manager who had guided ZZ Top to superstar status.

"Trying to play in a lot of different styles is a musical attribute, but it's also a marketing nightmare," he explained. "I was in a business situation where people, me included, spent too much time speculating on what to do and what not to do, instead of taking action. It was like sitting at the dinner table too long and the food wound up burning in the oven."

Tones finally spread the word about Johnson's talent, but the very eclectic nature of his album kept him from reaching a mass audience. He vowed to maintain his wide-ranging approach as much as his situation allowed.

"I strive to attain that goal, but unfortunately, that isn't the most commercially viable attitude," he said. "So you run into challenges and obstacles within the pop industry. I just hope I don't have to make the musical equivalent of Hula-Hoops—and then have to jump through them." ■

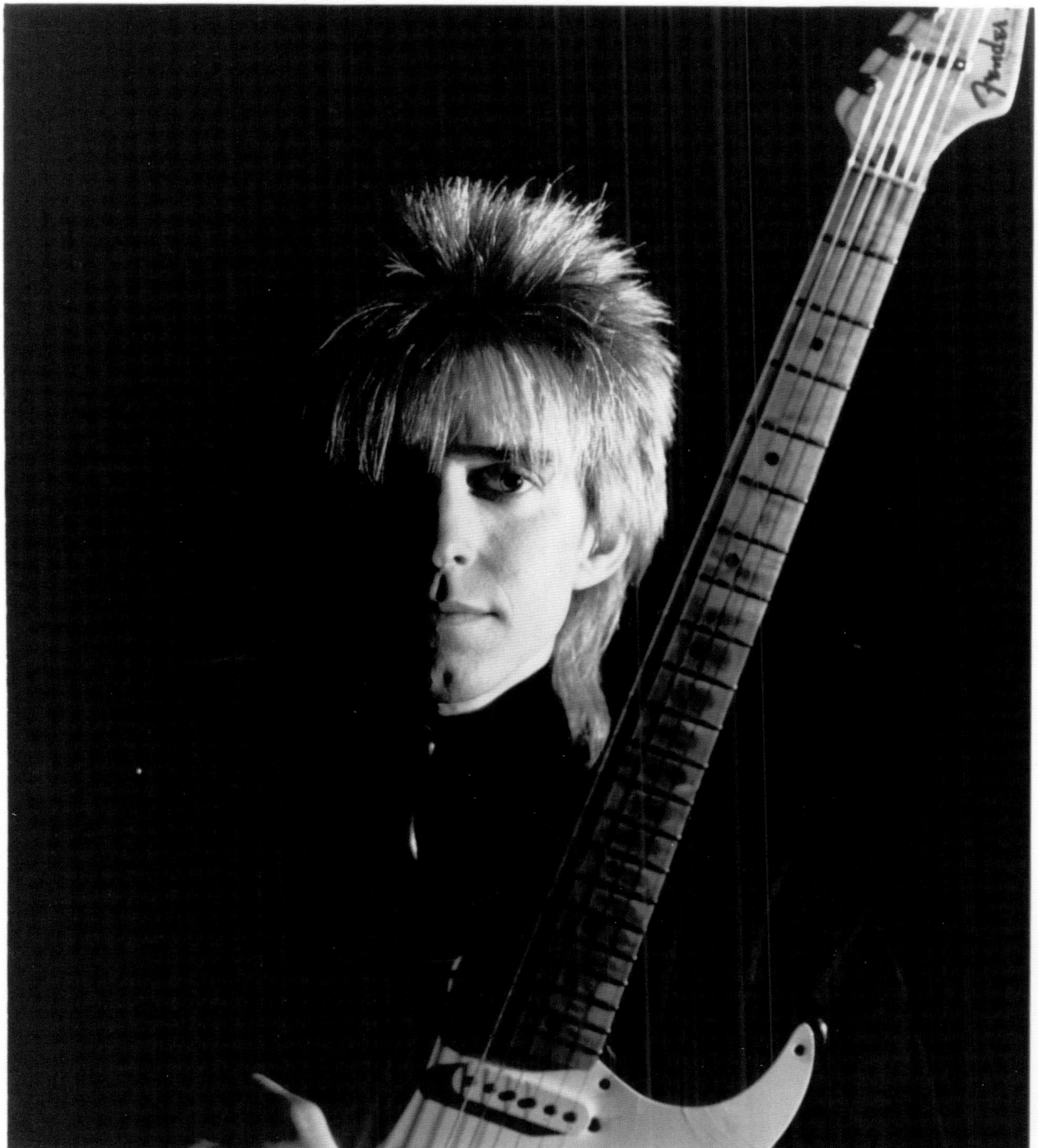

Photo Credit: Victoria Pearson

ERIC JOHNSON

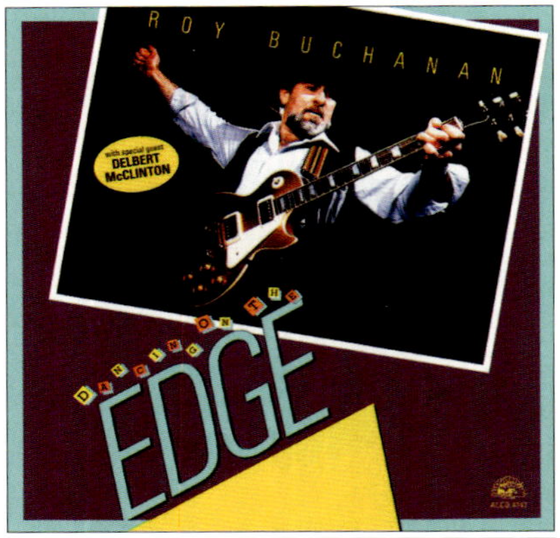

Billboard 200: *Dancing on the Edge* (#153)

Roy Buchanan's *Dancing on the Edge* featured a generous dose of his idiosyncratic and innovative guitar work.

A MASTER of the electric guitar, Roy Buchanan's controlled use of harmonics continued to influence musicians from Jeff Beck to ZZ Top's Billy Gibbons.

"Back in the Fifties, I started off as a Hawaiian guitar player—or steel guitarist, same thing," he explained. "I was used to playing up in that register, so when I switched off to regular guitars, I would try to imitate the sax players."

Searing solos, shimmering harmonics and a mixture of snarls, wails and squeals marked Buchanan as a wizard of the instrument. He first used the pinch harmonic technique on a 1962 record, "Potato Peeler" by drummer Bobby Gregg & His Friends. It became apparent that he could make a big name for himself as a guitar hero in various bands (the Rolling Stones once offered him their lead guitar spot), but Buchanan had stubbornly forged a criminally overlooked solo career instead.

"I can't really get involved in other stuff—I don't have the patience for going in the studio and playing something 50,000 times over and over," he shrugged. "I like a little freedom where I can play what I want to, not be a robot."

Buchanan also subscribed to a more relaxed work ethic than most other musicians. "For 10 years I lived and worked on a farm, and about four years ago I moved into town. I just like to play with my kids, and I like to practice, too—I can't play without it. It's like the old saying—'If I miss one day of practice, I know. If I miss two days, my wife knows. If I miss three days, my audience knows.'"

The live-sounding *Dancing on the Edge* album was one of the first records to place Buchanan's howling leads in a satisfying musical context, as evidenced on such sizzling tracks as "The Chokin' Kind" and an update of Bo Diddley's "You Can't Judge a Book by the Cover." Buchanan recruited Texas rock 'n' soul singer Delbert McClinton to sing those two tunes on the record, but Buchanan took his share of turns at the microphone—a move he'd historically been reluctant to make, despite the encouragement of fans who thought his vocals would help attract a wider following.

"I've never liked to sing—I'm a guitar player, not a singer," he said. "But people keep on going 'Sing! Sing! Sing!' I realize I don't have a good voice, so I've found a little talking style. It shouldn't irritate people too much, hopefully." ■

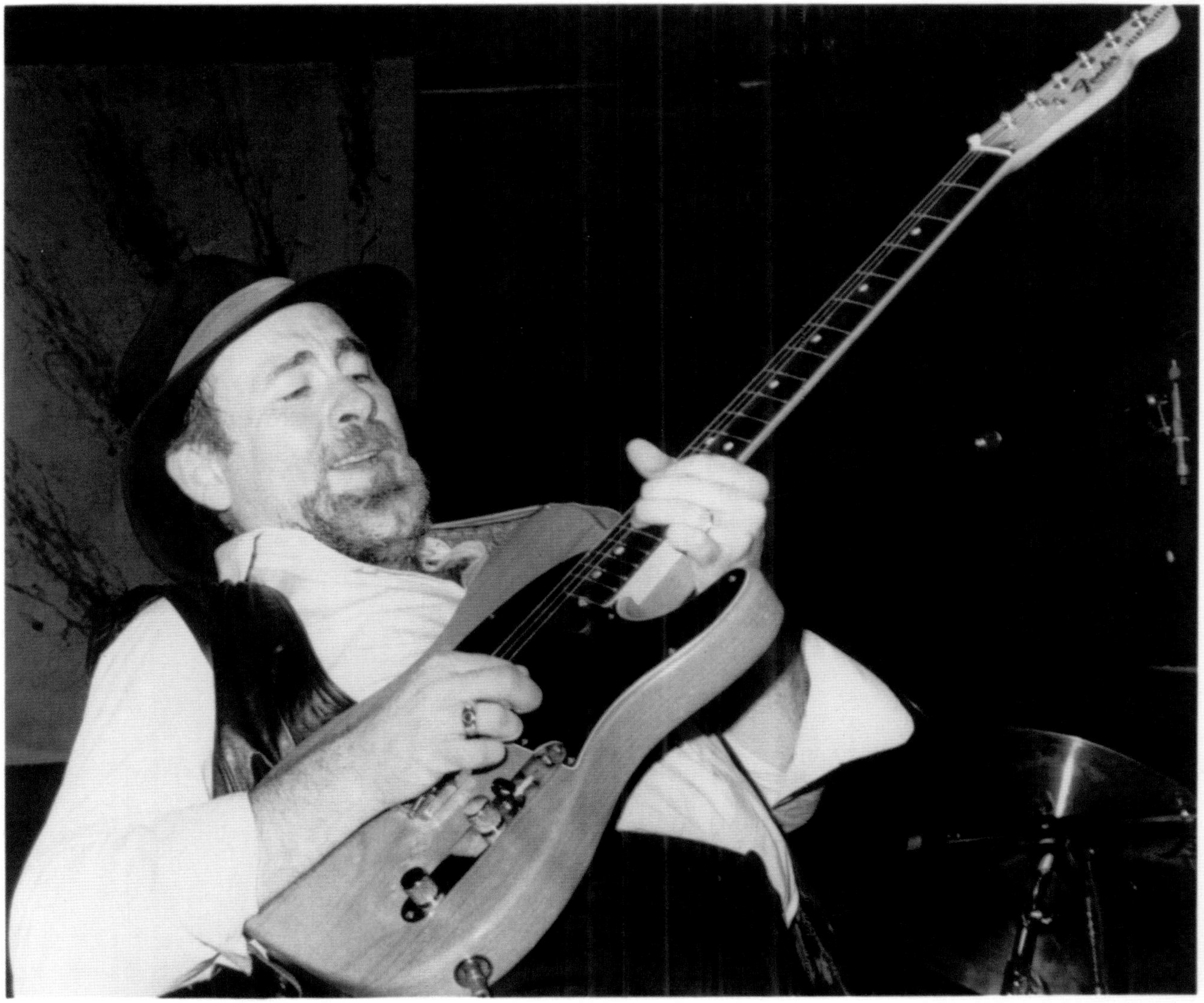

ROY BUCHANAN

Photo: Larry Kodani

Alligator Records
Box 60234
Chicago, IL 60660
(312) 973-7736

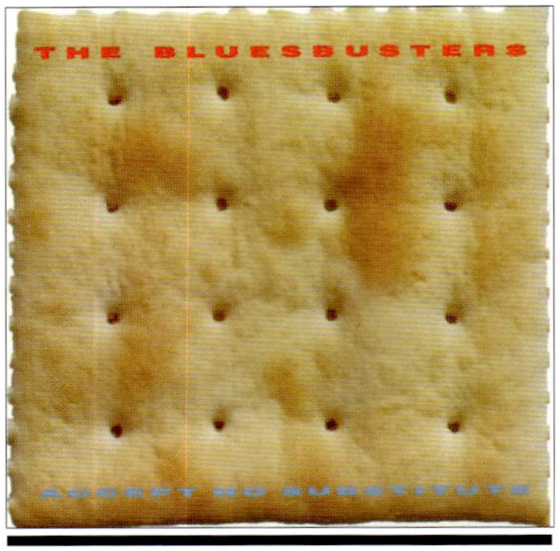

The Bluesbusters lived up to their impressive musical pedigrees on a debut recording, *Accept No Substitute*.

FIVE TALENTED players comprised the Bluesbusters. Guitarist Paul Barrere was a graduate of Little Feat, one of America's most revered groups of the Seventies. Singer Catfish Hodge had been a mainstay on the Washington, D.C. blues scene. T Lavitz once handled keyboard duties for instrumental whizzes the Dixie Dregs, while bassist Freebo accompanied Bonnie Raitt for more than 15 years. Drummer Larry Zack counted session and touring work with Jackson Browne among his credits.

Given their splendid individual backgrounds, did the Bluesbusters qualify as a new supergroup? "All you have to do is look at our bank accounts to know that's not the case," Barrere chuckled.

Barrere explained the unpretentious origins of the act. "Catfish and I basically started as a duet. We went out in July of 1984 and got dubbed the Bluesbusters by a friend—the *Ghostbusters* movie was big at the time. We did it basically to get out of Los Angeles during the Olympics, because I thought it was going to be a zoo around town."

Barrere and Hodge rediscovered the virtues of funky, good-time rock music "just by hitting honky-tonks and setting up our own gear." During their East Coast tour, Barrere divulged to Hodge that he had never been onstage without a rhythm section. So, upon their return to California, Freebo began sitting in on bass and tuba. Zack and Lavitz came aboard soon after.

Accept No Substitute, released on the independent Landslide label, spawned an underdog hit with the humorous "Phone Don't Ring." In light of the commercial success of the Fabulous Thunderbirds and Stevie Ray Vaughan, Barrere sensed a resurgence in the Bluesbusters' no-frills style.

"When Little Feat disbanded, I did two solo albums that went nowhere," he allowed. "That's why it's nice to be in this band, to be able to play in the Little Feat vein with fresh people and fresh ideas. Now I'm getting a lot of the same sensations onstage that I did back with Little Feat. You know—good feelings, feeling good." ■

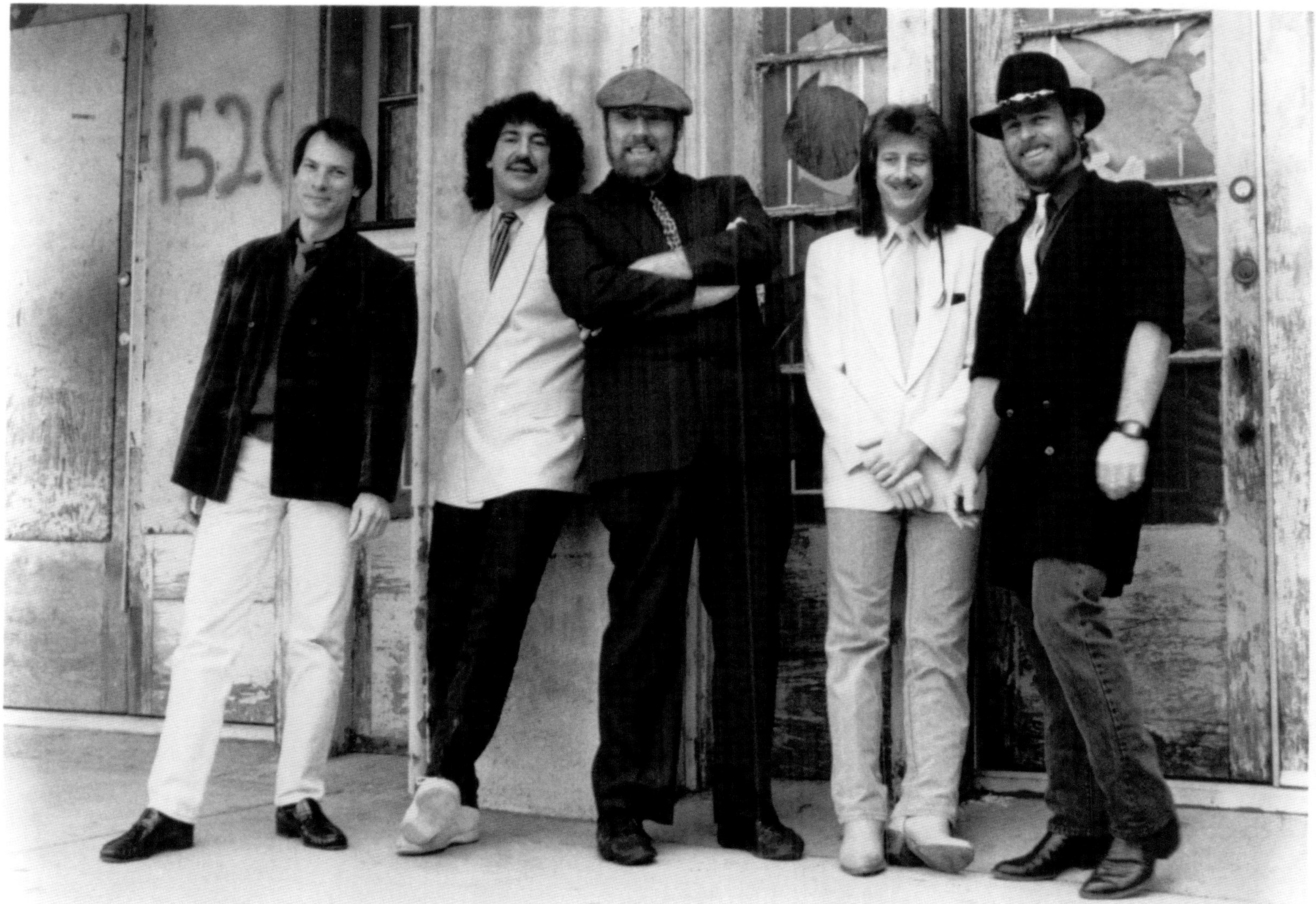

THE BLUESBUSTERS

LARRY ZACK FREEBO CATFISH HODGE T LAVITZ PAUL BARRERE

LANDSLIDE RECORDS

450 14th ST. N.W. SUITE 201 ATLANTA, GA. 30318 (404) 873-3918

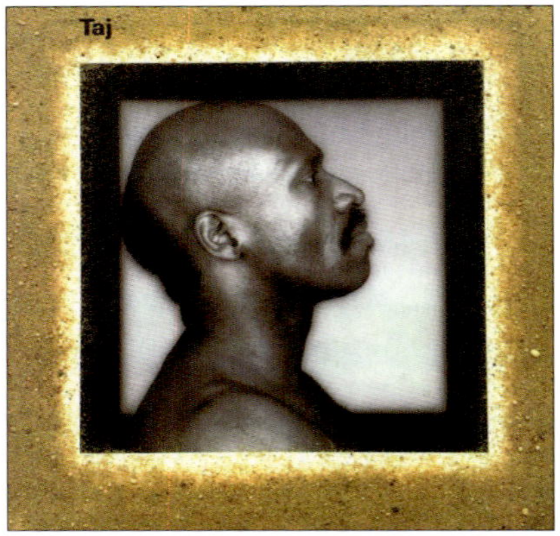

Immersing himself in the diverse roots of Hawaiian music, Taj Mahal returned with the highly acclaimed *Taj*.

VETERAN MUSICIAN Taj Mahal emerged during the mid-Sixties as a self-taught blues interpreter in the tradition of Sleepy John Estes. He formed the Rising Sons in Los Angeles (a band that boasted a young Ry Cooder) and continued to augment his natural ability on various instruments (including mandolin, banjo, bass, fife, piano and steel guitar) with his scholarly mind.

But his career as a "musicologist" hadn't fit the usual categories. "I've been involved in all sorts of musics and cultures, and it's been a long and winding road," the upbeat singer noted. "What pissed me off was that these corporate guys from major record labels treat my music like they're doing blues a favor—or doing anyone doing anything different a favor. And I don't particularly like that attitude."

The attendant lack of exposure wore him down at one point. And Mahal's recording career ground to a halt in the late Seventies.

"But I didn't want to feel bad about what I'd done—'Gee, they don't like me anymore, I guess I'm not worth anything.' I figured that was bullshit. I play music, and music isn't only when it's on the air or the big companies are making money off it. Music *is*. So, I went to places where people really hear music, where there's no Top 40—Africa, Europe, Australia. And that helped me feel better about what was going on. I took a little time off then and learned more about the business and recording technology."

In America, Mahal still fought the image of an old blues singer. "Why isn't Eric Clapton or Mick Jagger called a bluesologist then?" he wondered. "That's what those guys were doing, too—listening to old records and trying to make their music sound just like that."

Mahal felt more accurately represented on *Taj*, his first album in eight years. The record featured a variety of South Pacific musical influences, but Mahal maintained that the sound had nothing to do with his Hawaiian surroundings of the past five years (he made his home on Kaua'i).

"I've been into the Pacific music for a long time," he insisted. "Chuck Berry did 'Blues for Hawaiians' on his (1959) *Chuck Berry Is on Top* album—Chuck was playing slide on a lap steel guitar! When I was growing up, there was always a ukulele player on *The Ted Mack Amateur Hour*. And Arthur Godfrey was the big pusher of the ukulele back then—a Hawaiian lady woulc come out on his show to do the hula, wigglin' it around. It looked good to me! We forget about that stuff." ■

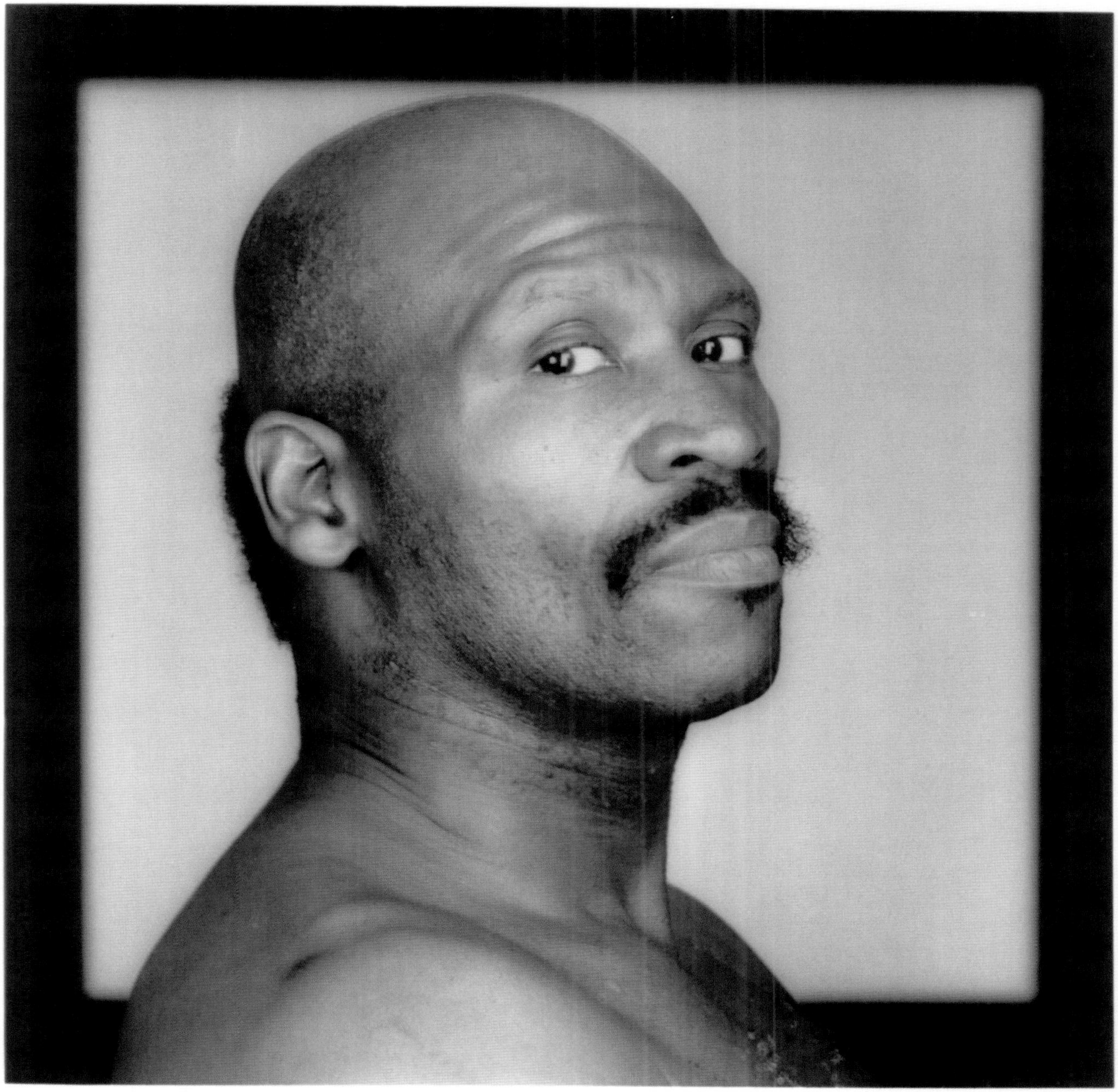

Taj Mahal

Gramavision Records
260 West Broadway
New York, New York 10013
212/226-7057

Photo: Robert Mapplethorpe

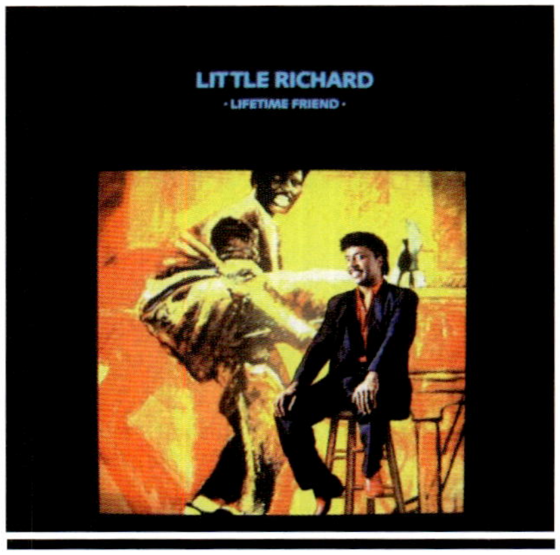

Billboard Hot 100: "Great Gosh A'Mighty" (#42)

Little Richard acted in *Down and Out in Beverly Hills* and performed the theme, "Great Gosh A'Mighty."

CERTAINLY ONE of rock 'n' roll's most colorful icons, Little Richard made showstopping appearances at awards ceremonies and television talk shows, where people dug his electrifying dazzle. But the steak was greater than the sizzle—more than three decades, earlier, his 1955 hit "Tutti Frutti" and its opening line "A-wop-bop-a-loo-bob-a-wop-bam-boom" forever changed the course of pop music.

"I am the emancipator, I am the innovator, I am the architect of rock 'n' roll!" Little Richard eagerly proclaimed when asked how history should view him. "A lot of people don't want to give it to me, but that's what it is. I never got what I should have got. But I thank God that I got what I got. It's better late than never."

Richard Wayne Penniman was steeped in gospel music while growing up in Macon, Georgia—"I sang so high, it was real hard for the church choir to sing with me!" He began to play the piano, and he also took note of R&B and boogie-woogie swing music popular with audiences of the era. He won a talent contest, but early recordings didn't receive notice. Then, in 1955, while he was washing dishes in a Greyhound bus station, Lloyd Price ("Lawdy Miss Clawdy") came through his hometown.

"He told Specialty Records about me. I took them a tape. They had me come to New Orleans and meet (producer) 'Bumps' Blackwell," Richard said. "I had a song I had been doing for a long time." As Little Richard, he recorded a slightly obscene ditty with slightly cleaned-up lyrics ("Tutti frutti, oh rooty" in place of "Tutti frutti, good booty").

In a remarkable three-year period, he registered the manic blasts that prescribed the fundamentally hedonistic, anarchic nature of the rock 'n' roll phenomenon—"Long Tall Sally," "Rip It Up," "Lucille," "Jenny, Jenny," "Keep A-Knockin'," "Good Golly, Miss Molly" and "Ooh! My Soul!" rolled out his pounding piano style, hoarse gospel-influenced screams and hollers, and ecstatic, trilling "wooo!"s in his giddy falsetto.

And Little Richard was a sight to behold, decked out in dazzling baggy suits, brandishing a processed sky-high pompadour, mascaraed eyes and facial makeup. For the time, it was more than a little threatening. "It was horrible," he said of the fear that his flamboyance inspired. "But God brought me through it."

At the height of his popularity, he suddenly quit show business to learn about the Pentecostal ministry and disappeared from the rock scene. Little Richard returned to rock 'n' roll performances several years later, and over time he swung back and forth between the church and his musical career.

He nearly scored a comeback hit in 1986 with "Great Gosh A'Mighty! (It's a Matter of Time)," the theme song from *Down and Out in Beverly Hills*. He "acted" in the film ("I just always be me!"), and it led to the release of the album *Lifetime Friend*, cut in England—"I call it 'message in rhythm,' because it's got good lyrics but not necessarily gospel." He hungered for an encomium as a king of rock 'n' roll. "I've never had a tribute done to me. I don't know why. Everybody knows me—omigod, I think so!" ■

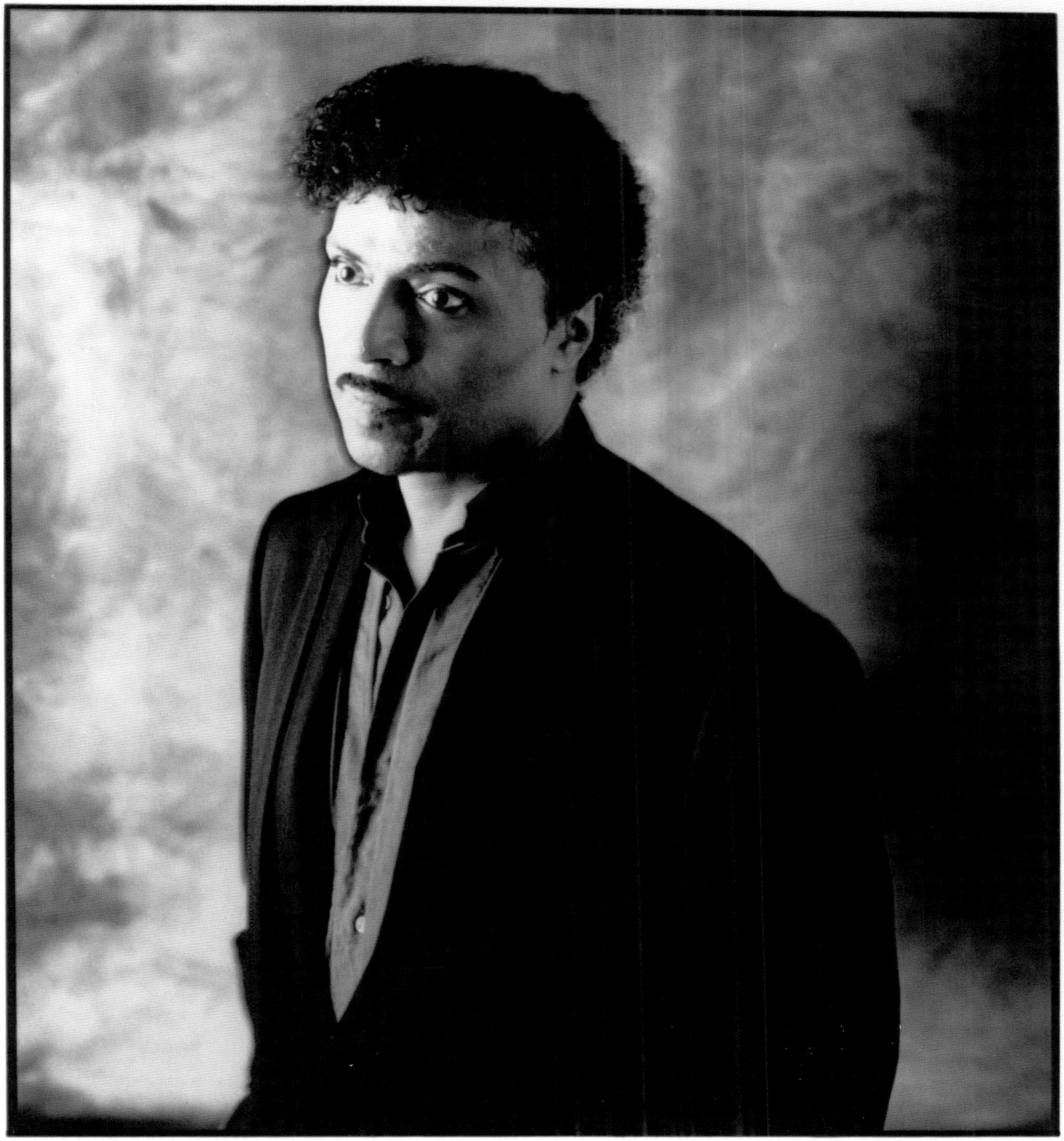

LITTLE RICHARD

WARNER BROS.

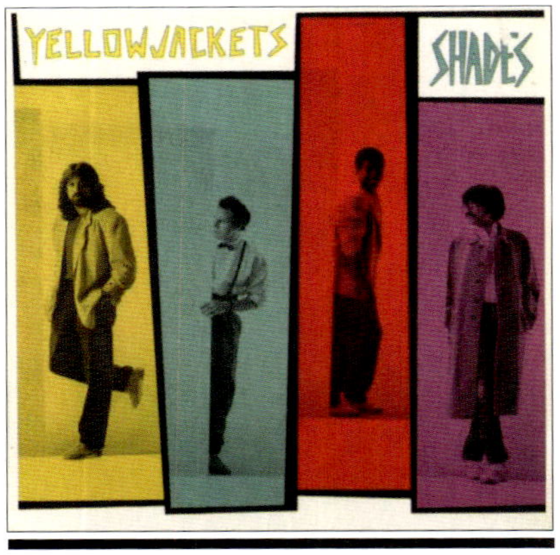

The four Yellowjackets brought together a variety of sounds under the banner of progressive instrumental music.

THE GROUP Yellowjackets still suffered from the petty is-it-jazz-or-isn't-it argument that raged between jazz purists and jazz fusion fans. The former camp wouldn't even acknowledge a contemporary instrumental act with a name like Yellowjackets. Yet the band members openly scorned the fusion tag.

"We avoid it because we feel we're playing jazz," bassist Jimmy Haslip insisted. "Our form includes a lot of jazz roots and improvisation. Music is always influenced by the times. Bands like us and Weather Report, Chick Corea, Steps Ahead—because we're playing high-tech electric instruments and stretching the boundaries of what preceded us, people say we're not playing jazz. That's not an open-minded opinion."

There was certainly no doubting the instrumental skills of Yellowjackets. The group of session players was initially assembled in the late Seventies by Robben Ford, who left after two albums to pursue a solo career. But the remaining members—Haslip, drummer Rickey Lawson and keyboardist Russell Ferrante—replaced Ford's signature guitar with the powerful sax of Marc Russo, an ex-Tower of Power horn player who sounded like he'd been taking soul steroids.

Shades was the latest Yellowjackets album, and the track "And You Know That" won the Grammy Award for Best R&B instrumental. But movie soundtrack work loomed—the band contributed two tracks to the film *Star Trek IV: The Voyage Home.*

"It's hard making a living just touring and recording as a jazz group, so we've gotta find some other avenues to promote our music," Haslip said. "Film seems to be a shoo-in because the boundaries are stretched a bit. You don't have to compete too much with the pop world when you're writing for film, you just have to conjure emotion—and we're really good at that stuff." ■

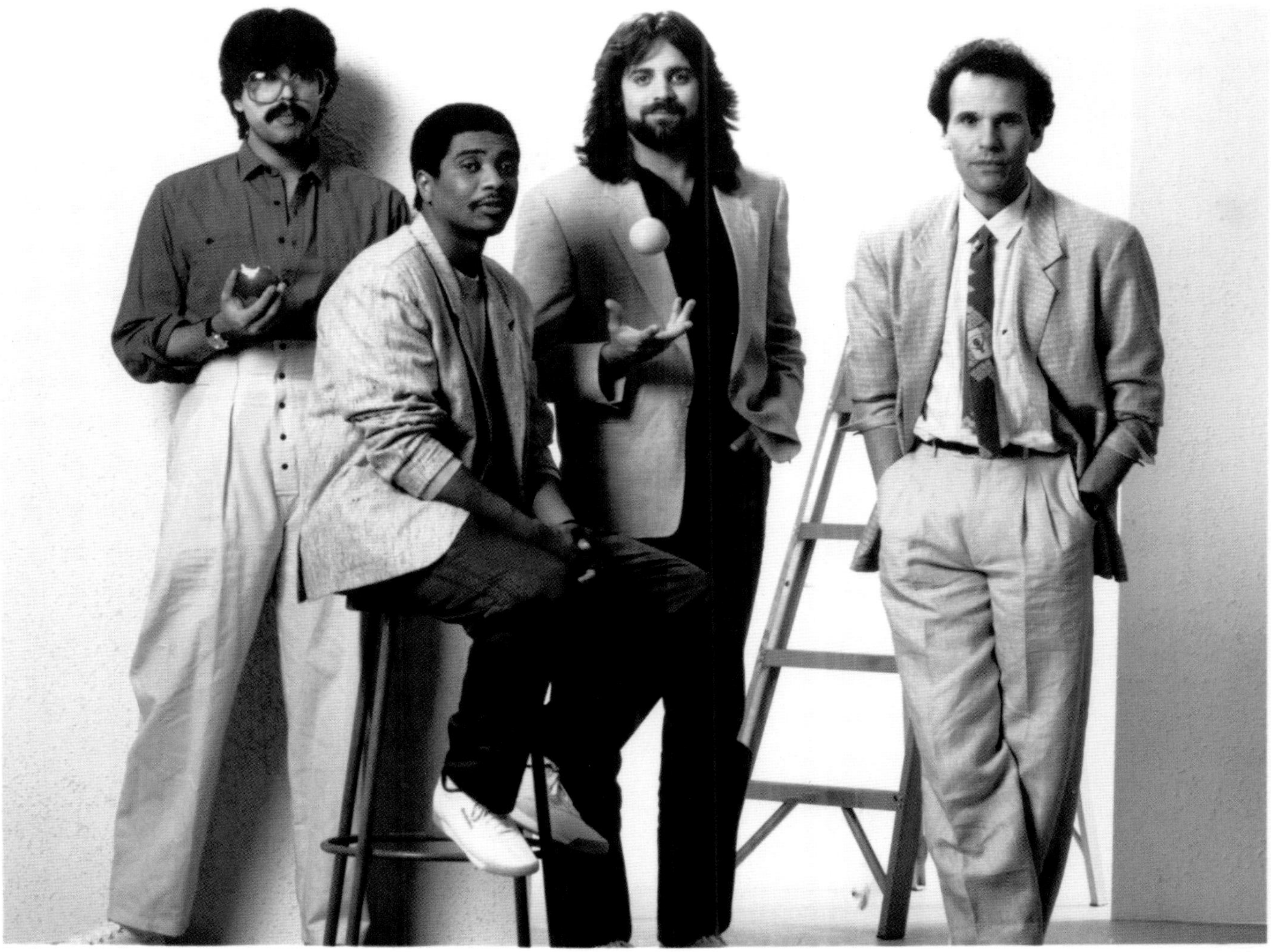

KRAGEN AND COMPANY
(213) 854-4400

YELLOWJACKETS

MCA RECORDS

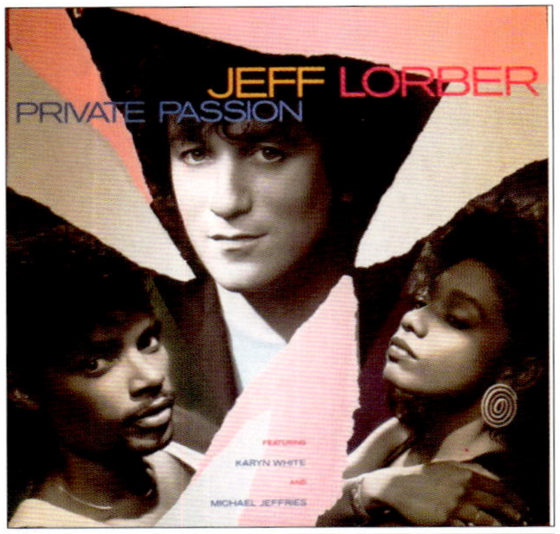

Billboard 200: *Private Passion* (#68)
Billboard Hot 100: "Facts of Love" (#27)

Probing crossover jazz, Jeff Lorber arrived at his commercial peak with "Facts of Love," vocalized by Karyn White.

IN THE late Seventies and early Eighties, Jeff Lorber established himself as an innovator in jazz fusion, issuing albums with his group, the Jeff Lorber Fusion. But the keyboardist had shifted his focus to rhythm & blues—*Private Passion* showcased a variety of vocalists and allowed Lorber to explore the sounds of urban contemporary pop. "I wanted to reach more people, because that makes music more fun," Lorber said. "So I got involved with singers and made records that were vocal/instrumental hybrids."

Lorber had been busy on other projects. Since he moved from the Northwest to Los Angeles in 1983, he had been in constant demand to work on other people's records. His résumé included studio work with the Pointer Sisters, Barbra Streisand, Eddie Murphy, Maurice White, Jeffrey Osborne and Patti Austin, among others.

"I'm not one of those session guys who gets hired for three different sessions in a day," he explained. "My role is to cut entire tracks with drum machines and sequencers, to create skeletons for songs that can be improved upon. It allows me to have a lot of control over every element of what I'm doing. I can hear the results instantaneously, instead of having to work with an entire band."

The contacts Lorber had made on the studio circuit had turned him into a developer of new talent with the musicians who had surfaced on his records. The title track of 1985's *Step by Step* album, a hit dance and R&B single, launched the career of singer Audrey Wheeler, and "One Step Closer to You" did the same thing for the voice of Gavin Christopher.

On *Private Passion*, "Facts of Love" featured his latest discovery, Karyn White, singing the lead vocal and other vocal cuts featured Tower of Power member Michael Jeffries. They both went on to record their own albums. And Kenny G, who was cracking the Top 40 with "Songbird," formerly played sax in Lorber's band. Lorber had signed him to a record label and produced his first album.

"I'd eventually like to become like Quincy Jones or Narada Michael Walden," Lorber said. "Those guys are producing artists all the time, but they're still involved in arranging, writing and playing. I enjoy all aspects of making music, and right now I'm glad that I get to work on a lot of different projects in different styles. I'm learning a lot, and I'm real grateful that I'm able to make a living as a musician. As long as I can figure out ways to pay the rent, I'm happy." ■

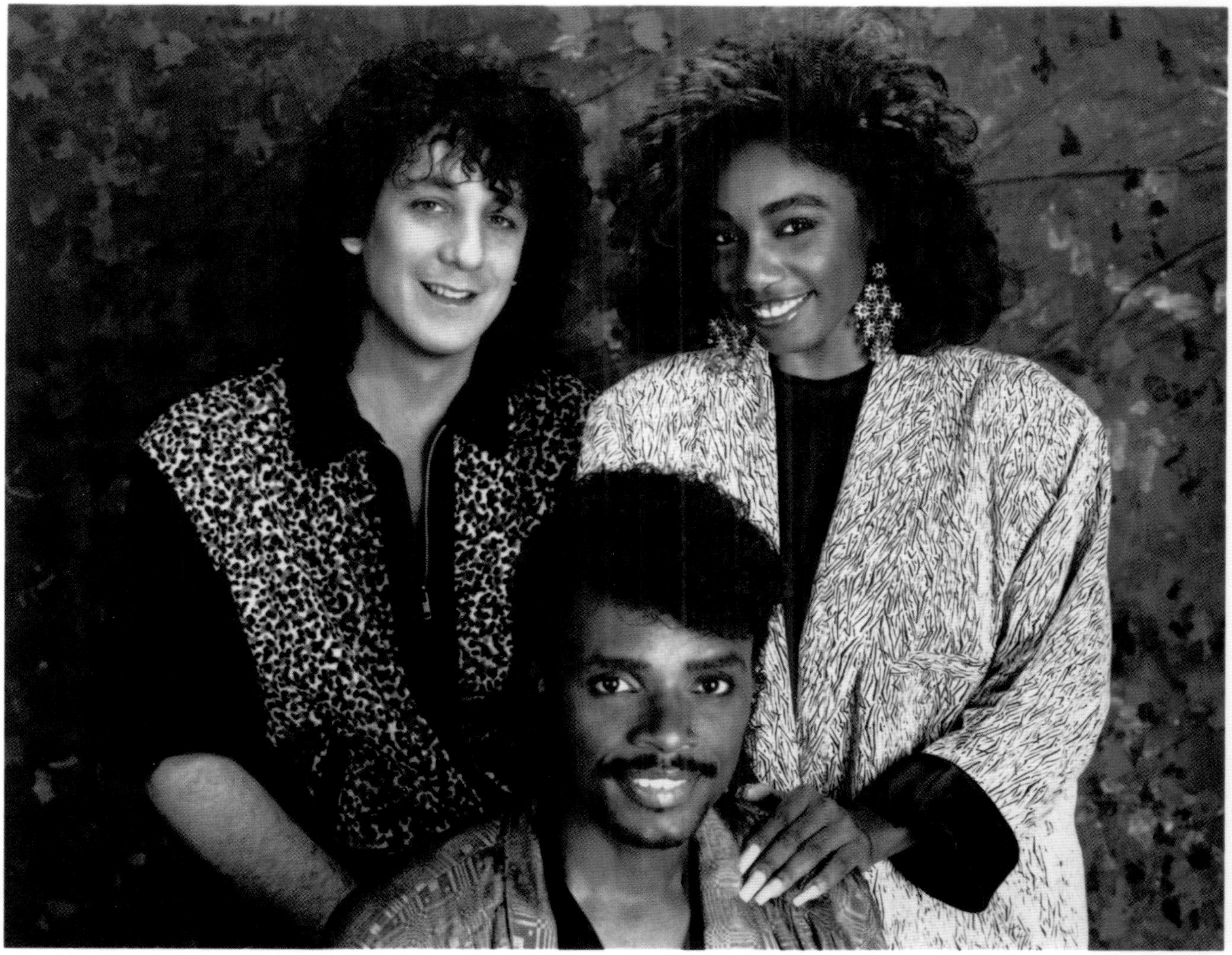

Photo Credit: Jason Dost

JEFF LORBER

FEATURING KARYN WHITE AND MICHAEL JEFFRIES

WARNER BROS.

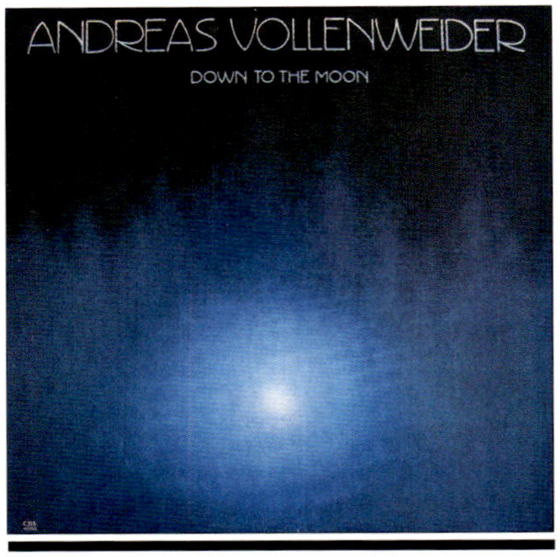

Billboard 200: *Down to the Moon* (#60)

Andreas Vollenweider's *Down to the Moon* was the first recording to win the Grammy for Best New Age Album.

SWIRLING, ATMOSPHERIC electro-acoustic harp music had made Andreas Vollenweider contemporary music's ultimate crossover artist. Riding a wave of popularity, the Swiss harpist's *Down to the Moon* album appeared on the pop, jazz and classical charts, and the accompanying "Andreas Vollenweider & Friends" tour sold out major venues.

"Any success surprises me because no one expected my music to be successful in any way," he said. "It was an experiment we originally did for ourselves just to try out new things. But we've received thousands of letters from people all over the world, personal letters reflecting dreams and hopes, about how they would like to go further to live a peaceful, worthwhile life. To us, it's clearly proved that we made the right step by just doing what we have to do and letting it go."

Vollenweider's previous three albums—*Behind the Gardens...*, *Caverna Magica* and *White Winds*—explored various fragments of fantasy. *Down to the Moon* was based on a unifying narrative, using the moon as an allegorical central image. Indeed, Vollenweider had achieved the full range of an orchestra by expanding on the natural character of his "instrument of brightness and light," liberating it from its associations with hovering angels and stuffy sentimentality.

"It's different from other harp music, because I don't know how the instrument is usually played," he said. "I've developed the technique by myself to serve what I like to do. I would play the harp upside down if it would sound better. There are much fewer limitations than we ever think. I added a damper to the harp which allows me to play more rhythmically, percussively. The amplification is a complicated, self-developed system that allows you to hear every string, clear and bright.

"But the music still has concrete reason to be the way it is, to trigger the imagination and build sensual emotions. It's just an initial description of a situation—it's up to the listener to dive into the scene and develop it. In this sense, it is functional music, not finished music—it just supports an activity by listeners. The structure of the music itself, the harmonies and melodies, are kept very simple so that you start with it and go from there."

Yet it vexed Vollenweider when his elevated mood music was lumped into the burgeoning new age category. "I cannot see any sense in the description," he sighed. "Astrologically, we're entering a new age, but I don't know anything about astrology! What counts is what takes place while the audience is listening, and I don't think anyone is thinking of new age. It should be like a journey, giving and taking together. And that's when I feel overwhelmed by this music." ■

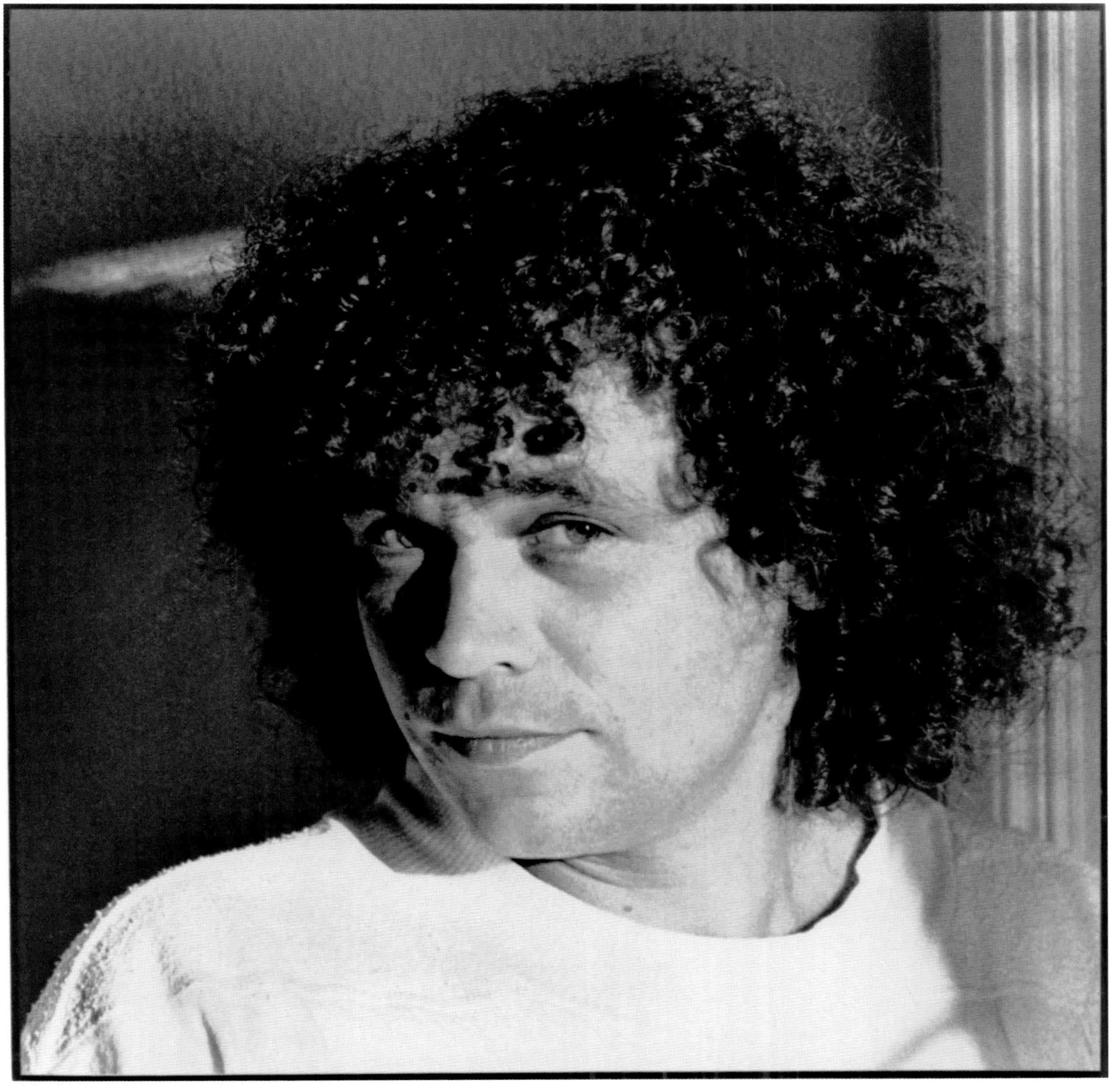

ANDREAS
VOLLENWEIDER

DOWN TO THE MOON

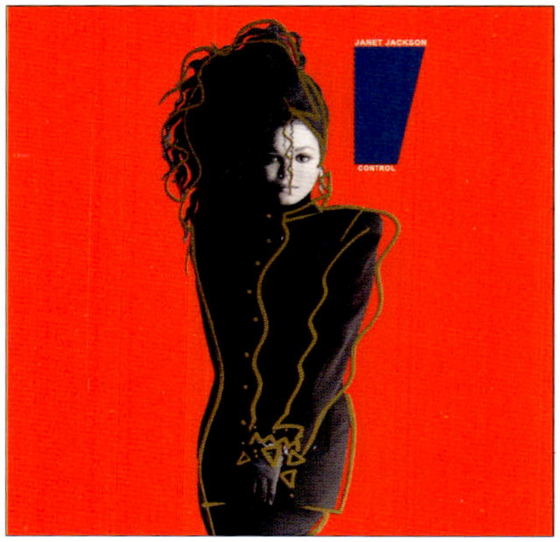

Fashioning the funky, sexy *Control*, which shot to No. 1 on the album charts and spun off five Top 5 hits, **Janet Jackson** attained predicted pop stardom.

Billboard 200: *Control* (No. 1)
Billboard Hot 100: "What Have You Done for Me Lately" (#4); "Nasty" (#3); "When I Think of You" (No. 1); "Control" (#5); "Let's Wait Awhile (#2); "The Pleasure Principle" (#14)

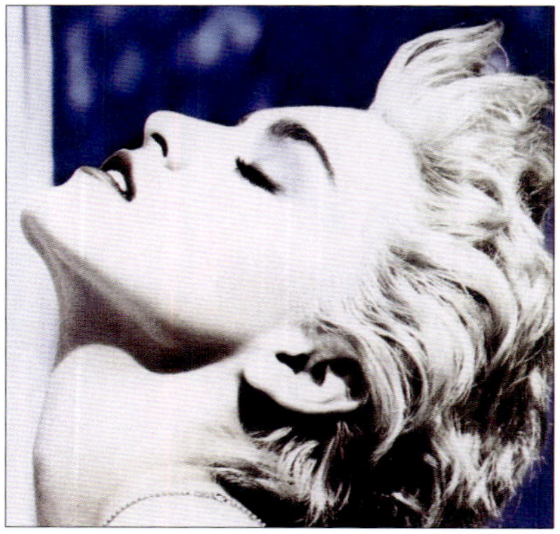

Five smash hits from **Madonna**'s third album, the best-selling *True Blue*, all reached No. 1 on either the *Billboard* Hot 100 in the US or the UK singles charts.

Billboard 200: *True Blue* (No. 1)
Billboard Hot 100: "Live to Tell" (No. 1); "Papa Don't Preach" (No. 1); "True Blue" (#3); "Open Your Heart" (No. 1); "La Isla Bonita" (#4)

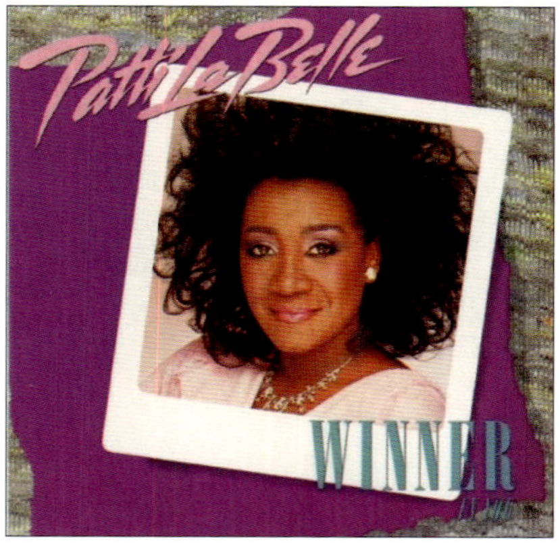

Soul diva **Patti LaBelle** scored with *Winner in You* and "On My Own," a duet with Michael McDonald, both of which got to No. 1 on pop and R&B charts.

Billboard 200: *Winner in You* (No. 1)
Billboard Hot 100: "On My Own" (No. 1); "Oh, People" (#29)

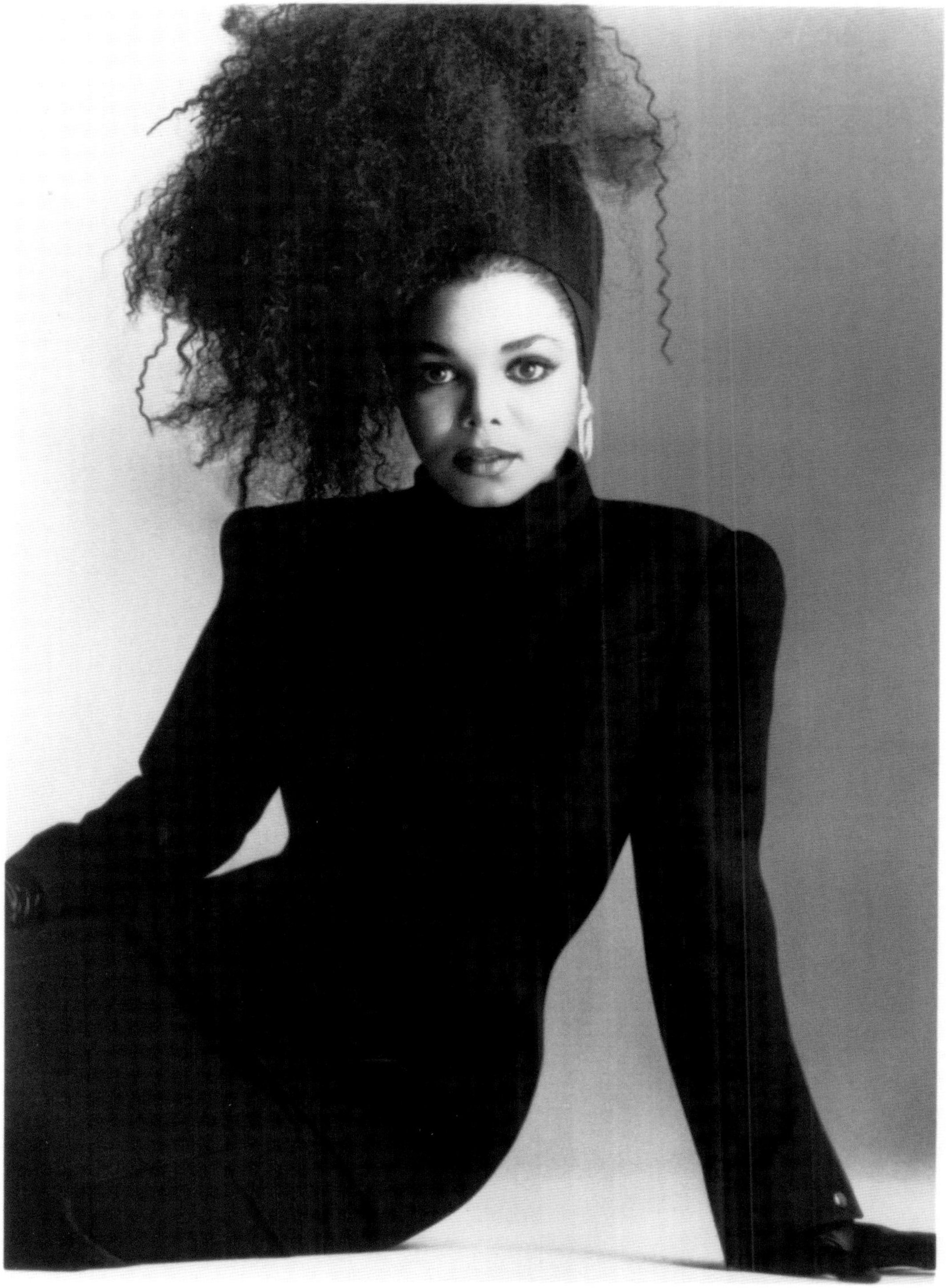

JANET JACKSON

A&M RECORDS
Printed in U.S.A.

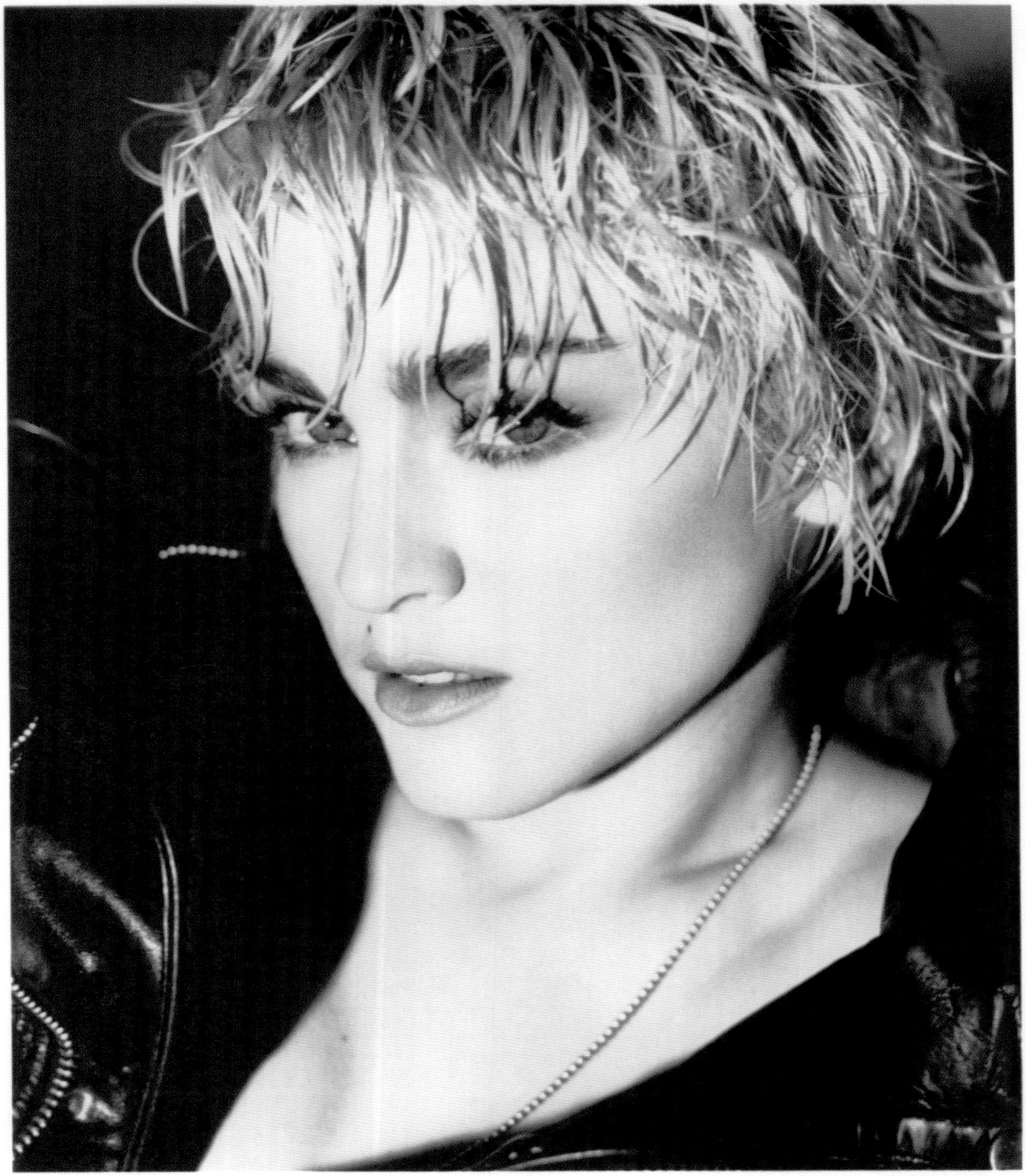

Photo Credit: Herb Ritz

MADONNA

SIRE™

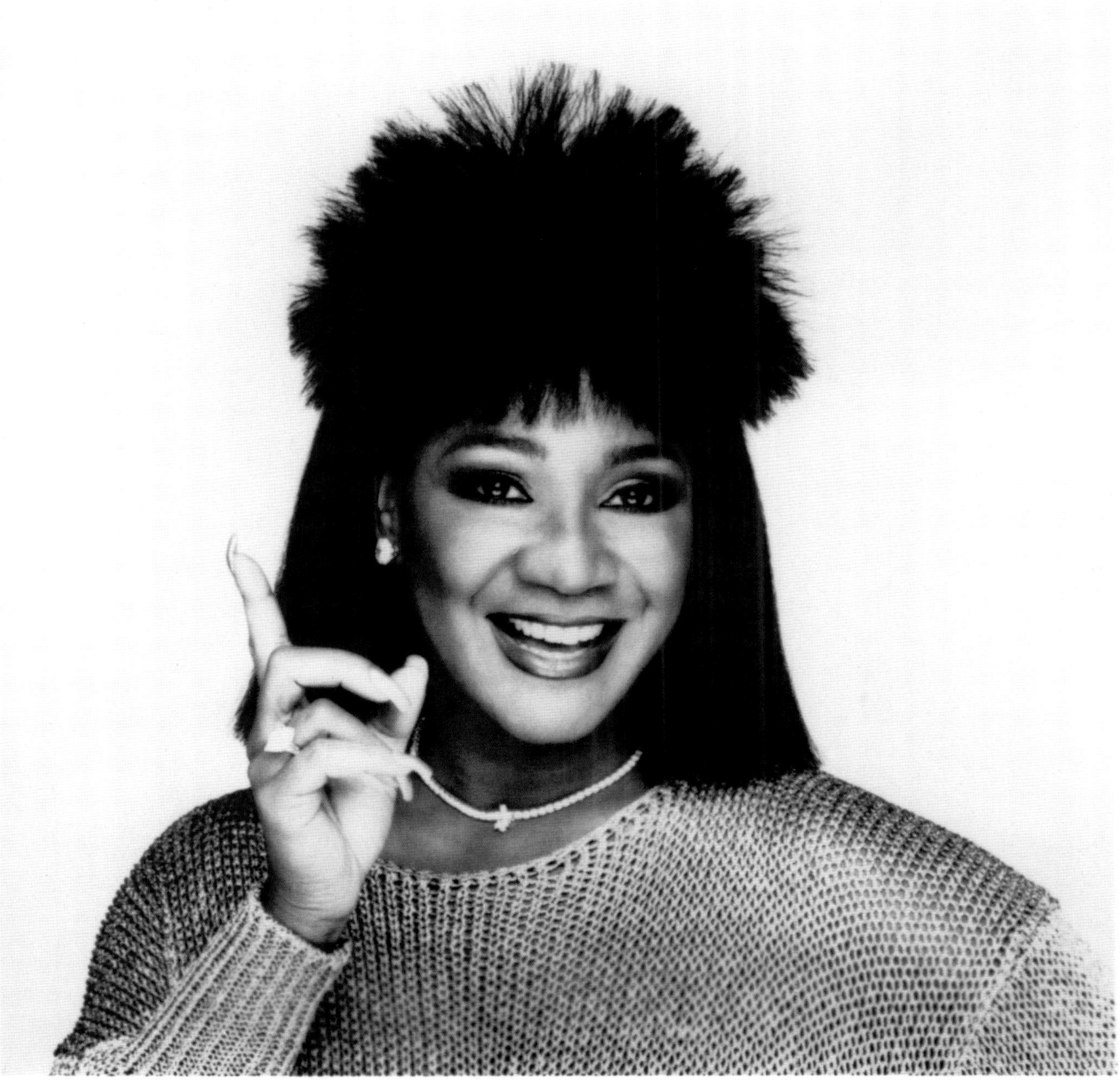

Patti LaBelle

MCA RECORDS

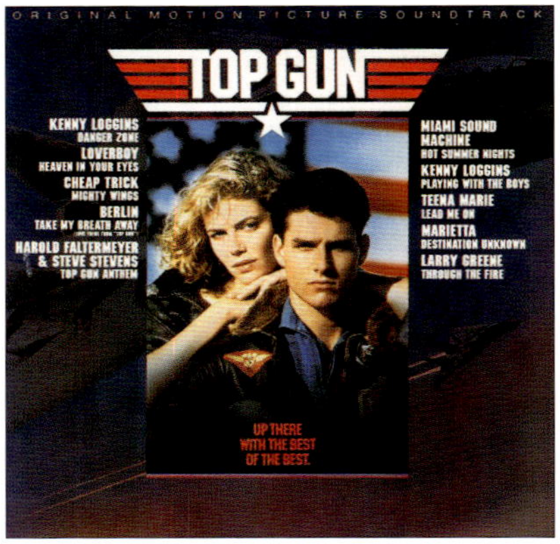

On the best-selling soundtrack to *Top Gun*, **Kenny Loggins** fired up "Danger Zone," and "You Take My Breath Away" sent Berlin to international acclaim.

Billboard 200: *Top Gun* (No. 1)
Billboard Hot 100: "Danger Zone" (#2); "Take My Breath Away" (No. 1); "Heaven in Your Eyes" (#12); "Playing with the Boys" (#60)

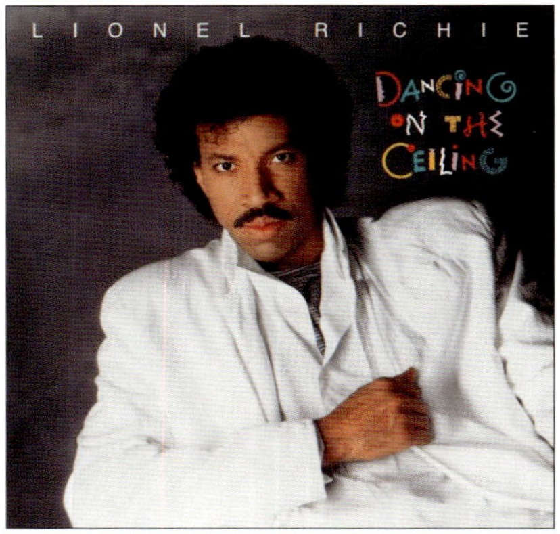

One of pop music's hot commodities, **Lionel Richie** issued *Dancing on the Ceiling*, an immensely popular album that boasted a run of five smash singles.

Billboard 200: *Dancing on the Ceiling* (No. 1)
Billboard Hot 100: "Say You, Say Me" (No. 1); "Dancing on the Ceiling" (#2); "Love Will Conquer All" (#9); "Ballerina Girl" (#7); "Deep River Woman" (#71); "Se La" (#20)

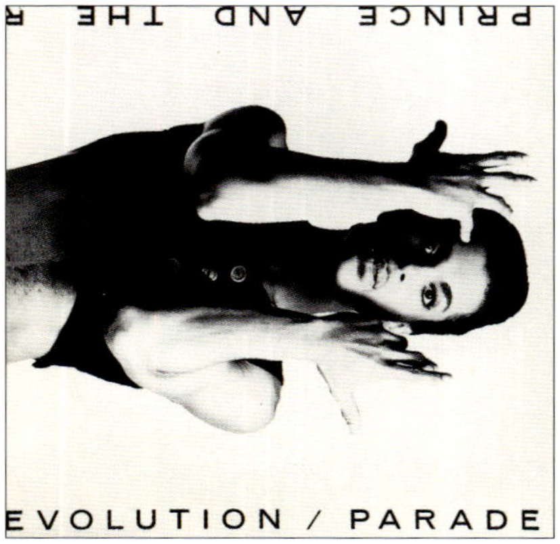

Parade, the last album billing **Prince & the Revolution**, served as the soundtrack for his second film, *Under the Cherry Moon*, and "Kiss" climbed to No. 1.

Billboard 200: *Parade* (#3)
Billboard Hot 100: "Kiss" (No. 1); "Mountains" (#23); "Anotherloverholenyohead" (#63)

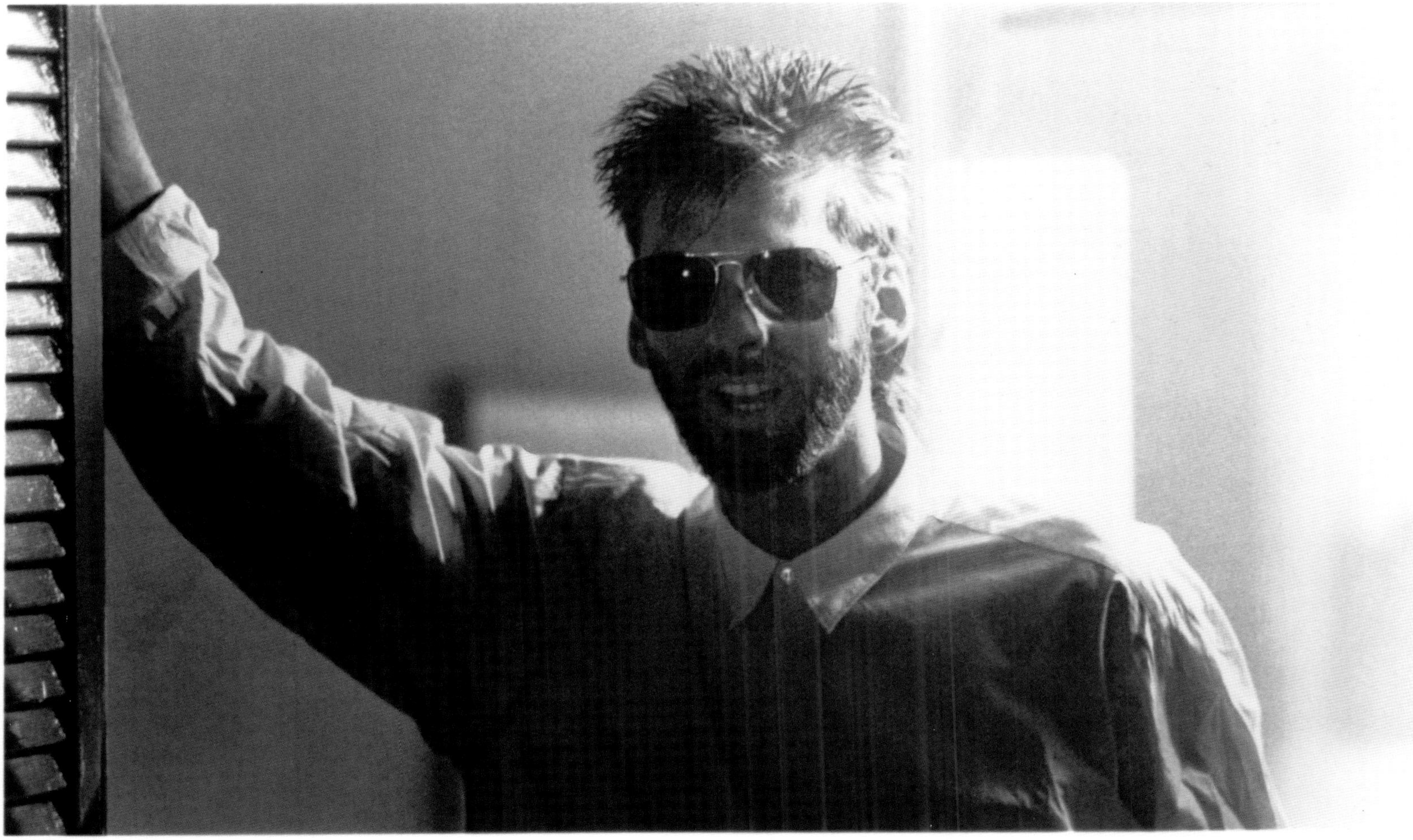

Photo: Brian McLaughlin

Columbia recording artist Kenny Loggins, performs "Danger Zone," the first single and video from TOP GUN, the original motion picture soundtrack album from the Paramount film, "TOP GUN "

Paramount
A Gulf Western Company ®

TOP GUN

Columbia
8605

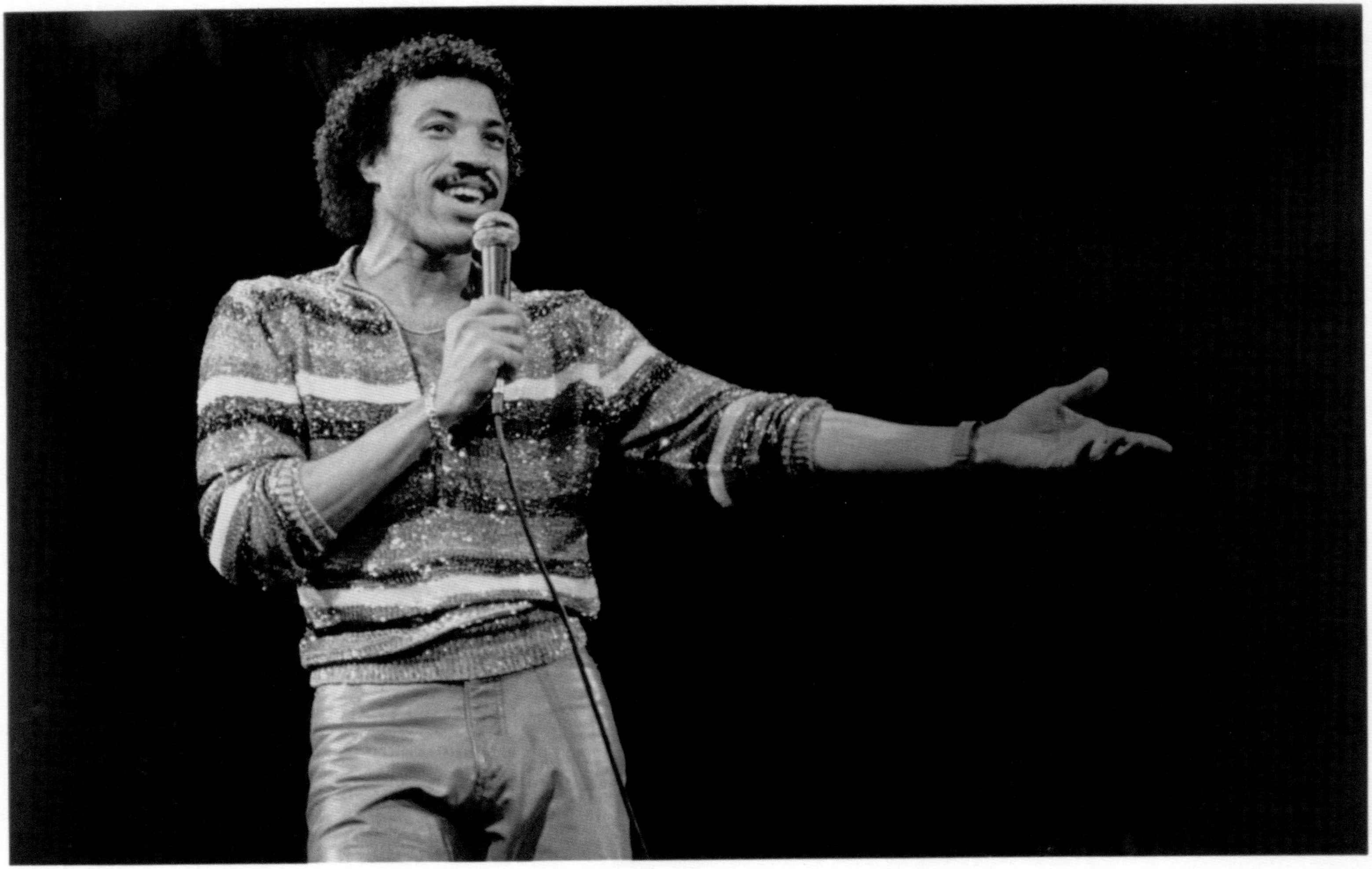

Photo by: PAUL NATKIN

KRAGEN AND COMPANY

MANAGEMENT/PUBLIC RELATIONS
(213) 854-4400

LIONEL RICHIE

MOTOWN

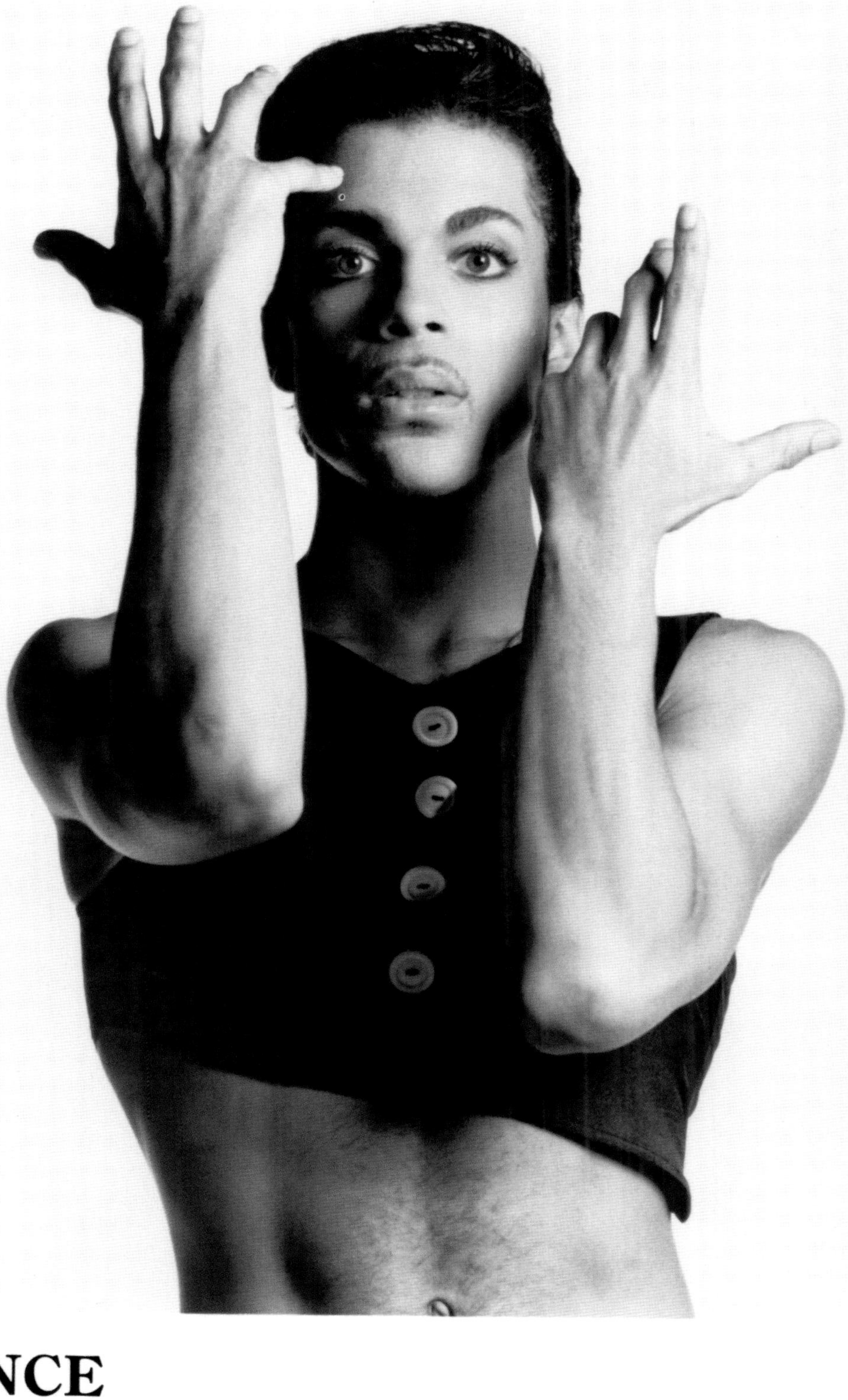

Photo Credit: Jeff Katz

PRINCE

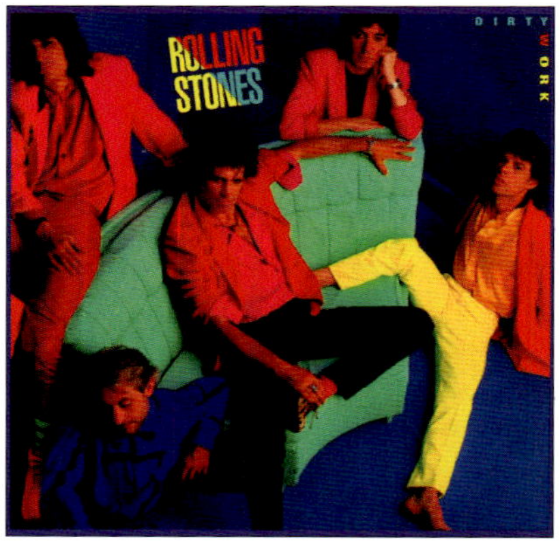

Featuring "Harlem Shuffle," *Dirty Work* was the first **Rolling Stones** album after the band signed a record deal with CBS, reportedly the biggest in history.

Billboard 200: *Dirty Work* (#4)
Billboard Hot 100: "Harlem Shuffle" (#5); "One Hit (To the Body)" (#28)

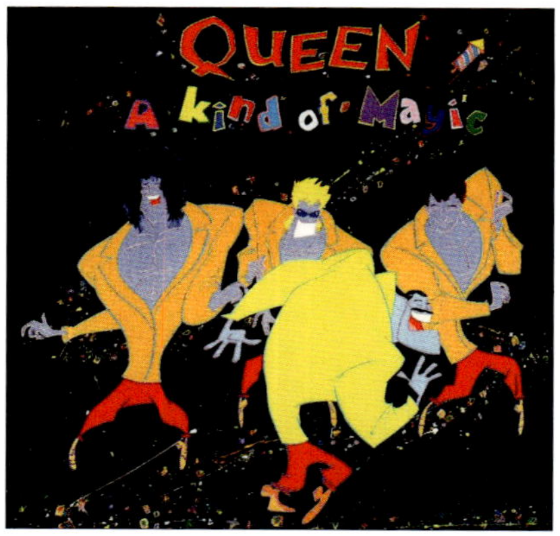

A Kind of Magic, **Queen**'s first album since an exalted set at Live Aid, went straight to No. 1 in the UK and sustained the band's rabid following in Europe.

Billboard 200: *A Kind of Magic* (#46)
Billboard Hot 100: "One Vision" (#61); "A Kind of Magic" (#42)

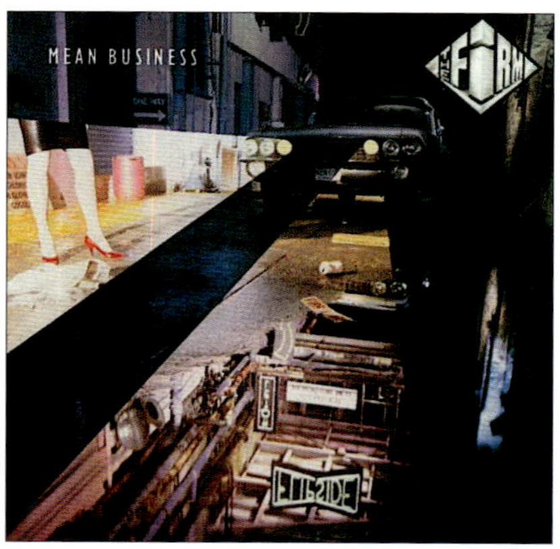

The Firm, a hard-rock supergroup featuring Paul Rodgers and Jimmy Page, released its second album, *Mean Business*, emphasizing "All the Kings Horses."

Billboard 200: *Mean Business* (#22)
Billboard Hot 100: "All the Kings Horses" (#61)

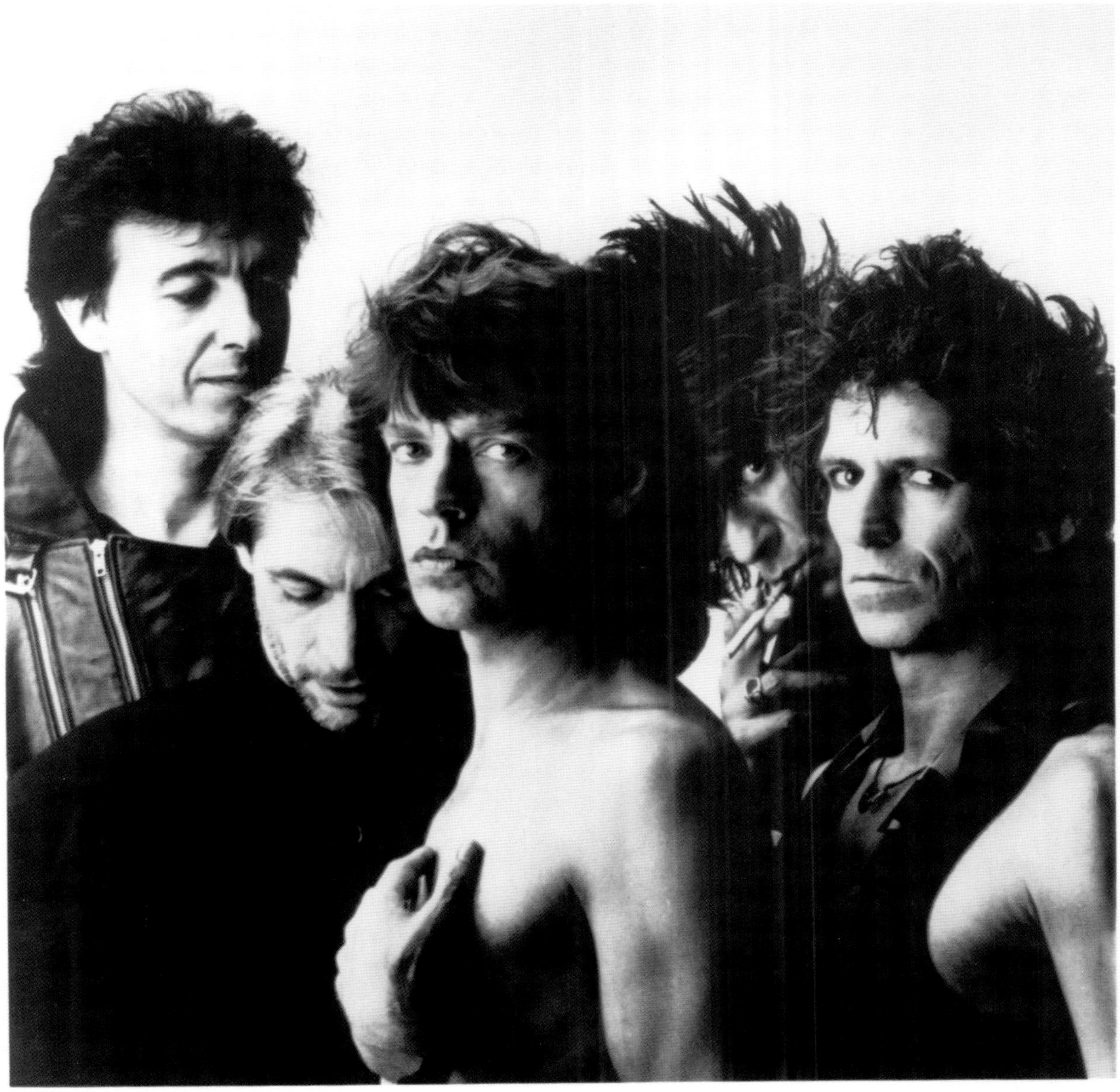

PHOTOGRAPH: ANNIE LEIBOVITZ © 1986 PROMOTONE B.V.

THE ROLLING STONES

8603

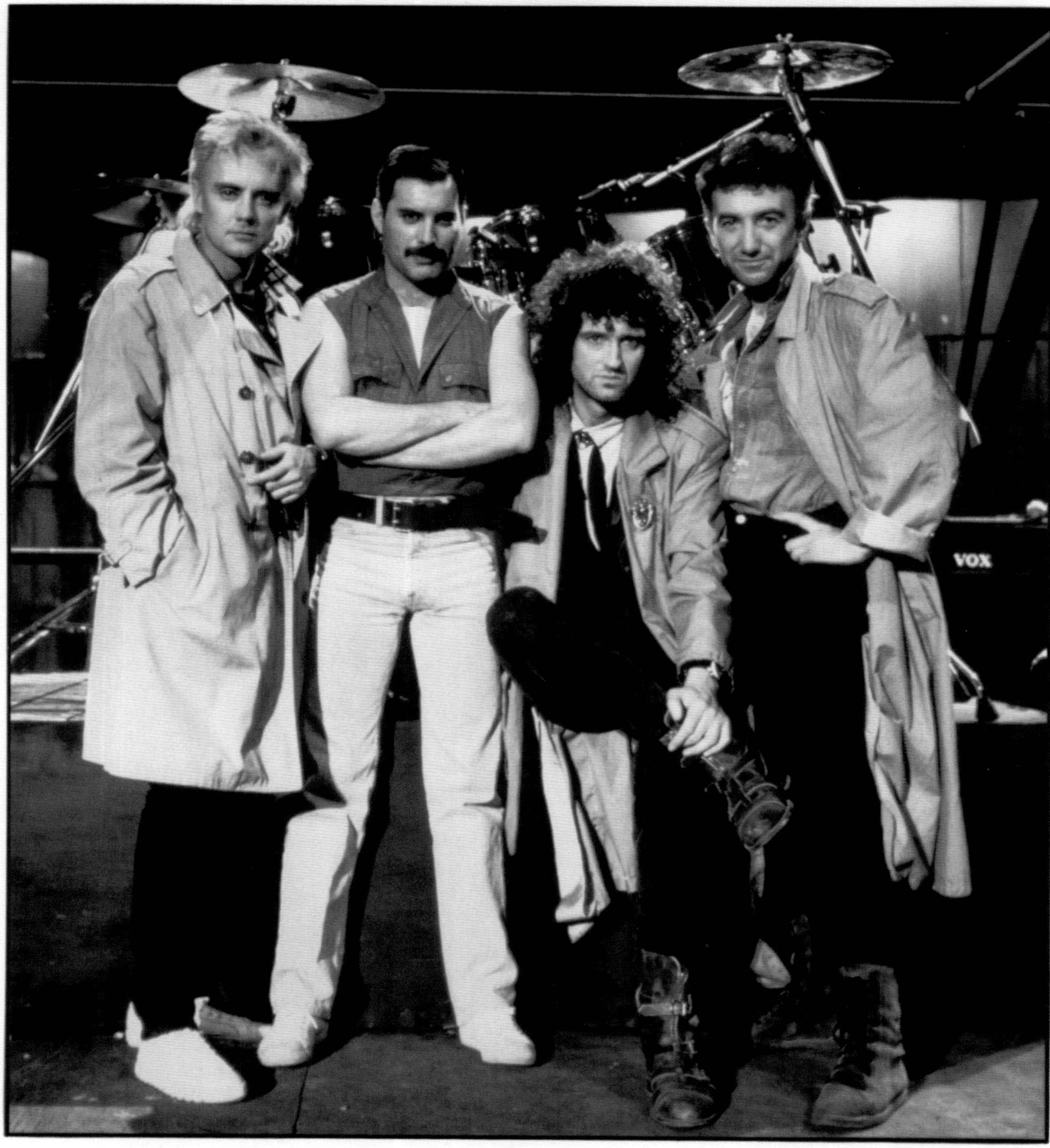

Photo: Peter Hince / 1986

Roger Taylor Freddie Mercury Brian May John Deacon

QUEEN

Capitol RECORDS

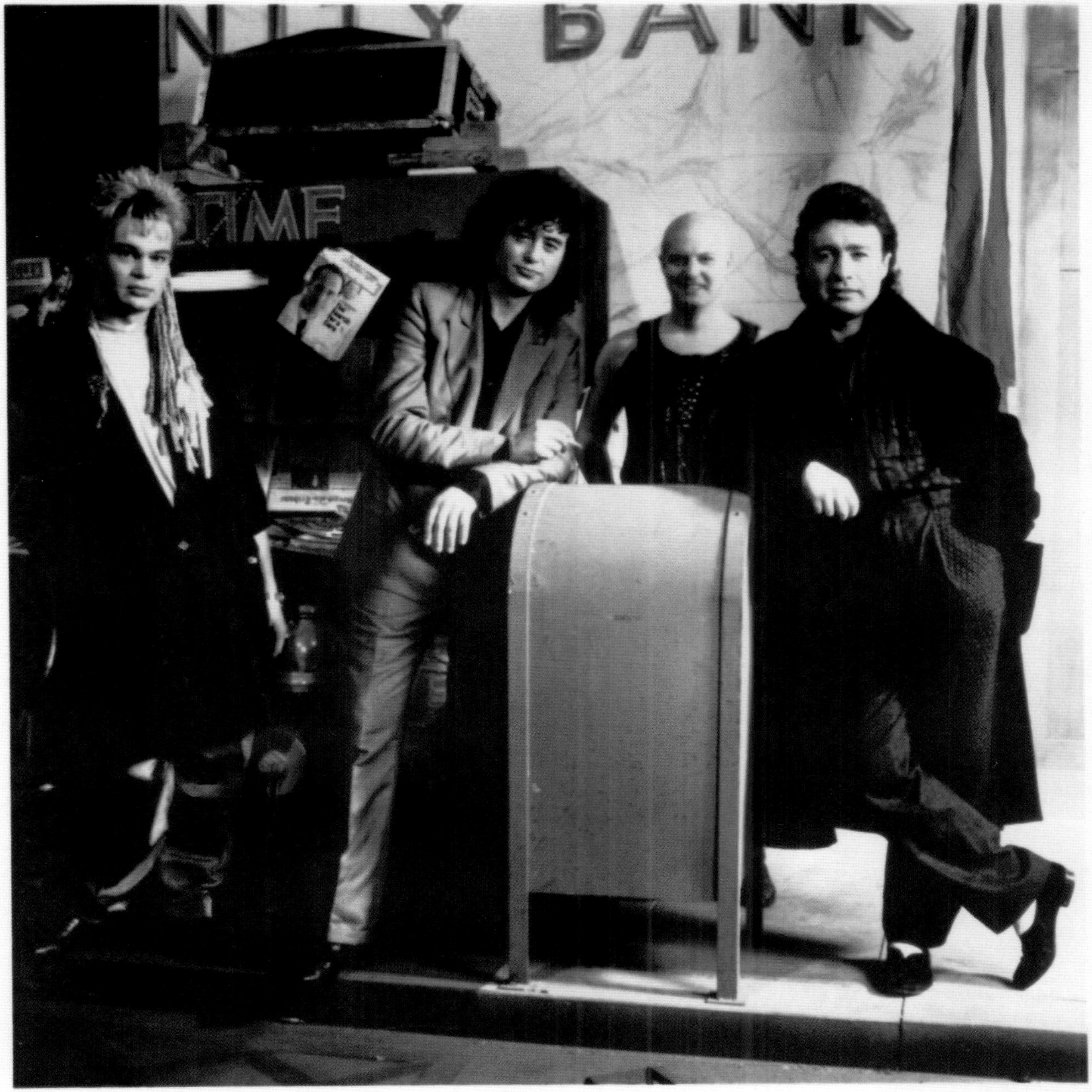

TONY FRANKLIN JIMMY PAGE CHRIS SLADE PAUL RODGERS

THE FIRM

ATLANTIC

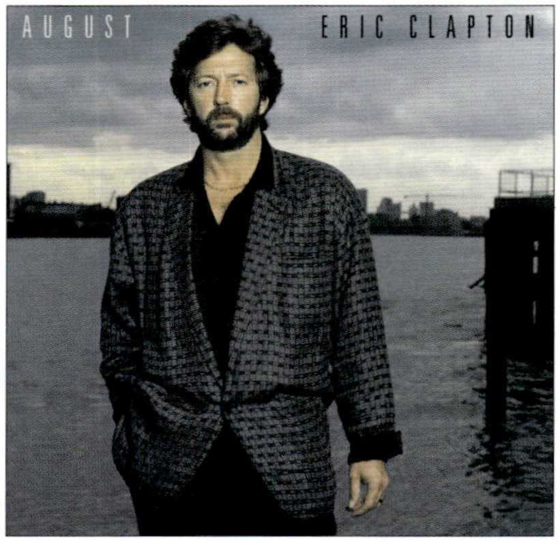

On *August*, rock guitar legend **Eric Clapton** produced a No. 1 mainstream rock hit, "It's in the Way That You Use It," heard in the film *The Color of Money*.

Billboard 200: *August* (#37)

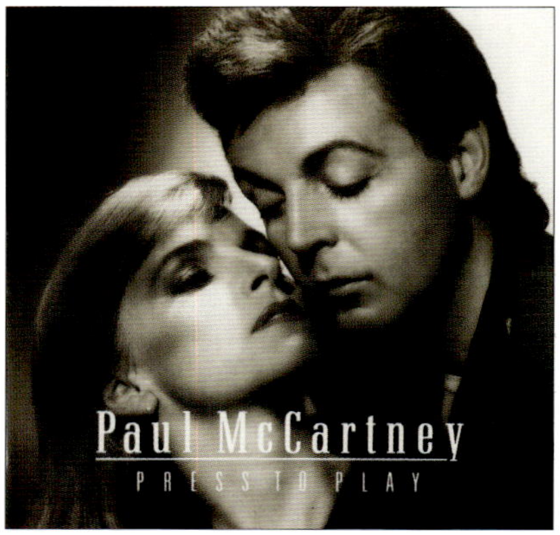

Hankering to re-establish himself on *Press to Play*, **Paul McCartney** hooked up with Eric Stewart, formerly of 10cc, who co-wrote six of the album's songs.

Billboard 200: *Press to Play* (#30)
Billboard Hot 100: "Press" (#21); "Stranglehold" (#81)

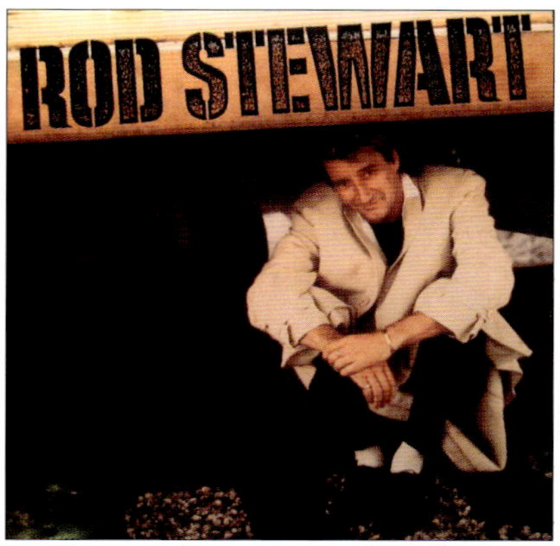

An auspicious if inconsequential **Rod Stewart** song, "Love Touch" was highlighted in *Legal Eagles*, a romantic comedy thriller by director Ivan Reitman.

Billboard 200: *Every Beat of My Heart* (#28)
Billboard Hot 100: "Love Touch" (#6); "Another Heartache" (#52); "Every Beat of My Heart" (#83)

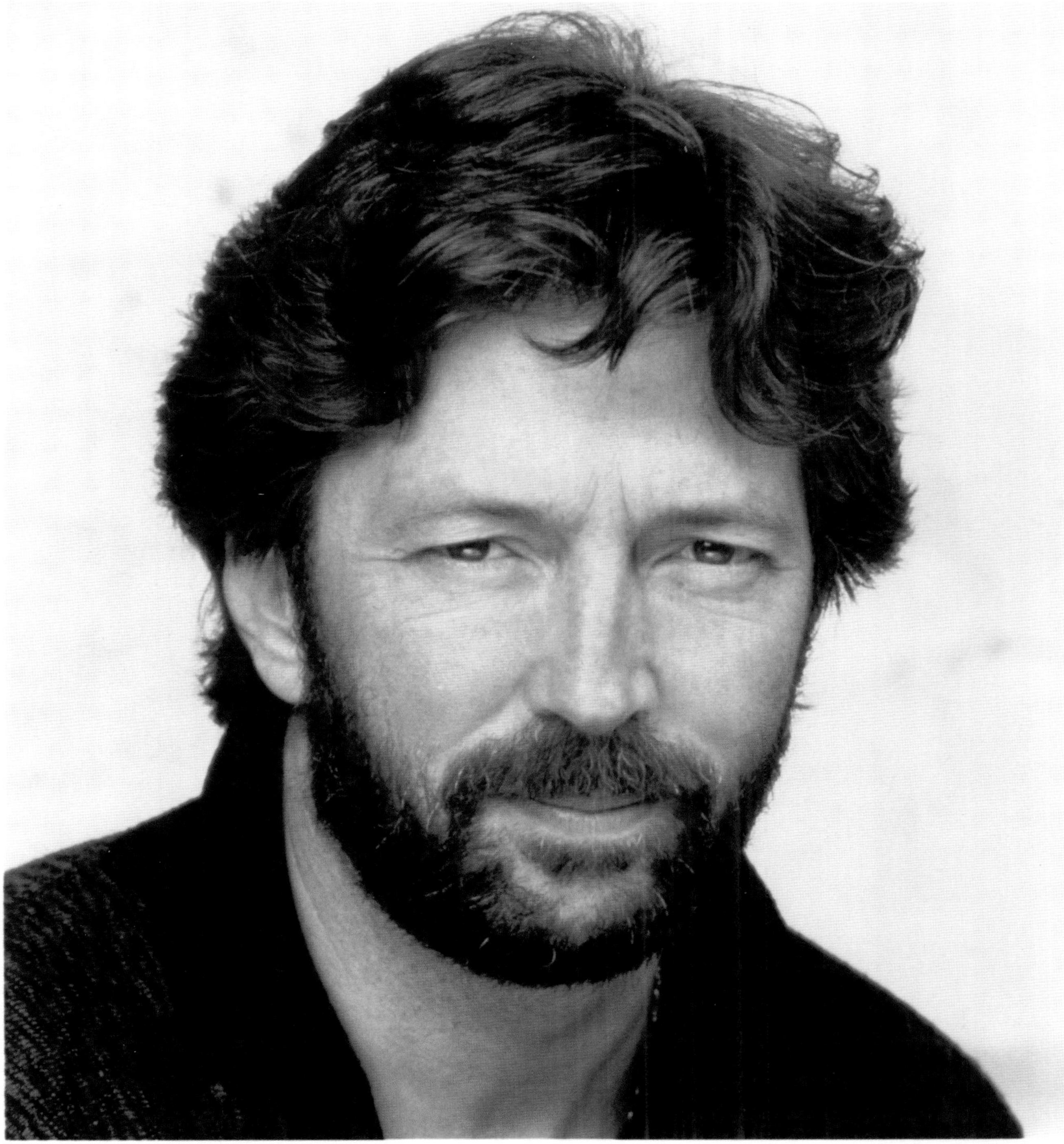

ERIC CLAPTON

DUCK RECORDS

WARNER BROS.

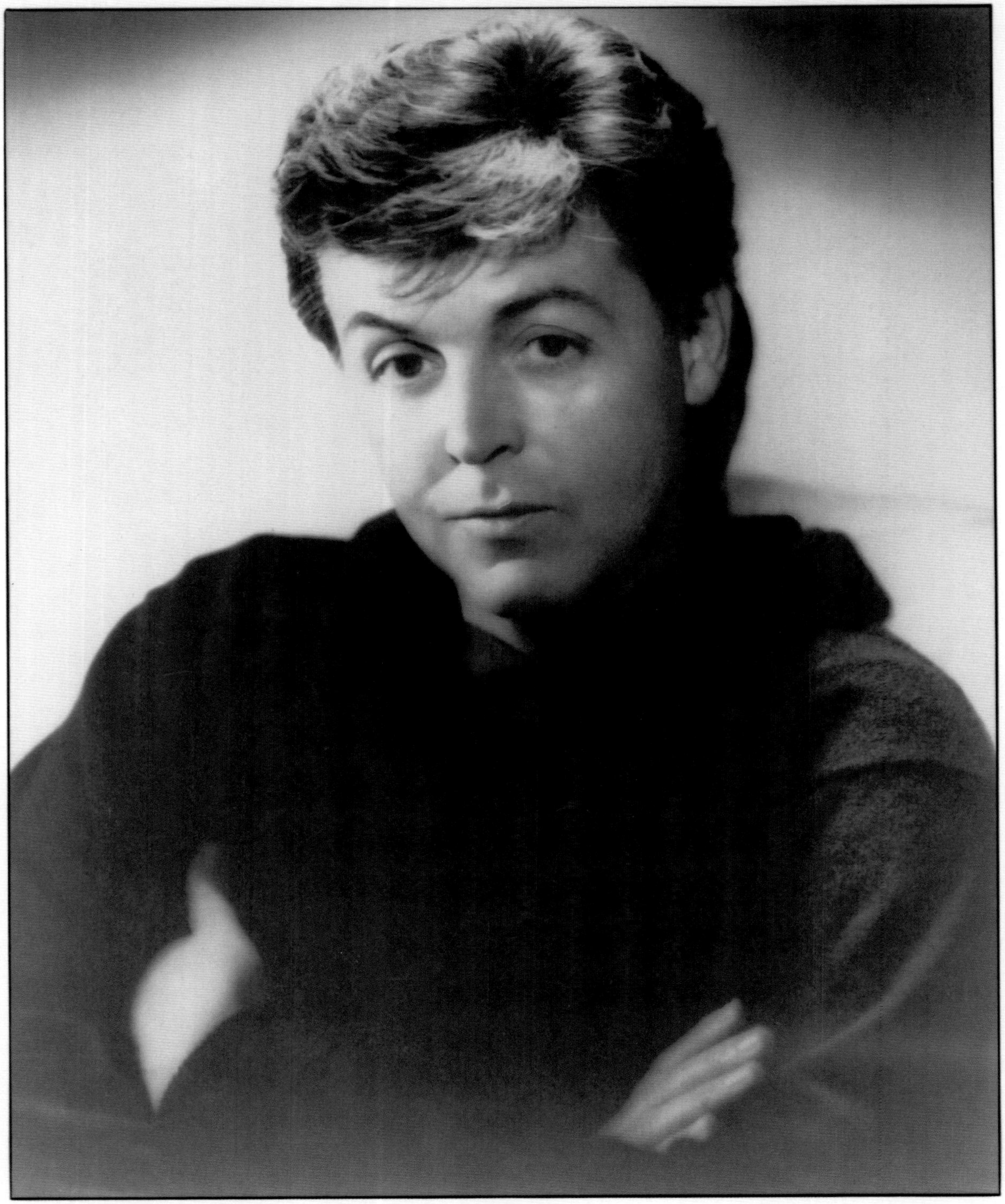

mpl

PAUL McCARTNEY

Capitol RECORDS

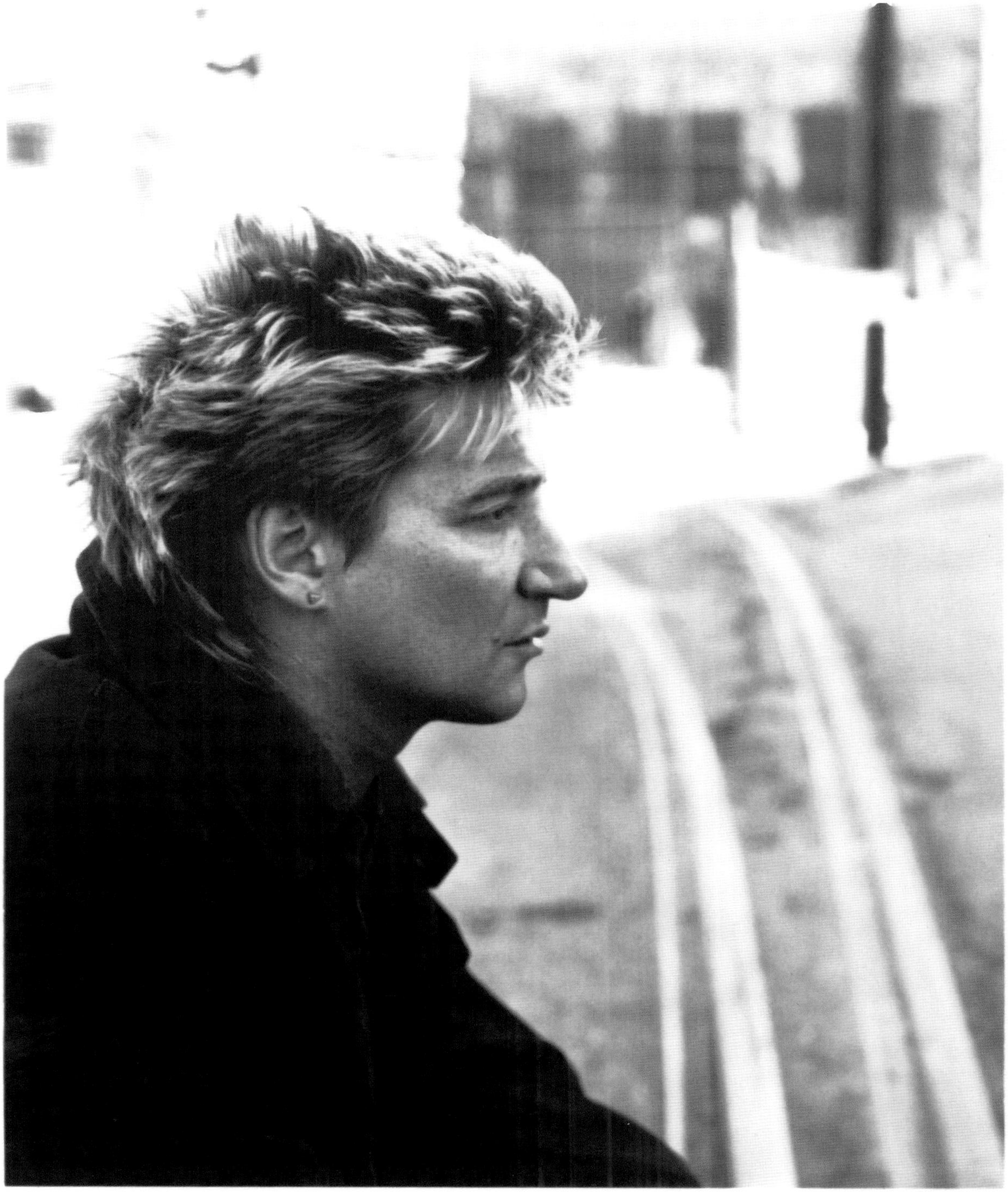

Photo Credit: Philip Dixon

ROD STEWART

WARNER BROS.

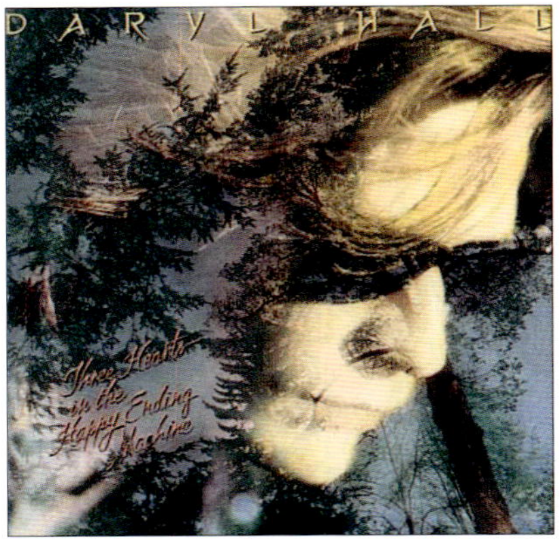

Offering *Three Hearts in the Happy Ending Machine* to cap Hall & Oates' hot streak of the early Eighties, **Daryl Hall** reaped a sublime solo hit, "Dreamtime."

Billboard 200: *Three Hearts in the Happy Ending Machine* (#29)
Billboard Hot 100: "Dreamtime" (#5); "Foolish Pride" (#33); "Someone Like You" (#57)

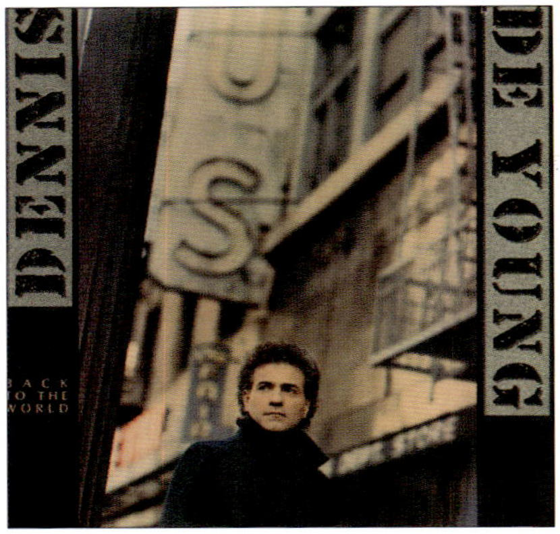

The keyboardist and vocalist of Styx, **Dennis DeYoung** sustained his solo career with *Back to the World* and the adult contemporary hit "This Is the Time."

Billboard 200: *Back to the World* (#108)
Billboard Hot 100: "Call Me" (#54); "This Is the Time" (#93)

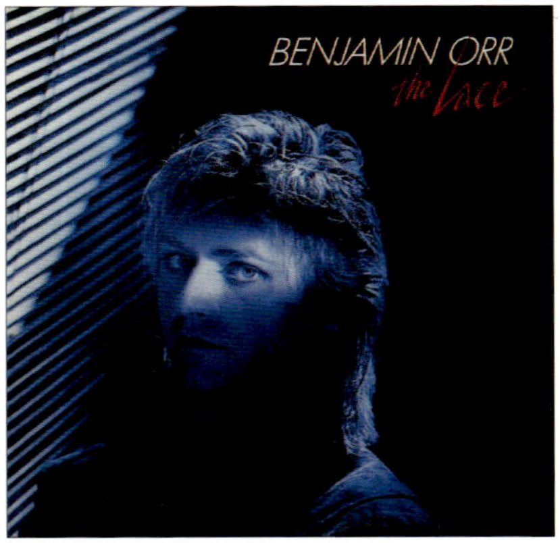

From his solo album *The Lace*, the Cars' bassist and vocalist **Benjamin Orr** scored a modest hit with "Stay the Night," co-written with his longtime fiancée.

Billboard 200: *The Lace* (#86)
Billboard Hot 100: "Stay the Night" (#24)

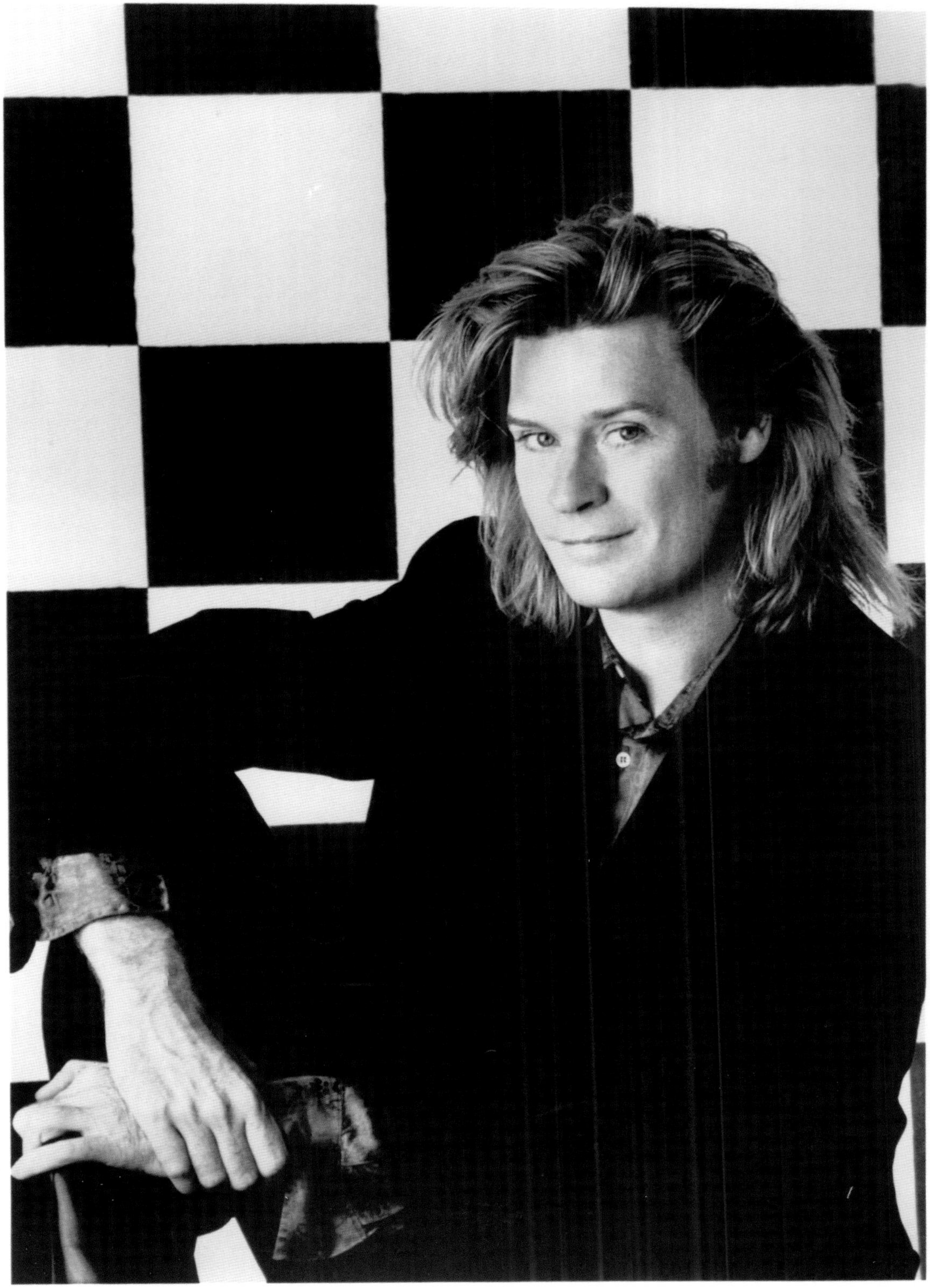

Photo By: Ken Regan/Camera 5

DARYL HALL

RCA Records and Cassettes

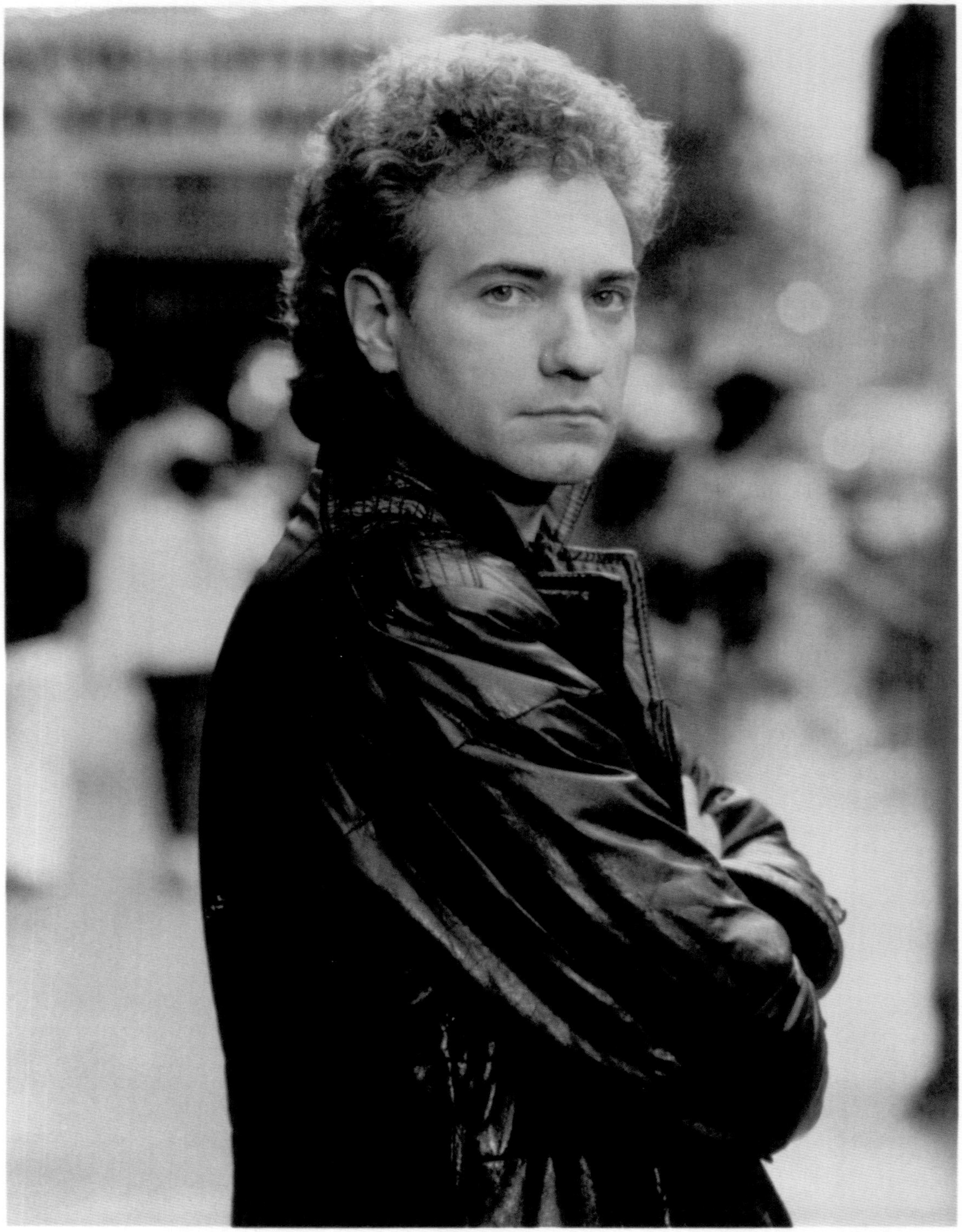

DENNIS DE YOUNG

A&M RECORDS
Printed in U.S.A.

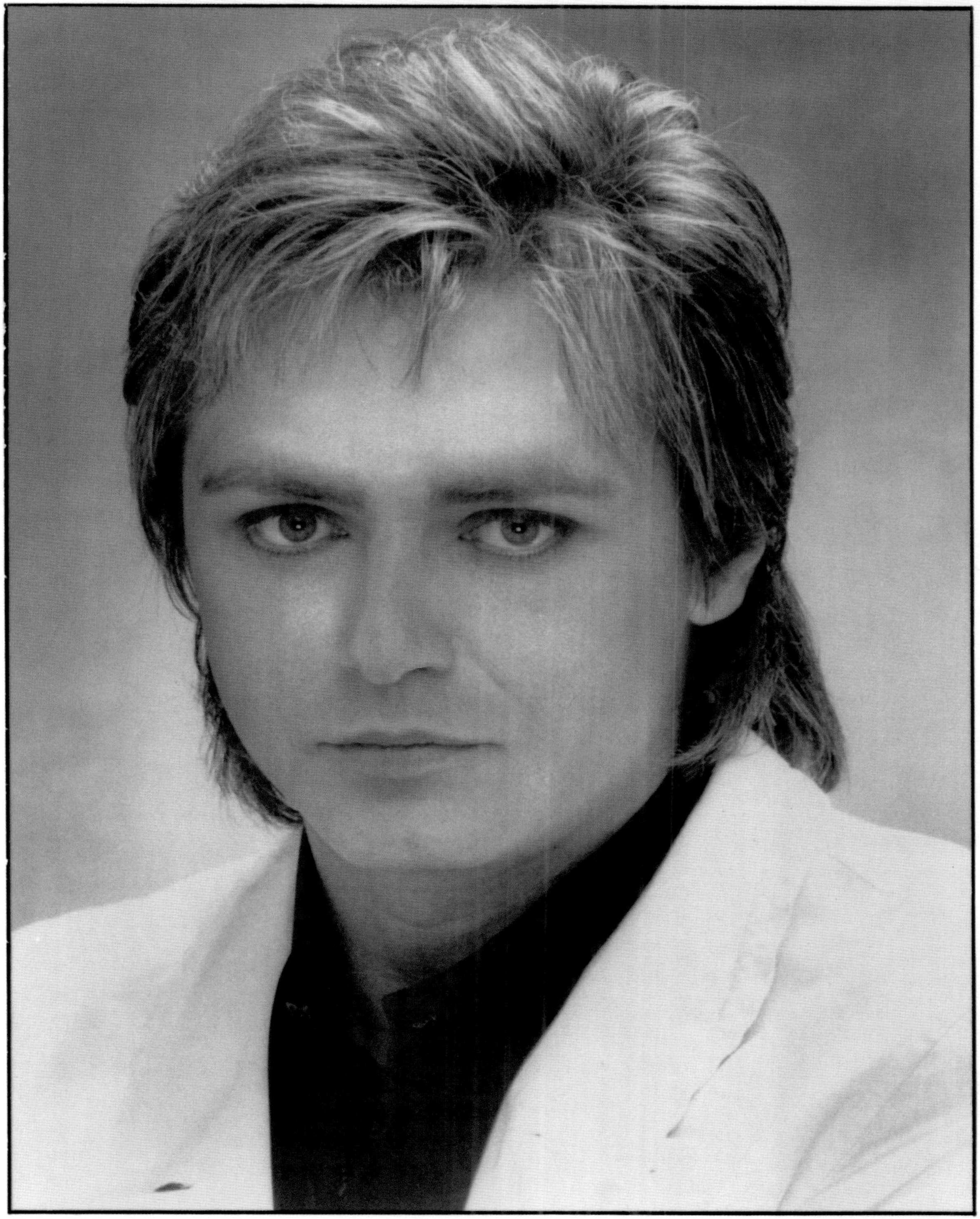

PHOTO CREDIT: JEAN RENARD/1986

BENJAMIN ORR

ELEKTRA

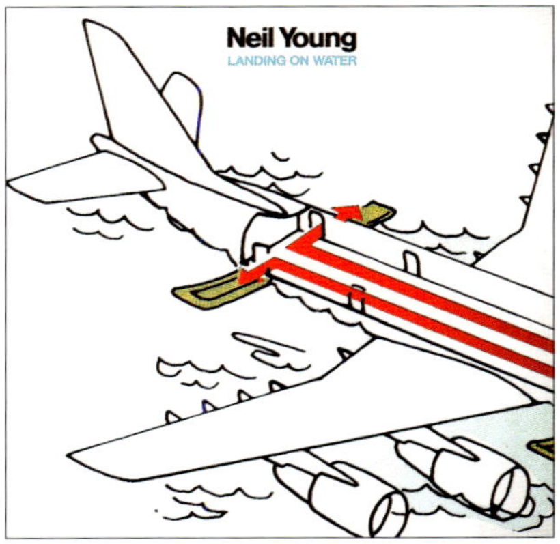

Recorded without his band Crazy Horse, **Neil Young**'s *Landing on Water* assimilated "technical advances," with synths and gated drums entering the mix.

Billboard 200: *Landing on Water* (#58)

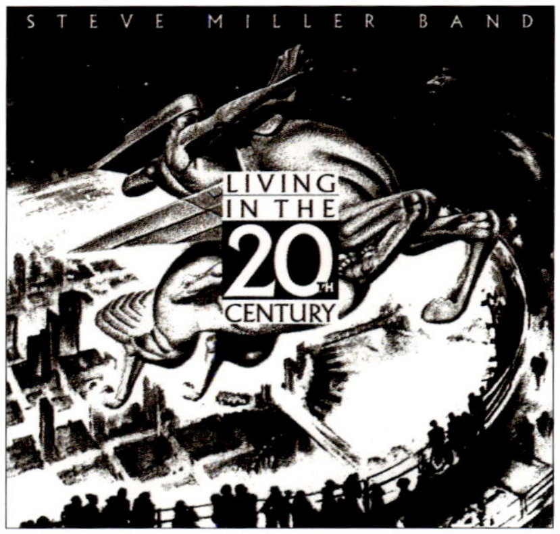

Steve Miller Band investigated the roots of his music, filling one side of the album *Living in the 20th Century* with Delta/Chicago/Texas blues-rock styles.

Billboard 200: *Living in the 20th Century* (#65)
Billboard Hot 100: "I Want to Make the World Turn Around" (#97)

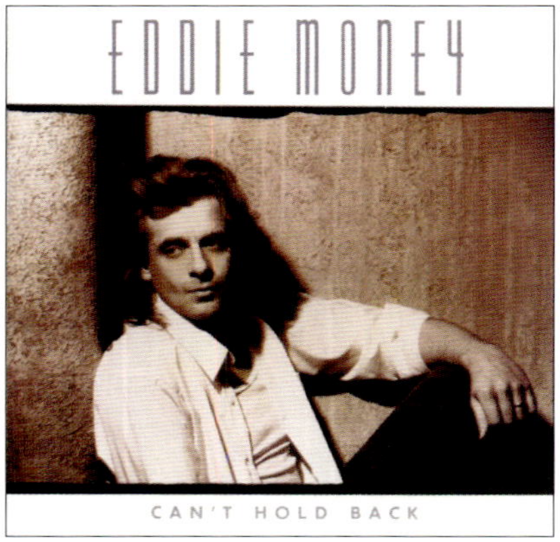

Eddie Money's *Can't Hold Back* netted a signature song, "Take Me Home Tonight," highlighted by legendary singer Ronnie Spector's guest appearance.

Billboard 200: *Can't Hold Back* (#20)
Billboard Hot 100: "Take Me Home Tonight" (#4); "I Wanna Go Back" (#14); "Endless Nights" (#21); "We Should Be Sleeping" (#90)

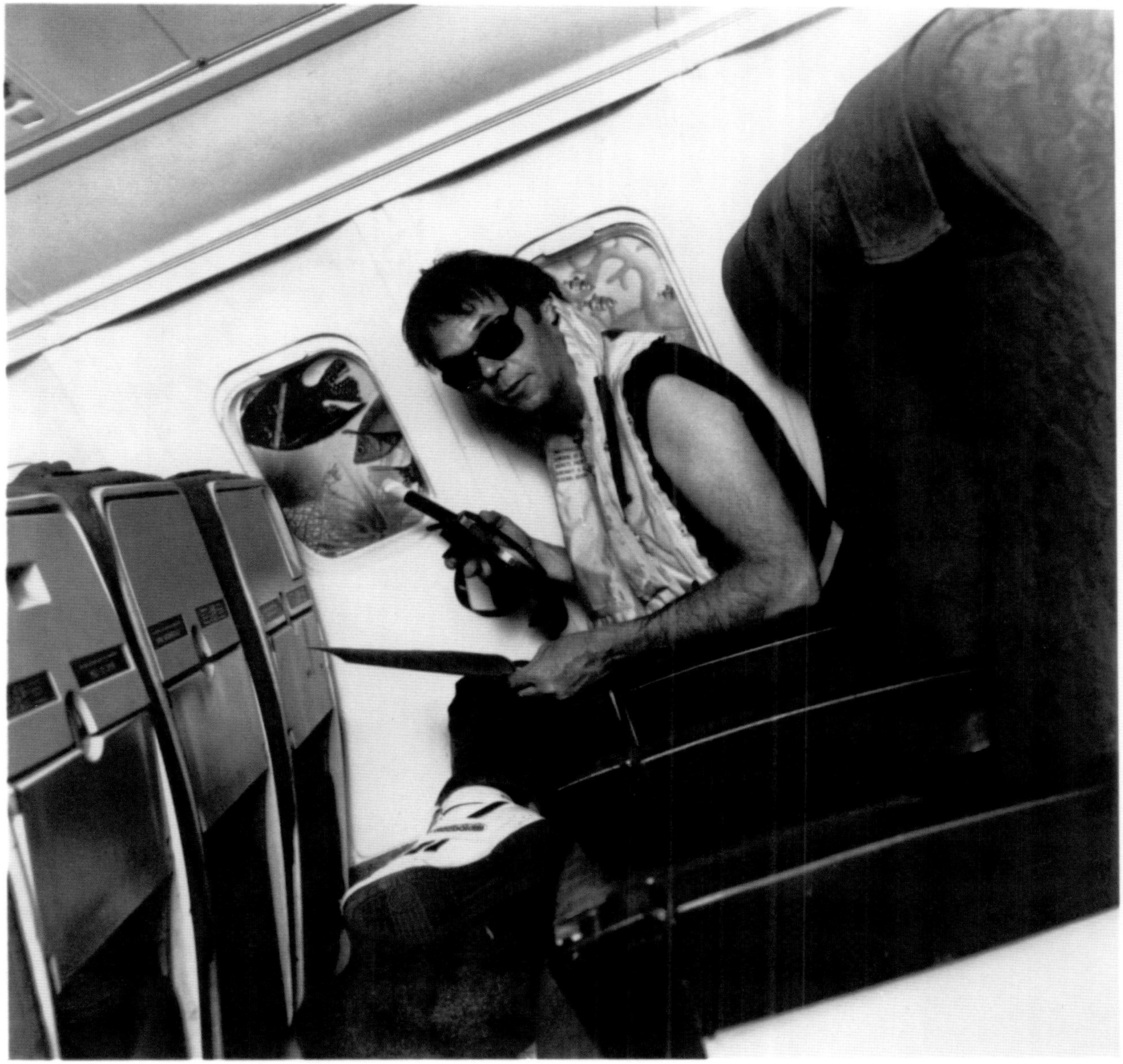

Photo Credit: Hugh Brown

NEIL YOUNG

JENSEN
COMMUNICATIONS
PUBLIC RELATIONS
(213) 841 3343

GEFFEN RECORDS

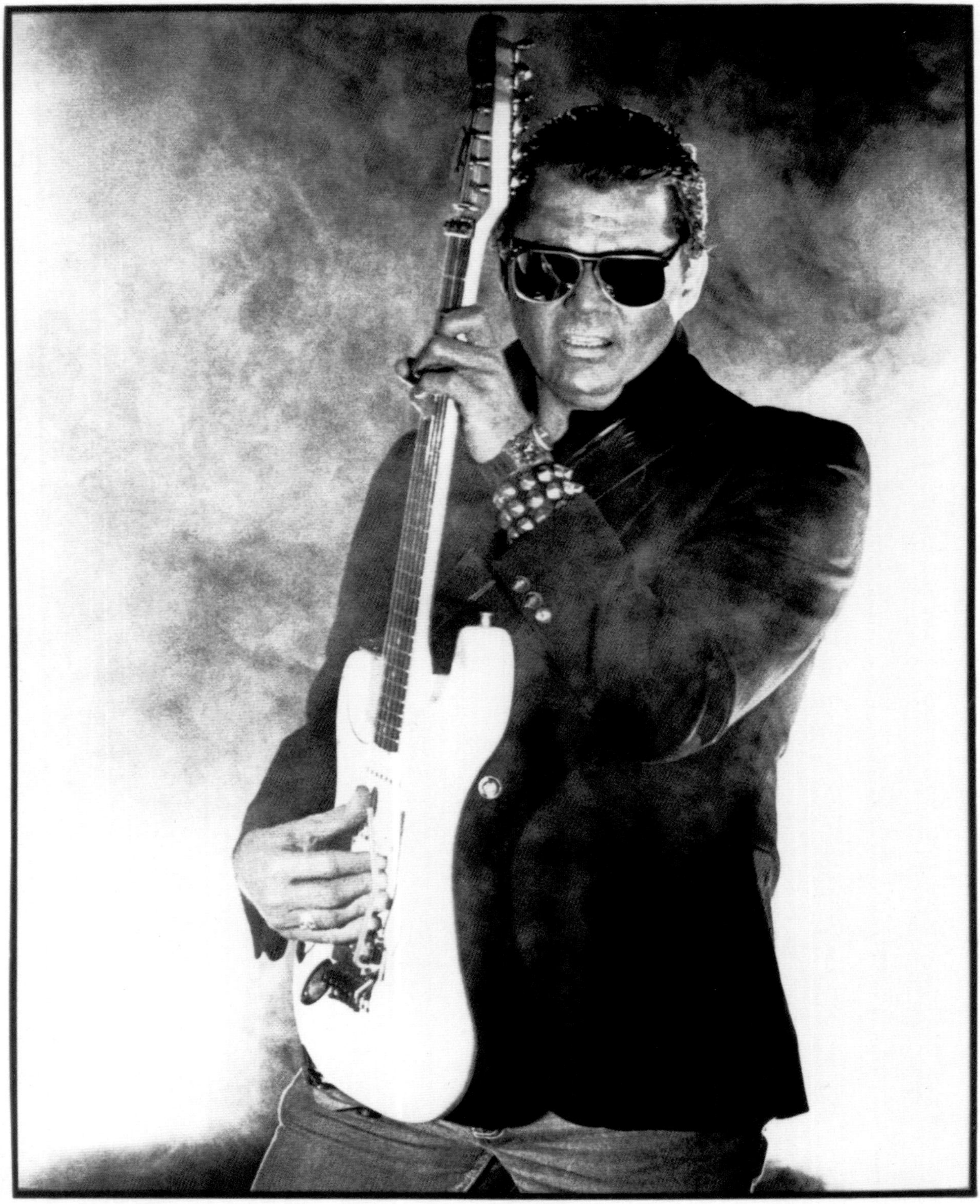

STEVE MILLER

Photo: Kimberly Smith / 1986

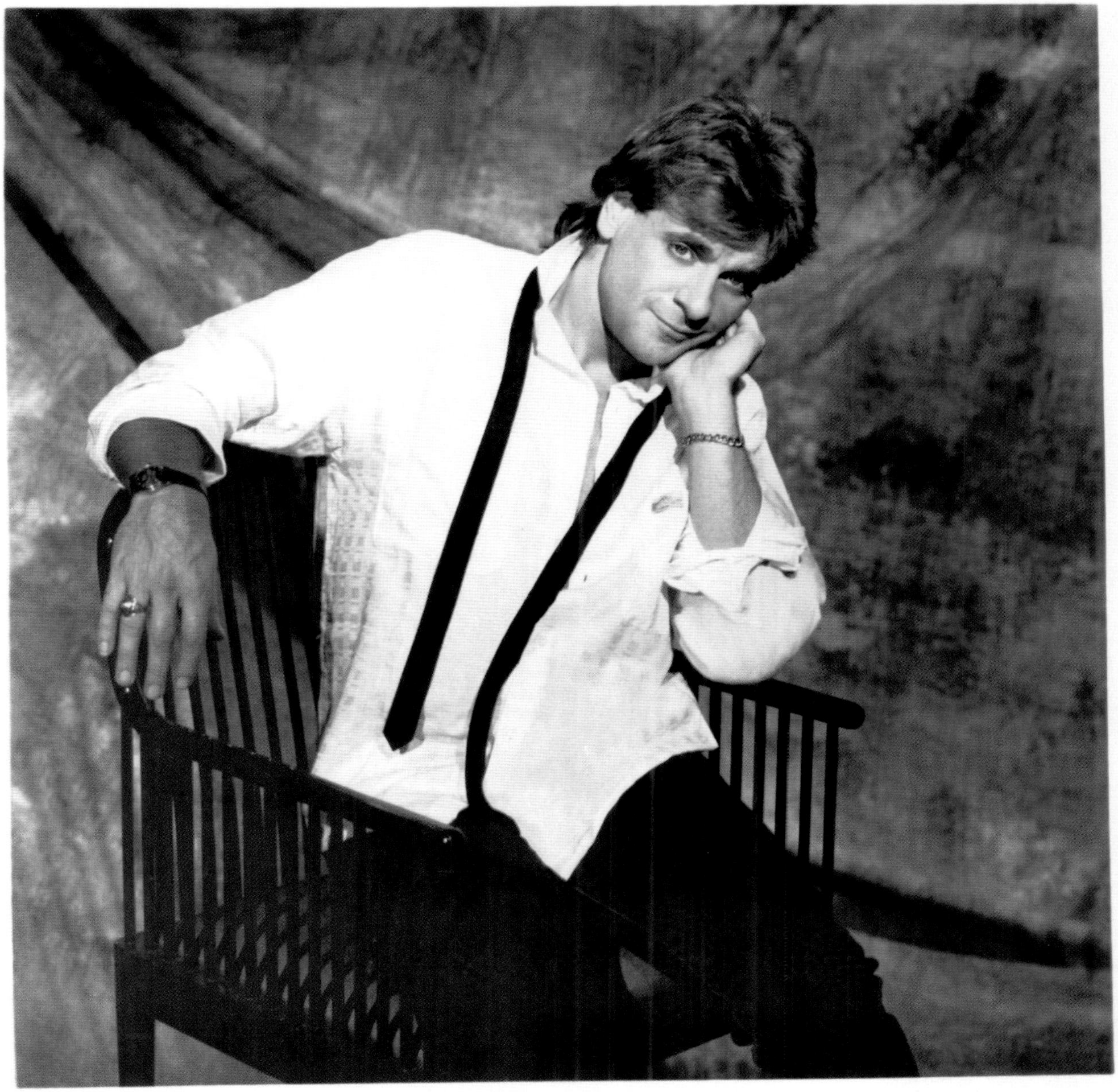

PHOTO CREDIT: BONNIE SCHIFFMAN

EDDIE MONEY

wolfgang

BILL GRAHAM MANAGEMENT
201 Eleventh Street San Francisco CA 94103
(415) 864-0815

Columbia

8610

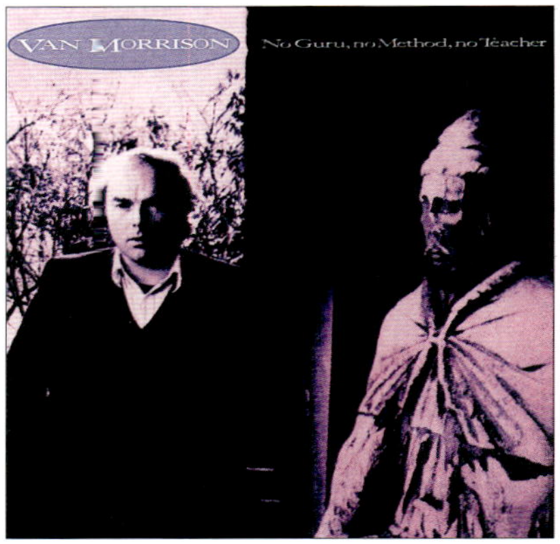

No Guru, No Method, No Teacher put **Van Morrison**'s standard for lyrical inspiration into effect, drawing upon various spiritual and philosophical teachings.

Billboard 200: *No Guru, No Method, No Teacher* (#70)

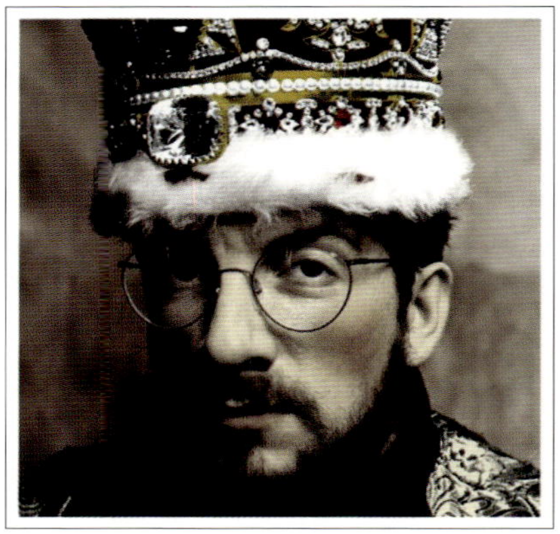

Elvis Costello and producer T-Bone Burnett assembled backing musicians, dubbed "Confederates," for a new version of "Don't Let Me Be Misunderstood."

Billboard 200: *King of America* (#39)

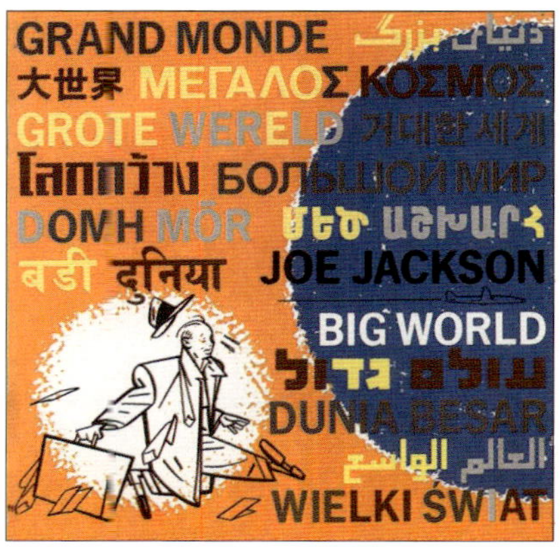

Joe Jackson recorded *Big World*, an album of all-new songs, in front of an invited live audience instructed to hold its applause during his performance.

Billboard 200: *Big World* (#34)

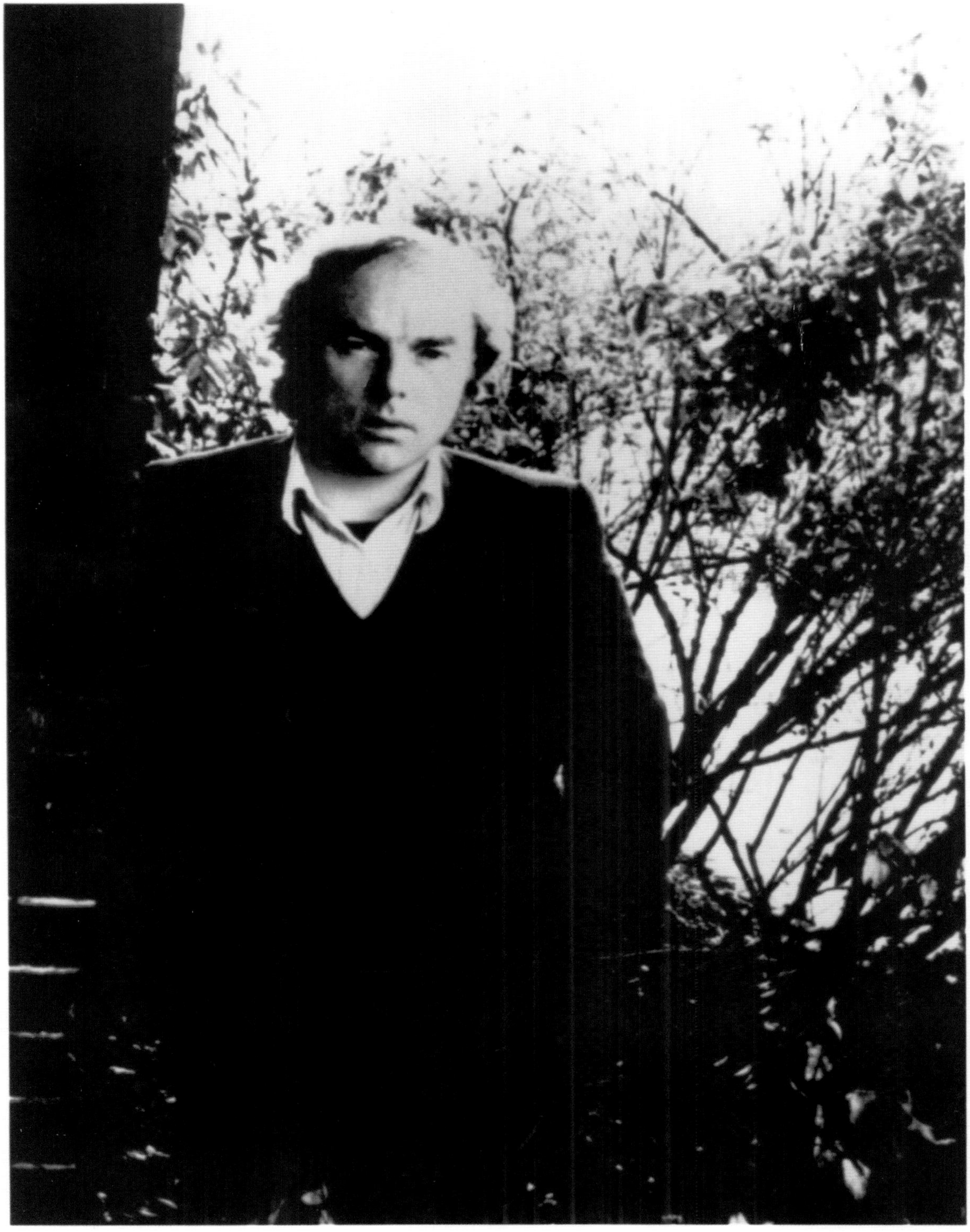

VAN MORRISON

PolyGram Records

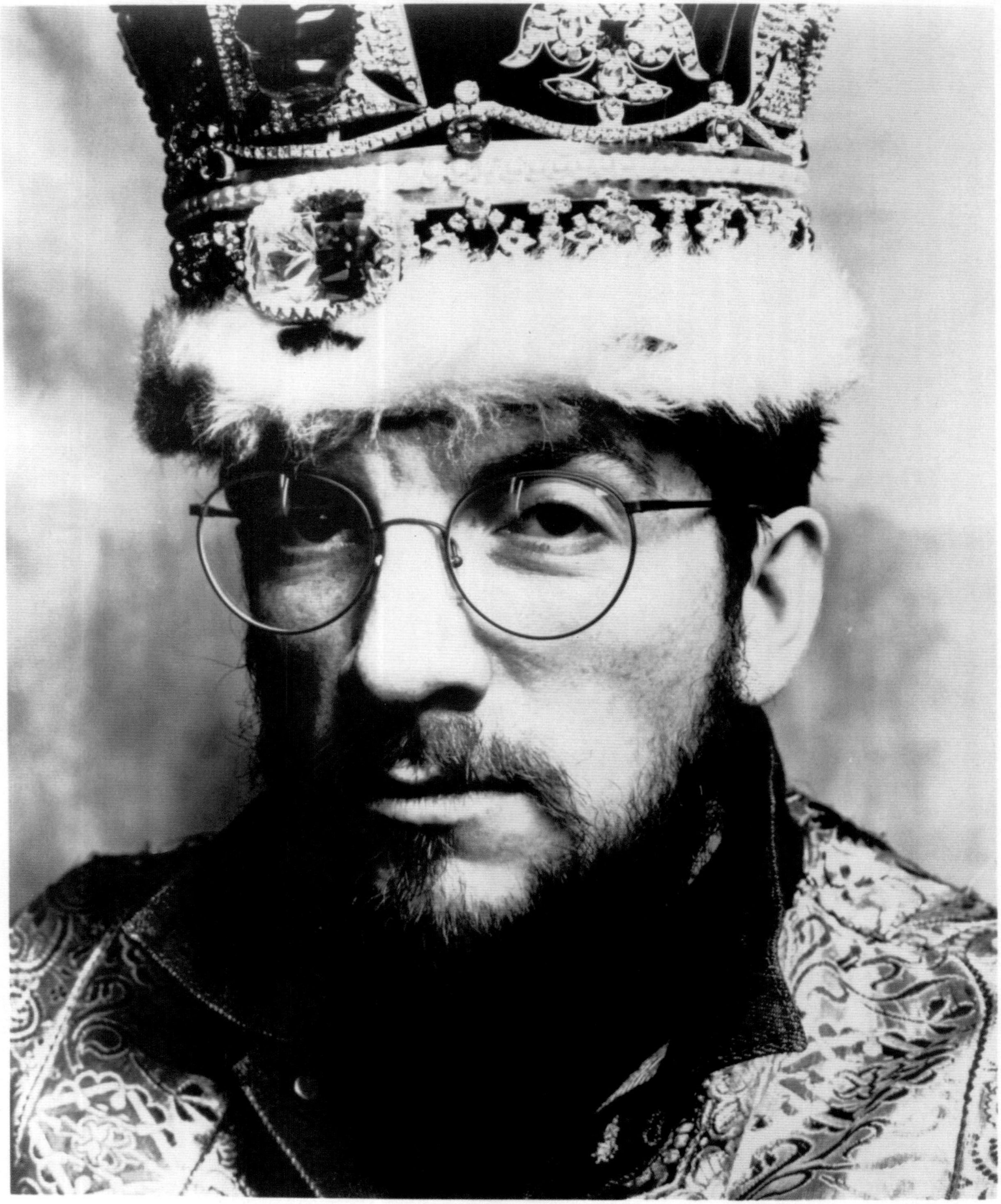

PHOTOGRAPH: TERENCE DONOVAN

ELVIS COSTELLO

Columbia

8602

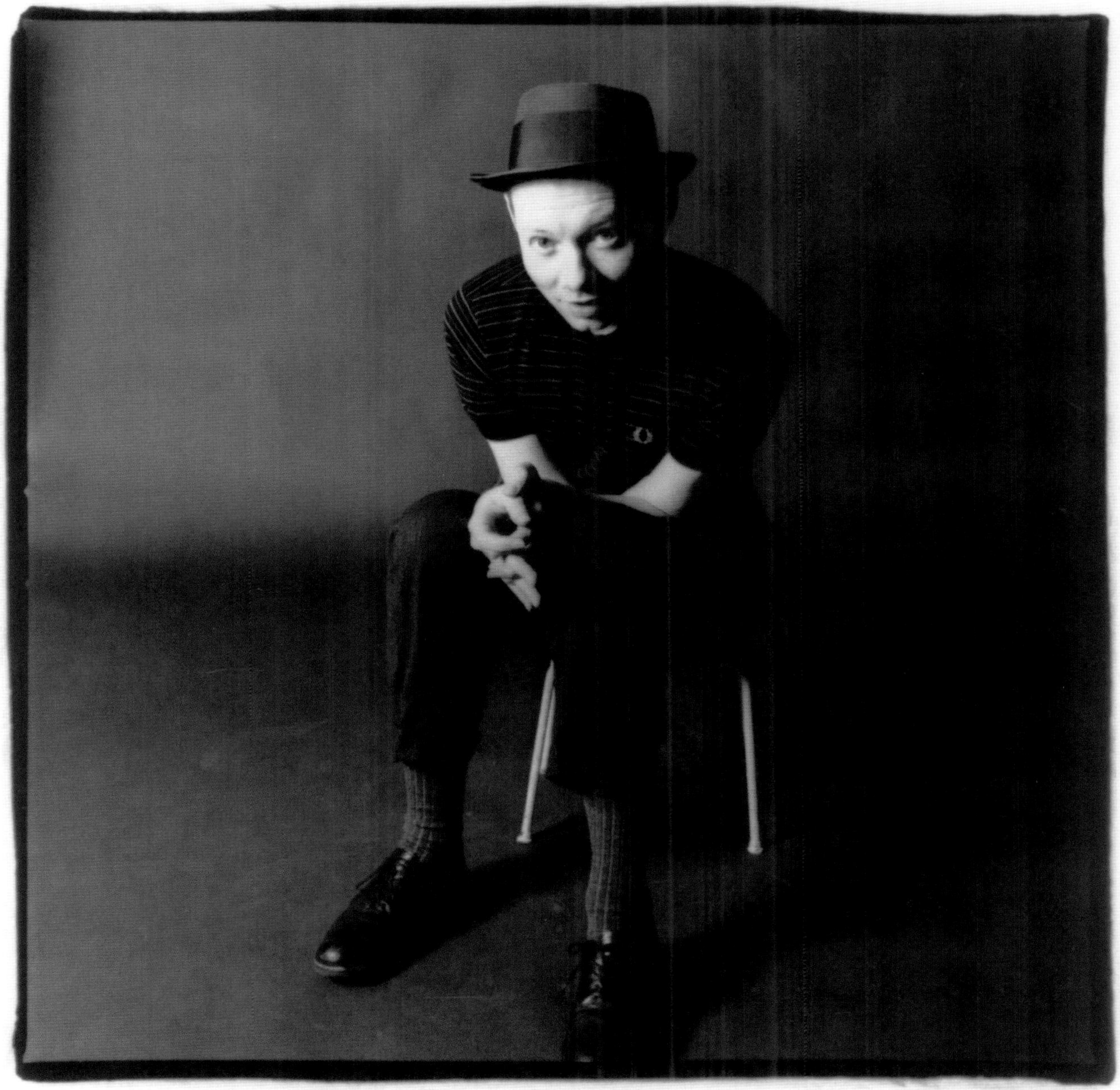

Photo Credit: Laura Levine

JOE JACKSON

A&M RECORDS
Printed in U.S.A.

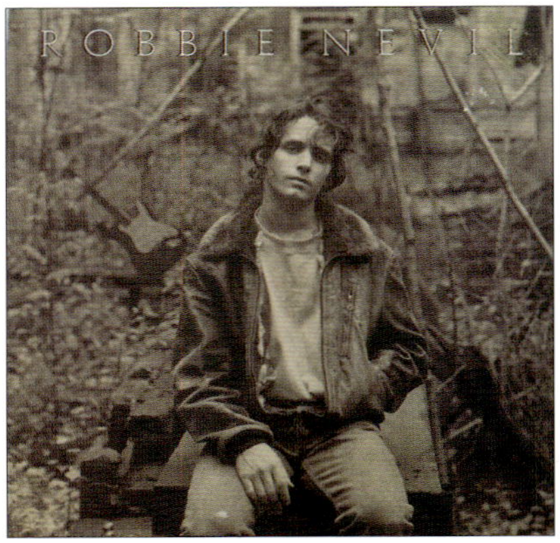

Songwriter and session guitarist **Robbie Nevil**'s self-titled debut album was buoyed by three Top 20 hits, "C'est la Vie," "Dominoes" and "Wot's It to Ya."

Billboard 200: *Robbie Nevil* (#37)
Billboard Hot 100: "C'est la Vie" (#2); "Dominoes" (#14); "Wot's It to Ya" (#10)

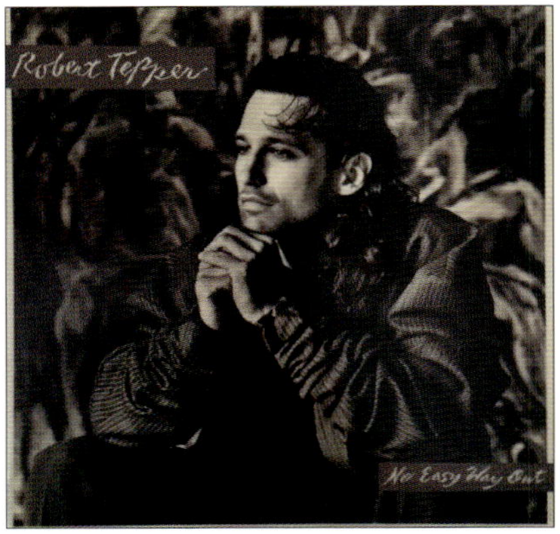

Director Sylvester Stallone fleetingly put singer **Robert Tepper** into the limelight as his "No Easy Way Out" appeared in the No. 1 box office hit *Rocky IV*.

Billboard 200: *No Easy Way Out* (#144)
Billboard 200: "No Easy Way Out" (#22); "Don't Walk Away" (#85)

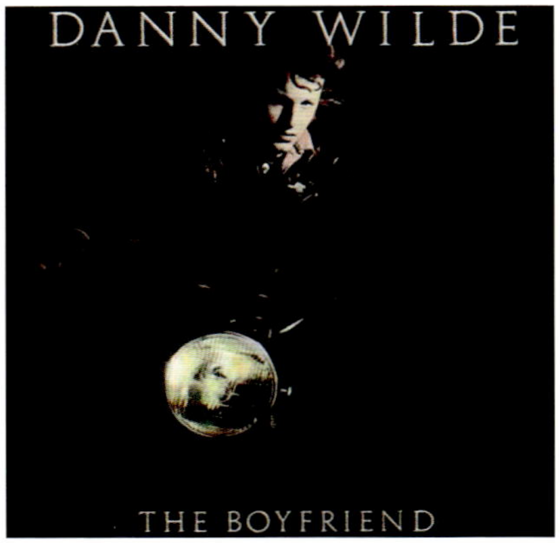

After parting with the Quick and Great Buildings, two overlooked power-pop bands, member **Danny Wilde** landed a minor solo hit with "Isn't It Enough."

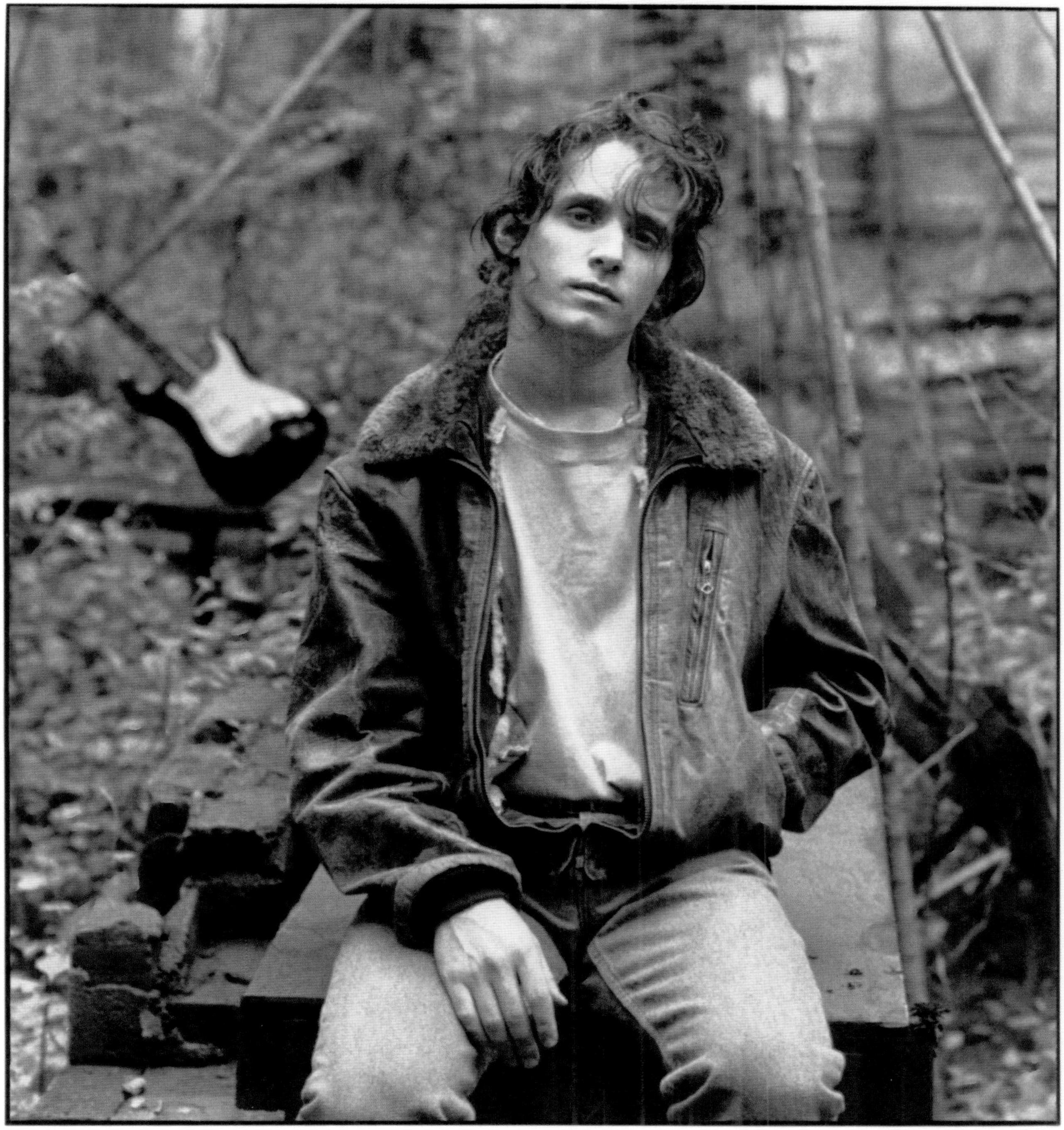

PHOTOGRAPHY: DUANE MICHAELS/1986

ROBBIE NEVIL

MAN
HAT
TAN

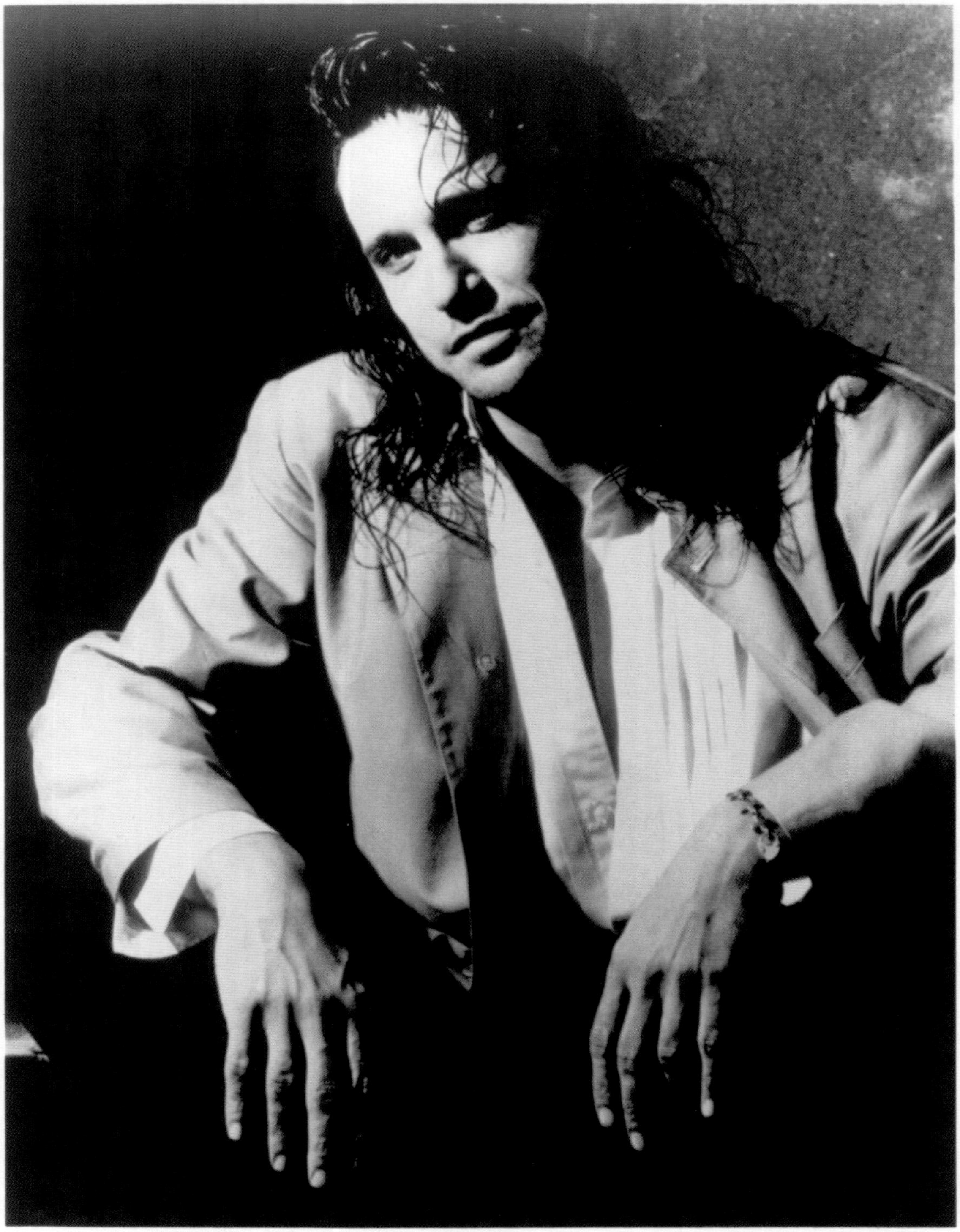

ROBERT TEPPER

Scotti Brothers™

EPA
EPIC PORTRAIT ASSOCIATED
8512

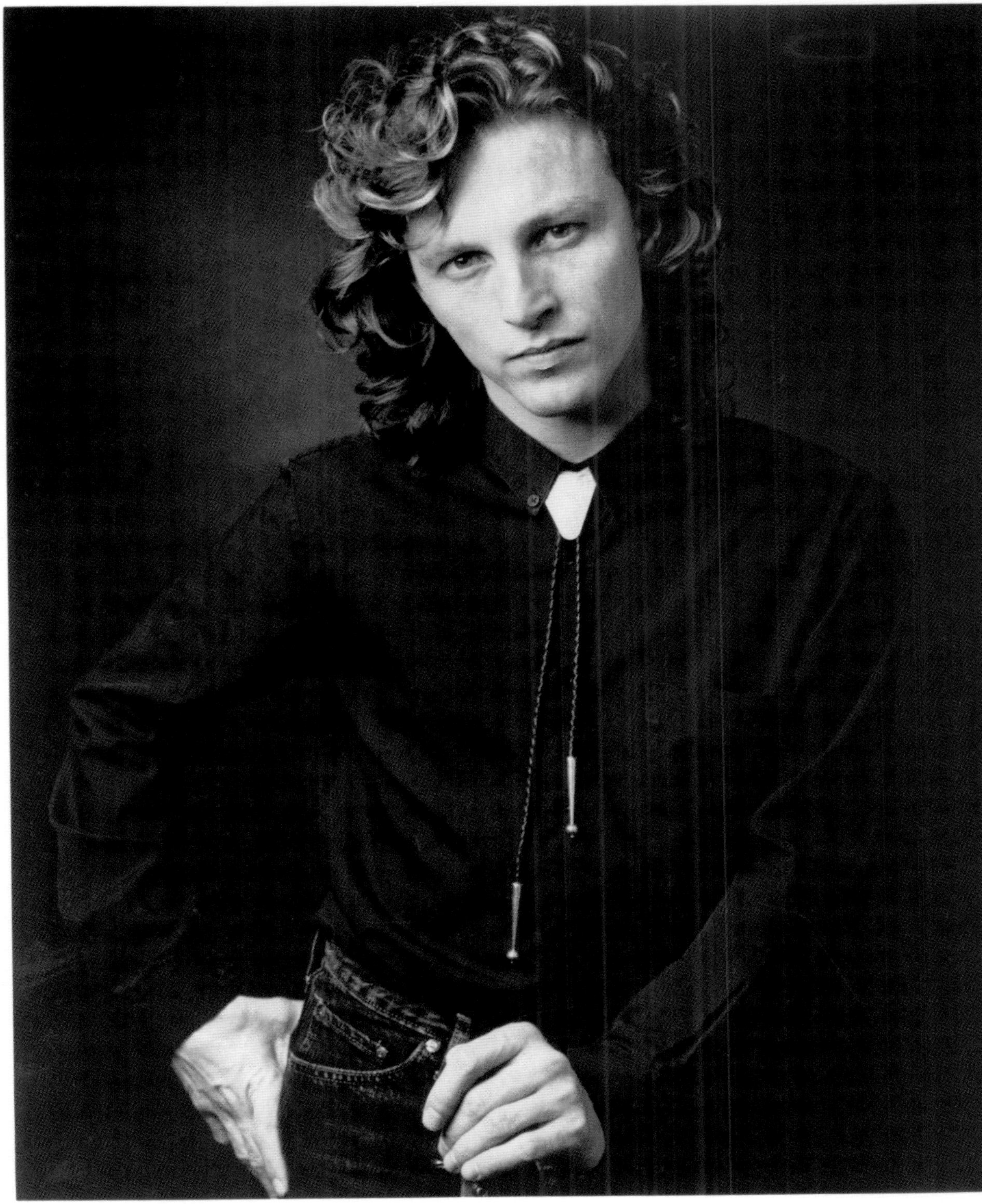

Photo: Keli Rogers

DANNY WILDE

ISLAND

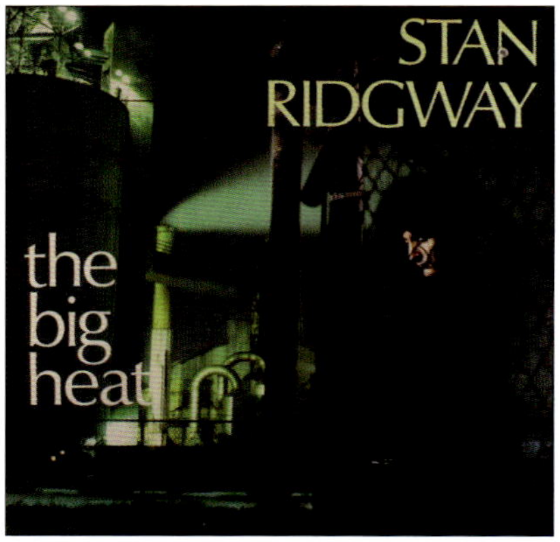

Former Wall of Voodoo singer **Stan Ridgway** issued *The Big Heat*, and "Camouflage," an epic Vietnam story tale, was an unforeseen hit in the UK and Europe.

Billboard 200: *The Big Heat* (#131)

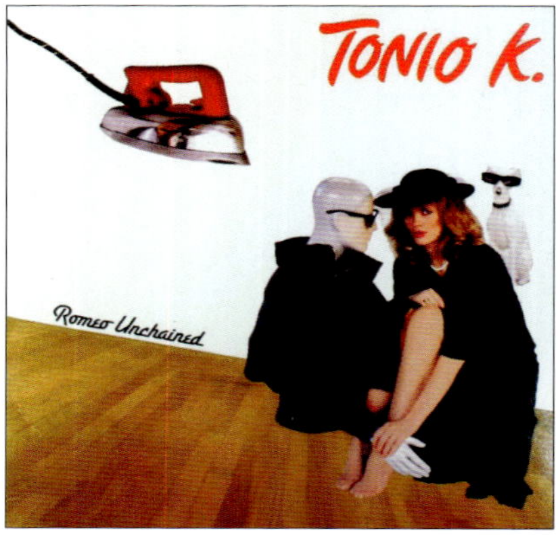

Singer-songwriter **Tonio K.**'s skewed seriocomic vision flashed in *Romeo Unchained*, which landed on numerous publications' "best of" year-end lists.

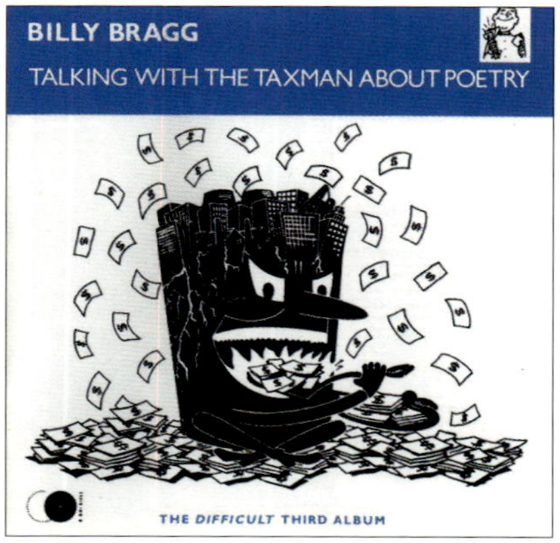

"Levi Stubbs' Tears," a stunning character study, appeared on British activist and singer-songwriter **Billy Bragg**'s *Talking with the Taxman about Poetry*.

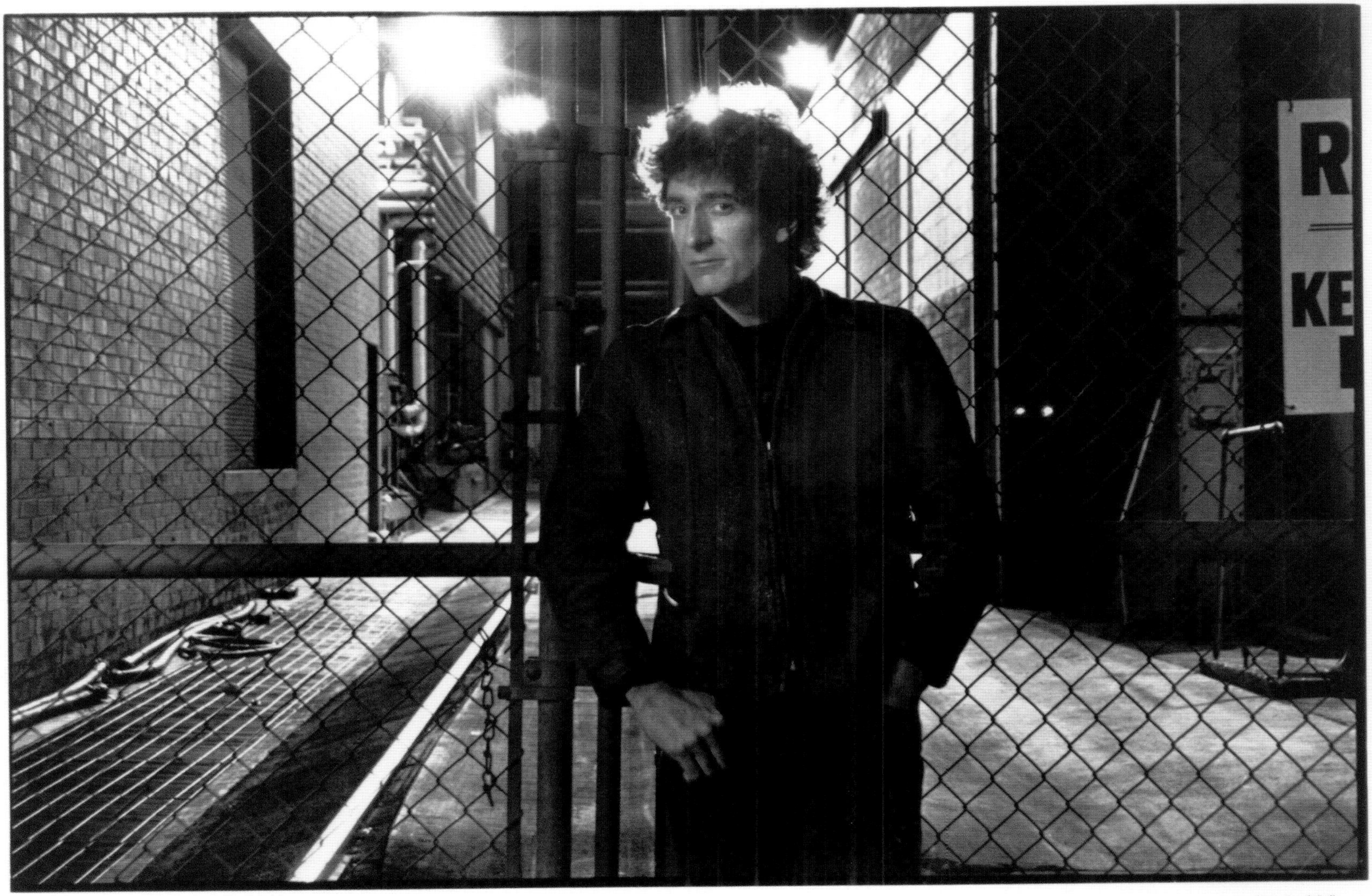

photo: Frank Delia

STAN RIDGWAY

I.R.S.

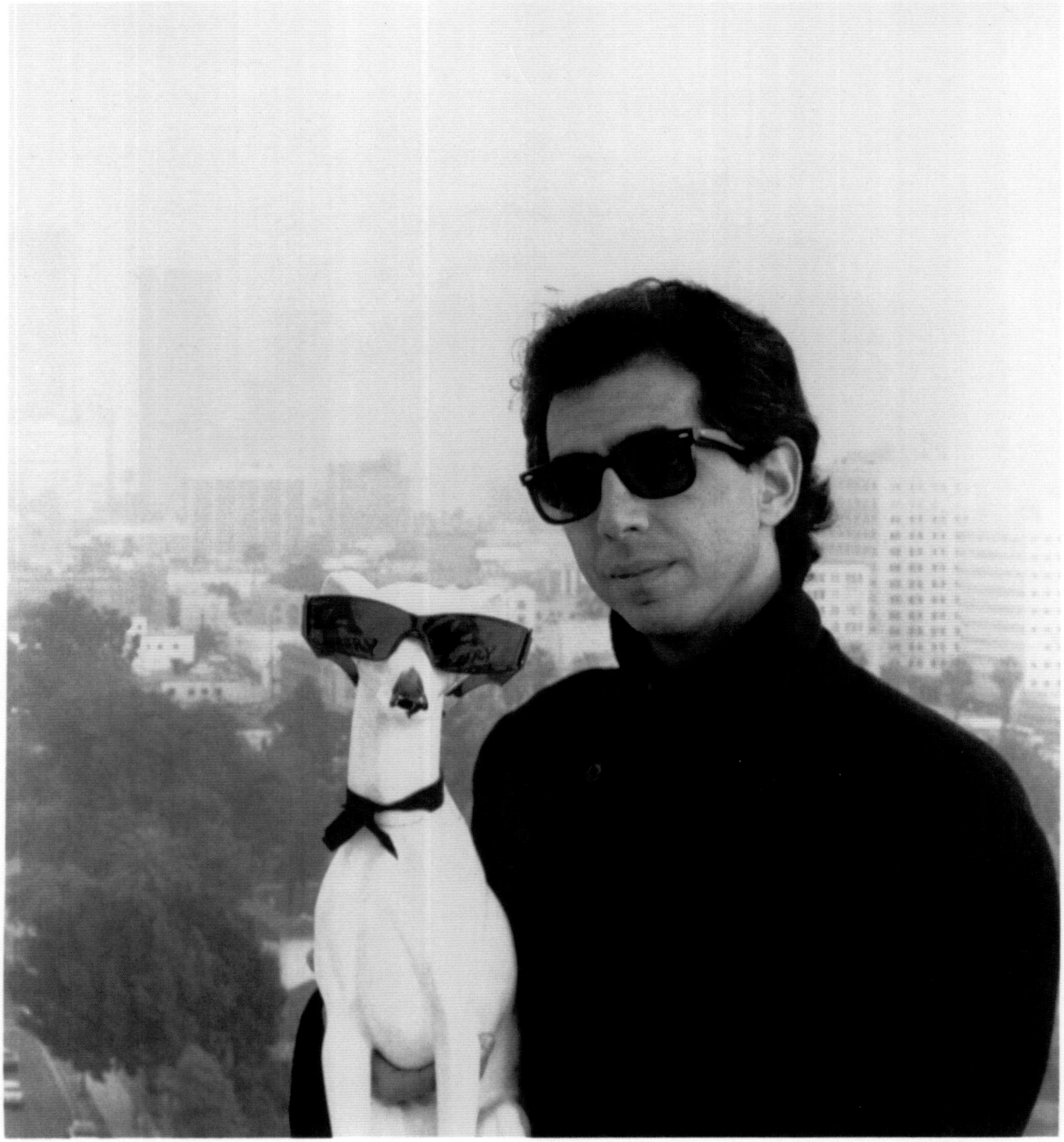

WHAT RECORDS

· 213 · 276 · WHAT

TONIO K.

A&M RECORDS

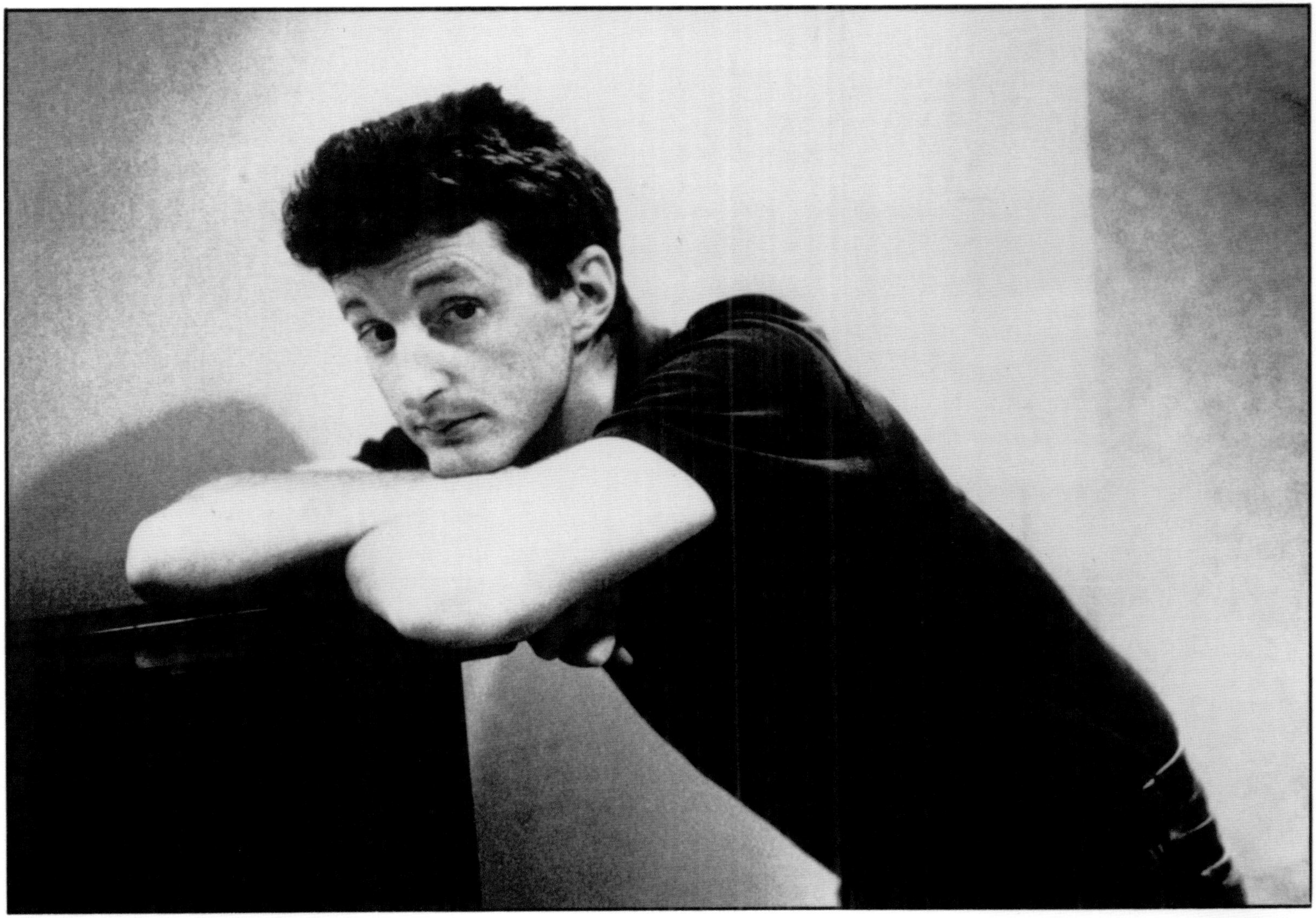

PHOTO CREDIT: PENNIE SMITH/1986

BILLY BRAGG

ELEKTRA

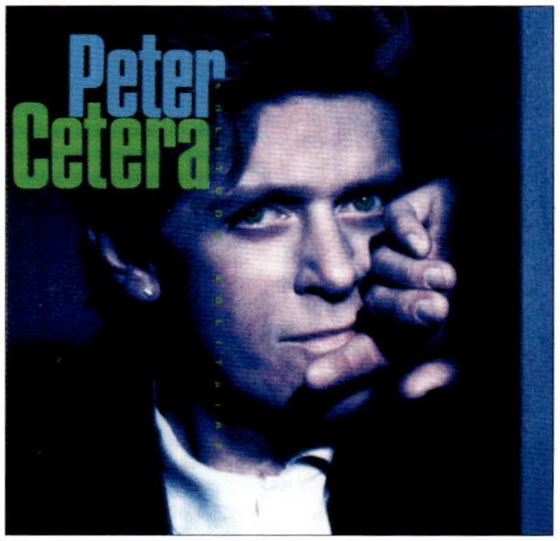

Upon exiting the band Chicago, veteran frontman **Peter Cetera** scored two No. 1 hits, "Glory of Love" and "The Next Time I Fall," a duet with Amy Grant.

Billboard 200: *Solitude/Solitaire* (#23)
Billboard Hot 100: "Glory of Love" (No. 1);
"The Next Time I Fall" (No. 1); "Big Mistake" (#61)

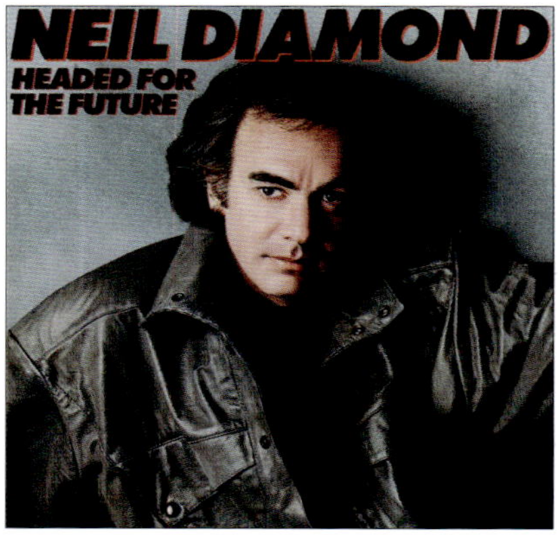

Designated by *Billboard* magazine as the year's most commercially successful solo act, **Neil Diamond** delivered *Headed for the Future*, a Top 20 album.

Billboard 200: *Headed for the Future* (#20)
Billboard Hot 100: "Headed for the Future" (#53)

"The Lady in Red," a languorous love ballad, pushed British-Irish singer-songwriter and instrumentalist **Chris de Burgh** to international prominence.

Billboard 200: *Into the Light* (#25)
Billboard Hot 100: "The Lady in Red" (#3)

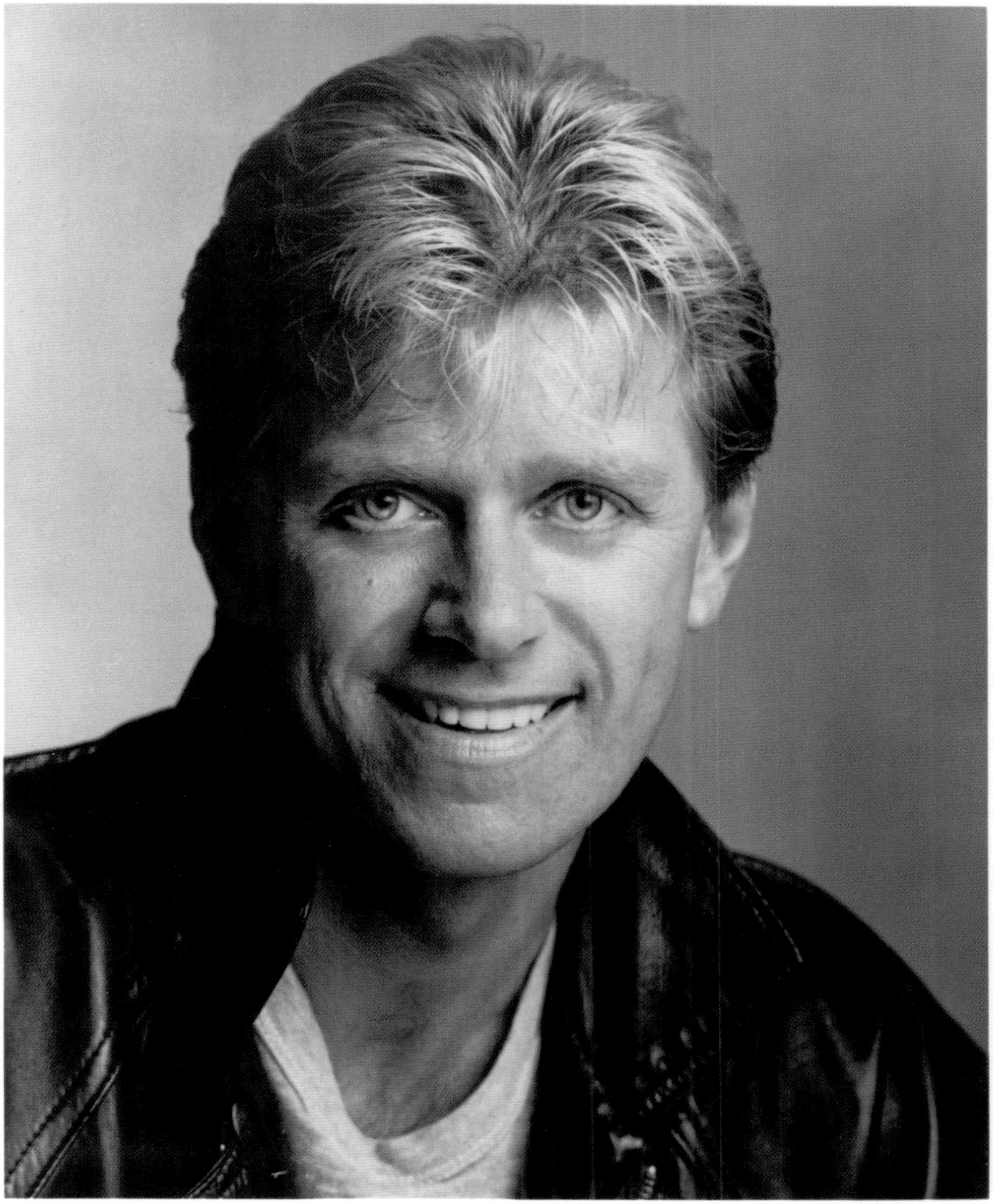

Photo Credit: Greg Gorman

PETER CETERA

WARNER BROS.

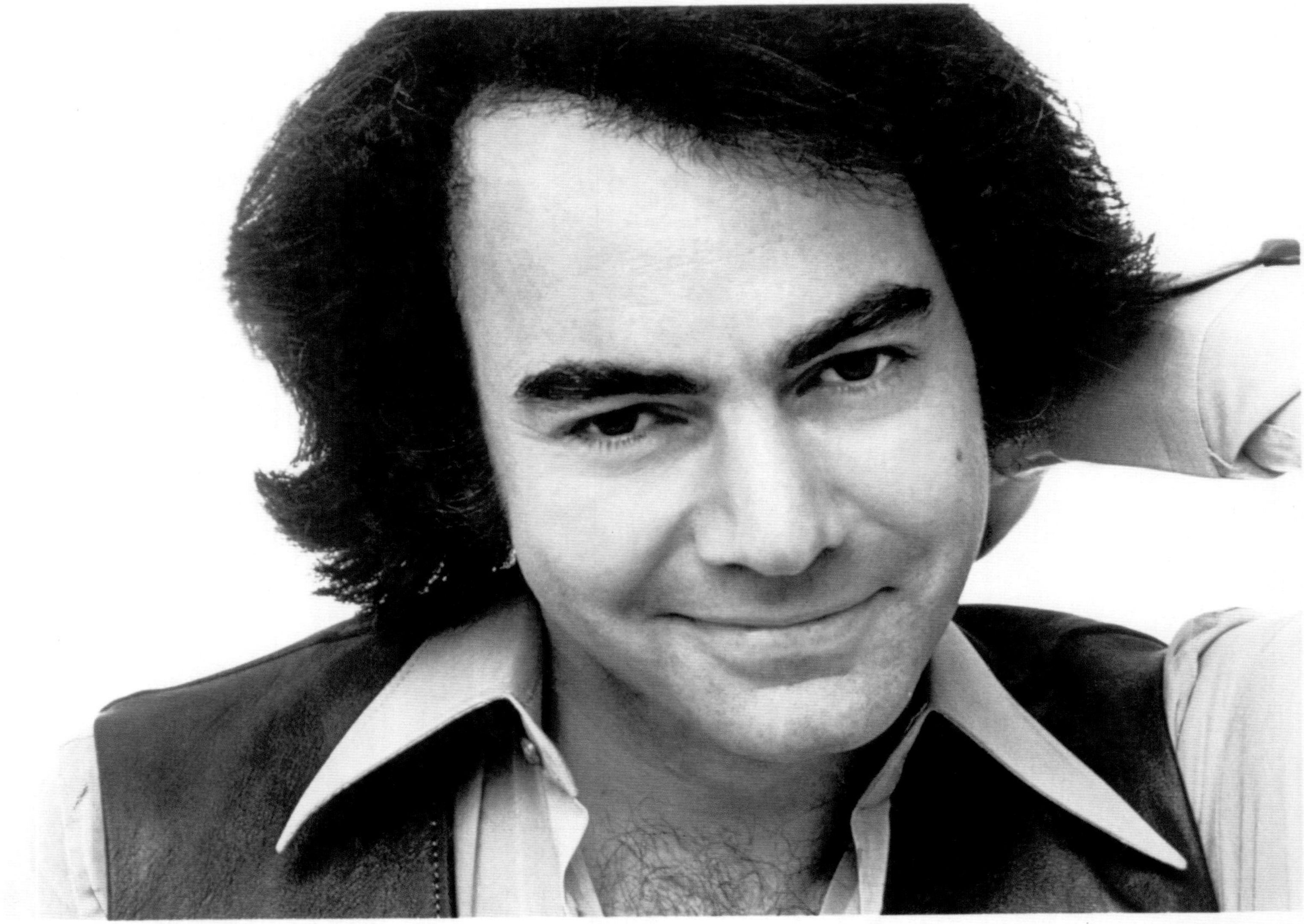

Photo Credit: Norman Seeff

NEIL DIAMOND

Columbia

8406

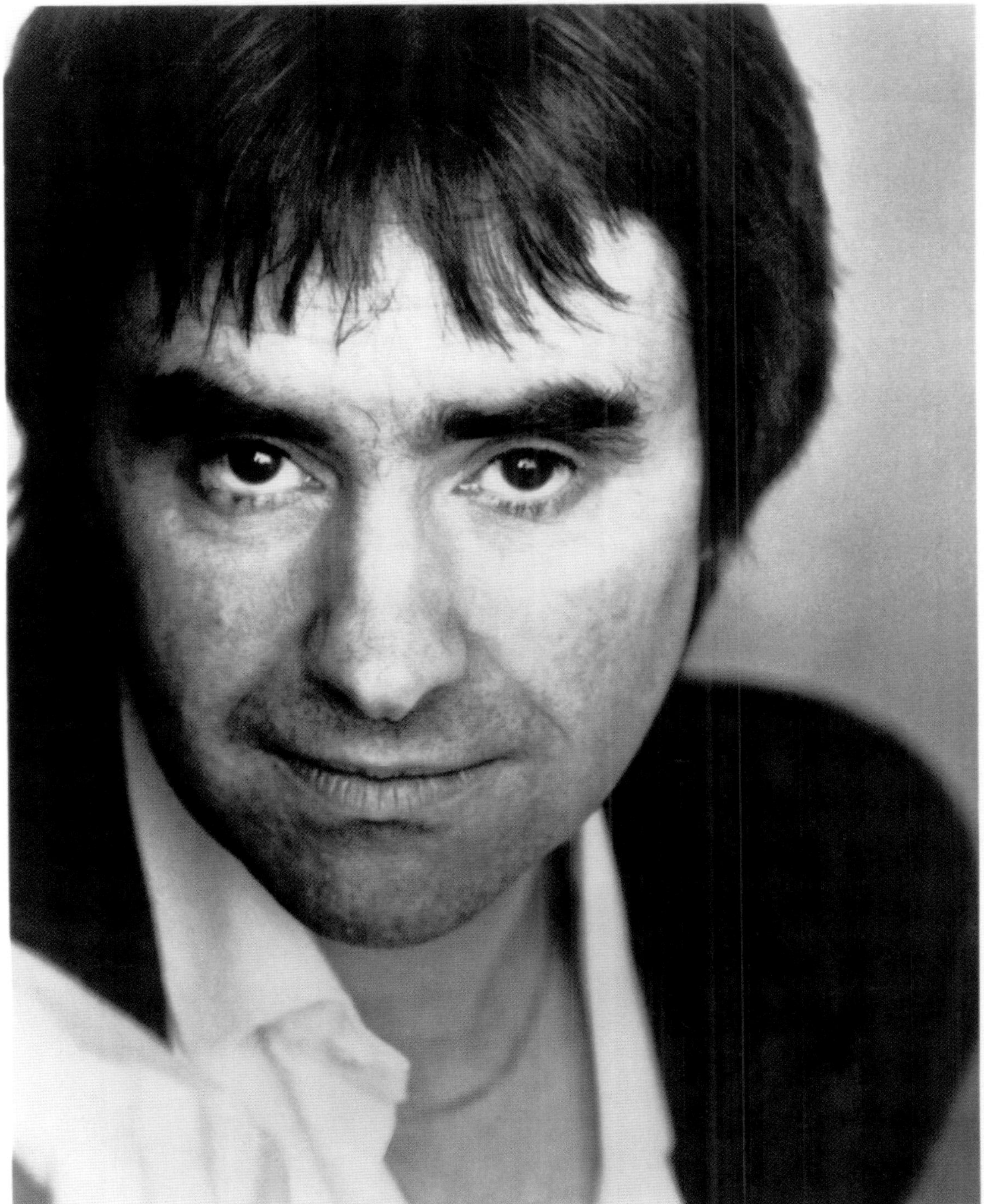

DIRECTION:
MISMANAGEMENT, INC.
01-731-7074

Chris De Burgh

A&M RECORDS
Printed in U.S.A.

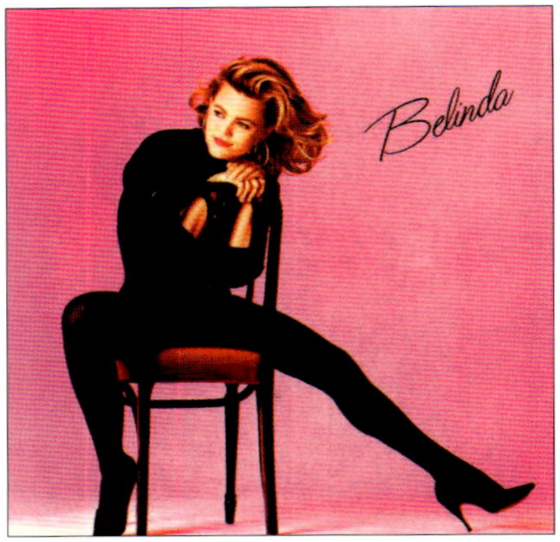

After the dissolution of the Go-Go's, lead vocalist **Belinda Carlisle** embarked on a fruitful solo career with "Mad About You," a radio-ready summer hit.

Billboard 200: *Belinda* (#13)
Billboard Hot 100: "Mad About You" (#3); "I Feel the Magic" (#82)

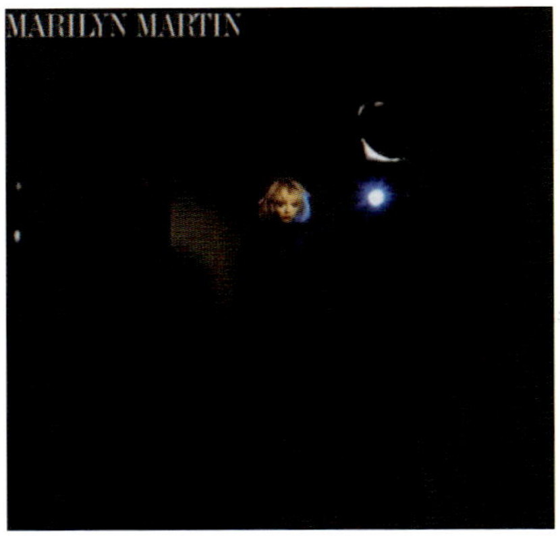

Having hit it big with "Separate Lives," a duet with Phil Collins that soared to No. 1, pop singer **Marilyn Martin** released her own self-titled debut album.

Billboard 200: *Marilyn Martin* (#73)
Billboard Hot 100: "Night Moves" (#28)

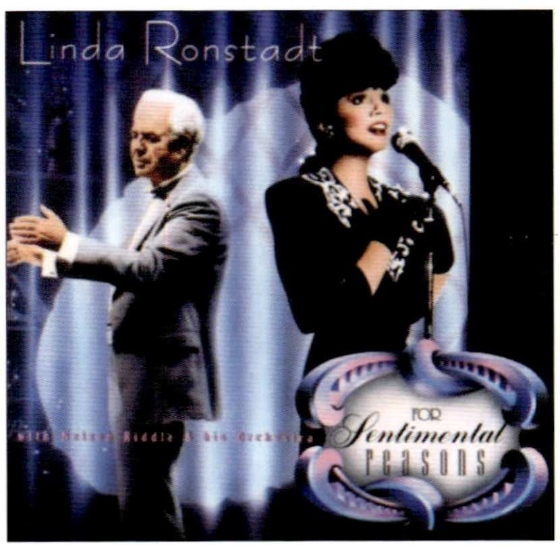

For Sentimental Reasons, singer **Linda Ronstadt**'s third collection of pop standards, contained the last masterful arrangements by the late Nelson Riddle.

Billboard 200: *For Sentimental Reasons* (#46)

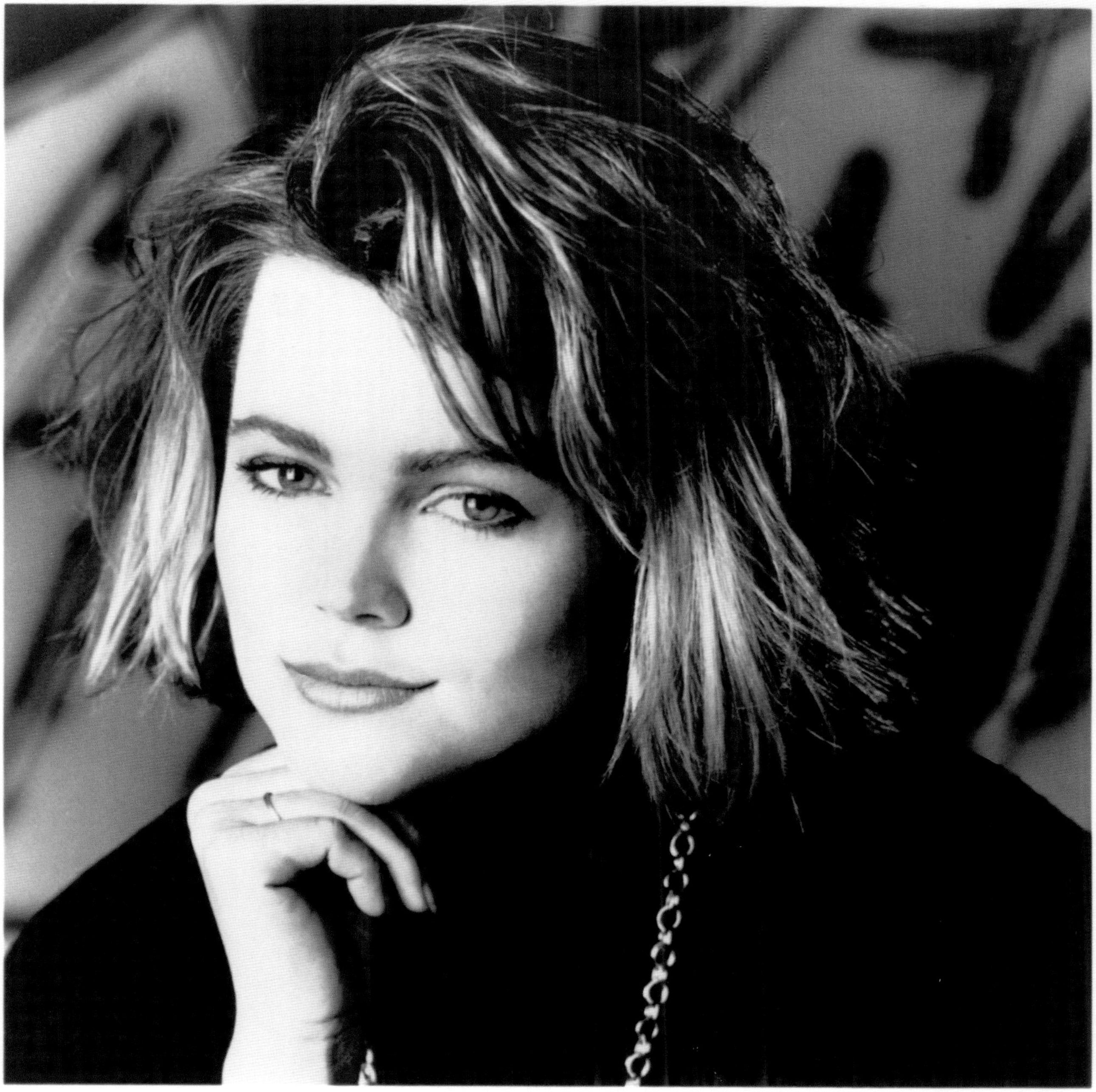

Belinda Carlisle

I.R.S.

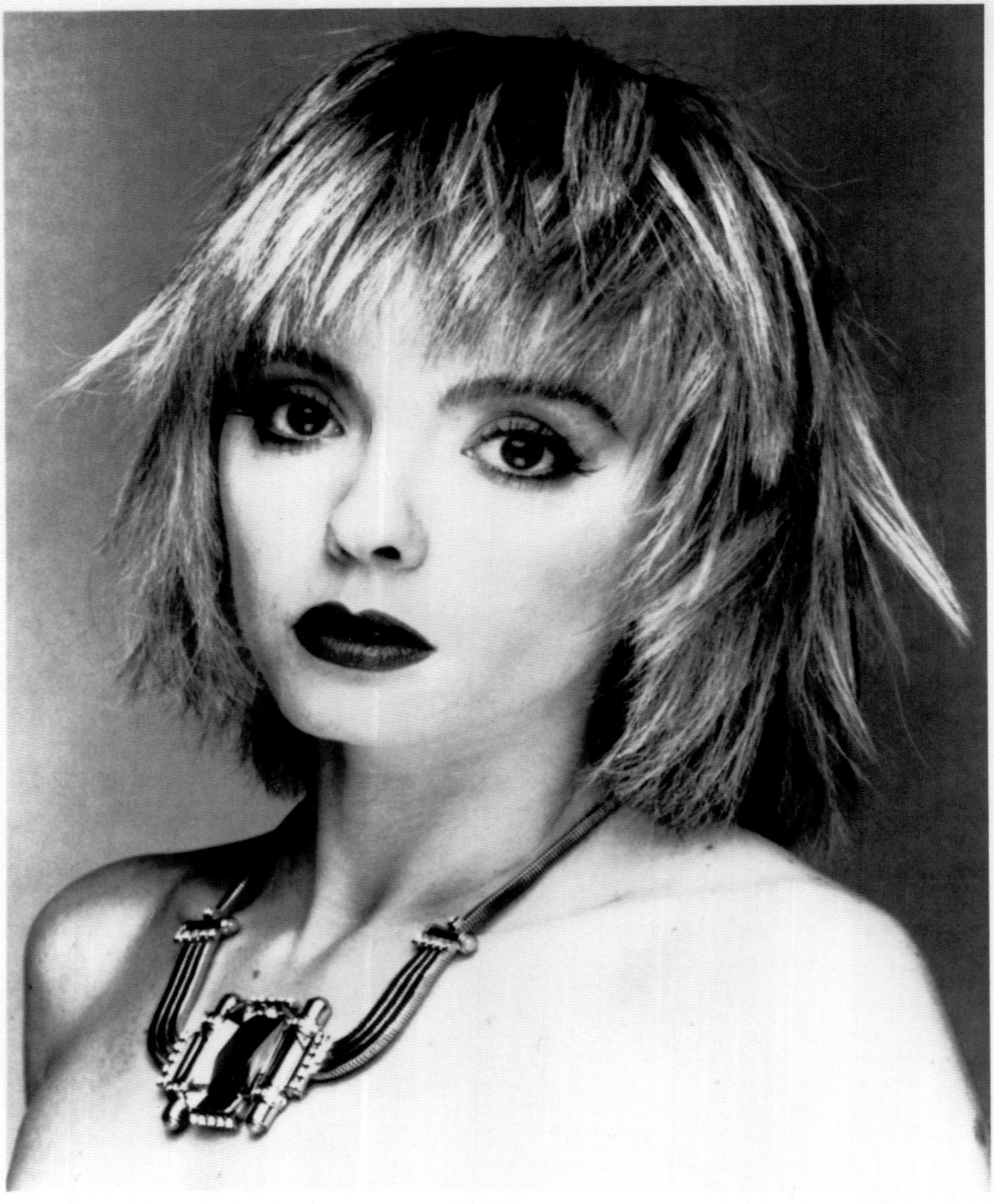

Brian Aris

MARILYN MARTIN

ATLANTIC

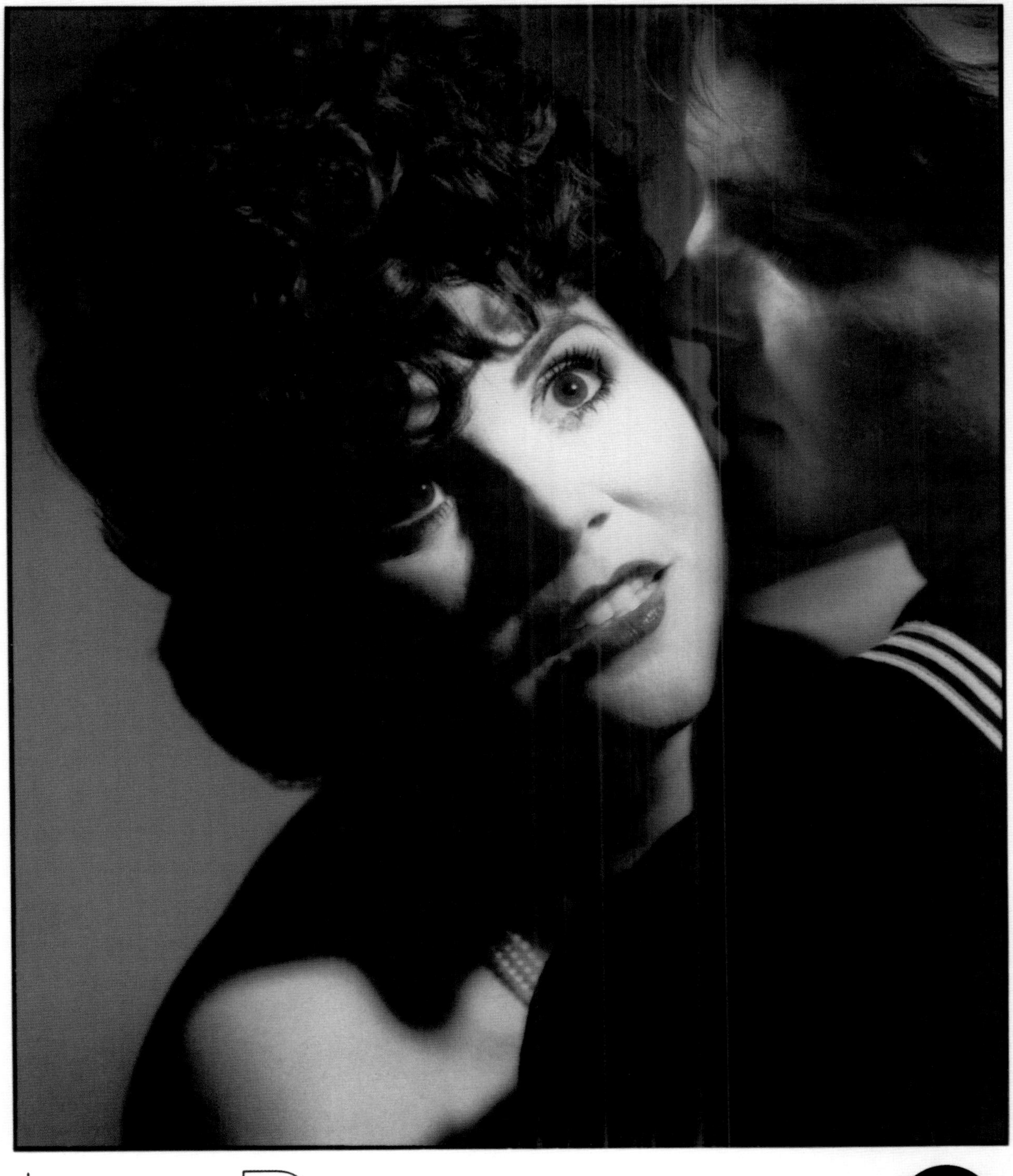

PHOTO CREDIT: MARK HANAUER/1986

Linda Ronstadt

ASYLUM

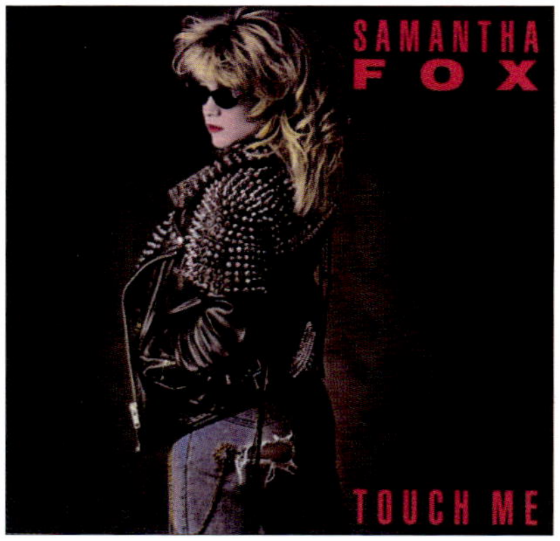

A topless model in a noted British tabloid, **Samantha Fox** began a pop music career with "Touch Me (I Want Your Body)," a No. 1 single in eight countries.

Billboard 200: *Touch Me* (#24)
Billboard Hot 100: "Touch Me (I Want Your Body)" (#4);
"Do Ya Do Ya (Wanna Please Me)" (#87)

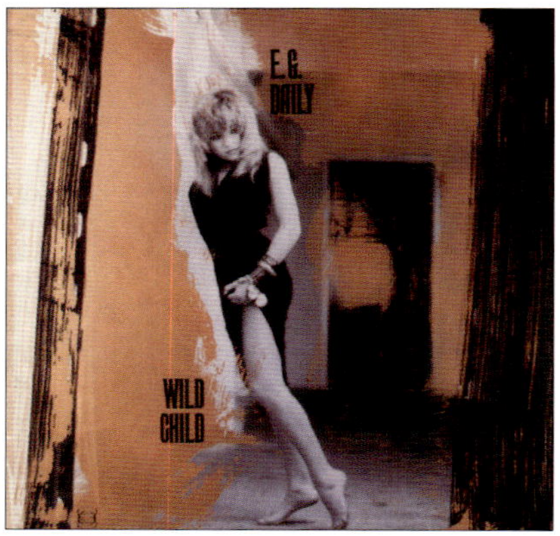

L.A.-based actress and musician **E.G. Daily** made it to the No. 1 spot on the dance club charts with "Say It, Say It," a track produced by Jellybean Benitez.

Billboard Hot 100: "Say It, Say It" (#70)

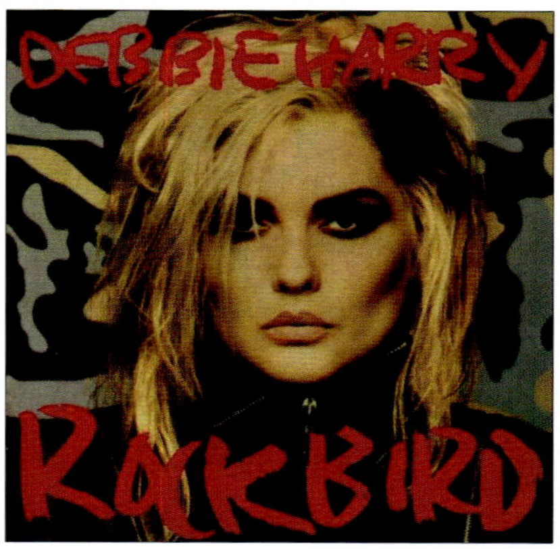

Four years after Blondie's split, singer **Debbie Harry** put out her second solo album, *Rockbird*, and "French Kissin'" emerged as her biggest hit in the UK.

Billboard 200: *Rockbird* (#97)
Billboard Hot 100: "French Kissin'" (#57); "In Love with Love" (#70)

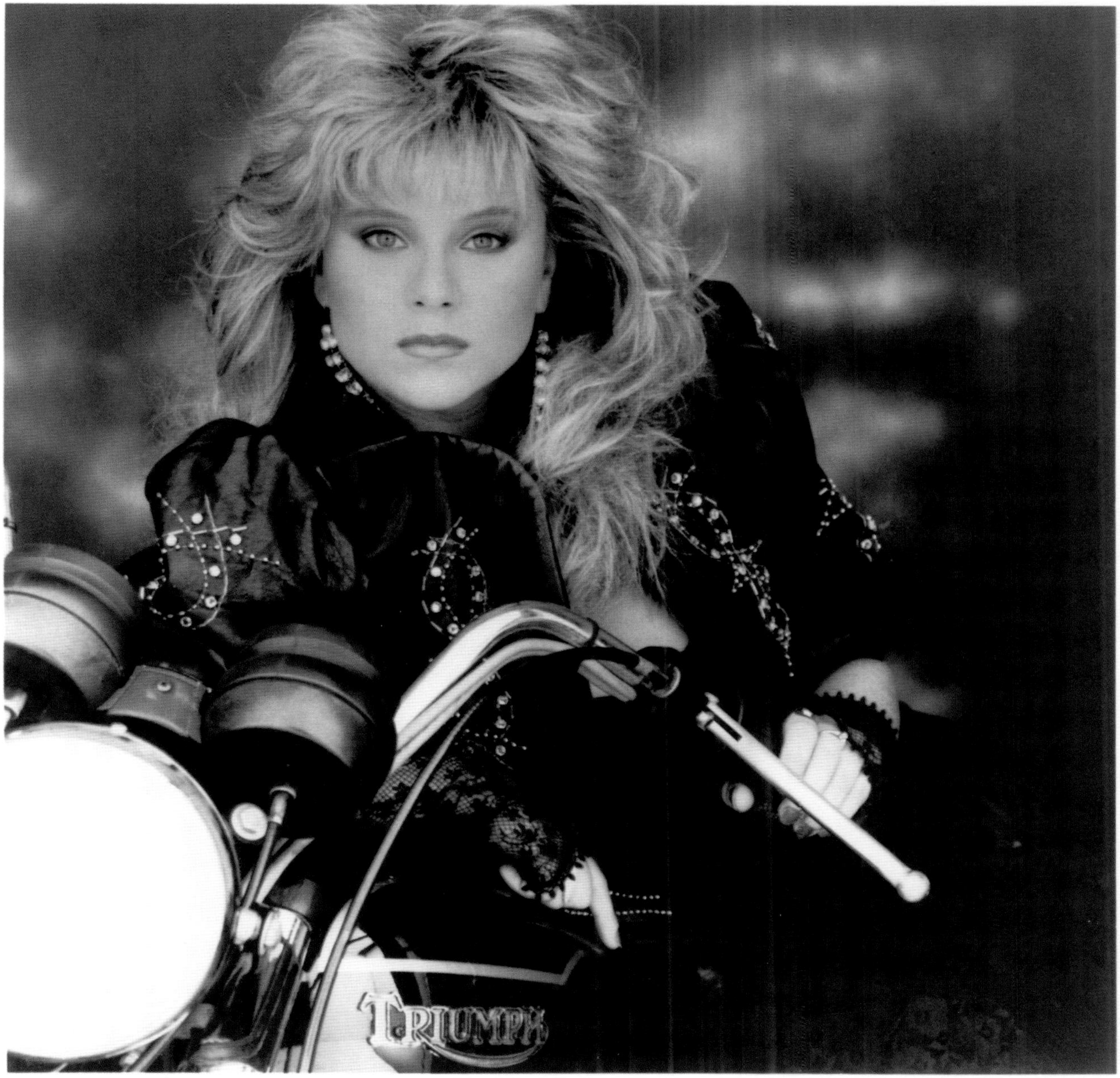

SAMANTHA FOX

J·I·V·E

Marketed and Distributed by RCA Records

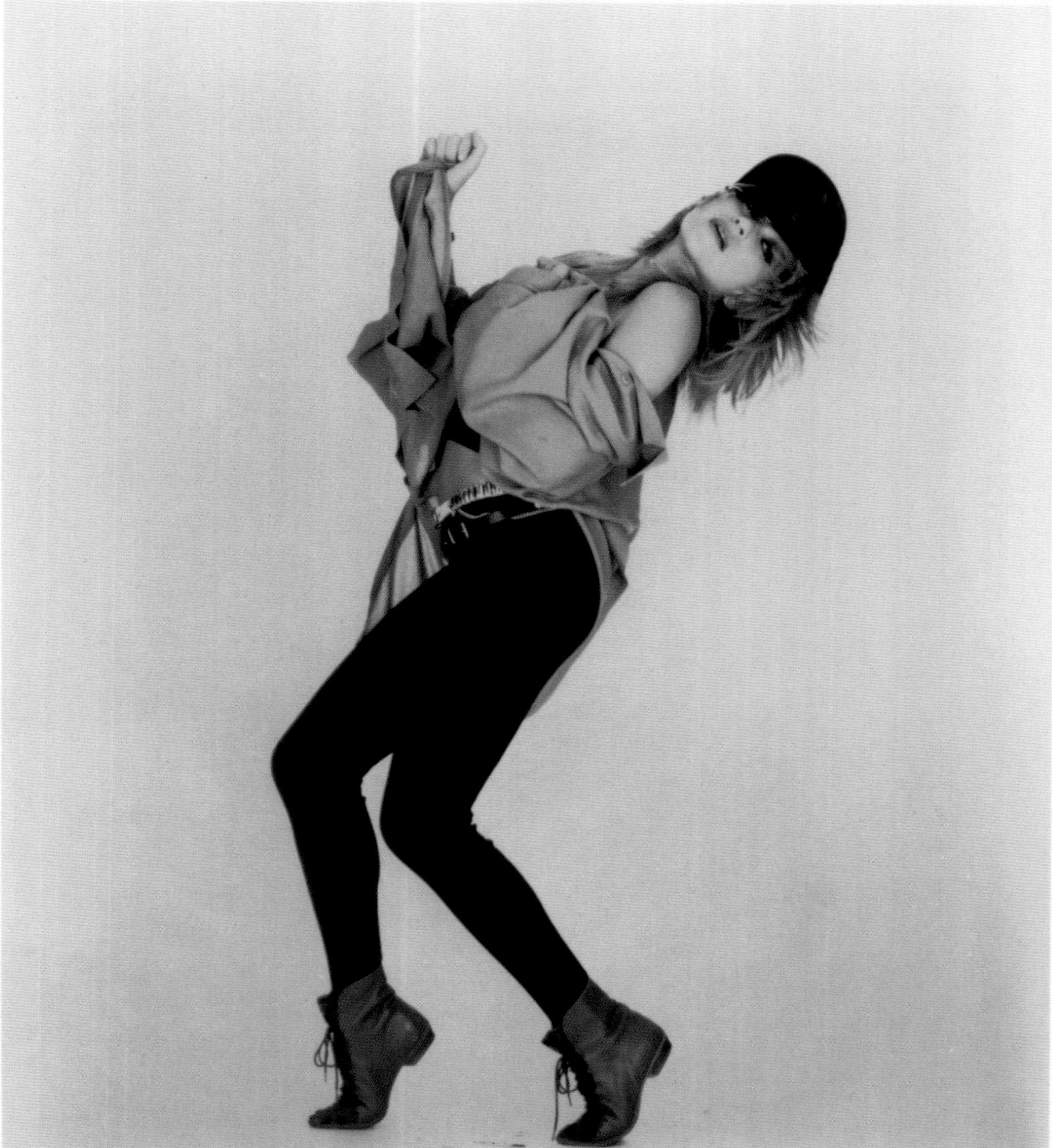

MANAGEMENT / DIRECTION:
GERBER • RODKIN
(213) 854-6693

E.G. DAILY

A&M RECORDS
Printed in U.S.A.

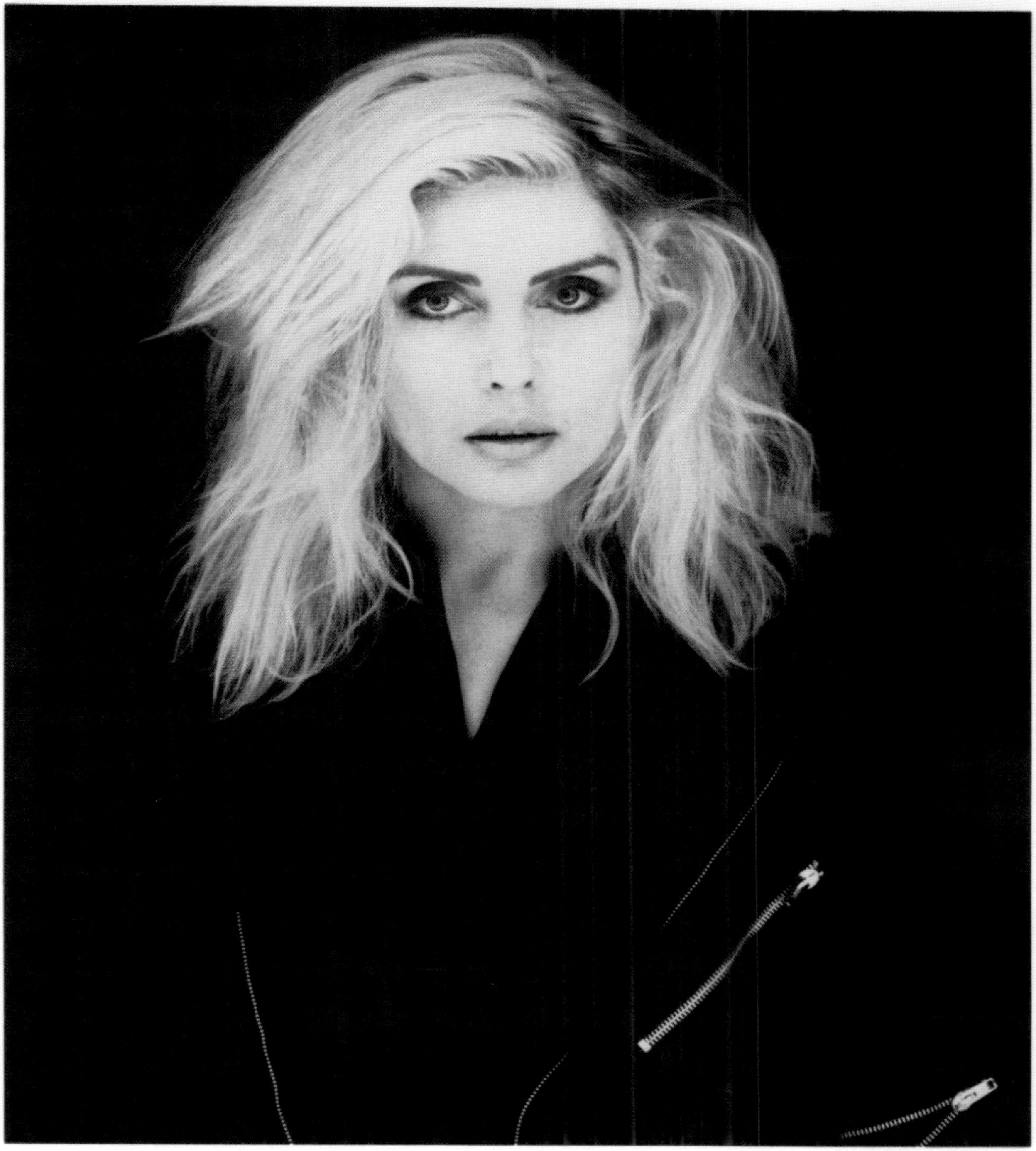

Photo Credit: Brian Aris

DEBBIE HARRY

GEFFEN RECORDS

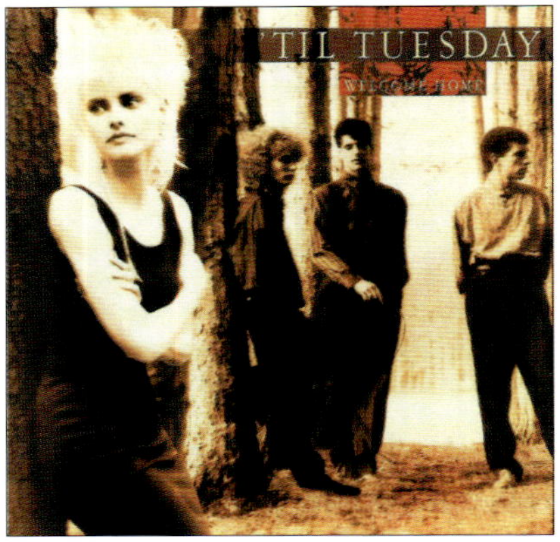

The follow-up to **'Til Tuesday**'s promising debut, *Welcome Home* saw the Boston act progress into the vehicle for lead singer Aimee Mann's songwriting.

Billboard 200: *Welcome Home* (#49)
Billboard Hot 100: "What About Love" (#26); "Coming Up Close" (#59)

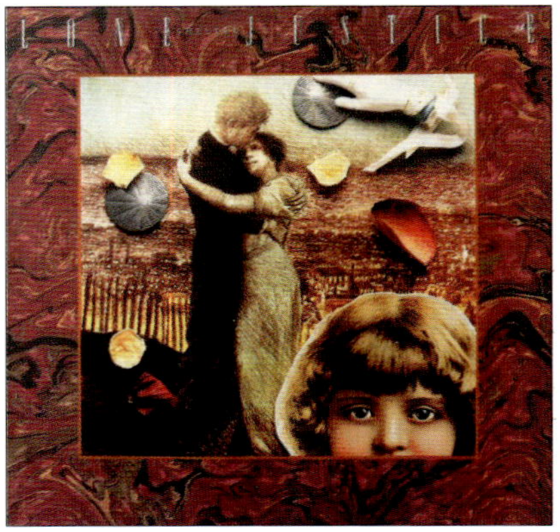

With a fresh lineup fronted by vocalist Maria McKee, **Lone Justice**'s second album, *Shelter*, delved into polished elements of modern and heartland rock.

Billboard 200: *Shelter* (#65)
Billboard Hot 100: "Shelter" (#47)

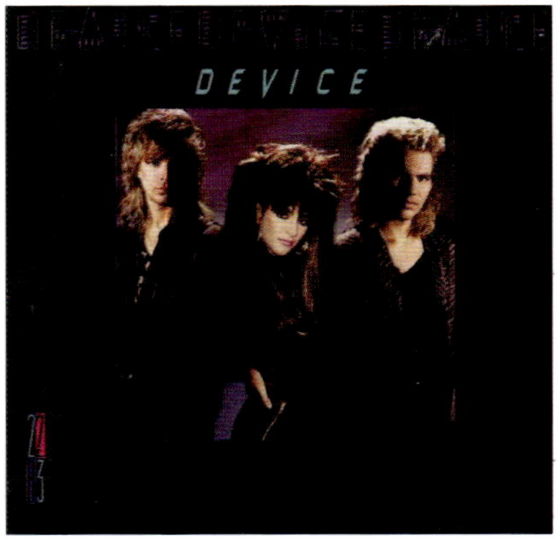

Songwriter Holly Knight's second band, the short-lived **Device**, bore a hit off *22B3* with "Hanging on a Heart Attack," crafted by hitmaker Mike Chapman.

Billboard 200: *22B3* (#73)
Billboard Hot 100: "Hanging on a Heart Attack" (#35); "Who Says" (#79)

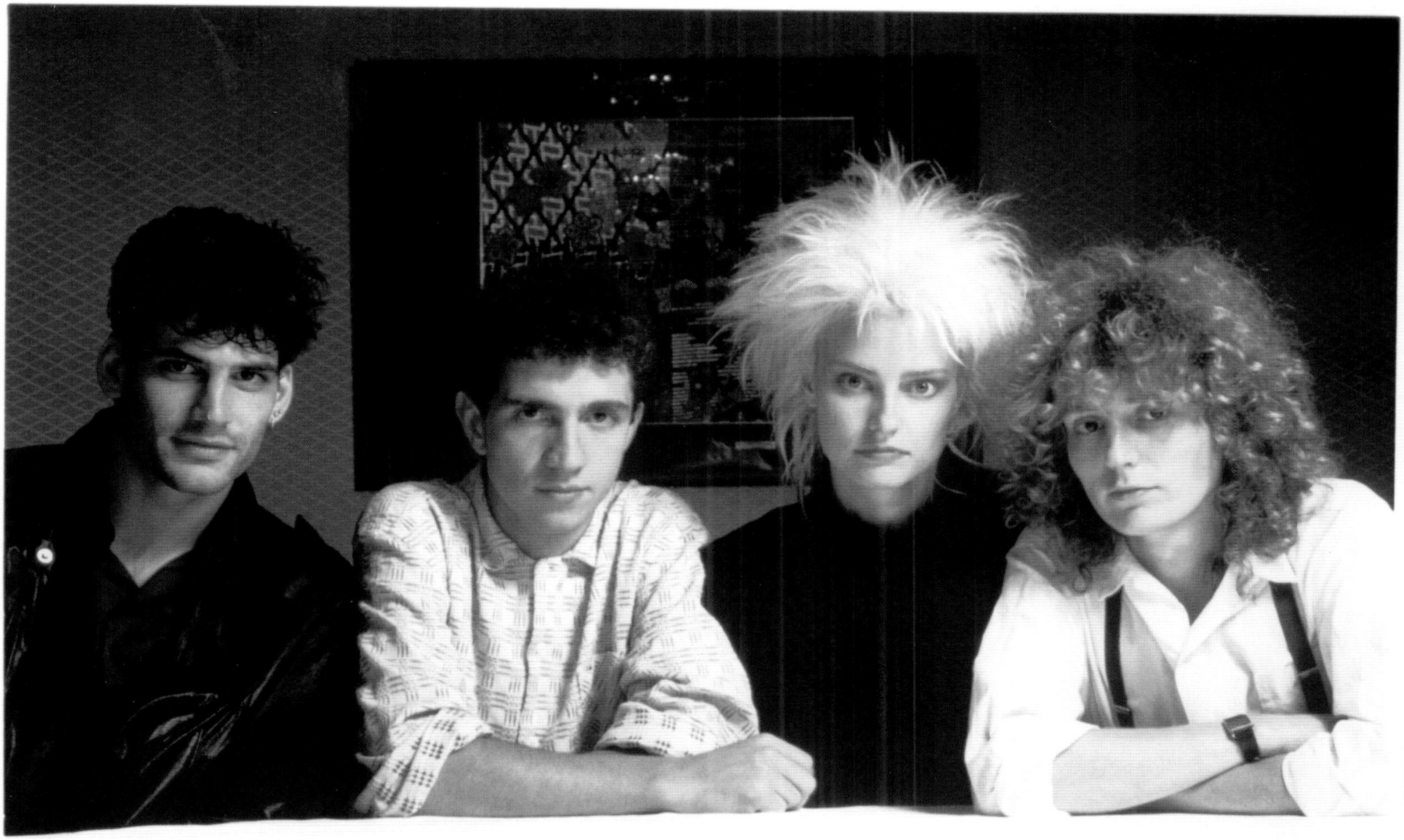

PHOTO: HIRO ITO

JOEY PESCE MICHAEL HAUSMAN AIMEE MANN ROBERT HOLMES

SYMMETRY MANAGEMENT

'TIL TUESDAY

Epic

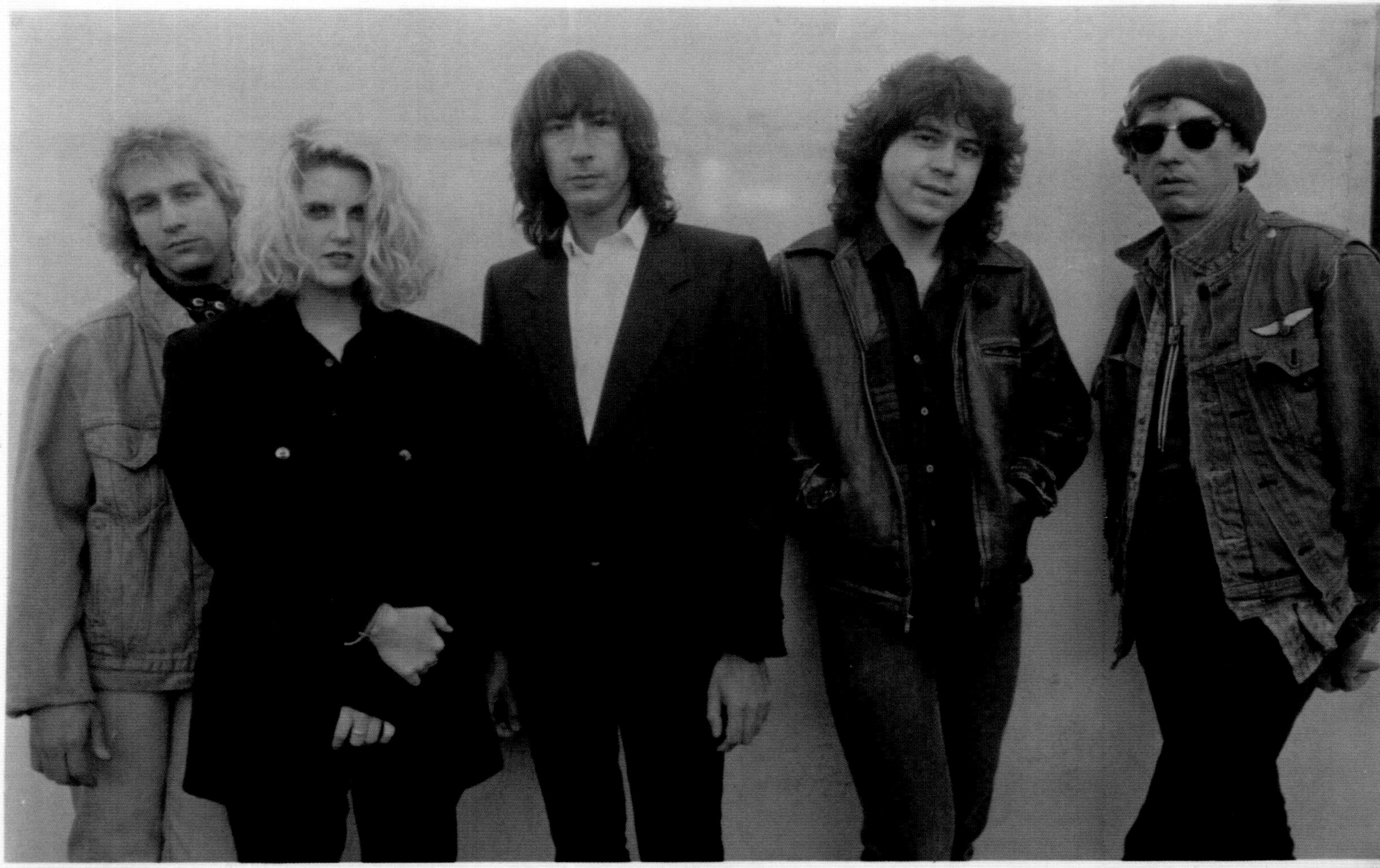

Photo Credit: Melenie Missen

LONE JUSTICE

GEFFEN RECORDS

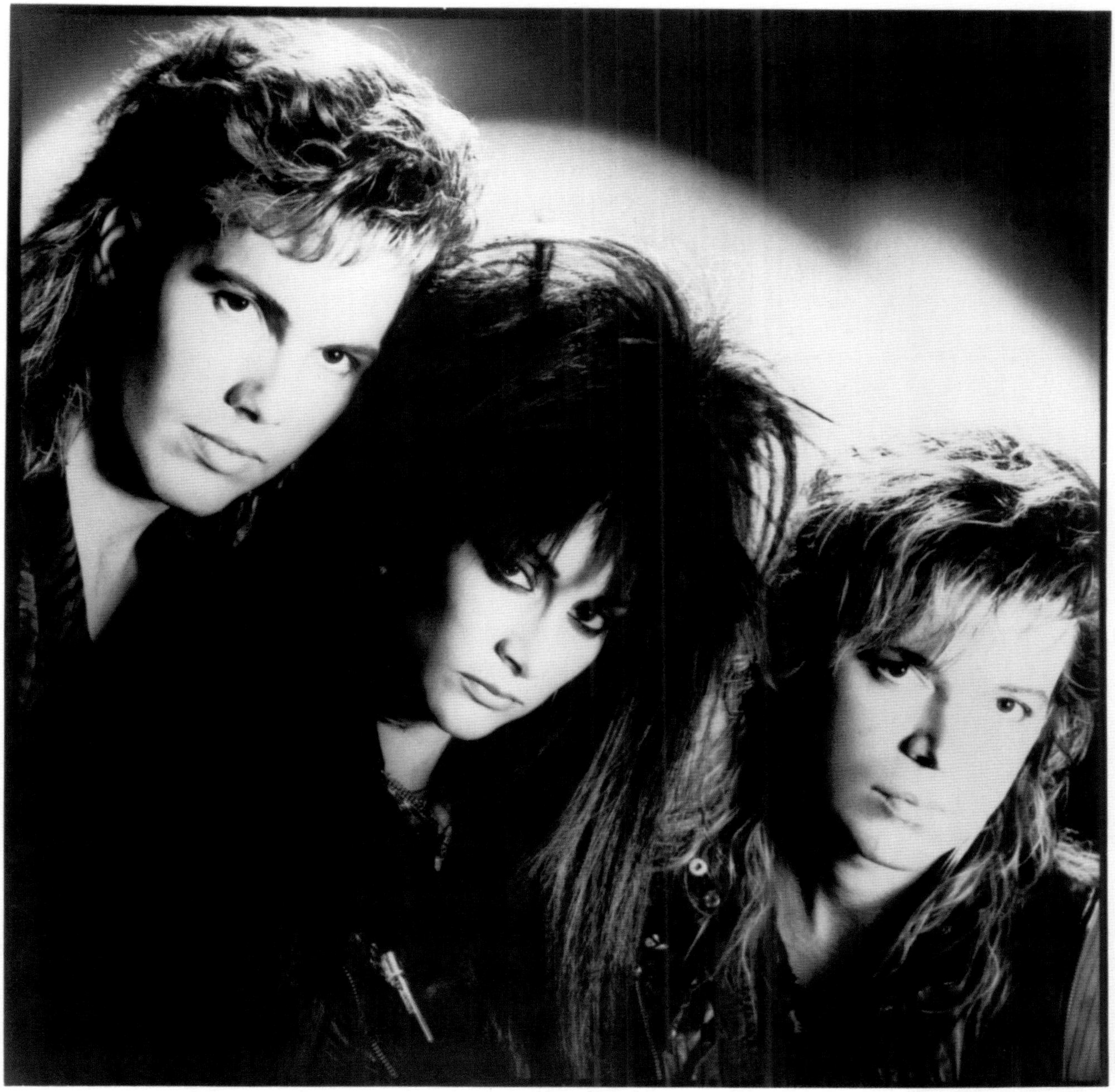

Photo Credit: Paul Cox

Paul Engemann   Holly Knight   Gene Black

DEVICE

Chrysalis™

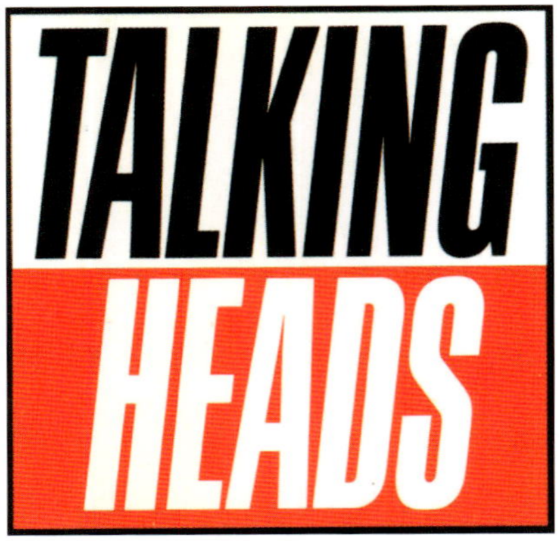

On *True Stories*, **Talking Heads** recorded all the soundtrack songs from lead singer David Byrne's outré directorial debut, hatching the hit "Wild Wild Life."

Billboard 200: *True Stories* (#17)
Billboard Hot 100: "Wild Wild Life" (#25)

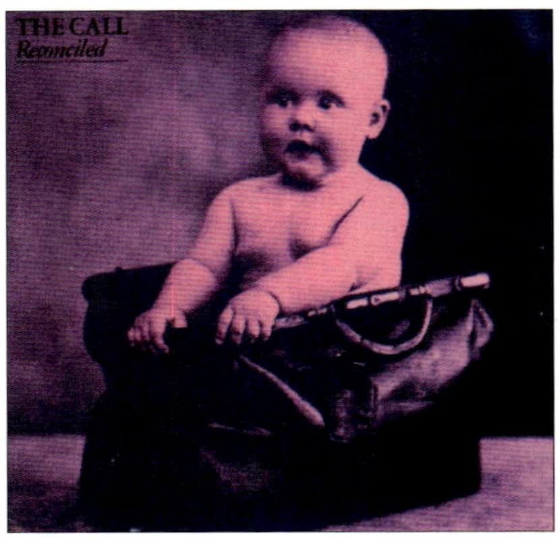

The Call's *Reconciled* begat a mainstream rock hit, "I Still Believe (Great Design)," and two more extraordinary tracks, "Everywhere I Go" and "Oklahoma."

Billboard 200: *Reconciled* (#82)

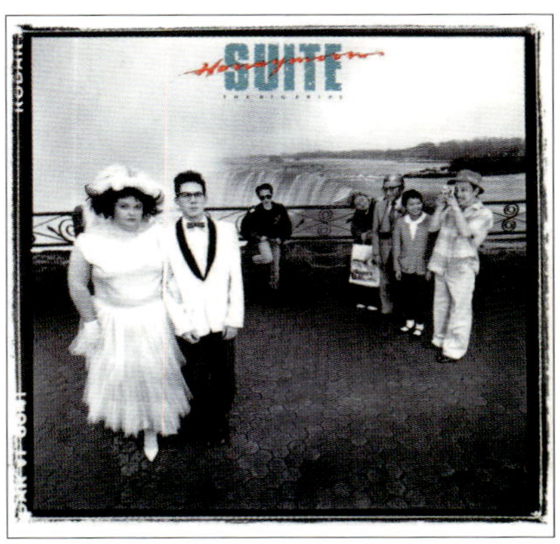

Honeymoon Suite's *The Big Prize*, produced by Canadian comrade Bruce Fairbairn, presented the keen hard-rock songs "Bad Attitude" and "Feel It Again."

Billboard 200: *The Big Prize* (#61)
Billboard Hot 100: "Feel It Again" (#34); "What Does It Take" (#52)

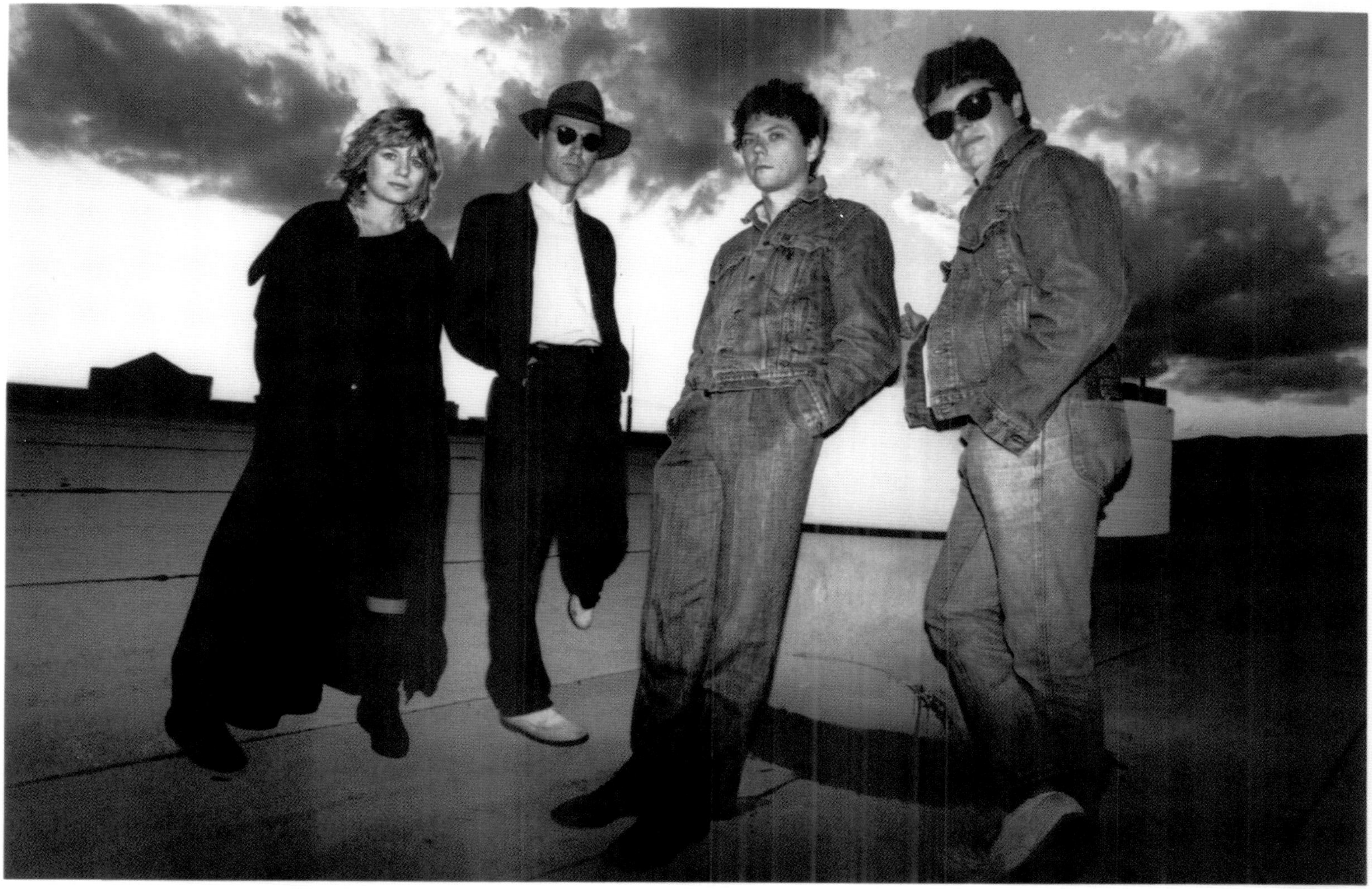

Photo Credit: Amy Etra

TALKING HEADS

SIRE™

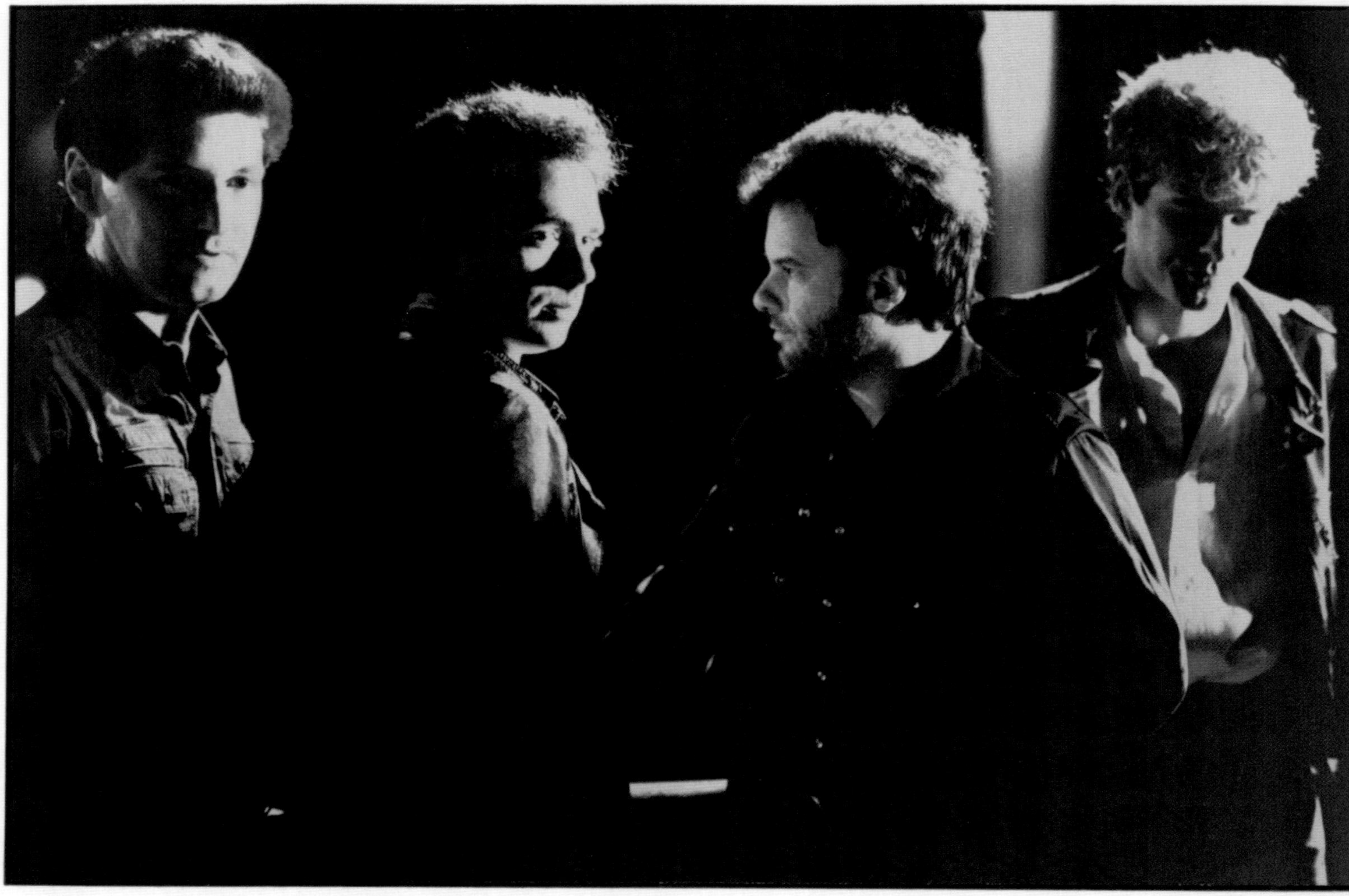

PHOTO CREDIT: ROBERT SPECTER/1986

TOM FERRIER SCOTT MUSICK MICHAEL BEEN JIM GOODWIN

THE CALL

ELEKTRA

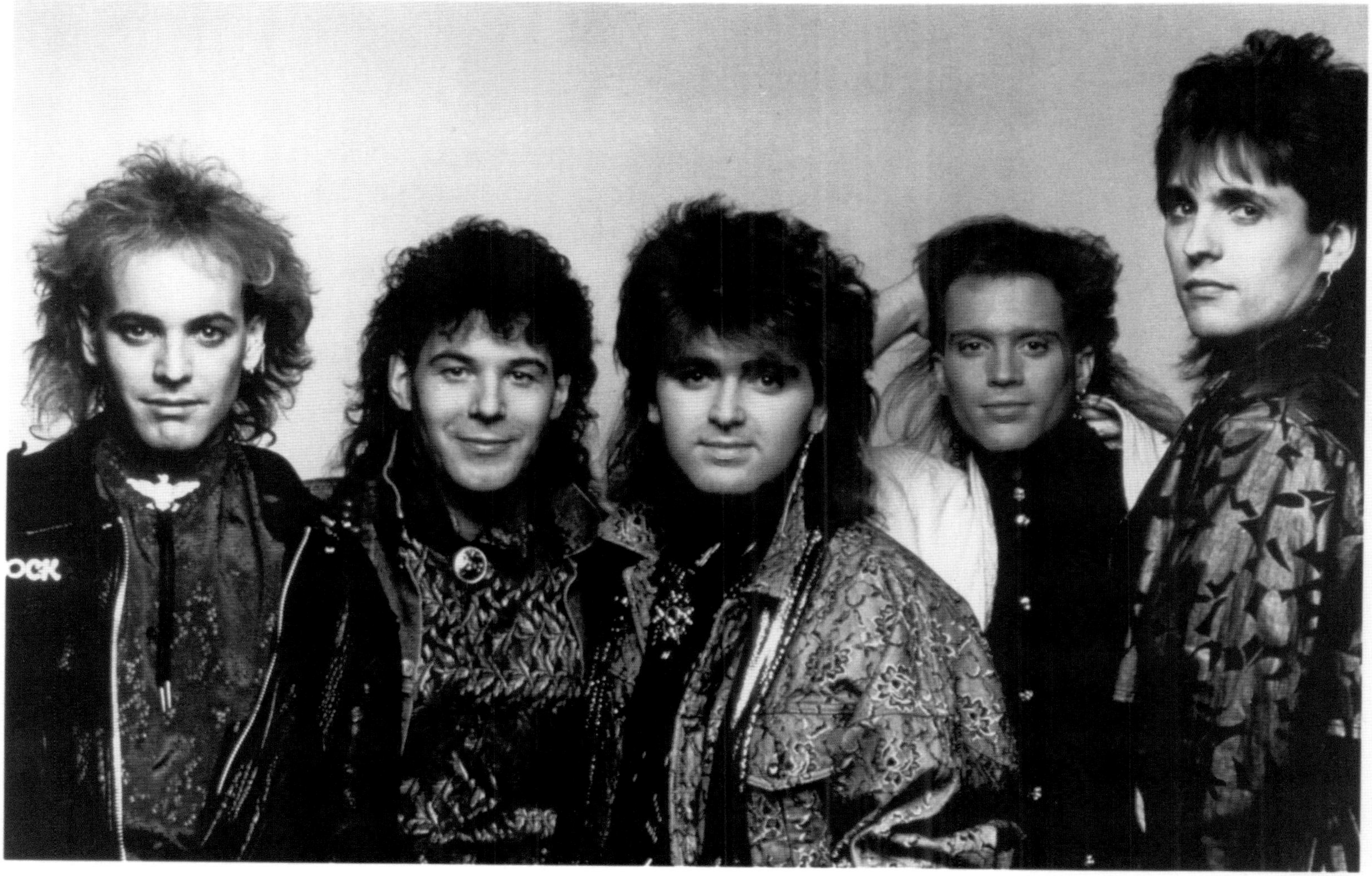

Photo Credit: Dimo Safari

Honeymoon

SUITE

WARNER BROS.

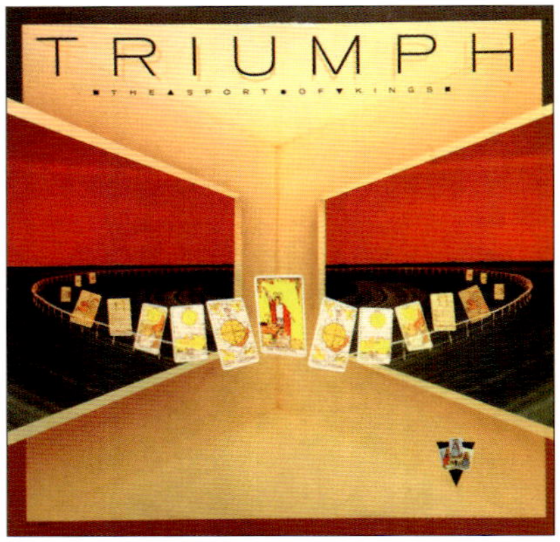

After nine albums, Canadian hard-rock power trio **Triumph** used an outside producer and wound up with a Top 40 hit, the ebullient "Somebody's Out There."

Billboard 200: *The Sport of Kings* (#33)
Billboard Hot 100: "Somebody's Out There" (#27)

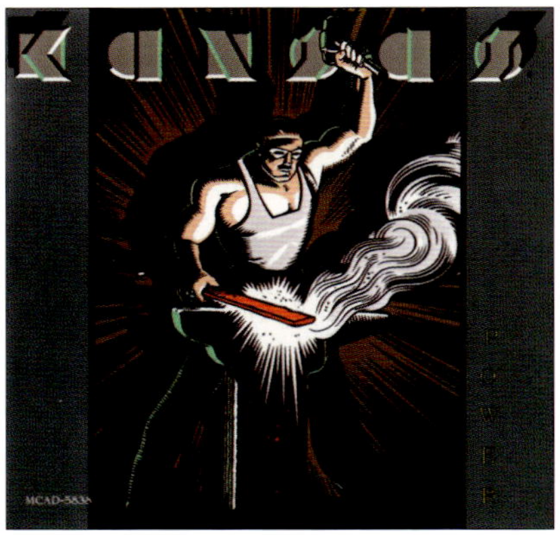

Kansas carried on with an overhauled lineup including famed guitarist Steve Morse, releasing *Power* and hitting the Top 20 one last time with "All I Wanted."

Billboard 200: *Power* (#35)
Billboard Hot 100: "All I Wanted" (#19); "Power" (#84)

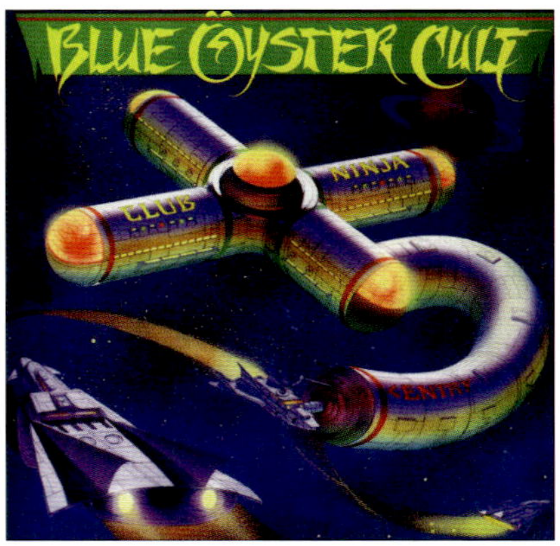

With the return of producer Sandy Pearlman, **Blue Öyster Cult** worked with outside writers on *Club Ninja*, scoring a modest hit with "Dancin' in the Ruins."

Billboard 200: *Club Ninja* (#63)

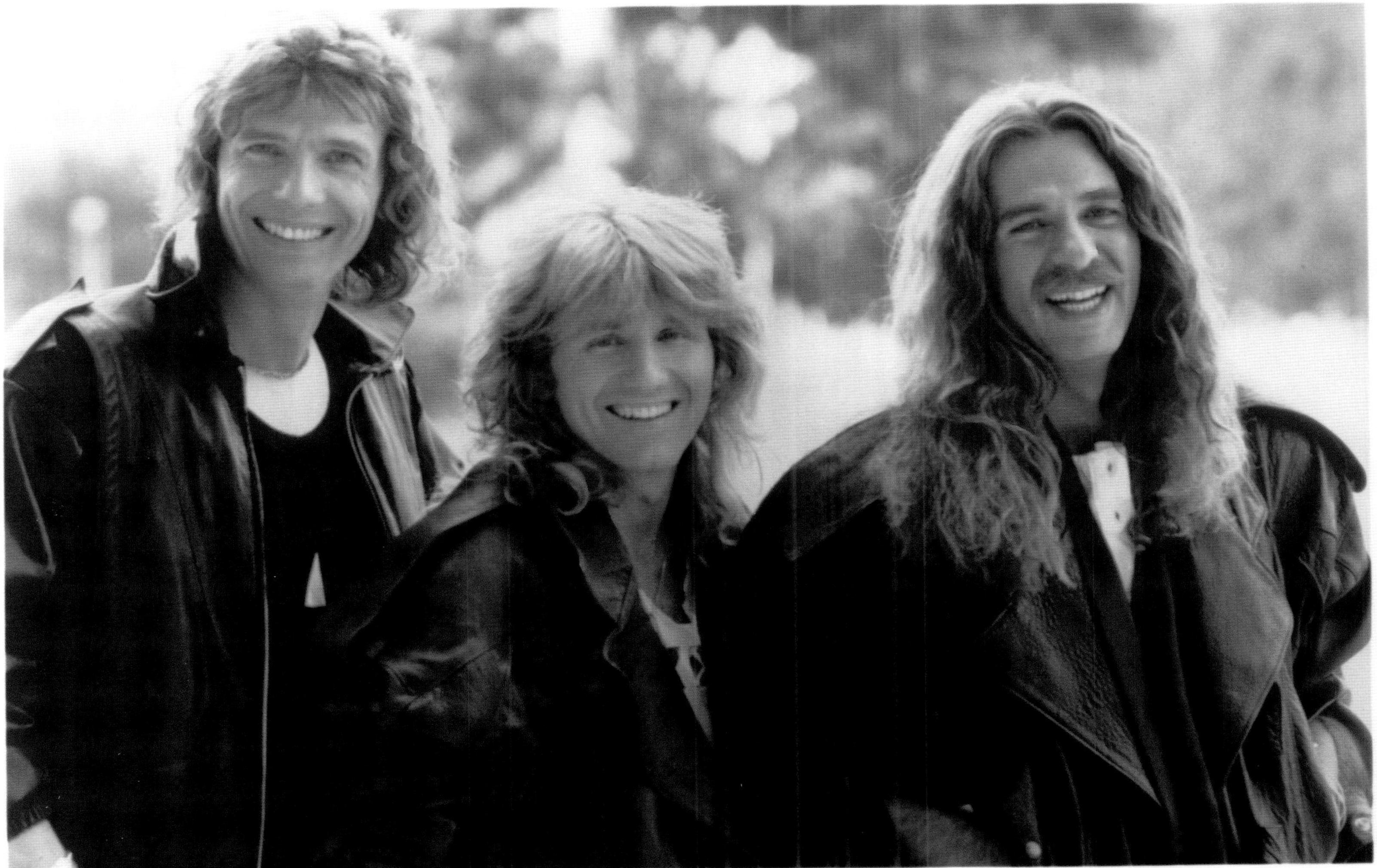

TRIUMPH

GIL MOORE **RIK EMMETT** **MIKE LEVINE**

MCA RECORDS

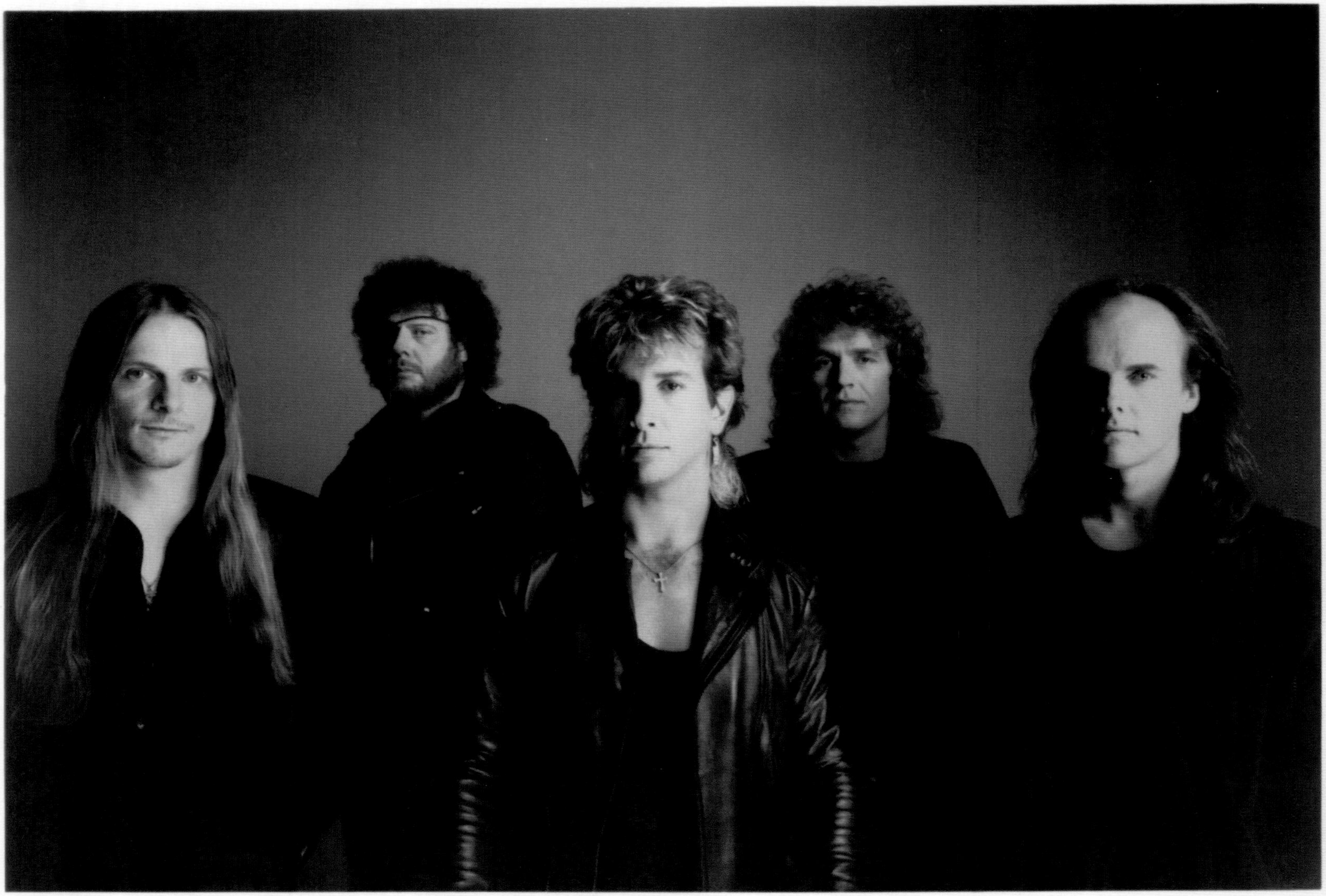

KANSAS

MCA RECORDS

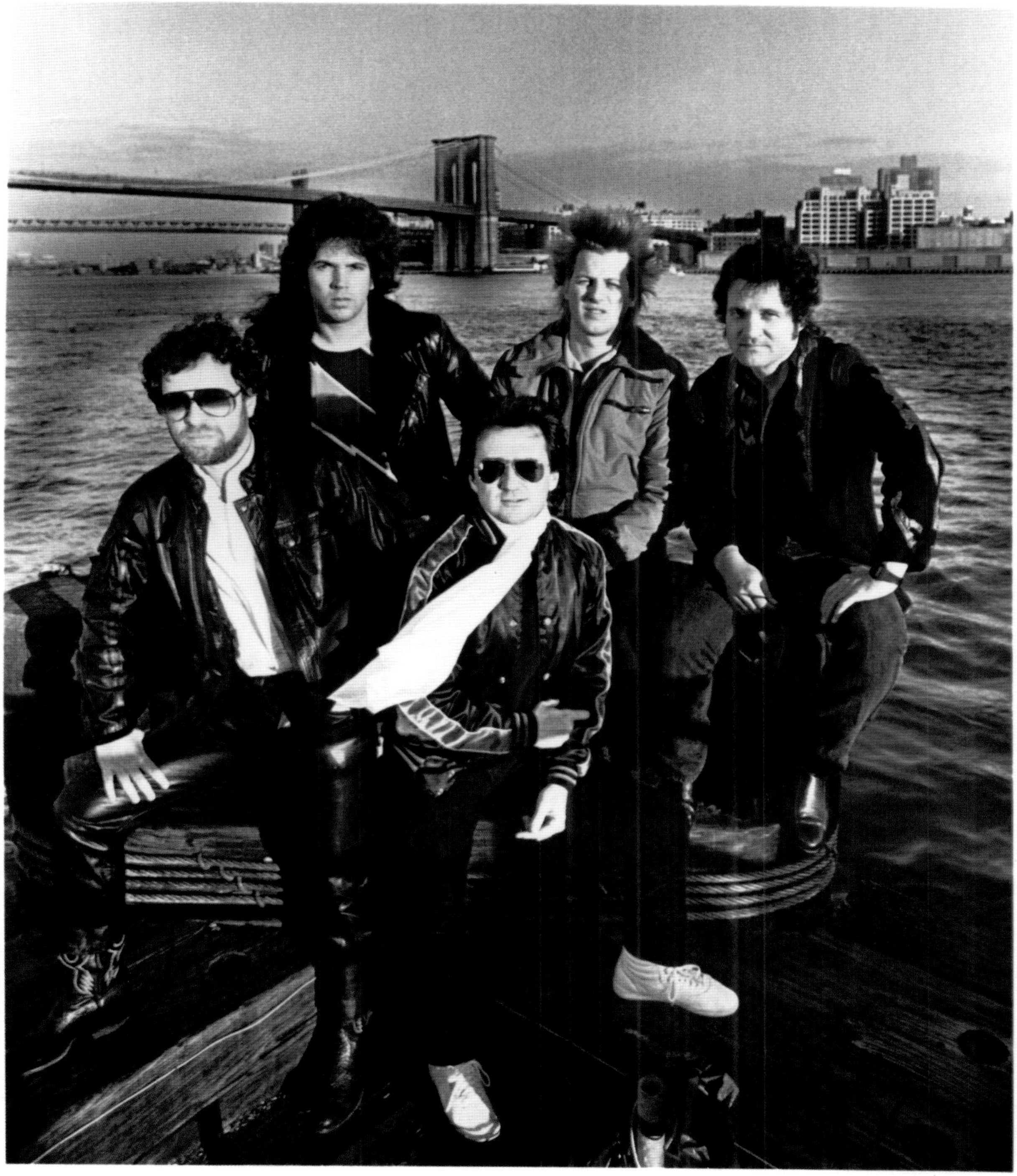

PHOTOGRAPH: STEPHENIE HOLLYMAN

From left ERIC BLOOM, TOMMY ZVONCHEK, DONALD ROESER, JIMMY WILCOX, JOE BOUCHARD

BLUE OYSTER CULT

Columbia

8511

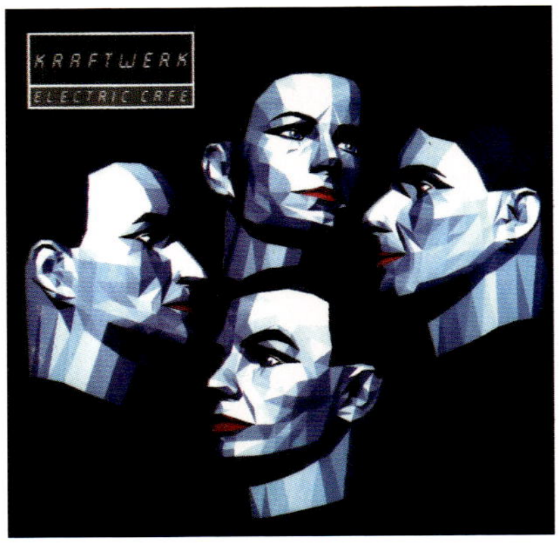

Kraftwerk's "Musique Non-Stop" and "The Telephone Call" were the German group's first "robot pop" songs to reach No. 1 on *Billboard*'s dance club chart.

Billboard 200: *Electric Café* (#158)

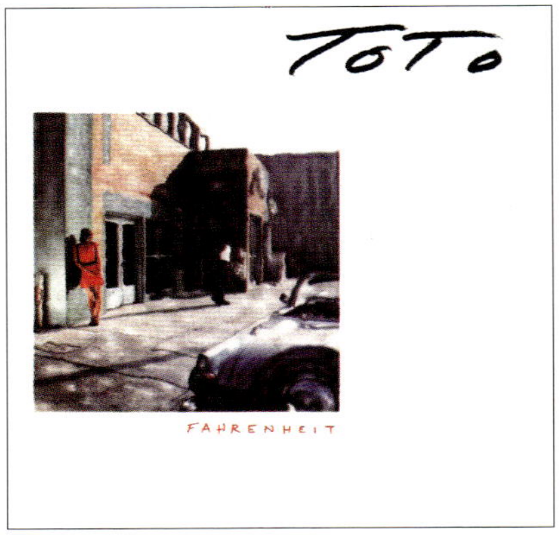

From **Toto**'s *Fahrenheit* album, "I'll Be Over You," with Michael McDonald adding a counterpoint vocal, reached the top of the adult contemporary charts.

Billboard 200: *Fahrenheit* (#40)

Billboard Hot 100: "I'll Be Over You" (#11); "Without Your Love" (#38)

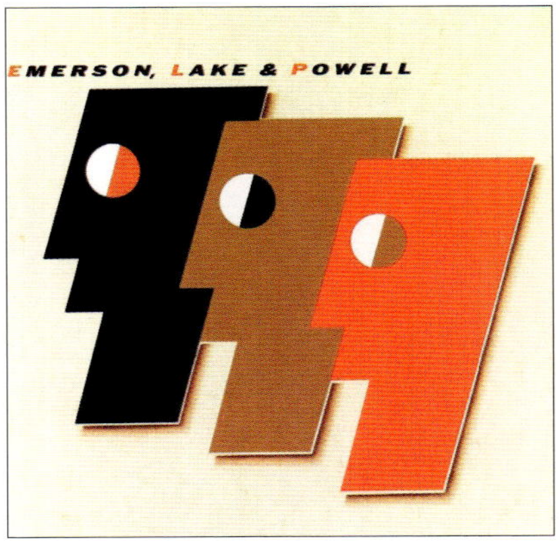

Using the ELP acronym, **Emerson, Lake & Powell**–Keith Emerson and Greg Lake with drummer Cozy Powell in lieu of Carl Palmer–arose with "Touch and Go."

Billboard 200: *Emerson, Lake & Powell* (#23)

Billboard Hot 100: "Touch and Go" (#60)

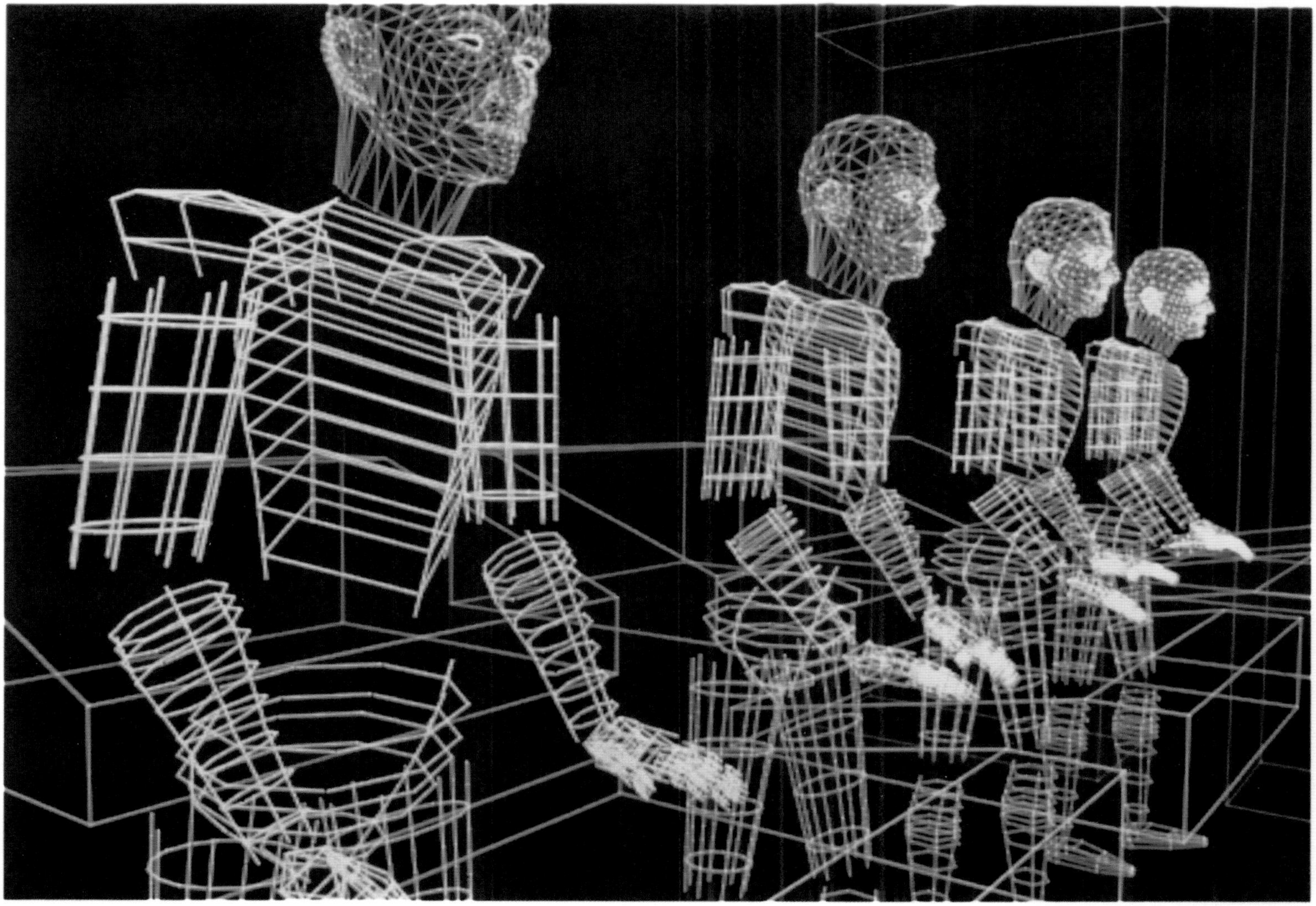

KRAFTWERK

WARNER BROS.

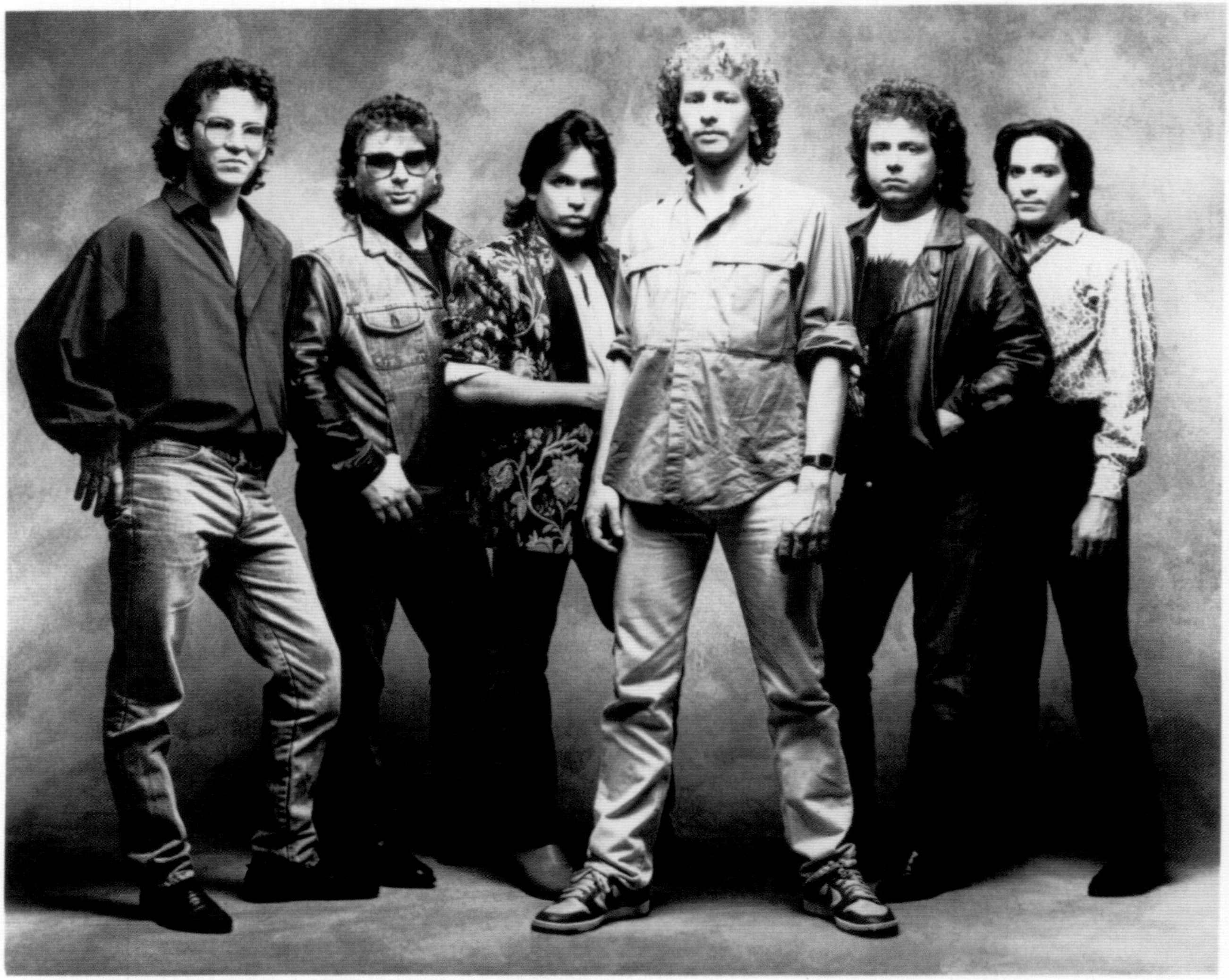

Photo Credit: Michael Going

STEVE PORCARO   DAVID PAICH   JEFF PORCARO   JOE WILLIAMS   STEVE LUKATHER   MIKE PORCARO

TOTO

The Fitzgerald Hartley Co
7250 Beverly Boulevard · Los Angeles California 90036
(213) 934-8002

Columbia
8608

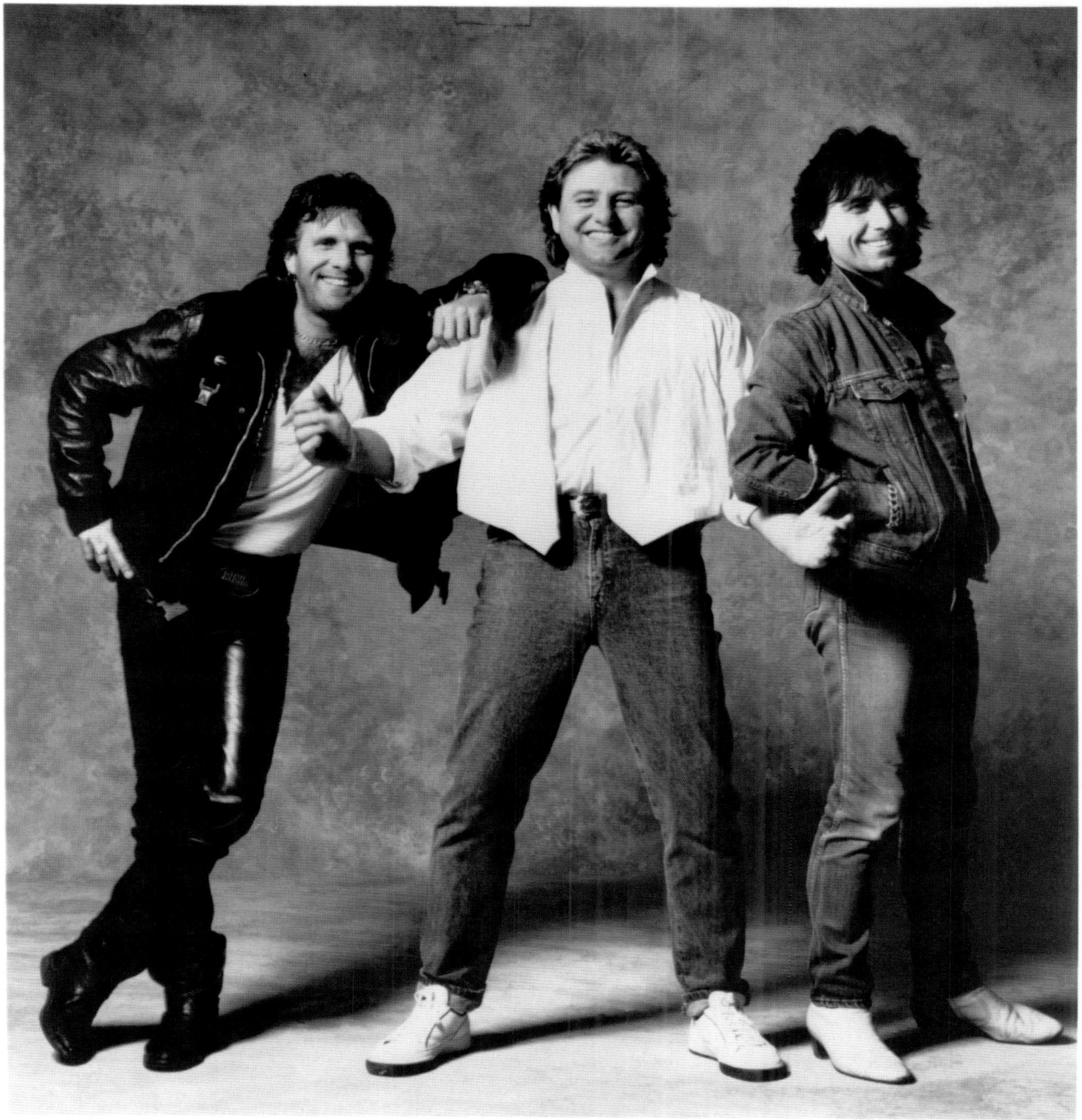

EMERSON, LAKE & POWELL

polydor

PolyGram Records

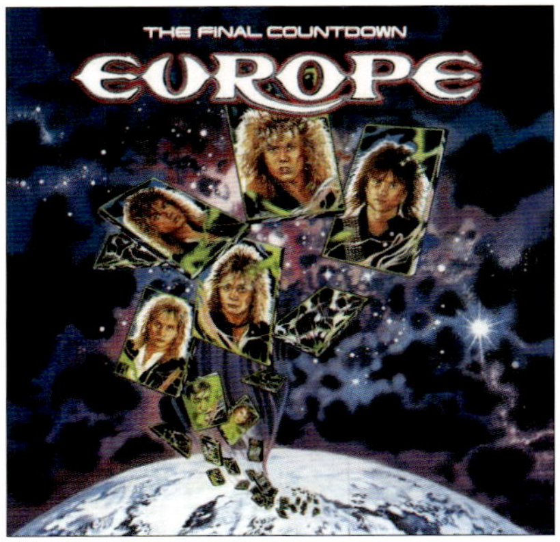

Lifted by "Carrie," "Rock the Night" and the epic title song, **Europe** met with global greatness on *The Final Countdown*, the Swedish rockers' third album.

Billboard 200: *The Final Countdown* (#8)
Billboard 200: "The Final Countdown" (#8); "Rock the Night" (#30); "Carrie" (#3); "Cherokee" (#72)

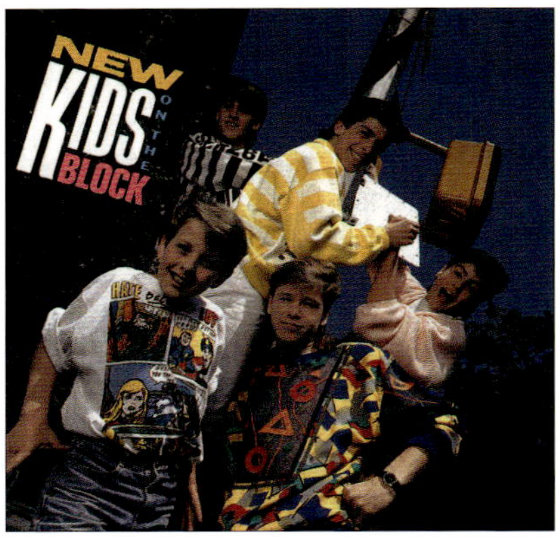

Largely ignored upon its release, **New Kids on the Block**'s self-titled debut album of "kid funk" caught the ear of the boy band's fan base three years later.

Billboard 200: *New Kids on the Block* (#25)
Billboard Hot 100: "Didn't I (Blow Your Mind)" (#8)

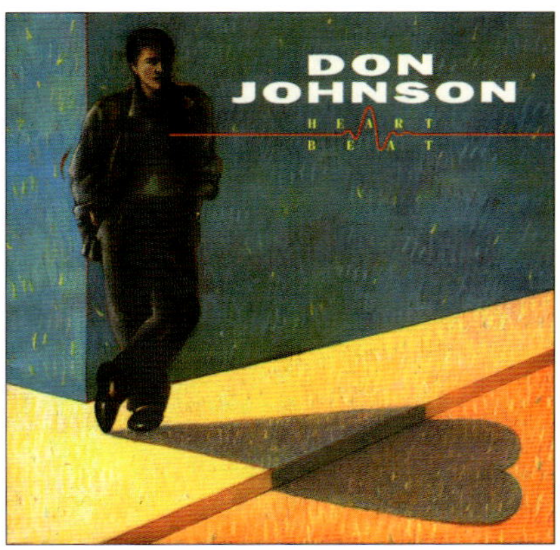

TV actor **Don Johnson** made his mark on the world of pop music with *Heartbeat*, the *Miami Vice* star's recording debut, and the title track, a Top 5 success.

Billboard 200: *Heartbeat* (#17)
Billboard Hot 100: "Heartbeat" (#5); "Heartache Away" (#56)

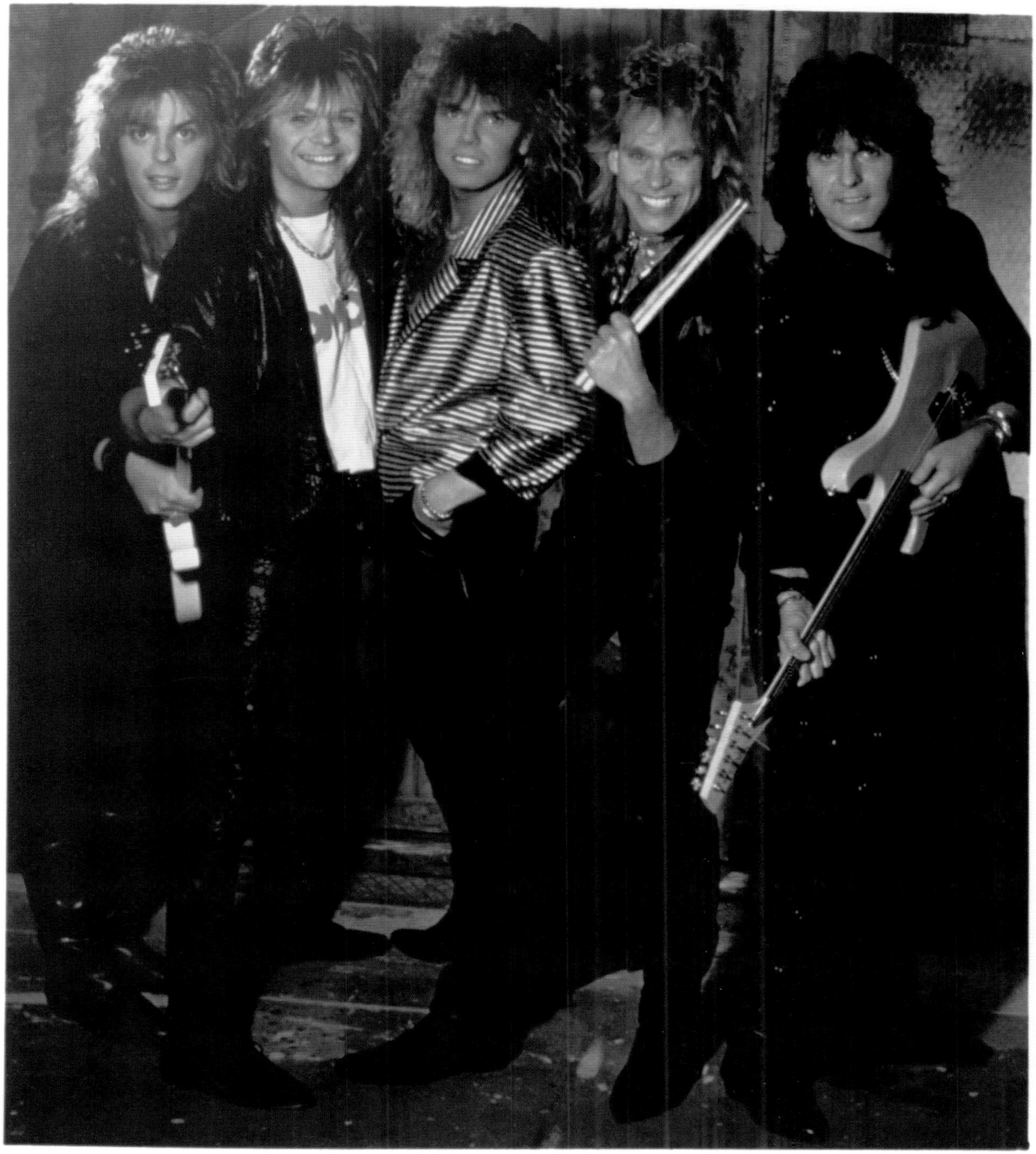

Photo:DiDi Zill

L-R JOHN LEVEN, MIC MICHAELI, JOEY TEMPEST, IAN HAUGLAND, KEE MARCELLO

EUROPE

Epic
8612

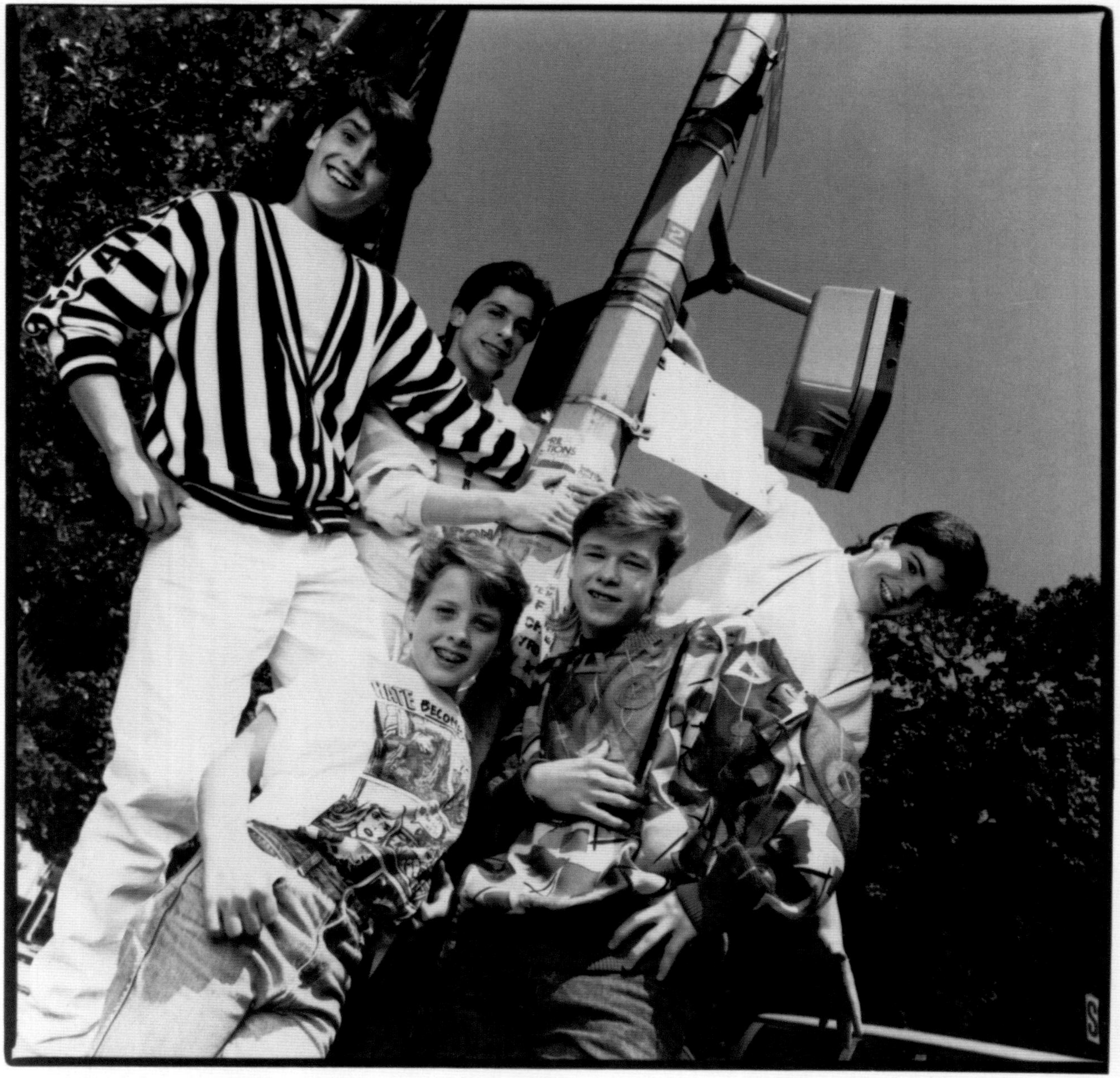

PHOTOGRAPH: CAROLINE GREYSHOCK

Clockwise from top left. JON KNIGHT, DANNY WOOD, JORDAN KNIGHT, DONNIE WAHLBERG, JOE McINTYRE.

NEW KIDS ON THE BLOCK

Columbia

8609

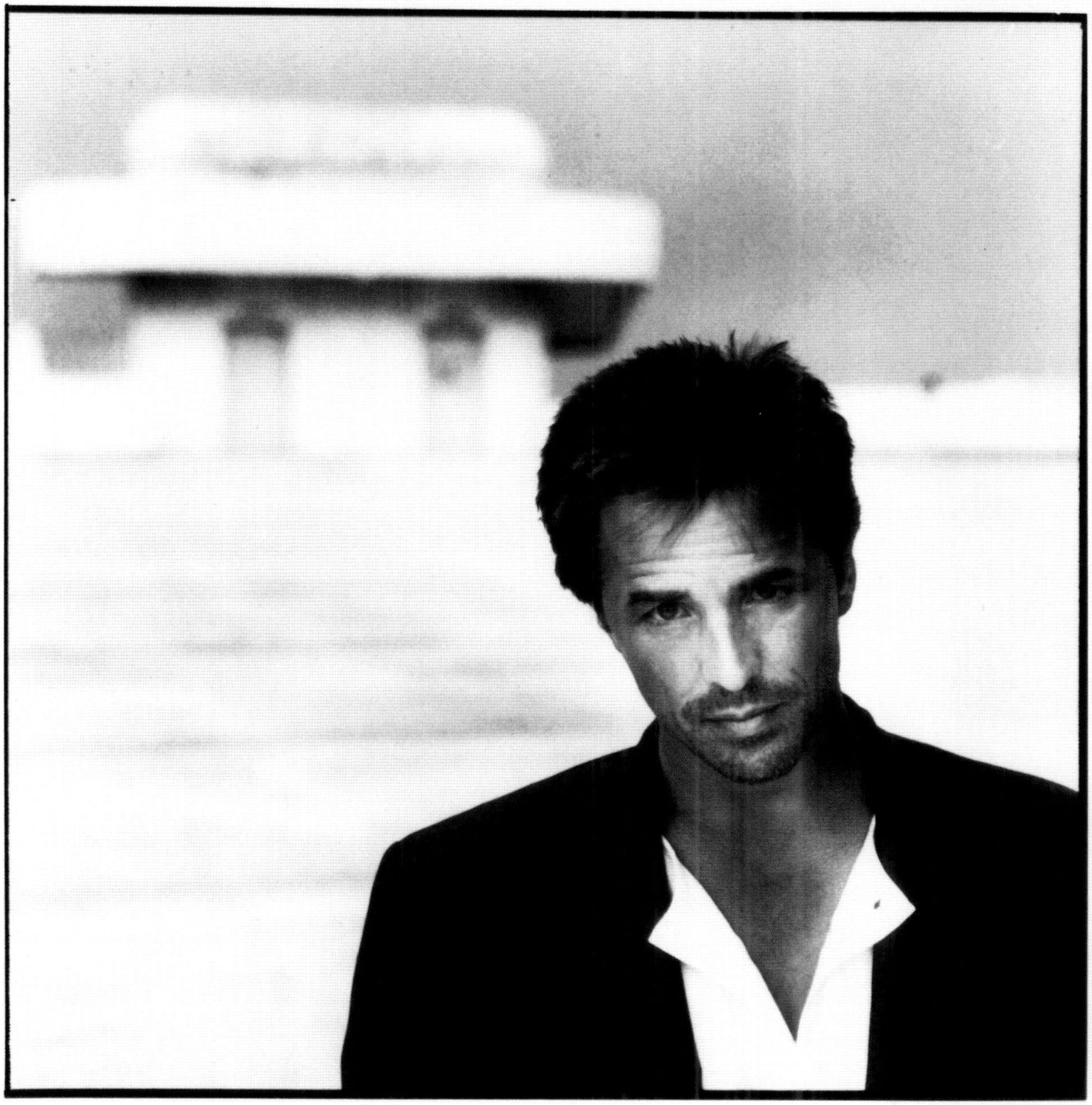

Photo: Mary Ellen Mark

DON JOHNSON

8608

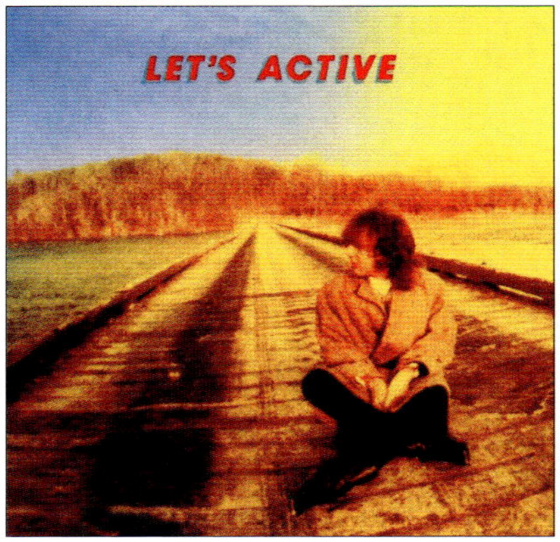

Big Plans for Everybody, **Let's Active**'s second full-length album, was largely a solo studio project for frontman Mitch Easter, known as R.E.M.'s producer.

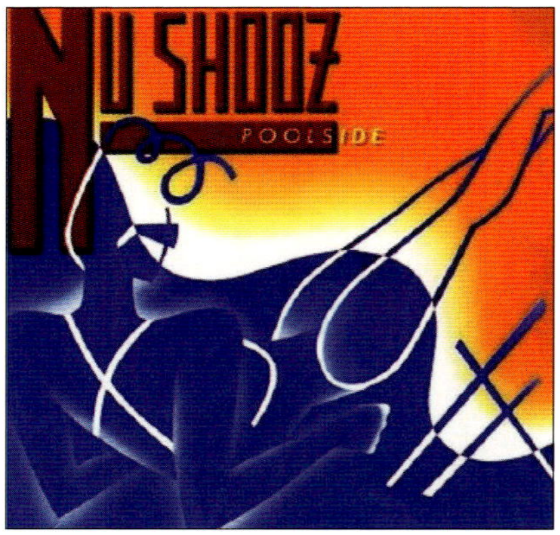

Portland-based **Nu Shooz**, fronted by the married duo of John Smith and Valerie Day, scored the pop and dance hits "I Can't Wait" and "Point of No Return."

Billboard 200: *Poolside* (#27)
Billboard Hot 100: "I Can't Wait" (#3); "Point of No Return" (#28)

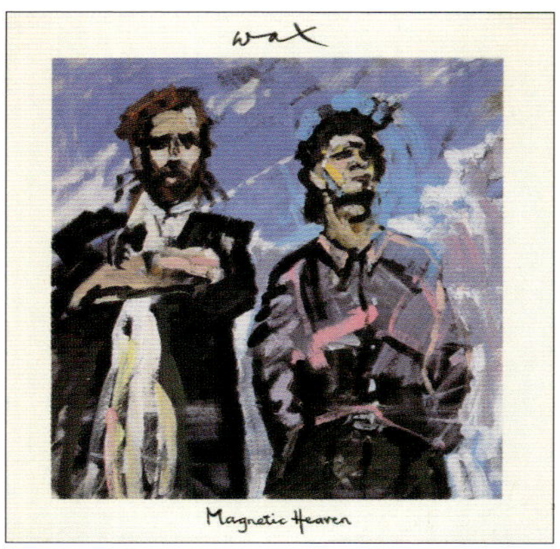

American singer-songwriter Andrew Gold and British pop veteran Graham Gouldman of 10cc teamed up as **Wax** and landed a hit, "Right Between the Eyes."

Billboard 200: *Magnetic Heaven* (#101)
Billboard Hot 100: "Right Between the Eyes" (#43)

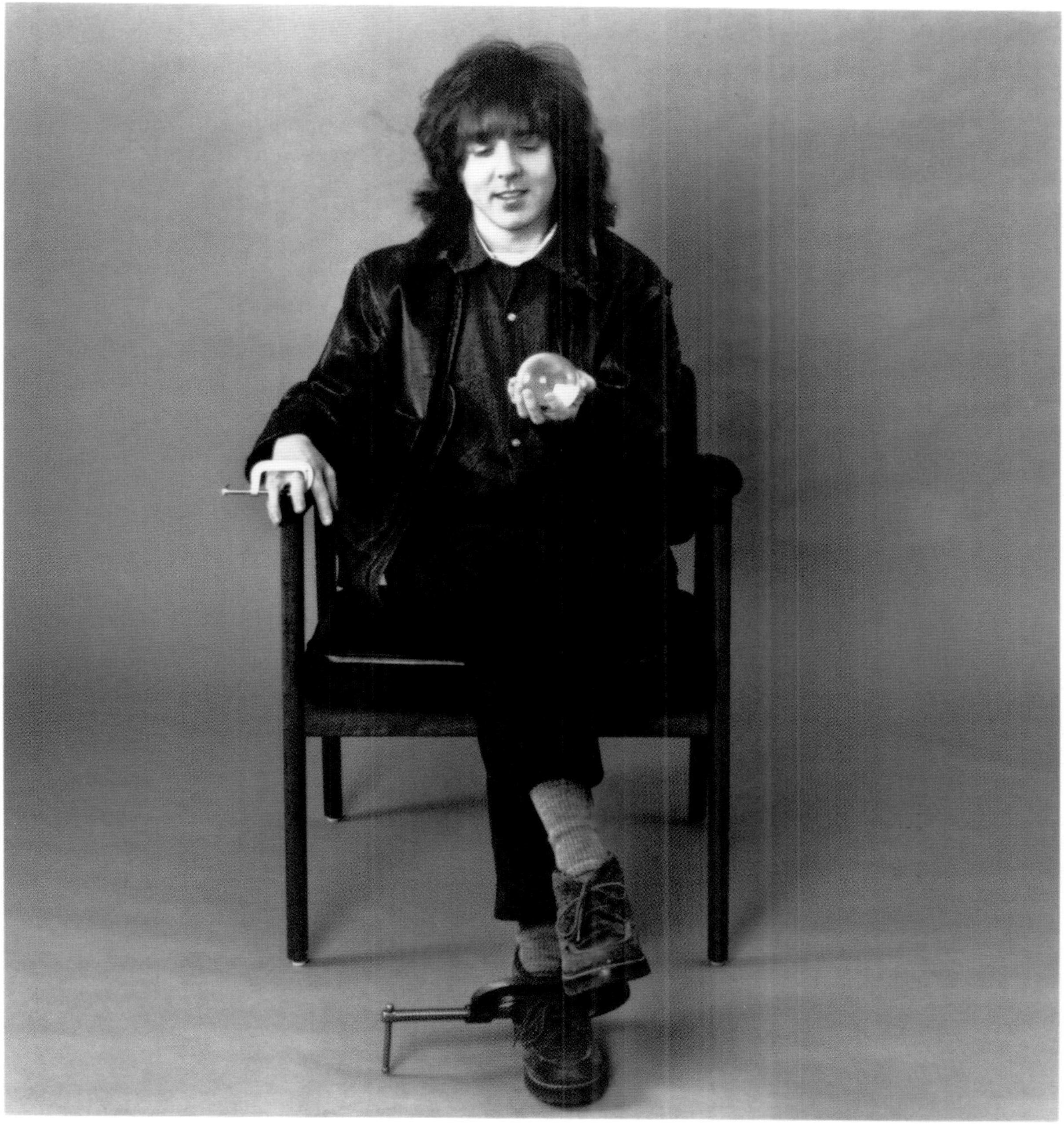

PHOTOGRAPHY: JOE LECHLEIDER

MITCH EASTER

LET'S ACTIVE

I.R.S.

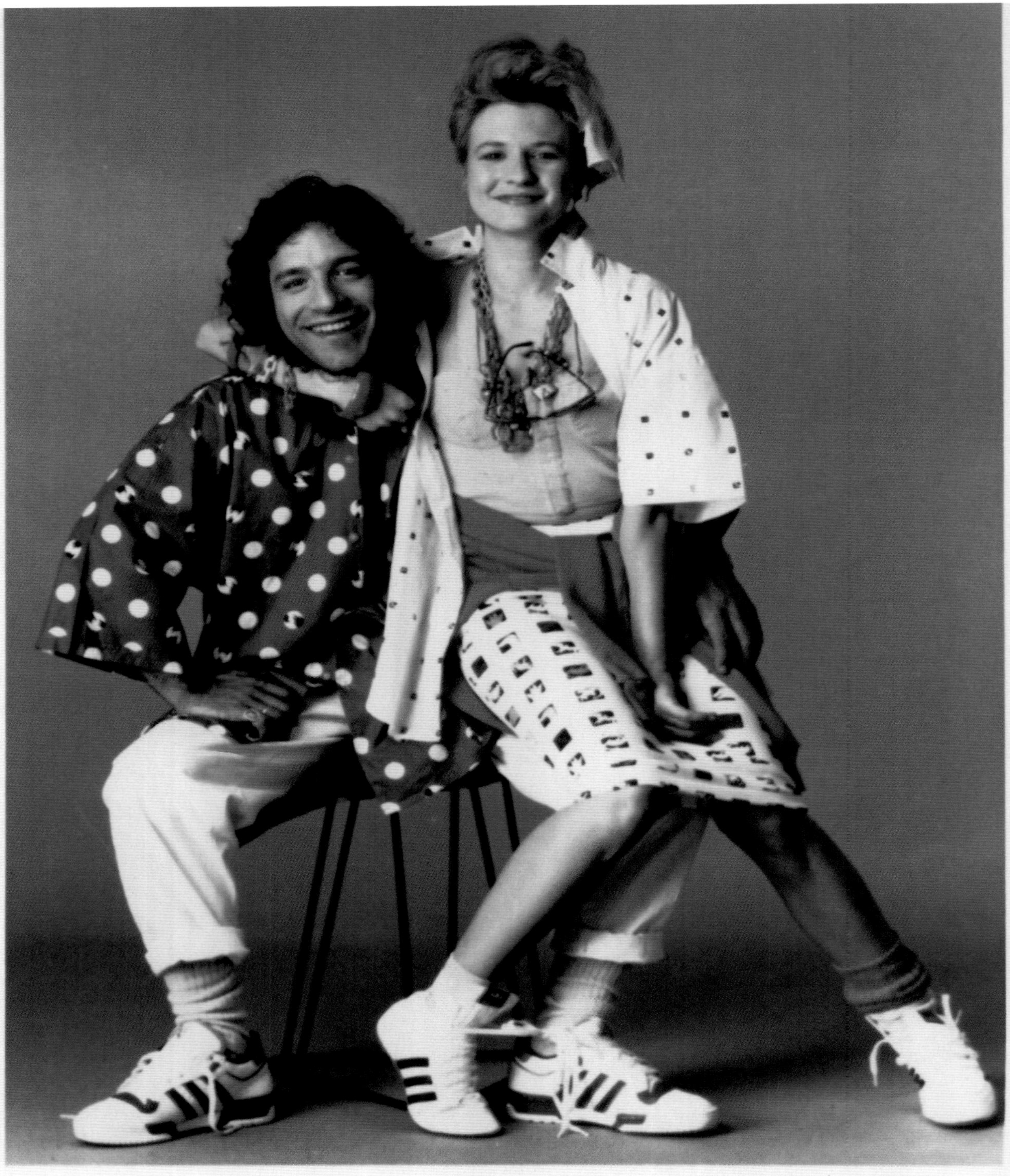

JOHN SMITH VALERIE DAY

NU SHOOZ

ATLANTIC

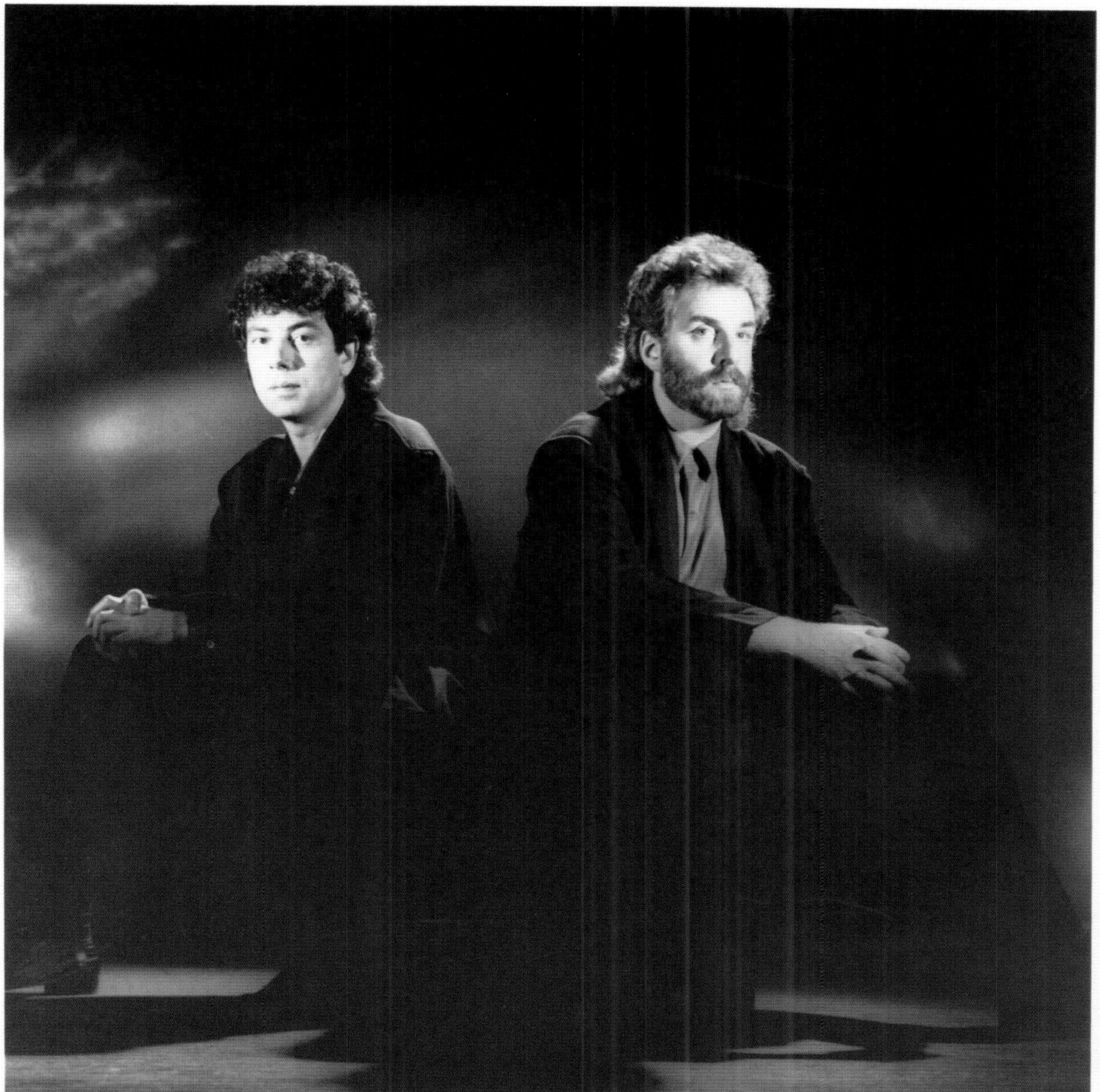

Photographer: SIMON FOWLER

wax

RCA Records and Cassettes

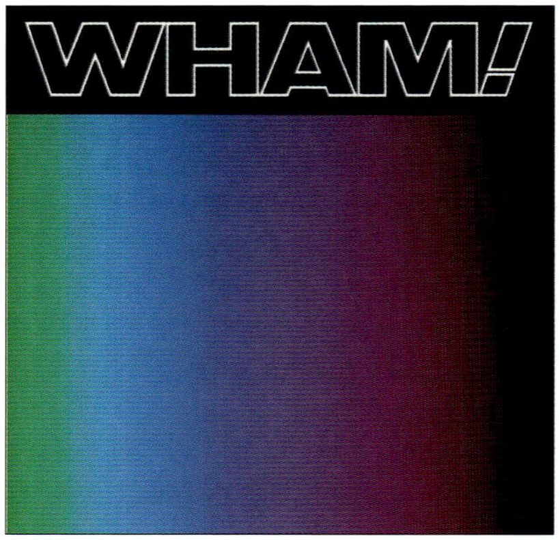

The final album by the UK pop duo **Wham!**, *Music from the Edge of Heaven* had the festive "Last Christmas" and "The Edge of Heaven," a farewell single.

Billboard 200: *Music from the Edge of Heaven* (#10)
Billboard Hot 100: "Last Christmas" (#11); "I'm Your Man" (#3); "The Edge of Heaven" (#10); "Where Did Your Heart Go?" (#50)

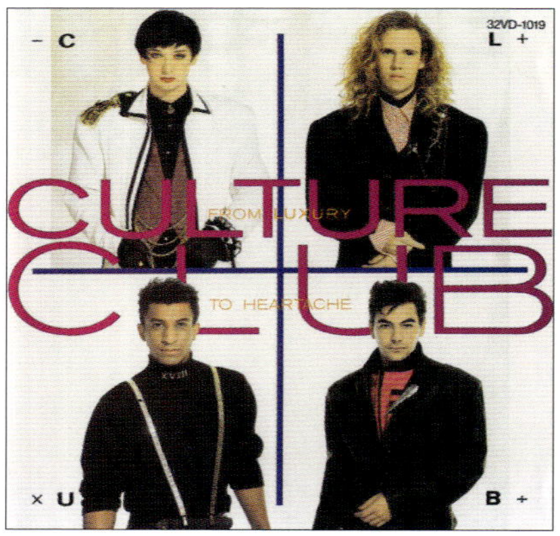

"Move Away," a song from **Culture Club**'s *From Luxury to Heartache*, was performed by frontman Boy George on an episode of *The A-Team*, a hot TV series.

Billboard 200: *From Luxury to Heartache* (#32)
Billboard Hot 100: "Move Away" (#12)

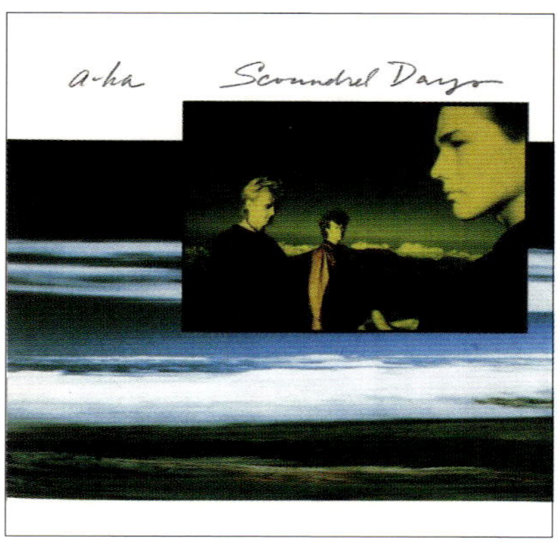

With its US success having wound down, **a-ha** issued *Scoundrel Days*, a high-charting hit in Europe, South America and the synth-pop band's native Norway.

Billboard 200: *Scoundrel Days* (#74)
Billboard Hot 100: "Cry Wolf" (#50)

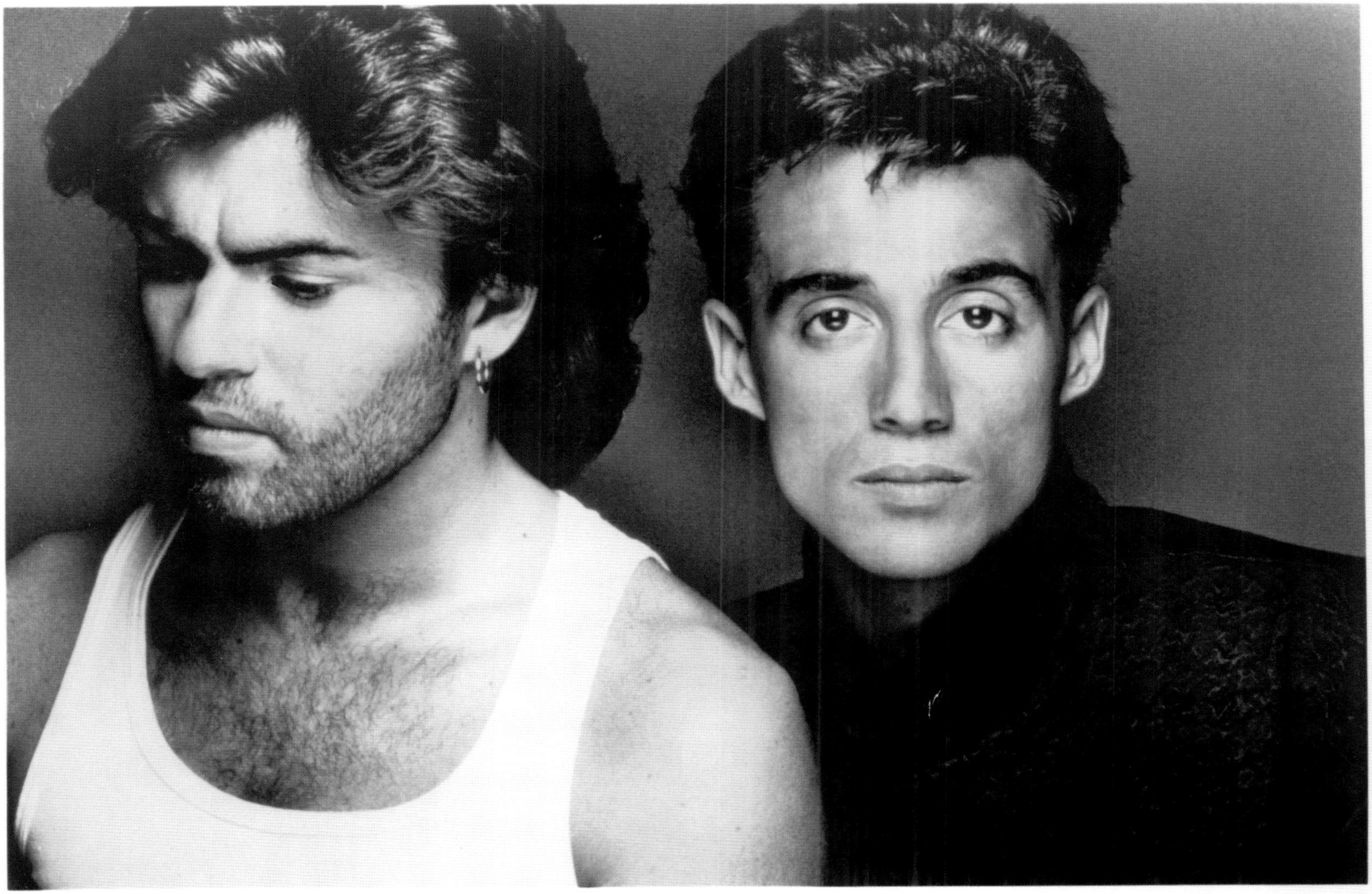

PHOTOGRAPH: TONY McGEE

WHAM!

Columbia
8606

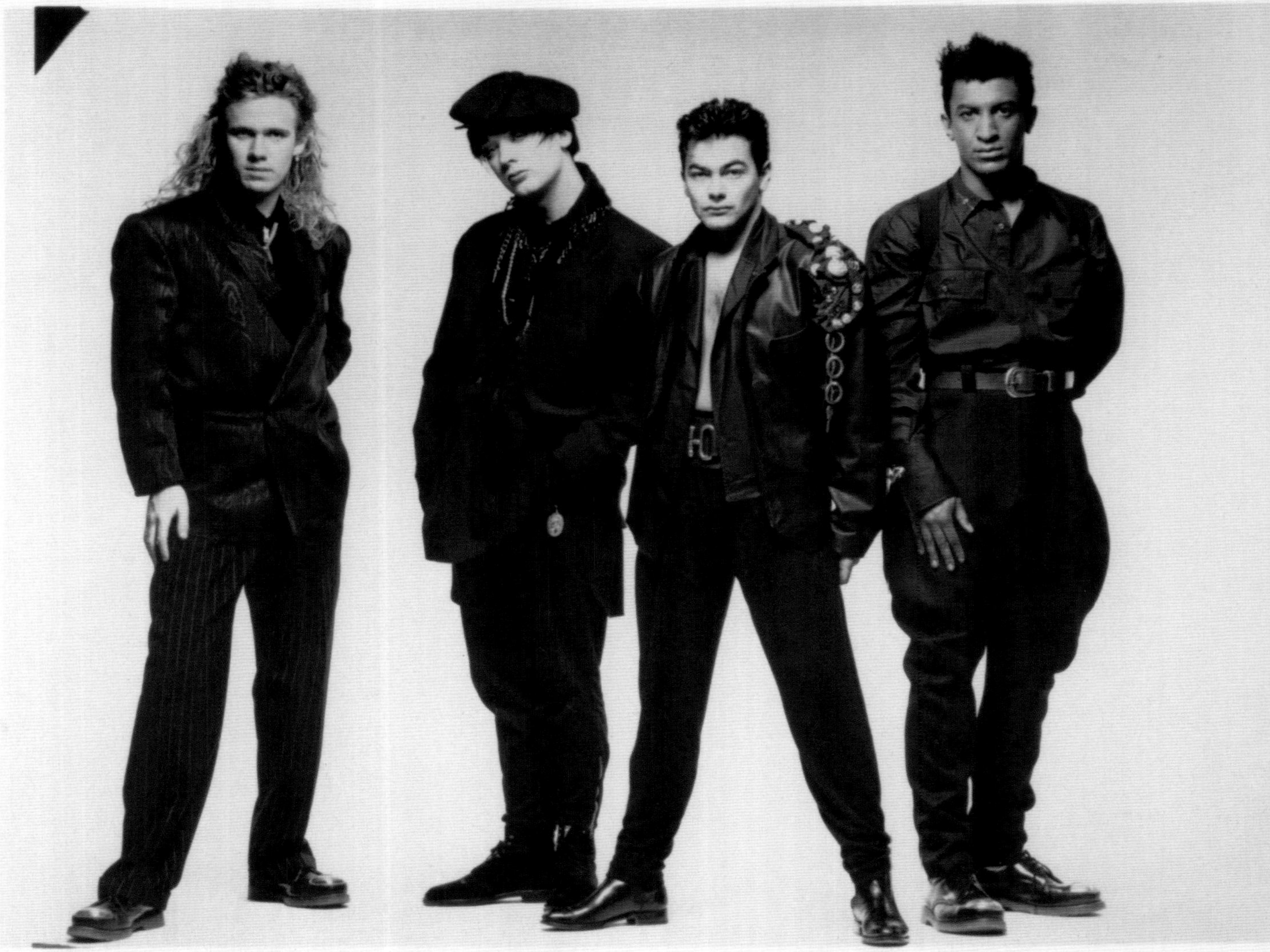

ROY HAY BOY GEORGE JON MOSS MIKEY CRAIG

CULTURE CLUB

Epic 8603

Virgin

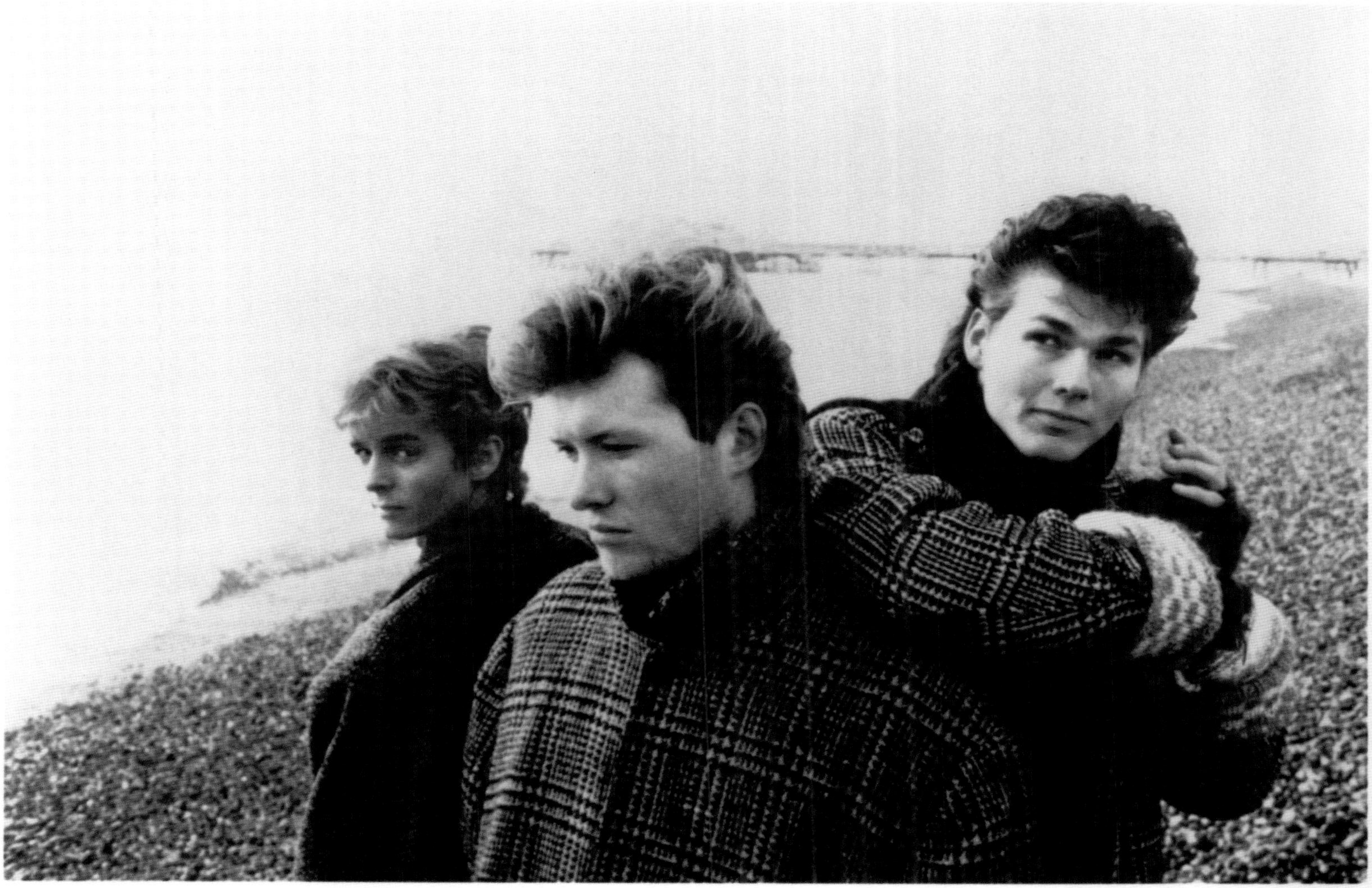

Photo Credit: Jonathan Leonard

A-HA

WARNER BROS.

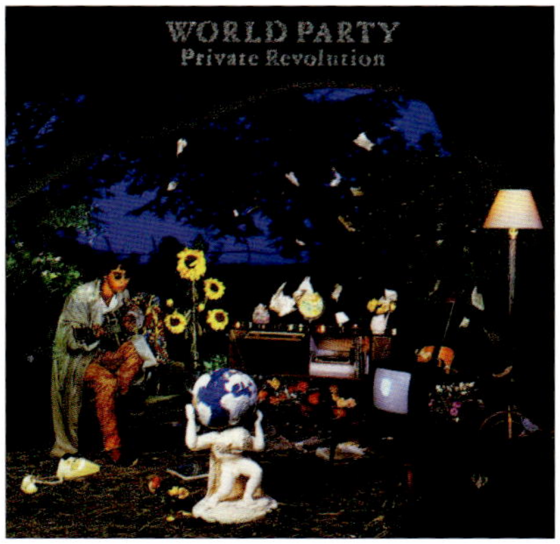

Karl Wallinger, the sole member of **World Party**, recorded *Private Revolution* in his personal studio setup, inspiring a perceptive global hit, "Ship of Fools."

Billboard 200: *Private Revolution* (#39)
Billboard Hot 100: "Ship of Fools" (#27)

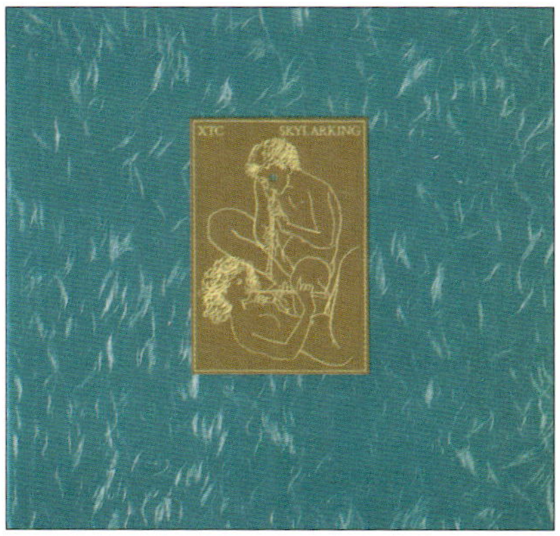

XTC's *Skylarking*, produced by Todd Rundgren, was later recalled and re-pressed to incorporate the controversial "Dear God," an unforeseen hit single.

Billboard 200: *Skylarking* (#70)

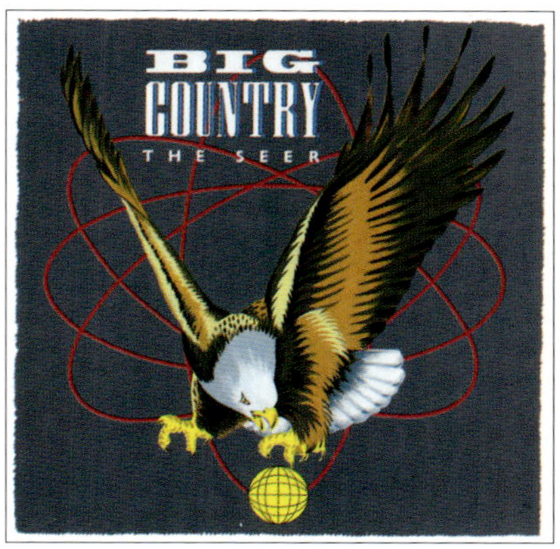

The Seer, **Big Country**'s third release, contained a magnificent single, "Look Away," the Scottish quartet's greatest accomplishment in the UK and Ireland.

Billboard 200: *The Seer* (#59)

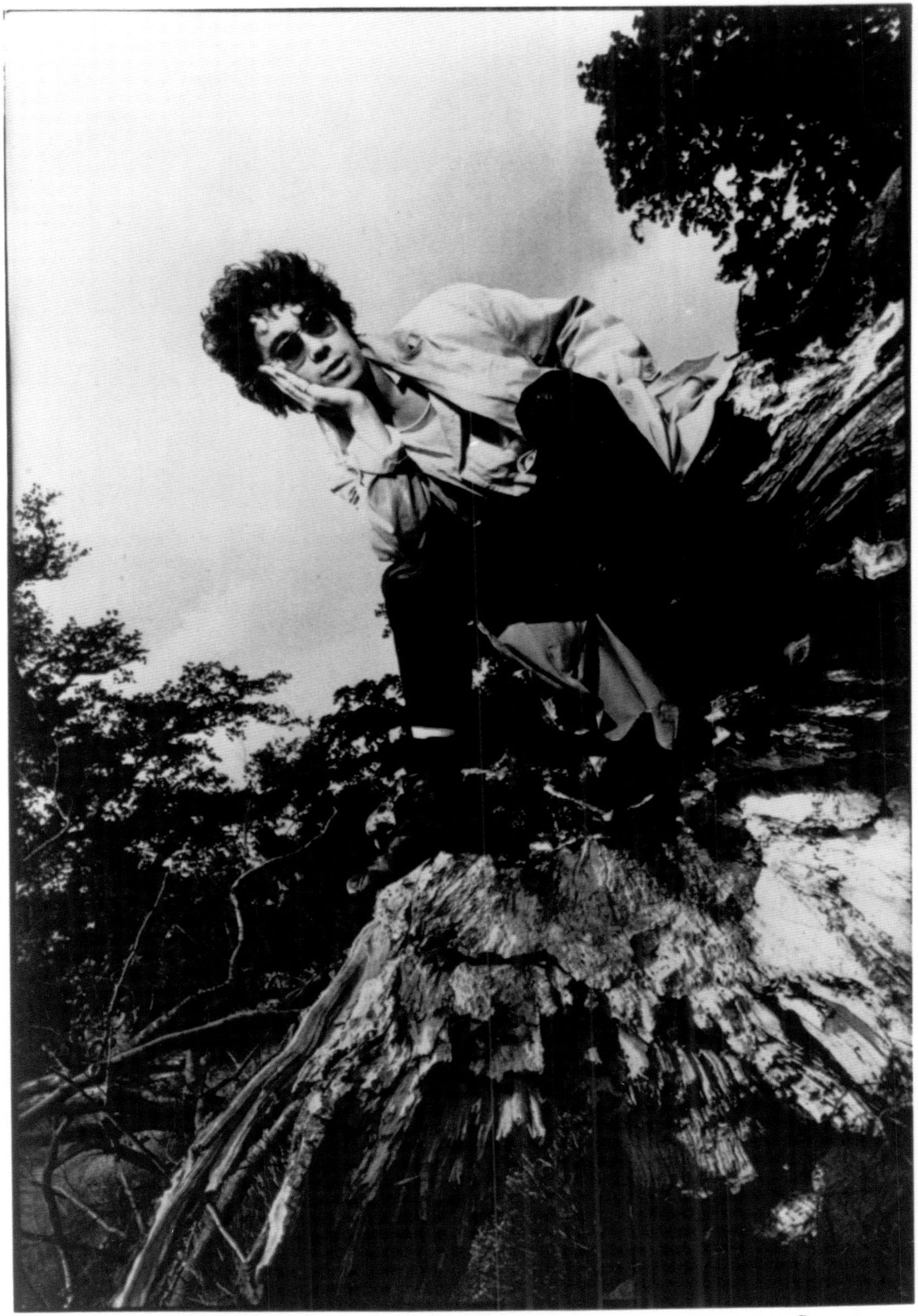

KARL WALLINGER OF WORLD PARTY

Chrysalis

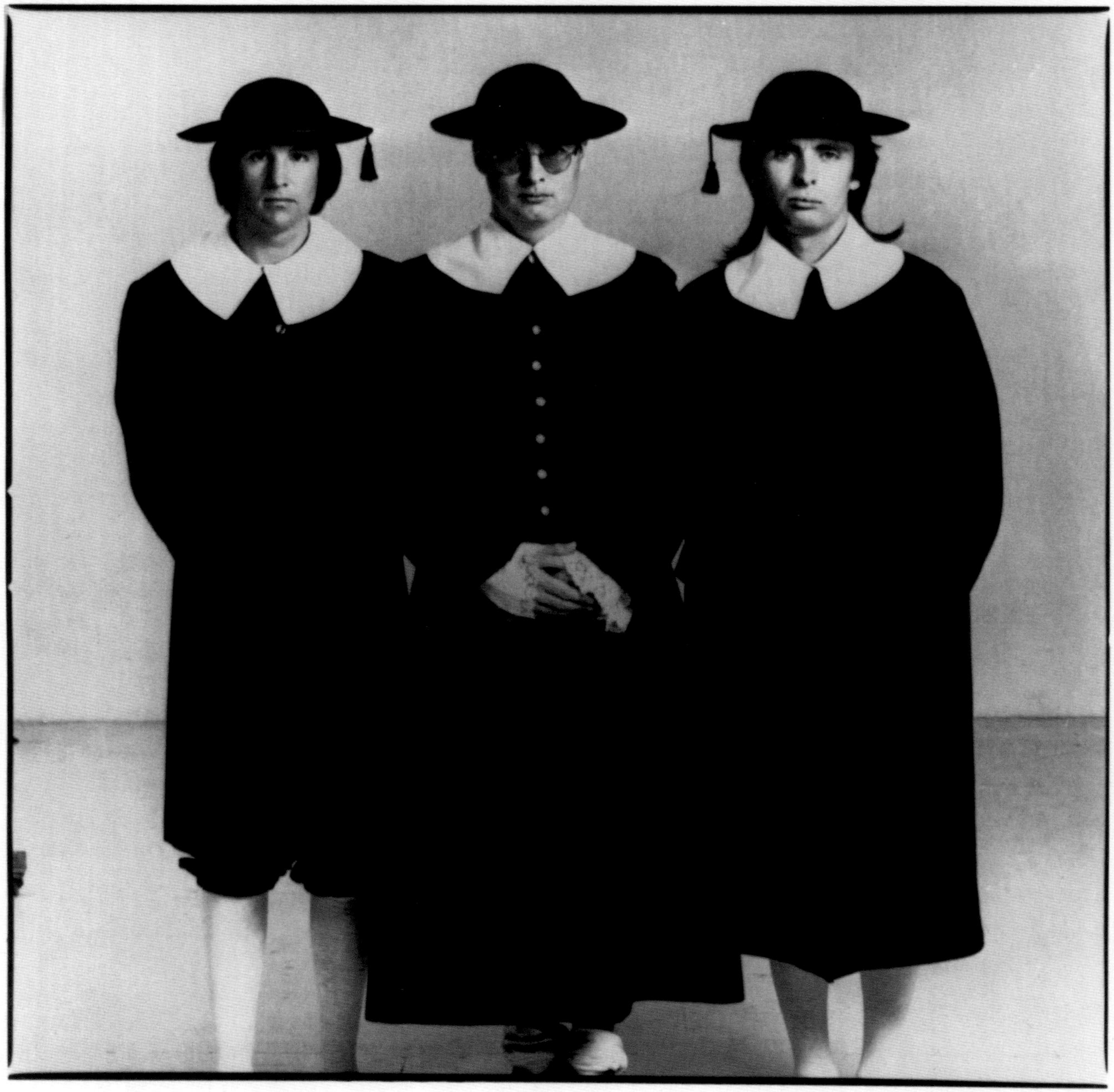

Photo Credit: Cindy Palmano

XTC

GEFFEN RECORDS

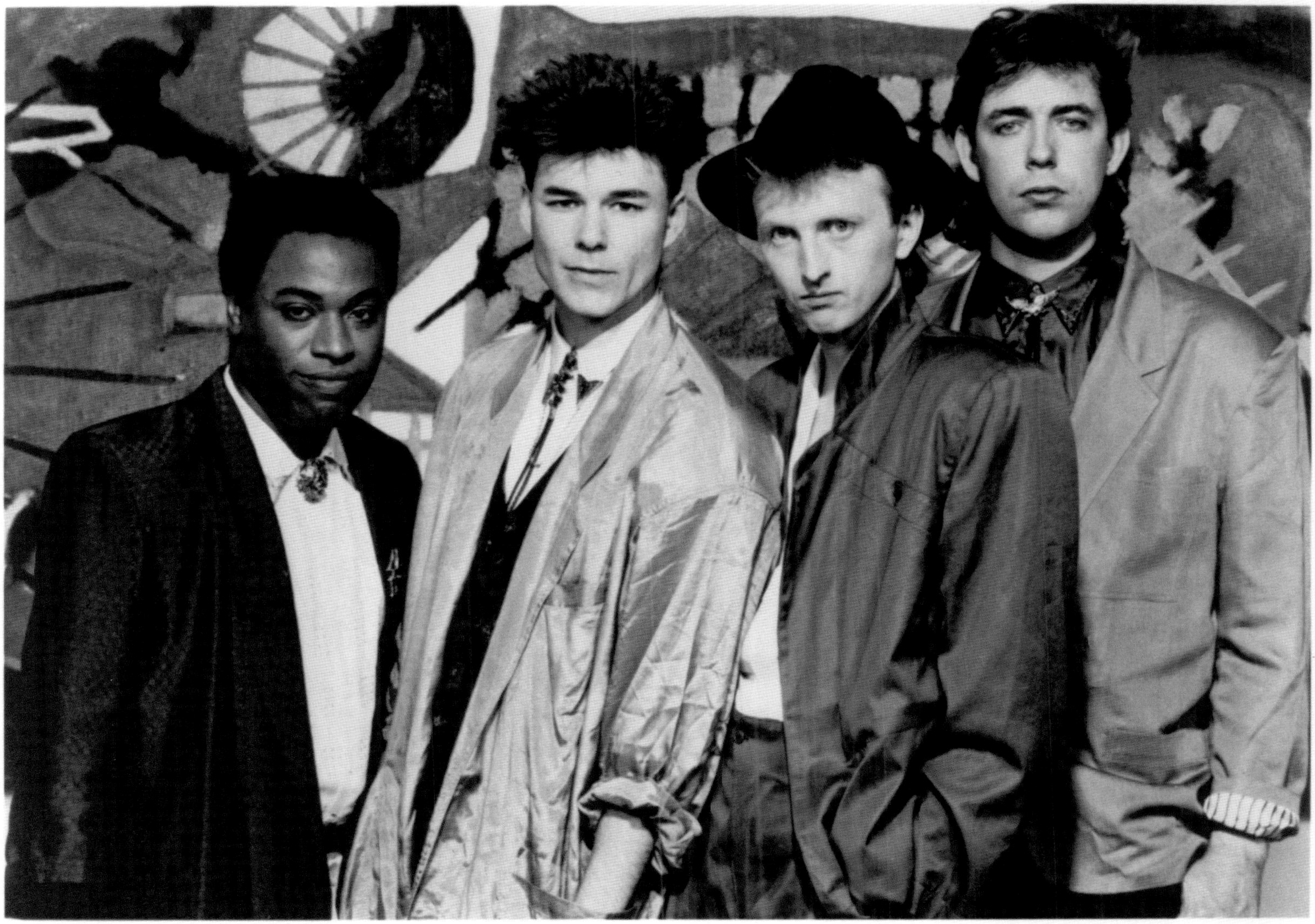

BIG COUNTRY

mercury

PolyGram Records

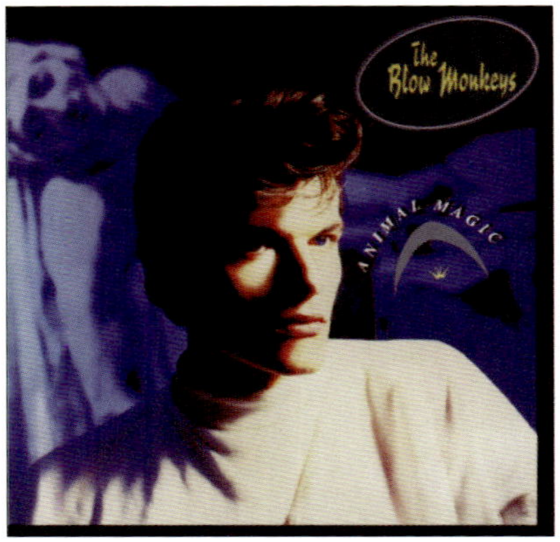

The Blow Monkeys emerged from the cluttered British music scene with a breakout hit from the *Animal Magic* album, the alluring "Digging Your Scene."

Billboard 200: *Animal Magic* (#35)
Billboard Hot 100: "Digging Your Scene" (#14)

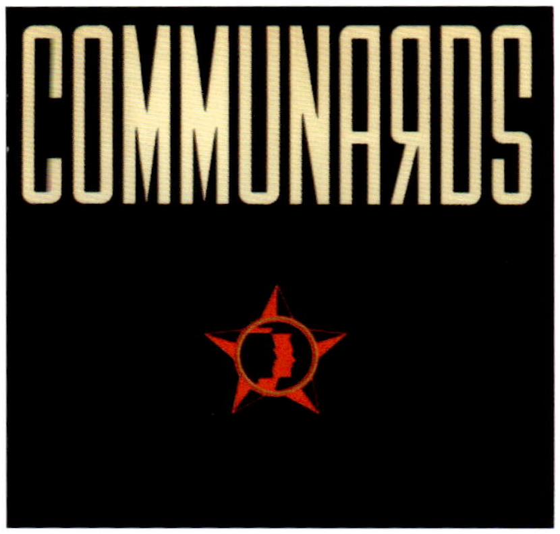

The UK pop duo **Communards** topped the US club play chart with a raucous cover version of Thelma Houston's disco staple, "Don't Leave Me This Way."

Billboard 200: *Communards* (#90)
Billboard Hot 100: "Don't Leave Me This Way" (#40)

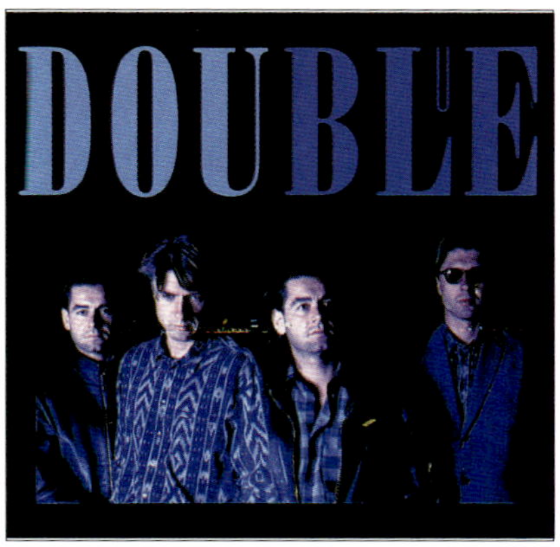

"The Captain of Her Heart" by Switzerland's **Double**, a pleasantly restrained ballad with a drifting jazz-pop piano line, attracted international attention.

Billboard 200: *Blue* (#30)
Billboard Hot 100: "The Captain of Her Heart" (#16)

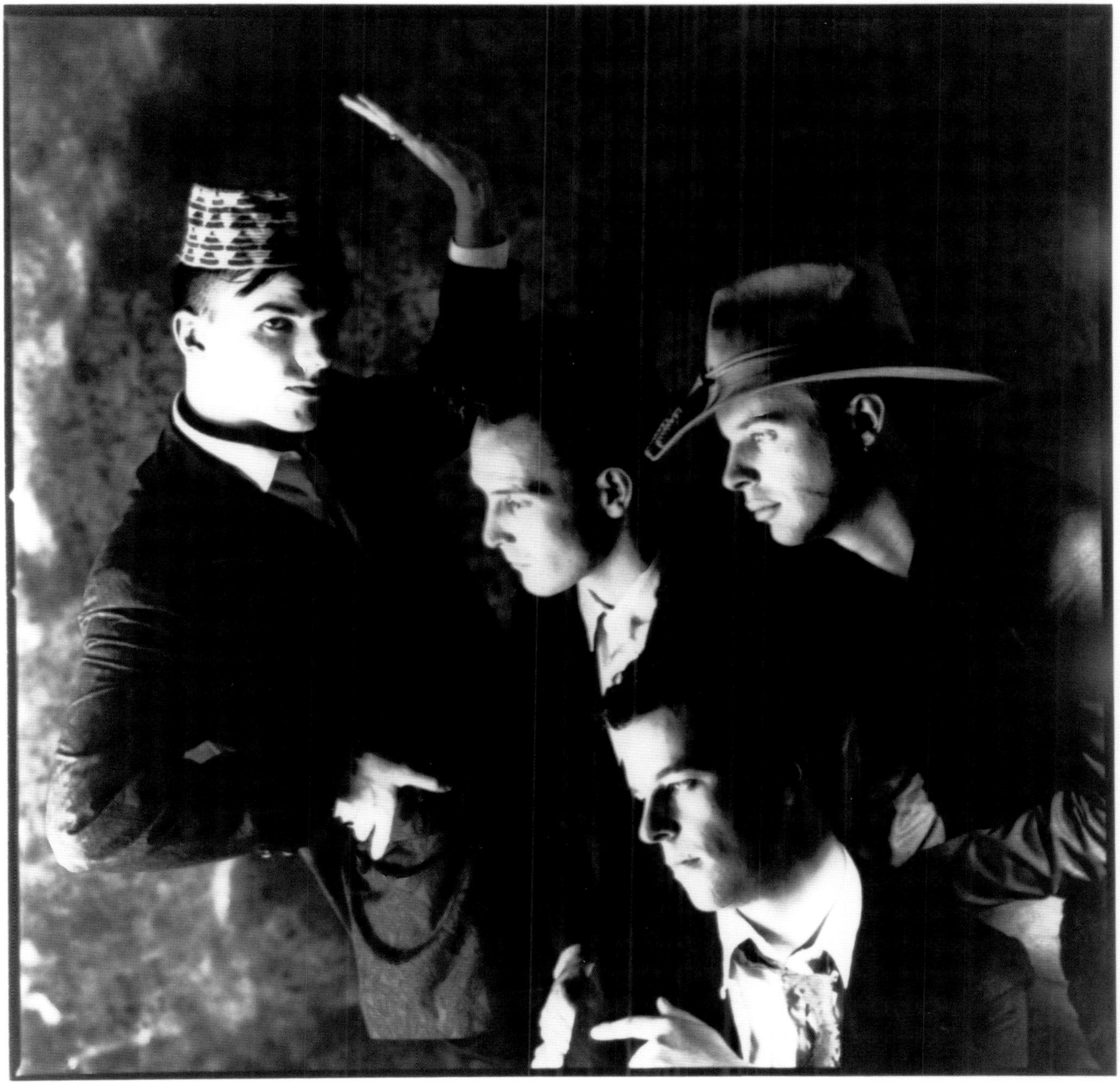

THE BLOW MONKEYS

RCA
Records and Cassettes

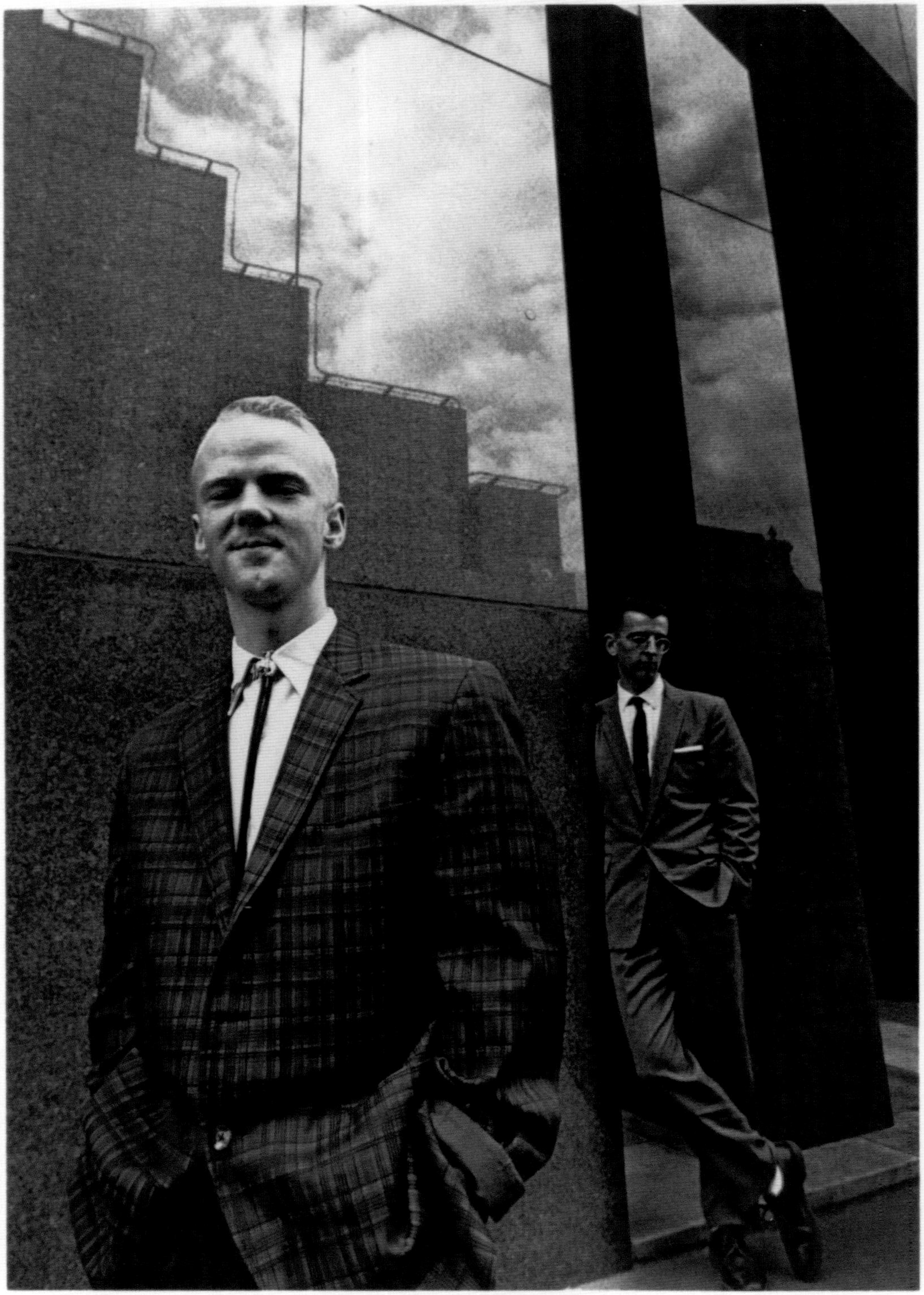

LONDON

COMMUNARDS

MCA RECORDS

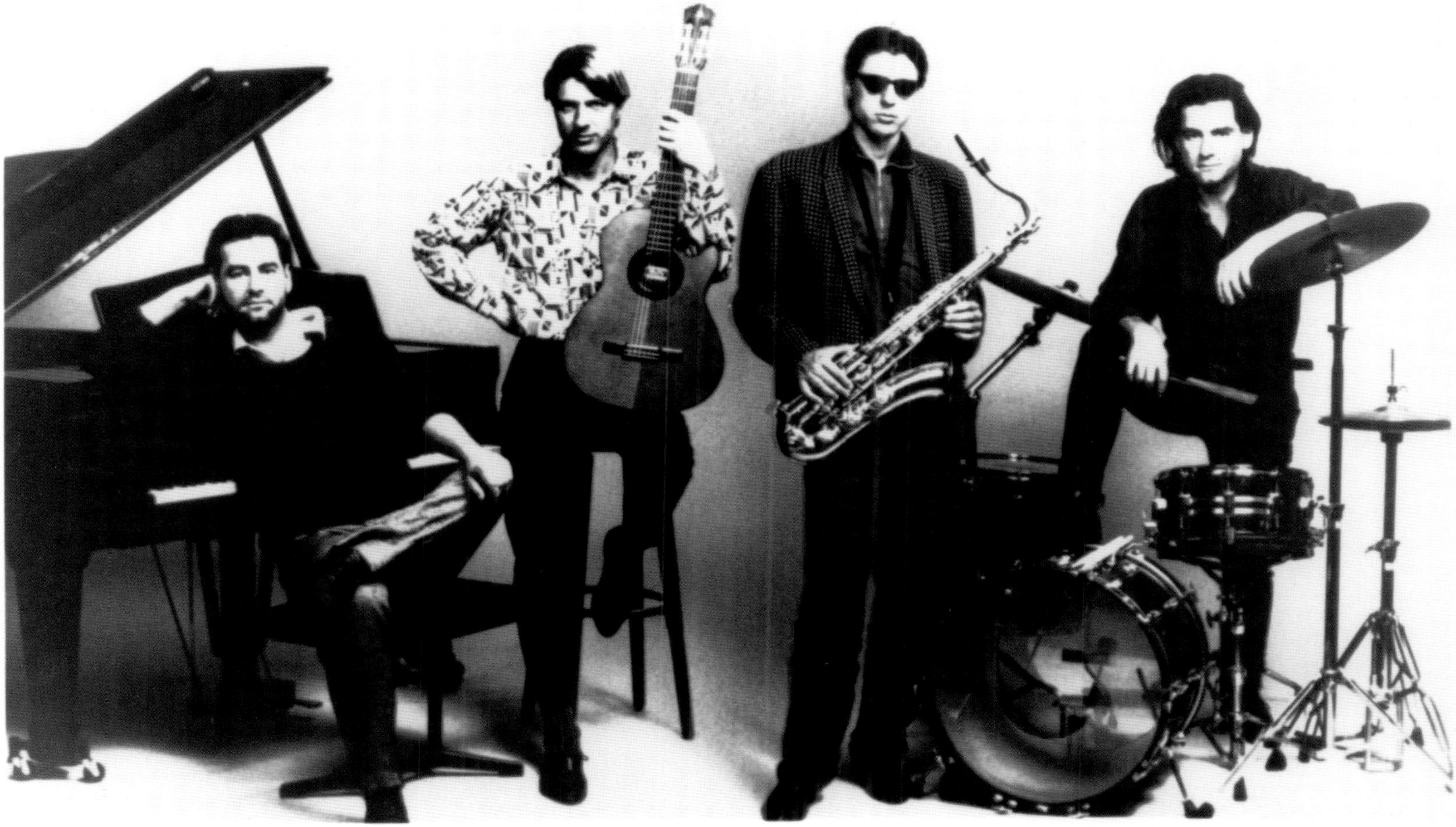

DOUBLE

A&M RECORDS
Printed in U.S.A.

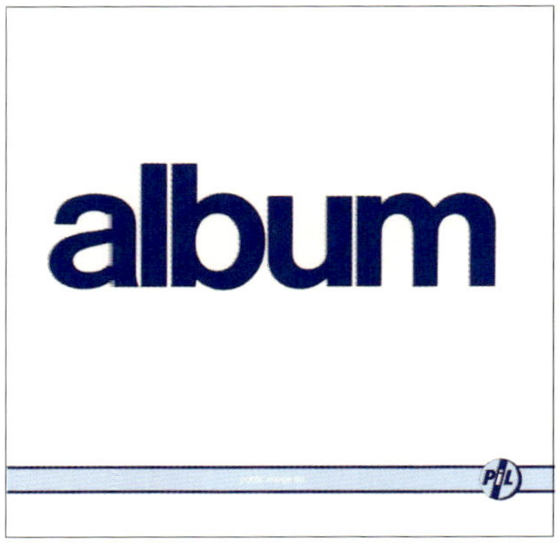

Essentially a solo vehicle for singer John Lydon, **Public Image Ltd** parodied generic brands on *Album*—or *Compact Disc* or *Cassette*, subject to the format.

Billboard 200: *Album* (#115)

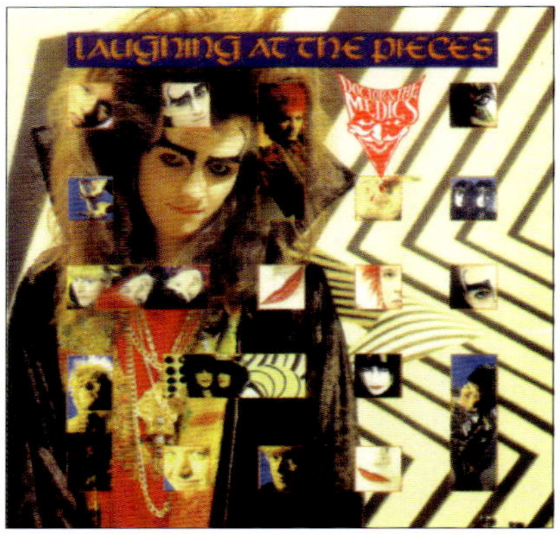

A wacky glam-psychedelic troupe, **Doctor & the Medics** saw their pulsating reading of Norman Greenbaum's "Spirit in the Sky" arrive at No. 1 in the UK.

Billboard Hot 100: "Spirit in the Sky" (#69)

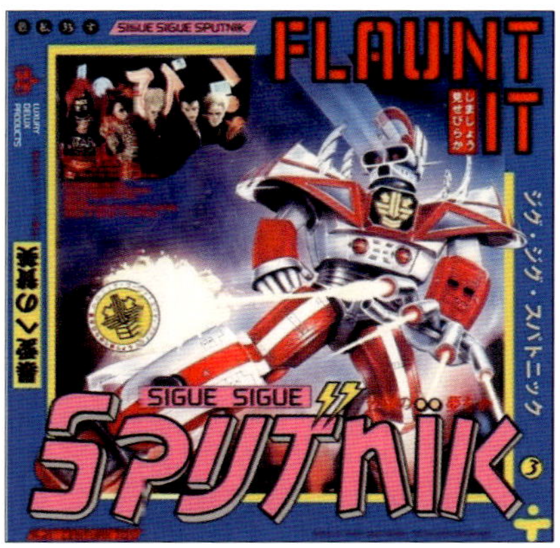

Sigue Sigue Sputnik's *Flaunt It*, which integrated paid commercials between songs, boasted the UK singles "Love Missile F1-11" and "21st Century Boy."

Billboard 200: *Flaunt It* (#96)

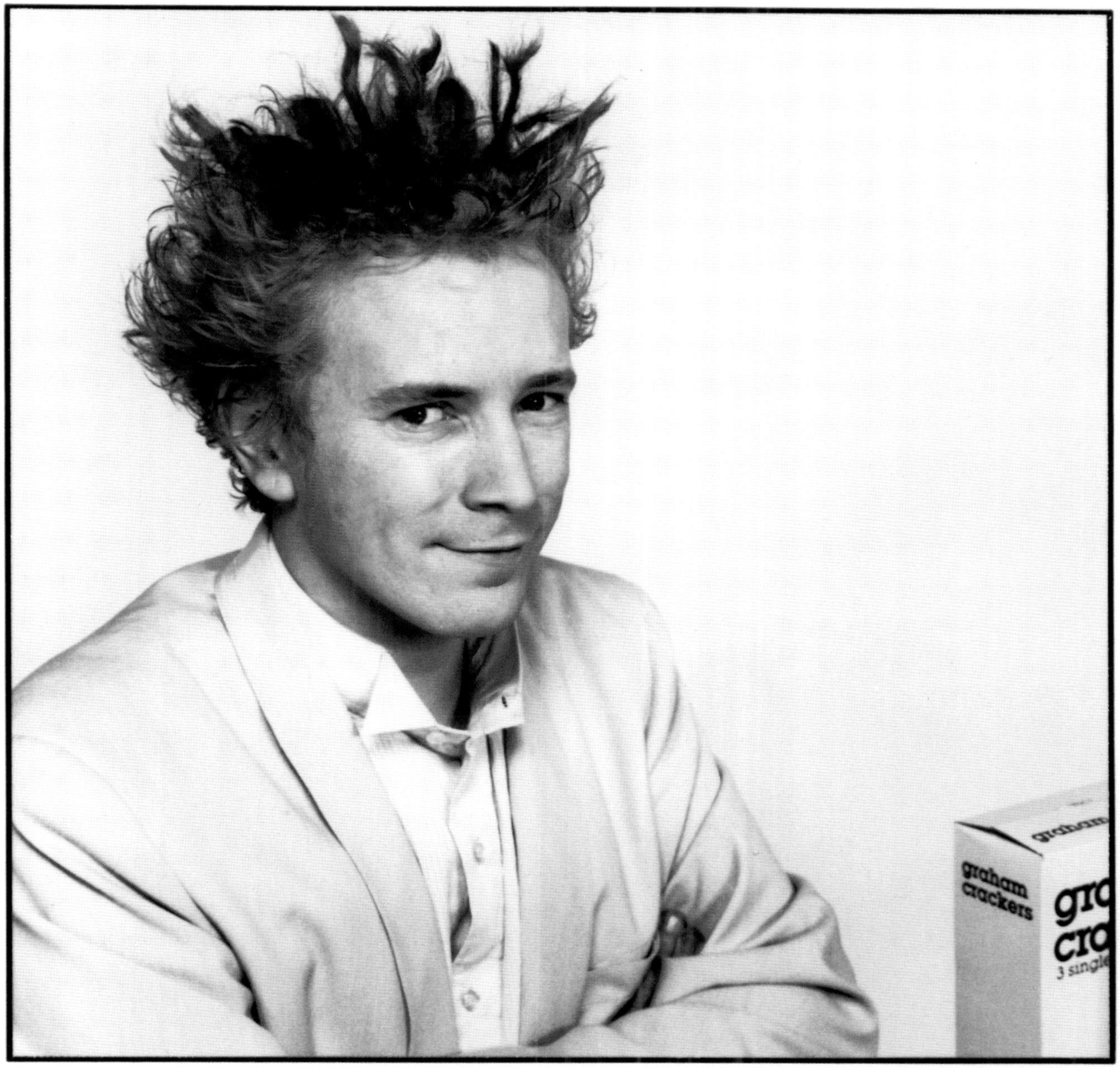

PHOTO CREDIT: JACKI SALLOW/1986

JOHN LYDON

ELEKTRA

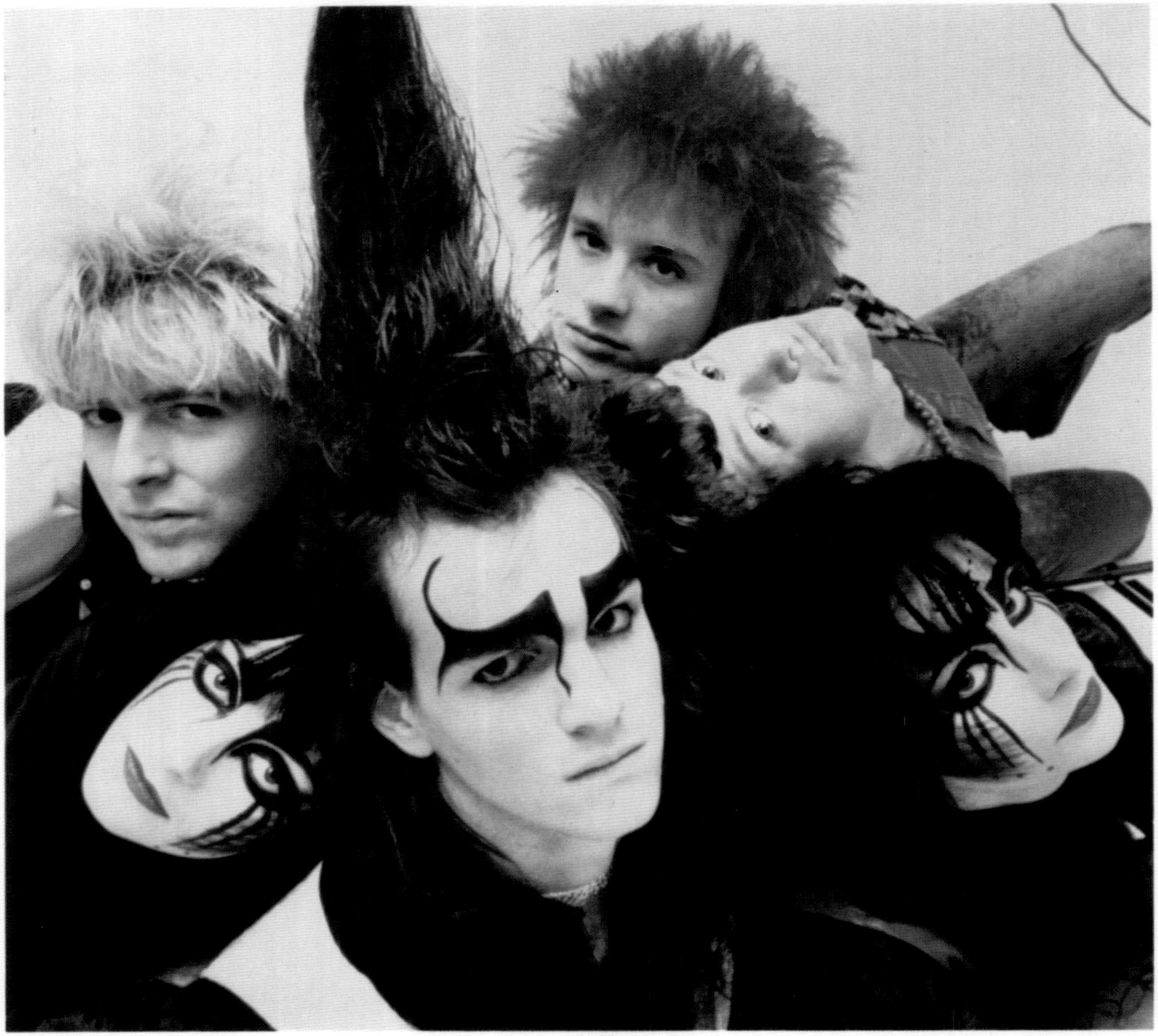

DOCTOR & THE MEDICS

I.R.S.

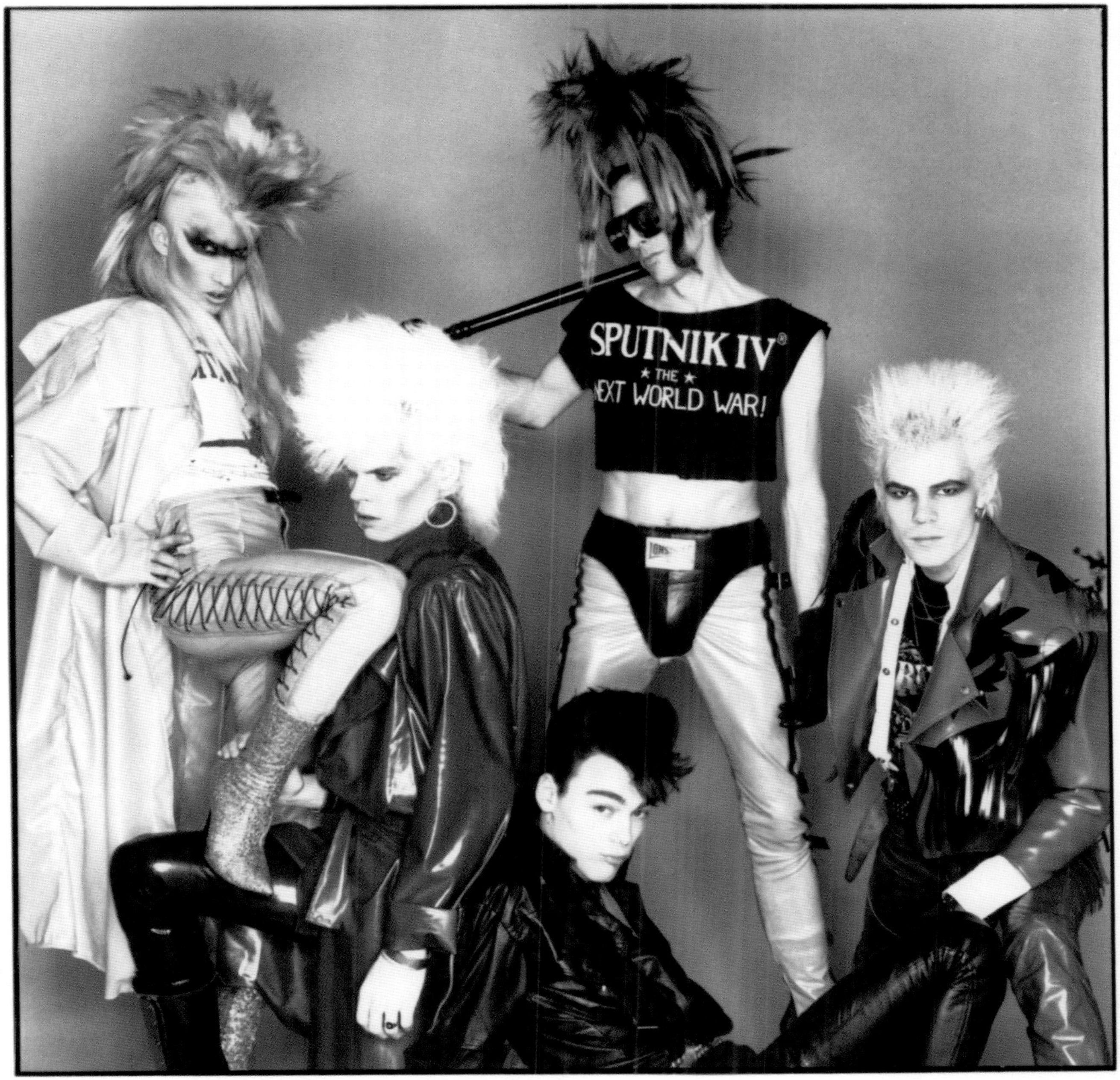

PHOTOGRAPH: JOHNNY ROZSA/1986

SIGUE ★ SIGUE ★ SPUTNIK

MAN
HAT
TAN™

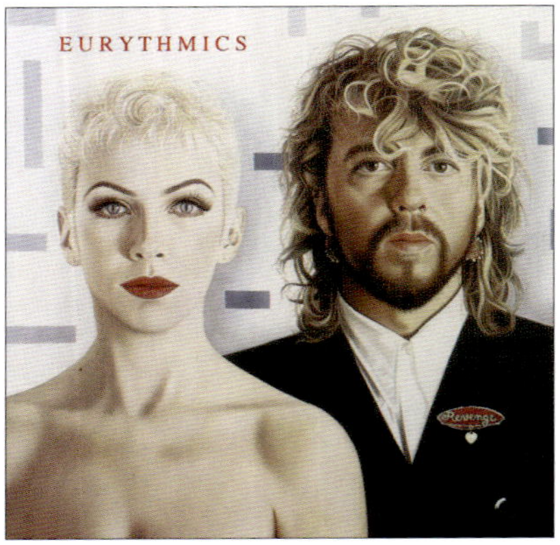

Propelled by an ear-grabbing harmonica riff, the insistent "Missionary Man" by the British duo **Eurythmics** flew to No. 1 on the album-oriented rock charts.

Billboard 200: *Revenge* (#12)
Billboard Hot 100: "Missionary Man" (#14); "Thorn in My Side" (#68)

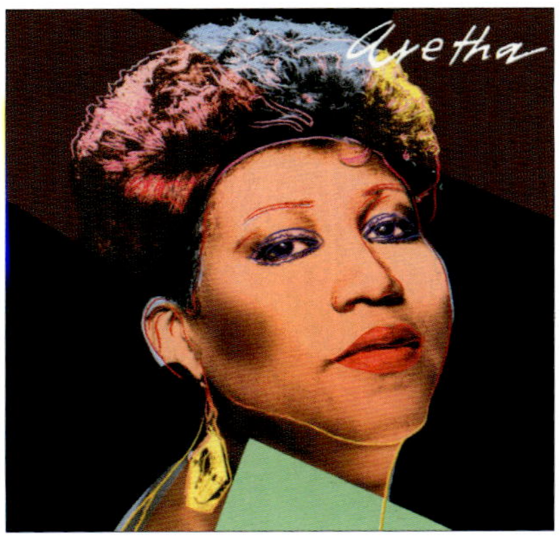

Soul giant **Aretha Franklin** scored smashes with a cover of "Jumpin' Jack Flash" and "I Knew You Were Waiting (For Me)," her duet with George Michael.

Billboard 200: Aretha (#32)
Billboard Hot 100: "Jumpin' Jack Flash" (#21); "Jimmy Lee" (#28);
"I Knew You Were Waiting (For Me)" (No. 1); "Rock-A-Lott" (#82)

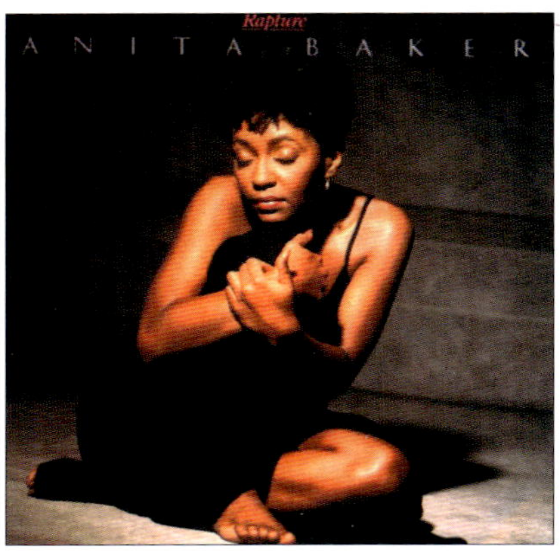

Romantic soul songstress **Anita Baker** rose to major stardom by dint of *Rapture*, a platinum-selling album, and "Sweet Love," a Grammy-winning pop hit.

Billboard 200: *Rapture* (#11)
Billboard Hot 100: "Sweet Love" (#8); "Caught Up in the Rapture" (#37);
"Same Ole Love (365 Days a Year)" (#44); "No One in the World" (#44)

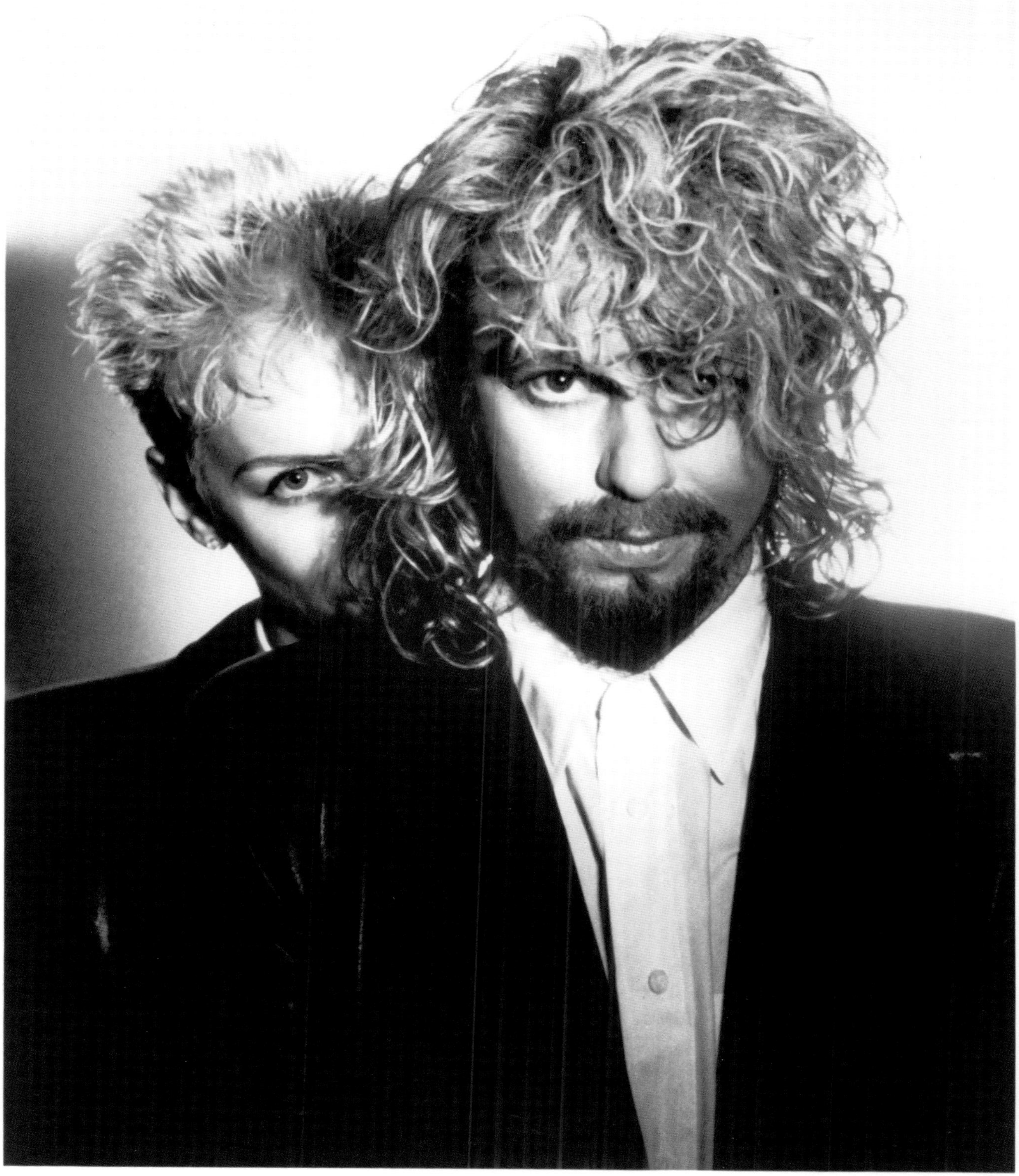

EURYTHMICS

RCA Records and Cassettes

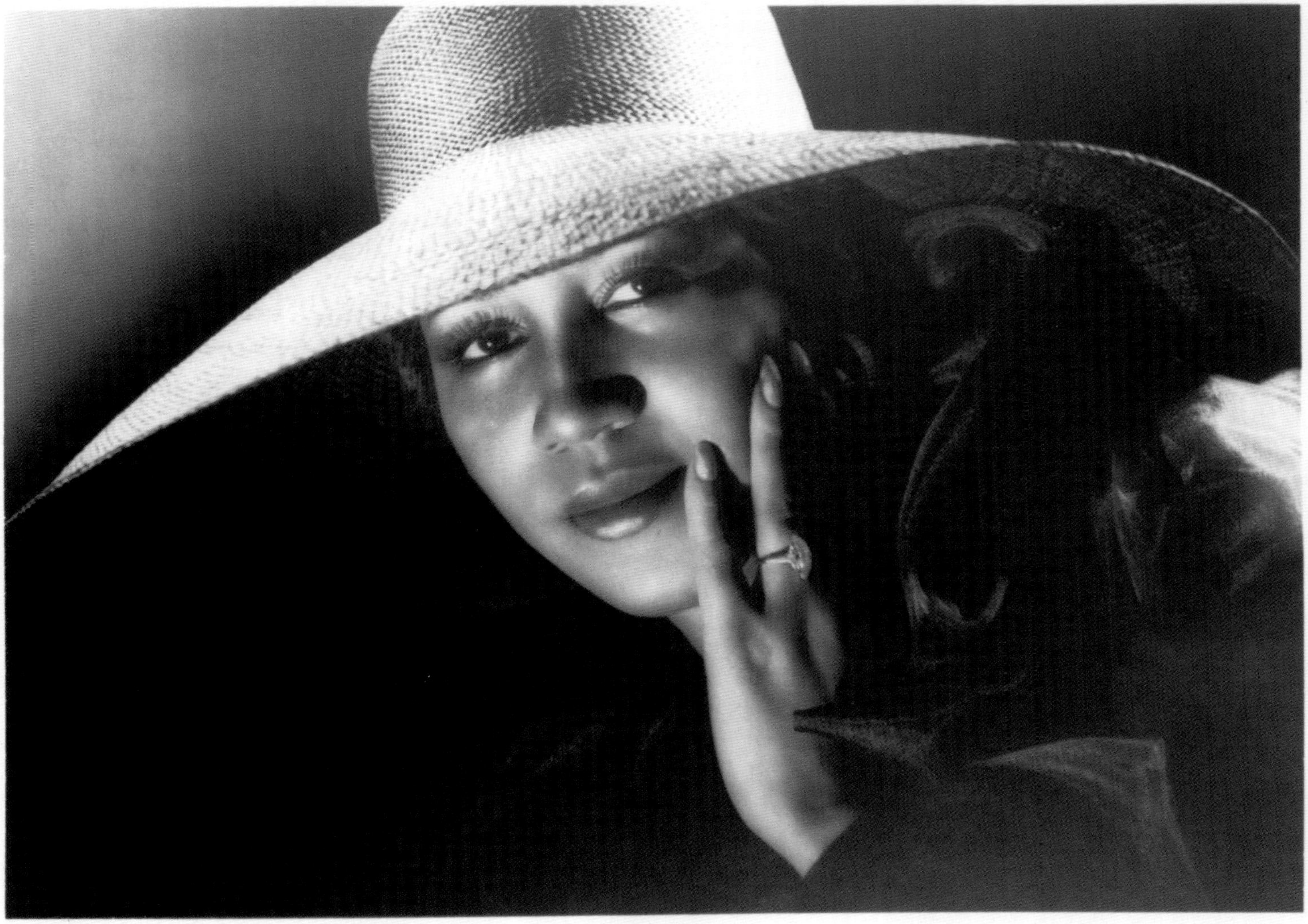

Aretha. Franklin

Management: Reverend Cecil Franklin
(313) 341-3743
Press Agent: Howard Brandy
(213) 657-7940

ARISTA™

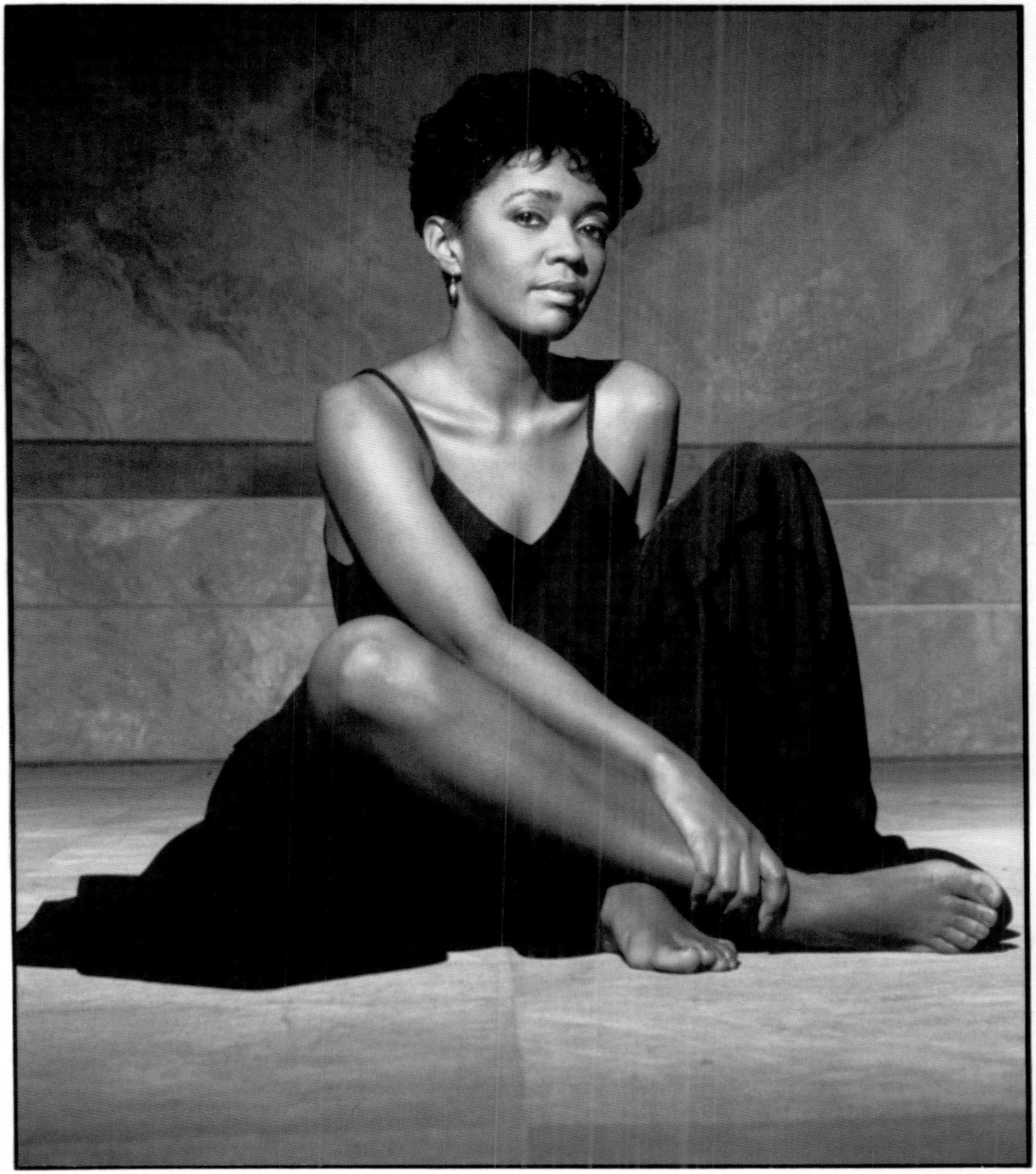

PHOTO CREDIT: CAROL FRIEDMAN/1986

ANITA BAKER

ELEKTRA

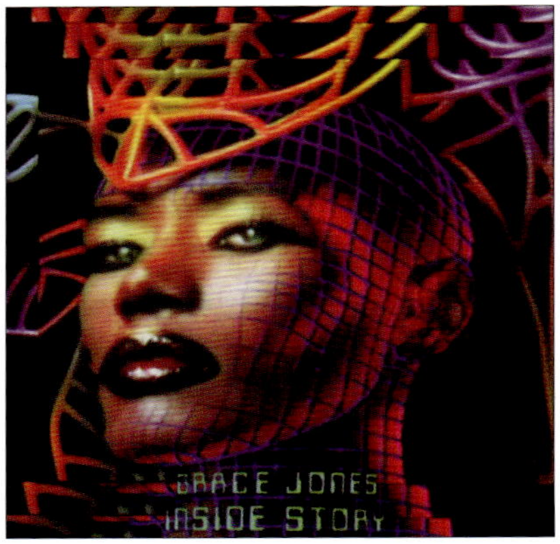

Grace Jones teamed with Nile Rodgers of Chic for *Inside Story*, and the album spawned the dance hit "I'm Not Perfect (But I'm Perfect for You)."

Billboard 200: *Inside Story* (#81)
Billboard Hot 100: "I'm Not Perfect (But I'm Perfect for You)" (#69)

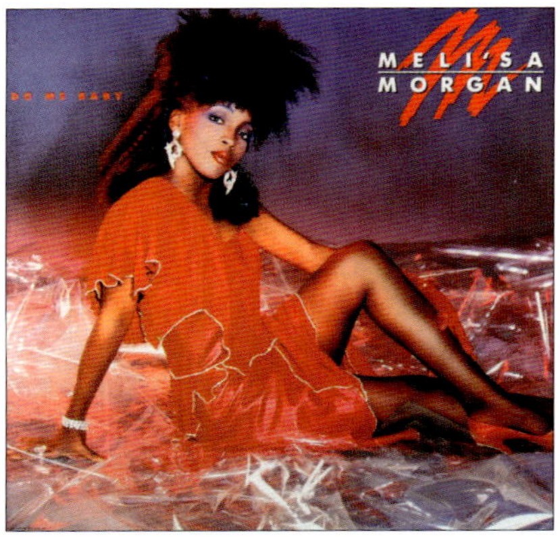

Meli'sa Morgan's solo career got off to an auspicious start, as the singer's sultry cover of "Do Me Baby," Prince's alluring ballad, topped the R&B chart.

Billboard 200: *Do Me Baby* (#41)
Billboard Hot 100: "Do Me Baby" (#46)

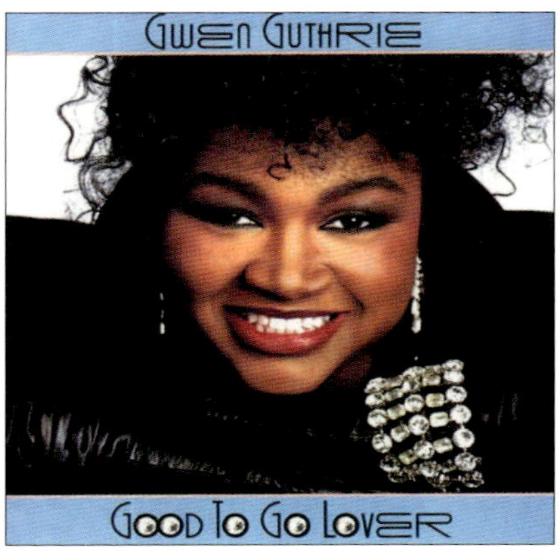

Soul diva **Gwen Guthrie**'s sassy "Ain't Nothin' Goin' On but the Rent," an anthem from *Good to Go Lover*, hit No. 1 on the dance club and R&B charts.

Billboard 200: *Good to Go Lover* (#89)
Billboard Hot 100: "Ain't Nothin' Goin' On but the Rent" (#42)

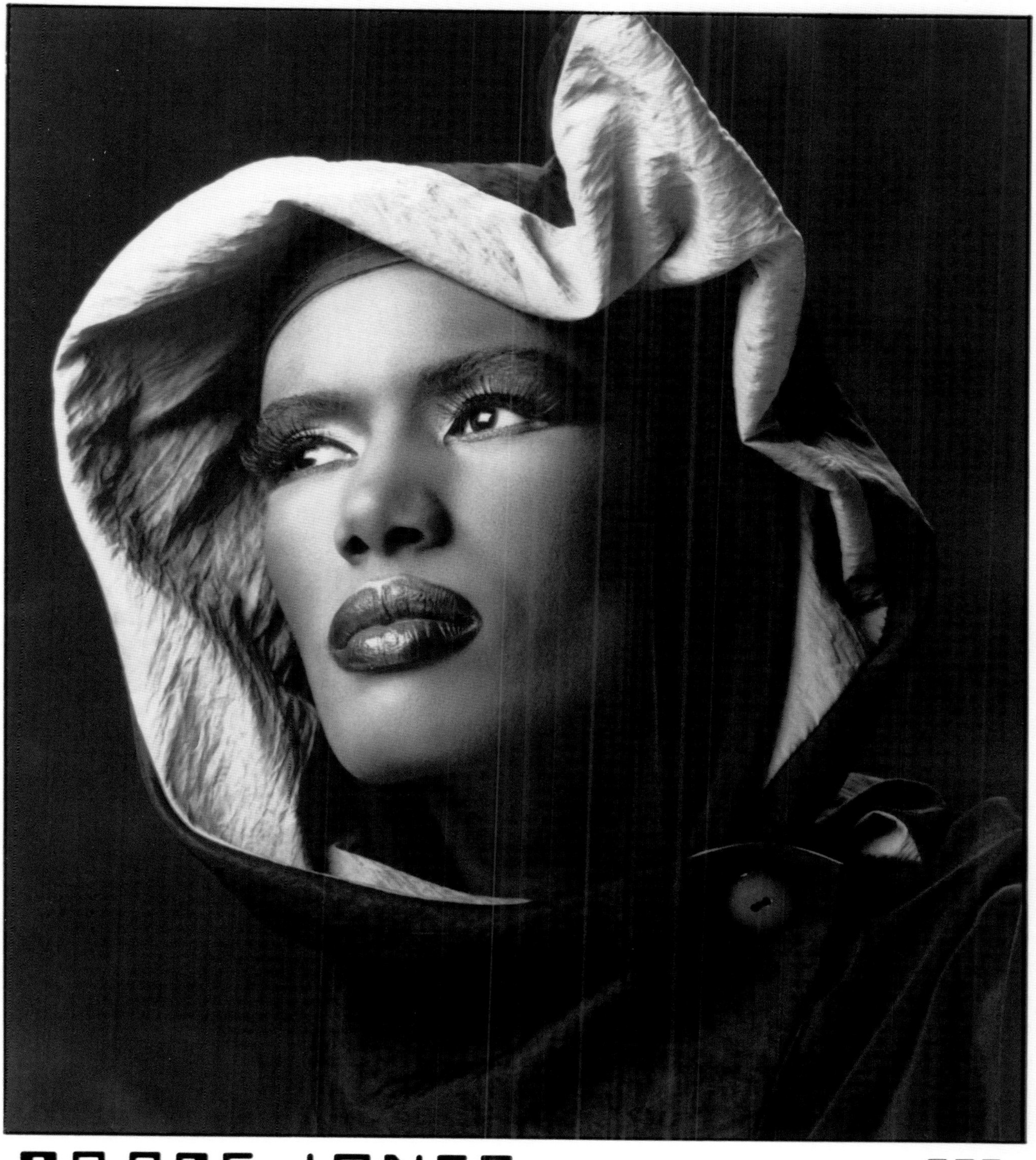

GRACE JONES

MAN
HAT
TAN™

Photo by Greg Gorman/1986

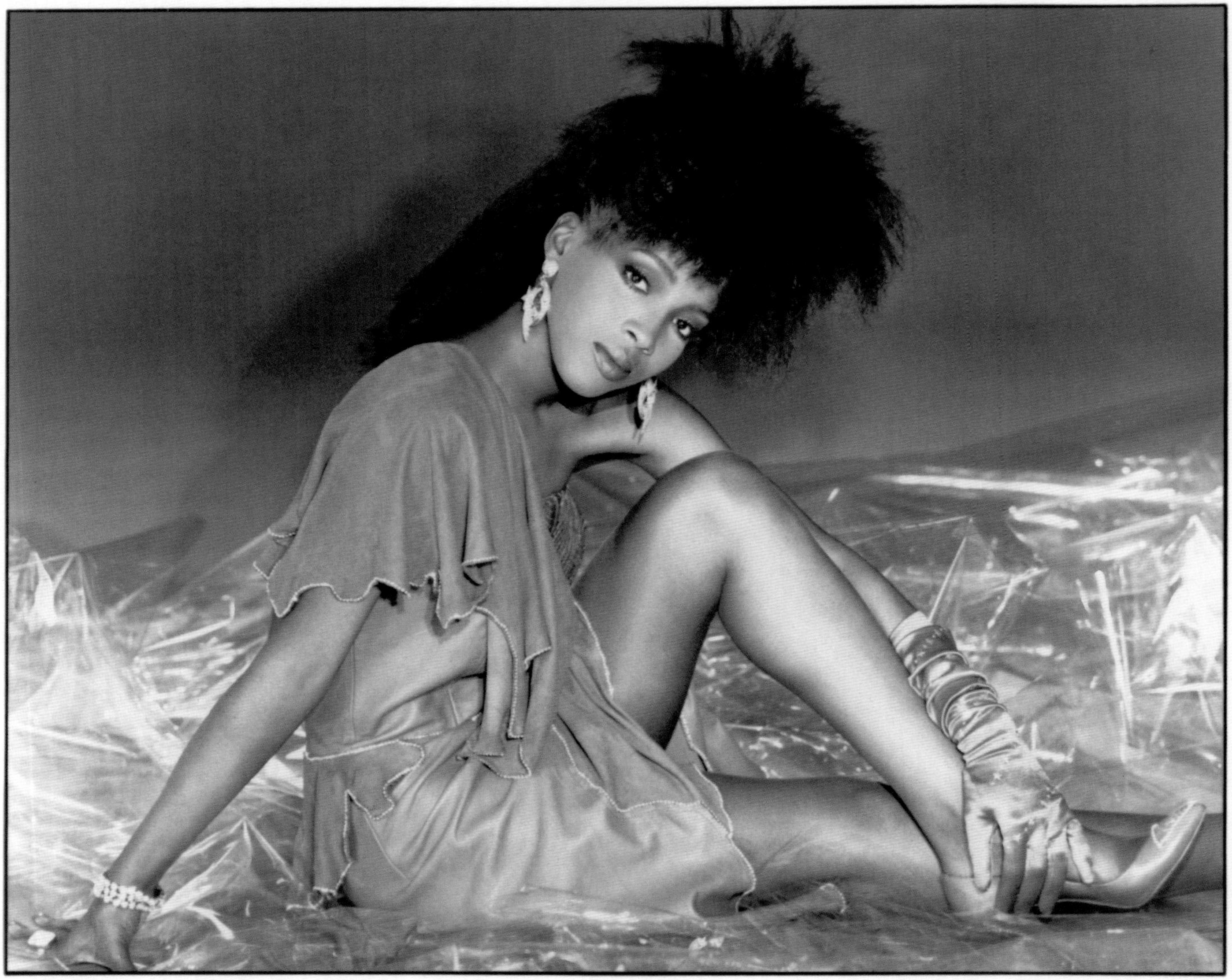

Photo: Carol Weinberg / 1985

MELI'SA
MORGAN

Capitol
RECORDS

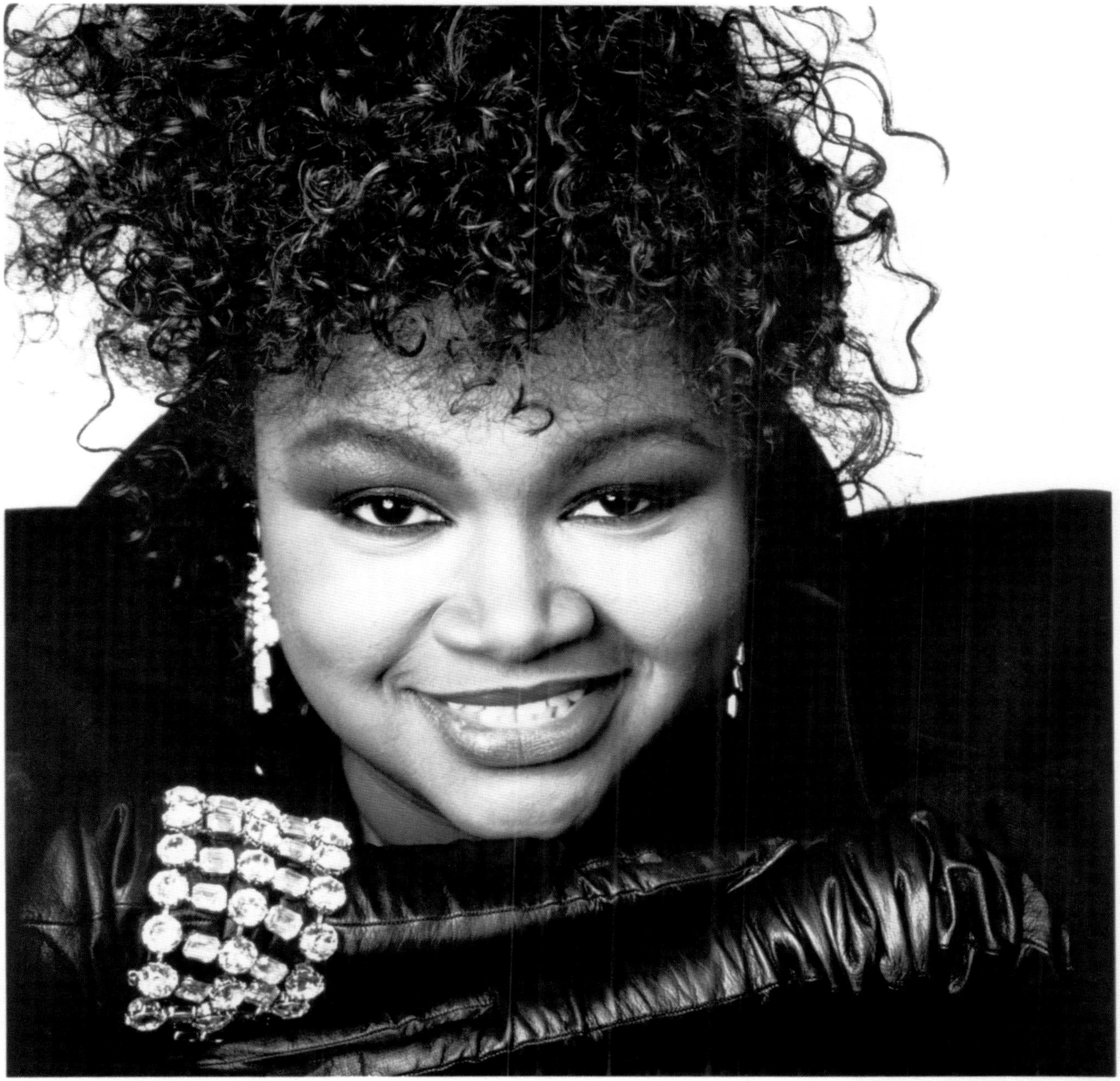

GWEN GUTHRIE

polydor

PolyGram Records

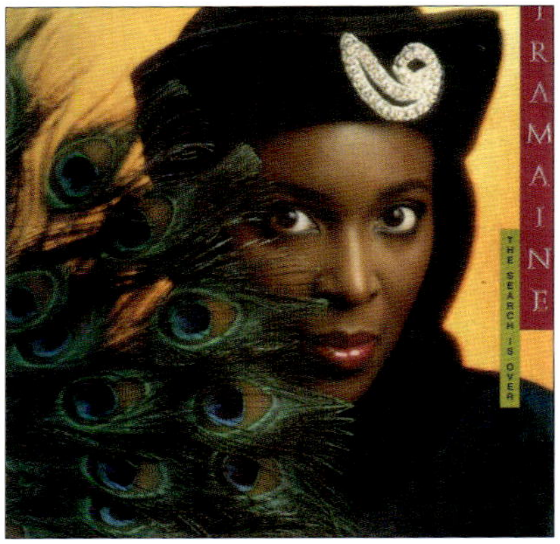

Gospel singer **Tramaine** crafted a monster club hit, "Fall Down (Spirit of Love)," the first inspirational record by a nonsecular artist to top the dance chart.

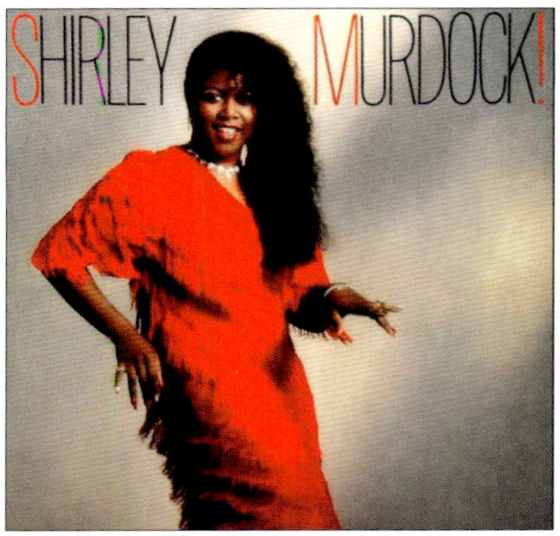

The power and tone of **Shirley Murdock**'s gospel grounding emerged in "As We Lay," a tender ballad that made the R&B, pop and adult contemporary charts.

Billboard 200: *Shirley Murdock!* (#44)
Billboard Hot 100: "As We Lay" (#23)

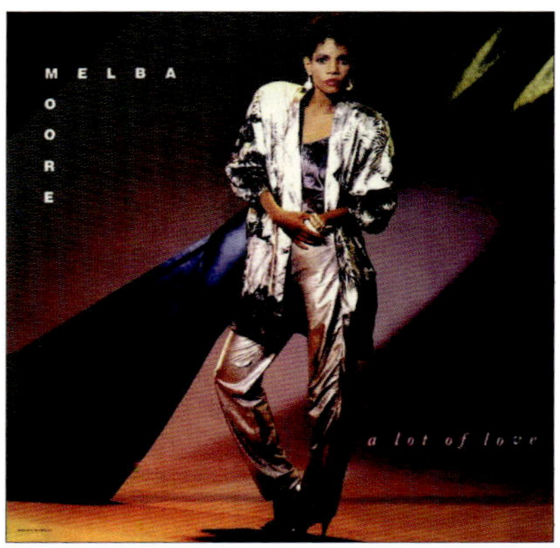

Singer and actress **Melba Moore** mustered two warm duets, "A Little Bit More" with Freddie Jackson and "Love the One I'm With (A Lot of Love)" with Kashif.

Billboard 200: *A Lot of Love* (#91)

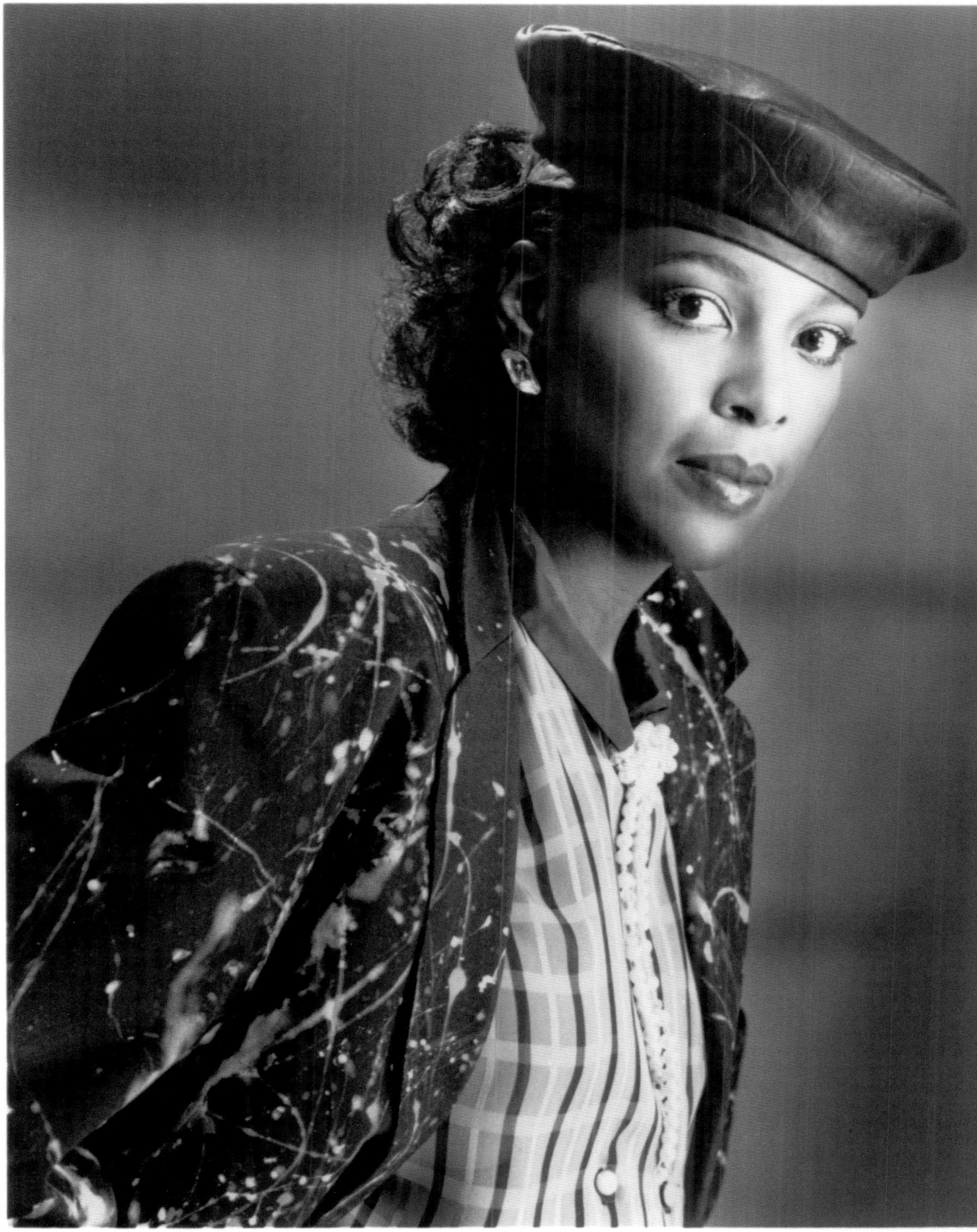

PHOTO CREDIT: NELS ISRAELSON

TRAMAINE

A&M RECORDS
Printed in U.S.A.

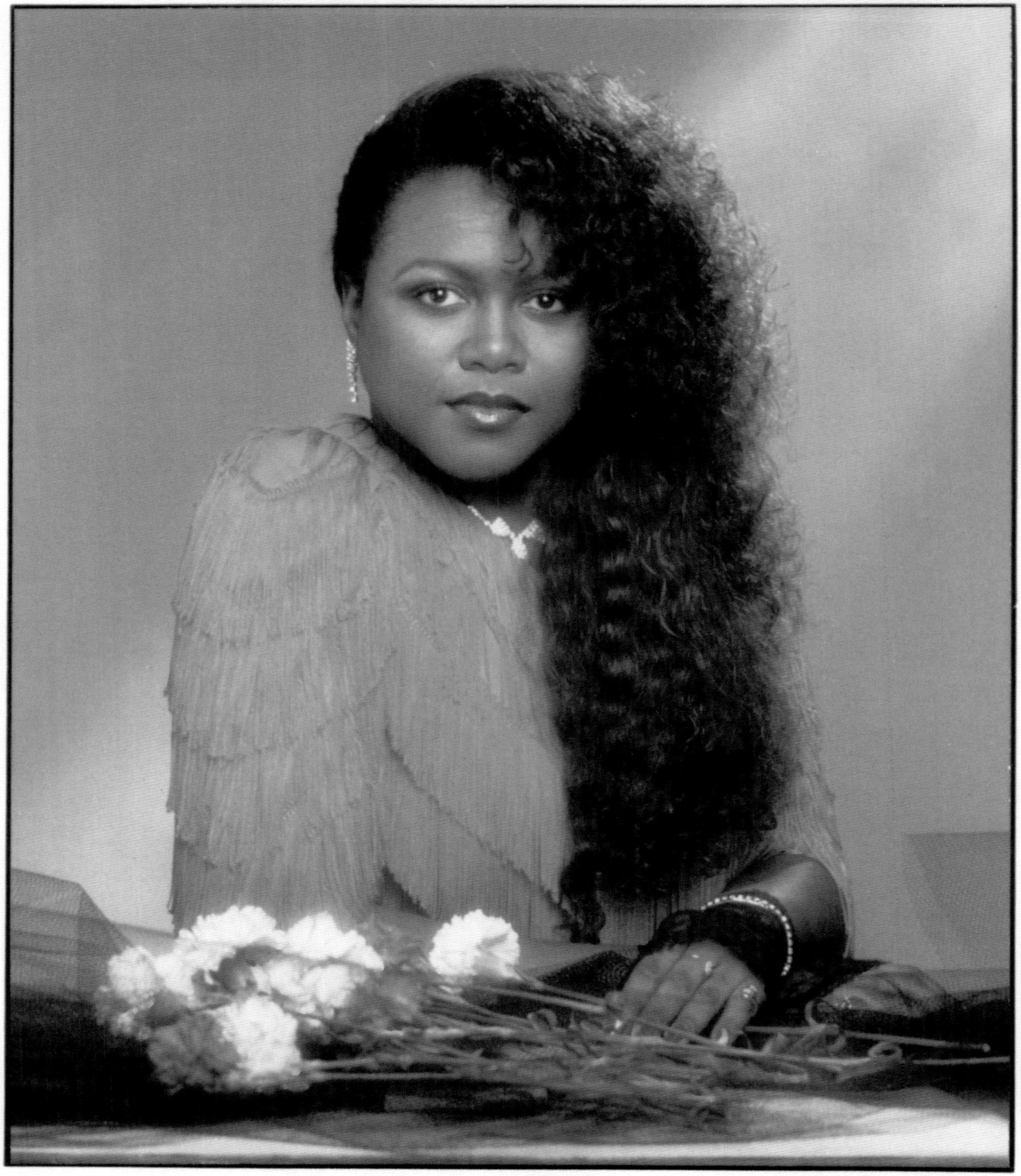

PHOTO CREDIT: MICHELE SINGER/1986

SHIRLEY MURDOCK

ELEKTRA

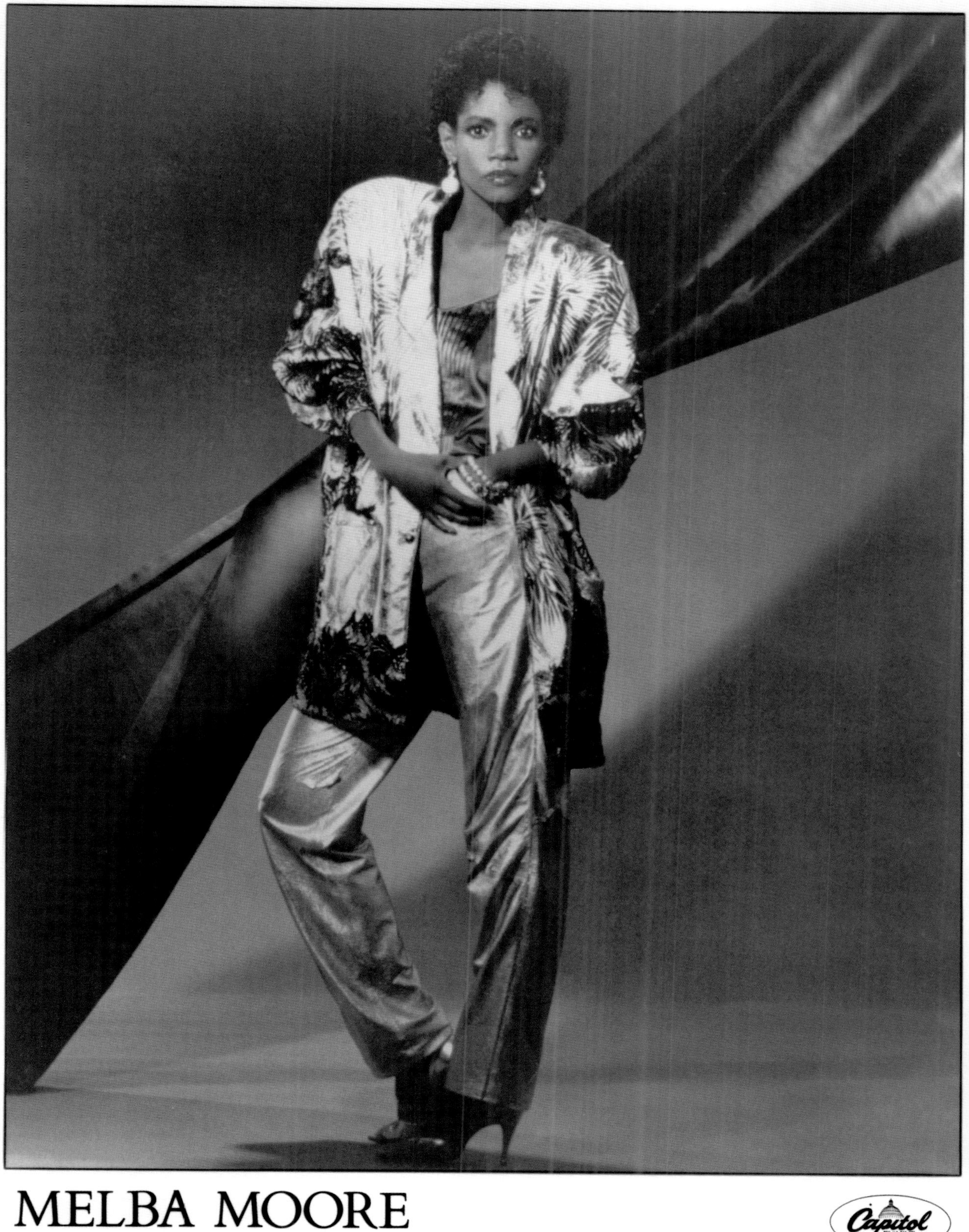

Photo: Carol Weinberg / 1986

MELBA MOORE

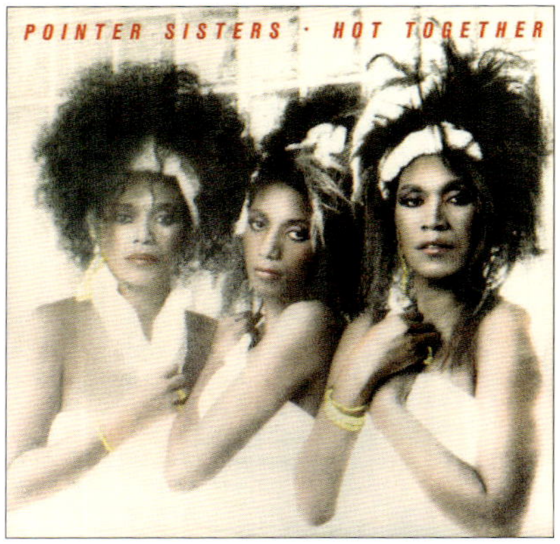

The versatile **Pointer Sisters**' run of Top 10 hits ended, but the feisty "Hot Together" found a spot on the soundtrack for the Mel Brooks movie *Spaceballs*.

Billboard 200: *Hot Together* (#48)
Billboard Hot 100: "Goldmine" (#33); "All I Know Is the Way I Feel" (#93)

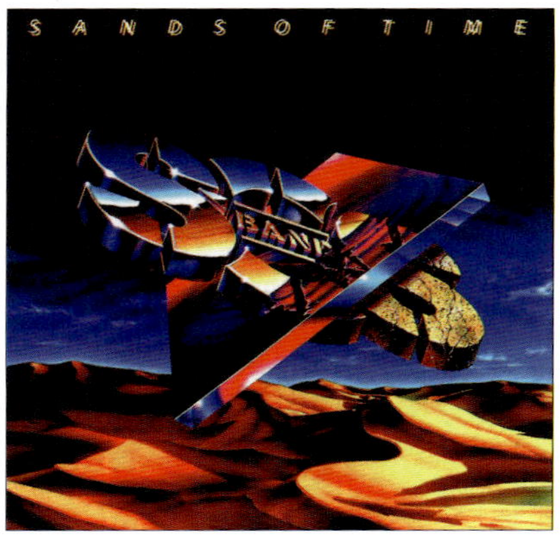

The funky **S.O.S. Band** served "The Finest," a track on the gold album *Sands of Time* and one of the group's last songs to showcase lead singer Mary Davis.

Billboard 200: *Sands of Time* (#44)
Billboard Hot 100: "The Finest" (#44)

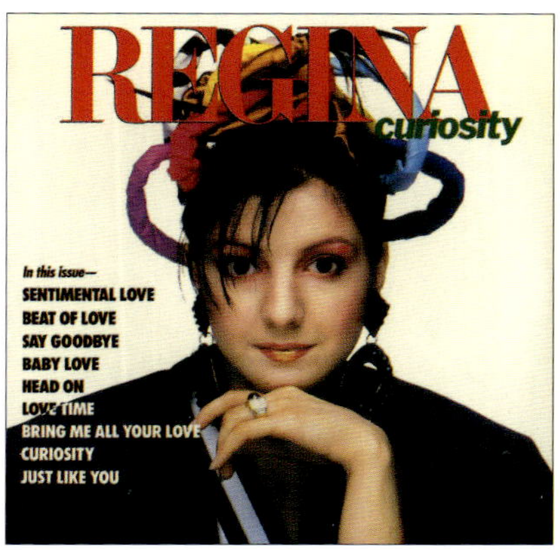

A songwriter for other acts, **Regina** sang the Madonna-esque "Baby Love" herself, hitting No. 1 in dance clubs and entering the Top 10 on the pop charts.

Billboard 200: *Curiosity* (#102)
Billboard Hot 100: "Baby Love" (#10)

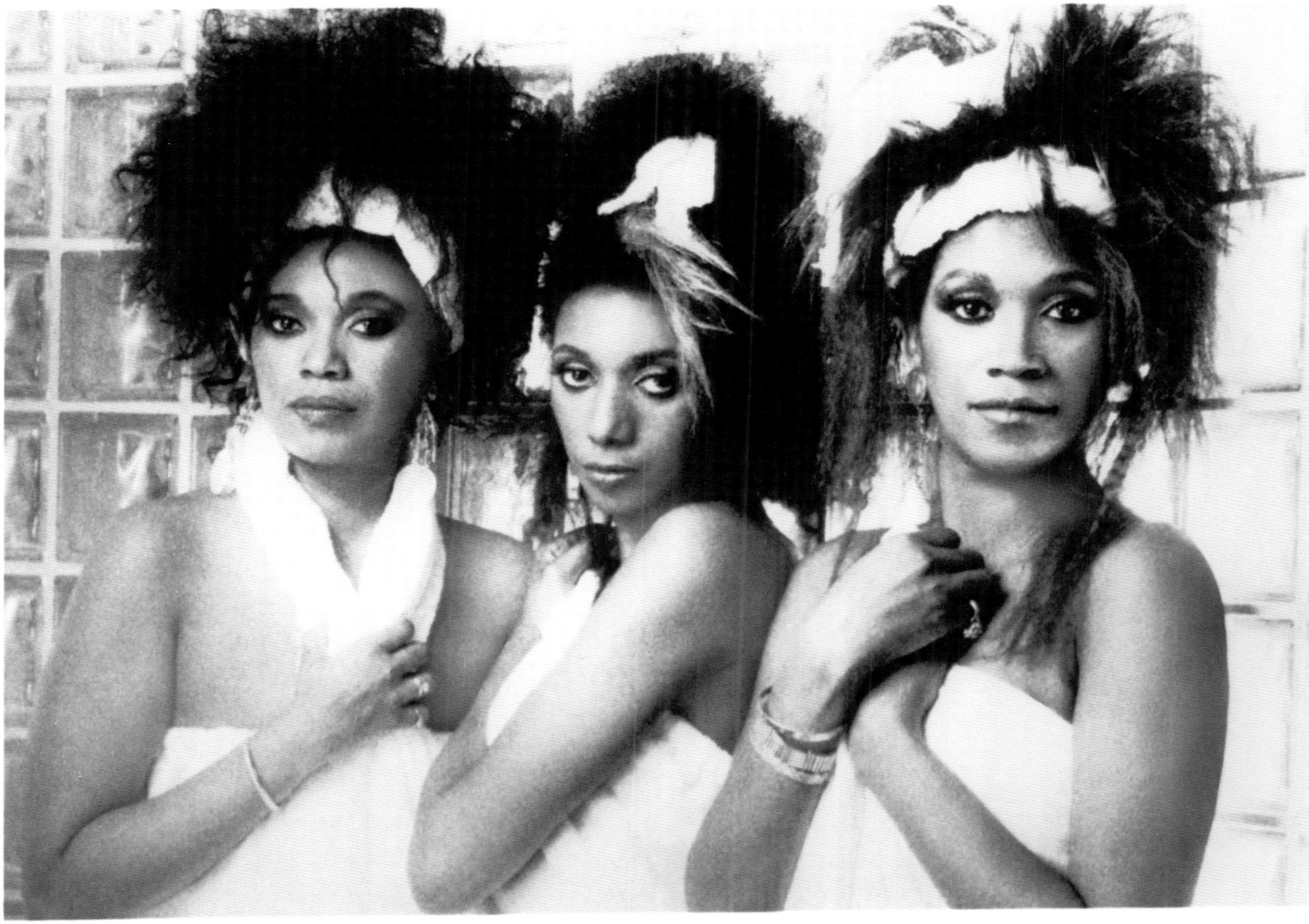

PERSONAL MANAGEMENT
GALLIN-MOREY ASSOCIATES

Pointer Sisters

RCA
Records and Cassettes

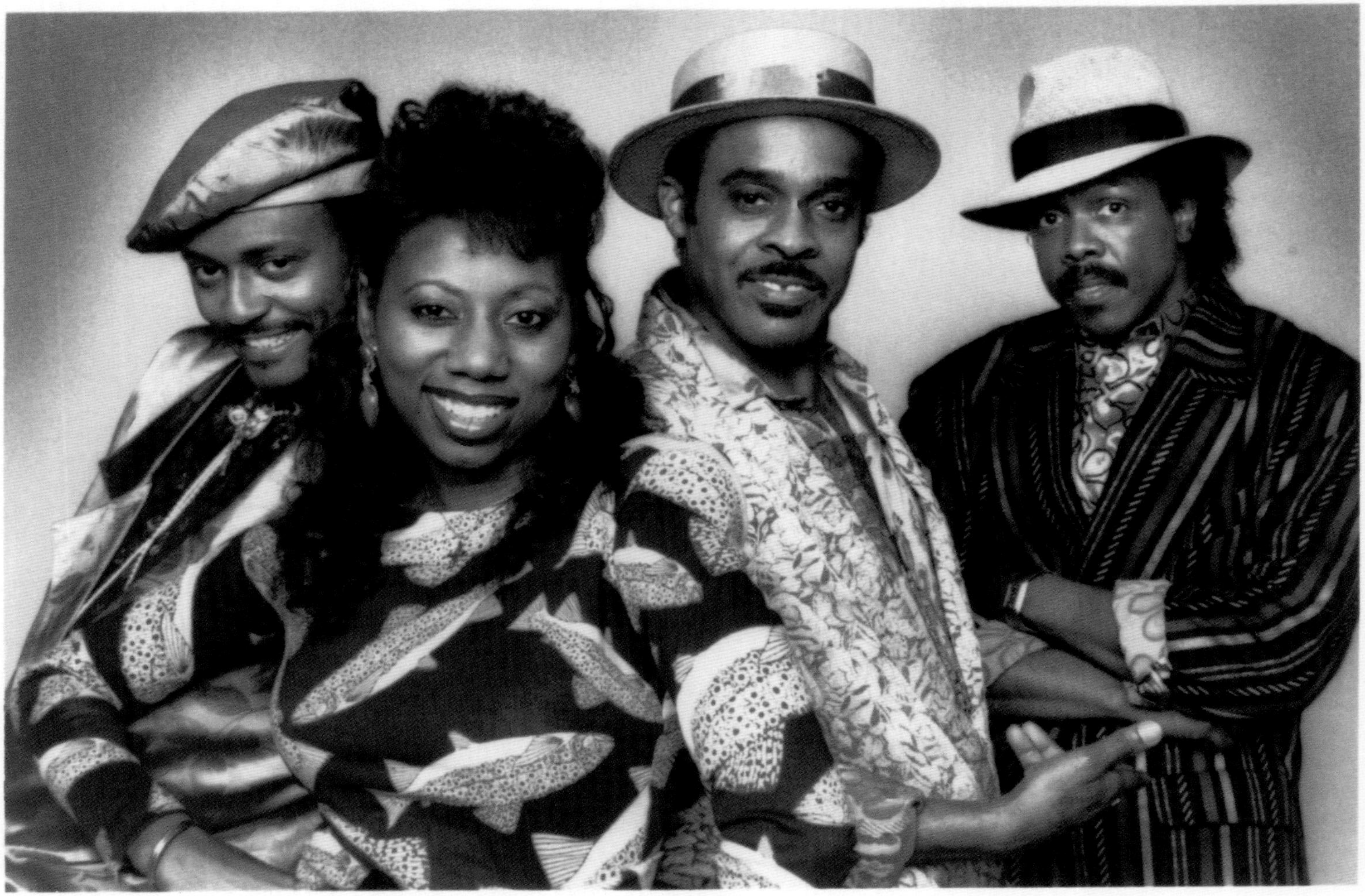

Photo: Rick Diamond

L-R: Bruno Speight, Mary Davis, Abdul Raoof, Jason Bryant

SIGHT & SOUND MANAGEMENT LTD
119 WEST 57TH STREET
NEW YORK, N.Y. 10019
(212) 541-5580

S.O.S.BAND

Tabu

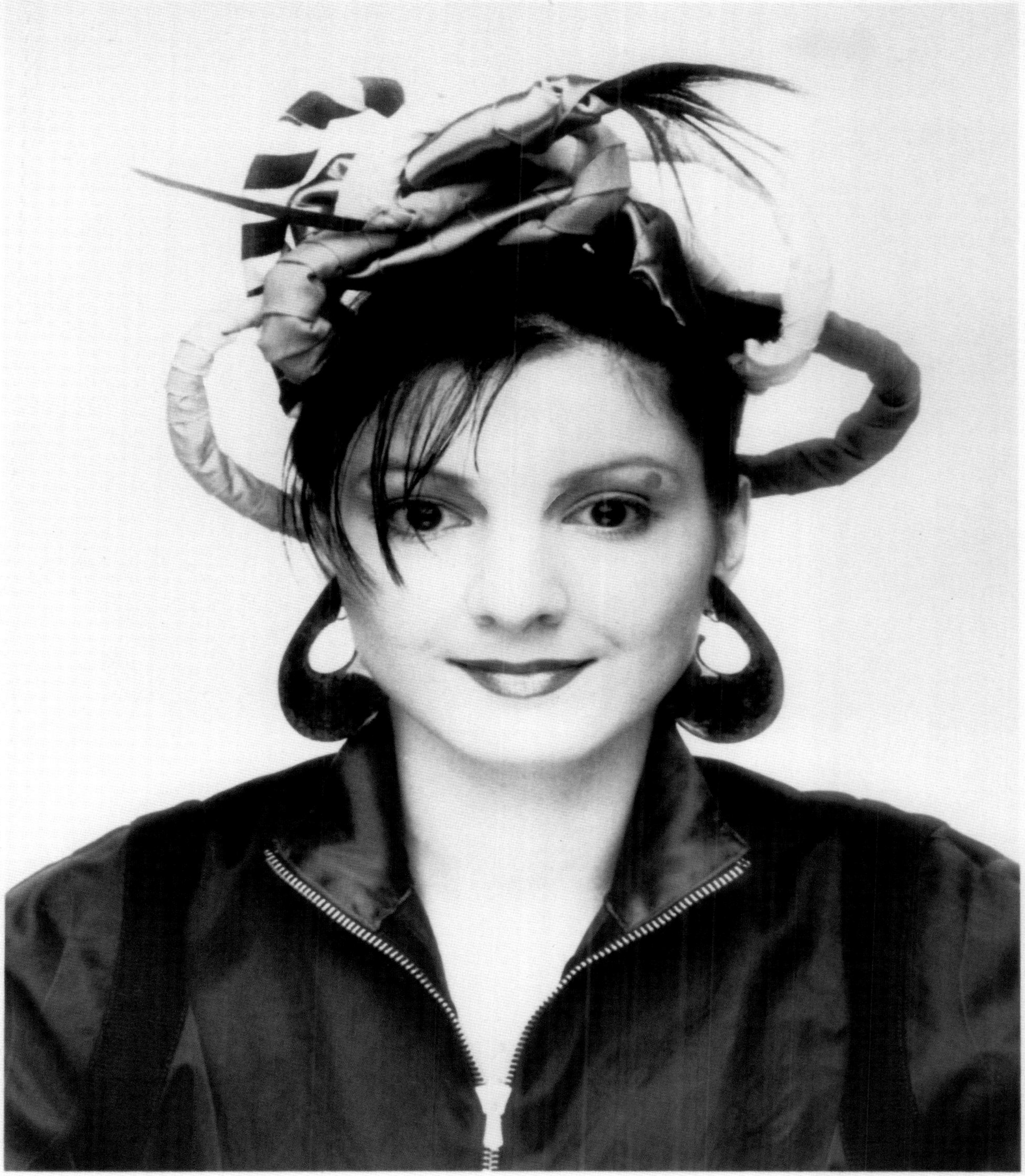

REGINA

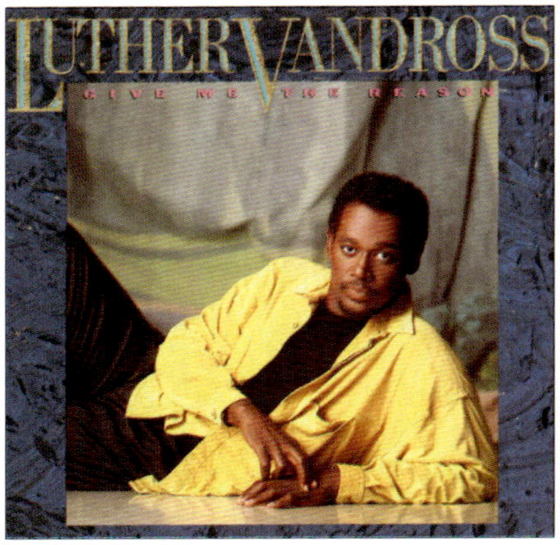

With *Give Me the Reason* and the crossover hit "Stop to Love," romantic balladeer **Luther Vandross** offered proof of his contemporary pop-soul mastery.

Billboard 200: *Give Me the Reason* (#14)
Billboard Hot 100: "Give Me the Reason" (#57); "Stop to Love" (#15); "There's Nothing Better Than Love" (#50)

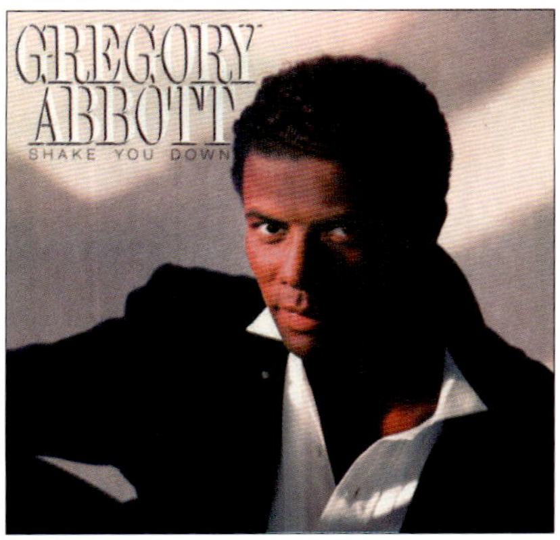

R&B singer **Gregory Abbott** roused the music industry, writing and producing the hit "Shake You Down," a platinum "groove ballad" from his first album.

Billboard 200: *Shake You Down* (#22)
Billboard Hot 100: "Shake You Down" (No. 1); "I Got the Feelin' (It's Over)" (#56)

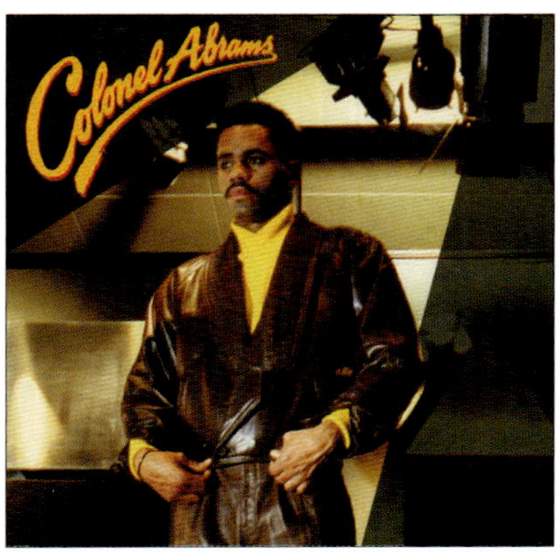

Growling and soaring, virile vocalist **Colonel Abrams** topped the dance charts with the worldwide hits "Trapped" and "I'm Not Gonna Let" from his debut.

Billboard 200: *Colonel Abrams* (#75)

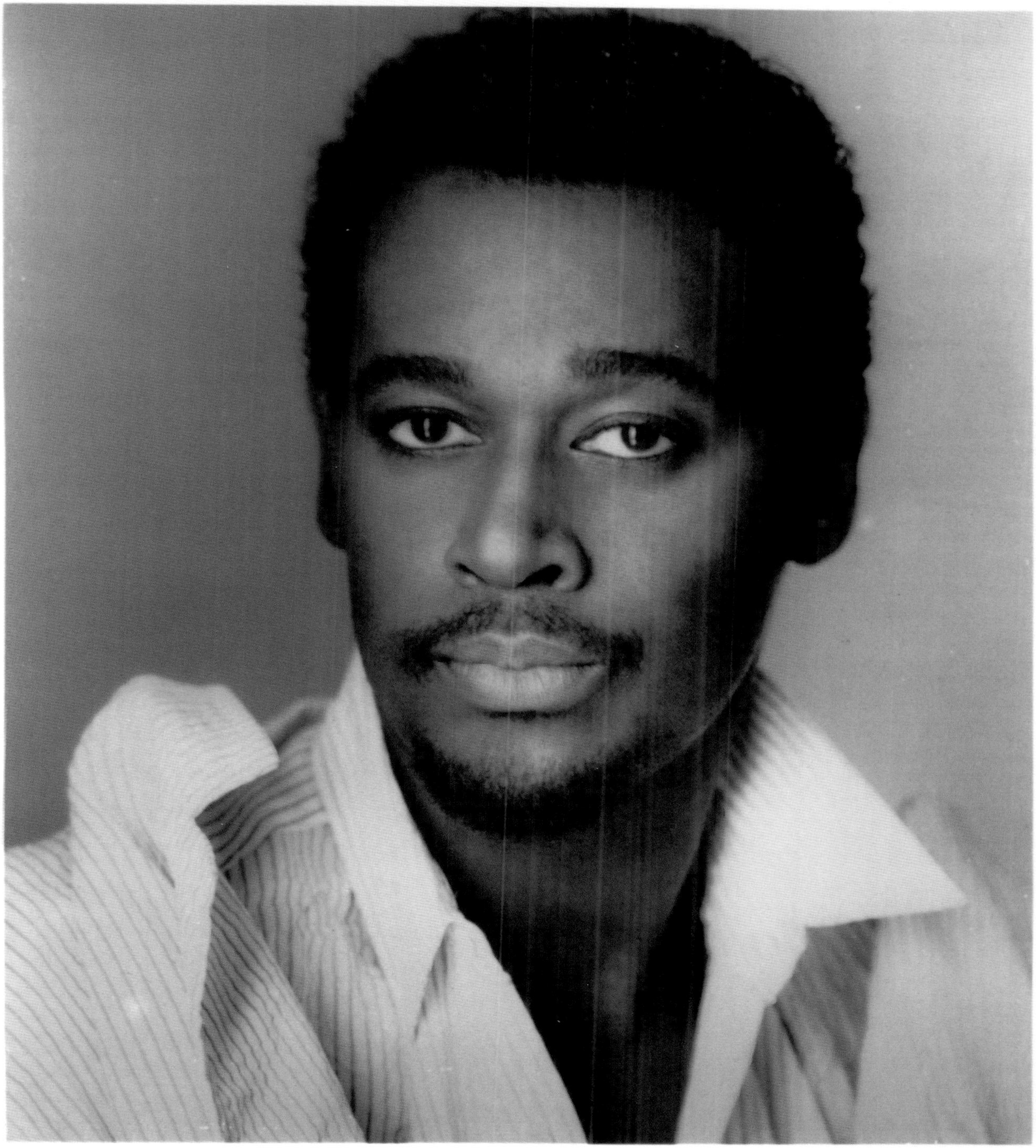

Photo Matthew Rolston

LUTHER VANDROSS

Alive

Epic

8609

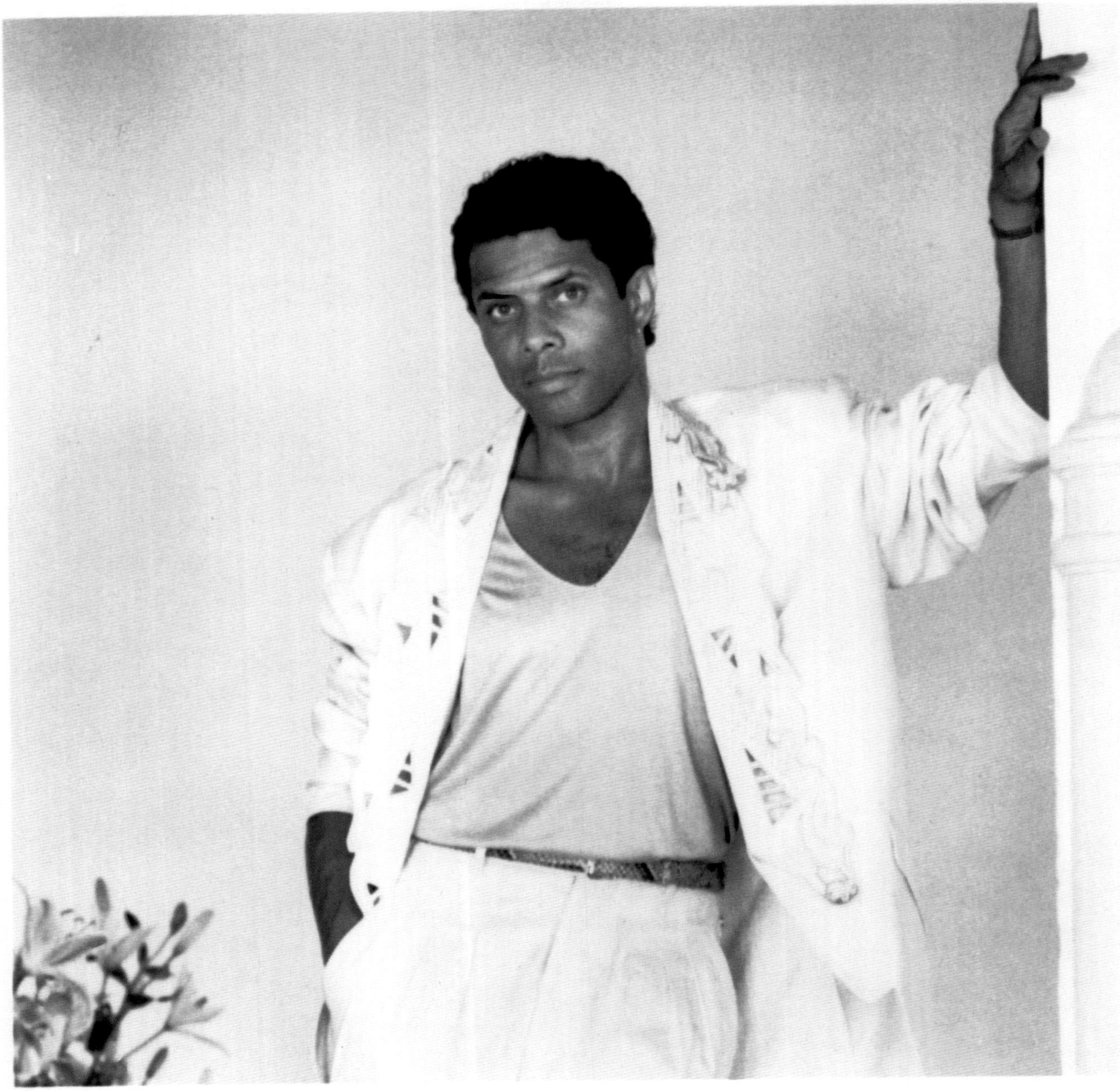

PHOTOGRAPH: RAUL VEGA

GREGORY ABBOTT

Columbia

8608

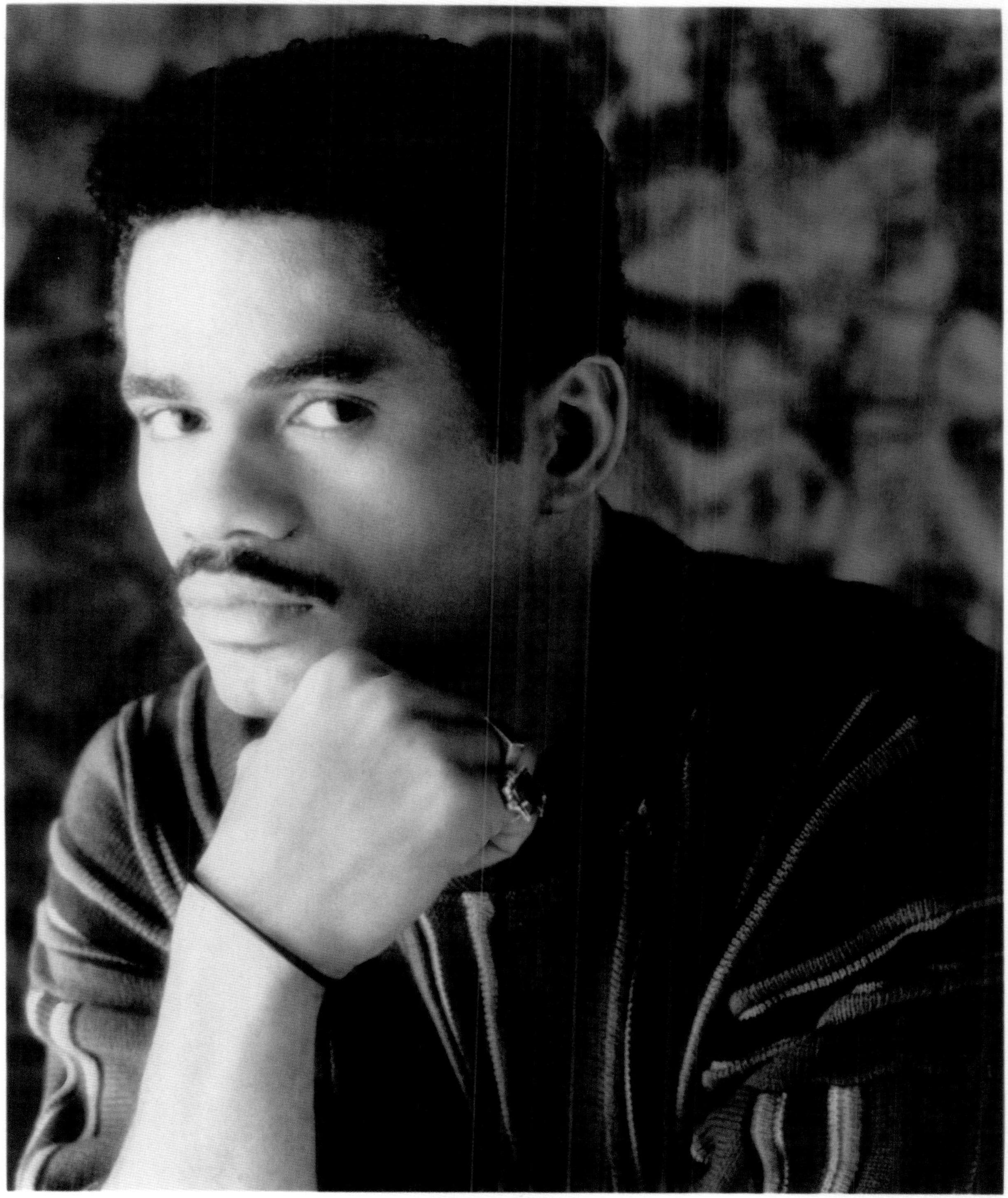

Colonel Abrams

MCA RECORDS

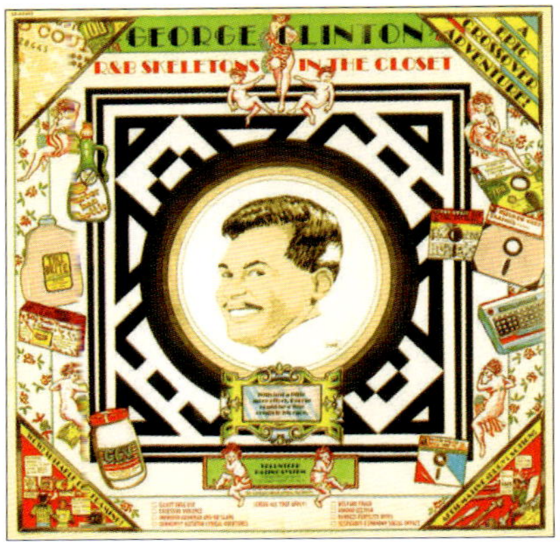

On his fourth solo project, Parliament-Funkadelic leader **George Clinton** cracked the R&B Top 20 again with the funk jewel "Do Fries Go with That Shake?"

Billboard 200: *R&B Skeletons in the Closet* (#81)

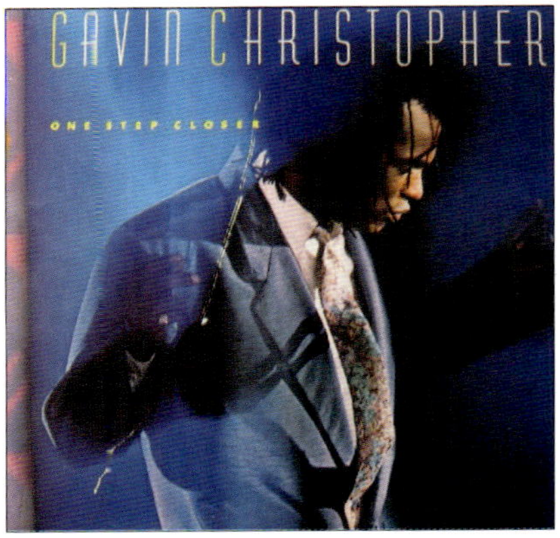

R&B musician **Gavin Christopher**, a vocalist, songwriter, keyboardist and producer, reached the pop charts with the soulful track "One Step Closer to You."

Billboard 200: *One Step Closer* (#74)
Billboard Hot 100: "One Step Closer to You" (#22)

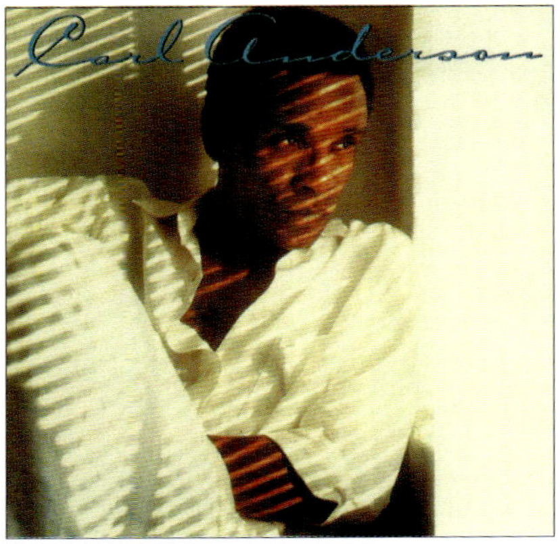

"Friends and Lovers," **Carl Anderson**'s smash duet with Gloria Loring, was first heard as the theme of a wedding scene on the soap opera *Days of Our Lives.*

Billboard 200: *Carl Anderson* (#87)
Billboard Hot 100: "Friends and Lovers" (#2)

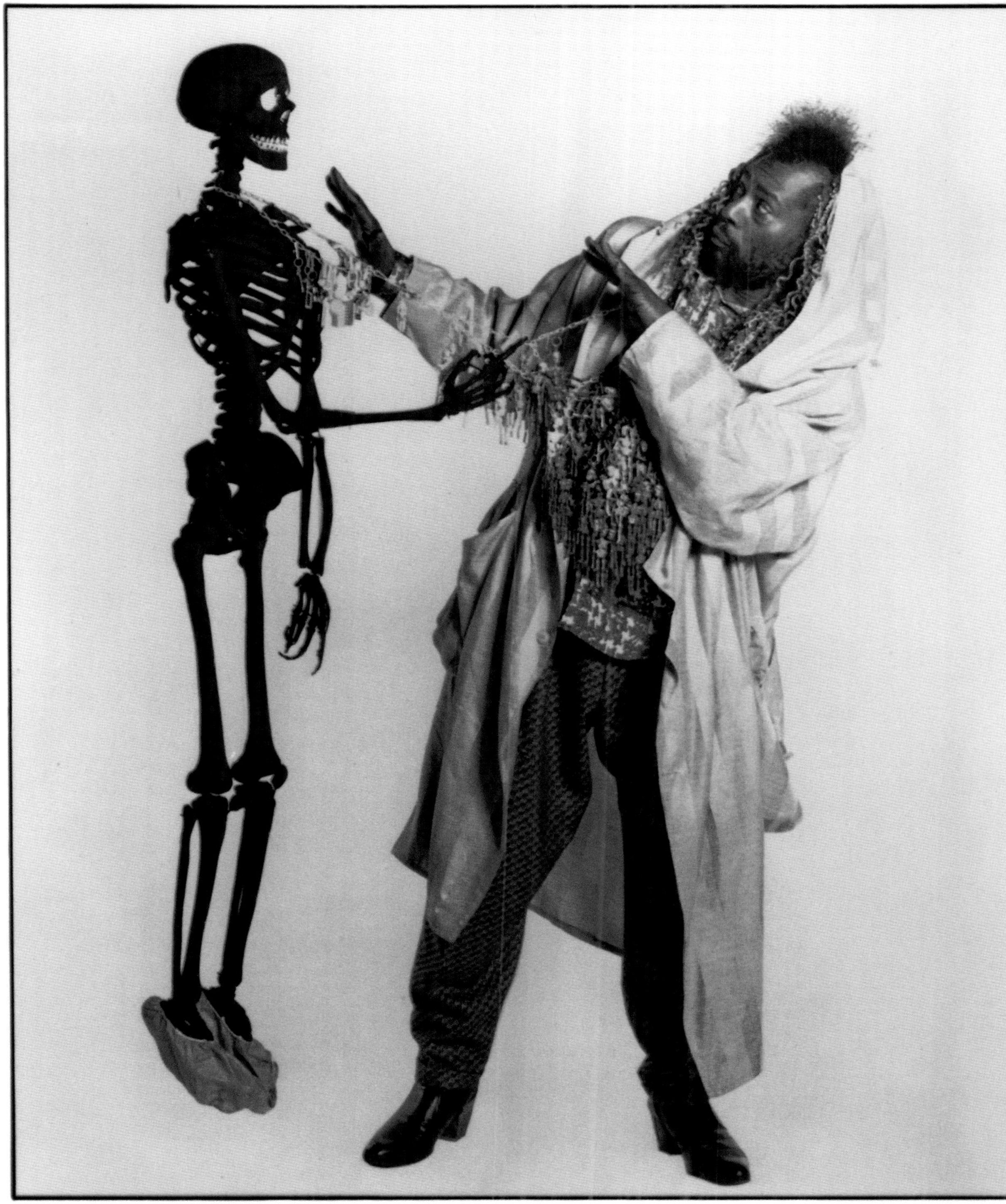

Photo: Diem Jones / 1986

GEORGE CLINTON

Capitol Records

GAVIN CHRISTOPHER

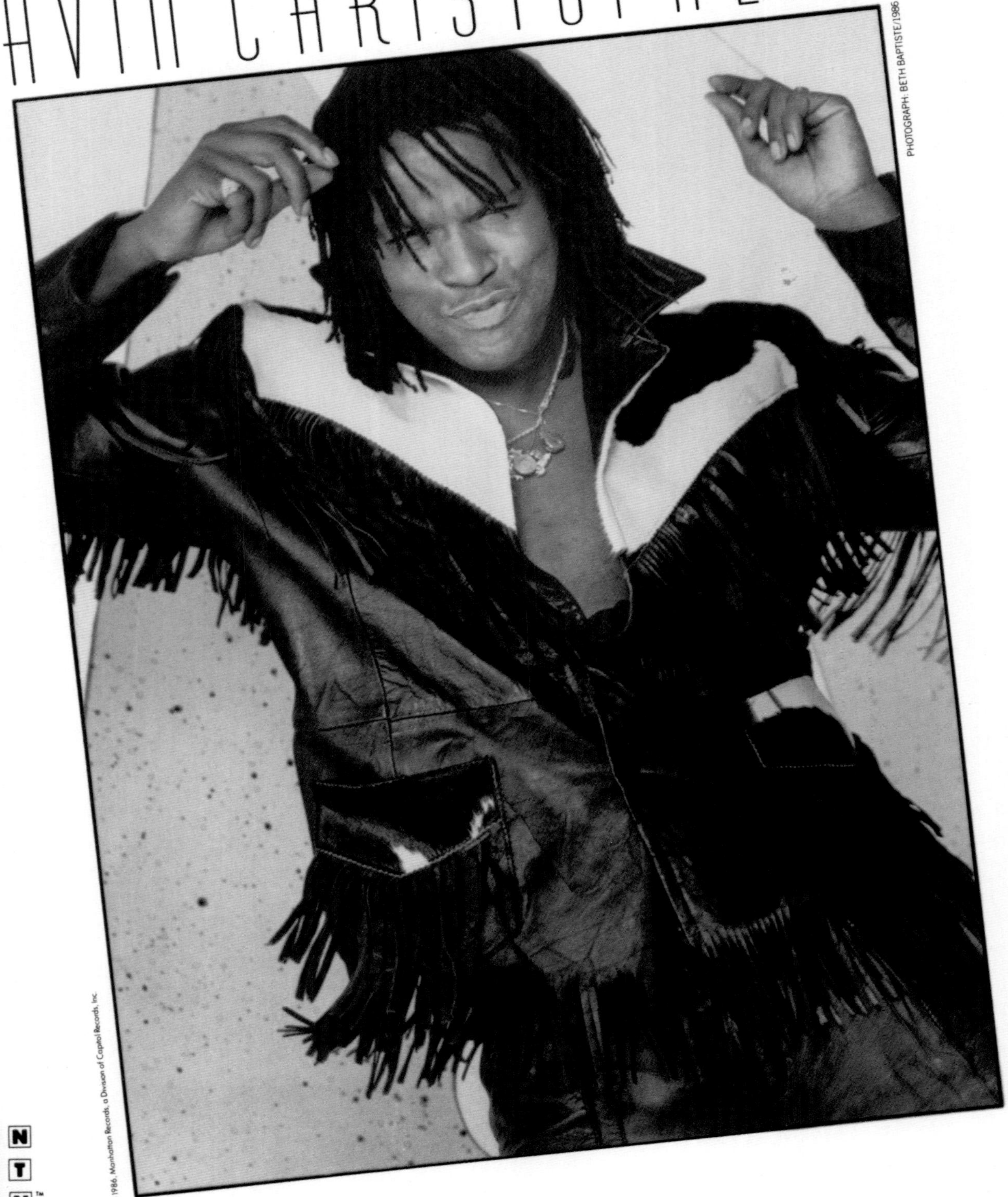

PHOTOGRAPH: BETH BAPTISTE/1986

MAN HAT TAN™

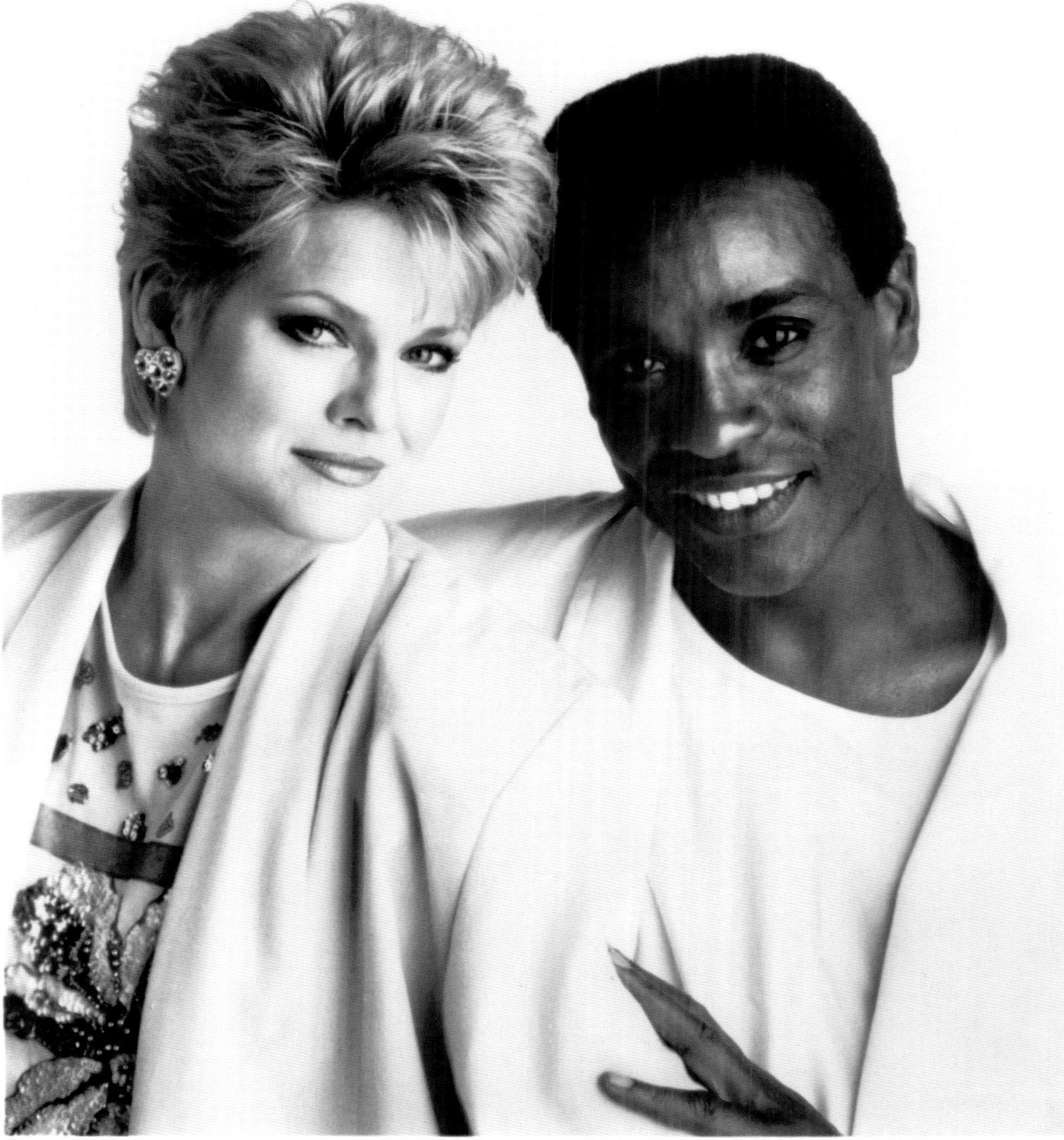

GLORIA LORING & CARL ANDERSON

CARRERE®

EPIC PORTRAIT ASSOCIATED

8606

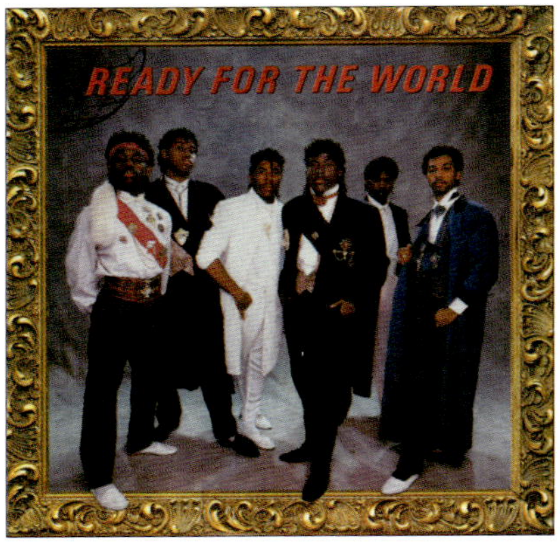

From the *Long Time Coming* album, **Ready for the World**'s "Love You Down," singer Melvin Riley's roguish move on an older woman, topped the R&B charts.

Billboard 200: *Long Time Coming* (#32)
Billboard Hot 100: "Love You Down" (#9)

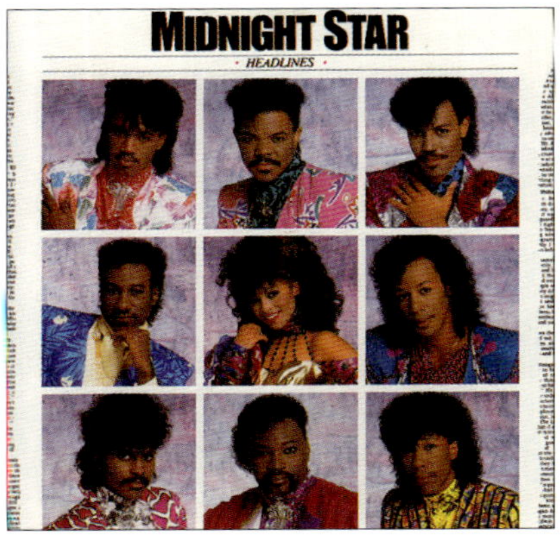

Headlines was the third album by **Midnight Star** to go gold, and the last to feature the R&B group's creative minds, brothers Reggie and Vincent Calloway.

Billboard 200: *Headlines* (#56)
Billboard Hot 100: "Headlines" (#69); "Midas Touch" (#42)

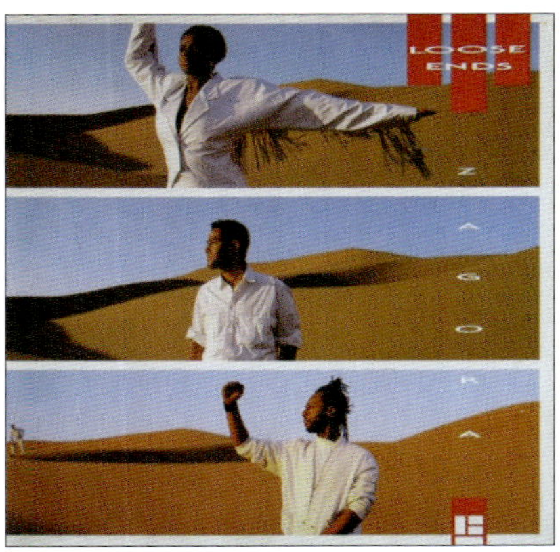

The British R&B trio **Loose Ends** topped the US R&B charts with "Slow Down," a huge dance-club smash, along with the punchy "Stay a Little While, Child."

Billboard 200: *Zagora* (#59)

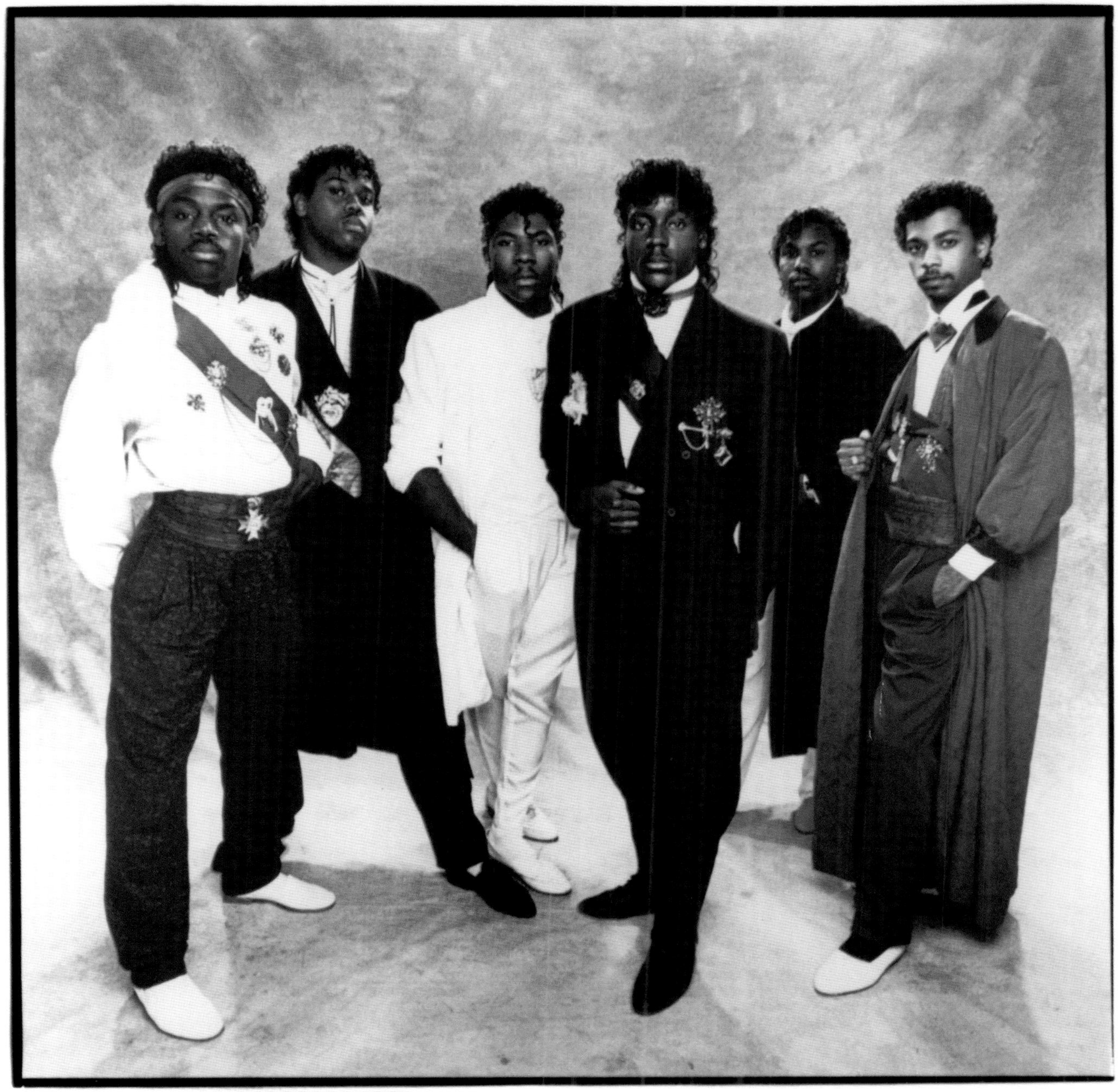

Left to Right: Willie Triplett, Gordon Strozier, Gerald Valentine, Melvin Riley, John Eaton, Greg Potts

Ready for the World

MCA RECORDS

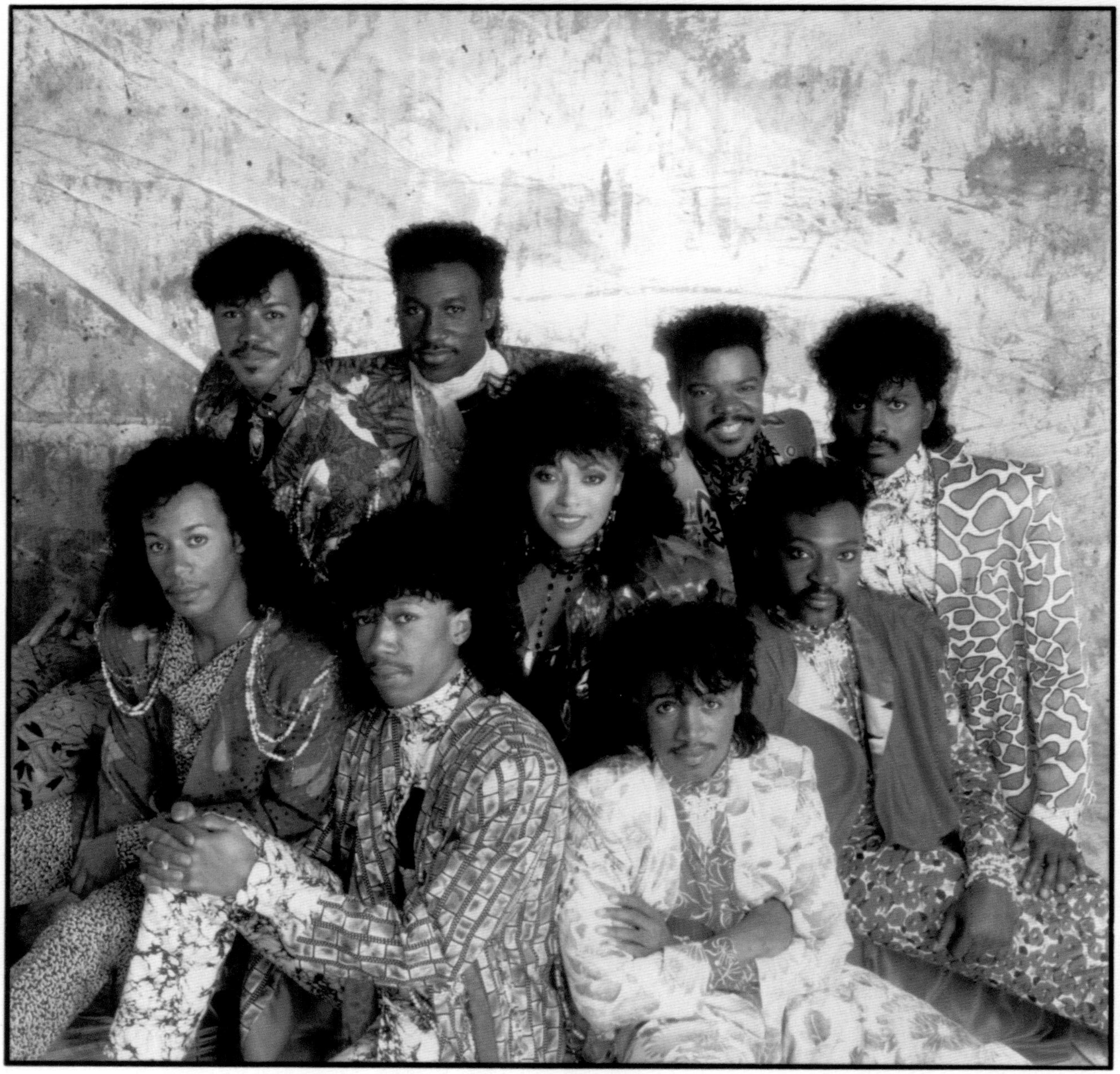

PHOTO CREDIT: RANDEE ST. NICHOLAS/1986

FRONT ROW: MELVIN GENTRY BO WATSON
MIDDLE ROW: VINCENT CALLOWAY BELINDA LIPSCOMB KENNETH GANT
BACK ROW: REGGIE CALLOWAY BOBBY LOVELACE BILL SIMMONS JEFFERY COOPER

Midnight Star

SOLAR
SOUND OF LOS ANGELES RECORDS
Distributed by Elektra/Asylum Records

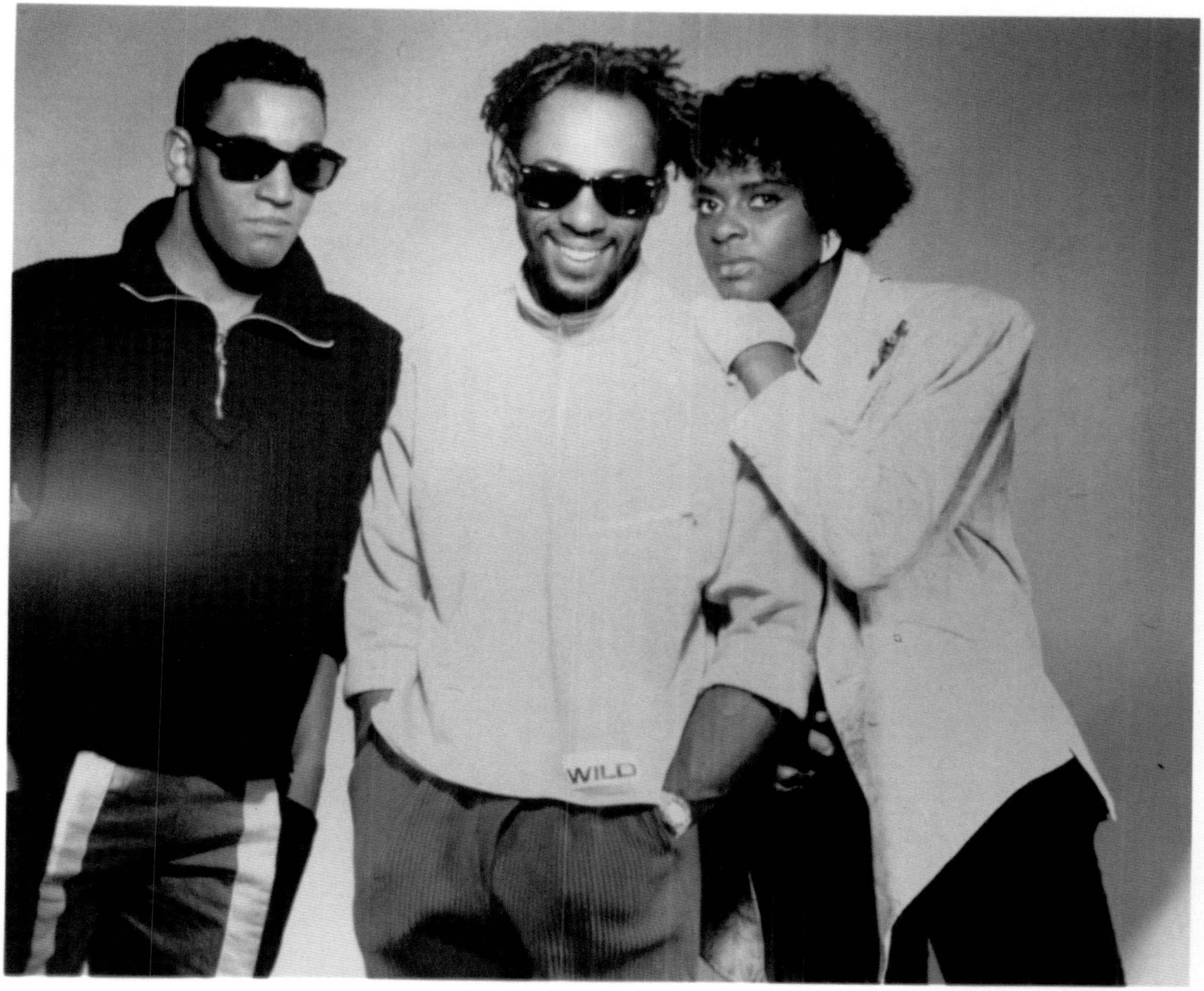

Virgin Records

LOOSE ENDS

MCA RECORDS

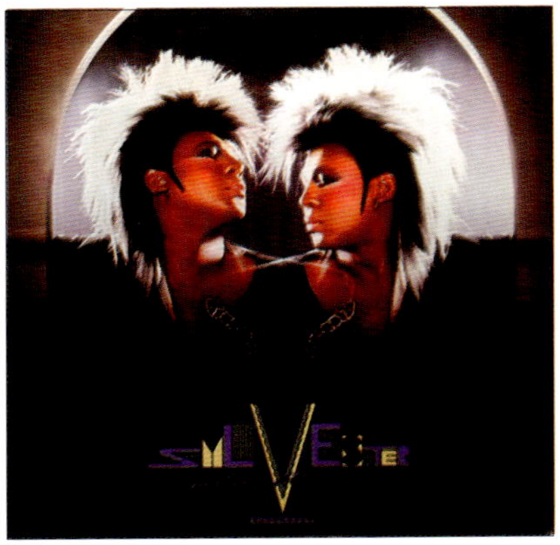

Sylvester, "the queen of disco," put out his last album, *Mutual Attraction*, and the dance hit "Someone Like You" before he died from AIDS complications.

Billboard 200: *Mutual Attraction* (#164)

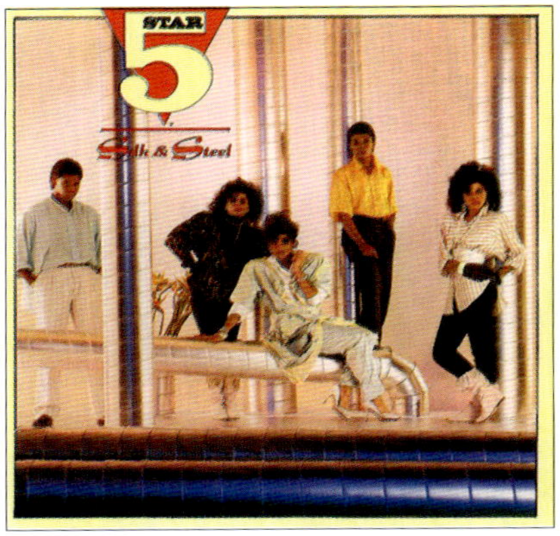

From **Five Star**'s *Silk & Steel*, a UK No. 1 album, "Can't Wait Another Minute" gave the British pop outfit a Top 10 single on the US R&B and dance charts.

Billboard 200: *Silk & Steel* (#80)
Billboard Hot 100: "Can't Wait Another Minute" (#41); "If I Say Yes" (#67)

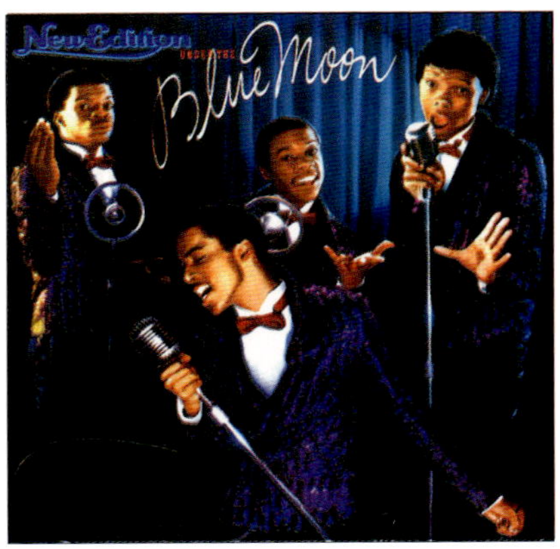

After Bobby Brown left for a solo career, teen-pop band **New Edition** continued as a quartet with *Under the Blue Moon*, an album of vintage doo-wop covers.

Billboard 200: *Under the Blue Moon* (#43)
Billboard Hot 100: "Earth Angel" (#21)

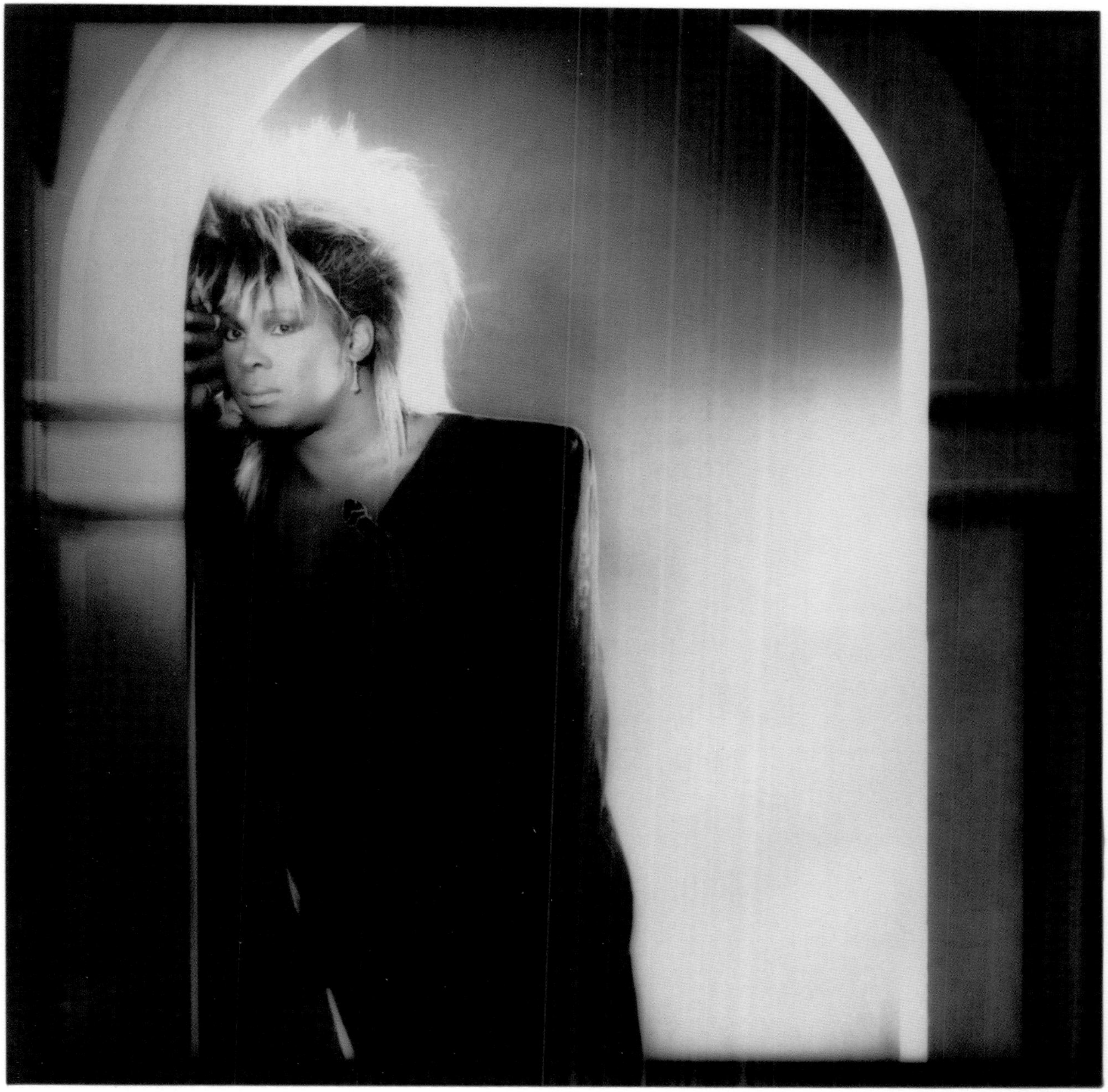

Photo Credit: Jeff Katz

SYLVESTER

WARNER BROS.

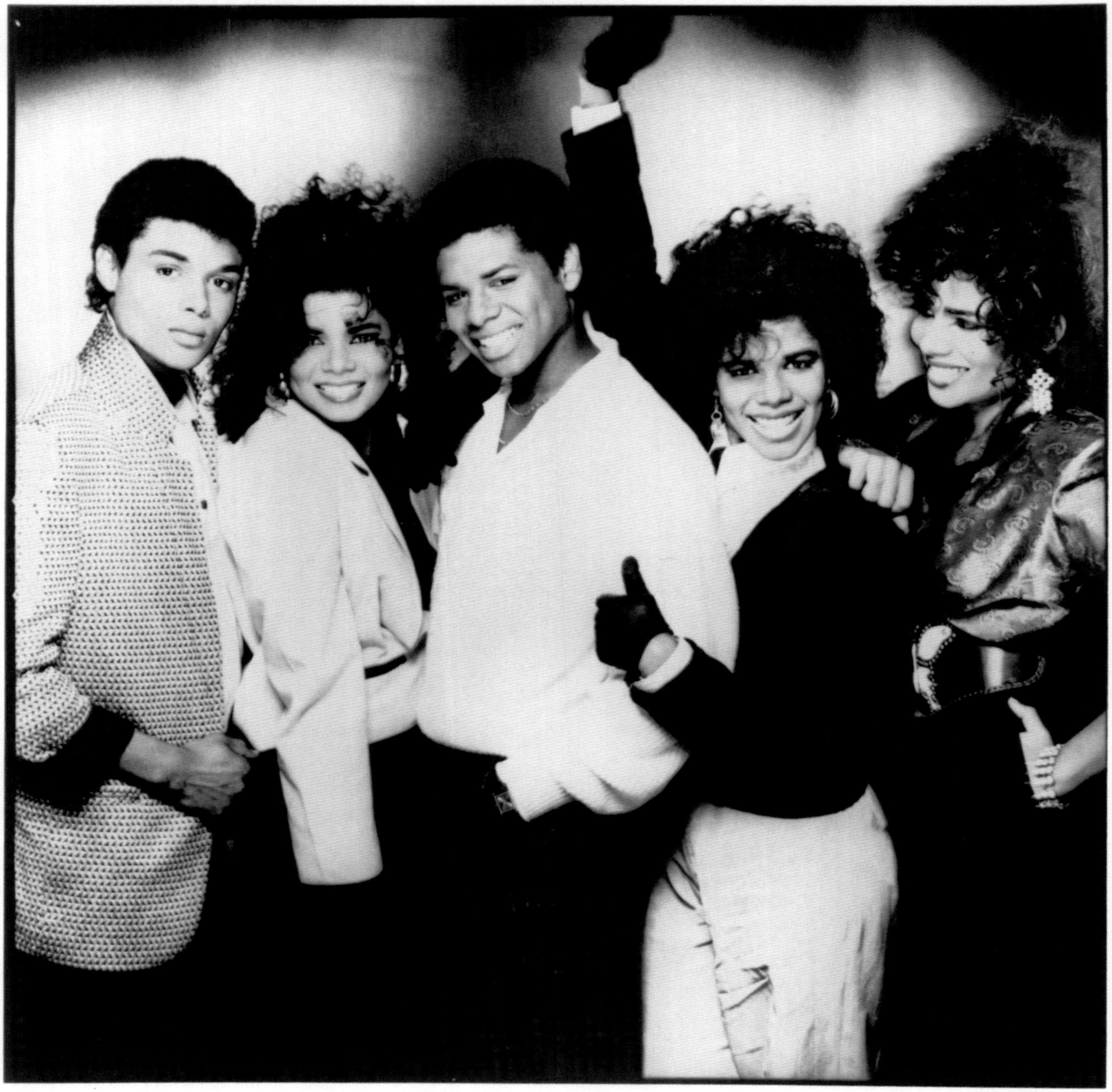

STAR 5

TENT

RCA
Records and Cassettes

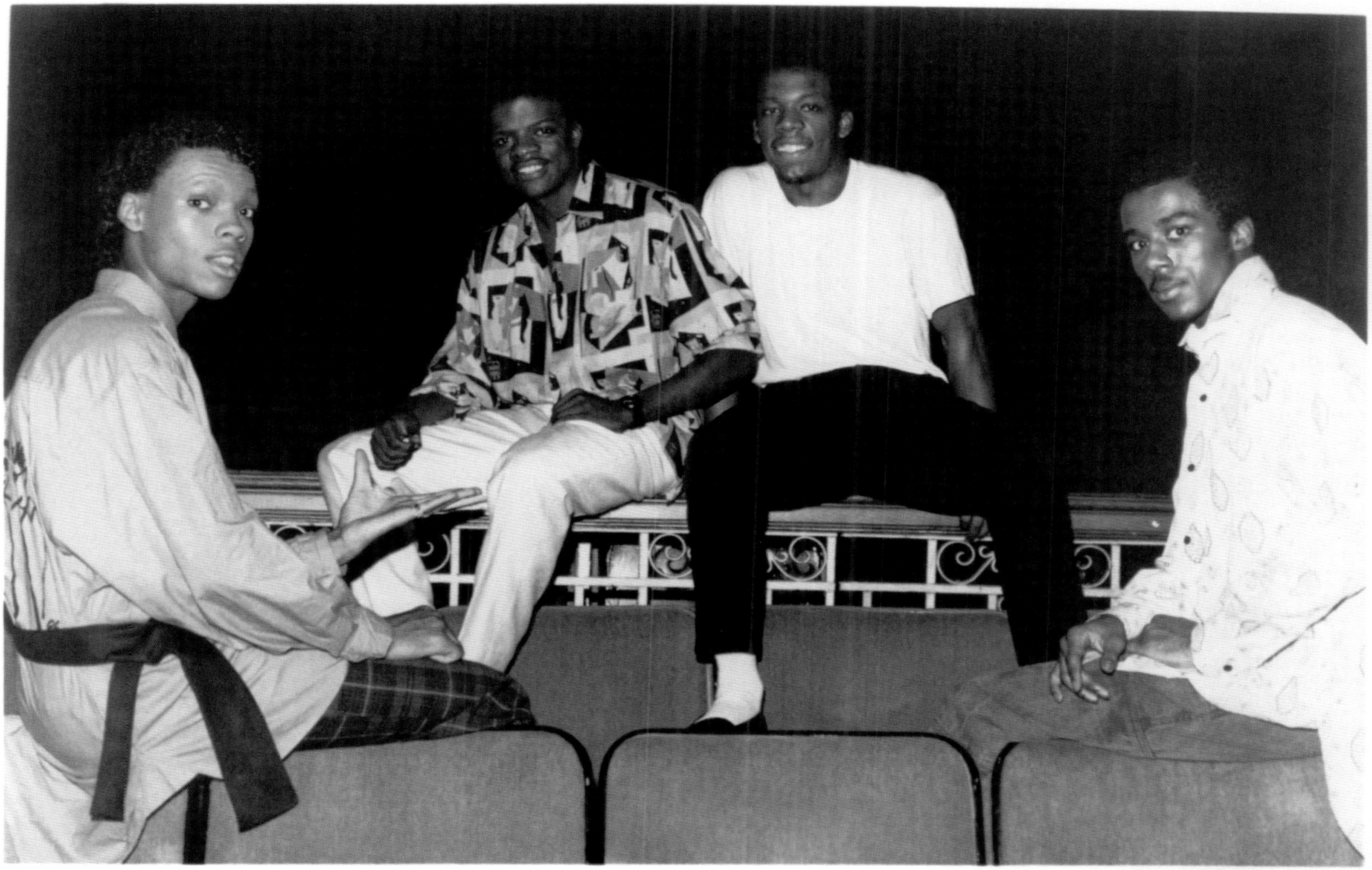

MCA RECORDS

New Edition

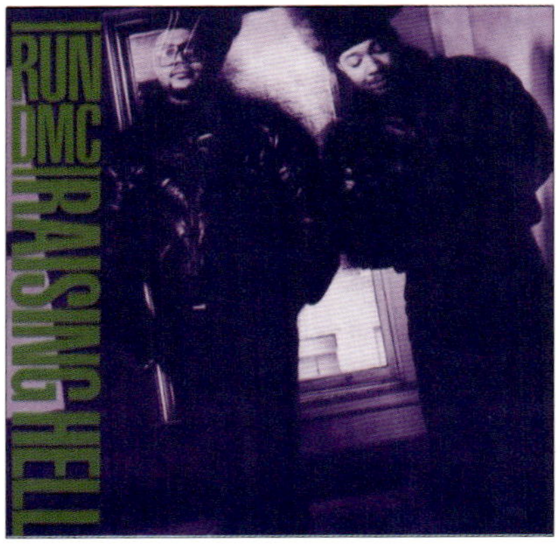

Run-D.M.C.'s *Raising Hell* provided a basis for the first duet between a rap act and hard-rock heroes, a remake of an Aerosmith classic, "Walk This Way."

Billboard 200: *Raising Hell* (#3)
Billboard Hot 100: "Walk This Way" (#4); "You Be Illin'" (#29); "It's Tricky" (#57)

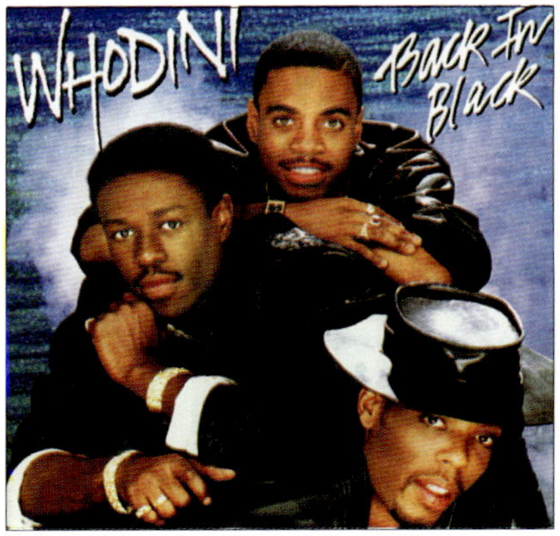

Back in Black, the third album by **Whodini**, a trio of young Brooklynites, charted a trio of hip-hop singles, "Funky Beat," "One Love" and "Growing Up."

Billboard 200: *Back in Black* (#35)

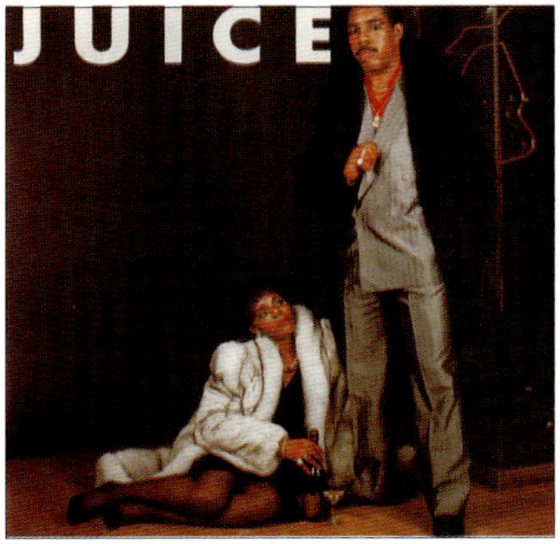

R&B singer Oran "**Juice**" Jones pulled off "The Rain" in falsetto as a tough-talking love man, and the waggish single made the Top 10 on the pop charts.

Billboard 200: *Juice* (#44)
Billboard Hot 100: "The Rain" (#9)

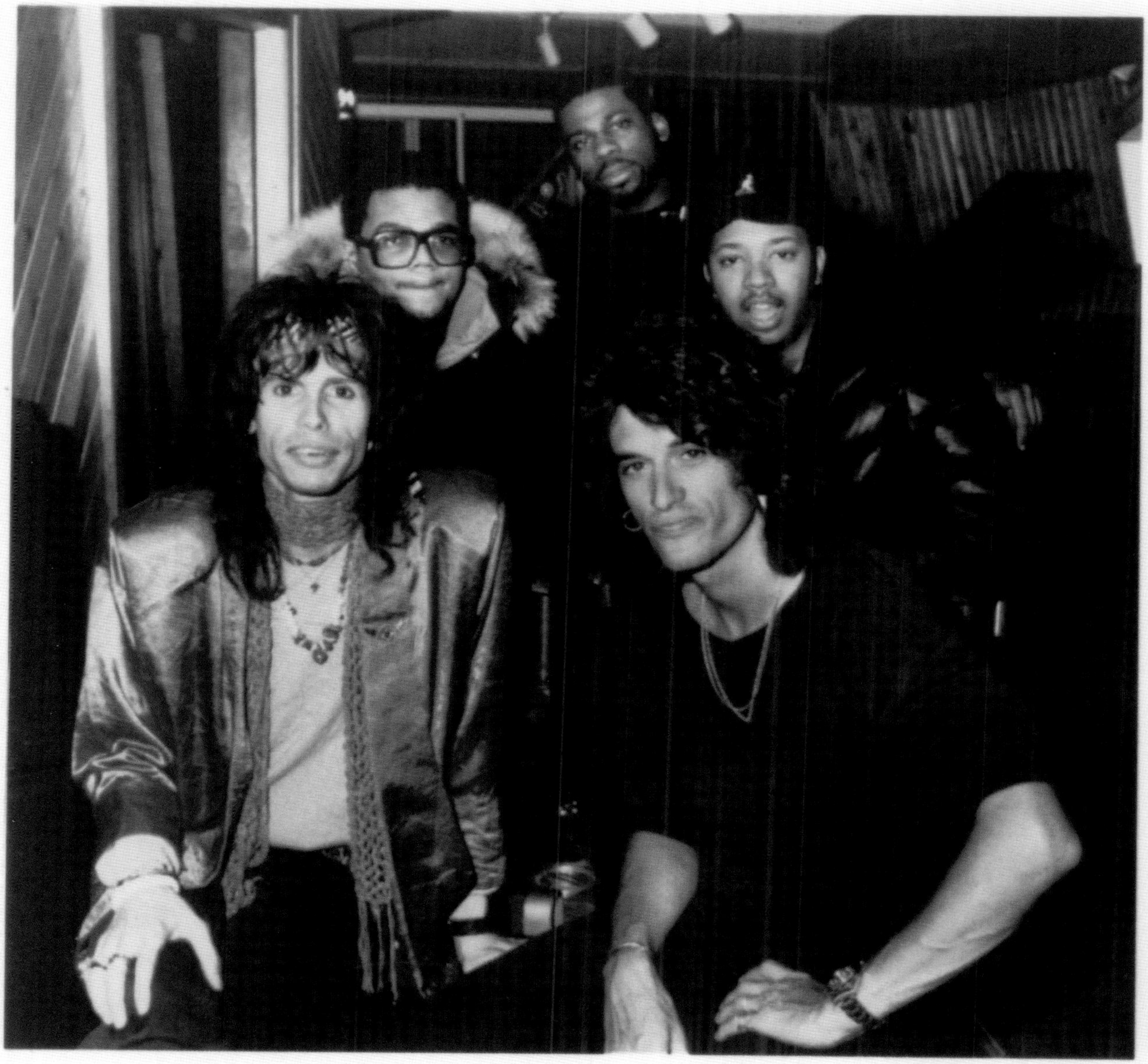

Pictured (clockwise from left) are: Steve Tyler, D M.C
Jam Master Jay, RUN, and Joe Perry

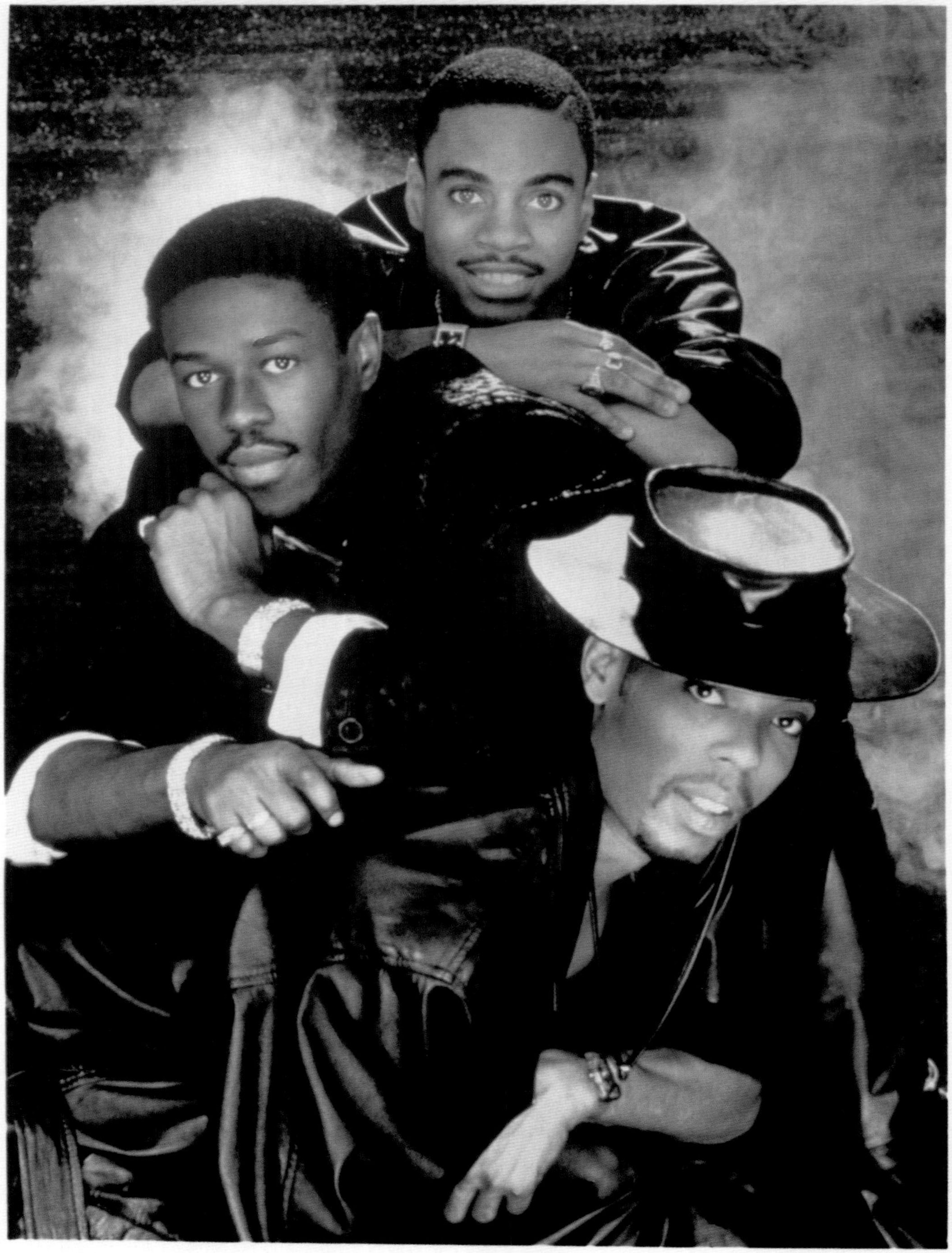

WHODINI

JIVE ARISTA

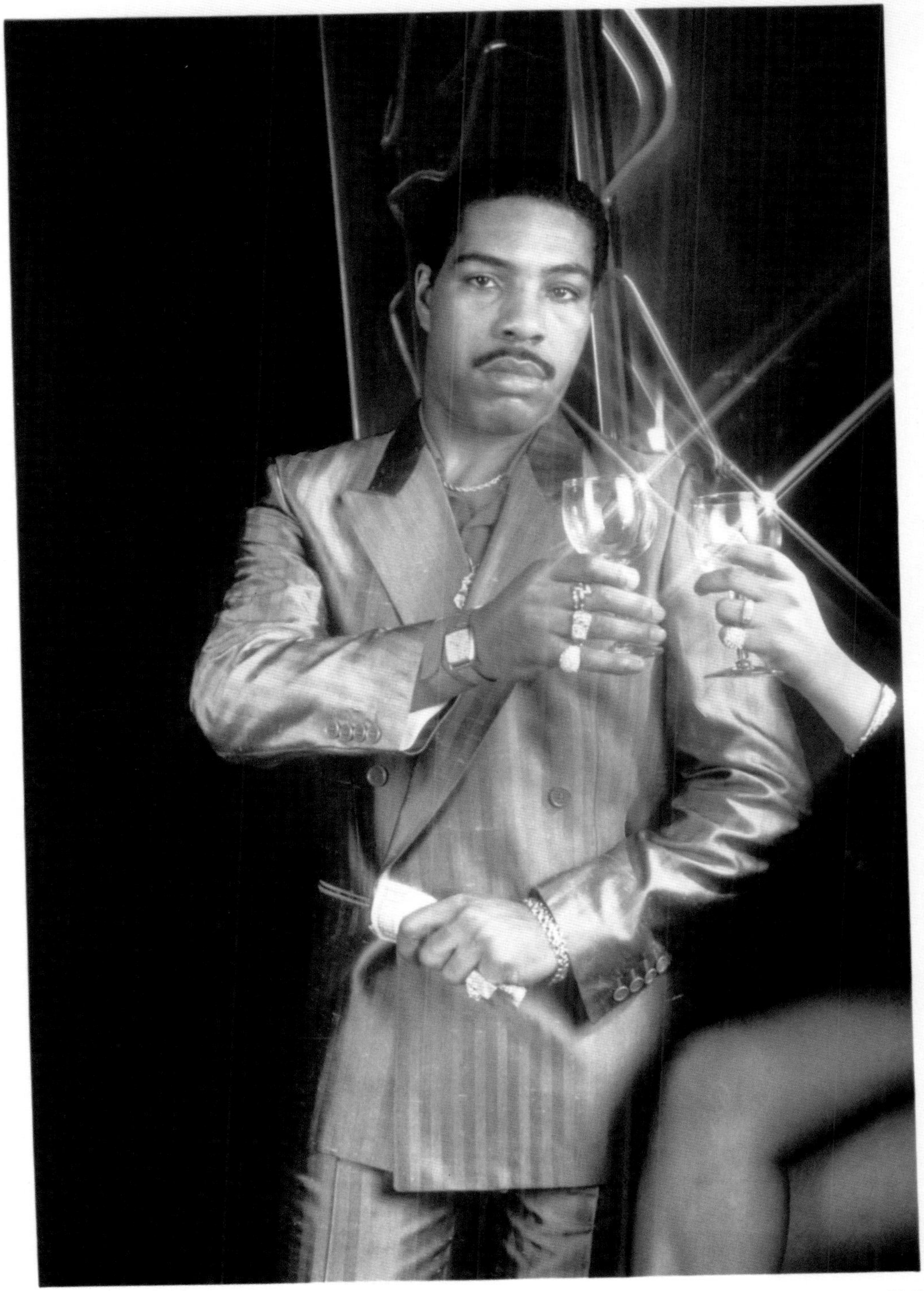

PHOTOGRAPH: LLOYD NELSON

Def Jam recordings

Rush Artist Management
40 East 19th Street
N.Y , N.Y   10003
212.420.4770

JUICE

Columbia
8605

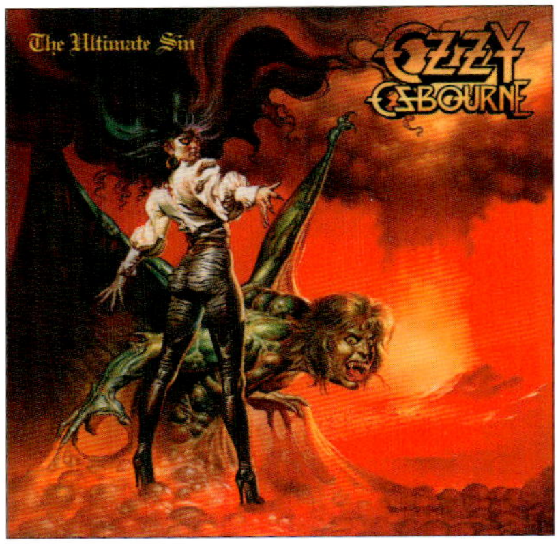

Hitherto the prevailing madman of heavy metal, erstwhile Black Sabbath frontman **Ozzy Osbourne** got flak for the streamlined sound of *The Ultimate Sin*.

Billboard 200: *The Ultimate Sin* (#6)
Billboard Hot 100: "Shot in the Dark" (#68)

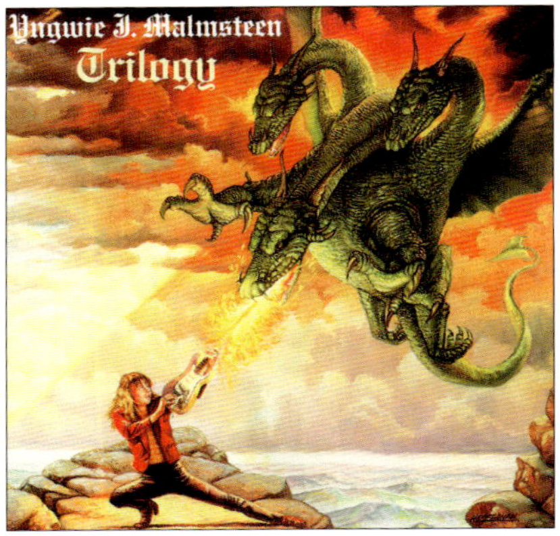

Turning in a dazzling display of neoclassical heavy-metal guitar work on his third album, *Trilogy*, **Yngwie Malmsteen** increased his stature as a composer.

Billboard 200: *Trilogy* (#44)

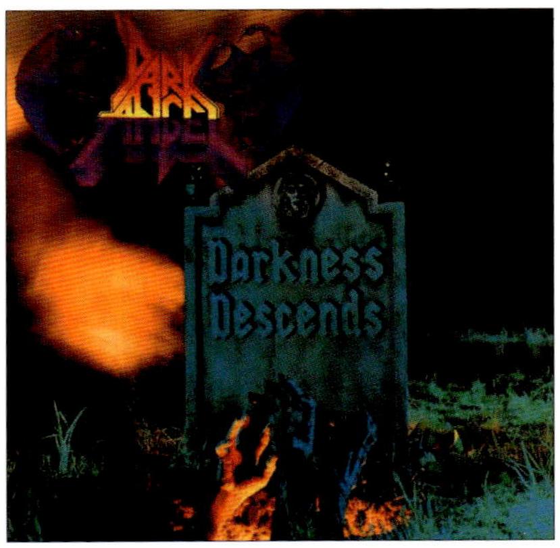

Dark Angel delivered a second album, *Darkness Descends*, that came to be viewed as the band's definitive statement within the thrash-metal underground.

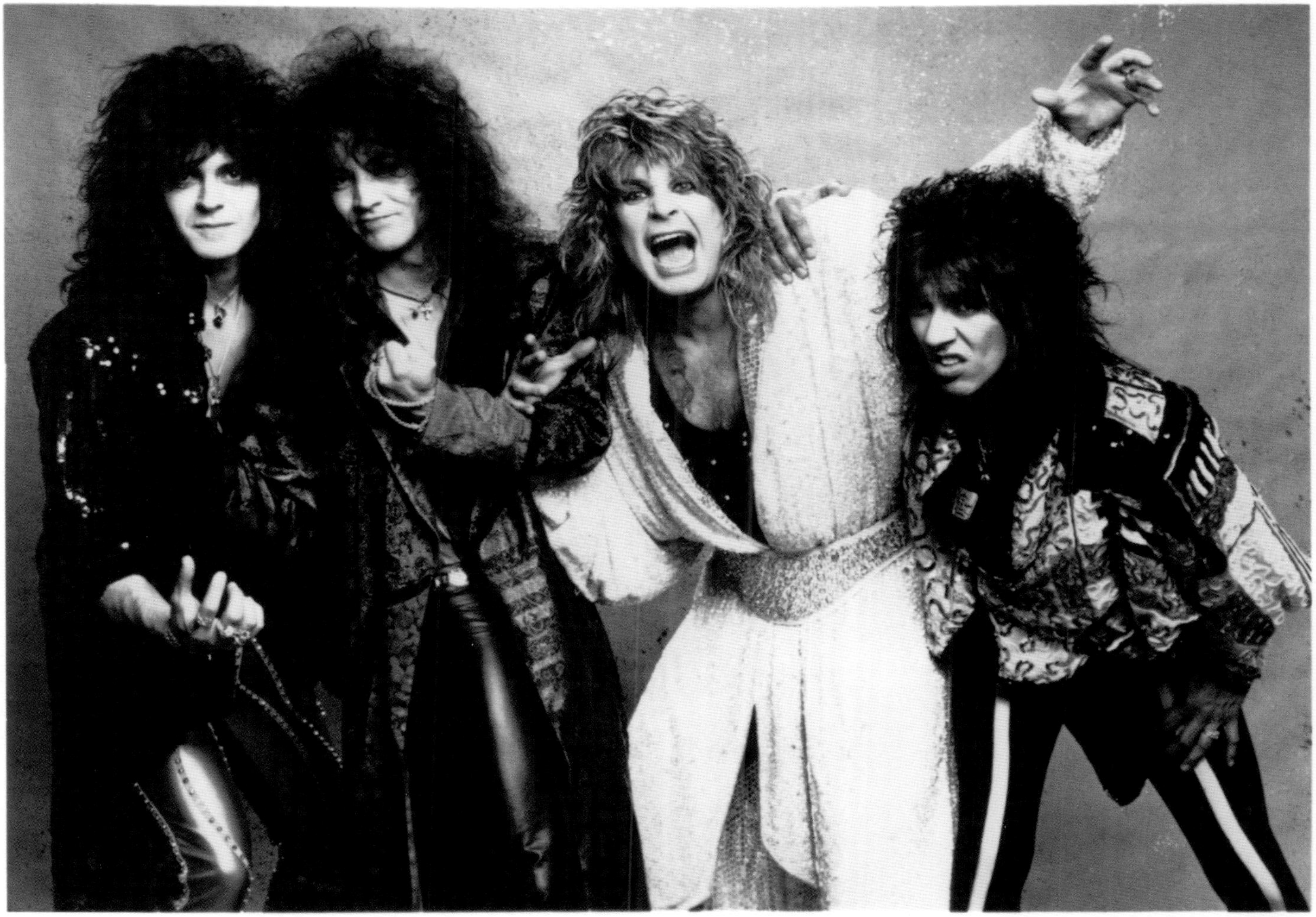

Photo: Mark Weiss

L-R: Phil Soussan, Jake E. Lee, Ozzy Osbourne, Randy Castillo

EPIC PORTRAIT ASSOCIATED

OZZY OSBOURNE

CBS
ASSOCIATED RECORDS

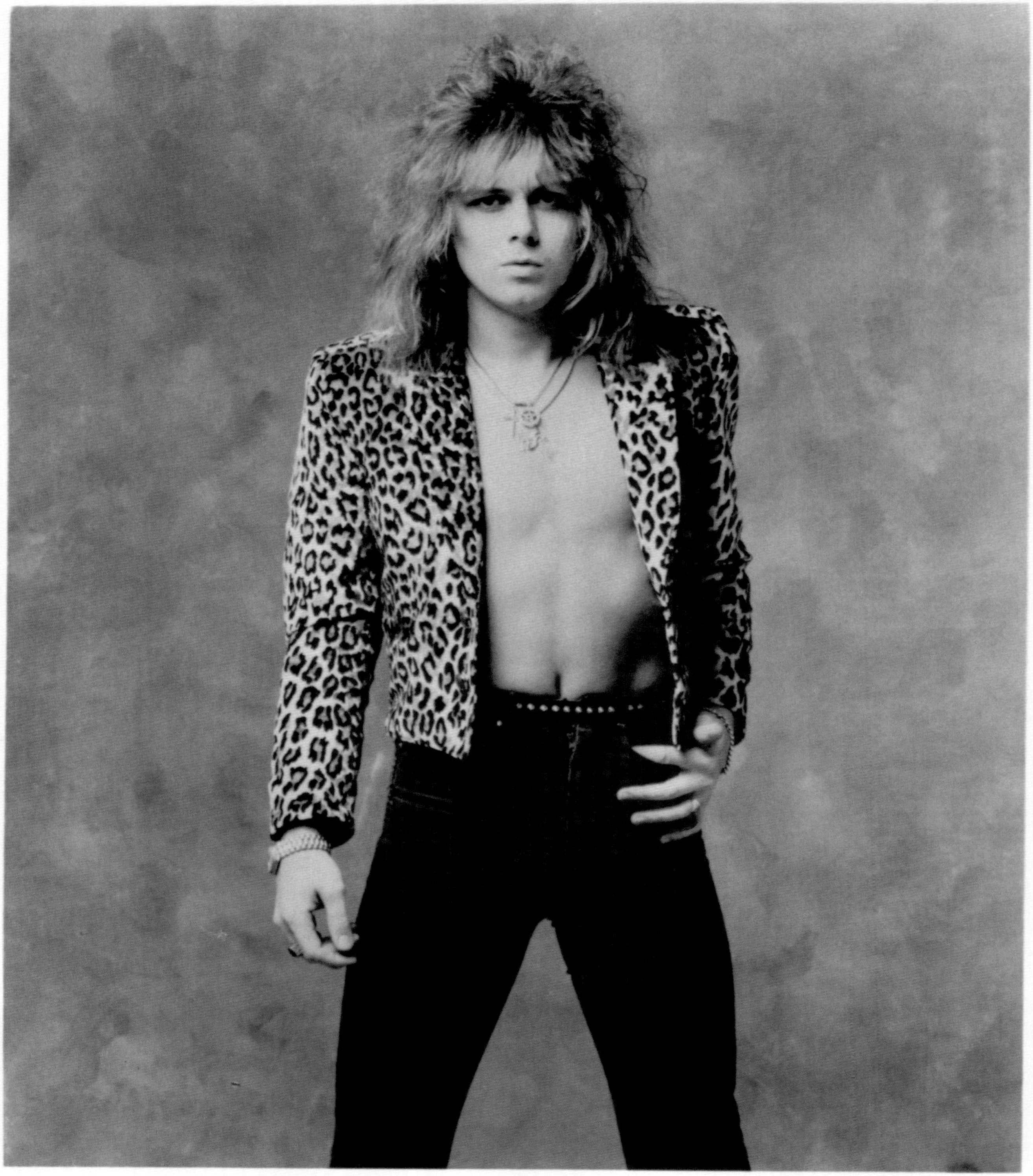

YNGWIE MALMSTEEN

polydor

PolyGram Records

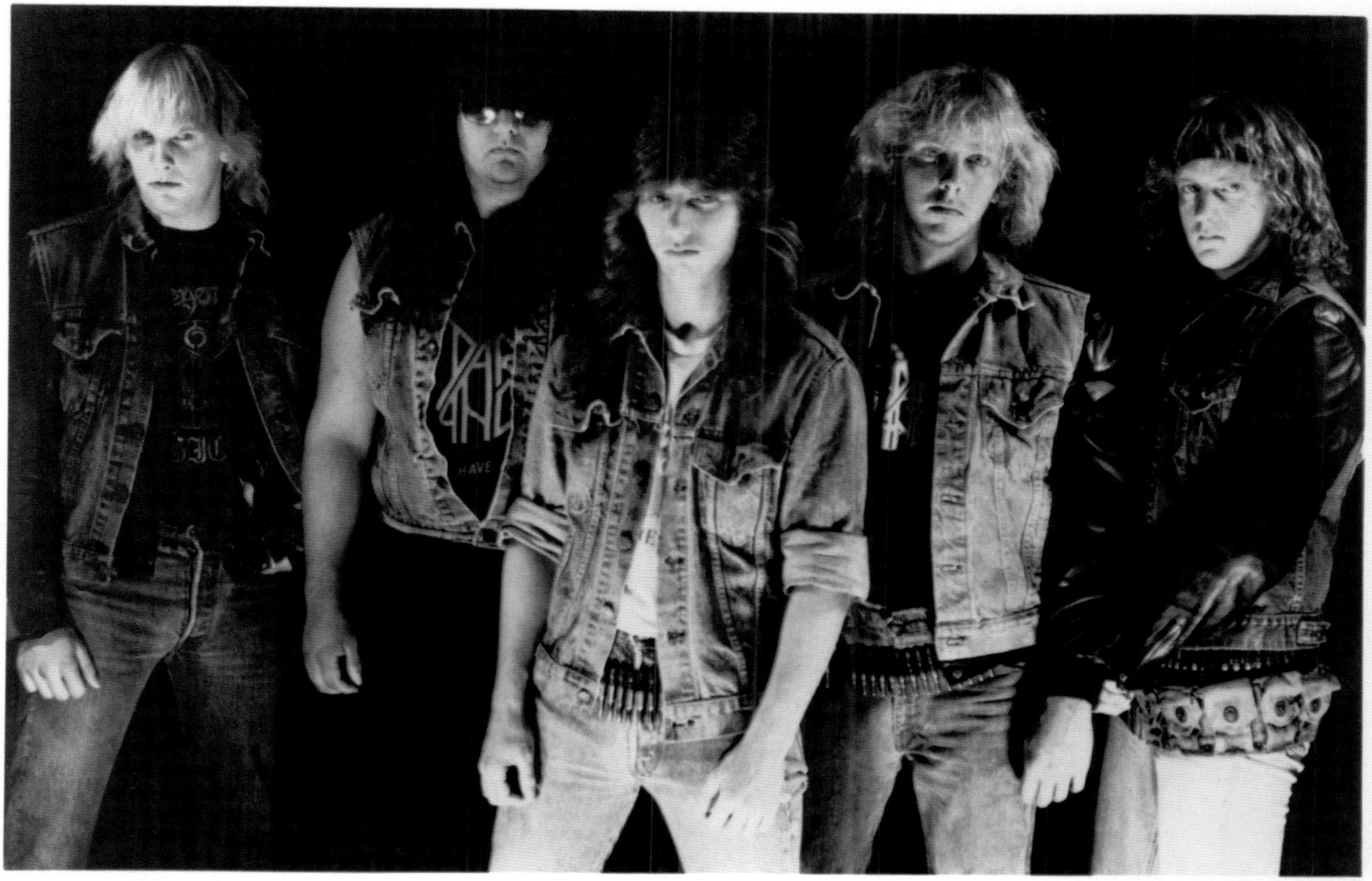

THE RELATIVITY LABELS
distributed by:
Important
RECORD DISTRIBUTORS, INC.
(718) 995-9200

DARK ANGEL

COMBAT

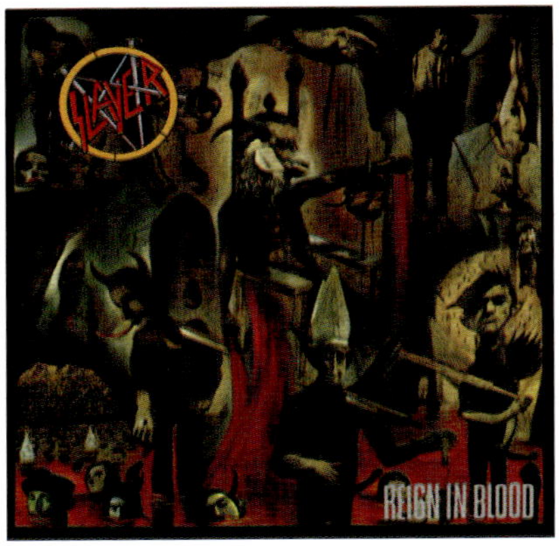

A joint effort with producer Rick Rubin, who tidied up the band's incendiary sound, **Slayer**'s *Reign in Blood* emerged as an influential thrash-metal album.

Billboard 200: *Reign in Blood* (#94)

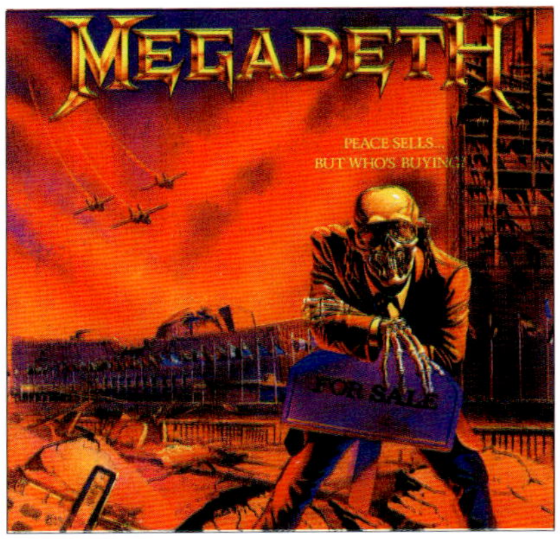

Within the underground metal scene, *Peace Sells...But Who's Buying?*, **Megadeth**'s first major-label album, signaled an upswing in the band's fortunes.

Billboard 200: *Peace Sells...But Who's Buying?* (#76)

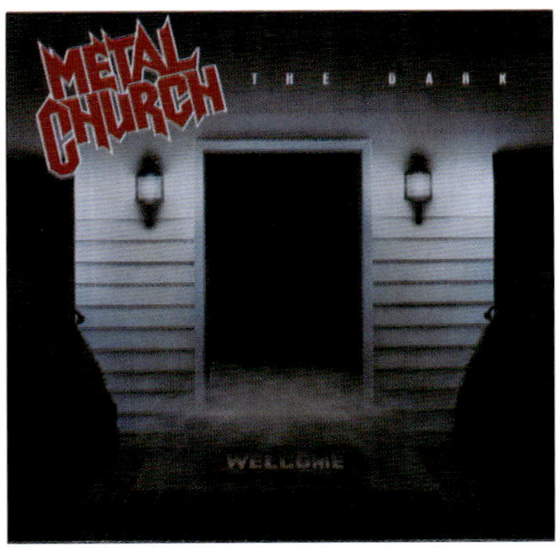

Hailing from the Northwest, **Metal Church** added a fierce entry to the heavy-metal genre with *The Dark*, getting a favorable response from headbangers.

Billboard 200: *The Dark* (#92)

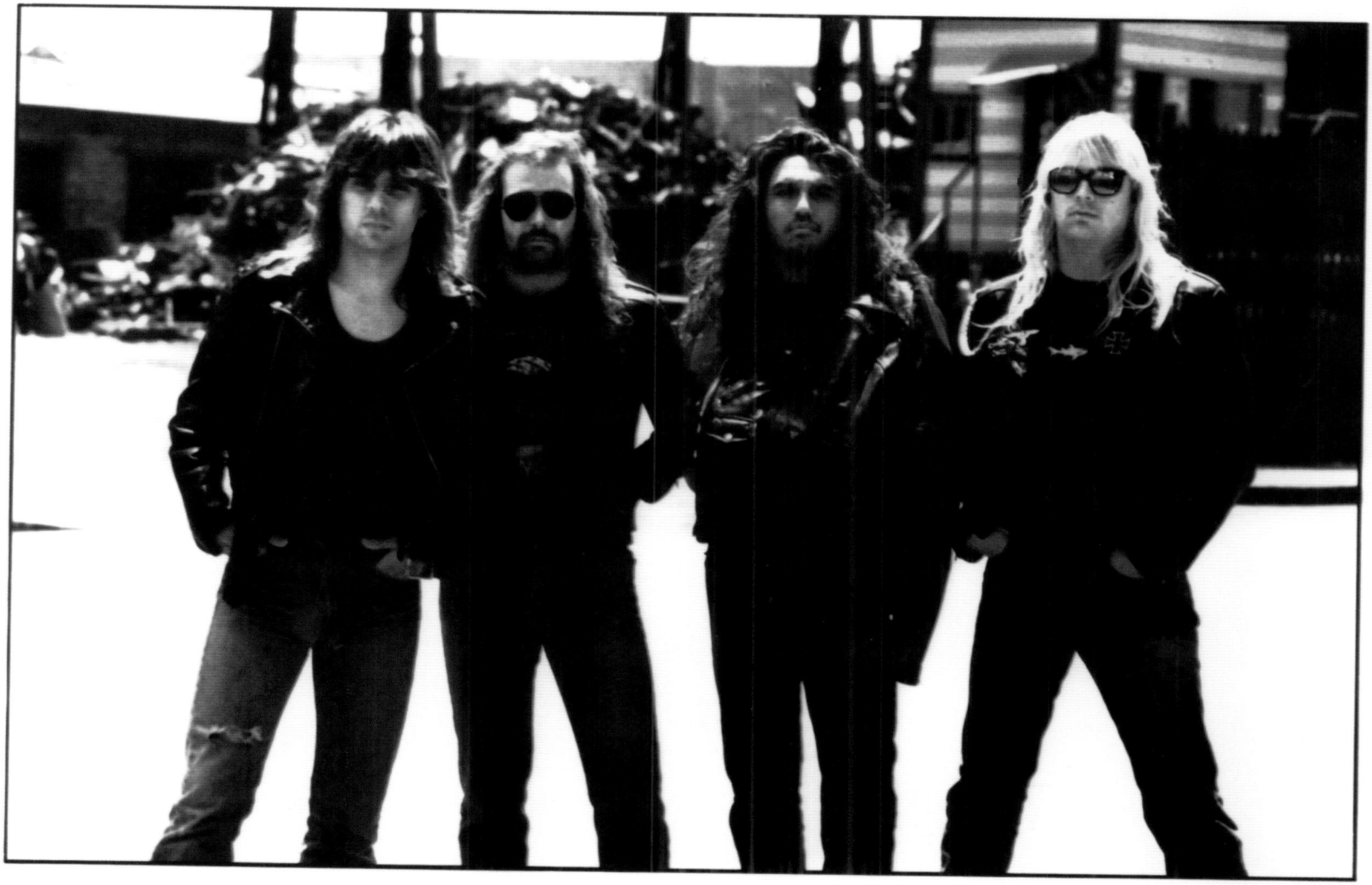

Photo Credit: Alex Socca

Def Jam recordings

GEFFEN RECORDS

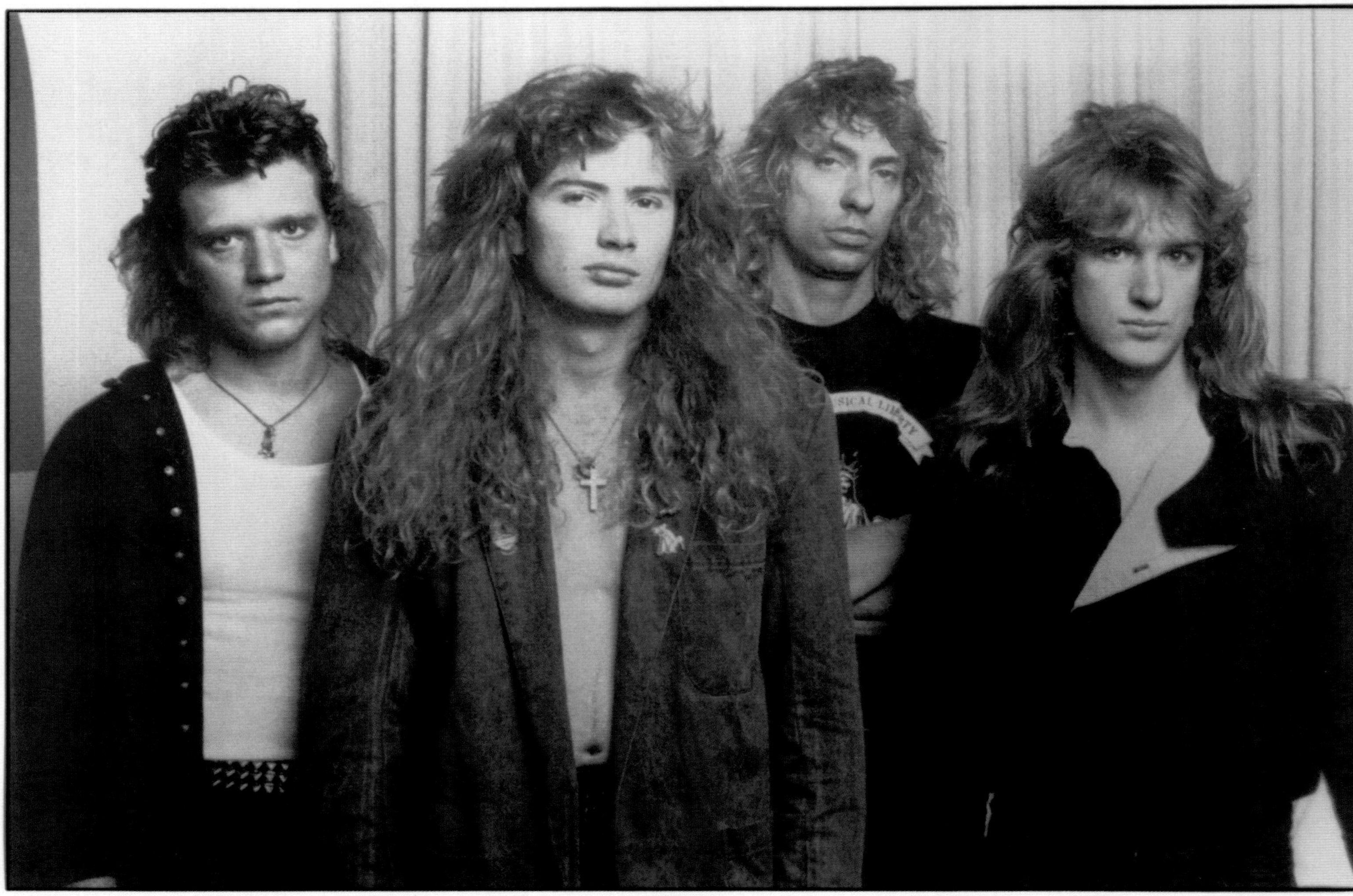

Photo: Dennis Keeley / 1986

Chris Poland Dave Mustaine Gar Samuelson Dave Ellefson

MEGADETH

Capitol Records

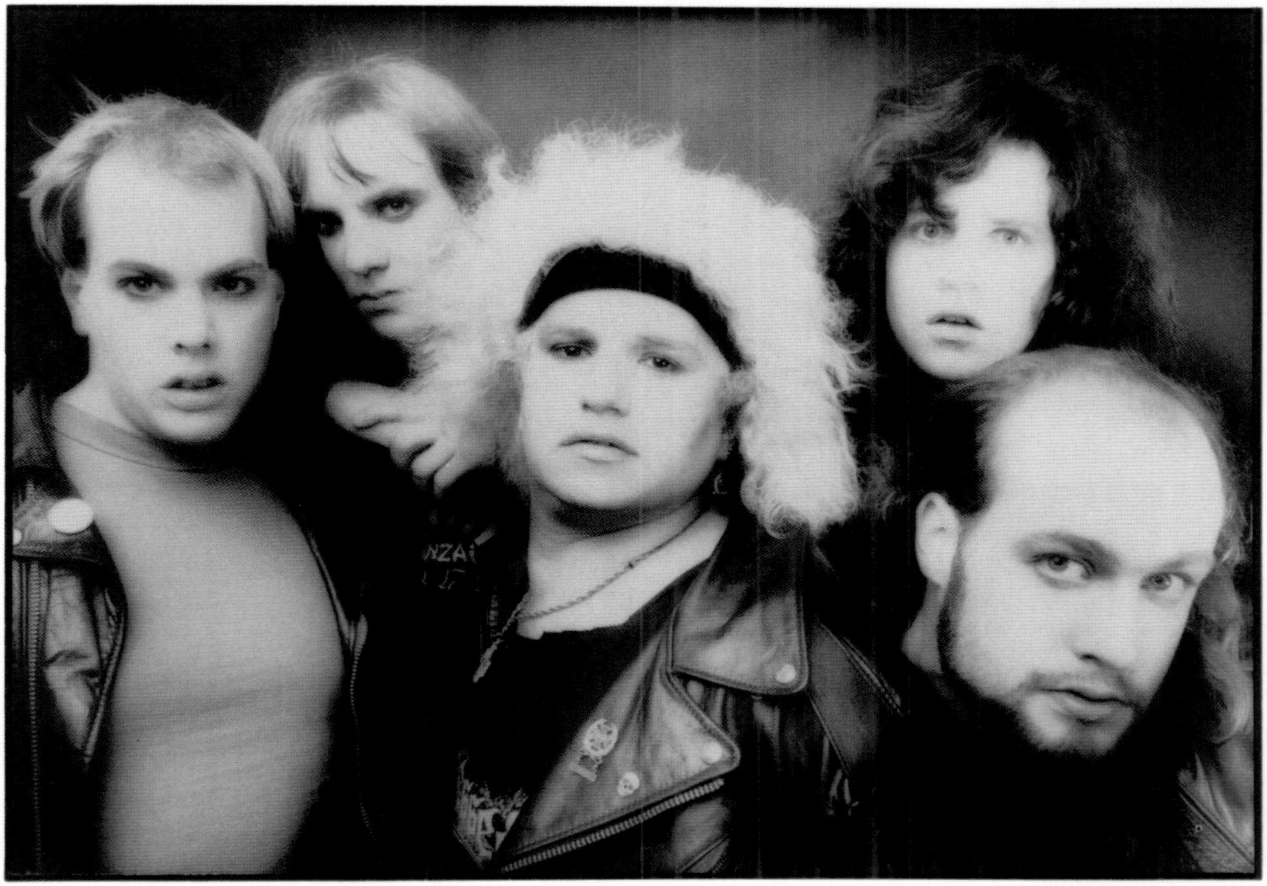

PHOTO CREDIT: SAULUIS PEMPE/1985

KURDT VANDERHOFF KIRK ARRINGTON DAVID WAYNE CRAIG WELLS DUKE ERICKSON

METAL CHURCH

ELEKTRA

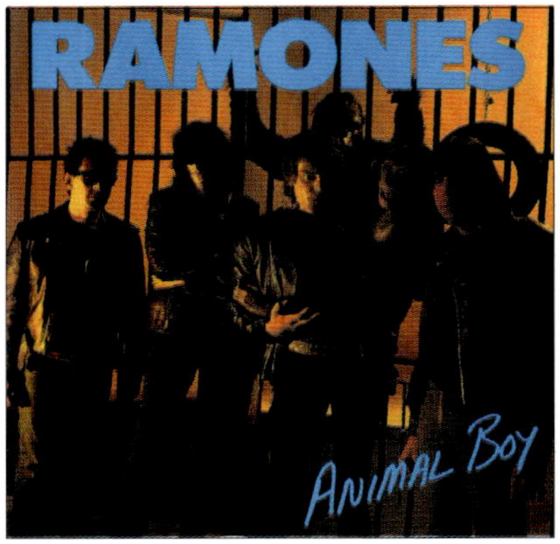

Ramones' "My Brain Is Hanging Upside Down (Bonzo Goes to Bitburg)" criticized Ronald Reagan's ceremonial visit to a German World War II cemetery.

Billboard 200: *Animal Boy* (#143)

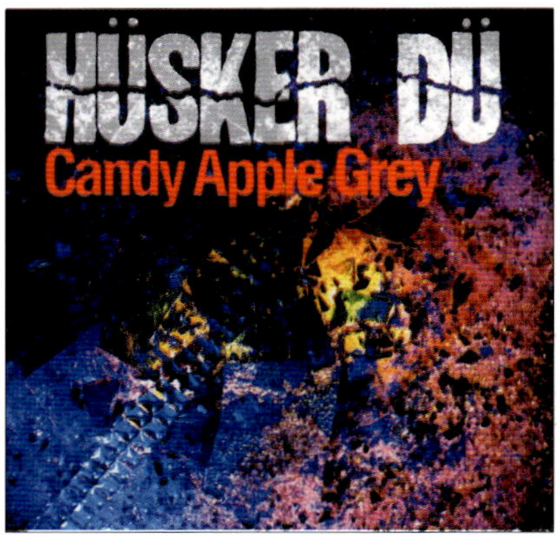

Signing to a major label to release *Candy Apple Grey*, **Hüsker Dü** progressed from a hardcore approach to the well-rounded punk-pop of "Sorry Somehow."

Billboard 200: *Candy Apple Grey* (#140)

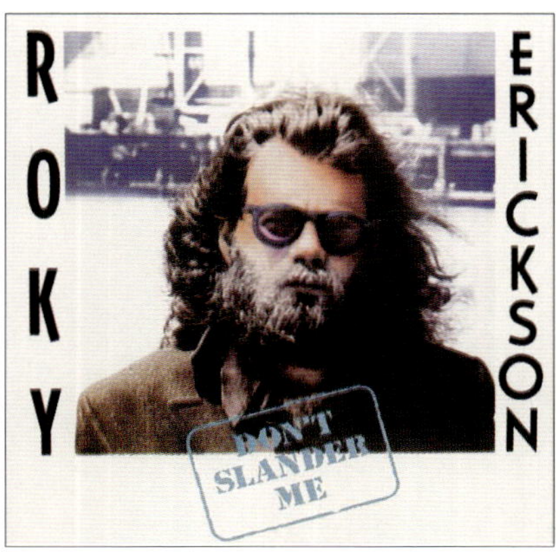

Roky Erickson delivered *Don't Slander Me*, the eccentric psychedelic-rock pioneer's most compelling album after his digressions in Texas mental facilities.

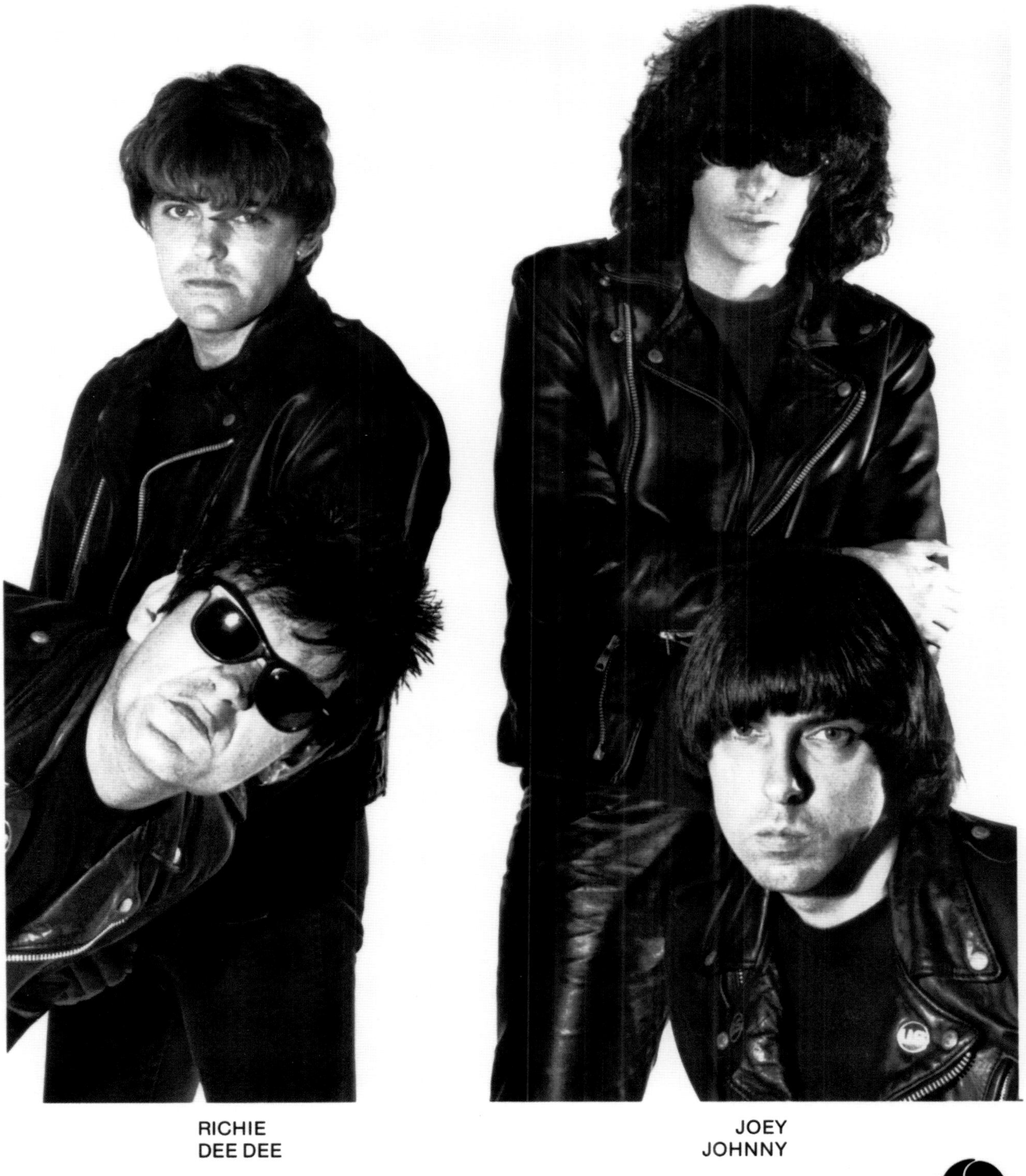

RICHIE
DEE DEE

JOEY
JOHNNY

RAMONES

SIRE

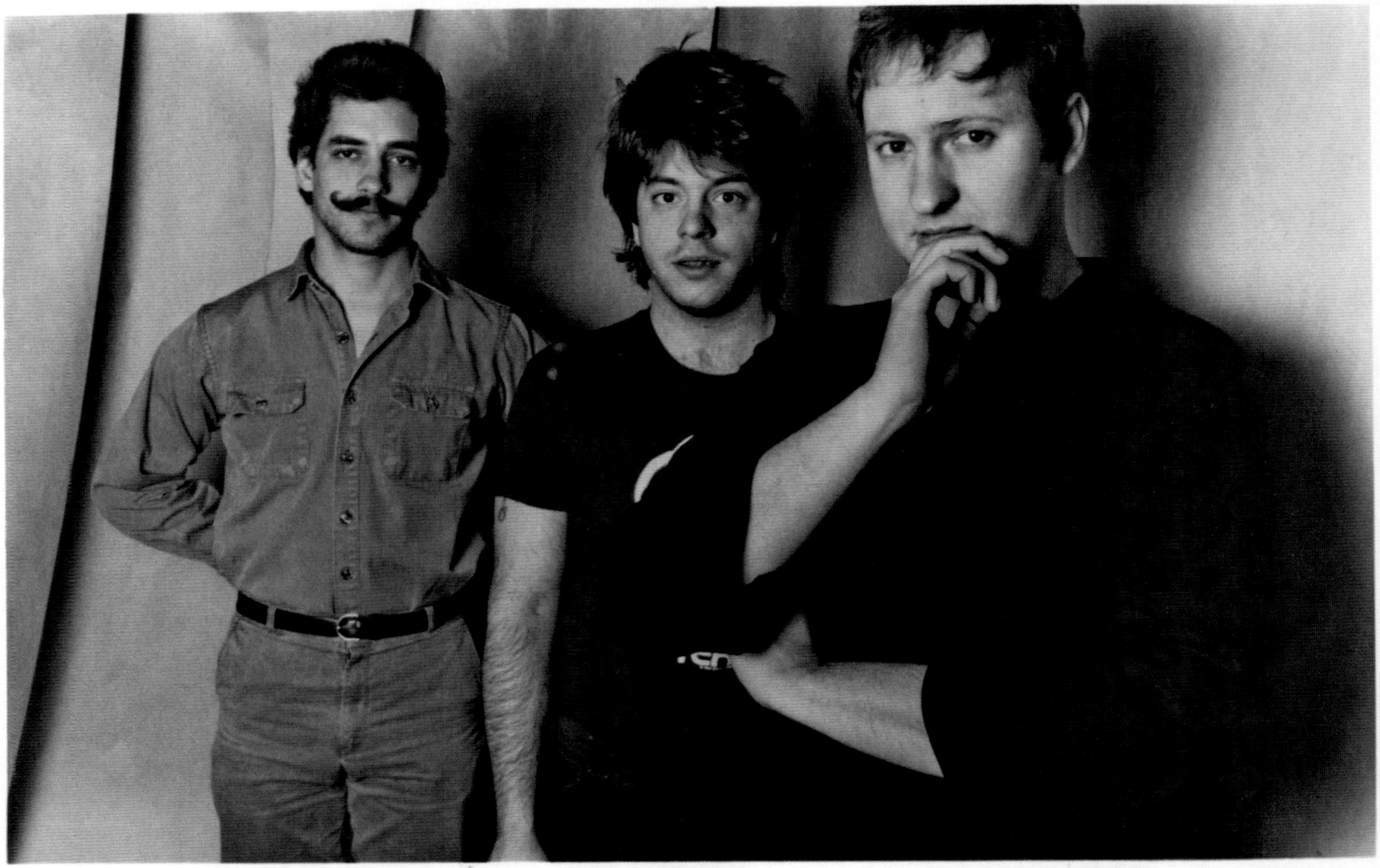

Photo Credit: Daniel Corrigan

GREG NORTON GRANT HART BOB MOULD

HÜSKER DÜ

WARNER BROS.

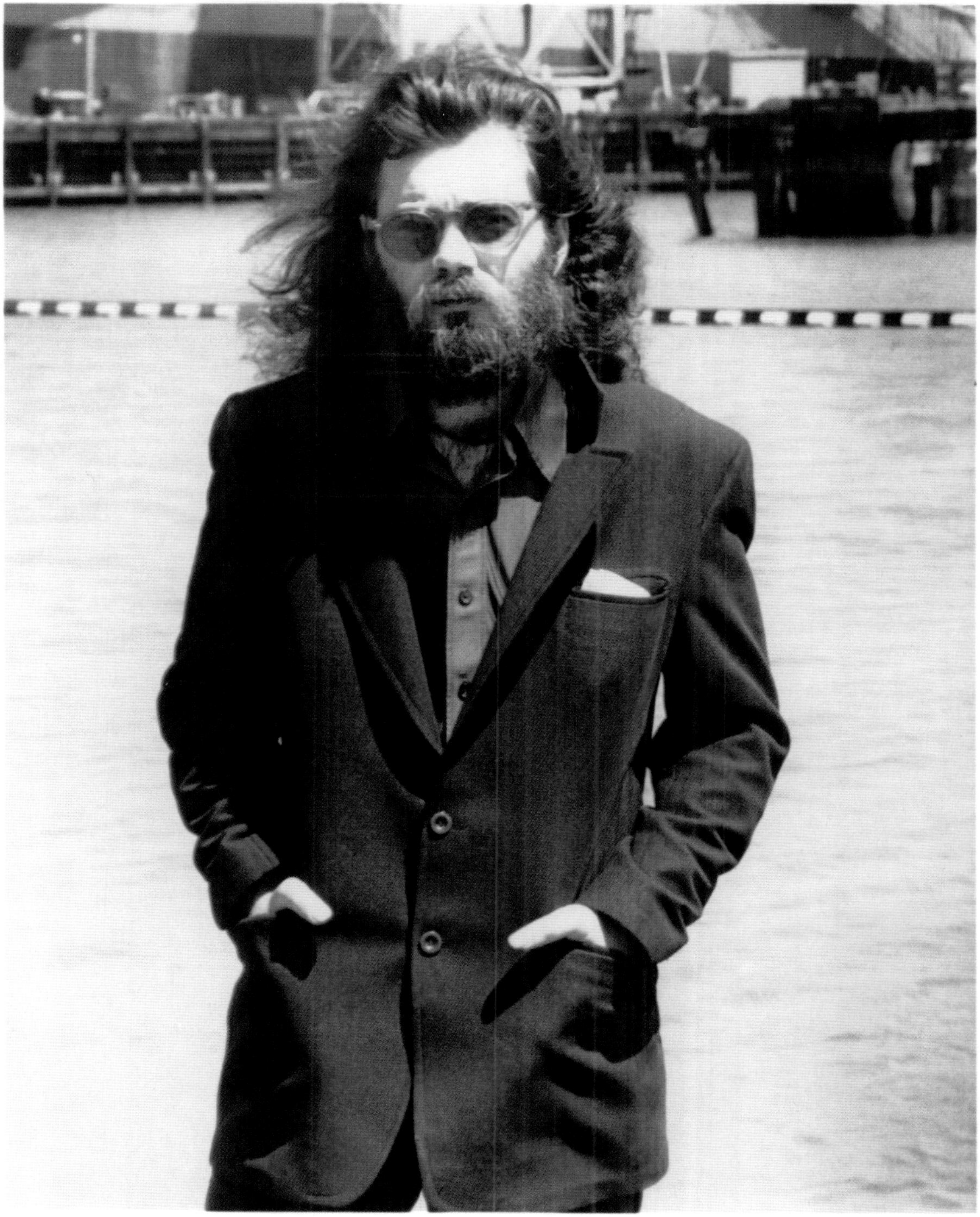

ROKY ERICKSON

PinkDust

PINK DUST RECORDS, a division of
The Enigma Entertainment Corporation
1750 East Holly Avenue, Post Office Box 2428
El Segundo, California 90245-1528 USA
(213) 640-6869

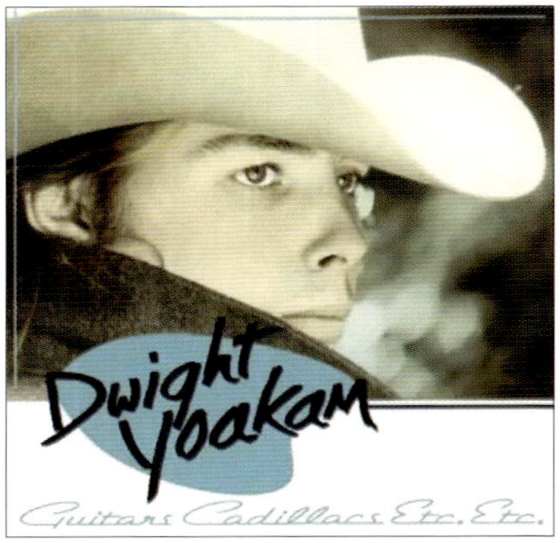

Country music's "neo-traditional" movement commenced when **Dwight Yoakam**'s Pete Anderson-produced *Guitars, Cadillacs, Etc., Etc.* hit the market.

Billboard 200: *Guitars, Cadillacs, Etc., Etc.* (#61)

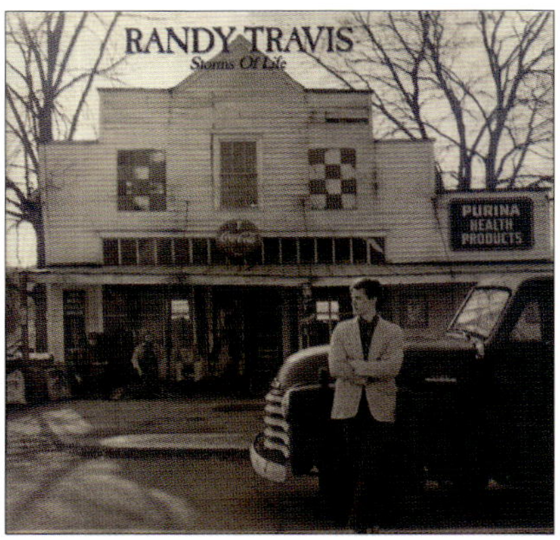

"On the Other Hand" and "Diggin' Up Bones,' from his grand debut *Storms of Life*, prevailed as **Randy Travis**' first No. 1 singles on the country charts.

Billboard 200: *Storms of Life* (#85)

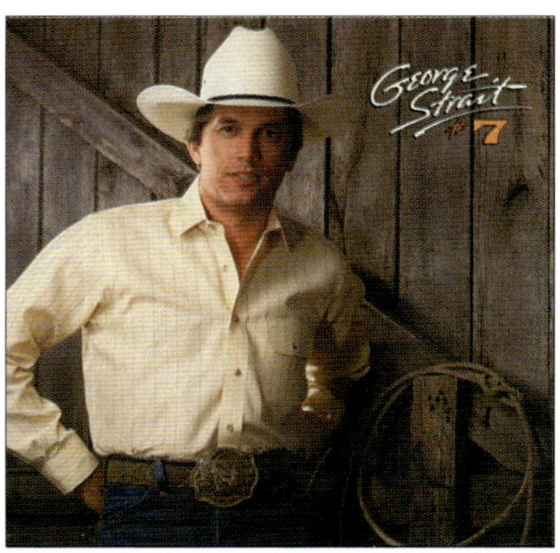

George Strait wore the country crown with two chart-toppers, "Nobody in His Right Mind Would've Left Her" and "It Ain't Cool to be Crazy About You."

Billboard 200: *#7* (#127)

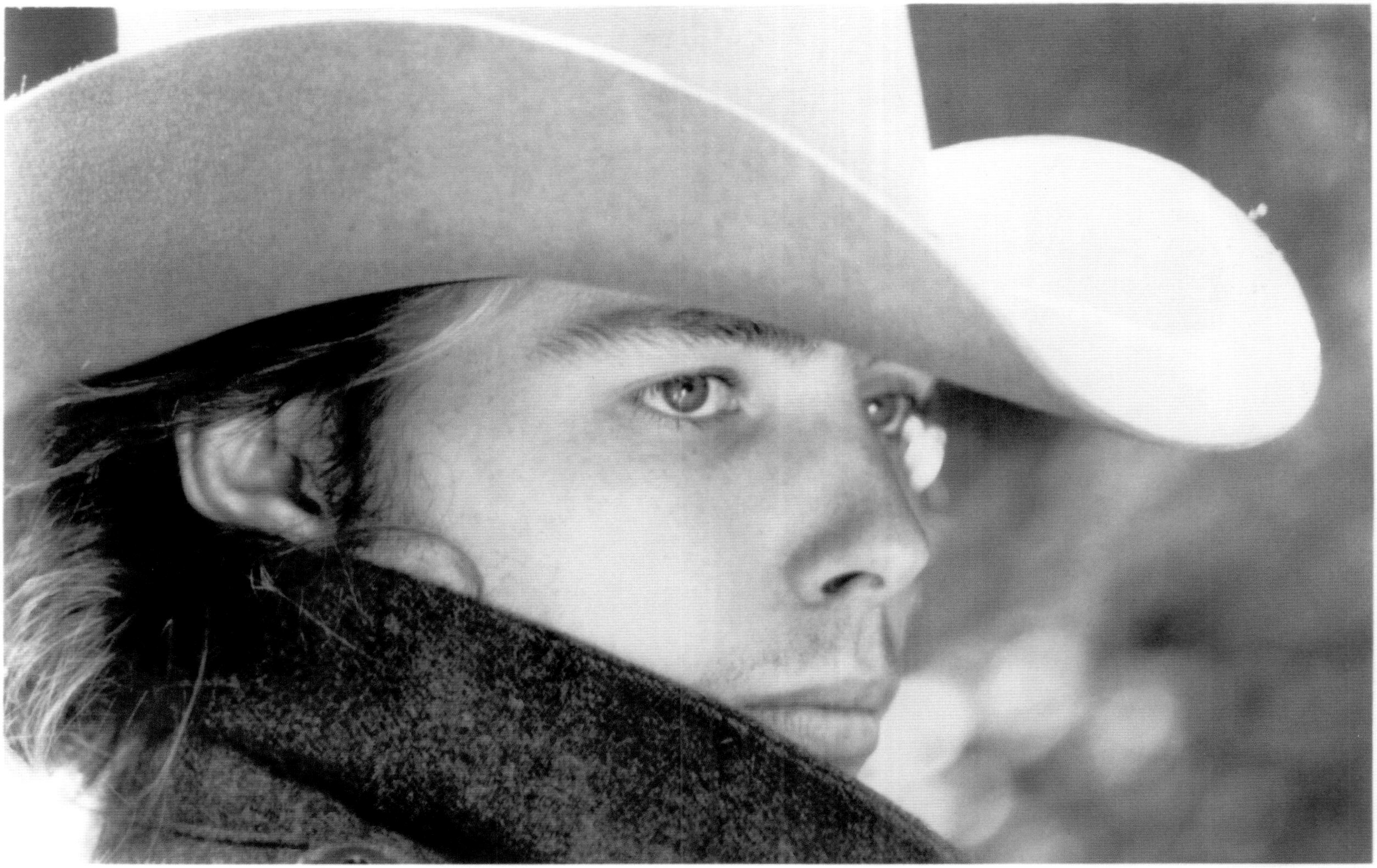

DWIGHT YOAKAM

WARNER BROS.

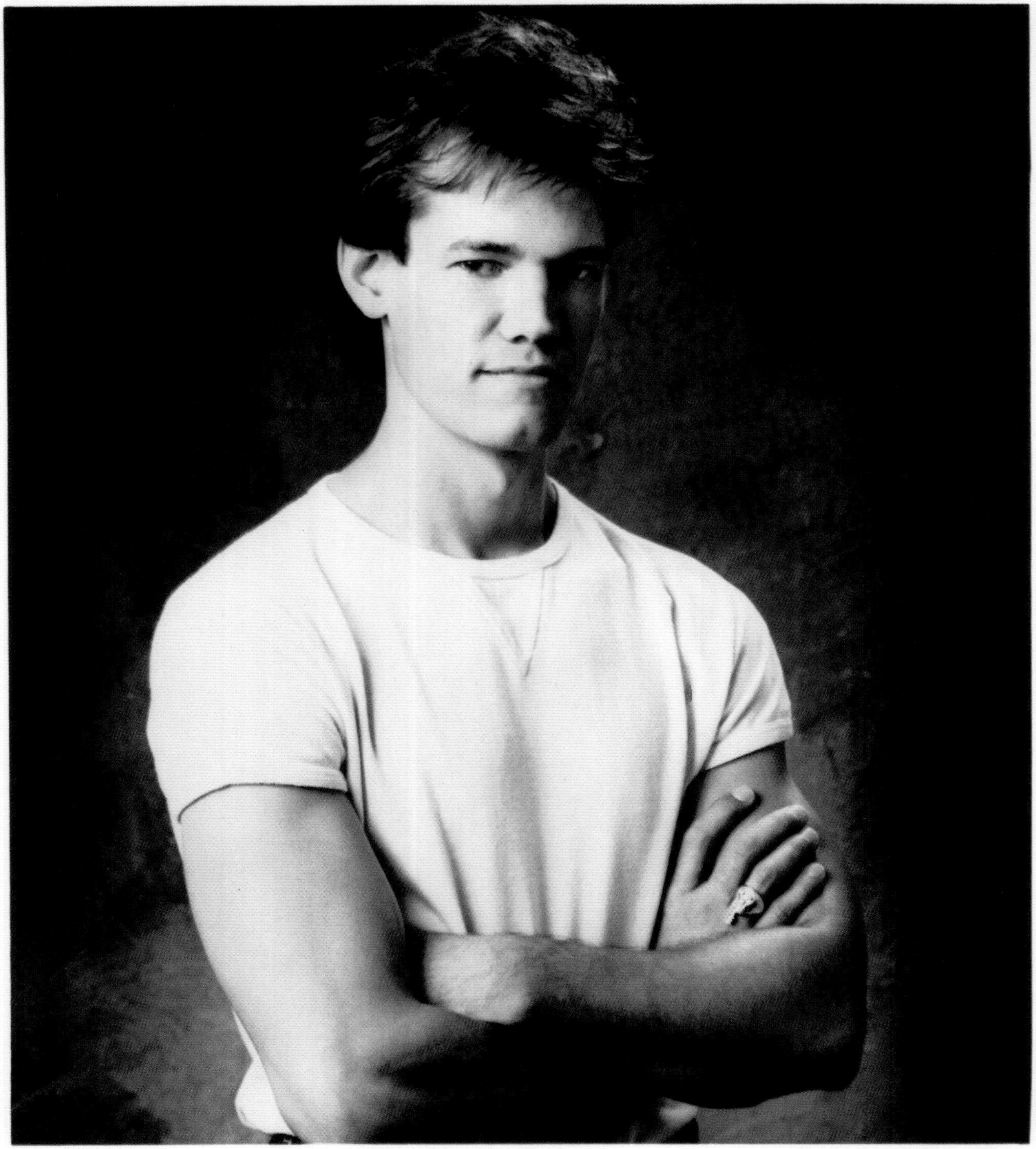

credit: Dean Dixon

RANDY TRAVIS

WARNER BROS.

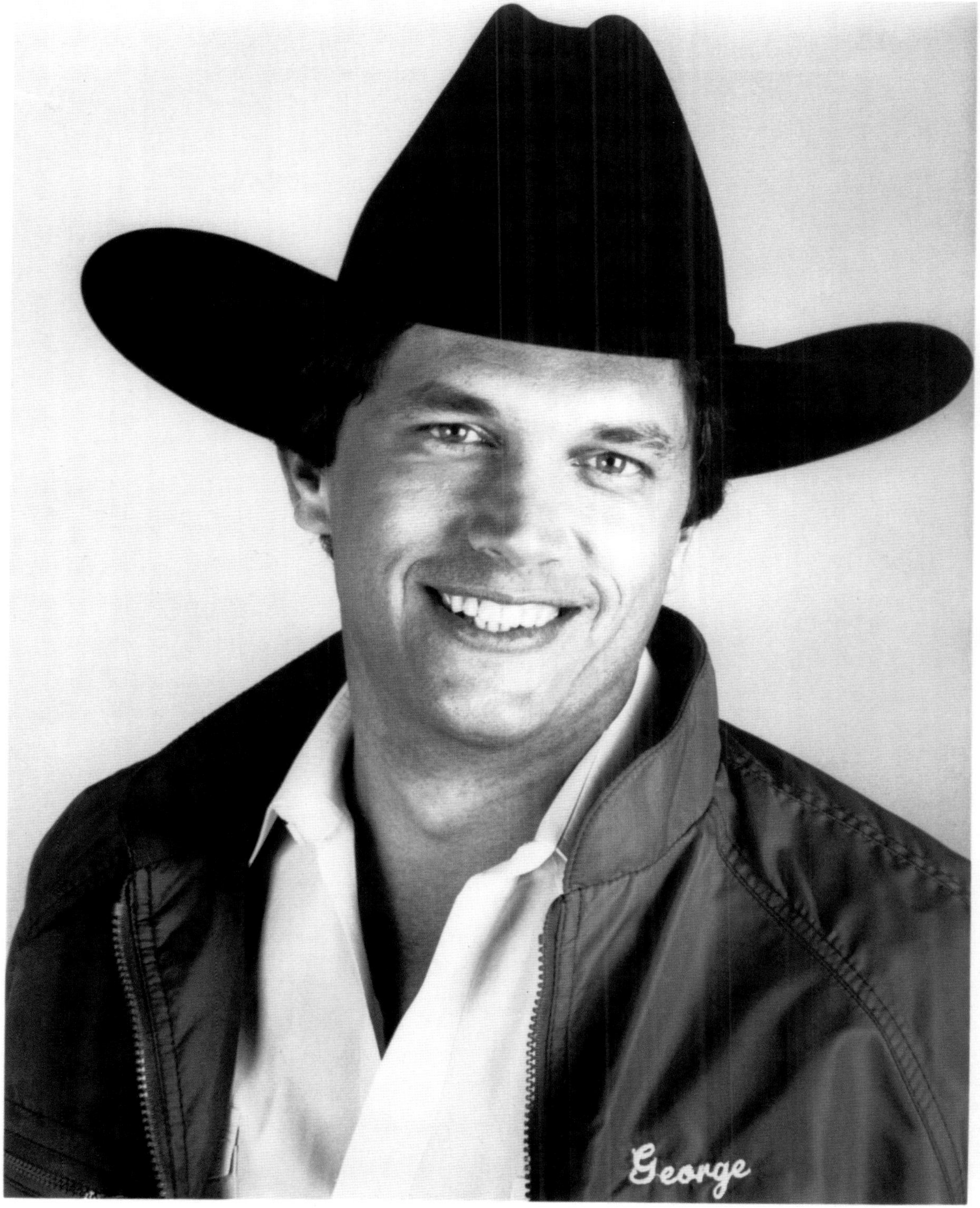

credit: Peter Nash

GEORGE STRAIT

MCA RECORDS

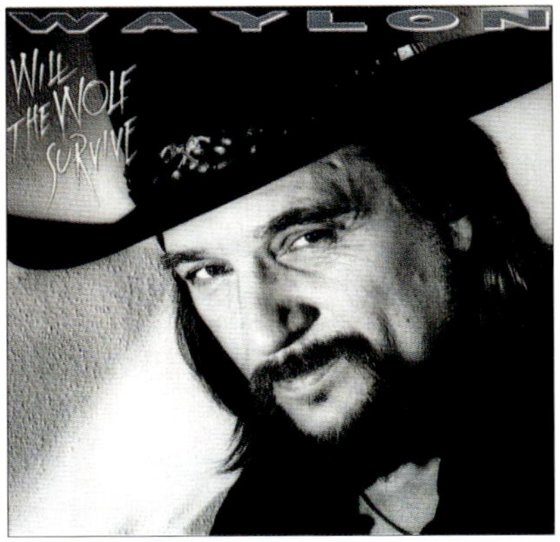

With producer Jimmy Bowen revising his outlaw country approach, **Waylon Jennings** bounced back to the top of the country charts with *Will the Wolf Survive*.

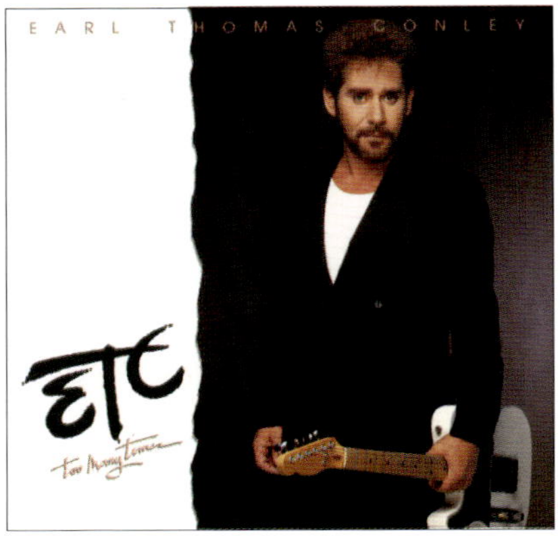

Duetting with R&B singer Anita Pointer on "Too Many Times," **Earl Thomas Conley** landed a #2 country hit and appeared on the television show *Soul Train*.

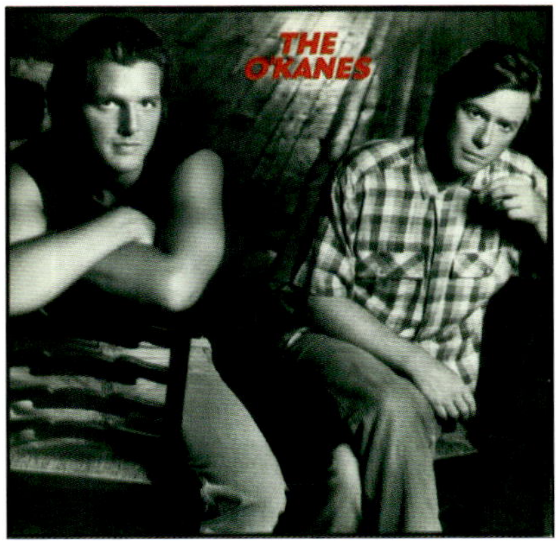

The O'Kanes, comprised of veteran Nashville songwriters Jamie O'Hara and Kieran Kane, got a No. 1 country hit, "Can't Stop My Heart from Loving You."

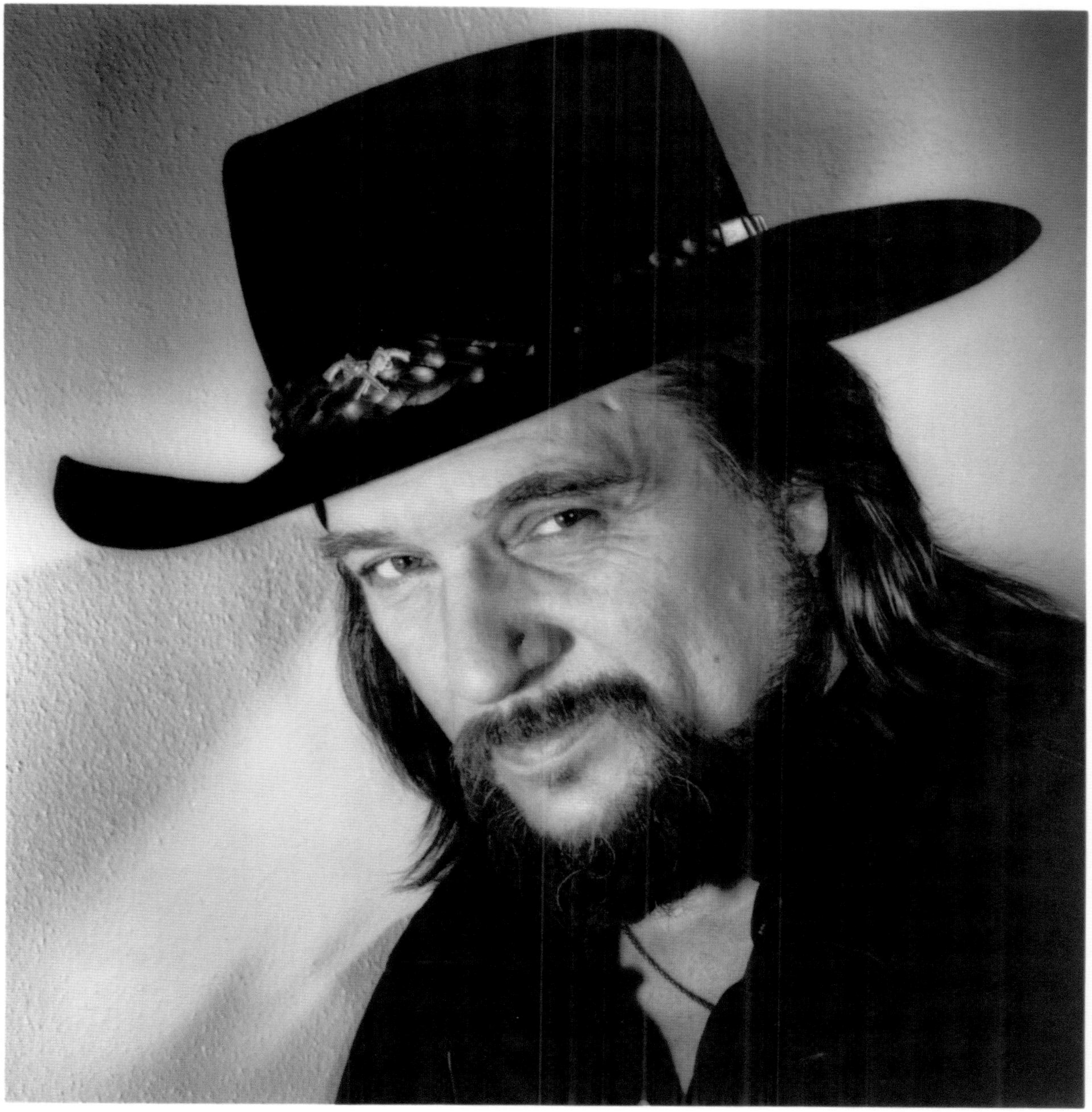

WAYLON

MCA RECORDS

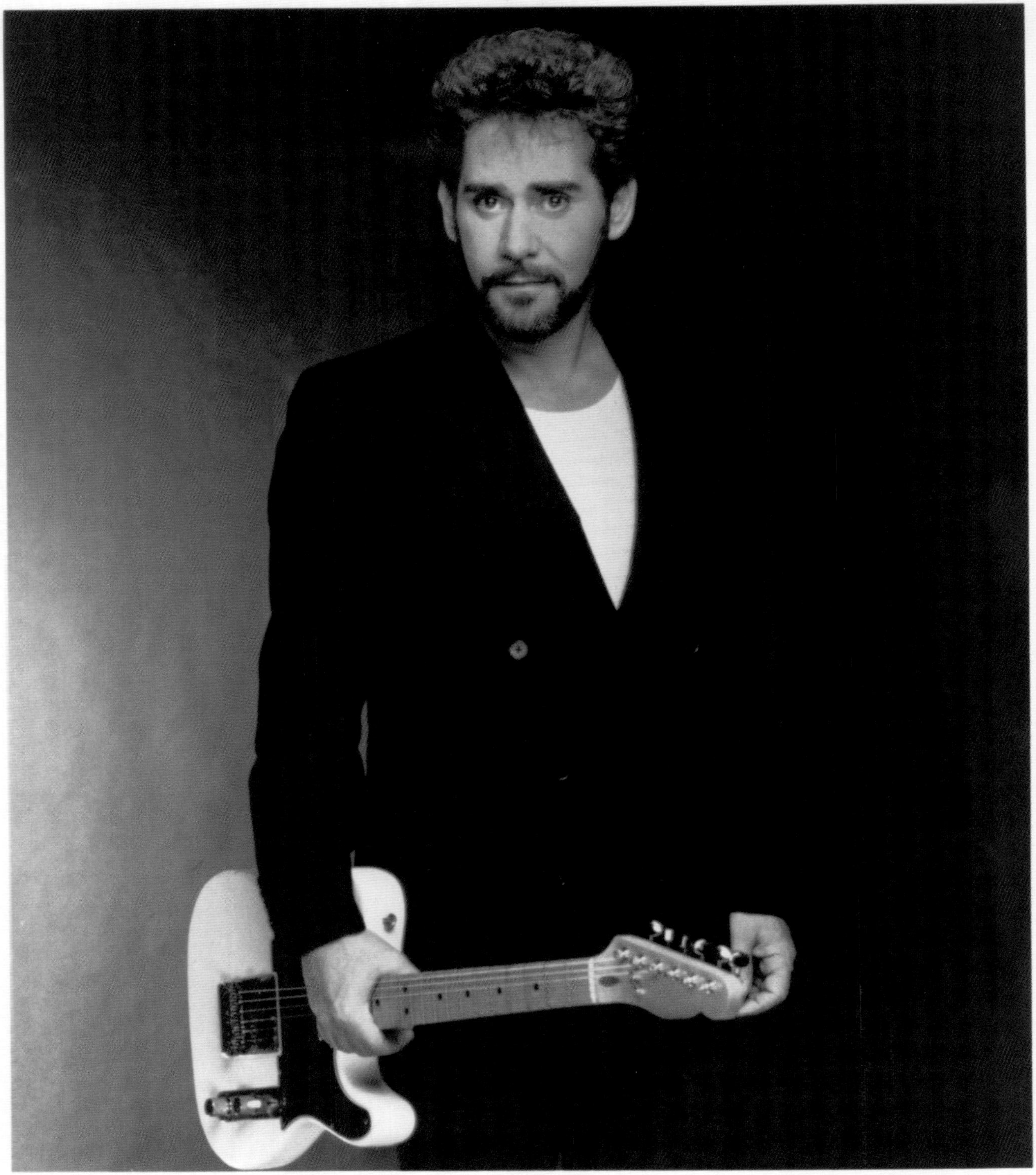

EARL THOMAS CONLEY

RCA Records and Cassettes
30 Music Square West
Nashville, TN 37203
Telephone (615) 244-9880

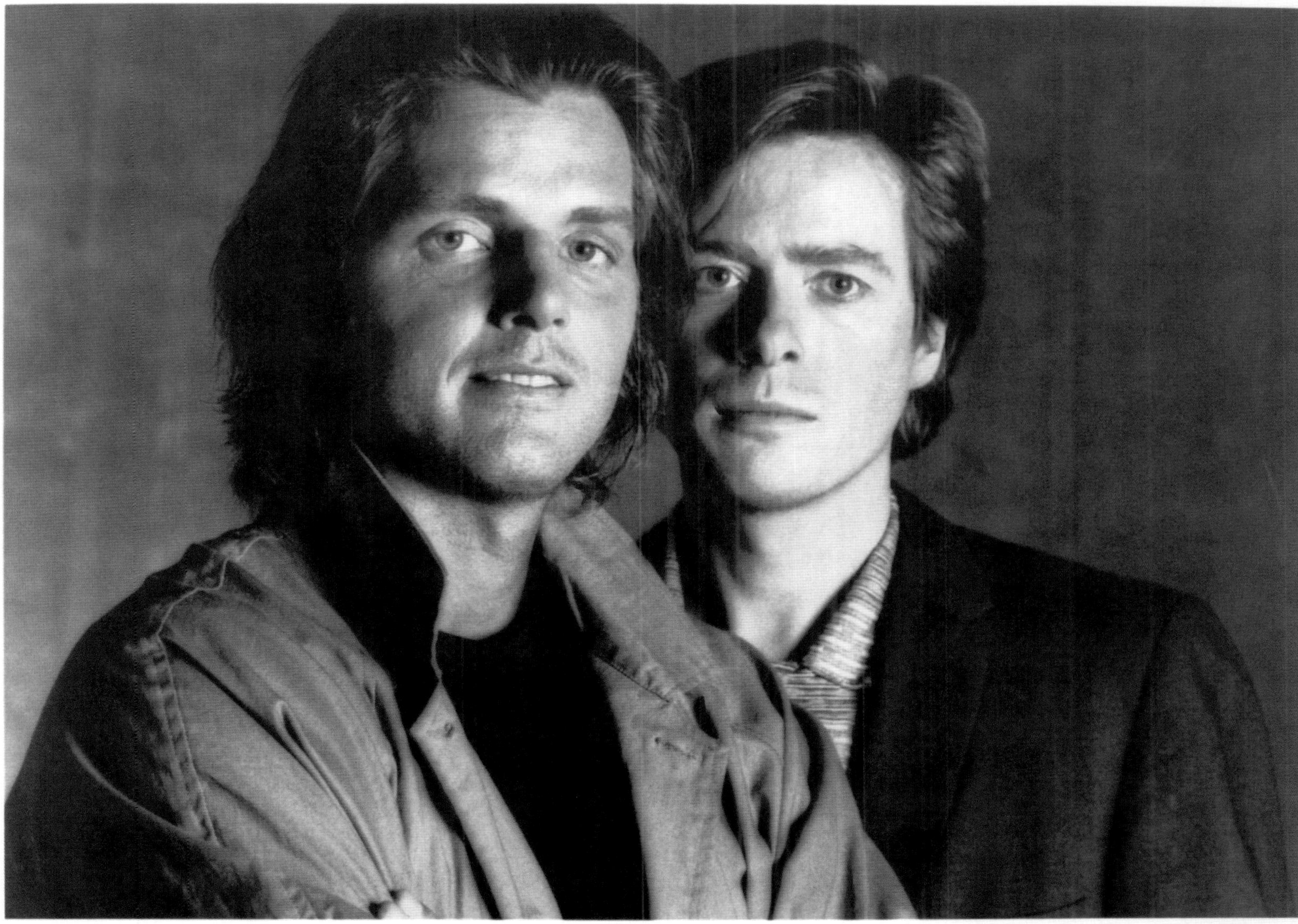

credit: Alan Messer

THE O'KANES

Columbia

8607

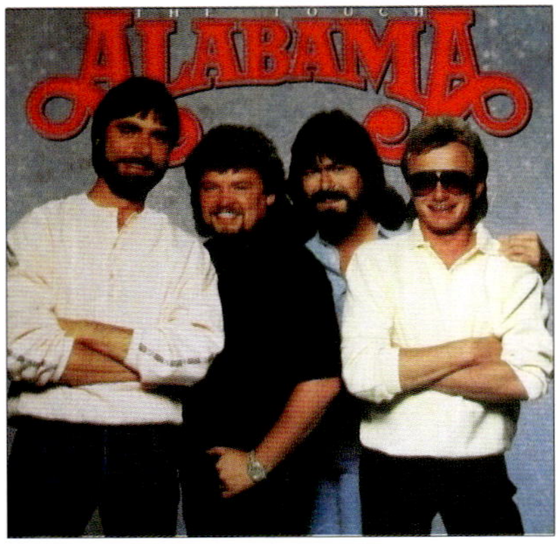

The Touch yielded "'You've Got' the Touch" and "Touch Me When We're Dancing," **Alabama**'s 20th and 21st chart-topping country singles in succession.

Billboard 200: *The Touch* (#42)

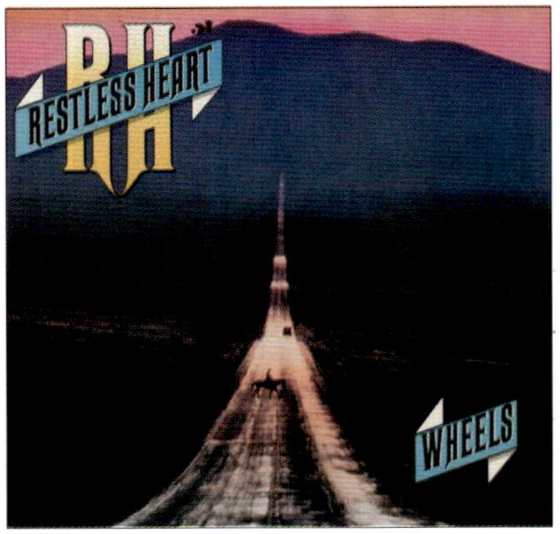

Wheels, **Restless Heart**'s breakthrough release, turned out four consecutive No. 1 country hits, with "I'll Still Be Loving You" extending to the pop charts.

Billboard 200: *Wheels* (#73)
Billboard Hot 100: "I'll Still Be Loving You" (#33)

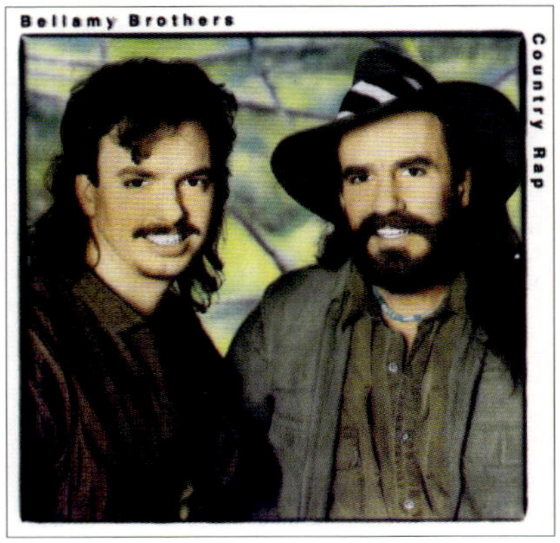

The Bellamy Brothers recorded "Too Much Is Not Enough" with the Forester Sisters and "Kids of the Baby Boom," continuing a run of No. 1 country tunes.

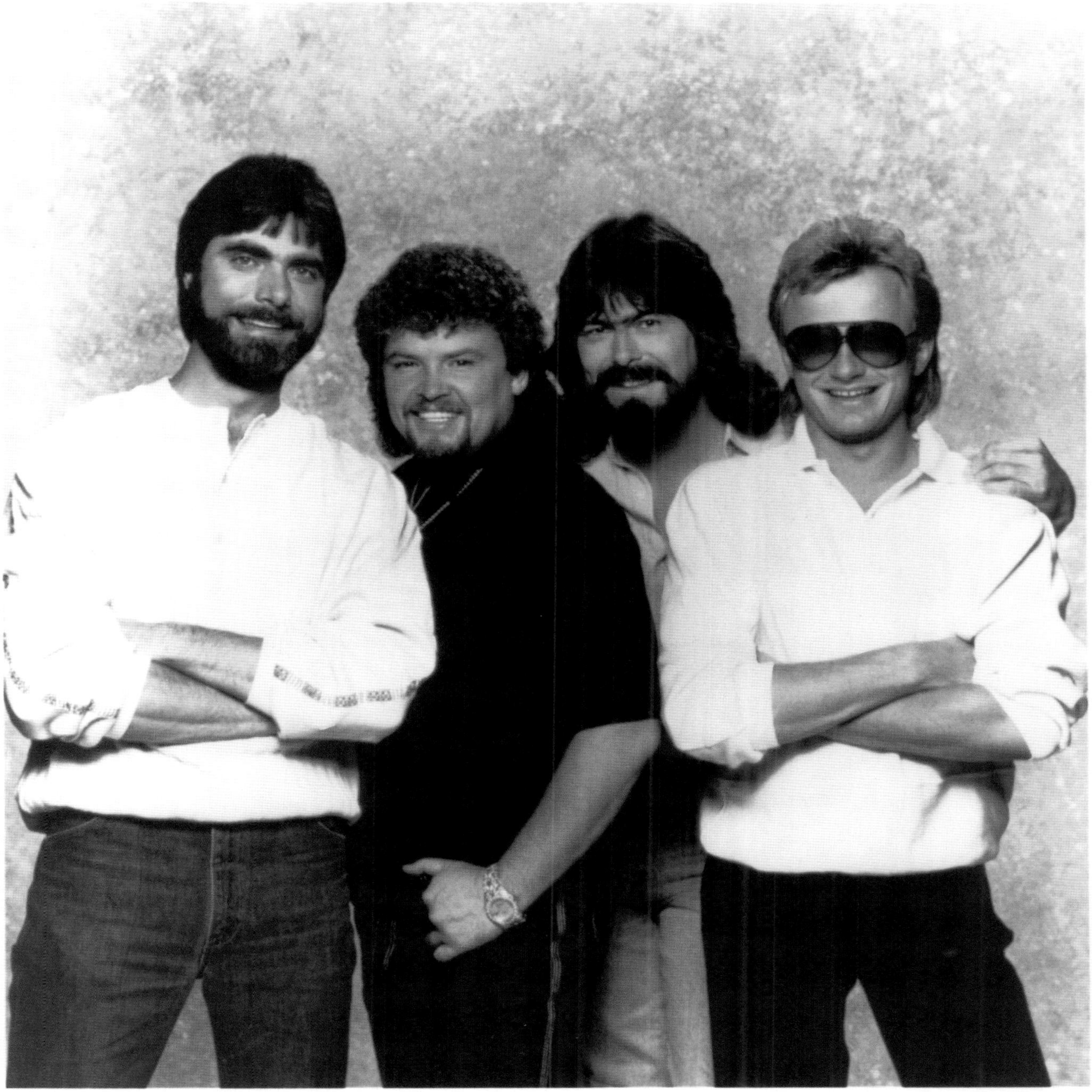

ALABAMA

RCA Records and Cassettes
30 Music Square West
Nashville, TN 37203
Telephone (615) 244-9880

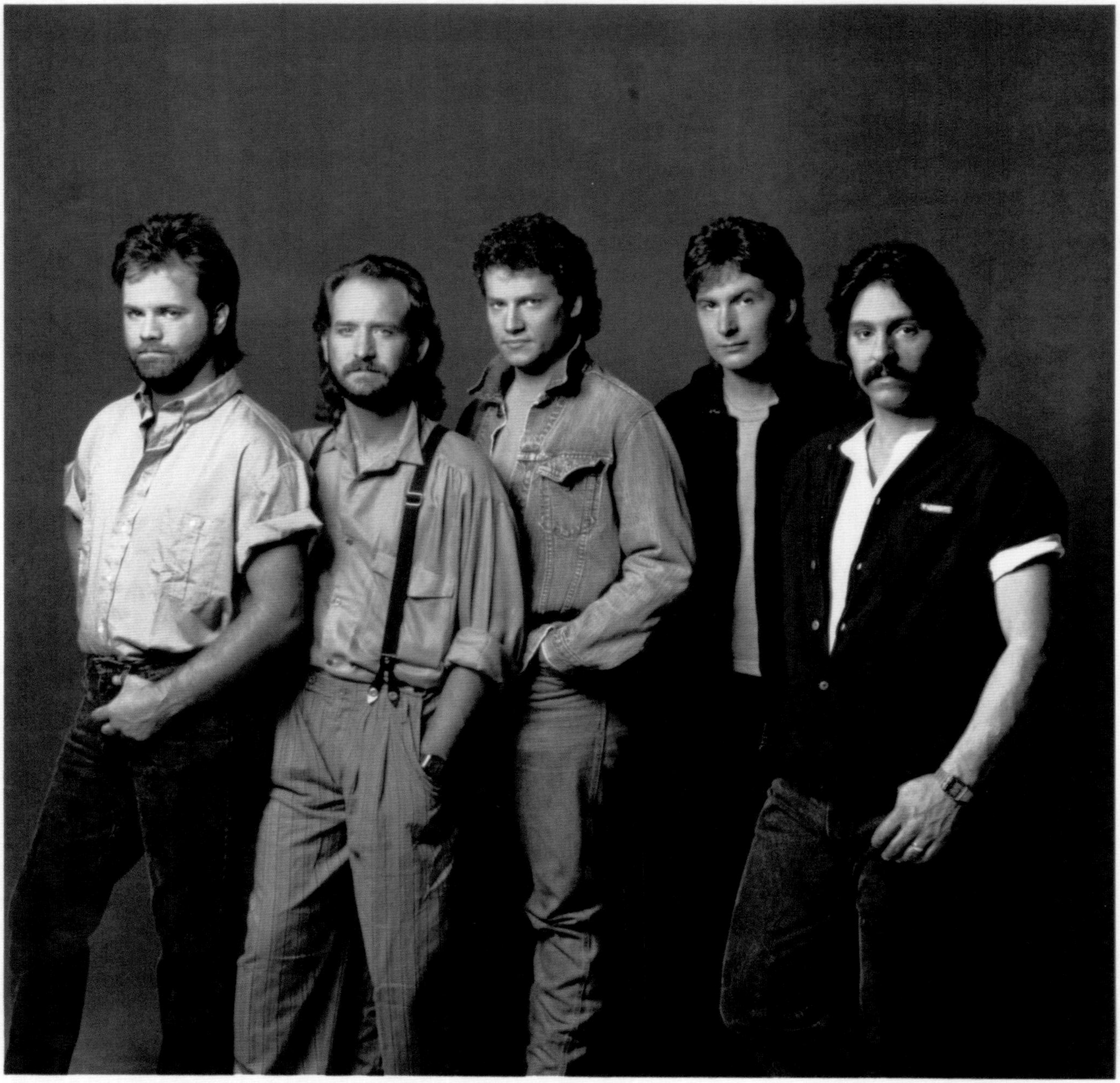

RESTLESS HEART

RCA Records and Cassettes
30 Music Square West
Nashville, TN 37203
Telephone (615) 244-9880

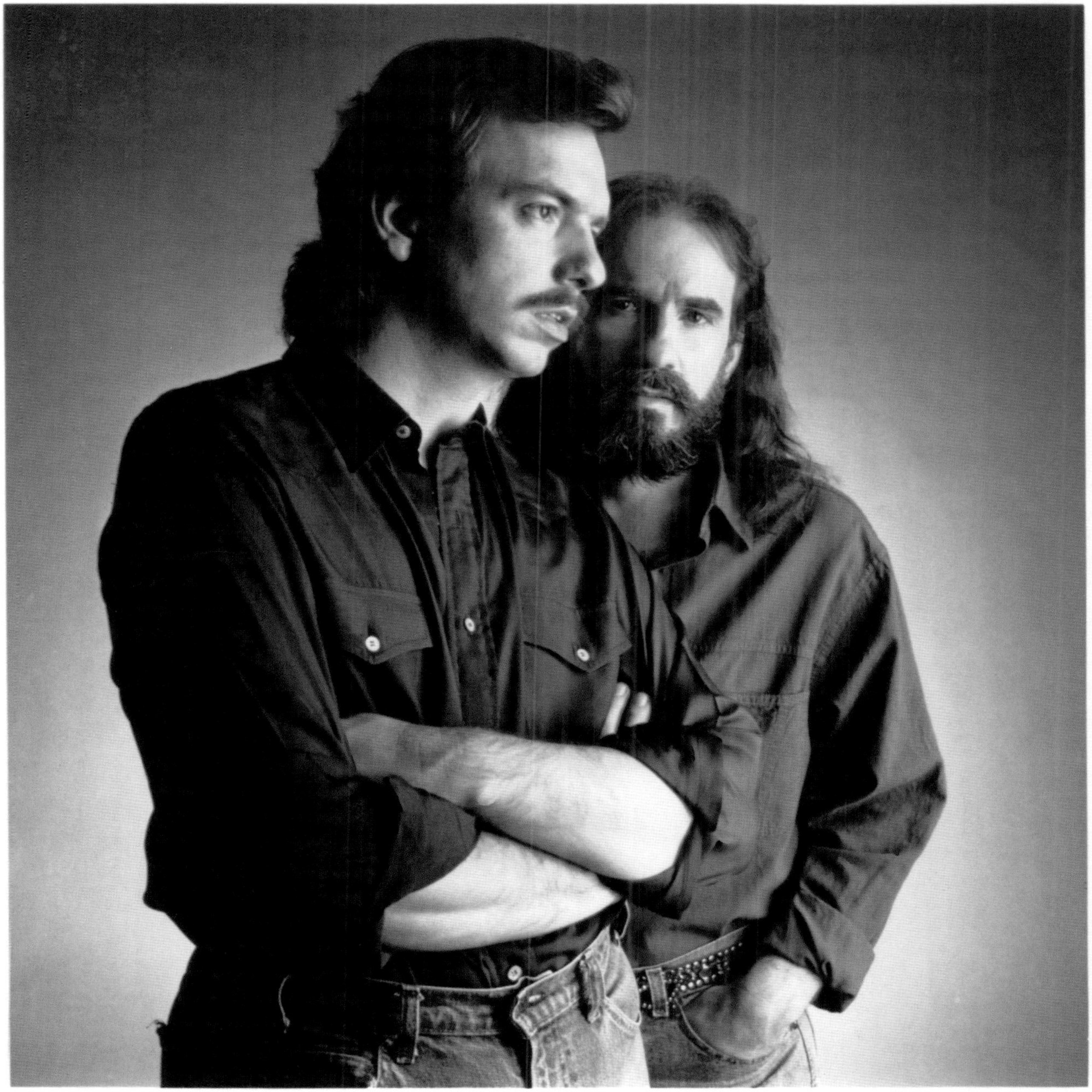

THE BELLAMY BROTHERS

MCA RECORDS
CURB
RECORDS

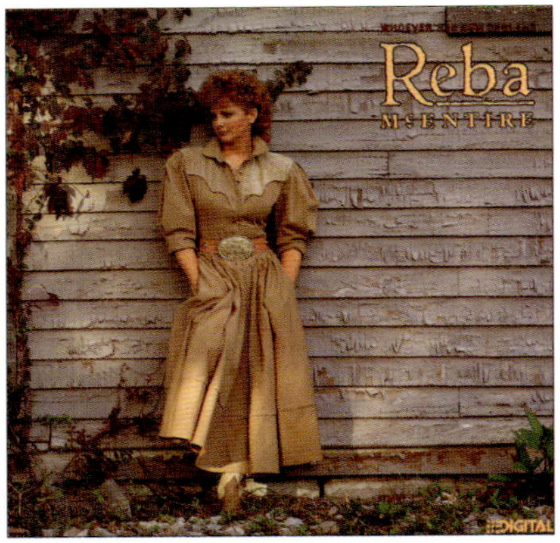

Incorporating a variety of pop content into her approach, **Reba McEntire** delivered the platinum *Whoever's in New England*, her first No. 1 country album.

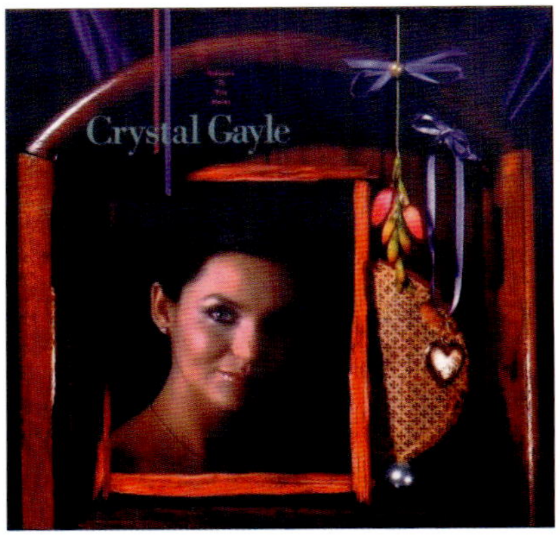

From her *Straight to the Heart* release, **Crystal Gayle** achieved her 17th and 18th No. 1 country hits, a remake of Johnny Ray's "Cry" and the title track.

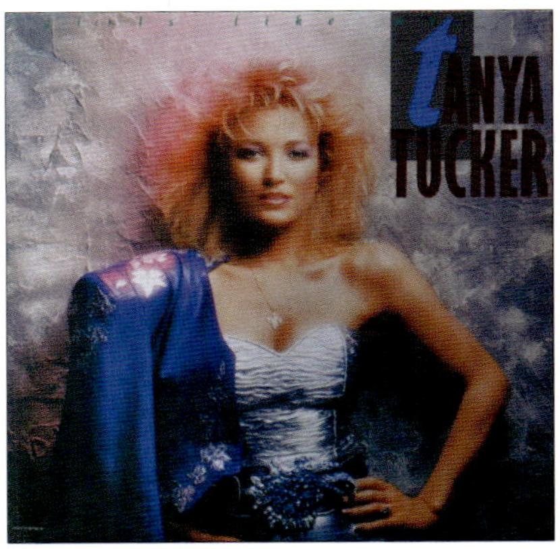

A 13-year-old country music wunderkind in 1972, singer **Tanya Tucker** rejuvenated her career with *Girls Like Me*, an album producing four Top 10 singles.

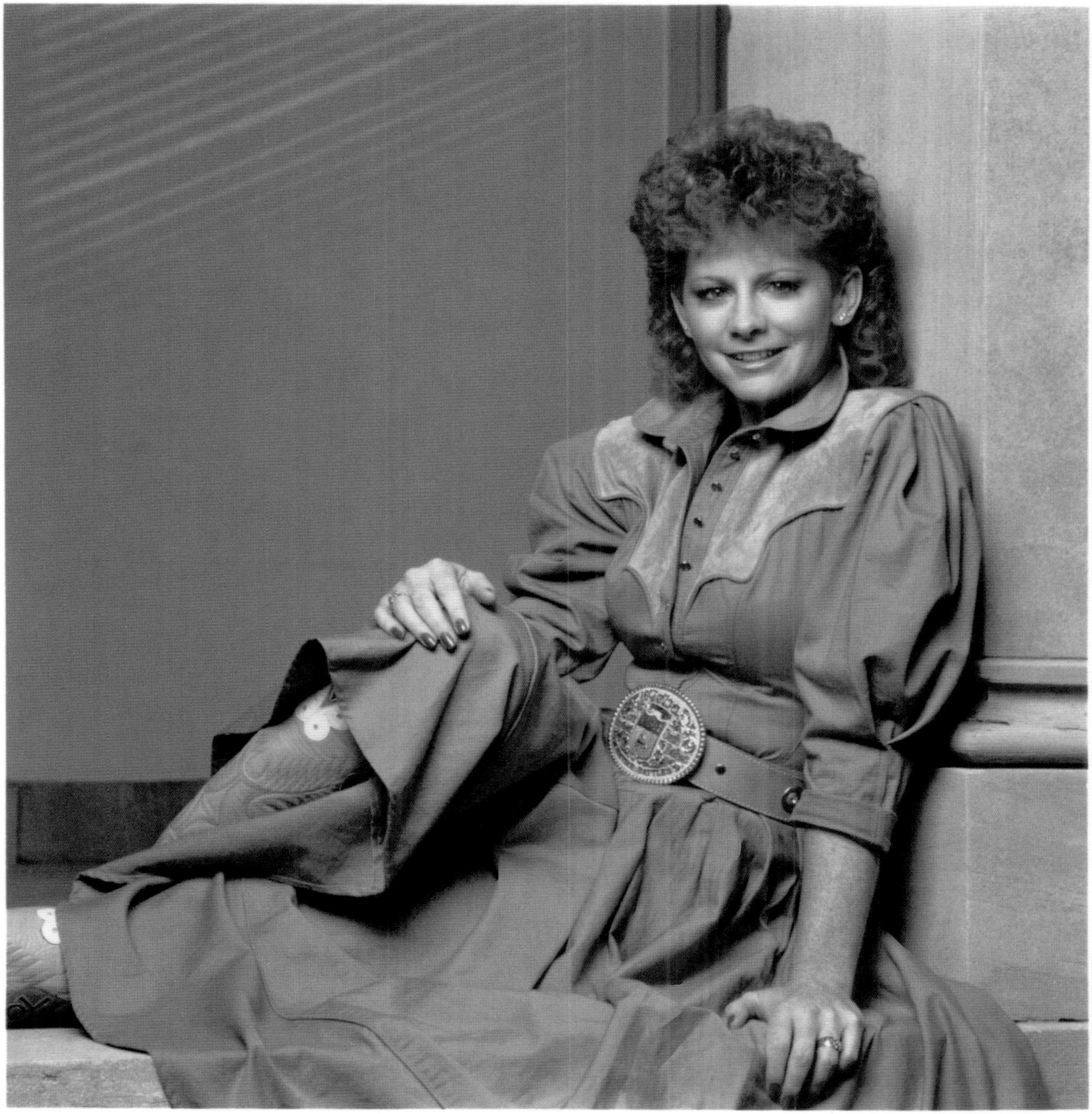

photo: Jim McGuire

Reba McEntire

MCA RECORDS

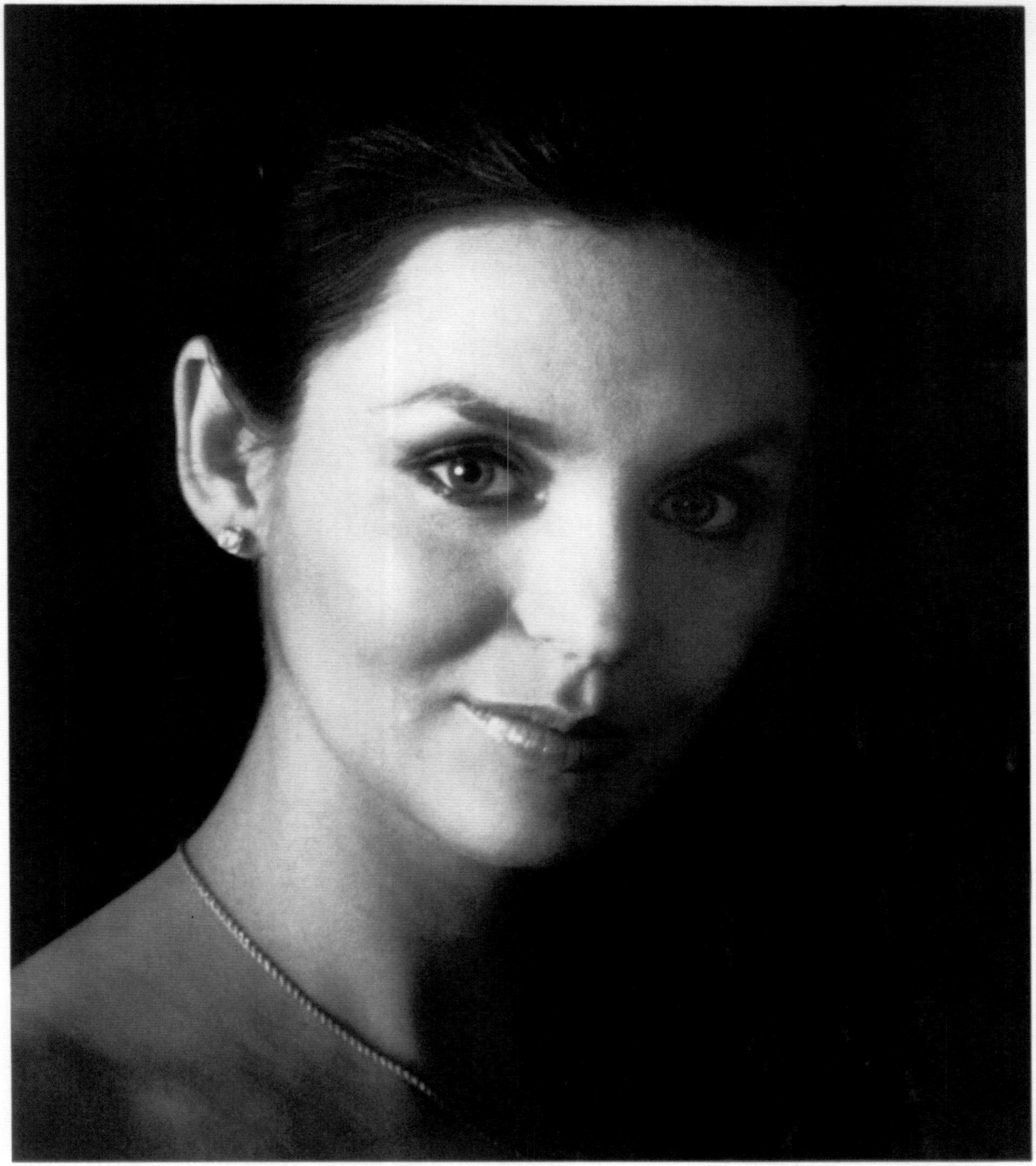

Photo Credit: Stuart Watson

CRYSTAL GAYLE

WARNER BROS.

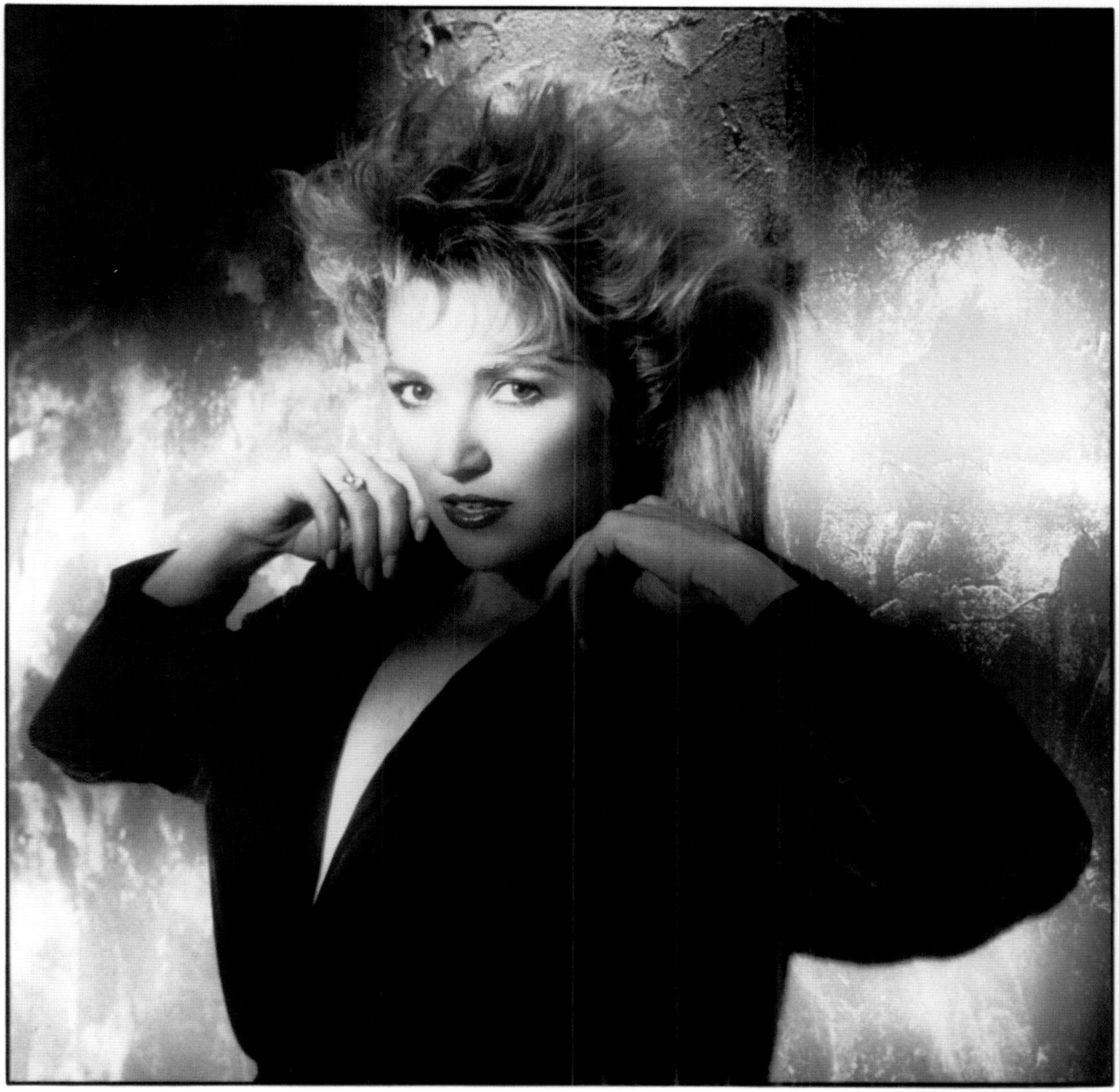

Photo: Dick Zimmerman / 1986

TANYA TUCKER

Capitol RECORDS

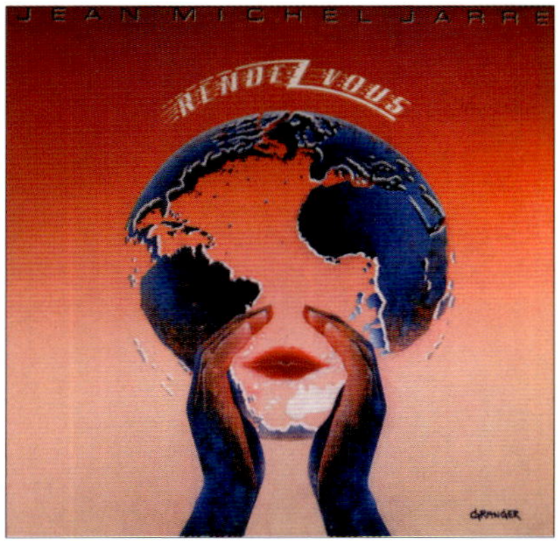

Electronic music master **Jean-Michel Jarre** honored Houston's sesquicentennial and the silver anniversary of NASA's Johnson Space Center on *Rendez-Vous*.

Billboard 200: *Rendez-Vous* (#52)

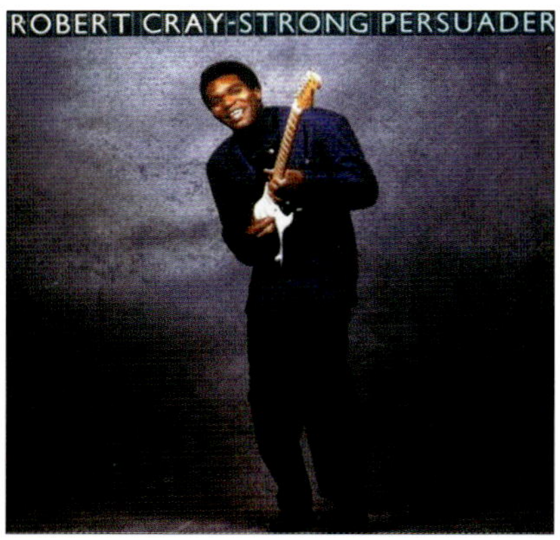

Strong Persuader snagged a Grammy Award, and the single "Smoking Gun" brought blues guitarist and vocalist **Robert Cray** a mainstream breakthrough.

Billboard 200: *Strong Persuader* (#13)
Billboard Hot 100: "Smoking Gun" (#22);
"Right Next Door (Because of Me)" (#80)

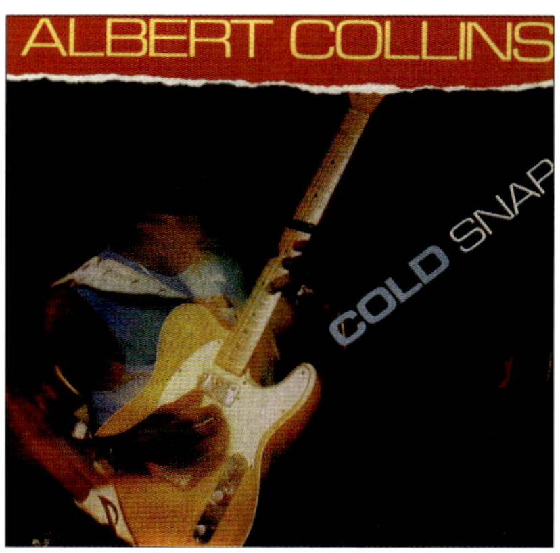

Electric bluesman **Albert Collins**, "the Master of the Telecaster," dropped *Cold Snap*, featuring an appearance by distinguished jazz organist Jimmy McGriff.

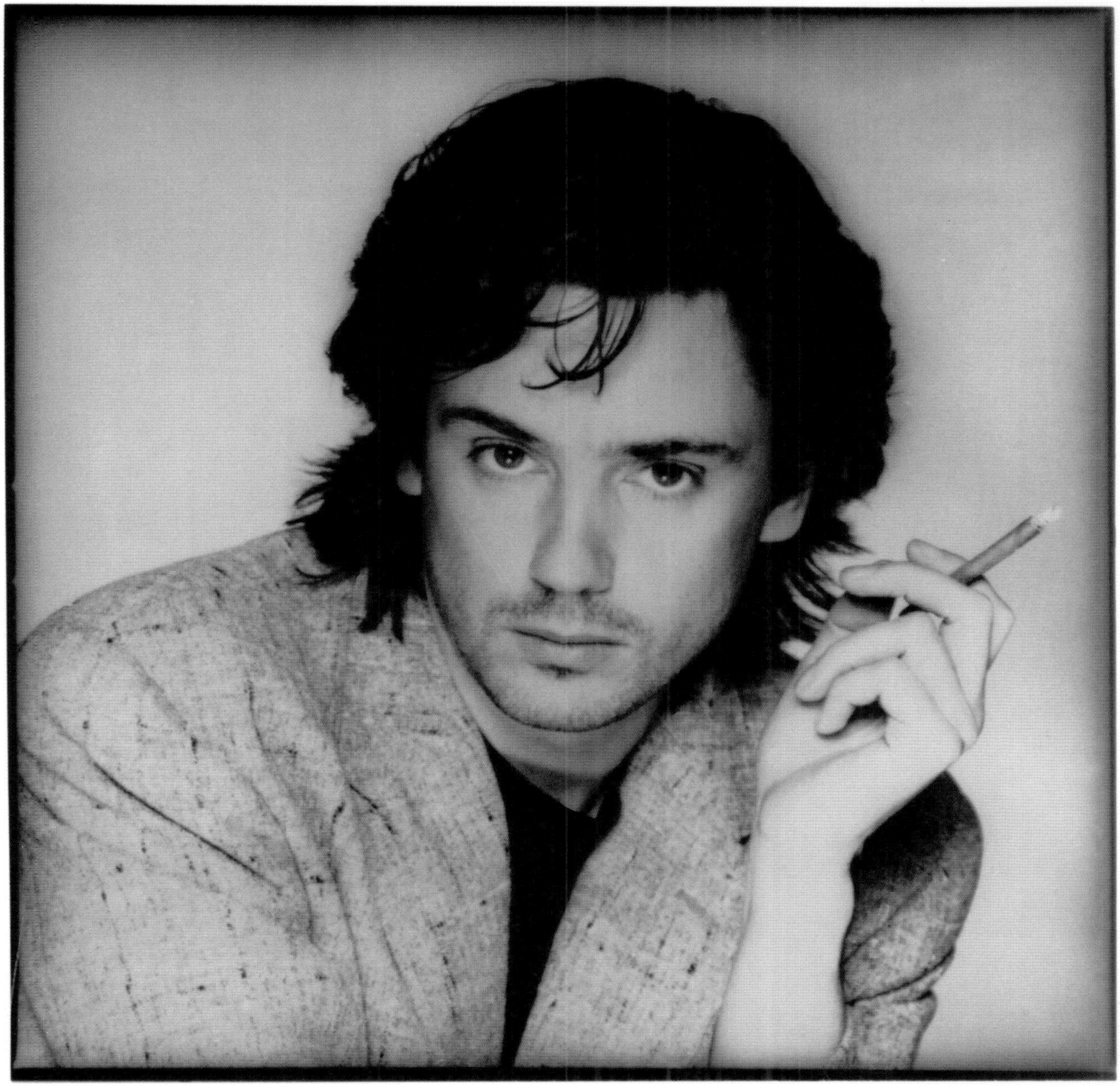

JEAN-MICHEL JARRE

PolyGram Records

polydor

DISQUES dreyfus

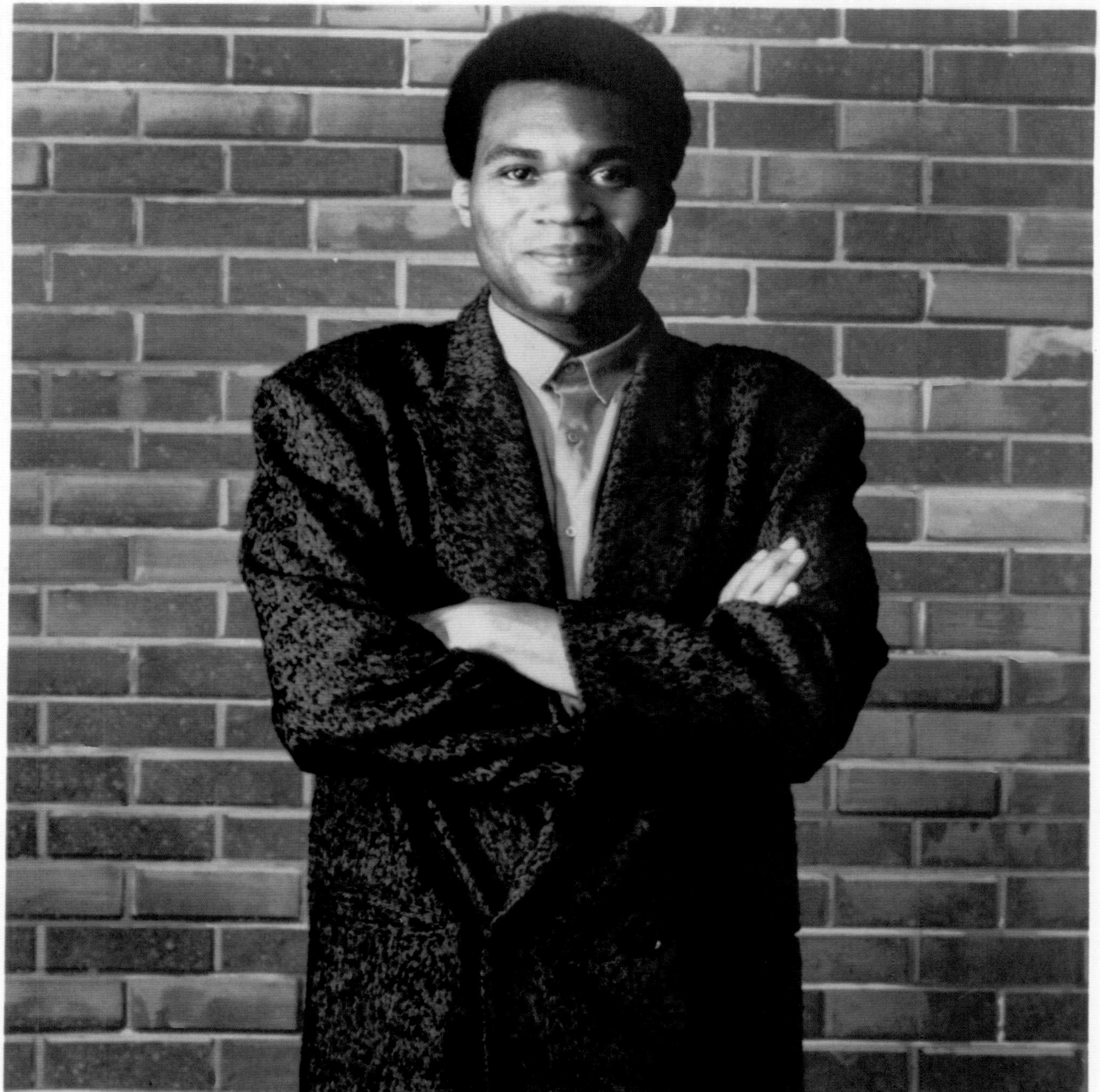

ROBERT CRAY

TOUR DIRECTION

the rosebud agency

P.O. Box 210103
San Francisco, CA 94121
415-386-3456
Telex: 340815
ROSEBUD SFO

mercury

HIGHTONE RECORDS

PolyGram Records

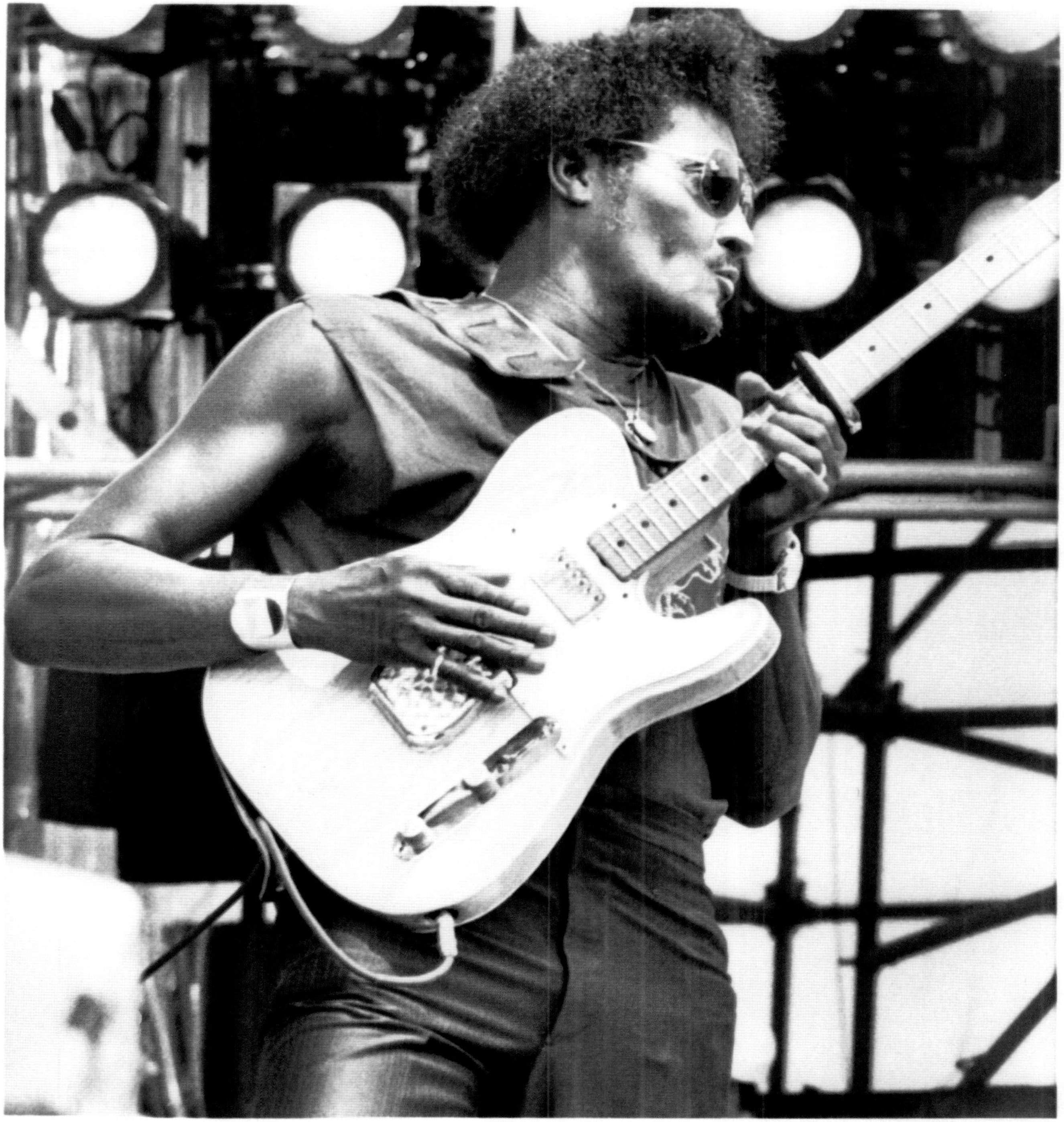

ALBERT COLLINS

Photo: Ebet Roberts

Alligator Records
Box 60234
Chicago, IL 60660
(312) 973-7736

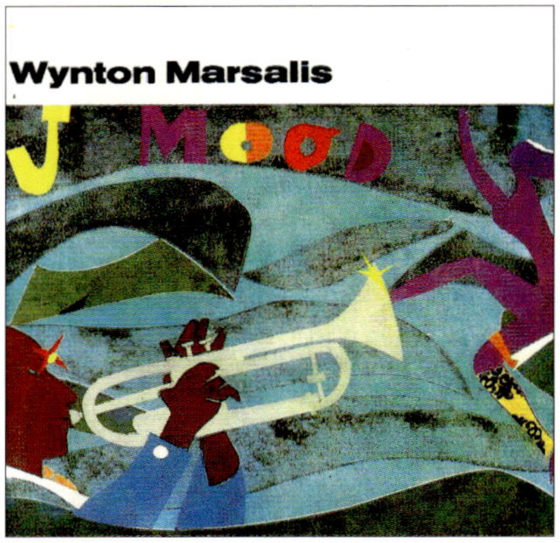

J Mood by trumpeter and composer **Wynton Marsalis**, the most extolled young man in jazz, won the Grammy for Best Jazz Instrumental Performance, Group.

Billboard 200: *J Mood* (#185)

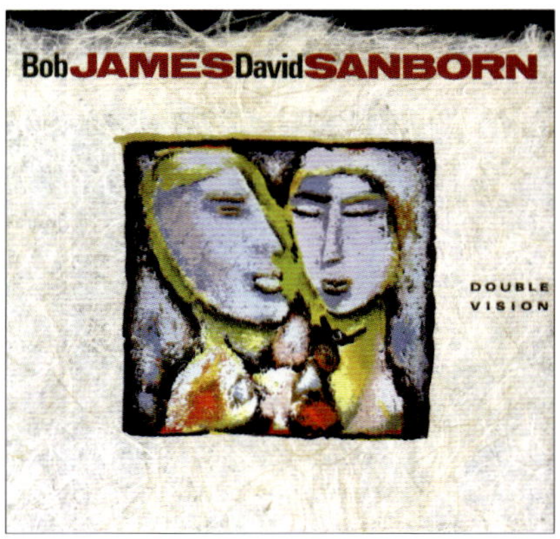

A **Bob James/David Sanborn** collaboration, *Double Vision* earned a Grammy Award for the instrumentalists, in the Best Jazz Fusion Performance category.

Billboard 200: *Double Vision* (#50)

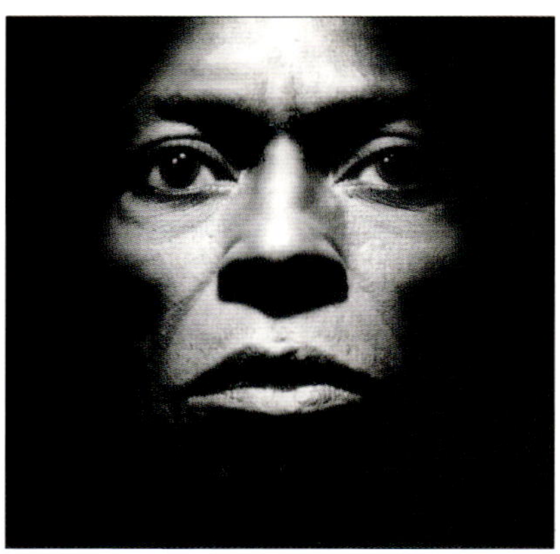

On *Tutu*, jazz trumpeter **Miles Davis** used younger artists and modern studio tools, from synthesizers and MIDI keyboards to aural exciters and drum loops.

Billboard 200: *Tutu* (#141)

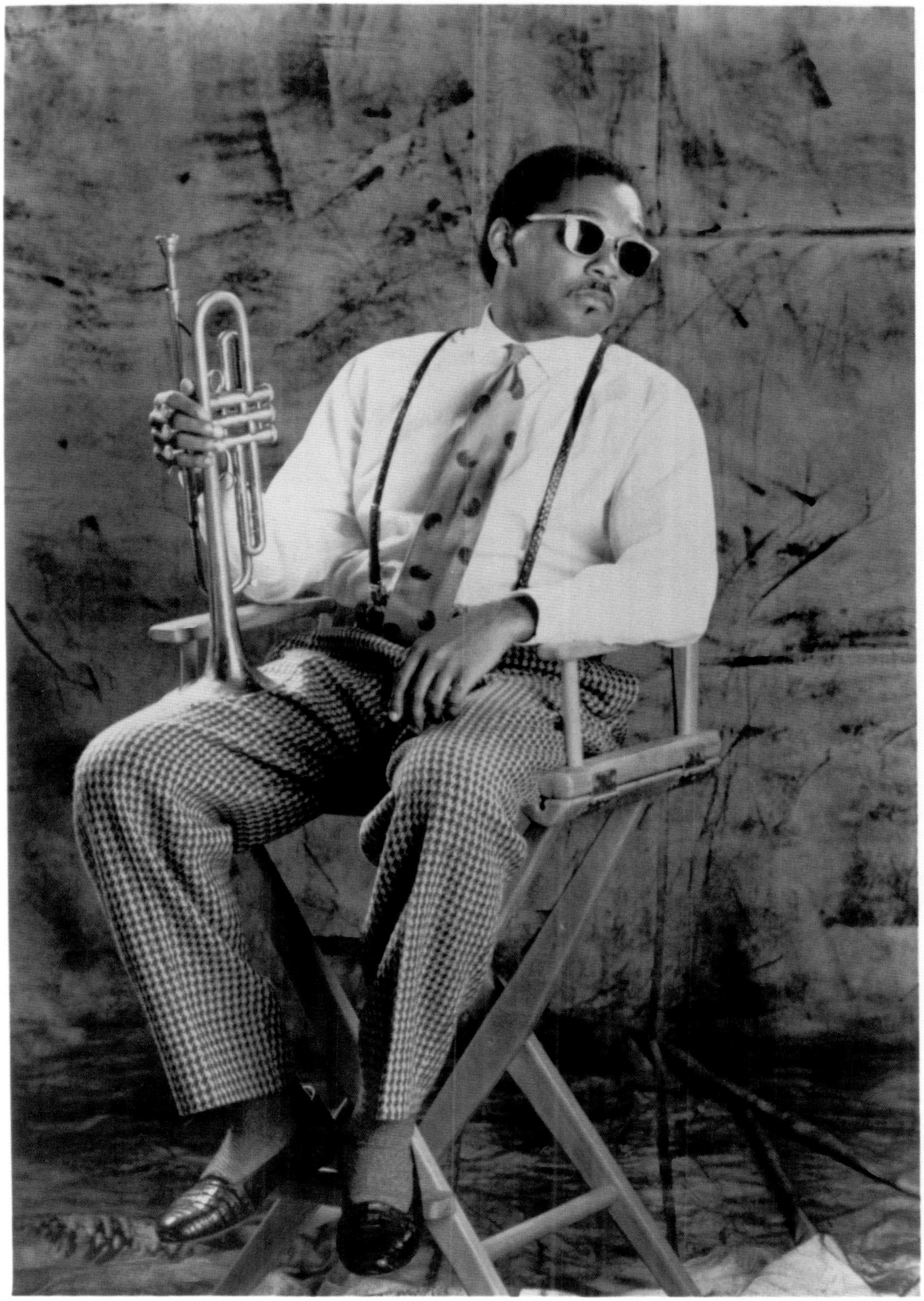

PHOTOGRAPH: ROBB JOHNSON

WYNTON MARSALIS

Columbia

8609

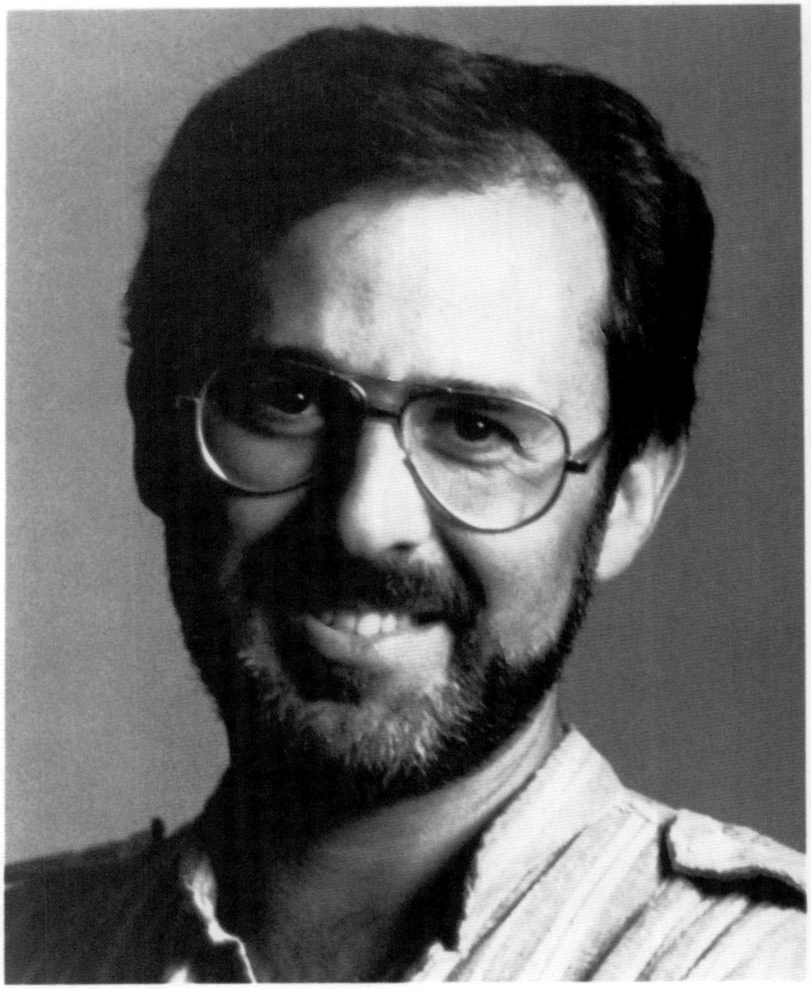

BOB JAMES

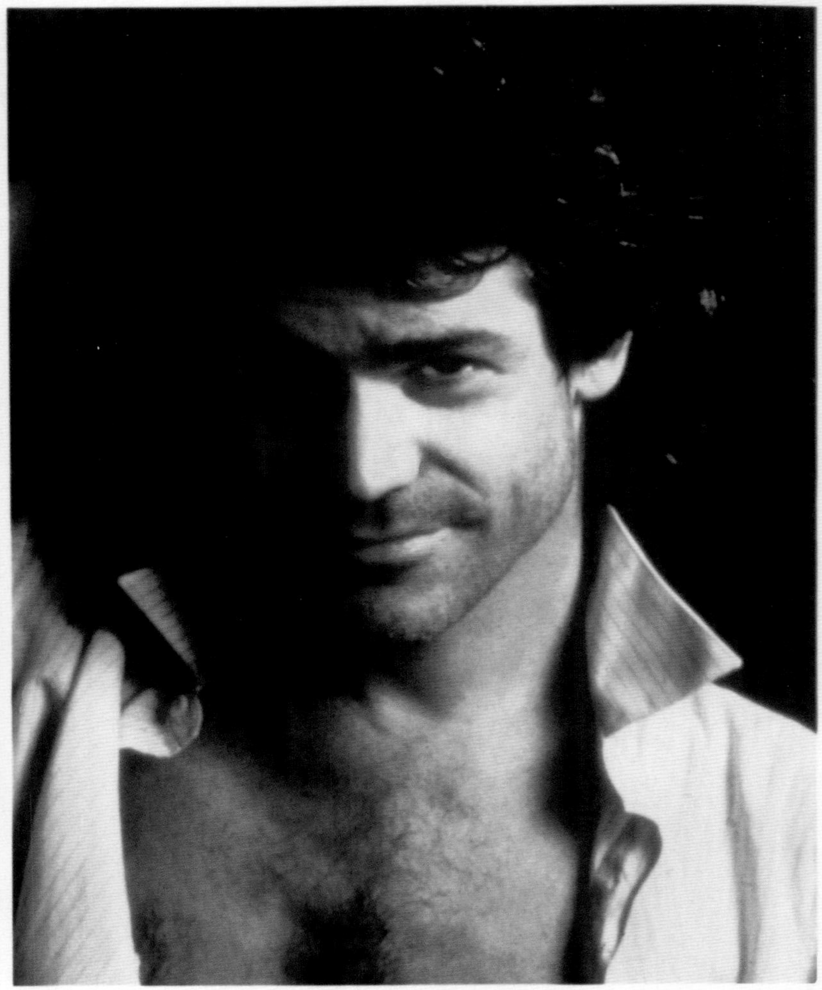

DAVID SANBORN

WARNER BROS.

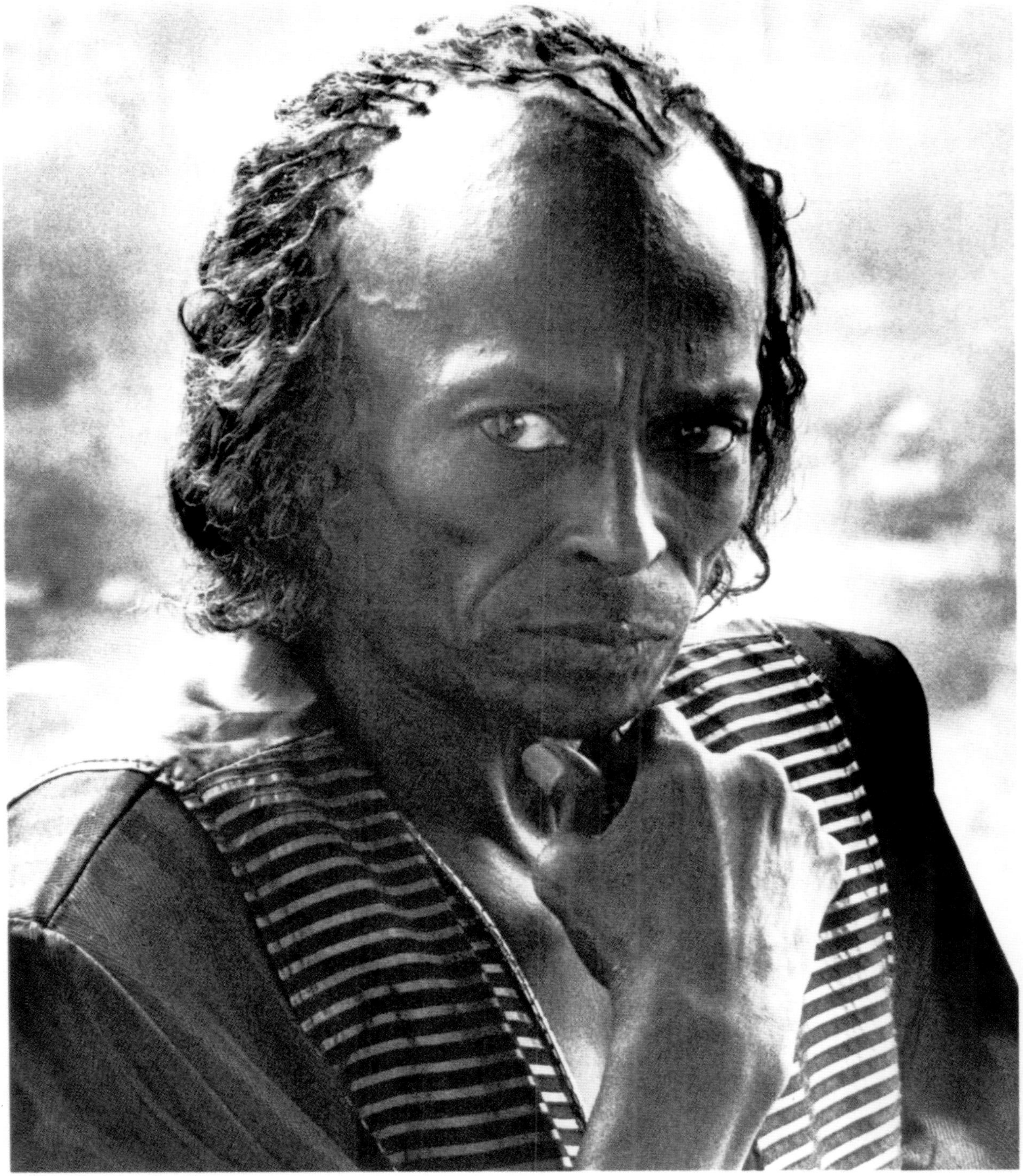

PHOTOGRAPH: KEN FRANCKLING ©1986

MILES DAVIS

WARNER BROS.

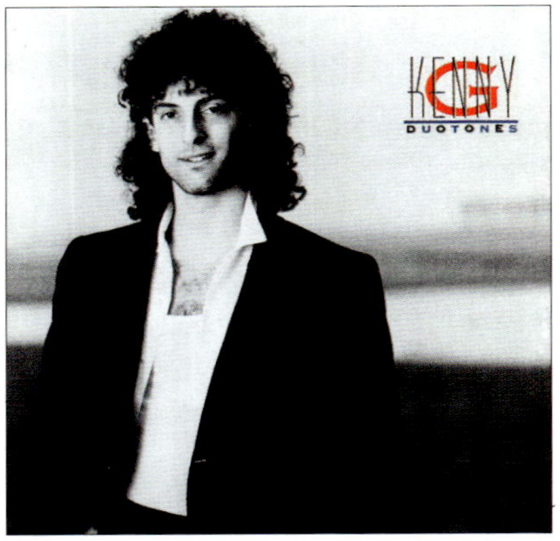

Identified by his signature song, the instrumental "Songbird," sax man **Kenny G**'s *Duotones* album made him a star, peaking at No. 1 on the jazz charts.

Billboard 200: *Duotones* (#6)
Billboard Hot 100: "Don't Make Me Wait for Love" (#15); "Songbird" (#4)

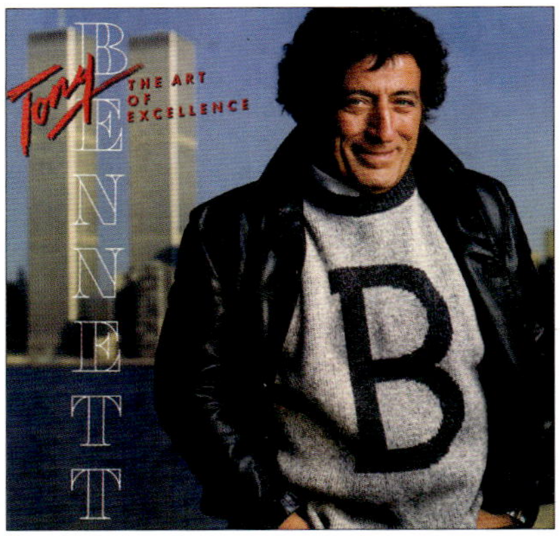

A noble pop and jazz singer of his generation, **Tony Bennett** had a resurgence with *The Art of Excellence*, his first album to reach the charts in 14 years.

Billboard 200: *The Art of Excellence* (#160)

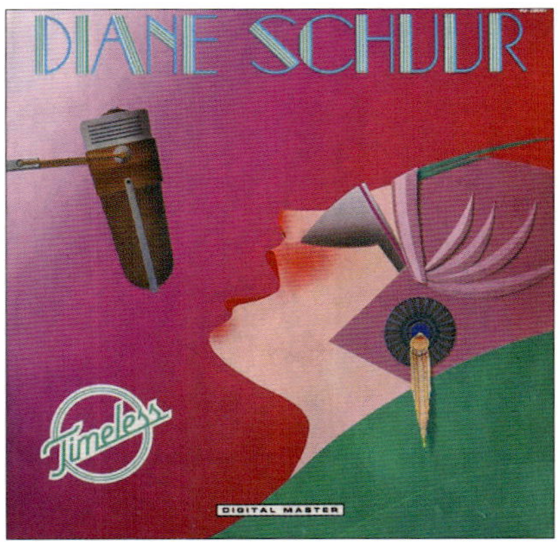

Blind from birth but gifted with perfect pitch, jazz singer **Diane Schuur** won her first Grammy for *Timeless*, her recording of standards from the big band era.

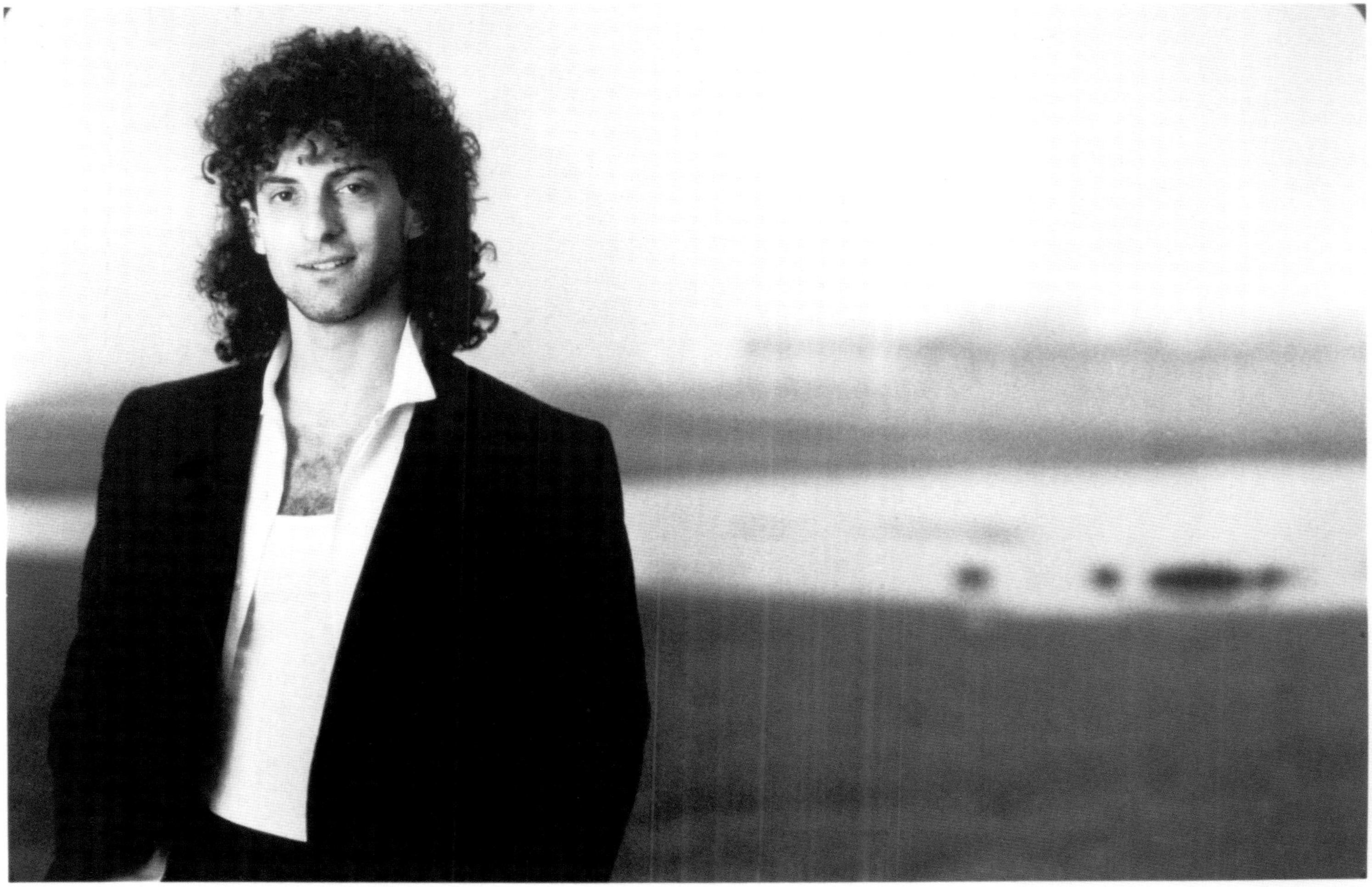

TURNER FRITZ

KENNY G

ARISTA™

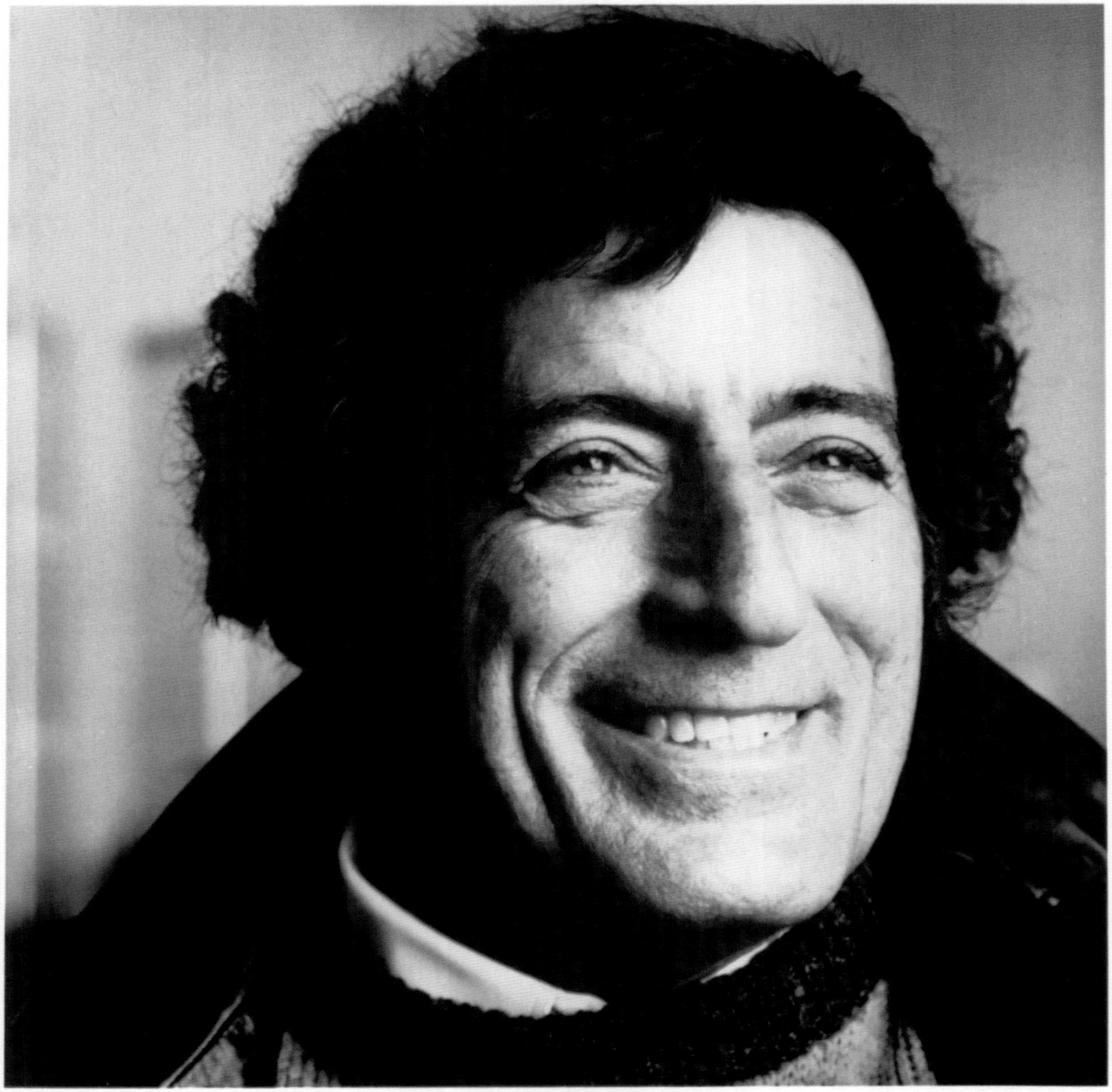

PHOTOGRAPH: ANNIE LEIBOVITZ

TONY BENNETT

Columbia
8604

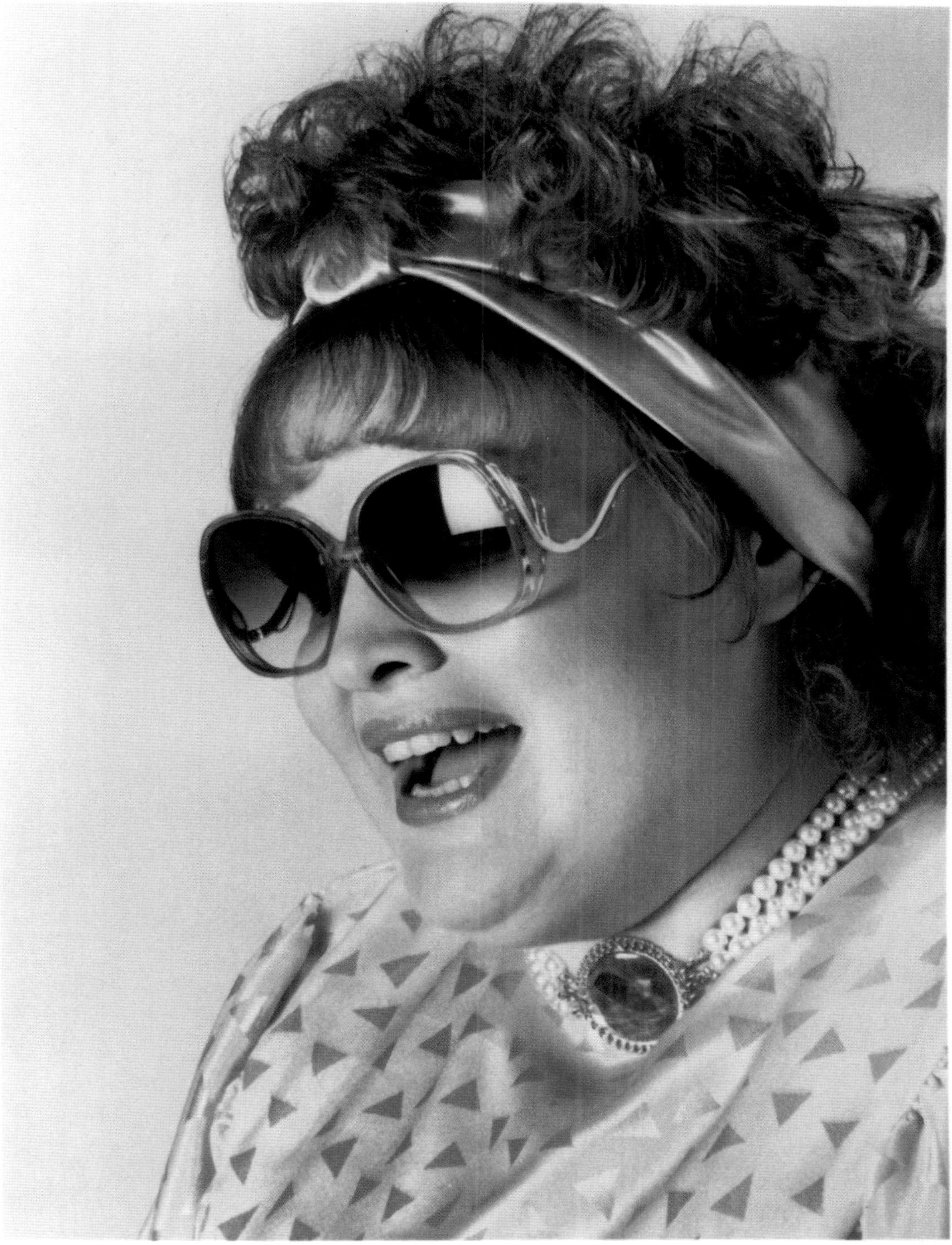

DIANE SCHUUR

GRP Records

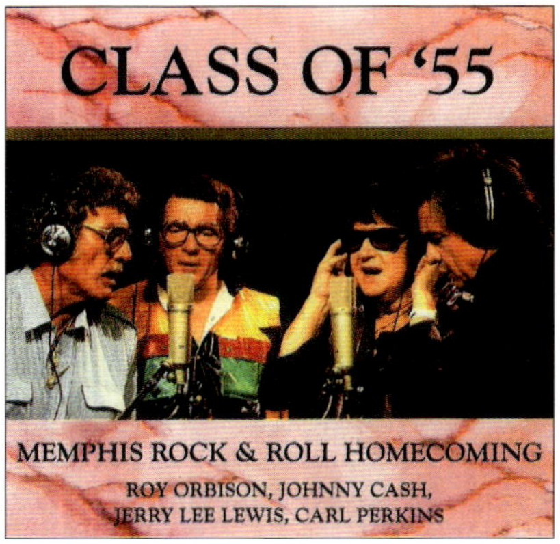

Memphis Rock & Roll Homecoming reunited rock 'n' roll legends Carl Perkins, Roy Orbison, Jerry Lee Lewis and Johnny Cash—**Class of '55**—at Sun Studio.

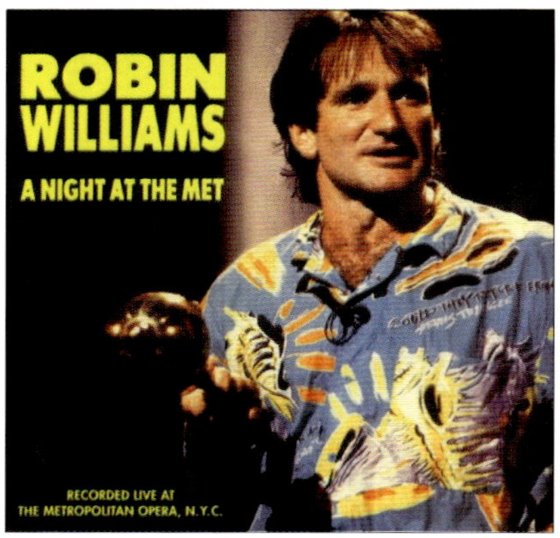

Robin Williams recorded his third comedy album, *A Night at the Met*, at an unlikely location for a stand-up routine, the Metropolitan Opera House in NYC.

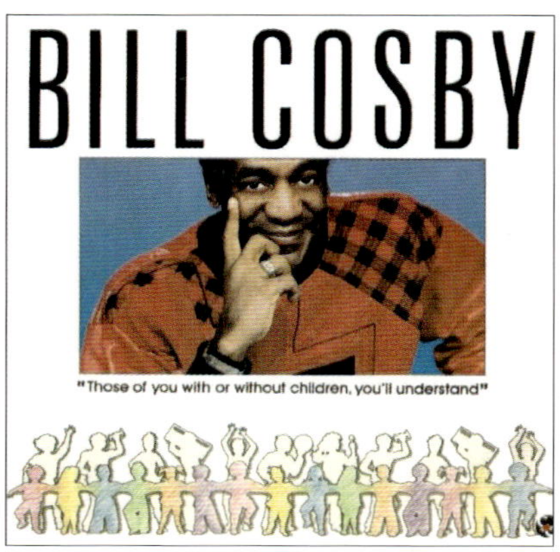

Those of You With or Without Children, You'll Understand earned the Grammy Award for Best Comedy Album, the seventh for actor and comedian **Bill Cosby**.

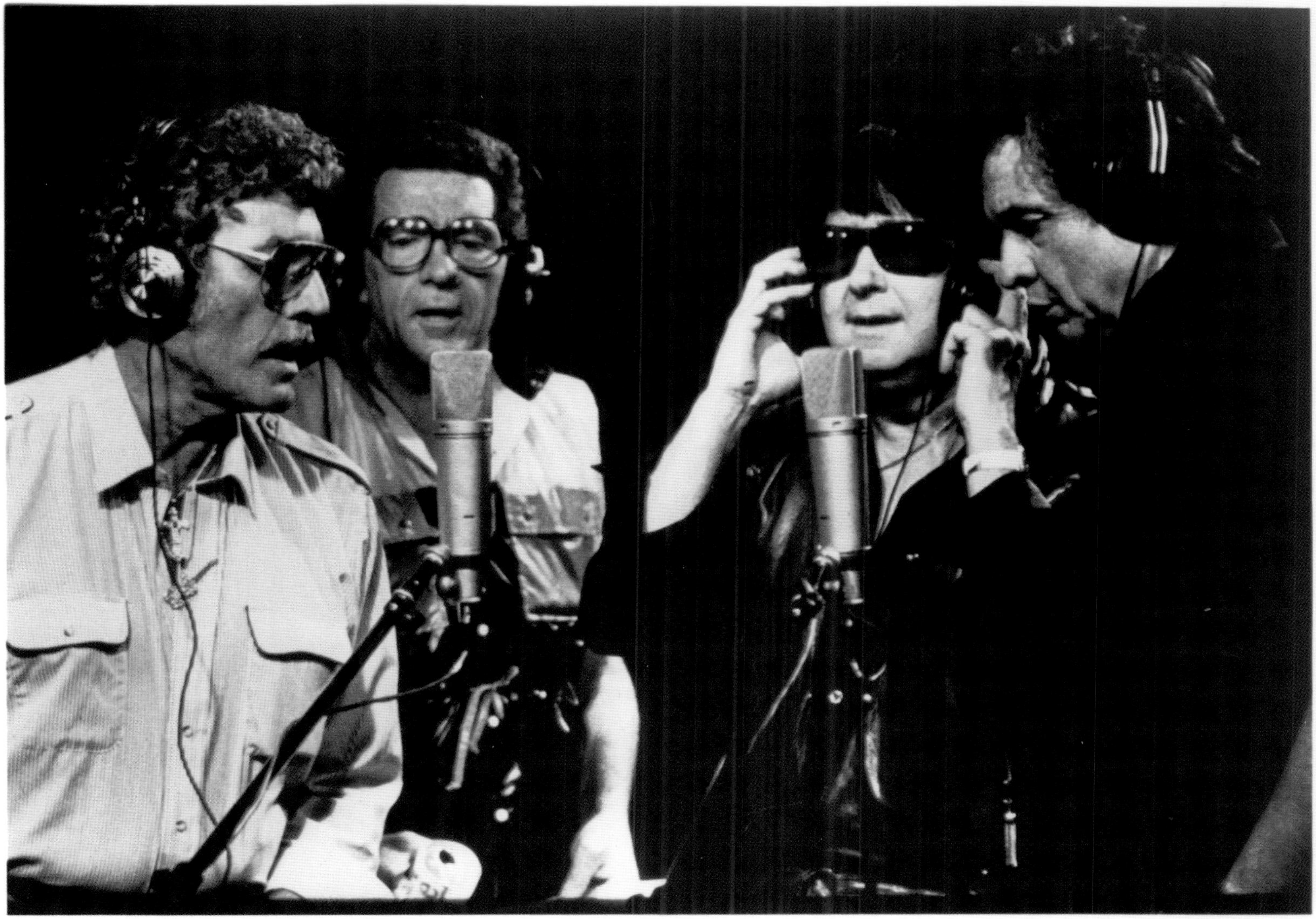

CLASS OF '55

AMERICA
SMASH
RECORDS

PolyGram Records

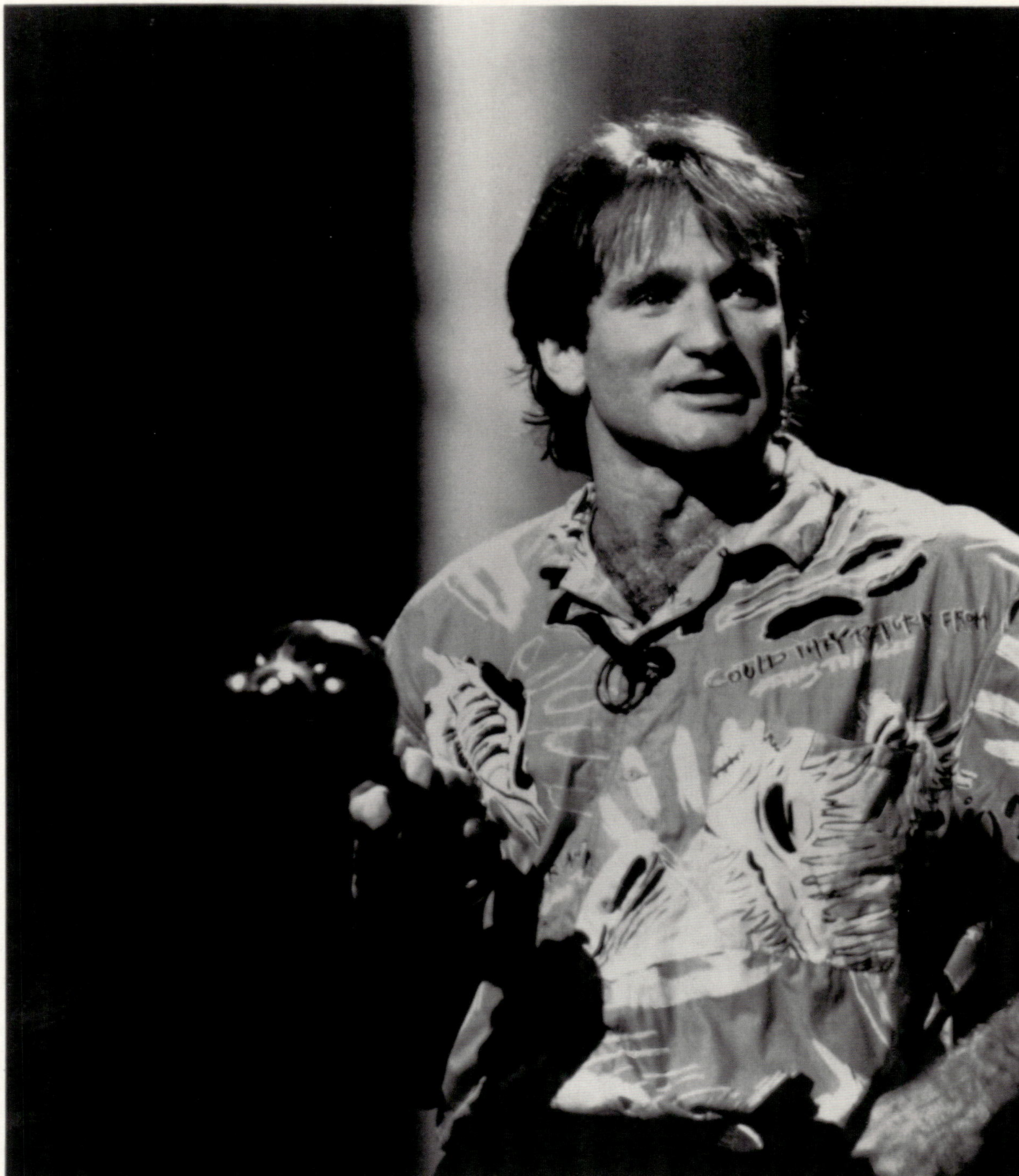

PHOTOGRAPH: ARTHUR GRACE

ROBIN WILLIAMS

Columbia
8610

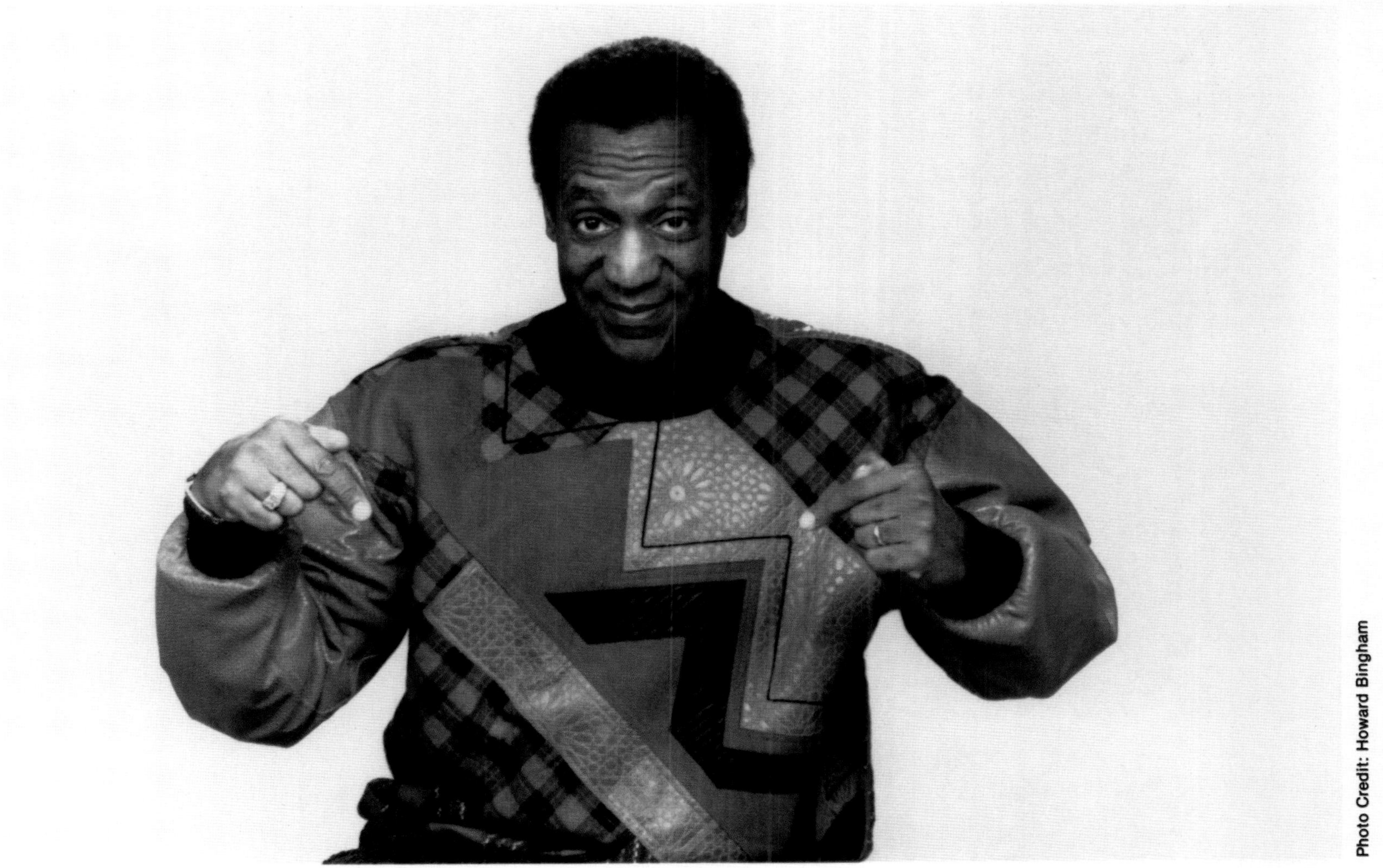

Photo Credit: Howard Bingham

BILL COSBY

GEFFEN RECORDS

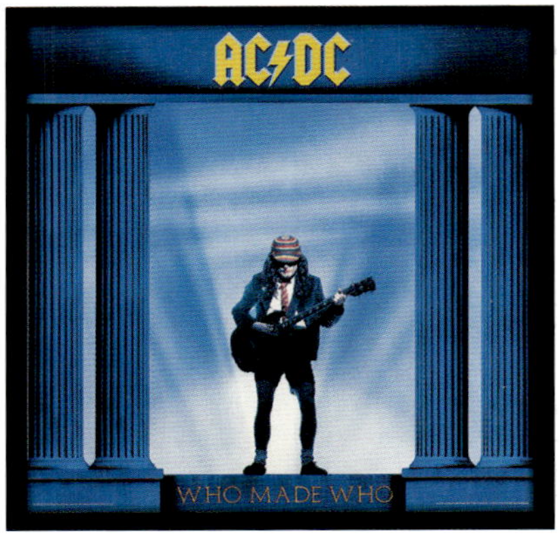

AC/DC's *Who Made Who*, the soundtrack to Stephen King's film *Maximum Overdrive*, combined classic tracks, the pounding title tune and two instrumentals.

Billboard 200: *Who Made Who* (#33)

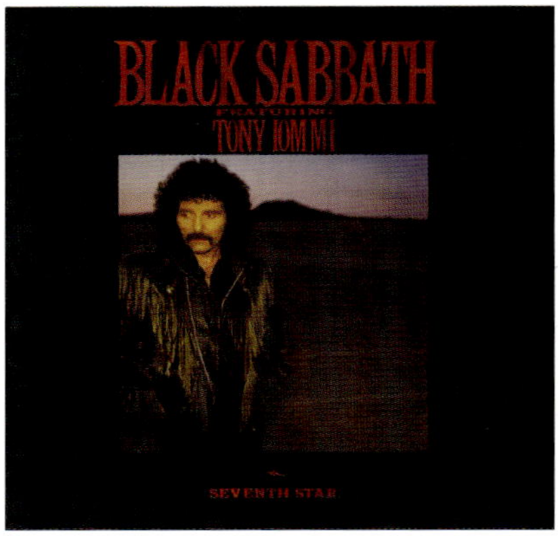

Founding **Black Sabbath** guitarist Tony Iommi intended it to be his first solo album, but *Seventh Star* was issued as "Black Sabbath featuring Tony Iommi."

Billboard 200: *Seventh Star* (#78)

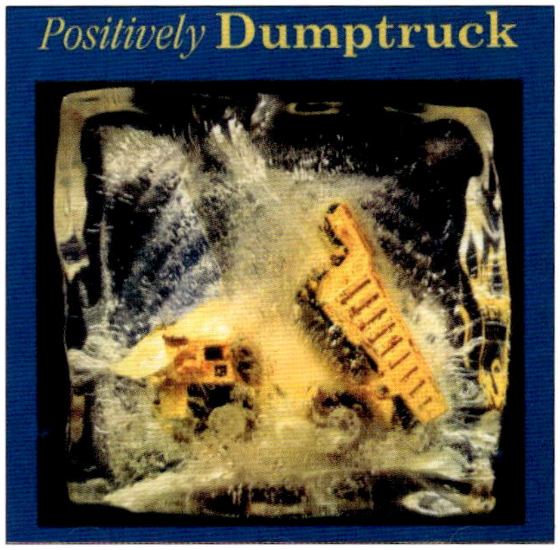

An indie pop band led by Seth Tiven and Kirk Swan, **Dumptruck** released a jangly second album, *Positively Dumptruck*, that became a college radio pick.

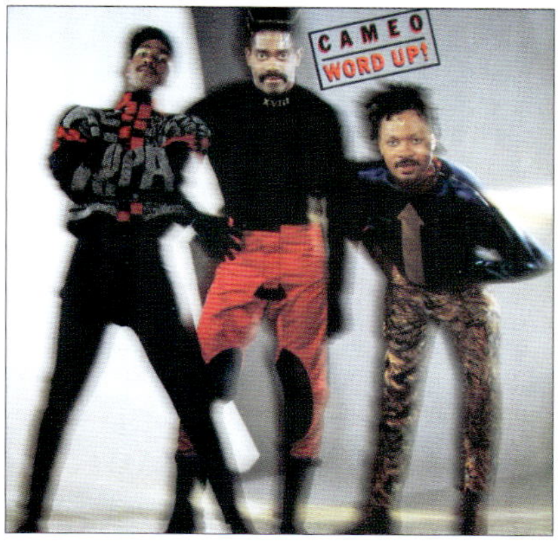

Fronted by Larry Blackmon, **Cameo**'s *Word Up!* album, featuring the wildly funky title track and "Candy," held down the No. 1 spot on the R&B charts.

Billboard 200: *Word Up!* (#8)
Billboard Hot 100: "Word Up!" (#6);
"Candy" (#21); "Back and Forth" (#50)

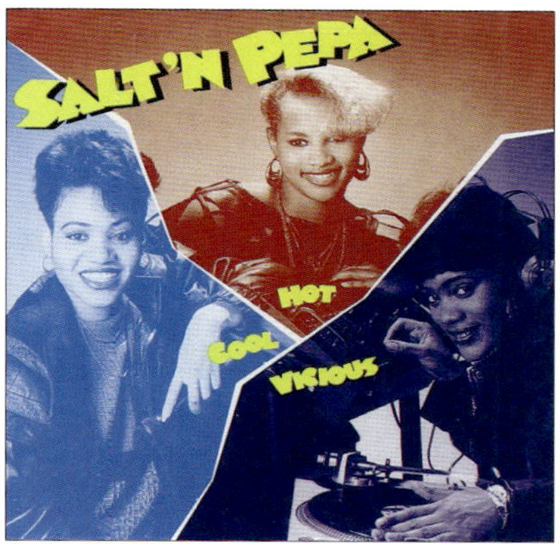

Hot, Cool & Vicious, **Salt 'N Pepa**'s debut, was paced to platinum status—a first for a female rap act—by "Push It," a single added to subsequent pressings.

Billboard 200: *Hot, Cool & Vicious* (#26)
Billboard Hot 100: "Push It" (#19)

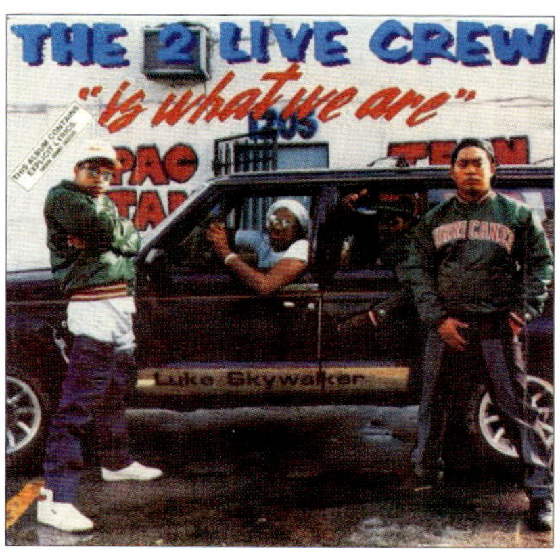

The 2 Live Crew stirred much controversy—a debut album of X-rated booty rhymes was deemed legally obscene in Florida and was promptly certified gold.

Billboard 200: *The 2 Live Crew Is What We Are* (#128)

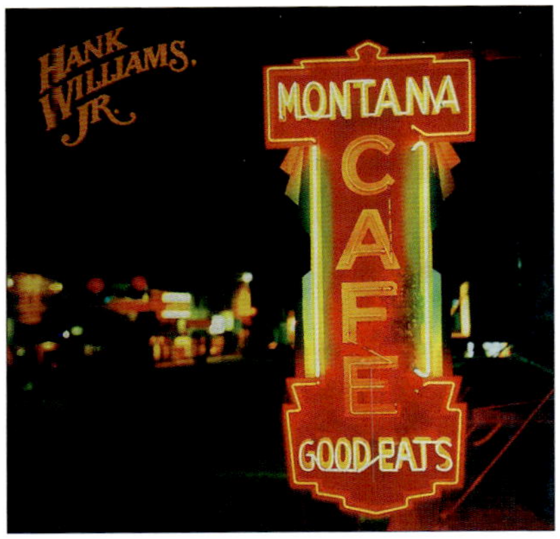

Covering his dad's 1949 hit "Mind Your Own Business," **Hank Williams, Jr.** enlisted the help of Reba McEntire, Tom Petty, Reverend Ike and Willie Nelson.

Billboard 200: *Montana Cafe* (#93)

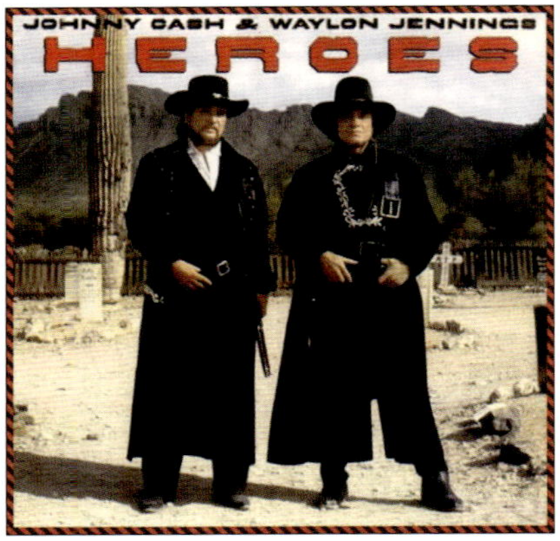

Johnny Cash & Waylon Jennings, who had hitherto teamed up as part of the all-star quartet the Highwaymen, recorded *Heroes*, their first album of duets.

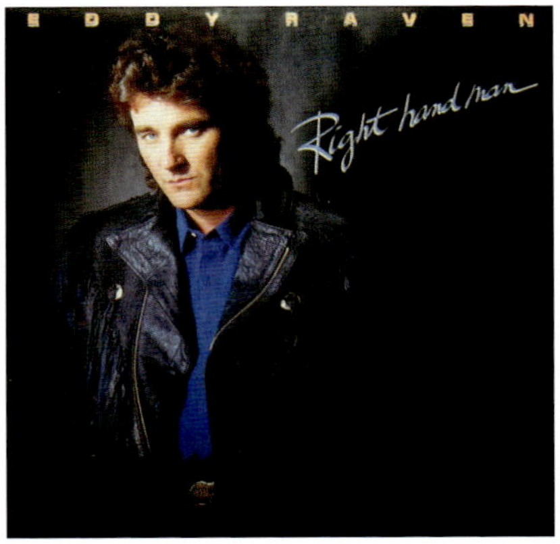

From the album *Right Hand Man*, "Shine, Shine, Shine" became singer-songwriter **Eddy Raven**'s second single to achieve No. 1 on the country charts.

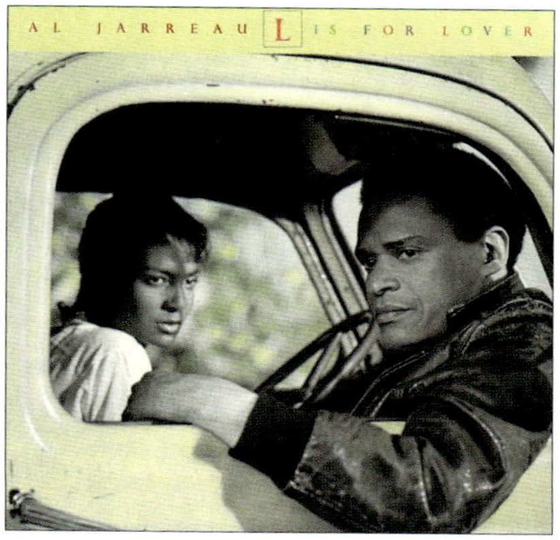

A joint effort with dance-music maven Nile Rodgers of Chic, **Al Jarreau**'s *L Is for Lover* evinced the jazz vocalist's versatility, substance and genuine joy.

Billboard 200: *L Is for Lover* (#81)

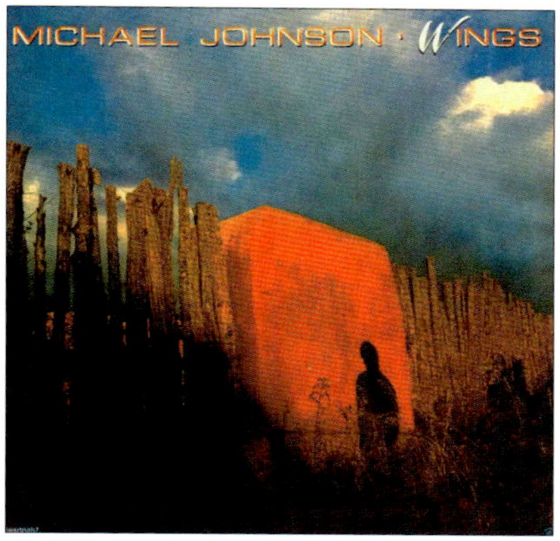

Wide-ranging pop singer-songwriter **Michael Johnson** charted two No. 1 country hits, "Give Me Wings" and the tender "The Moon Is Still Over Her Shoulder."

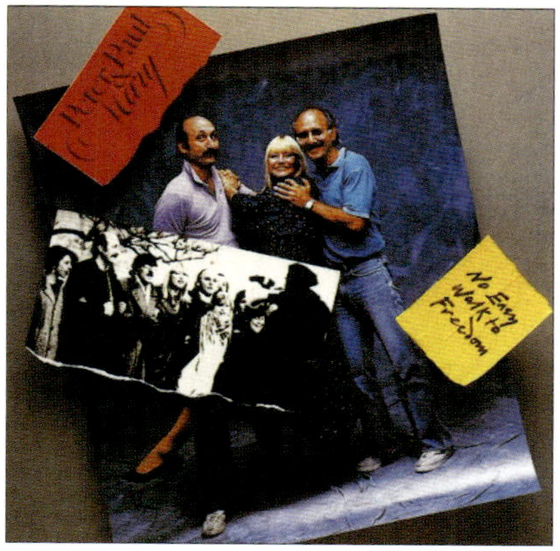

The release of *No Easy Walk to Freedom*, **Peter, Paul & Mary**'s first selection of songs in more than six years, dovetailed with the folk trio's 25th anniversary.

Billboard 200: *No Easy Walk to Freedom* (#173)

{ IN MEMORY OF JAY GRANT }

ACKNOWLEDGMENTS

Many people were essential to the creation of this book. My first thanks go to my amazing publishing team—Jon Rizzi for bringing his special brand of editorial wit and intelligence, and Kate Glassner Brainerd for her design artistry and unflagging pursuit of excellence. Special appreciation goes to Eric Pirritt's The Love We Bring Foundation and the Michael & Patricia Matthews Fund, whose facilitation was indispensable, as well as John Cerullo and Kevin Votel.

Mike Dickson, Chip Garofalo, Jennifer Soulé, Mark Zaremba, Peter Marcus, Matt Rue, Jay Elowsky, Dave Zobl and Mark Lewis contributed expertise and resources. I am especially indebted to my dear friend Michael Jensen, as well as Sue Satriano, Janice Azrak, Bryn Bridenthal, Byron Hontas, Kathy Acquaviva, Shelly Selover, Sue Sawyer, Glen Brunman, Rick Ambrose, Bob Merlis, Bill Bentley, Heidi Ellen Robinson, Les Schwartz, Rick Gershon, Jim Merlis, Judi Kerr and Susan Blond—all of whom supported my efforts.

I specifically treasure the beneficence of Dave Rothstein, Greg Phifer, John Tope, Kevin Knee, Dick Merkle, Jeff Cook, Michael Brannen, Zak Phillips, Rich Garcia, Jason Minkler, Burt Baumgartner, Mitch Kampf, Don Zucker, Carl Walters, Charlie Reardon, Robin Wren, Jimmy Smith, Sharona White, John Ryland, Geina Horton, Michael Linehan, Mike Prince and Jeffrey Naumann, who all graciously furnished information and assistance.

I gratefully acknowledge the editing and reviewing skills of Dick Kreck, Tom Walker, Diane Carman, Mike Rudeen, Ed Smith, Jay Whearley, Mark Sims, Jeff Bradley and Peggy McKay.

I also salute David Gans, Leland Rucker, Steve Knopper, David Menconi, Jon Iverson, Gil Asakawa, Mark Bliesener, Butch Hause, Ricardo Baca, John Moore, Justin Mitchell, Michael Mehle and Harvey Kubernik, whose writings formed a vital index for the music-obsessed.

Finally, I would like to acknowledge with gratitude my beloved wife, Bridget, for her constant devotion and kindness. I cherish her—the love of my life.

EDITOR | **JON RIZZI**
ART DIRECTOR | **KATE GLASSNER BRAINERD**

ISBN 979-8-9885329-1-0 PRINTED IN CHINA | Asia Pacific Offset

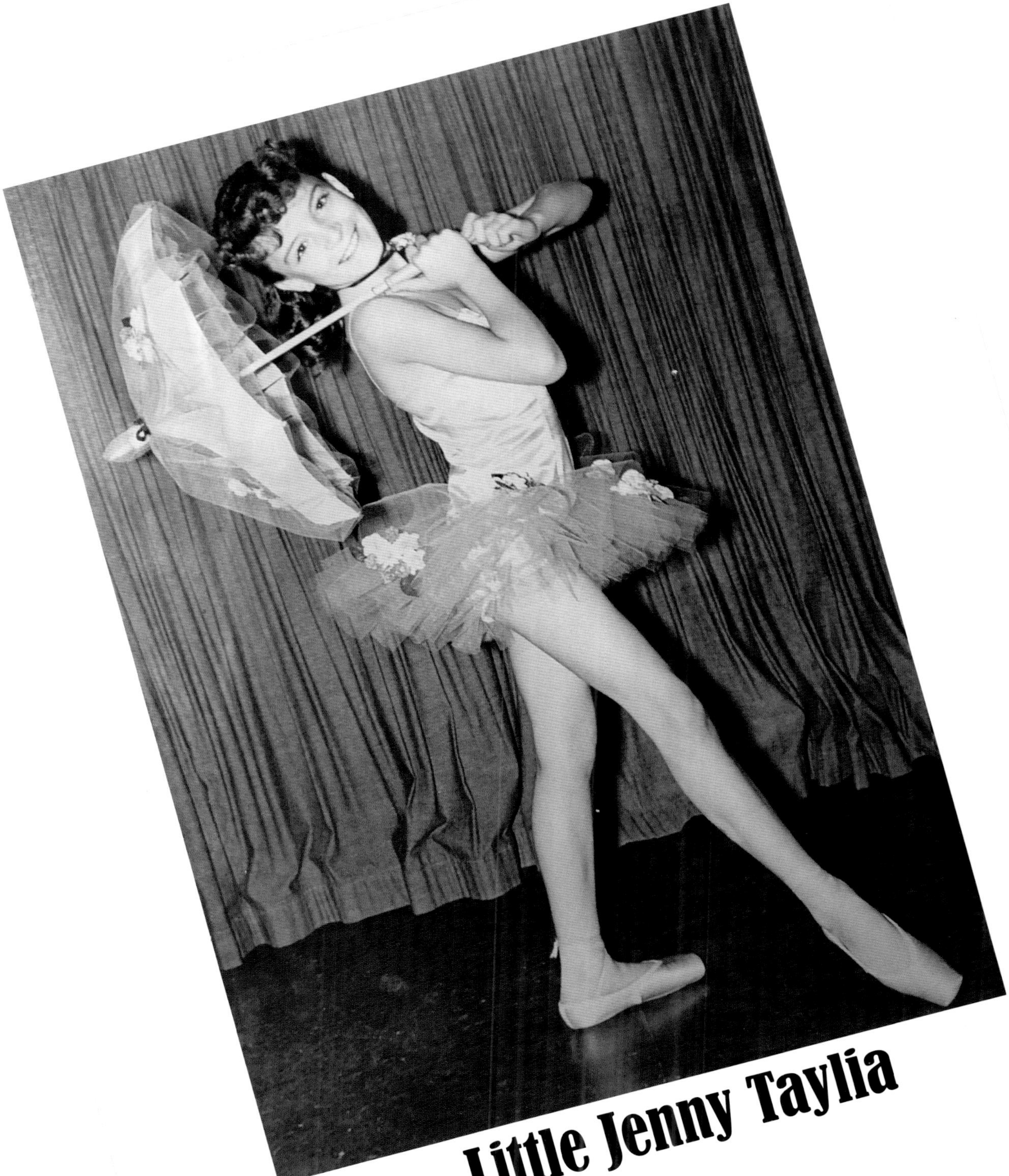

Little Jenny Taylia

Laetrile Records
"its the pits"

Next in the *ON RECORD* book series

Vol. 9 1992

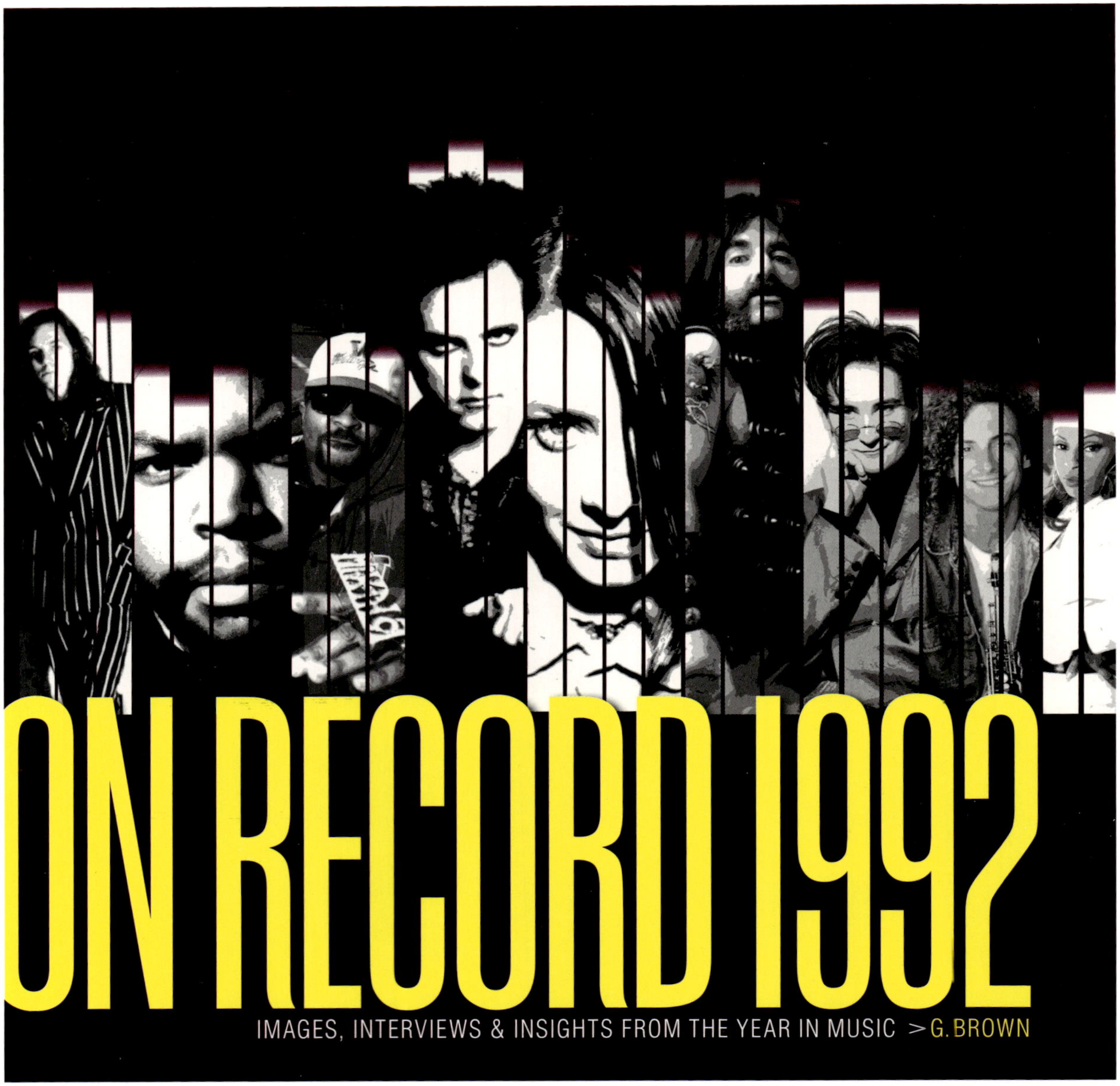